MAYBE A SECOND SPRING

MAYBE A SECOND SPRING

The Story of the Missionary Sisters of St. Columban in China

Edward Fischer

CROSSROAD · NEW YORK

1983

The Crossroad Publishing Company
575 Lexington Avenue, New York, N.Y. 10022

Printed in the United States of America

Library of Congress Cataloging in Publication Data

Fischer, Edward.
Maybe a second spring.

1. Missionary Sisters of St. Columban—China—History.
2. St. Columban's Foreign Mission Society—History.
3. Missions—China. I. Title.
BV2300.M53F57 1983 266′.251 83-15080
ISBN 0-8245-0615-4 0-8245-0617-0 pbh

Contents

MAYBE A SECOND SPRING

CHINA
KOREA
JAPAN
TOKYO
YELLOW SEA
PEKING
TIENTSIN
SHANSI
SHANTUNG
KANSU
SHENSI
HONAN
R. HWANG-HO
KIANGSU
NANKING
SHANGHAI
ANHWEI
HUPEH
HANKOW
WUCHANG
HANYANG
KIUKIANG
CHEKIANG
NINGPO
SZECHWAN
R. YANGTSE KIANG
CHUNG KING
NANCHANG
HUNAN
FOOCHOW
FUKIEN
KIANGSI
KWEICHOW
TAIWAN
KWANGSI
R. SI-KIANG
KWANGTUNG
CANTON
HONGKONG
YUNNAN
KATHA
MANDALAY
BURMA
HAINAN ISLAND
THAILAND
VIETNAM
SOUTH CHINA SEA
MANILA
PHILIPPINES
MINDANAO
SHANGHAI
HANYANG
NANCHENG

·1·

Seed Time

In a small flat in an elegant Georgian house at 119 St. Stephen's Green West, in Dublin, two women were discussing the purpose of life. Lady Frances Moloney, a widow at forty-six, said that she was considering joining the French Sisters of Charity to work in foreign missions. Her friend, Anneence Fitzgerald-Kenny, reminded her hostess that Irish women might soon be forming a new sisterhood to work in China.

This turned the conversation to a talk given six months earlier, on October 11, 1917, across the Green, at Mansion House, on Dawson Street. In that graceful eighteenth-century structure, Father John Blowick had told the Catholic Truth Society some plans that would reshape thousands of lives.

Straightaway, it influenced some Irish, Australians, and Americans—changed the lives of Chinese, Filipinos, and Koreans—and eventually reached Peruvians and Chileans.

Because of that speech dozens of women would, in time, go to the heart of China. They would face a civil war, bandits, war lords, Communist guerrillas, and Japanese invaders, to say nothing of opium addicts, lepers, floods, famine, and plague. Their time there must have been the most hectic that part of the world had seen since the days that Peking man lived in a cave on the North China Plain, some 360,000 years ago.

The twenty-nine-year-old Father Blowick spoke, at Mansion House, of how he and a few others were forming a society of priests to work among the Chinese. In the closing minutes he told of the work that medical missionaries might do. Women doctors are especially needed, he said, because Chinese women have a deep-rooted objection to having male doctors treat them, an objection that was cultural rather than feminist.

Father Blowick suggested that Irish women start a community of sisters who would prepare themselves as doctors, midwives, and nurses. He warned that since the mission would be China, those who volunteered must be prepared "for a lonely, often solitary life, and must be satisfied with little more than the necessities of life."

Lady Frances Moloney and Anneence Fitzgerald-Kenny concluded their conversation in the house on St. Stephen's Green by deciding to look into the possibilities of helping start a new sisterhood for such work. Two weeks later, on May 11, 1918, they took a train from Dublin to Galway, the first lap of a trip to Saint Columban's College at Dalgan Park.

Lady Moloney was definitely interested in a vocation as a nun. She wrote to the Bishop of Galway, "I am very hopeful that this mission work is really God's will for me, as I have had a hankering after it since my husband's death five years ago."

Miss Kenney was more inclined to remain a laywoman doing volunteer work that would be of help to religious.

That two remarkable women should show an interest gave encouragement to John Blowick. They helped keep alive his plans for a new sisterhood at the time he was overwhelmed by the strain of founding a society of priests.

Later he wrote to Lady Moloney saying that he thought God had chosen her to start a religious community. She responded by urging him to make enquiries about her character "so that you do not accept one who might be a hindrance instead of a help. My own bishop of Dublin had a very poor opinion of me and some of the public bodies with whom I have worked probably consider me rather aggressive."

Lady Moloney was not one to be happy with talking theories; she was soon restless. "I feel being such a broken reed. My spirit chafes at the restraint and delay, but I recognize that the discipline is good."

Her first inclination was to take her training in a novitiate at one of the Galway convents so as to be near Dalgan where plans were being made for the new congregation. She changed her mind, however, and enrolled for nurses' training at Mater and at Hollis Street hospitals in Dublin.

When Frances Moloney passed the final examination at the hospital with distinction, Teresa McCollum, also preparing for the missions, wrote to Father Blowick: "No one can know how well she earned her distinction in every way. Many a poor timid soul has 'got through it' a great deal easier on account of her gentleness and encouragement."

As a child Frances had sent pocket money to help children in China. As a young girl she did volunteer work with the French Sisters of Charity in Boulogne-sur-Mer. It was there that one of the sisters was a lasting inspiration: "Here among the sick poor, Sister Joseph introduced me to her friends in whose joys and sorrows she participated. No work was too sordid for the humble sister to do. Up and down the steps we trudged on our daily rounds. It was a valuable apprenticeship to be of use in later years."

The apprenticeship was of value when Frances, as a young society woman in England, spent an evening a week with the "sweated needle-women" of East London factories. Upon her family's return to Ireland, after being presented at Buckingham Palace, she made frequent visits to the Hospital for Incurables at Donnybrook. Still later, when her husband, Sir Alfred, was governor of the Windward Islands, she worked hard to bring some amenities into the lives of lepers.

The death of Sir Alfred at the Blue Nuns' hospital in Fiesole, in 1913, ended her sixteen years of marriage to a colonial official. By then her interest in helping others was so well known that Pope Pius X predicted that she would find a vocation in charitable work.

This mature woman, of wide experience, was ideal when it came to working with Father John Blowick to determine the spirit which would characterize the Missionary Sisters of St. Columban. Their interplay of minds was such and their attitudes so complementary that it was difficult to say which one had a certain idea and which echoed it.

The bond of sympathy can be surmised from something the priest wrote to a friend: "Lady Moloney is everything that is included in the word *decent* to the superlative degree." Just before his death in 1972 he said that "she was the first live spark" that ignited the flame for a new sisterhood.

From Dublin, Frances sent Father Blowick frequent notes describing the kind of spirit she would like to see encouraged. In one she said, "All spirit of criticism, either of superiors, equals, or others, must be avoided. Anyone showing such a spirit should not be retained in the congregation."

On December 13, 1918, she wrote: "I trust the novice mistress will realize that we want this wide and happy spirit, as straight as a die, but not tending to crush the individuality of anyone, or to turn out all our members into one pattern or mould."

The kind of spirit she valued in a woman is indicated in something she said about a possible candidate: "She is a girl of deepest piety and great love of the poor and has the necessary sense of the ridiculous which carries one over the small difficulties and worries of daily life."

In referring to one who might be a future mistress of novices she said: "She has a big mind and a big heart and I think would not worry us with all the pettiness which we would wish to avoid."

The constitution for the new congregation was issued in 1924. When it was revised in 1981 the first sentence in the introduction said: "It was because two people shared a vision and answered a similar call that the Missionary Sisters of St. Columban came to be."

Whenever people expressed the belief, as some did in the beginning, that the superiors for the priests were also the superiors for the sisters, Father Blowick pointed out that canon law forbids such an arrangement. The two branches of the Columbans were linked only in spirit and in purpose, he said.

Just as Father Blowick had merely suggested a new sisterhood in his talk at Mansion House, the idea to start a missionary society of priests had been planted nearly as haphazardly six years earlier. That happened in 1911 when Father John M. Fraser, a Canadian, arrived in Ireland from Chekiang, China.

Years later Father Blowick recalled: "He visited many ecclesiastics in Ireland and preached in many churches to large congregations with the purpose of stimulating, or rather creating, interest in China. He met with little success at the time beyond arousing the interest of some of the ecclesiastics whom he visited.

"But the one act of his destined to bear most fruit was a lecture which he delivered to the students at Maynooth College. He forced us to realize that China was a pagan nation, that priests were so few as to be practically powerless in their efforts to cope with the enormous task they had set themselves.

"Of the effect of that lecture in Maynooth, I can speak with personal knowledge. It brought before the future priests of Ireland the fact that there was still on earth a large nation which was practically altogether pagan, and many were the heart-searchings that followed that lecture among the more serious-minded men who had heard it. And even among priests to whom accounts of it had been given during the long summer vacation which followed."

Father Fraser's talk at Maynooth came at one of the most critical times in the history of China, for it was in 1911 that the revolutionaries overthrew the imperial system under which China had been ruled for two thousand years. The new republic promised everybody everything including religious freedom. The missionaries took heart.

Religious freedom had suffered under the old dynasty. Father Fraser spoke of the horrors of the persecution during the Boxer Rebellion. The cruelties had not been the same in every province, he said, but varied with the hate of each mandarin.

Father Fraser decided that on his way back to China he would travel across the United States collecting funds for the Lazarist fathers, a French missionary society working in the Orient.

While in New York he was invited to dine with Monsignor James McEnroe and his assistant, Father Edward Galvin, at Holy Rosary rectory in Brooklyn. At the close of the meal the Canadian priest asked the monsignor if he might speak to the parishioners at all of the Masses on Sunday.

"You may not!"

The blunt answer shocked Father Galvin. It puzzled him, for the monsignor was usually a gracious and generous man with any guest who came to the house.

To ease the blow, Father Galvin asked the visitor if he would come to his room for a talk. He didn't find this easy, for Father Fraser was not a likeable man. His manner was remote and intense; his voice harsh and monotonous.

After the guest was seated on the only chair in the room, Father Galvin sat on the bed and began by saying he had long wanted to be a missionary in China. Although the visitor punctuated everything with disparaging remarks, Ned Galvin felt compelled to tell the highlights of his thirty years from the day he was born in County Cork.

As a boy he had talked of becoming a missionary but was discouraged by parents, pastor, friends, and bishop. Go to Maynooth, they said, it is the best seminary in Ireland. He knew that Maynooth prepared priests for work in Ireland and not for the foreign missions, but still he accepted their advice.

When Edward Galvin was ordained June 20, 1909, in the college chapel at St. Patrick's, Maynooth, something unusual happened: the bishop of Cork had no vacancies in his diocese, the first time that had ever happened. This was not sad news for the newly ordained Galvin; for the time being he would be escaping the treadmill of a curacy in an Irish parish.

Go to America, the bishop advised, and come back in three years.

The three years were almost up. Galvin told Father Fraser that in the Brooklyn public library he had read most of the books about China. Would the missionary take him along on his return to China?

Fraser showed no enthusiasm for the idea. With cold manner and dead voice he said, "If you want to go with me you'll have to hurry. I'll be leaving in a few weeks, about the first of March. You'll need permission from your bishop."

That night Ned Galvin walked down a dark Brooklyn street to post two letters: one to the bishop of Cork and one to Mary Lordan Galvin, his mother. The bishop responded with enthusiasm; his mother with dismay, "The tigers will eat you!"

What a dreary trip to China. Father Fraser would not permit Father Galvin to tip for any service on the long train ride across Canada or on the longer voyage across the Pacific. Even though Ned Galvin had money of his own, the missionary kept him on a semi-starvation diet. Fraser said not to speak with strangers and offered little by way of conversation himself. At times while the severe missionary slept the priest from Cork cried with loneliness.

Upon arriving in China in mid-April of 1912, Father Fraser turned the young Irishman over to the Lazarists and disappeared with scarcely a goodbye. The Lazarists spoke only Chinese and French, and since Galvin spoke no Chinese and only a little "Maynooth French," he faced lonely days.

Every step of the way to the missions was crowded with discouragement. And yet Ned Galvin felt this was the place he should be.

Until he learned Chinese he could be of little help, and so he enrolled in a language school in Hangchow. Because of a good ear, and the ability to mimic various tones, he did well; so well that the Lazarists sent him to Shanghai to perfect himself in the language.

Within six months he was hearing confessions and preaching sermons. At last he was working among the people.

Long letters home, describing life in China, were more effective than Ned Galvin realized. They were read and reread, passed along, discussed, and printed in small county newspapers. They helped awaken Ireland to an enthusiasm for the missions.

Two Maynooth men, Fathers Joseph O'Leary, of County Cork and Patrick O'Reilly, of County Meath, arrived in Shanghai, at Christmas of 1915. While still standing on the hectic Shanghai dock, they told Father Galvin that his letters had helped them decide to become missionaries. There is now an intense interest in Chinese mission work at Maynooth, they said.

The two new men had hardly unpacked when they were urging Galvin to return home to start a mission society. The man from Cork would hear none of it, but they kept at him. Finally, after a novena asking for guidance, he agreed to give it a try.

Back in Ireland wherever Galvin went he heard the name of John Blowick. He was intrigued by the thought that the brilliant student, who at twenty-six held a chair in theology at Maynooth, was willing to turn his back on all of that academic security to become a missionary in China. He must meet him.

Blowick was anxious to meet Galvin, too. Here was an Irish priest, a Maynooth man, who had spent four years in China—surely he would have some suggestions.

A mutual friend, Father Ronayne, brought them together on September 4, 1916. The priest invited them to his mother's home at 16 Langford Terrace, Monkstown.

Since both men were given to promptness they met at the front door at the appointed hour, eight o'clock. By the soft light of a gas lamp they sized up each other. What a contrast!

Blowick, small and elegant, almost delicate, dressed in a well-fitting coat and a high top hat. Galvin, big and rangy, roughhewn, in a rumpled suit, a too-large Roman collar, and cap—only his shoes were polished, as they always were.

Father Galvin later described the contrast as ranging "from the ridiculous to the sublime."

The two men had hardly settled in front of the fire in the parlor when they discovered a startling coincidence: both had been inspired by Father John Fraser. And what an unlikeable man!

Blowick spoke in some detail of the lecture that Fraser had given at Maynooth in June of 1911. It had caused so many young men to want to become missionaries.

"The strange thing," said Galvin, "is that Father Fraser can't stand a mission himself. He spends all of his time traveling, recruiting, raising funds, organizing, almost anything but living on the mission. Yet here we are tonight talking about an Irish mission to China because of him."

Before the evening was well along, Galvin knew that he wanted Blowick to join him in founding a mission society. The young man not only had a good mind for organization, he was also known and respected by the priests of Ireland.

Blowick, willing enough to resign his chair at Maynooth, took pause when considering all the things that would have to come to pass before anyone could so much as pack a trunk for China. The mission society would need to build a seminary, staff it, and prepare a program of studies suitable for men destined for the Orient. Even before that the society would have to have the backing of the bishops of Ireland and the approval of church authorities in Rome. What if the hierarchy thought that this was merely a wild-eyed scheme that could embarrass the Church?

It was not just a matter of starting. Once started the organization would need to be sustained. Where would all of that money come from? Galvin felt he knew the answer to that.

By dawn the two priests were talking about a meeting of the bishops of Ireland scheduled for Maynooth five weeks hence. The first priority would be to organize a committee of clergy and laymen, men held in high regard, to formulate a request that would be presented to the bishops.

After some to-do the bishops approved the request. Go ahead and start a mission house to train priests for China—after you have the approval of Rome.

Even before Rome's approval, everybody involved worked at a hectic pace. Father Edward J. McCarthy, one of the first to volunteer for the society, wrote:

> We spend most of our time traveling by train, sidecar, bicycle. We take on as many churches as we can ourselves. Ned told me the other day that China is nothing to the work we are doing at present. You can guess what it is to go around and interview parish priests, preach three sermons on Sunday, lecture in schools and convents during the week, visit every priest in the diocese as we go along organizing lectures, etc., not a moment to ourselves.

One suspicious old pastor well out in the country was not too sure he wanted Ned Galvin to speak to his parishioners. He circled the missionary several times before asking if he really had spent four years in China. When Galvin said that he had, the old man sighed, "Well, the ways of God are not our ways," and allowed the visitor to preach at all of the Masses.

Nine months passed and no word from Rome. Father Blowick, himself a canonist, had some sense of how the Congregation for the Propagation of the Faith took the long view of centuries. Father Galvin, however, was always aware of minutes passing, and so was beside himself with frustration.

The two priests, knowing that German submarines threatened everything afloat, sailed for Rome in June of 1917. Ned Galvin was pessimistic all of the way, saying that even if they received approval for their plan, they would not be assigned favorable territory in China. "They will save that for the Italian missionaries."

The Irish priests were in Rome a week before receiving an appointment with Cardinal Serafini, Prefect for the Congregation for the Propagation of the Faith, and two weeks before being granted an audience with Pope Benedict XV.

During these meetings it was evident that Father Blowick had a sense of diplomacy and that Father Galvin knew a great deal about China. Galvin seemed familiar with every mission in the Orient and with the status of every town. He refused to consider starting missions in remote mountain areas that were full of bandits, suspicion, and anti-foreign hatred.

Father Galvin told Pope Benedict that religious orders were trying to hold onto many sections with too few priests. The time has come, he said, to divide those sections and staff them with younger men.

The day after the papal audience, June 18, 1917, Cardinal Serafini wrote a letter to Cardinal Logue in Ireland saying that permission was granted for "a college to be founded in Ireland for Foreign Missions."

(At this time the new organization was being called the Maynooth Mission to China; it would later be known as the Society of Saint Columban).

In Ireland the word China began appearing in the press and flying from mouth to mouth as never before. In county after county young men were expressing a wish to become missionaries.

Within a few days after Father Blowick had given that effective speech in Dublin, Father Galvin sailed for the United States on a darkened liner with guns mounted on the foredeck. His friends, and especially his mother, feared he might be a victim of U-boats, for this was November of 1917 and the United States had been at war with Germany since April.

The Irish priest received some encouragement from John Cardinal Farley in New York, William Cardinal O'Connell in Boston, George Cardinal Mundelein in Chicago, and Archbishop John Glennon in Saint Louis. But not one of them could see his way clear to invite another missionary society into his archdiocese.

On Saint Patrick's Day, 1918, Father Galvin arrived in Omaha and thought, as he walked to the episcopal residence, how fitting it would be if on this day the new Irish society could find a new home in the United States. That is exactly what happened when Archbishop Jeremiah J. Harty expressed pleasure at the thought of having missionaries open a headquarters in his diocese.

After all that rejection, at last Ned Galvin felt accepted. With less than $300 in his pocket he hurried down the street to rent a one-room office, hire a sign painter to letter on the door The Irish Mission to China, and locate a printer for his new magazine, the *Far East*.

In April of 1918 Rome made an offer of a mission territory in China—the vicariate of Kweichow. Galvin replied with a firm rejection: too many mountains, too few people, and too remote.

The official birthday of the society came on June 29, 1918, when Bishop O'Dea of Galway canonically erected the Maynooth Mission to China. Twenty priests took the oath of membership that day.

The Society was making headway in Ireland and in America, and now began directing attention to Australia and New Zealand. Encouraging letters from the bishops of Maitland and Wellington made it clear that Irish priests would be welcome there to prepare young men for China.

During all of this, a strange silence emanating from Rome got on the nerves of priests eager to be on the way. The society waited with impatience from April of 1918, when the offer to Kweichow was refused, until November of 1919, when Rome offered the city of Hanyang and some surrounding countryside.

Galvin said he would prefer Hankow across the river. Yet he made no point of this officially when he and Blowick hurried to Rome to accept the offer.

On Saint Patrick's Day of 1920 a farewell party was held at Dalgan, in County Galway, and two days later eleven priests sailed for the mission in China.

·2·

Time of Cultivation

With the priests off to China, Father Blowick could give added attention to working with Lady Moloney to start a congregation of sisters. He had received more than a hundred letters from women asking about the possibility of a mission to China. Some even volunteered outright. A few, anticipating the founding of a new congregation, were training in hospitals.

For advice Father Blowick sent letters to Catholic medical missionary headquarters in India, France, Italy, and the United States. What advice he received was long in coming and mostly mistaken. He was so impressed with the achievement of women doctors among Protestant missionaries that he sought help from Dr. Agnes McLaren and Dr. Margaret Lamont.

Who should prepare these young women for religious life until members of the new congregation would be ready to do this for themselves, is a question he and Lady Moloney discussed. Both knew that no matter what the constitution said, the women training the first members would have leeway in shaping the spirit of the new sisterhood.

Finally, on May 6, 1921, Father Blowick wrote to Mother Agnes Gertrude, superior general of the Irish Sisters of Charity, asking, "Would you be prepared to admit a number of selected ladies to your postulancy and novitiate to prepare them to be the nucleus of the new congregation?"

Three days later, Mother Agnes Gertrude suggested that he renovate one of the houses on the Cahiracon estate for the novitiate, and promised to send a few sisters to train postulants and novices.

Father Blowick was pleased for he knew that the Sisters of Charity base their training on an adaptation of the Rule of Saint Ignatius. He and Frances Moloney liked their stress on personal discipline, asceticism, and acceptance.

On a bleak February 1, 1922, with the hills of Clare under snow, three Irish Sisters of Charity—Camillus, Alphonsus, and Bartholomew—reached Cahiracon to prepare for the aspirants who would arrive shortly. The three sisters no sooner entered the building than they named it Saint Brigid's Convent, for they had arrived on the feast day of the saint.

The estate on the banks of the Shannon, near Ennis, in County Clare, had been purchased in 1920 when the Columban fathers found that their college at Dalgan, near Galway, was getting too crowded. At Cahiracon the priests established Saint Senan's College where seminarians could study philosophy for two years before moving on to Dalgan for four years of theology.

On February 7 the first young woman to arrive, later to be known as Sister Brendan Walsh, apologized for being early, explaining that she had taken a short cut by crossing the Shannon by boat.

Others came by train to Ennis and traveled the remaining fourteen miles by car. Eventually their names in religion would be Sisters Patrick Moloney, Finbarr Collins, Brigid McSweeney, Mary Joseph McKey, all Irish, and Francis Xavier Mapelback, an Australian.

Seven others arrived at that time: Elizabeth Brannigan, Peg McDonnell, Vera Lees, Kathleen Brennan, Elizabeth Dalton, Mary Elizabeth Scanlon, and Teresa McCollum.

Approaching the estate the postulants found it nicely set on the river bank well covered with great gnarled oaks and entanglements of ivy, brushwood, bramble, holly, and fern. They passed beyond the main house, Saint Senan's, and continued down the road for a mile to Saint Brigid's, a sturdy, two-story stone building that had probably been a dower house. In the days of the lord of the manor many estates had a house built for the dowager to live in during her declining years, leaving the affairs of the mansion to a younger generation.

The house stood exposed with no tree, plant, or shrub to screen it from view. It was a low-roofed, grey, bleak place, with a wing running back on one side. The only note of color in the picture was the green door of the house and the red roof of a farmer's barn some distance down the road.

The convent was situated at the point where the Shannon takes a definite turn westward toward the ocean. From the upper-story rooms, under sloping ceilings, the nuns could look out of small windows to see, at times, "white horses" covering the river, and in rough weather heard the low surge like a distant sea beating on the rocks.

The land behind the house descended to the river in graceful undulations. On the opposite shore rose a wooded cliff with a Celtic cross on its summit. In the distance, low blue hills defined the horizon on a clear day.

The Sisters of Charity planned a pattern of activity, a calm rhythm, that would bring tranquility to the day. The postulants, and later the novices, too, arose at five o'clock. All gathered in the chapel fifteen minutes later, arriving well before the start of prayer to give the mind time to prepare for worship.

After an hour of prayer the women went to their rooms to "tidy up" and returned to the chapel at seven. By now a chaplain had arrived to say Mass, having traveled by pony cart from Saint Senan's.

After breakfast at a quarter to eight the day passed in a cycle of prayer, manual work, and classes, with two periods of recreation. It came to an end with night prayers at nine o'clock and lights out at ten.

Among the men who came to Saint Brigid's Convent to teach dogma, scripture, and theology were Fathers John Blowick, Michael O'Dwyer, Patrick Cleary, Patrick Connolly, Timothy Harris, John Henegan, and Ronan McGrath.

A half-century later some sisters could still recall the "contagion" of John Blowick's lectures. What he knew and felt he passed on readily to his listeners.

He stressed, time and again, that the postulants were preparing themselves for a difficult life: "It will be hard, hard work, and it is not the chaplain or the confessor, or the sisters who can do it for you. It is all in yourself. Christ living here in the tabernacle will give you all the grace and strength you need.

"All missionaries must realize that it is God's work they are called to do and that of themselves they can do nothing. They must get this point well into their minds even if years are spent in realizing it."

Father Blowick never let them forget that they were breaking new ground: "Remember that this is the beginning of a new Order. You have not realized the terrible responsibility on you as the first members. Future generations will look to you."

Father O'Dwyer continued this theme: "I hope that each one of you will act as if she alone were responsible for the spirit of the congregation. It is a great responsibility resting on each one of you."

Through the years the sisters remembered Father O'Dwyer for his common sense, his impatience with people who go through life talking theory but doing little: "With certain people there is a big danger in the spiritual life," he said. "They form great ideals for themselves, but, splendid as they are, they never come to anything and this for two reasons—first, because their ideals are entirely their own and not of God, and secondly, because they never take the trouble to carry them out. Theirs are the ideals that are buried in churchyards.

"There is such a thing as feeling good in the abstract: we have this feeling and are very enthusiastic. But do we recognize good in the concrete? Are we able to keep our enthusiasm alive and *do* good?"

Balance was a great concern for Father O'Dwyer: "Too much prudence will keep us from doing anything," and "In obedience as in everything else there must be common sense."

Father O'Dwyer was fascinated with the mystery of a vocation: "I must constantly ask myself and carefully examine the motive that brought me here. Was it the wave of enthusiasm that swept over the land that brought me, the glamour and heroism surrounding it? If it is only this then my house is built on sand.

"The most important factor in testing your vocation is the testimony of your own conscience. God does not look to superiority of the intellect, but to the disposition of the heart."

Father O'Dwyer was interested in hearing how the novices at Saint Brigid's came upon their vocations.

One young woman, for example, who lived with her parents while her brother attended Maynooth, sometimes considered becoming a nun. When her brother spoke of the mission being planned for China, it struck a responsive chord. She tried to put this from her mind and heart, so much so that whenever she saw a copy of the *Far East* magazine lying around the house she hid it away in a table drawer. In time she became Sister Leila Creedon and gave years of service to the Far East.

Another young woman was working in the Dublin office of Lever Brothers during the civil war in Ireland when there was talk, in the 1920s, of boycotting English goods. She decided not to get caught in the boycott and so answered a newspaper advertisement for a secretary who spoke Irish. She felt qualified, having been in the Gaelic League. Through the want ad she became secretary to the Columban fathers, and later, as Sister Columban Kennedy, went off to China.

A girl went to a funeral in Clare and there met a woman who spoke of nuns preparing themselves for mission work in China. The woman said she would like to meet them, but hesitated to visit the convent by herself. The girl who volunteered to accompany her later went off to China as Sister Michael Mongey.

After a postulancy of six months at Saint Brigid's, the aspirants received the religious habit. Following two years in the novitiate, they took the vows of poverty, chastity, and obedience. These vows were for three years, and after that final vows were made for life.

The first postulants received the habit of the Missionary Sisters of Saint Columban, October 4, 1922, in the chapel at Cahiracon. On the occasion, the Most Reverend Michael Fogerty, bishop of Killaloe, concluded his sermon: "The future history of the new congregation is still Heaven's secret. May the religious habit you are the first to wear become famous for its conquests in religious history. It descends upon you with the blessings of Saint Columban. May his virtues adorn your lives and make glorious the habit you wear, until Christ calls you home to receive the virgin's or the martyr's crown."

Those last two words echoed something Bishop O'Dea had said to the Columban priests a few years earlier: "You are not apt to amount to much until you are hit over the head a few times out there in China. Some day you may want to establish a martyrs' room here at Dalgan."

Had such a room been established it would now hold twenty plaques.

Father Patrick O'Connell returned from China to conduct classes at Saint Brigid's in Chinese language, culture, and history. He started by telling the postulants that the Catholic Church had fifty vicariates, each almost as big as Ireland, and nearly three times as densely populated. There were 2,370 priests caring for about 2 million Chinese.

Protestantism was represented by 103 sects, he said. Although its followers numbered only 300,000, they were served by 5,186 foreign missionaries, two-thirds of whom were women.

In his talks Father O'Connell also made it clear that the sisters faced a life of hardship and danger. Letters coming out of China certainly confirmed his warning. The postulants and novices read them carefully.

One that they spoke of often had come from Father John O'Leary. While visiting in the home of a parishioner, at a mission stop called Ling Wha Seh, the Columban retired to a small room with a mud floor. He noticed several holes here and there but paid no attention; he was more aware of the bed which was a door placed atop several bricks. The only other object in the room, a box in the corner, seemed a good place to put his clothes, but he changed his mind upon finding three hens caged in the lower level, and a rooster on the upper level.

No windows graced the tiny room, but it needed none because thin bamboo laths let in plenty of light and air. The missionary could look through the wall to see three pigs grunting in disagreement outside. Beyond one wall was a kitchen which sent out thick cooking odors.

"No sooner was the candle extinguished than I began to experience something creeping all over me," wrote Father O'Leary. "Up and down it ran. Instead of taking shelter under the bedclothes I jumped up and stood in the middle of the room. The whole floor seemed alive. Rats! Rats! Rats! The Rodent Congress of Ling Wha Seh was in session.

"I was very awake. All night rats kept pouring in and out on their way to the kitchen. In the early morning the rooster began to broadcast."

The rats were as bad the second night as the first. Out of exhaustion the missionary was able to sleep a couple of hours.

"The third night I had a beautiful, long, sound sleep," he said. Not even the rooster awakened him.

Another letter that made an impression on the sisters came from Father Peter Fallon describing his first sick call. The call had come on a bitter winter morning with six inches of snow on the ground and a piercing north wind coming in off the river. Even indoors the air was icy. It was one of those times when missionaries delayed writing for several weeks because the ink was frozen in the bottle.

An old woman was dying ten miles away in a village of four hundred Catholics. Father Fallon tried to hire a sedan chair, but could find no one willing to go out in the blizzard. After much discussion two pagans consented to make the journey provided their passenger gave a handsome bonus above the ordinary fare.

"Everything went well," wrote Father Fallon, "until we reached a sharp hill. In the effort to ascend, the man in front who was carrying the chair slipped and fell. A general mix-up ensued. The two coolies exchanged hasty words, and then set off again. They hardly started when a similar accident occurred. This time, instead of blaming each other they turned on me, and decided that I was the cause of all the misfortune.

"They refused to go another inch and demanded their money. This I refused to pay, as they had failed to carry out their part of the contract. So I left them and determined to finish the journey on foot. I had not gone very far, however, when they overtook me once more, and gave me a cordial invitation to resume my seat. I accepted the offer, and this time things went well, and we were soon at our destination."

Father Fallon was surprised at the reception. Scores of people, hearing that a priest was coming, assembled to bid him welcome. Torches flared, firecrackers exploded, children yelled. Everybody had something that would make noise—a drum, cymbals, bamboo flutes, tin cans, clappers. One old lady slapped a pair of bricks together.

The house where Father Fallon stayed was poor. Old pieces of clothing covered the floor and the dust and cobwebs of ages were thick on the wall. The only adornment was a picture of the Sacred Heart with a taper burning in front of it, one that gave off a pungent odor and a blinding smoke. The furniture consisted of four rickety chairs and a three-legged table propped against the wall.

For all of its misery the room was soon converted into a chapel. When the excitement subsided outside, parishioners assembled to offer a prayer for the dying woman. Father Fallon administered the sacraments of Penance and of Extreme Unction.

Under the curious gaze of a hundred spectators the priest ate pork, vegetables, rice, and fruit, and retired for the night. He wanted to close the door, but, alas!, there was no door.

"I got into bed, but not to sleep. For no sooner had everyone retired than a new sort of intruder put in an appearance. Rats, cats, dogs, young pigs—all seemed to have free access. The greater part of the night was spent in vain attempts to rid myself of those unwelcome visitors. Finally, however, I abandoned despair, and resigned myself to rest as well as I could in their company."

At the coming of a welcome dawn, Father Fallon said Mass, gave the sick woman Holy Viaticum and the Apostolic Benediction, and commended her soul to the Divine Mercy.

And then something happened that surprised the missionary: "On my way home I experienced the joy and happiness that more than compensated for the difficulties of the preceding day and the discomforts of the night."

The sisters enjoyed the optimistic letters Fathers Richard Ranaghan, Thomas Quinlan, and Patrick Dawson had sent back to Ireland. A few paragraphs from one of them will evoke the mood:

"Our welcome to Tsao-Su was one we can never forget. It was a very trying ordeal. A huge procession was formed, small boys dressed in gaudy silks rode on ponies ornamented with ribbons and silk bows, another crowd of boys carried placards with Chinese signs which translated into Irish might read *Cead Mile Failte* (A Thousand Welcomes).

"Two sedan chairs were provided for us. A batch of them with large silk umbrellas and square canopies gave another touch of color to the parade. The military brass band and the Tsao-Su Catholic Guild band headed the procession. At times when the cymbals and brass and tin instruments got into motion together the din was terrific.

"In fact the two of us were the only ones who seemed not to have been caught up in the thrills of excitement. There we were seated in our chairs with black silk canopies, being whirled along, praying that the end might soon come.

"A large number of pagans joined the procession and hundreds of men and women watched from windows. Members of the city council, army, navy, police, and railway companies were present. It was a great day for Tsao-Su and I am glad it is only one in a lifetime for me.

"When we arrived at the priest's house we thought we had escaped from the bulk of the throng. A spacious reception-room was waiting for us. Tea and cigars were offered. We did not feel the least inclined to drink the tea, yet it is part of the ceremony. Not only did we drink the tea but we kept smiling, though the reception-room was densely packed.

"The hugh multitude commenced bowing to us. So we stood side by side and bowed alternately. I never felt stiffer. It was great fun for the children who were laughing and cackling like young ducks.

"Soon the Catholics from the outlying districts began to swarm in. Father Dawson's patience was giving out and the remark somehow slipped out. 'Had I known all of this was before me I would rather have stayed two nights in a sampan on the river.' I was delighted that he came along for his genial presence helped me a good bit in getting through the longest and biggest ceremony I ever assisted at."

Why all of the rejoicing? The people of Tsao-Su had no resident priest for many years. Now they were expressing their gratitude that one would stay and work among them.

Every letter had in it enough adventure to make interesting reading; however, those that spoke of bandits brought fear to the heart. One such arrived in the fall of 1923 telling of the experiences of Fathers Walsh and McHugh.

At four o'clock in the morning on August 14 a Chinese servant had awakened Father Walsh at his mission station saying that bandits were near. The Columban escaped the village by pony and rode for two days to reach the Han River. On a steamer bound for Hanyang he met a confrere, Father McHugh, also escaping a roving band who had, as he said, "the easy conscience of the brigand."

Father McHugh had arisen at one o'clock on the morning of August 16 to say Mass at his mission station before leaving for Hanyang when in the middle of the service he heard sounds of heavy firing. After consuming the Host, he fled to the little river that flowed near the house. Almost immediately the house was surrounded by fifty men who asked for the "foreigner." They looted the house, sprinkled kerosene on the floors, and set fire to the place.

These were the bandits who two months earlier had captured Father Melotto and held him for ransom. The priest, then well into his sixties, begged the bandit chief to have mercy on the parishioners of Teian mission, where he had served for thirty years. When soldiers attacked the brigands, the chief put his revolver to the old priest's head and murdered him.

It was not just Christianity that suffered. People, buildings, and symbols dedicated to any religion were apt to feel the ire of bandits. Father Dawson wrote from T'ai-lin-miao that brigands burned a Buddhist monastery near his church and extracted a ransom from the Buddhist monks who were living there.

The women at Cahiracon found some consolation in a letter that arrived early in 1925 from a French sister in Su-tchuen: "Don't worry about us. China is a volcano; hatred of the European is deep-seated and general, and an eruption may occur at any time. But the people do not extend anti-European hatred to the sisters. We are a class apart in their eyes, and, far from molesting us, they go out of their way to be kind and respectful."

In recalling all of this in 1974, the last year of his life, Father O'Dwyer said of the first Columban sisters who prepared for China: "Those women were characterized by a spirit of adventure. There was no knowing what was coming. They faced the total unknown. But they had great faith and were always good-humored. They were good-humored because they saw the effort for what it was."

Those early Columban sisters always gave credit to the women who had trained them in the good attitudes of a religious life. In a letter to Father O'Dwyer, in 1930, Mother Finbarr, then superior general of the Sisters of Saint Columban, recalled: "All three Sisters of Charity had that peculiar charm of mind and manner that goes with what we recognize as holiness."

In recalling Mother Camillus, the first mistress of novices, a Columban said: "She trained her novices by the interior law of charity and love which frequently formed the subject of her exhortations. One never-to-be forgotten day, Mother gave us an exhortation on love. The charity of which she spoke flowed straight from the heart and radiated from her. The spirit of the gentle Christ shone from within. The impression lasted for days. In some it was reflected by a deeper thoughtfulness. In others it blossomed into a beaming alacrity for duty and hard things."

Mother Alphonsus, who succeeded Mother Camillus as mistress of novices, was a severe woman. Frequently she pointed out that only the disciplined and selfless would be strong enough for the China missions. Her severity must have been tempered with some gentleness because Mother Finbarr wrote to Father O'Dwyer who had also known Mother Alphonsus: "I have often asked myself even while she was with us what made it possible for her to be so faithful herself in the least things, yet so understanding and indulgent for others."

The third Sister of Charity who had arrived in Cahiracon on the feast of Saint Brigid was Sister Bartholomew. After only a brief time she was replaced by Sister Eucharia, who, in turn, was replaced by Sister Joseph Conception, an English aristocrat. The irony was that she, born Evelyn Vavasour at Hazelwood Castle, brought inspiration to Irish women at a time when English aristocrats were not held in high regard in Ireland.

Her spirit of poverty was striking. A nun who knew her in the novitiate said: "Everything she brought with her or used was of the poorest kind. I remember being particularly struck by her poor little writing desk and wondered at it—but I never saw her use anything else in the after days. We could not help wondering who she was—but it was many years later before I knew anything of her family. Even at the reception of the holy habit when we dressed as brides hers was the simplest gown and veil of all."

After becoming a nun she worked for a short time in a children's hospital in Dublin. Eventually, her major work was with the blind at Merrion, an estate between the Irish sea and the Dublin hills.

Whenever Columban priests visited Merrion she asked about their missions in China. The more she heard of the work, the more she urged her superiors to become more mission-minded. It was almost inevitable that Sister Joseph Conception should, sooner or later, become involved in the formation of the new sisterhood.

After reaching Cahiracon in 1924 she gave an example of dedication that could not be ignored. Knowing that the mission field would demand rough manual work, she set an example at milking cows, polishing chapel floors, cleaning kerosene lamps—all performed with zest. Even while taxing her own gaunt, ascetic body, she kept a careful watch to prevent any over-straining among the postulants and novices.

Fifty years later, Sister Malachy McPolin recalled: "Sister Joseph Conception feared no work. And my, how she loved the poor! I used to go with her when she visited them. What an exceptionally good model for foreign missionary Sisters!"

Sister Mary Moroney added, "She was very understanding; she knew when you wanted to explode. She was easy on others, but hard on herself. She would never complain, and all through the years you would remember that, and when you began to complain you would think of her and feel ashamed."

The Sisters of Charity felt a sense of accomplishment when they saw the first seven Sisters of Saint Columban for the Mission to the Chinese professed. It was on September 29, 1924, the feast of St. Michael the Archangel, that Bishop Fogarty of Killaloe performed the ceremony and appointed Sister M. Finbarr the first superior general.

The new novices were dressed in their recently designed habit of black serge, with a guimpe of the same material, and a white linen collar and a black cincture. The headdress consisted of a white linen cap with a black veil. A silver crucifix hung from the neck and a rosary hung from the cincture.

Now they looked more like sisters outwardly. Inwardly, they still would have to prepare themselves for two more years at Cahiracon. They were becoming aware of the truth of something that Father Galvin had written from China to a nun in Cincinnati. When she wrote to him telling of her program for a more severe spiritual life, he had discouraged her from excessive devotions: "Remember that sanctity is a slow growth."

·3·

To the Field

While the first six Columban sisters were packing, preparing to leave Cahiracon for Hanyang, a cablegram arrived from Father John O'Leary: "No casualties, no looting, no disorder." He was referring to a victory in the civil war when the southern forces (Cantonese) captured Hanyang on September 6, 1926.

The morning of Saturday, September 11, the small chapel at Cahiracon was crowded. After singing a Te Deum, everyone left except the six sisters who remained behind to ask, one more time, for blessing on their new work:

Mother M. Finbarr (Nora Collins, Cork)
Sister M. Patrick (Lady Frances Moloney, London)
Sister M. Theophane (Johanna Fortune, Wexford)
Sister M. Lelia (Mary Creedon, Kerry)
Sister M. Agnes (Irene Griffin, Australia)
Sister M. Philomena (Helen Woods, Sligo)

The sisters not leaving for China gathered in front of the convent and as the cars started sang, "Go Ye Afar." One of them wrote, "Only a few of the more stoical amongst us succeeded in reaching the last verse." One of the sisters noted in her diary, "a hard parting."

As the three cars reached the gate at Saint Senan's College, students, priests, and workmen were gathered there to cheer. At Kildysart, three miles down the road, villagers stood in their doorways calling, "God speed!"

Waiting at the railroad station at Ennis were six Columban priests also on their way to China: Fathers John Loftus, Charles Donnelly, Joseph Hogan, Peter Fallon, John Lalor, and Daniel Houlihan. Father Blowick was there, too; he would accompany the group as far as Hamburg. Mother Finbarr, the congregation's first superior general, would go all the way to China, but planned to return to Ireland soon after seeing the sisters settled at Hanyang.

The train rides to Limerick and to Cork were short, familiar steps on a journey that would stretch into long, unfamiliar ones.

In the cathedral of Cork a solemn Benediction was held on Sunday evening. At the close of the service the Columban sisters remained in their pews to give the parishioners time to depart. A surprise was waiting at the door—as a guard of honor, hundreds of well-wishers flanked the sidewalk all the way to the convent.

"God bless you, sisters!" rolled long the line.

How the church bells rang!

At three o'clock Monday morning the Columbans boarded the tender which would take them to the *Bremen* anchored far out in deep water. Friends and relatives went along on the two-hour trip to say goodbye. Emotions were strong, but the new missionaries made a special point of smiling.

As the lighted ship sailed, a German band played Irish melodies.

With dawn reaching the receding shores, Father Blowick began Mass at a makeshift altar in the ship's smoking room. Religious services for the rest of the trip would be conducted by six priests on their way to the missions.

When the *Bremen* reached Germany, the Columbans had several days to explore while waiting to board the *Coblenz*. Some were impressed with the spic-and-span of it all, and others felt that such tidiness would get on the nerves. One wrote in her diary: "We had a solid German tea—everything in Germany seems to be solid, even the flowers."

In the dining room of the *Coblenz,* Sister Agnes, the Australian, kept recalling a German expression, one she had heard as a child. She asked its meaning of Sister Mary Patrick, who as Lady Frances Moloney had become familiar with several languages while living abroad.

"You must not say that, it is very wicked."

The young sister felt embarrassed, especially when noticing how much the German waiter blushed.

In Holland the thing that most impressed Sister Agnes was the visit to the missionary college of the Belgian fathers.

"We were warned that the rector liked to dress up like Santa Claus, and so we nearly laughed when he appeared, not dressed up, but exactly like old Father Christmas with a long white beard. He is called the Father of Missionaries, and has been about forty years in China where he left his heart. The old father had just started his retreat, but said it was as good as a retreat to see missionaries on their way to China. He has some of the things worn by the martyred Bishop Hamer who was killed by the Boxers in 1900. Two priests of this missionary group were martyred only a fortnight ago at Pekin, so we are approaching holy ground—with wonderful possibilities, if only one were worthy of such a fate."

On to Genoa, Port Said, Colombo, and Singapore. On November 3 the diarist wrote: "About 8 p.m. we came to Hong Kong, and for the first time met the Chinese on their native shore." Probably not one of the sisters had any intimation of how large Hong Kong would eventually loom in the history of the Columbans.

Shanghai was startling. That immense city, stretching back from the waterfront lined with towering granite buildings, wide streets and palatial homes. Behind the grandeur sprawled a Chinese city with narrow tortuous streets where the senses were bombarded with seething commotion, the smell of bad sanitation, and the sound of all of those rising and falling inflections. A heady experience!

Suddenly, a Dublin accent fell on the ears, and there stood Sister Gabriel Plunkette, a Vincentian Sister of Charity. Just behind her was Father John O'Leary, regional director of the Columban mission in Hanyang. He had arrived from the interior to escort the new missionaries on the six-hundred-mile journey up the Yangtze.

In a Shanghai hospital, conducted by the French Sisters of Charity, the women from Ireland had a preview of the afflictions they would face through the years. One of them wrote: "We visited the dispensary which is in the convent grounds. The cases that we saw would break your heart. The men seemed to suffer mostly from sore legs and eyes. There was one case of elephantiasis; it is very common in this country.

"The worst sight of all was the poor leper woman who sat apart on a bench. Her face was very disfigured, and when we approached her she glided away as if afraid of us. The lepers do not live in the city, but they manage to pass the police by covering their hands, and so come to the dispensary."

On the crowded wharf at Shanghai the sisters learned that the river boat, *Luen Ho,* would need four days to take them up the Yangtze to Hankow, the port of Hanyang. The reverse, downstream took three days. Along the route were four large ports—Kiukiang, Nanking, Wuhu, and Anking.

While waiting to go aboard, the sisters were surrounded by the everlasting chanting that is inseparable from heavy work in China. Coolies could not function unless droning a singsong. Where there were no cranes or machinery, all lifting and carrying was done by coolies.

While on the wharf, Father O'Leary said that daily the new missionaries would be amused at the way things are done in China, but their way of doing things would be just as amusing to the Chinese. Only recently an elderly Chinese gentleman had said to him: "You take off your hats in company instead of keeping them on. You mount a horse on the left side instead of the right. You begin dinner with soup and end with dessert, and we do the opposite. You drink wine cold instead of hot. Your books all open at the wrong end and the lines on a page are horizontal instead of vertical."

The *Luen Ho* steamed out into the Yangtze, which was ten miles wide for about forty miles and then suddenly narrowed to five, and, in time, to one. Like all rivers in China it is both a joy and a sorrow, carrying supplies and passengers and providing irrigation, but also bringing floods that destroy much of the good that has been done.

In a poem, Father Galvin had written of the Yangtze, "with long voiced murmur." He might also have mentioned how yellow it is, for each year it carries down millions of tons of clay to discharge into the sea. "We longed for a glimpse of the sparkling Shannon," a sister wrote. Father O'Leary did not help matters when he pointed to the murky water and said, "That is what you will be drinking for the rest of your days."

The sisters were delighted with the show at every town where the loading and unloading process was much the same. A small boat crowded with passengers approached the steamer; somebody tossed down a rope which was grasped and made fast at the stern of the junk. Since the steamer had not completely stopped, merely slowed down, when the boat was made fast all of a sudden it inevitably went into a jig threatening to precipitate Chinese galore into the water.

When the ladder was let down from the lower deck of the steamer the bustle, confusion, and noise began. Some passengers were clambering up while others were sliding down. Some yelled "*man man-tee*" (take your time) and others shouted "*quai-quai tie*" (get down quickly). Bundles, baskets, and baggage flew overboard onto the junk, often landing atop passengers below. Beyond making a wry face and rubbing the hurt there was no protest.

During the first frenzy of excitement women passengers who wished to disembark stood by in absolute silence with a tense look on their faces. When all the men had gone, it was their turn to "shoot the rapids," a descent of great velocity thanks to two husky Chinese who stood at the head of the gangway.

The shipping company did not deal directly with Chinese passengers, but sold second- and third-class space to a Chinese middleman for a lump sum and allowed him to put as many passengers as he pleased on board. Hence passengers were crowded into a pitiable huddle, with only a few having planks for beds. All brought a blanket padded with cotton as bed clothing and curled themselves up near baggage piled at random on deck. Some even set up business, offering fruit, candy, and cigarettes. Others ran card games and thus drew dense crowds of spectators.

On the whole it was a cheerful crowd.

Once when the steamer lay at anchor a crowd of women beggars put out from the shore in little tubs not more than six feet in diameter. The women, using short paddles and square pieces of board, propelled their tipsy crafts, which threatened to turn turtle at any moment. No such accident occured and soon they were alongside, grasping the mooring cables and calling out for money. Coins began to fall into the tubs, but many missed the mark.

On the first day out, Father O'Leary unfolded a map to give the sisters a quick lesson in geography. "Our vicariate is the Hupeh Province," he said, "in the heart of China. The vicariate is 156 miles long, about the distance from Cork to Sligo. The width varies from fifty to ninety miles. The area is over a fourth of Ireland, larger than Leinster or Connaught. It contains over five million inhabitants, considerably more than Ireland."

Hupeh is a somewhat mountainous country, as Father O'Leary described it, with a small but fertile plain between the Han and Yangtse. The flat country is intersected by hundreds of rivers and streams, the largest, of course, is the Yangtze, the mightiest river in Asia. He said that its thirty-five-hundred-mile length is fourteen times as long as the Shannon.

At Hanyang, where the sisters would live, the Yangtze is a mile wide and deep enough to be navigable by ocean-going steamers. The next river of importance, the Han, is a tributary of the Yangtze.

Except for the Nile delta no other river in the world can match the Yangtze or Han for irrigation. With water so plentiful the land is expected to yield three crops in a good year.

The riverboat was moving toward the point where the Han joins the Yangtze. On the three wedges of land at that juncture are Wuchang, Hankow, and Hanyang, known as the Three Sisters. Together they form the metropolis of Wuhan with its three million people.

The nuns were at lunch when the boat docked at Hankow, on November 15, 1926. Between them and Ireland stretched two months and thirteen thousand miles of water. Through an open door they could see a welcoming committee composed of Sisters of Loretto, Christian Brothers, and Columban priests.

Amid the excitement everyone boarded launches for the short trip across river to Hanyang. Upon reaching shallow water they had to transfer into sampans for the final hundred yards to "the miserable flight of steps." Getting into the dancing sampans took some doing because the travelers still had the boat motion in them and so lacked balance.

The arrival was recorded in the diary: "Across the dirty water stretched a few rickety planks, which creaked beneath our weight and a watery grave seemed imminent. As we crossed we saw a woman bathing her child's feet in a dish of divers colored rags and muddy water. Another child led a blind musician by the hand."

Rickshaws were waiting with wheels sunk several inches into mud. Although Hanyang means "the sunny side of the Han," darkening skies threatened a downpour at any minute.

From the rickshaws the sisters could look up over the waterfront to see Hanyang sitting atop a hill. Like most Chinese cities it is surrounded by an enormous wall, twenty feet tall and so thick that four people can walk side by side along its top. On the river side is the enormous *Tung Men* (East Gate), a massive wooden structure studded with great bolts. An ancient patina covers all, as well it might for the wall was ancient the night that Christ was born.

Through the great gate, guarded by soldiers, the rickshaws rattled into the industrious ant hill, the perforated honeycomb, called Hanyang. They raced through narrow streets that had been made by people accustomed to walking in single file, each taking his turn in an endless line.

The rickshaw coolies darted back and forth miraculously avoiding collisions along the Shing Mah Road. Although only eight feet wide it was wider than most; such are called *ma loo* (horse street) because they are wide enough to accept a horse drawn vehicle.

Most of the route was so narrow that the nuns felt they could have helped themselves from the open store fronts on each side. Chickens and ducks scattered and pigs grunted. An old lady was using a live pig for a footstool while she did her mending.

The rickshaw men yelled, "Hi! Ho!," varying the crescendo depending upon how annoyed they were with the coolies carrying buckets of water, fish, or excrement. They vented their ire on a woman limping along on tiny, bound feet, on a child eating a stick of sugar cane, on an old man carrying a basket of greens, and on a deformed beggar thrusting out a straw basket for alms.

In spite of the commotion the nuns were noticed. Shopkeepers ran to the entrances of their stores and called to their neighbors to hurry to see the foreigners, for Chinese are fascinated by *wi-gwei-ren* (people from outside the kingdom). If the neighbors were too slow to see the first part of the procession, they stared at the last of it, or hurried ahead of the rickshaws and turned back to get a better look.

Finally, someone shouted, *"Sho Tah lai Liao!"* (Sister has come), and the lead rickshaw swung through the gate of the convent of the Sisters of Loretto. Catholic Chinese were crowded into the mission compound to stage a deafening welcome with firecrackers.

The sisters went directly to the chapel to sing a Te Deum.

·4·

A Quick Uprooting

The Sisters of Loretto were in China because of a letter that Father E. J. McCarthy had written from the Columban headquarters in Omaha to Father Galvin in Hanyang. Impatient with Father Blowick's delay in founding a congregation of nuns, Father McCarthy had recommended: "I would try very hard to get what I consider the best and most progressive Order in America and I feel fairly certain that we could succeed if we go about it in the proper way. It would be a very great privilege to get them for they are in demand all over the country. Every bishop and priest who wants to put up a decent academy and high school wants to get the Loretto Sisters."

Father Galvin kept this in mind, so that when, in May of 1922, he was on his way from Hanyang to New York to meet Father Blowick he stopped at the motherhouse of the Lorettines, near Bardstown, Kentucky. His talks with Mother M. Praxedes, the superior general, were so auspicious that two months later she sent a cablegram saying the order would finance the travel and support of six sisters. The six arrived in Hanyang on October 19, 1923.

Now, three years later, the Lorettines were serving refreshments to the newly arrived Columbans. On both sides there were so many questions to ask; so many stories to tell.

Right off the Columbans met the cat called Our Lady's Tumbler, because whenever the church door opened she ran in and made directly for Our Lady's altar, and there tumbled on the rug to her heart's content.

And Jeff, the dog, had just been rescued from a Chinese feast. Father Quinlan's houseboy had saved him from dissection; the black coat was divided like a map—legs painted red, ribs green, ears blue, and head white.

In recalling her first night in Hanyang one of the Sisters of Loretto told the new arrivals that she had awakened gripping something soft, about the size of a mouse. She held on, afraid to let go. When she tried to throw it out the window her bedspread flew past her. She had been holding a tassel on her spread.

Sister Agnes asked about rats; she recalled that Father Galvin had written: "They have been running over the Chinese for centuries. They are a fact of life. They do not expect you to try to do anything about them and if you aren't hostile to them, the chances are they won't be hostile to you."

The Lorettines said that they had considered extinguishing their kerosene lamps at night to save money, but could not bring themselves to do it. One of them confessed: "It's a comfort to have a light because the rats come in through the holes in the brick walls, armies of them. They race over the floors and onto the bed and pillows, if the room is dark."

In each bedroom a kerosene lamp and a crucifix stood on the table, beside the iron bedstead. The other furnishings were a chiffonier, washstand, and chair.

Now that the welcoming crowd was gone, the Columban sisters stepped outside for a better look at the Lorettines' convent. It was two Chinese houses with three rooms in one and four in the other; a kitchen adjoined one house and a church the other. A cement courtyard stretched in front of the buildings, all surrounded by a high white brick wall. The visitors found it "quaint."

An ancient attendant swung open the huge gate where Fathers Edmund Lane and Thomas Quinlan waited with a line of rickshaws to take the new arrivals to their convent. Just as the nuns were climbing aboard a torrent of rain broke and they were hurriedly covered with waterproof rickshaw rugs.

The convent, a mile outside the west gate, had been the home of a British engineer connected with the Hanyang Iron Works. It stood in a row of European-style houses on the reedy shore of the mystic lake of Bai-ah-tai, supposedly haunted by the spirit of a wandering minstrel. The lake, surrounded by golden *tung-tun* trees, was filled with the sound of ducks by day and of frogs by night.

Before the nuns could unpack, Father Lane, the Columban bursar, gave them some orientation. They would have to keep a few native servants, he said, to keep "face." Almost daily they would need to send a boy across the river for supplies. In a small book Father Lane made entries for the first day's order: bread, tinned butter, veal, onions and rice. Water would be supplied from the Yangtze, quite a distance to carry two buckets on a pole that fitted across the shoulders. It was to be stored in a large earthenware jar and treated with alum so that the mud would settle to the bottom. The priest's admonition, "always filter and boil it," was not needed, for the sisters had seen the Yangtze from the riverboat.

The nuns looked through the house to choose a room for a chapel. Immediately they made arrangements with Father O'Leary about vestments, candlesticks, and other things needed for Mass and Benediction. Father O'Leary promised to return the next morning to reserve the Blessed Sacrament. When asked what kind of Mass they would like they requested a votive Mass of Our Lady, saying they had decided to place the convent under the patronage of Our Lady of Good Counsel.

Just before departing, Father Lane introduced the sisters to a boy who would do various chores and to a woman who would sleep in the house, answer the door, and do odd jobs. With uneasiness the nuns faced Pedro and Malia, for they did not have a word of any language in common.

Fortunately, the Christian Brothers had a college next door to the convent. Whenever Pedro became too confused with what the sisters were saying, he could run to the school to seek help.

The brothers happened to be there because when Father Blowick returned to Ireland from China in early 1921, he had asked the superior of the Irish Christian Brothers to send some of his men to start a school. By November three brothers were in Hanyang and four others arrived a few months later. Now, five years later, they were conducting a school for two hundred teenage boys, fifty-six of whom were boarders who paid ninety dollars a year.

Large playing fields belonging to the brothers' college stretched in front of the sisters' compound. On the fields military troops drilled, for the civil war was at its height. A few months earlier the brothers had watched skirmishes that lasted several days at the very gate of the mission compound.

After their first night in Hanyang the sisters were surprised to see how soon the day gets under way in a Chinese city. In Ireland they were accustomed to towns that make a lethargic start at nine or ten o'clock, but here the streets were crowded by seven with all shops open and the river alive with junks.

The first Sunday was an uneasy time for the new arrivals. Accustomed as they were to quiet and rest on that day, they found it difficult to accept open shops with business in full course and buildings under construction alive with slaters, masons, bricklayers, and hod carriers.

Sunday afternoon, however, brought a lift in their spirits when they attended the Stations of the Cross recited by the students at the Christian Brothers' College. Especially pleasing were the Chinese prayer chants. How those plaintive melodies originated no one seemed to know; one of the brothers suggested that liturgical hymns taught by early missionaries had evolved into Oriental melodies.

Each Sunday afternoon, two boys selected as chanters passed from station to station accompanied by an altar boy carrying a crucifix. The first chanter announced the station and recited the meditation; the second read a short prayer, both intoning their parts in a loud voice similar to the tone used by the deacon at High Mass. The congregation responded in a plaintive chorus of two hundred voices, chanting the Our Father and the Hail Mary, alternating from the epistle and gospel sides.

The devotion took the greater part of an hour, closing with a litany, the rosary and Benediction. The sisters were told that Orientals are accustomed to give more time to public devotions than Occidental Christians. One of the brothers recalled that a Columban father had tried to shorten his Sunday service, which traditionally lasted two hours, but after three Sundays of the short version a delegation of parishioners came to the vestry to request a return to the longer liturgy.

During a tour of the school building the brothers said that their curriculum included the natural sciences, history, bookkeeping, typing, Chinese literature, and church doctrine. The program was planned to prepare students for matriculation in any university in China, the United States, or Europe. Chinese students are apt at mathematics, the teaching brothers observed; they have a knack for numbers. They also star when it comes to taking brush and ink to form those elegant characters of the Chinese language. Their ability with English composition was another matter.

The brothers offered to take the Columban sisters on a tour of the neighborhood. Upon leaving the mission compound they passed through a three-thousand-year-old pagan cemetery and were soon in a narrow winding street that emerged into an open square dominated by a massive Buddhist temple.

Inside the gate was a large pond, the home of sacred turtles well fed by visitors. Before the great statute of Buddha, lamps and incense burned. In a long hall stood statues of five hundred gods, a god for any one of many petitions.

This great change from the life the sisters had known in Ireland brought a dreamlike quality with it. The unreal feeling did not pass quickly. The women had to keep reminding themselves that this is real life and not a fantasy; this is where they were to work out their destiny.

Just as the Christian Brothers had taken over a school begun by the Columban fathers, so, too, the Lorettines had taken charge of one founded by the priests. In their embroidery school 131 young women were learning to make sets of liturgical vestments to be distributed by Benziger Brothers of New York, an arrangement made by Father Galvin on one of his trips to the United States.

When the Columban sisters visited the embroidery school they were, of course, greeted by firecrackers at the gate and found refreshments waiting inside. Eating native food prepared in the native way is often the first trial a missionary encounters. The Columbans were aware, as one wrote later, that "the good people will be insulted if one does not partake of everything present."

The nuns glanced toward Mother Finbarr who indicated that they make the sign of the cross, and Sister Mary Patrick suggested that they "eat in the name of the Lord." So they ate "brown cakes, dried fruits similar to dates, salted peanuts, rice candy, dark nougat, watermelon seeds, cakes that resemble noodles, tangerines, fruit which looks like tomatoes, and tea." As for the watermelon seeds one sister, in her eagerness to please, ate shell and all before the Chinese hosts showed her how to remove the shell.

At the Lorettines' grade school the Columbans found the children so enchanting that they wished they could begin teaching right away. They were delighted with the cry that went up whenever a teacher entered the school yard: *"Sho Tah lai liao! Sho Tah lai liao!"* (Sister has come! Sister has come!)

Immediately the children came running to *Sho Tah* with all their troubles, ranging from sore eyes to broken pencil points. They also asked help for ailing members of the family: "My mother has sore finger. . . . My brother cough. . . . My sister itch." Before long the *Sho Tah* would become acquainted with the whole family.

The children were so attractive that Sister Mary Patrick wondered how the Chinese ever developed the saying: "A teacher requires two stomachs, one to hold food and the other to hold anger."

They must have been something of a problem though, judging from a few sentences in one of the Lorettines' letters: "Sister presides in the refectory three times a day to see they do not beat one another with their chopsticks, demonstrate with their bowls, throw rice on the floor, or scream at the top of their voices. They are a lively, jolly crowd, good-natured and brimful of fun—always ready to enjoy a joke."

At the close of the school day all of the nuns accompanied the children to the front gate. As the pupils sang out, "Glood blye, sis-si-ter," quite a crowd gathered in the narrow street. Coolies and rickshaw men became tangled in the crowd and they too, stopped to stare at *Sho Tah*.

Inquisitiveness is an outstanding Chinese characteristic, the Columbans decided during those first days in Hanyang. It was not just staring, but also the interminable questioning: Where are you going? Where are you coming from? How old are you? What have you in that parcel? How much did you pay for it?

The Columbans were painfully aware that they could neither teach, nor answer questions, nor have any real influence until they had learned the language. How frustrating it was! For instance, when one of them wanted to get two chickens for dinner she attracted the cook's attention, raised two fingers and crowed. When she put a kettle of water on to boil, she told the cook to boil milk also, only to return to find the milk mixed into the water.

The woman who came daily to conduct language study had a theory that first you train the ear and then the tongue, and finally the eye. If the ear can hear meaning, speech will follow, and, in time, the eye will be ready to deal with reading and writing. It is the progression that a child passes through.

The sisters had a textbook in which sentences ranged from easy to difficult. The teacher read these aloud, repeating each a few times. After copying them down phonetically, the sisters repeated them until the teacher said they sounded correct, or nearly so. While learning to count to ten one of the Columbans observed, "Some of the numbers sound just like being seasick."

The sisters learned that all literate Chinese read and write the same language, but speech ranges widely. Perhaps half of the people understand Mandarin, the national tongue, but millions depend on dialects and languages too numerous to count. Such variety causes bewilderment; for instance, a Cantonese cannot understand his neighbor, a Fookenese, and neither of them can communicate with a native of Shanghai, except perhaps in a Pidgin Chinese.

Speaking the language is difficult enough, the nuns learned, but reading and writing it are even more so. Written Chinese has no alphabet with which to form words; rather than having twenty-six letters as in English, the Chinese have a different character for each word so that thousands of symbols must be memorized. While the written language had the advantage of being the same all over, only about one in every two hundred Chinese could read and write.

The Columbans found that they picked up language best by being in the midst of where it was spoken. As Sister Theophane observed, "When you are listening to Chinese all day long it gets into the ear and suddenly it comes to you."

The Lorettines, sure of themselves, enjoyed showing the new arrivals around so that they might become saturated with the language. In the past three years the sisters from Kentucky had become known in Hanyang, Hankow, and Wuchang as "the Sisters with white collars."

On one such brief excursion the Columbans found Hanyang and Hankow to be cities of remarkable contrasts. In Hanyang there were no railroad stations, trams, motorcars, electric lights, or steam heat.

Although Hanyang was exceedingly shabby, Hankow, just across the river, had the general appearance of order and neatness, with its foreign quarters, spacious thoroughfares, and well-built houses. This order was mostly imposed by Sikh policemen from India, employed by foreigners.

They were handsome, those Sikhs, tall and well-built. No scissors touched their hair done up in bright turbans, usually red, causing the Chinese to call them *hoong to'ou* (red head).

No love was lost between foreigner and native, especially not between the Indian policeman and the Chinese common people, most of whom regarded lawmen with awe and fear. The Sikhs spoke the language well and had a wonderful assortment of choice phrases to use when any rickshaw man contributed more than his share to the confusion.

The six Columban sisters were especially delighted to be taken to a nearby town on fair day. In each place they found the scene and the action much the same.

For miles around country people came with their produce. Wheelbarrows were soon tangled with carts, and carts with mules, donkeys, and peddlers. All traffic was hoplessly confused, and yet the Chinese seemed uncommonly patient for they had been schooled in the manners of Confucius, manners still practiced in the country but now largely ignored in the cities.

Things to be sold were spread out on the ground, displayed on boxes, and arranged on the steps of a disused temple. Nobody scattered things in a haphazard way, but all was arranged with a feeling of good order. Venders displayed crockery to show niceties of shape and glaze, aligned peanuts in rows of compact little heaps, and hung tobacco leaves in neatly tied bundles. They bound raw cotton into white packages and arranged long narrow strips of spun cotton into flower-like patterns.

Such a variety of things! Iron shoes for the donkey and satin shoes for village girls; books, paper, brushes, and inks for writing; soaps, candles, toys, and looking glasses.

Stall after stall displayed grapes, yellow corn, sweet potatoes, turnips, carrots, and eggs. Chickens squawked inside their crates and pigs with feet tied together squealed.

The aroma from the kitchen enticed a crowd, for the Chinese have long worshipped Tsao Wong Yeh, the god of the kitchen. One Columban wooed by the aroma wrote home: "Their goods look very appetizing—pastries in great variety, cakes hot and cold, baked, steamed, and fried, plum cakes and seed cakes. And there are hot stews and cold pickles. The children, wearing strings of large red hawthorne berries around their necks, crowd around the candy man and munch loads of crab apples."

Inns and hotels did brisk trade. Attendants kept busy refilling kettles of boiling water for tea and replenishing bowls with rice and millet. Their patrons—mule drivers, bearers, and countrymen—having traveled all night crowded the long narrow benches at hostel doors.

Jugglers, acrobats, and fortune-tellers competed for attention with players who, in an open theater, enacted once again the folk dramas of China. An old storyteller sitting in an impressive chair broke off in the middle of an exciting event with all of the cunning of a serial writer, and only after collecting from his audience, resumed the narrative.

Money changers sat throughout the market place behind bowls of copper coins and mounds of silver dollars, for farmers preferred hard currency. Everyone was suspicious of paper money no matter how well it was decorated and endorsed by a banker's signature.

And well they might be suspicious. Warlords issued their own money as fast as the presses could run, and the Nationalist government also covered expenses by keeping the printers working all night. The time would come when the face value of bank notes would fall below the cost of printing them.

Besides listening to Chinese in the normal flow of life the sisters continued to fill the air with sounds of *chu*s and *deu*s and *su*s, hoping to get a few *ding-how*s (excellent) from their teacher. They knew what Sister Theophane had said about the language suddenly coming to you was true, but the long awkwardness was frustrating.

They felt especially inept just before Christmas when two Sisters of Loretto were selected to go to Hwan-Ja-Shan to take care of the victims of famine. There was little satisfaction in merely going to the landing to watch the two nuns climb aboard a little steamboat on which every cubic foot was occupied. When Father Jeremiah Pigott suggested that the two climb onto the roof of the engine house, they inched their way through the crowd and one of the sisters stepped on the cloth slippers that gave scant protection to a Chinese man's toes. He exclaimed, sotto voce: "My, those foreign women have big feet!"

One of the Lorettines wrote back to Hanyang: "The soldiers stopped us several times but did not bother us. One of them had a consignment of a hundred bugles with which they will torture sleeping Tsai-Tien for months to come."

After riding eight miles by pony from the landing to Hwan-Ja-Shan, the two nuns were put to work feeding three hundred refugees twice a day. They measured rice and doled out medicines. "A regular mixture of hospital, orphanage, school, and convent rolled into one," one of them wrote.

The letter concluded: "All of us had a happy Christmas, thank God—Christmas dinner of water buffalo for our three hundred charges. My, how they enjoyed it! Sister and I shared the buffalo with them—tough enough, but still not bad."

Strangely enough the two sisters on the remote mission at Hwan-Ja-Shan attended Midnight Mass, something that those in Hanyang were unable to do. The city was under martial law and activities of all kinds had to cease at nightfall.

At Christmas in Hanyang the Columbans, for the first time, experienced anti-Christian feeling. Communist students pasted posters of hate on convent walls and stood at the church door handing out anti-Christian leaflets to parishioners.

A charwoman hurried to the convent in tears to tell of wicked things being said about missionaries. "Don't mind what we do tomorrow," she said. "We may be told to do things, but our attitude has not changed."

In the normal course of events Chinese still treated missionaries with deference. When the sisters used the traditional greeting, "Did you eat your rice today?" the answer was, "Yes, I am sorry you could not join me." Upon parting the Chinese would say, "Go slowly, we love your company."

Shortly after Christmas Hanyang began preparations for the Chinese lunar year, a movable feast which begins some time between January 21 and February 19, and is celebrated through the following twenty-eight days.

The Columbans were thrilled when first they heard the cry, *Go Nien!* (Happy New Year). The words were on the lips of thirty thousand inhabitants of Hanyang jostling each other in the narrow streets. The air vibrated with expectation. Shoppers bought chunks of beef, pork, and chicken galore. They found attractive wild ducks and geese from the broad marshes, sleek pheasants from the woods, and green vegetables from trim little plots. Lake and river also provided an abundance.

Shops featured parcels of confectionary brilliant in color and bottles of rice wine with alluring labels. Little red scrolls and streamers proclaiming "joy" hung on wall and window.

By time-honored custom all bills were paid at New Year's. Anyone not paying could say by way of excuse that he avoided troubling the merchant with bookkeeping at this festive time.

Members of families from near and far merged into a unit which showed that the ancient patriarchal instinct still prevailed. This is what held together China's millions despite war and revolution.

On New Year's Eve family doors were bolted and barred, windows sealed, and hearth swept. Wood, brass, reed, and wind instruments proclaimed the advent of the day. No one retired to rest.

On the morning of New Year's Day everyone put on the best of silks and gathered for the feast. The streets were deserted, not even a stray dog appeared. The sudden appearance of a human being would be an evil omen. All day long festivities went on behind closed doors, nothing riotous, just the joys of a sweet and happy reunion.

On the following morning, doors and windows burst open and streets were crowded with beautifully gowned people. Everyone was going to and fro visiting friends, exchanging gifts, and bearing messages of joy and goodwill. With smoking incense and dainty dishes almost everyone worshipped the shades of ancestors. The rich distributed alms among the poor.

On the next day, many directed their worship toward the more important deities in the temples. The elderly offered clouds of incense to the gods of health, and young women begged for the gift of many children. Crafty fortune-tellers predicted a happy future for their patrons.

Actors presented plays on sloping hillsides. Acrobats delighted. Conjurors astonished.

The dead, sleeping among the rice and corn fields that they had cultivated, were not forgotten. Relatives came to their graves to bow with deep deference and burn ceremonial paper money. Incense glowed in little local shrines. Beneath all of the joy, the Columbans felt, there was an unrecognized hunger for an Unknown God.

Slowly and with hesitation life began to return to normal. Shops opened but little was sold because the "hands" had gone to their homes, and almost all had found an excuse to prolong the stay.

The major spell of *Go Nien* lasts for weeks. The nuns noticed that pupils tended to prolong revelry. Winds at that time of year are especially right for flying kites, and so small boys filled the sky with their handiwork.

As the moon grew to a full, pure splendor unknown in the West, children bought paper lanterns shaped like the head of a dragon. These, with lighted candles inside, they carried in procession through streets and country lanes. Amidst scraps of songs there was much laughter until some child's lantern went up in a sudden flame and then lamentation filled the night.

A festive mood prevailed until the sixteenth day of the moon when children reluctantly searched out their discarded books and returned to school, with hearts filled with regret. And adults, too, from the Great Wall to Yunnan Province settled down to the drabness of daily chores.

The Chinese New Year celebration was hardly past when Saint Patrick's Day arrived. That meant nothing to the Chinese but it did to the sisters from Ireland. Several days before the feast, a shamrock arrived from Cahiracon.

"Our grateful thoughts flew home to the packers," one of the nuns wrote. "The moss was as fresh and wet as when growing on the bog, but the sharmrock seemed to have died before it was drowned. We supplemented it with some Chinese trefoil of similar shape."

The celebration was cut short by a serious alarm of fire. A block from the convent a grain shop was set ablaze by soldiers. The buildings seemed doomed as hot charcoal rained into the mission compound.

"We went to church and prayed for help. Saint Patrick was reminded of his skill in putting out the pagan flame at Tara! Nothing happened to us, thank God."

Anti-Christian feeling intensified in the spring of 1927. Two years earlier the Anti-Christian Union had demanded that the minister of education prohibit the teaching of Christianity in mission schools. The minister replied that this was impossible because at the establishment of the republic, thirteen years earlier, religious freedom had been proclaimed, and besides such freedom was included in treaties that China had with foreign powers.

By the spring of 1927, an organization called Young China, with a membership of eight million students, was fighting Christianity as a foreign influence. The union had a policy of supporting students who abandoned Christian schools and of showing special favor to those coming to them from Christian missions.

Some of the radicals threatened to take over the embroidery school because the nuns would not turn it over to them. The girls in the school held a meeting to decide that if they were beaten they would bear it, but if the nuns or priests were harmed they would attack the attackers even though it meant instant death.

The girls recalled how Fathers Galvin and Pigott had risked their own lives to make sure that the students at the school were safe when the Cantonese army had stormed Hanyang the previous fall. While mission buildings were being riddled with bullets, the two Columbans came out into the crossfire and hurried along the city wall to the school.

They also recalled that in the previous fall, during the forty-day siege of Wuchang, just across the river, Brother O'Donoghue had helped care for four thousand refugees, rationing thirty bags of rice to hold off starvation as much as possible. Even so the brother had written, "Within the city there is no burial ground and the supply of coffins has been long exhausted. Along the street, corpses lie around any old place."

And now, in the spring of 1927, a mob of fanatics appeared daily at the Christian Brothers' College, next door to the Columban convent. The schoolyard was filled with grimacing, passionate faces, each framing a gaping mouth.

The brothers felt unrest inside the school, too, and before long defiance spread to the domestic staff. At this point the superior made what appeared to be a sudden decision to withdraw his community. All plans were kept so secret that the brothers were nearly gone before anyone knew it.

Their departure left the Columban sisters feeling isolated. Father

O'Leary decided that they should no longer remain where they were, not even for another night. He sent Father William Walsh to help move them with speed and secrecy.

The nuns hurriedly dismantled beds, packed crockery, and tied clothes into bundles. A table turned upside down formed a carriage for kitchen utensils. Several coolies hung things from the end of poles and went trotting off through the gate into the city.

It was a hurried procession that arrived at the convent of the Sisters of Loretto. Fortunately, the Lorettines were completing a new convent and so moved to it the same day that the Columbans occupied their old one.

Life was still uneasy. Soldiers felt free to come and go in the mission compound. Several threatened to take over the church, saying it would be a pleasant place to sleep. The organ especially attracted them and they spent hours making noise on it.

During Lent the Columbans decided to make a retreat and Father William Devine agreed to conduct it. Although he was as new to China as the nuns, he was not new to the priesthood. Before joining the Columban fathers he had served as a chaplain in the British Army during the First World War.

So that the sisters might make their retreat with complete attention, Mother Finbarr volunteered to perform all housekeeping chores. When they protested their superior general explained that she would be making her retreat upon returning to Ireland later in the year, just before her final profession.

Before the retreat was well begun the quiet was disturbed by soldiers firing indiscriminately in all parts of town. Anxiety increased with the passing days of Lent. Soon it was time to whisper once more the old Irish prayer: "May God stand between us and harm."

Father O'Leary used such words as "extortion," "cliques," and "chaos" when describing the situation. Was he making too much of it, the sisters wondered, or was his awareness of history better than theirs? He was very aware, and made sure that they were too, that the first Irish martyr in China was a Sister of Charity of St. Vincent de Paul, Louise O'Sullivan. She and nine other sisters were murdered in the Tai-ping rebellion of 1870.

Sister Louise, while nursing the Chinese in Shanghai and Peking, could not overcome her repugnance to their customs and manners. She said as much in a letter to the superior general of the order, and when authorized to return home set out to visit a sister community on the way in Tientsin. Upon finding too few nuns and too many patients at the hospital, she volunteered to stay even though her antipathy for the Chinese character remained.

The sisters in Tientsin were regarded with suspicion by Chinese fanatics who named them "white devils." They were charged with stealing children, whose eyes and hearts were used in the concoction of medicines which worked wonders. This charge had such an inflammatory effect that when the sisters visited the sick of the city they were openly insulted. They ceased their visits and stayed in the convent hoping the storm would blow over.

The fanatics, however, were out for blood and determined to exterminate the "child stealers." On June 19 and 20 havoc in the city was of such violence that the missionaries knew they were in for trouble. On the twenty-first the mob attacked the mission station of the Lazarist fathers, put the priests to death, and burned the buildings. The sisters, seeing the flames from their convent, prepared for what they felt was inevitable.

During a hot June day they spent hours in anxious suspense. Toward evening there was a lull but they knew that the storm would soon break with redoubled fury. After the usual period of spiritual reading the nuns assembled in the chapel and brought the children with them.

Suddenly the doors burst open and a mob came in search of the bodies of the "murdered" children.

The superior, Sister Marquette, offered herself, but asked mercy for the children. The answer was a blow from the assassin's saber, and she fell dead before the altar.

Each sister shared her fate. Several had their eyes and hearts torn out, and two were roasted over a fire. Sister Louise made an escape through the side door of the chapel. In the kitchen she met one of the mob who seized a pot of boiling water and scalded her with it. She ran back to the chapel and was stabbed to death at the altar.

The recollection of such events haunted Father O'Leary. He was not alone in his concern. The American consul in Hankow insisted that Sister Mary Jane, the superior of the Sisters of Loretto, come to the consulate. He urged that she take the Americans to Shanghai immediately.

She responded that when the feeling was running high against foreigners in Hanyang, in 1925, the sisters had been advised to cross the river to Hankow where they would have the protection of foreign soldiers and gunboats. They had refused, preferring to remain in their convent surrounded by people whose goodwill they had won.

Since the American consul did not force the issue now, Sister Mary Jane took for granted that he was giving his reluctant consent for the sisters to stay where they were.

On April 5, however, the American consul sent for Father Thomas Quinlan. While crossing the river from Hanyang to Hankow, the missionary saw gunboats on the Yangtze, symbols of the uneasiness that foreign governments felt in China.

The American began by saying, "A thousand marines landed in China a month ago to protect property in the civil war, and yet the Nationalists looted the U.S. and British consulates only last week. It is about a mile from the landing stage in Hanyang to the sisters' convent. There are at least ten soldiers' barracks along the route.

"To land a party of marines might lead to bloodshed. And yet, if you don't send the American nuns from Hanyang immediately, I'll send in marines to bring them out!"

Confronted with such an ultimatum, Father Quinlan said that all of the sisters, Lorettines and Columbans, would leave at once for Shanghai. From the consulate he went directly to the two convents and announced that all should be ready to depart by noon the following day.

On the morning of departure, the teacher arrived as usual for the Chinese lesson. To keep the flight a secret, Sister Agnes sat with patience through the lesson and so avoided starting rumors.

"It was a rush to be ready in time," said Sister Theophane. "Many little things were left undone. There was no time to wash up or clear away the remains of the meal which we had so little heart to eat. Father O'Leary was anxious to get us off. We did not know of the threatening strike among the coolies, how pressure was put on the rickshaw men to refuse to carry us."

When the nuns came out of the convent, each carrying one small bag, the children rushed upon them. "Where are you going, Sisters?" "We want to go with you." "Will you soon come back?"

During the rickshaw ride through the streets of Hanyang, the nuns were once more impressed with the teeming population. One of them wrote: "It was just the same as the day we came and now we are going away."

At the landing steps a crowd gathered and urged the boatmen to refuse to carry the foreigners across the river. Father O'Leary became angry, but he respected the Chinese saying, "If you repress a moment's anger you will avoid the sorrow of a hundred days." So he used some Irish blarney and the tenseness eased.

Rather than have the Lorettines ride through Hanyang in rickshaws, Father O'Leary marched them round the back of the city and down to Suwan compound on to the East Gate where he had no difficulty in finding boats to take them across the river.

Instead of landing at Hankow, the usual plan, all sisters were taken directly to the S.S. *Kungwo,* the largest of the riverboats. On board were seventy Protestant missionaries and three Jesuits. Another refugee boat leaving at the same time carried fourteen Jesuits.

During the trip downriver to Shanghai a Columban sister wrote: "The Jesuits have suffered severely. Fifty-four of them have had to leave their missions—everything seized.

"One of the three on board has a broken leg. Coming down from a distant part on horseback, a wooden bridge gave way under him, plunging horse and rider into the water.

"A Spanish lay brother, who operated a dispensary, traveled five days to reach the crippled Jesuit. By that time all kinds of Chinese remedies had been applied and gangrene threatened. The brother managed to set the leg and disinfect the wound.

"While making their way down the Han in a sampan, bandits attacked their boat and took every penny. The priest and brother reached Hanyang with only the clothes they wore.

"Of the fifty-four Jesuits all have come away except one who was too far to be reached. All their houses and property have been seized. Two Jesuit fathers have been killed in Nanking. May God protect our priests who are remaining with their flocks in Hanyang."

·5·

An Uneasy Season

While the sisters were taking refuge in Shanghai, at Easter of 1927, the Columban priests in remote areas were living in danger. Monsignor Galvin sent out letters, on April 20, to each Columban in his vicariate saying that with the exception of one priest in each parish, the others were to come at once to Hanyang.

About the time the letters were delivered, bandits looted Father Patrick O'Connell's presbytery; soldiers occupied Father Jeremiah Pigott's premises, and fanatical members of the Workers' Union bludgeoned Father Ulick Burke.

In describing the latter incident, Monsignor Galvin wrote that just as the workers were leaving the church, they were confronted by an opposing gang from the Peasants' Union: "One of the workers ran into the church pursued by the peasants. They wounded him in the church, then dragged him out into the presbytery yard, and killed him before Father Ulick's eyes. Seven other workers had taken refuge in the basement of the presbytery, but the peasants found them, too, dragged them up and killed them in Father Ulick's presence. He says that, in all, fifty men and three women belonging to the Workers' Union were killed in and around the place."

Such horror stories were becoming usual throughout the provinces. In its vast stretches of history, China had never been in greater disarray.

When the Columban sisters took refuge in a Chinese hospital in Shanghai, run by the Franciscan Missionaries of Mary, they saw enough of the great city to find it a contrast with the walled cities of the interior where gates were closed at nightfall. Here they observed reflections of western culture—golf courses, universities, motorcars, trams, race tracks, and publishing houses.

The difference, though, was mainly superficial, for even in the sophisticated international seaport the ancient social fabric remained intact: many objects were still produced by craftsmen, family relationships were firm, and religious practices continued, at least for the time.

Side by side with this foreign city of Americans, English, French, Russians, and Portuguese, almost dovetailing into it, was the Chinese city. In passing from a European street into a Chinese street the nuns felt they were stepping into another world. Blind musicians playing flutes or elongated string instruments moved slowly along the passages. The most mournful cry in the world, "*Low ui ba wo chen*" (Give me a little money) came from every side. Children, turned old by poverty at seven, huddled almost naked in the cold rain, making the sounds of beggars.

Anyone not begging was trying to sell something. The traveling restaurateur announced his approach by shaking a small wooden box with dry peas inside. A yoke across his shoulders bore a large box at each end—in one box was a kettle of rice and vegetables with a wood fire beneath it, and in the other were chopsticks, bottles of sauce, and a tub for washing dishes.

Itinerate tradesmen crowded the streets. When they arose in the morning they attached their wares to each end of a bamboo stick and took off for the most desirable locations. A Columban observed that such tradesmen seemed always smiling whether business was good or not. With great good will they bargained over each sale, never refusing a reasonable offer. Perhaps they were so high-spirited because they had no bills for gas, rent, or insurance.

The Columbans and the Lorettines expressed delight in how well the Chinese hospital was being administered. This had not always been the case, said the Franciscan Missionaries of Mary.

Lack of education made it difficult for the orderlies to grasp the scientific basis of modern nursing, and so many things went wrong. In their anxiety to please patients they often failed to enforce medical instructions: Why should not a sick man get out of bed, if he wished? Why should he not remove the bandage and scratch the wound, if he felt an itch? Why should not the typhoid patient eat, if she feels hungry?

The sisters soon saw that the solution was to train Chinese girls as nurses. By 1927 many hospitals were well staffed with Chinese nurses, but there were still fewer than three hundred foreign nurses in the country.

Shanghai hospitals were burdened with soldiers and filled with war talk. It was not just a civil war with the northern army of Peking fighting the southern army of Canton; the complications were much more chaotic.

Warlords, many of them vicious brigands, had their own armies. To finance campaigns they taxed and mistreated peasants beyond endurance. In Amoy, for example, a warlord collected seventy-one different taxes, seven levied on swine alone: a standard pig tax, a slaughter tax, a swine-raising tax, a tax on pig inspection, a surtax on breeding, a tax on cooked pork, and a tax on the sale of pork.

And then there were the exhorbitant tolls on cargo moving across canal or river. Each toll was set at the whim of greedy officials at each point along the route; this was especially true of tolls levied on a shipment of silk. The result was that foreign merchants could go into the interior, bribe petty officials, buy silk at a minimal price from the farmers, ship it to Shanghai, and sell it for ten times as much as paid.

The Chinese had so much "squeeze" applied to them that they were ready to join anything. The Workers' Union, the Peasants' Union, and an assortment of radical student groups thrived. The Reds who had been with the army of the south were now forming guerrilla bands of their own.

Add to all of this the free-lance bandits. They fought for no cause excepting their own, and were often seeking trouble for its own sake. They held individuals for ransom and would loot a city unless paid to leave it alone.

As an old man said, "When an army has passed, nothing grows but brambles."

Nature conspired to increase the confusion. Floods, droughts, and plagues of insects brought starvation to the provinces of Shantung, Yunnan, Szechuan, and Hupeh. Relief boats, sent by charitable organizations, were looted by bandits who themselves were starving. Rice sold at eight times the normal price and in many places could not be had at all, for if it was put on sale in the shops, starving soldiers seized it and killed any shopkeeper who protested.

All such tribulations were much discussed in the hospital with its own rounds of hurt, fear, and death. While the Columbans, with their skills in nursing, were of great help to the Franciscan sisters, they still kept working at language studies, and tried to be in touch with the Chinese life that throbbed all around them.

Although they were being useful, they continued to feel uneasy that they had been forced to leave Hanyang. One of them wrote home: "The priests console us for being down here by telling us that everyone was surprised that we stayed in Hanyang so long."

In Shanghai the sisters experienced the Feast of Ancestors, on the first day of the Seventh Moon, which usually falls in July and marks the beginning of the summer heat. On this day, the Chinese say, the gates of Hades open and all souls get a two-week holiday. They rush to their old haunts, often in a vindictive mood, and so must be appeased.

For appeasement a large table is set before the altar covered with vegetables, rice, fish, clam chowder, roast pig, beef, mutton, chicken, ham, nuts, birds' nest pie, and the stomachs of Cantonese trout made into jelly and served with turtle sauce. Chopsticks are kept within easy reach and even a pipe with a supply of the poppy is at hand.

The family retires, is very quiet, and in spite of the heat keeps under covers so as not to be seen by visiting spirits. In the morning the family moves on tiptoe to form a semicircle around the altar of ancestors feeling that the ghosts enjoyed the feast since nothing dreadful happened in the night.

A nun who had been stationed at the hospital for years told the visitors: "Paper boxes containing paper clothing are prepared for the ghosts and burned. Even paper coolies are dispatched in the same way. Some even send them houses made of paper and bamboo. If the ghost was a soldier, paper rifles are sent; if a sailor, a paper ship."

That each ancestor might get the gifts intended, deeds are drawn and signed and stamped with thumb, or palm of right hand, or sole of left foot. These deeds which might list lakes, or a river, or even trout to stock them, are thrown into a fire, to fly to Hades via smoke.

Since most of the ceremonies for the Feast of Ancestors took place within the home, the sisters witnessed only the appeasement of the water gods. The Chinese spent days making boats of sheets of paper pressed into the shape of a dish with a cotton ball soaked in vegetable oil atop each. On certain nights of the festival thousands floated on rivers and lakes, guiding the spirits to safe harbor. All of those lights blinking in the darkness reminded the nuns of fireflies, and of childhood back home.

It was during the Feast of Ancestors that Mother Finbarr was recalled to Ireland. On the mother general's last day in China, the diarist wrote in Singapore: "Hearts were heavy but everyone was too fully occupied to have much time for thinking long. Mrs. O'Brien motored Mother Theophane and Sisters Mary Lelia and Mary Patrick to the Jesuit workshop at Siccawai to buy some wee presents for Mother General to take to Cahiracon. It was difficult to find anything quite suitable. At length a very plain wooden stationery case was selected for Mother Mary Alphonsus—so plain that it could not possibly conflict with her high standard of Holy Poverty."

On the next day, July 2, the diarist noted: "Mother General broke down as she tried to say a few last words to the community. A lonely figure she looked, still, white, and thin from her recent illness."

Years later Sister Theophane recalled, "She left us lonely and in a state of great uncertainty about the future."

The sisters talked of Cahirocon and sent frequent letters. One of them wrote: "Shanghai is gradually losing its warlike appearance. The barbed wire entanglements have gone rusty, and the sandbags at the crossings, unable to contain themselves any longer, have begun to spill their insides into the street.

"We found the heat trying at first and the mosquitos had a few choice meals off us until we provided ourselves with nets. Things are much better now, rain has been falling copiously—a welcome change, although it means that walking through the city streets is like wading through soup.

"China is a great place in spite of its drawbacks. I am quite in love with it and my heart fills with gratitude when I think that I am really here at last."

Not long after Mother Finbarr's departure for Ireland the sisters in Shanghai had their spirits lifted by good news from Hanyang. On July 14, 1927, Father Michael O'Dwyer, superior general, sent a cablegram from Ireland to China saying that Edward Galvin was being raised to the rank of bishop.

When Father John O'Leary delivered the message to Monsignor Galvin he was about to say congratulations, but saw the monsignor's face and kept quiet. The trappings of bishop—mitre, cross, and crosier—meant little to the man from Cork who later said, "I was never meant for such things, but the one thing I am rather anxious about is the motto, and what I want is *Fiat voluntas tua* (Thy will be done). I hope that might constantly remind us here in China that we are here not to convert China but to do God's will, and we don't know twenty-four hours ahead what that is."

This honor in 1927 really had its root back in 1921 when, on November 21, Father Blowick had cabled from Rome to tell Galvin that the Columbans would now be in charge of a vast territory, a vicariate, that included not only Hanyang but also Mienyang, Tienmen, Anlu, Chunghsiang, Kingshan, and a part of Hanchwan. (It was at this time that Rome suggested that the priests change the name of their community from the Chinese Mission Society to Saint Columban's Foreign Mission Society.)

Because of this extension of territory, Father Galvin was appointed prefect apostolic of Hanyang, on October 29, 1924, and given the title of monsignor. He disliked the world of pomp, ceremony, and protocol and wrote to Father O'Dwyer: "The appointment came to me not as a blessing but as a burden and a cross. I tried to escape it and failed. I cannot remember any time in my life when I felt more miserable than I do at the present moment."

In mid-August the sisters received their greatest emotional jolt so far. Word came that Father John O'Leary had died, August 13, 1927, at age thirty-five. The intelligent young priest, so alive with interests and information, had been their mentor on the trip up river to Hanyang and had been the one to hurry them out of town when the mood darkened.

Before suffering the fatal sun stroke at the mission station of Sung

Ho, he had written: "It was a very hot day—so hot that I threw myself on a chair and gasped for breath. I had just returned from a long journey, a visit to the pastor over in the adjacent district. The air was full of the noisy buzzing of cicadae, and all about was the hot and sleepy lethargy of an August day."

The sisters would miss him, as would the editors of the *Far East* magazines published in the United States, Ireland, and Australia. Father O'Leary, a natural-born journalist, was faithful in sending them information. He wrote in a clear, picturable way, as instanced by his final article describing the flood in Sung Ho, less than a month before his death.

"Concrete pillars were literally torn up by the roots, and three-foot steel beams that span the arches of the bridges were lifted and carried fifty yards by the flood.

"When the waters were rising, men were sent out to beat gongs and warn the people. They knew the flood was coming, but many refused to move. They said it was the Dragon on the rampage: he would get them anyway. So there were some four or five hundred drowned. All the low-lying lands were flooded. More than half the crops were ruined.

"I have seen hundreds of houses demolished by the flood. Men found their chairs and tables in their cornfield, and they fished cups and saucers out of the duck pond. I saw boats in the middle of the rice fields and a plough or two in the river-bed. It is no wonder that the Chinese fear the River Dragon and that they charge him with the damage.

"It is very hot, even here. For the past few days the thermometer has stood round eighty-five, but it felt worse than that owing to the damp. The Chinese feel the heat as much as we do."

In this summer of 1927 the sisters were able to say that they had experienced the extremes of a full-cycle of weather. January, February, and March had been bitter: eggs froze and ice had to be broken in the water bucket before one could bathe. In June, July, and August a terrible humidity weighed down on the cities, tar bubbled in the streets and not a leaf stirred.

Sister Mary Moroney, in retirement, recalled the weather of China: "The cold was preferable to the heat. In cold you could be active; you could do your work. In heat all of the energy was drained from you. The thirst was terrible. It was dangerous to drink anything cold; it could give cramps. Hot Chinese tea was best in the heat."

When hot weather arrived it found the sisters still in the heavy black habits designed for the chill of Ireland. Mother Finbarr said that without delay they must have new habits, white and light.

Mainly because of the debilitating effect of the weather, the Columbans were plagued with illnesses. Mother Theophane and Sister Philomena ran high temperatures. The doctors diagnosed their illness as "Shanghai fever."

Sister Agnes was confined to Saint Mary's Hospital for five months with typhoid. A Columban wrote of her condition: "One day the Sisters were allowed into the sick room for a moment. She lay in a stupor, the lips parted and white. The Sisters, grief stricken, saw death written all over her."

When word reached Shanghai that November 6, 1927, had been set as the date for Monsignor Galvin's ordination as bishop, the Lorettines and the Columbans applied immediately for permission to return to Hanyang for the occasion. The American consulate granted the request with such dispatch that the Sisters of Loretto were back in time to decorate the church for the ceremony. British authorities were so dilatory that the Columbans were still in Shanghai and so missed the occasion when the Most Reverend Celso Constantini, papal delegate, performed the ritual, assisted by the bishops of Hankow and of Puchi. For the Chinese, Edward Galvin was no longer *Shen Fu* (priest) but now *Gao Ju Chao* (bishop).

A few days after the ceremony the British consulate finally cut the red tape and the Columbans made hurried preparations for a return journey up the Yangtze.

All afternoon on the last day of the four-day trip the ship passed Ho Chen's troops on the march to Hankow. One of the sisters wrote: "Marching in single file they seemed never ending, and one wondered how there could be another army—never mind five more—even in a country of four hundred millions. As they stepped along the bank of the river you could see them quite plainly and almost distinguish the umbrellas and teapots! You might say it was rather a thrilling experience watching an army on its way to battle—only, as usual, there was no battle.

"When we arrived in Hankow we heard that the army which had been in occupation there had decamped, leaving a free walk-in to the newcomers. If only they had a few battles, the thing might come to an end sometime. The soldiers don't seem to mind to what side they belong and change about every day according as it suits them."

Since the ship docked late, the nuns remained on board overnight. Shortly after dawn Fathers Thomas Quinlan and Peter Fallon arrived to take them across the river by launch. By coincidence they climbed the ancient steps to enter Hanyang on November 15, the Feast of Saint Gertrude, the day they had entered the city a year earlier. The place seemed dirtier and the smells more plentiful than when they had left seven months earlier.

"One wondered how anything could be done to uplift people in such surroundings," a sister wrote. "The one who first entered Hanyang and thought it was possible must have possessed the faith that moves mountains."

On the rickshaw ride through the streets the nuns met with no animosity. For the most part the people merely stared with indifference.

"As we neared our own little place where the people knew us we got a warm welcome and as soon as we alighted from the old rickety rickshaws the little ones gathered round us, seized all our available hands and escorted us into the compound. Then the elder ones gathered round and it was nothing but, "*Dho shay Tien-Dieu, shodah lie liao*" (Thank God, the sisters have returned).

To say thanks for a safe return the nuns went directly to the old church and there found a great transformation. The place had been renovated for the ceremony of Ned Galvin's ordination as bishop. The old blue wooden pillars now encased in cement pretended to be stone. Over the high altar a statue of Christ stood where once had been a picture. Stained glass windows flanked the sanctuary and tiny ones glistened in the domes that had risen out of the roof.

Some things had not changed. Pedelo was still there, dusting first and then sweeping. No one had been able to convince him that it should be the other way around.

Old Rosa still knelt on a little cushion in back of the church to keep under her eye the whole congregation. Woe betide the girl who forgot her veil, or the boy who pulled girls' plaits.

An old *popo* (granny), stouter than she imagined, tried to squeeze between bench and pillar and became lodged there. Several women went to her rescue. When extricated she insisted on kneeling on the seat of a bench. Jallah, Rosa's second-in-command, poked her in the back until she got down.

Outside, the rose bushes were in full bloom. Sister Mary Patrick observed that there would be plenty to decorate the church on the eighth of December.

In approaching the convent the Columbans found a Sister of Loretto trying to hold a chimney pipe in position with a dilapidated broom. The old chimney had always toppled whenever there was a fuss.

"The Loretto Sisters were goodness itself as usual," a Columban wrote. Although only home a week or so before us, they had left their own work and put our house in order for us."

In the kitchen they found that Lou-ja was back at the stove. Each nun glanced to note the state of his fingernails, which, a year earlier, had been the subject of some concern.

Lou-ja had terribly long nails as was the fashion. One of the sisters felt a delicacy in approaching him on the subject, but at the same time he had to learn to make the bread. The Columbans held a council meeting on the matter and it was decided that Sister Agnes should collect all of the ingredients on the table, and, as if it was a part of the proceeding, get a basin of water, wash her hands and clip her own nails, then place a basin of clean water before Lou-ja and make a sign to him to do likewise. It worked. Lou-ja made the sacrifice without a word, even of the nail that indicated the length of his ancestry!

Upon returning to Hanyang one of the first things the sisters did was to visit Bishop Galvin. They admitted to him that they had felt frustrated during their first year in China. War and illness and ignorance of language had kept them from doing the things they had hoped to do.

He said that he understood the feeling, but that they should see the experience of being refugees as part of their training. Because of war and famine and floods they would, sooner or later, be dealing with refugees beyond number. Now they would have a deeper sympathy with the emptiness of the uprooted and the terror of uncertainty.

Bishop Galvin said that there were eighteen thousand Catholics and four thousand catechumens in the vicariate. He was especially interested in having the Columban sisters open catechumenates, schools of religious instruction for women and children. These were not attracting as many effective catechists as they would like.

Bishop Galvin told the sisters he wished they would also open a dispensary. He said that when he arrived in Hanyang in 1920 there was not one qualified doctor of medicine in the city. There were plenty of quacks; some served as undertakers, selling medicine in one part of the house and coffins in another.

In 1921 Dr. Robert Francis arrived from New Orleans to assist the Columban fathers. Bishop Galvin recalled how appalled the American had been by the way the Chinese lived. He quoted the doctor as saying: "I see boatmen and farmers stop to drink out of their hands from a polluted flow. Nearly every well in a large settlement is grossly polluted. The river water far out in the stream is good, but too often it is bailed near the shore, near a neighborhood of native houseboats which continually pollute it. And the houses! They are built to shut out thieves. So they shut out light and air and shut in dirt and damp."

As the nuns were leaving the bishop's house, Bishop Galvin reminded them that they were not here to convert the Chinese but to be at God's disposal. Yes, he understood how much they wanted something definite to show for their time in China. Especially when the second group of sisters arrived from Ireland, which he hoped would be soon.

·6·

Learning the Land

While visiting the sick and dying the Columban sisters learned their way about Hanyang. In the beginning they accompanied the Lorettines, but, in time, were on their own.

On the first such call, a typical one, a Lorettine and a Columban, Sister Mary Patrick, set out to visit a sick woman at Mung-ja-nin, in the suburbs.

Heavy rain, mixing with two feet of melting snow, turned the route—the one the Irish called O'Connell Street—into a quagmire that encouraged more wading than walking. Carefully, the two nuns picked their way through jostling crowds, swerving rickshaws, and an unending procession of coolies staggering beneath heavy loads. At one point they were confronted with live pigs swinging upside down from poles and giving out a sound that grated on Occidental nerves, but not Oriental ones, for the Chinese seem to enjoy anything adding to the uproar of the day.

In open store fronts dry fish hung next to skinned carcasses. The nuns glanced at the latter and speculated as to whether or not the cat, missing from the convent for several days, might not be gracing an aromatic stew.

After thirty minutes of slipping and sliding the destination came in sight, a hut set among graves and surrounded by a vastness of exceedingly slippery mud. How to reach the door without falling, or losing a shoe, or dropping precious bottles of medicine? For the benefit of a watching crowd, the sisters kept laughing, for they had been told that no matter what the predicament if one keeps laughing one does not lose "face."

Just inside the door, in the most conspicuous place on the wall, hung a large unframed picture of the Sacred Heart. Under it, on a small table, were two bottles holding pink artificial flowers. This surprised the nuns for they knew that the husband of the dying woman was the only Catholic in the house. The two or three other families living there were pagan.

Everyone received the two sisters with deep Oriental courtesy. A woman with a lighted candle brought them to the sick woman's dark, cramped room. The Lorettine did what she could to comfort the patient who could no longer speak and was scarcely conscious. Sister Mary Patrick standing there holding the medicine bottles felt something knocking against her head in the darkness; finally, peering into the deep gloom she decided it was a piece of pork suspended from the rafter.

As the nuns were leaving, Shu Peter, a neighbor, arrived. He wanted medicine for his sick baby. The Lorettine told Sister Mary Patrick that Peter was burdened with troubles. Last week his wife was so ill that she would have died had not mother superior taken her to the doctor. He himself was dying of consumption. His family barely existed on the money he earned making matchboxes.

On the way back to the convent the sisters stopped to visit another patient, old Mrs. Dsong. Her daughter, a widow, had two children, Joseph and Frangego, who greeted the nuns with, "Good Morning," although it was half past four in the afternoon. While the Lorettine looked after the grandmother, Joseph pulled a low stool from under the table and urged the Columban to sit on it. She soon discovered he wanted to reach her crucifix. He kissed it and urged Frangego to do the same.

When the nuns returned to the convent caked with mud they found the lost cat in front of the stove licking himself. They chided each other for having had such ghoulish thoughts.

As the sisters went about visiting in homes they noticed that in China each family was a strong, independent unit. Although the father was spoken of as head of the house, it was the mother who ruled the home. The father's authority was theoretical, but the mother made the important decisions: When should the children start schools? When should they marry? With the soothsayer, she set the days for weddings and funerals. With the fortune-teller, she selected the time to begin a journey, start a business, or select a building site. She insisted that all ceremonies of birth, marriage, and death be in accord with tradition.

A Chinese woman was adept at the arts of cooking, sewing, weaving, and embroidering. Although she might not read or write she could recite a poem of eight hundred lines with unerring accuracy. It was a common practice for women, while at work, to listen to some aged storyteller recite in a singsong tone the classics of poetry, romance, and legend.

The women handled the money. Since the Chinese wife was responsible for maintaining the home, all wages earned by members of the family came to her. No one lived or worked for himself alone, but for the sake of the family.

The system was effective because filial piety was the first law of family life. Confucius said: "Parents ought to bear one trouble, that of their own sickness." At the mother's knee every child was instructed: "Be filial at home, and respectful to your elders when away from home. Be circumspect. Be truthful. Let your love go out freely towards all. Cultivate goodwill to man."

It was this natural inclination toward a religious spirit that helped the Columbans in their work among the Chinese.

Since the mother dominated the home, the work of the Columban sisters with women and girls was especially important. If a man converted the chances were that he would fall away after marriage. If a woman became a convert she often brought an entire family into the church with her.

While working to preserve life, the sisters almost daily visited the dying and so learned the customs surrounding death; for instance, the Chinese usually join a coffin club, contributing an annual fee, so that on the day of death a coffin will be provided.

As soon as someone appears near death, or is incurable, the patient is dressed in "death clothes." The clothes worn in life are thrown away. The belief is that garments being worn at death will accompany the spirit.

Scarcely had the dying person ceased to breathe than a messenger hurried to a magician whose first function was to decide at what time the relatives should don mourning attire. After the magician had spoken other messengers departed to announce the death to relatives living at a distance. Soon friends arrived at the house to kowtow before the corpse on the bier.

At one part of the ceremony mock money, houses, and utensils, all made of paper, were burned, in the hope that all of these would be delivered for use in the next life. For the same reason a few coins were placed on the coffin when the body was buried.

Customs were so many and so varied that the nuns were constantly learning new ones. Each day in the convent they exchanged newly found customs the way philatelists exchange stamps.

Soon Sister Mary Patrick, who as Lady Moloney had learned her nursing skills in a Dublin hospital, started a small dispensary. She wrote of her patients: "Most of them would require a first class miracle to cure them, and think it should be no trouble to the foreigners to perform one. Though the cure of the body is not always accomplished, our little dispensary affords us many opportunities of drawing souls to God, as the poor people get to know that we are anxious to help them, and this breaks down the prejudice against foreigners."

In Dublin no one had taught Sister Mary Patrick what to do for cases of opium poisoning, something now encountered often. She tried emetics, and if they were not effective she used strong solutions of permanganate of potash. This often worked wonders.

Shortly before Christmas of 1927 Chiang Kai-shek expelled the Communists from the Nationalist Army and broke diplomatic relations with Russia. This drove many Reds from Hankow, Hanyang, and Wuchang.

The sisters benefitted from this move for they no longer had to endure anti-Christian demonstrations. The Columban fathers in country parishes, however, suffered all the more because when the Reds fled to the country they joined bands of bandits to track down all foreigners, especially Christians.

Even the gentry began to hold missionaries for ransom, defending their actions by saying that they themselves had to pay large sums to soldiers for protection from Communist terrorists. The protection money was high because most soldiers were occupied fighting in the civil war between armies of the north and south.

People felt so put-upon that they began to take matters into their own hands, forming self-protection societies with such names as Big Swords, Ironsides, and Sharp Daggers. Since Catholics did not join these societies, which indulged in occult pagan rites, the missionaries were fair game.

Father Loftus divided the groups of brigands into major and minor bands. A major one might number ten thousand and minor ones might range in size from eight to sixty. Most of the bands found recruits from army deserters who brought rifles and ammunition with them.

The Columbans were often surprised at the bandits' personal appearance. Father Luke Mullany wrote: "My conception of a Chinese bandit was a rough, uncouth fellow, covered with martial implements, with tousled hair, scarred face, and clad in dirty clothes. These three men, however—and I believe it can be said of the majority of China's bandits—were very well groomed. Over their well-made long garments they wore satin jackets. All had on foreign felt hats, one carried a nicely carved walking stick, and another wore pince-nez glasses. They displayed no weapons, though one had a yellow cord slung across the shoulder ending in his side pocket, and to which I presumed was attached a revolver."

These three took Father Mullany hostage at Ko-Chia Dzae and said that unless he produced $3,000 within two weeks he would be shot. Bishop Galvin reported this to authorities who sent a military company to capture the bandits.

At the same time, Christmas of 1927, other priests in the field were being harassed more than ever. Fathers John O'Carroll and William Walsh had to flee Yuin Lung. When Father Frank O. McDonald visited Father Patrick O'Connell, the pastor at Ko Kia Tsui Mission, a mob broke into the rectory to beat them. The two Columbans, bruised and bleeding, were forced to watch the mob wreck the church and were then marched off assured that they would be beheaded. For a month they were held captive until Bishop Galvin persuaded a magistrate to send soldiers to rescue them.

Three Communist bandits ordered Father Lalor and his catechist to dismount when on their way from Yo Kow to Yuen Ho, on May 5, 1928. They broke open the priest's boxes to scatter the contents on the ground and took $300 from the kit bag. Father Lalor snatched back the money just as nine other bandits arrived. One put a revolver to his ribs, threatening to shoot him if he did not give up the money. Meanwhile they took his watch, fountain pen, and spectacles.

The bandit with the revolver demanded that the Columban write a letter to the Yo Kow Catholic Mission asking for $20,000. When he refused, his catechist was so sure the brigands would murder his pastor that he volunteered to hurry to Yo Kow and ask for the ransom. The bandits made it clear that if the catechist was not back within twelve hours with money they would shoot the priest.

After dragging the priest to a village the bandits shoved him into the back room of a house where they ordered him to write a letter asking for money. When he refused, six men held him at pistol point for an hour. He still refused.

After dark the Reds ordered the missionary into bed and the six got in with him. Since it was overcrowded they forced their captive to get out and spend the night under the bed.

Father Lalor was in that house from Sunday night until Tuesday morning with nothing to eat. On Tuesday night the bandits again threatened to kill him if he did not write a request for money, and again he refused.

Later the same night he was taken to another house a mile away, but the owners objected and the band moved to another place in the same village. Here they kept the priest for six days, giving him three buns a day for subsistence.

Toward the end of the week the bandits forced a lump of opium down Father Lalor's throat. He struggled, but he was so weak from hunger that he was easily overpowered and when nearly unconscious from the opium the bandits, thinking he was dying, stretched him on the ground. Villagers objected to his being left there to die, fearing they would be blamed. So the captors wrapped the Columban in matting, carried him to a field, dropped him onto a pile of wet straw, and departed.

A crowd of men, women and children gathered around for an hour until they got tired of looking and left. The Columban sprawled there all day under a strong sun too weak even to crawl.

At sunset a man from the village brought some hot tea. After darkness the peasant and three others carried the priest to a house, provided food and drink and a bed for the night. At daybreak the Good Samaritan led Father Lalor to the home of a Catholic, who took him to the mission in Tai Lin Meao.

At Christmas of 1928 three Columbans, Fathers John O'Carroll, Francis McDonald, and John Cowhig were on the run from bandits. To make matters worse, China was having its most severe season in sixty years.

It was evident that with so many people living dangerously sooner or later something truly serious would happen, and so it did. At dawn on July 15, 1929, bandits of the Red Army captured Father Timothy Leonard while he was saying Mass. As the assailants rushed the altar the priest reached for the ciborium. A bandit struck his arm with a rifle butt scattering the consecrated particles. Other bandits trampled on them.

After ripping the priest's vestments from him, the fanatics bound him with ropes. They also bound the Mass server. Upon their demand for money, Father Leonard said that he would give them all he had, about $100, if they would release the boy, which they did.

While the priest knelt in prayer the Reds smashed tabernacles, broke vases, and shredded vestments. They jeered at him and jerked on his ropes with such vehemence that he fell forward to the floor striking his face, receiving the first of many wounds.

The Reds marched Father Leonard up to the mountains, twenty miles from the church, and there he and a dozen other captives were put on trial. The judges were the commander of the Communist detachment, age twenty-six; his chief of staff, age twenty, and the head of the political bureau, age twenty-nine.

The judges accused the missionary of having broken the law. When he asked what law, the judges said he was guilty of the practice of religion, and that his Church had "hooked on" with the Kuomintang. The Columban said his Church had nothing to do with politics, but the judges marked his sheet, "condemned."

All captives were held in one room, and as each name was called the prisoner was led out to be stabbed to death at the door. Father Leonard's head was nearly severed from his body. An elderly Chinese gentleman, spared because he paid a ransom, told three Catholics of what had happened. They put the dead priest in a coffin, on July 20, and carried him to Nan Feng where Fathers Patrick Dermody, Patrick Quigley, and a Chinese priest said a Solemn Requiem Mass. A vast crowd, pagan and Christian, assisted. A Chinese girl at the Mass eventually became a Columban.

The murder was the topic of conversation a week later, when Bishop Galvin visited the Columban sisters in Kuling, a mountain retreat where they had gone to recover from the heat of Hanyang. The bishop spoke of the eleven foreign priests who had been killed in China since the sisters' arrival three years earlier.

Just before leaving, his tone changed. Here is some good news, he said. A letter from Mother Finbarr promised that six more Columban sisters would be ready to leave Ireland for China in about three months.

A few months earlier the bishop had written to his superior general, Father O'Dwyer: "I need—and the need is urgent—at least two central catechumenates for women in the country just at present. I want about four Sisters in each catechumenate. Let me say right away that I want only strong, healthy Sisters—frail Sisters are of no use in the country districts. I propose that we build a very simple housing for these Sisters—Chinese style, which is, we find, the proper thing for the country.

"I'd like to know if the Sisters can come and about when they can come. If you say that our Society couldn't finance the scheme, I believe I could get Sisters of another Order to come and do it, but I much prefer that our own Sisters would work side by side with us, and I am very keen on giving them every possible chance."

As soon as the bishop departed Kuling, Sister Theophane wrote to Mother Finbarr that everyone was studying Chinese with renewed vigor so as not to lose too much "face" when the new sisters arrived: "Our teacher, Anna, confided to me that we are getting too old to study any more and that 'when the new Sisters come it will be fine.' "

Sister Theophane concluded: "We can hardly think of anything but the arrival of the six from Cahiracon. Won't we be delighted to see them again! We will be quite a big community—for a little time at least. And besides we shall have some nice fresh jokes for recreation—our old ones are almost worn threadbare from being trotted out regularly once a week for months and even years—although there is something new to laugh at every day in this delightful country."

The Columban priests were pleased, too. In a letter home, Father John Loftus spoke for the rest: "We are all very glad to hear that a new batch of the Sisters are coming from Ireland to us here. We really must do something for the women if we are to keep things going properly in our district.

"Mixed marriages are a terrible danger and a pagan wife will not only ruin a whole family but even a whole mission. And she need not be a demon to do it. A Catholic husband with a pagan wife will do nothing, or next to nothing. He does not wish to quarrel with her. He becomes lukewarm and careless and finally falls off—a dead branch.

"In such circumstances the children do not know whom to worship—God or Buddha. Hence the vital importance of sending us more Sisters to help to make converts of the women."

By now the Columban sisters were gaining confidence. It was evident that they were needed and wanted.

·7·

More Helping Hands

On a page headed October 15, 1929, the Feast of Saint Teresa, a nun at Cahiracon, Sister Ignatius, wrote in her diary: "We can guess that the quiet peaceful days at the Mother House will never come again for us, that never again will we be surrounded by the loving care of Mother Alphonsus or edified by Sister Joseph Conception's boundless zeal for souls. In taking leave of Mother General we envy the first band of sisters, for they had her with them to keep up their courage and spirits, and help them by her example to face every hardship."

A few hours later the second group left for China: Sisters Ignatius O'Keefe, Basil McBrearty, Michael Mongey, Dolores Callan, Columban Kennedy, and Colmcille McCormack. All from Ireland, except Sister Basil who came from England.

The diarist reported, "All of us kept up wonderfully even after the 'goodbyes' were said."

Six sisters boarded the *Malawa* on the eighteenth, the feast of St. Luke. The ship, all black and brown, they found somewhat gloomy, but were pleased that the crewmen were lascars. Watching the dockhands load cargo was good fun, and as one nun observed, "I am afraid the language is not technical."

The reticence of nuns in those days is evident in a comment: "We have the end table, which was the best they could do. The people are extremely nice; no one notices us."

Daily the sisters attended Masses at 7, 7:30, and 10 o'clock and sang a Te Deum in the afternoon. Someone asked Sister Colmcille, who had been choirmistress in Cahiracon, should the Te Deum be sung in Latin or in English and she answered, "Oh, Latin, we'd be only stumbling over the English."

The *Malawa* steamed from Southampton through the Bay of Biscay and past the Andalusian Range: "No wonder Spain is a land of mystics—one would not need aids to mental prayer with such uplifting scenery."

At Port Said the diarist commented: "We bless Mother General for her forethought in providing white habits, they are a real boon. We are not suffering at all from the heat since we put them on this morning. Even the butter in the dining saloon has ceased to spread over the dish—is the effect due to our cool appearance, or to the lump of ice sitting on top of each bit?"

The Columbans searched out churches and visited convents in Marseilles, Aden, Columbo, Penang, Singapore, Hong Kong, and Shanghai. At one place they met a mother superior from Kilkenny who had been on the missions twenty-eight years "and she looked grand, though a bit washed out." They met a priest from Derry, thirty-five years on the missions, "who is as merry as a school boy." Wherever the ship stopped they met missionaries from Cork, Kerry, Ennis, until they began to realize that the tiny space called Ireland was providing missionaries for the remote parts of the world.

In Penang a sister from Cork wanted to show the visitors her school, and so she asked the children in her classroom if they would work in silence when left alone. They promised they would.

"You know I trust you, don't you?" she said.

Out in the hallway she told the Columbans, "Always trust the Chinese children, and let them know it."

One of the visitors recalled, "Each class we went to was a fresh surprise. Such happy, intelligent, nice mannered children! The wee ones were especially lovable—little mites in trousers, or little things looking like old women with their topknots, with a chrysanthemum stuck in it."

While going from the school to the ship the sisters stopped to visit a snake temple.

"Here we alight, screw our heads on straight and tight and go in. We ought to have been horrified and frightened at the sight of snakes of all sizes, curled around branches and on the frames of pictures, but we just take it all for granted, like everything else these times. They are all asleep but later on they begin to wriggle. There are a few old gods in glass cases, one of which the little boy who shows us around says is his grandfather! Outside in a cage is a big python, twenty feet long. We ask if he bites and the boy says, 'No, squeeze.' Judging from the look of him it would not be well to get into his embrace."

The sisters boarded the river steamer in Shanghai for Hankow. In spite of their Irish brogues and Irish complexions, the purser tacked to their cabin doors the sign French Sisters.

Just after the boat departed Shanghai, Sister Mary Ignatius had a chance to do the kind of thing that she had come this far to do. A small boy approached with some alum and asked, "Please, this good for eyes?" She said, yes, and told him the amount to use. He returned with a cup and spoon to ask, "This right?" She reduced the quantity by half. It was evident from the look he gave her that she had gained "face."

On the five-day trip the Columbans heard old China hands speak with admiration of the Chinese farmer. One man who had spent much of his life in the Orient pointed to the riverbank where a farmer was breaking ground with a kind of wooden plow and lethargic buffalo, used from time immemorial.

"The Chinese farmer may not be much to look at," he observed, "but you Sisters will change your opinion at close range. You will see at first glance that his life is a hard one. His frame is wiry and his muscles stand out like cords, and not without reason.

"He often carries on his back the water to irrigate the land or the manure to fertilize the farm. The harvest he reaps by hand and trudges with it miles to the nearest market.

"The hardships do not interfere with his good humor. He can laugh and joke better than many in more prosperous circumstances."

The old China hand spoke of famines he had observed. A lack of water usually causes the problem, he said. At the first sign of a drought the farmer carries water day and night until the wells dry up. The sun beats down on withering stalks which lose their refreshing green and turn a sickly yellow.

The worst he had seen was in 1920 and 1921. Peasants somehow survived on makeshift food: flour made from leaves, chaff from grain, poplar buds, corncobs, thistles, flower seeds, sawdust, tree bark, peanut shells, cotton seed, sweet potato stems, and roots of all kinds.

The interesting old man spoke of some unusual customs the sisters might expect to find among their pupils: "The first time a child goes to school he arrives very early in the morning carried on his mother's back. His head is covered by a veil and he clutches a stick of celery. The veil is to hide him from evil spirits; the celery signifies industriousness, from the word *kan* which means both celery and diligence.

"When the class begins, the first pupil leaves his seat to stand before the teacher who reads aloud a certain passage. The child repeats this and returns to his seat where he continues singing the passage aloud, oblivious to all around him. The second pupil does the same, and so on until the whole school is finally shouting away, each at a different lesson in pandemonium. You Sisters may need quiet for study, but not the Chinese."

When the study hour is ended the children stand before the teacher to hurl their memorized passages at his head. Woe to the one who hesitates or has forgotten the text. The rod is nearby.

The boat arrived at its destination on November 27, 1929, a day earlier than expected. Two Columban fathers, Joseph Hogan and John

Mackay, reached the wharf well after docking, disappointed and embarrassed, explaining that they had been told that the boat would not arrive until the next day because of fog.

Hankow with all of its lights was a lurid sight. A sister said it was "like a cinema screen with hundreds and hundreds of people all rushing toward you."

Two small boats arrived to take the missionaries across the river to their convent in Hanyang. Sister Columban used her umbrella to poke her way into the shaky boat and steady herself until she could sit down. In no time the party had crossed the river into a different world, more Chinese and less Western. No electric lights here; torches and an occasional lamp lit the shops.

"Everything is weird," wrote the diarist. "In rickshaws we bump over rickety streets which seem in the process of reconstruction or destruction or something. All the time we are enjoying the full measure of smells, the like of which were never smelt in Ireland.

"We race along the edge of the river with nothing between us and a watery grave save the skill of the rickshaw-man. Round corners and through narrow dark streets, through smells and smells and smells, and over more broken stones. I would not have missed that ride through Hanyang for anything. There was such a gorgeous element of uncertainty about it—the real mysterious East. At last we stop.

"Home! Deo Gratias!

"Friendly faces peep out and friendly hands catch ours to bring us through the doorway. Mother Superior and the sisters are all around us. Firecrackers are going off in the background and it looks like a Christmas tree."

After Benediction in the chapel the sisters returned to the convent. Soon questions filled the air. The old hands wanted to hear about Ireland and the new ones could not get their fill of China.

The fresh arrivals told of how they had moved from the old dower house, Saint Brigid's, to the main house, formerly Saint Senan's College, when the priests bought a place at Navan, County Meath. It was in the chapel of the new location that Mother Finbarr had taken her final vows upon returning from China in the fall of 1927.

Sister Mary Patrick was amused to observe Sister Michael's eyes turning to the stove from time to time. After taking down the pipes for cleaning the coolie had reassembled them with all the seams turned toward the front instead of toward the wall. While this had nothing to do with the stove's efficiency the sight of all seams wrong side foremost was aesthetically disconcerting.

Many things in China will seem awry, Sister Mary Patrick assured the newcomers. For a time they will think they are in the land of topsy-turvy, for in almost every action and thought the Chinese are their direct opposites.

A Chinese shakes his own hands instead of clasping the hand of visitors. His manner is cheerful when he tells you of a death in the family. A bride wails and does not smile. A man may show you with pride the coffin his son has given him.

Since the new arrivals had just ended a six-week journey, the conversation turned naturally to travel. The pioneers spoke knowingly of trains, ponies, and the *joudza*.

"What is that?" the six newcomers asked in unison.

A *joudza* is a chair set onto two parallel bamboo poles, about sixteen inches apart, Sister Theophane explained. The passenger rides until the four coolies tire and then the passenger becomes a pedestrian. Good carriers can cover thirty miles a day over rough paths.

Sister Michael recalled that when Father O'Dwyer returned from China he had spoken with enthusiasm about the ponies. "I take my hat off to the Chinese ponies," he had said. "They are small but for speed and endurance I would back them against any pony in Ireland."

The superior general had traveled by pony hundreds of miles. Sometimes he rode on wide paths, sometimes on the tops of narrow banks, but never once, though the pace was rapid and the ground uneven, had he the least reason to complain of the fleetness, surefootedness, and endurance of the little animals.

"Of course, there are 'weeds' among them," he had said, "But give me a Chinese pony which has been properly cared for, and I will undertake a sixty-mile journey with light heart."

The five Columban sisters who had been in China for three years agreed that riding a train is hectic. The cacophony and acrobatics of passengers transferring their baggage is a shaking experience, they said.

The beggar boys jumping onto the train are problems, too. Give one a coin and dozens swarm all over you. The safest system is to give the coin as the train is leaving the station, just as it reaches the speed where it is too late for others to jump aboard. Every town has its quota of beggars who come to meet all trains.

Being able to speak with such authority was good for the morale of the nuns who had been in China for three years. They had been learning from the Sisters of Loretto, Franciscan sisters, Columban priests, and Chinese teachers. Now, at last, they were teaching somebody else. The six new arrivals were stimulated by all of those exotic stories and eager to make a start.

Years later Sister Mary Moroney said, "In China while we were having breakfast at seven it usually happened that a ring would come at the door. People would be asking that we visit their homes to look after the sick."

That is what happened the day after the arrival of the new sisters. Sister Theophane suggested that they follow around behind the old hands for a few days to get the feel of the work. Off they went in three small groups.

No matter how early the sisters began their rounds they found Chinese shops open. The newcomers commented on this and were told that the shops would stay open until far into the night, for the Chinese system of bookkeeping is so choked with detail that the clerks are busy recording sales and balancing entries long after the sun has set.

The Chinese have a great awareness of money, Sister Philomena said. She told of an old Chinese woman, hobbling along on bound feet, who had said that she was going to a relative's to die. "He lives near the family graveyard. I will avoid the expense of coffin bearers for such a long distance."

In visiting the sick the newcomers felt an ache of empathy when they saw what the Chinese use for a pillow—a roll of bamboo, a block of wood, or a brick. They were assured that the patient would not sleep in comfort using the pillows that foreigners prefer.

They also noticed that Chinese kitchens lack bread pans, cake tins, jelly moulds, pots, pans, and skillets, so taken for granted back home. In most kitchens one concave metal bowl with a capacity of several gallons was the lone utensil. It seemed someone was always at the fire to feed fuel and cook one dish at a time. Smoke and steam filled the room, not enough to blind or suffocate but enough to cause eye trouble throughout the land.

So many houses were shabby—a patchwork of any materials available. Floors were often earthen. Chickens, ducks, and pigs had the run of the place.

Chinese home life was not attractive to the women from a Western culture. And yet the happiness of the children was a splendid advertisement for it. A happier lot could not be found in the world. Many were beautiful with olive faces and sparkling eyes.

The ability of the Chinese to bear pain was something that the nuns never ceased to admire, as they made their rounds. Dr. Reid told of eleven hundred operations that he saw performed at Nanyuan barracks on soldiers wounded in the civil war. Three operations were performed simultaneously in the same room until all cases were dealt with. No anaesthetics were used. Each patient was quite conscious on the operating table from which he could see two other operations in progress. And yet not a soldier raised any objection, or uttered a sound while under the knife.

The nuns often found themselves in the presence of death and lowered their voices, but not the Chinese. A funeral is a loud affair.

At the start of a Requiem Mass the newcomers were startled by the pop of firecrackers, clash of symbols, and wheeze of the harmonium, all joining into something related to jazz. All through the service the congregation sang prayers as loud as possible, except at the Consecration when a salvo of firecrackers took the place of the traditional bell.

At the end of Mass women began a wailing lament, throwing themselves on the coffin. When the procession had formed they were rudely pulled from the coffin which was placed on a bier and carried on a magnificent catafalque, richly embroidered with red the predominant color.

In the procession children carried white banners on which were printed important episodes in the life of the deceased. Men carried tables with ornaments atop them. Others bore long poles with thousands of tiny firecrackers wrapped around each. Then came a magnificent choir bearing gigantic photographs of the deceased.

The procession passed through the city with clashing cymbals and trilling flutes. A fusillade of firecrackers and harmless bombs competed. All along the way the population paused to witness and to wonder.

The new sisters were not long in Hanyang when one of them, Sister Ignatius, a nurse, was able, along with Mother Theophane, to save the life of a missionary. It began when Father Ulick Burke trudged for ten miles through the snow on Christmas Eve. Although he had only Chinese cloth shoes and no change of clothing he endured a blizzard because he had promised to visit an old mission center for Christmas and did not want to disappoint the Christians.

Upon arriving, wet to the knees and lacking dry clothing, he sat in a cold church hearing confessions until time to say Midnight Mass. The next day he felt ill, but was able to walk the ten miles back to his headquarters, Tsan-Dan-Kow, where he began to run a high fever.

On December 29 he sent for Father Patrick Laffan, who finding Father Burke in poor condition, decided the only hope of saving his life was to take him to Hankow for medical attention. The journey, over one hundred miles, had to be made in a small boat. On the way the Columbans were caught in a blinding snowstorm which delayed them two nights and a day. Believing his patient was near death, Father Laffan anointed him, and had him carried—with repeated falls—on a bamboo bed across snow-covered country to the mission presbytery at Hwan-Ja-San.

From there Father Laffan wrote to Father Thomas Quinlan, Bishop Galvin's vicar-general, telling him that Father Burke had neither eaten nor slept for twelve days and that his temperature ranged between 102 and 104. Would Father Quinlan send help as soon as possible, for the patient could not complete the journey to Hanyang?

Upon receiving the message, Father Quinlan tried to get a doctor to accompany him to Hwan-Ja-San but the weather and roads were so terrible that none would consent to go. The Columban and Loretto sisters offered to risk the journey, but Father Quinlan feared they might get lost in the storm. The sisters gave Father Quinlan medicines and instructions which he sent along to Fathers Laffan and Maguire who were nursing Father Burke. When the weather improved a bit Fathers Quinlan and Devine set out with Mother Theophane and Sister Ignatius.

"The journey was pretty bad, but the Sisters were heroic," wrote Father Quinlan on February 3, 1930, six weeks after Father Burke had taken ill. "We set out at seven in the morning and crossed over to Hankow, whence a motor car took us part of the road. Then the Sisters walked a bit, boated a bit, and did the last ten miles in sedan chairs. The paths were in slush and the coolies were slipping at every step."

Once the sisters had to get out and walk through mud. In crossing a one-plank bridge Sister Ignatius slipped and suffered a bad fall. Her habit was in a fearful state after that. The four missionaries arrived at Hwan-Ja-San at six that evening.

The sisters took up duty at once and cared for the delirious patient for ten days until he was ready to be moved to a hospital in Hankow. It was a hard fight to save him. The elements were against him all of the time.

Father Quinlan concluded his letter: "The greatest credit is due to Father Laffan, the man who brought him in the rowing boat and cared for him and kept him warm through a wind and snow storm on the river for two nights and a day. How he kept him from catching a fresh cold is beyond my comprehension. But when we remember that Father Laffan sat in a corner of that little open boat all that time without a blanket or overcoat and ate nothing, except a crust of half-baked bread, we are not surprised that the Lord spared the life of his comrade.

"Fathers Laffan and Maguire kept the life in him until the Sisters arrived. But their best care would not have been sufficient to pull him through without the Sisters. He was gradually weakening and was pretty far gone the evening the Sisters got in and took over the case."

This was heady stuff for the six young women who had spent the past few years in the tranquility of Cahiracon, on the banks of the Shannon.

·8·

An Abundance of Adversity

At Christmas of 1929 there came a calm before the storm. The sisters celebrated the great feast in Hanyang with a poignant awareness of how far they were from home, but with a sense of safety. No crowds jeered outside the church and no one posted a sign saying Death to Christians, as in the past.

The Columban priests in remote areas also knew the peace of Christmas. Father Edward Byrne said that in Lichwan he and Father Thomas McCarthy enjoyed "the happiest Christmas we have ever had." He told of how he felt on Christmas Eve: "What a heartening spectacle! Here in a remote corner of China—pagan China—we had our little church packed with devout souls giving honor and glory to God. Many of these poor souls had suffered to be present on this night, and it was a joy to me and to Father McCarthy to be present with them, to help them prepare to receive their Eucharistic Lord."

Unaware that this would be his last Christmas, Father Cornelius Tierney wrote that he and Father Eugene Duffy had found life peaceful in Kiangsi during the holidays, because bandits and soldiers, for the moment, behaved themselves. There was also a marked increase in the number of the faithful receiving the sacraments. In the central mission, Kien Chang, the increase was one-third over the previous year, and in some places the number doubled.

Columbans all over the vicariate agreed that the night before Christmas was exceedingly cold. Parishioners arrived bearing little hand stoves filled with glowing charcoal. Such tiny furnaces, resembling earthenware buckets, combined to raise the temperature inside the churches just a little, but the air was still icy as Midnight Masses began.

Anti-Christian bias reemerged just after Christmas. On New Year's Day of 1930, for example, a Catholic Chinese professor at a military school in Nanning, having paid a courtesy call on a priest, was summoned before the director of the school and told never to do that again.

Besides, he was to discontinue going to church on Sundays. All of this despite the state's declaration of religious freedom.

The brief lull in troubles had given Bishop Galvin a false sense of confidence, causing him to do something he soon regretted. The bishop, anxious to learn how effectively nuns might work in smaller communities, sent five Columban sisters to Sien Tao Chen, a seemingly safe community. After all, four hundred militiamen were stationed there.

In Sien Tao Chen, 150 miles northwest of Hanyang on the Han river, Fathers Patrick Laffan and James Linehan had one of the vicariate's best churches, a gift from Cardinal O'Connell of Boston. Most parishioners were descended from families who had been in the faith for more than two hundred years. An ideal place to try the experiment, or so it seemed.

At the start of Holy Week in 1930, Mother Lelia and Sisters Mary Patrick, Dolores, Michael, and Columban left Hanyang by steamer. On the trip up the Han, in whichever direction they looked, fore or aft, port or starboard, they saw Chinese junks with high decks, two enormous eyes in the bow, and a single square sail fitted with bamboo laths to prevent its "bellying." Such an exotic setting and a new challenge had everyone in high spirits.

The sisters arrived in the morning just in time for the ceremonies on Wednesday. That ritual and the remainder of Holy Week were heightened by their participation. Easter Sunday in the church in Sien Tao Chen was the biggest day the Catholics remembered. The church was packed; many could not get in at all. An organ was lent by a pagan in the street, so Sister Mary Patrick played. The other sisters formed the choir and Father Lane, after hearing confessions for five and a half hours, sang a Missa Cantata. The Church was at its height in Sien Tao Chen. Catholics and pagans alike rejoiced to see the sisters among them. Father Walsh said that the next day when he and Bishop Galvin and Fathers Quinlan, Laffan, Linehan, and O'Collins were together, "We concluded that the coming of the Sisters to the country was the crowning of our Mission."

On Thursday night, April 24, Communist bandits secretly surrounded Sien Tao Chen and waited for dawn. At first light they rushed the town from four points, shooting as they came and shouting "*saar*" (kill). The defenders, still in bed, gave scant resistance, and so the brigands took possession and began looting.

When rifle fire began, Bishop Galvin was at the Communion of the Mass. With him were Father Walsh and Sisters Columban and Michael. Soon Fathers O'Collins and Linehan, having scaled the wall at the rear of the compound, went to the altar to consume the Blessed Sacrament. Mother Lelia hurried out, followed by Sister Dolores, who instantly returned to the convent for Sister Mary Patrick. When all priests and nuns had gathered in the church, they went into the sacristy, for it afforded the best protection against bullets.

A commotion outside drew Bishop Galvin to the church door. Two dozen Reds shouted for admittance at the front gate. Suddenly, they broke into the compound.

The bishop moved to the center of the church to stand his ground. The young bandit leader, Wang, came forward with a smile. He was neatly dressed in a military uniform and spoke with the politeness of a gentleman.

Wang assured the bishop that there was nothing to fear. "We are only against the rich people who oppress the poor. We have no quarrel with the Catholic Church. You priests are good people who help the poor."

The chief had a look around the church and posted guards so that no Columban might escape. Little by little the firing ceased outside the building, or rather shifted to another part of town.

All of the Columbans left the sacristy and went to the women's catechumenate behind the church. There they found the Chinese women huddled together in a dusky room. The bishop said later, "I distinctly recall the terror which was pictured on their faces."

Sister Mary Patrick suggested that since there was a lull at the moment, why not have some coffee and she went to the kitchen for it. Father Linehan took the sacred vessels from the church and buried them in a heap of sand.

Bishop Glavin wrote: "I had a cup of coffee in my hand—into which Mother Lelia had put a fistful of sugar—and was stirring it with a knife when Father Walsh came in to ask that I go to interview the bandit leader. I met him in front of the church. Again, he was friendly and polite, and I, too—however I may have felt—tried to be likewise. For we were completely in the man's power; any show of harshness might have irritated him and his followers and perhaps cost us our lives."

The bishop said, "You must be very tired. Come have some breakfast."

Soon the bandit chief was having tea and toast and eggs and chatting with the bishop, as though it were a reunion of old friends.

The bishop asked where the Reds had come from and the young chief said that he could not tell, but that it was a distance of ninety li (thirty miles). This marching all night is wearing, he said.

"The Sisters are frightened," the bishop told him. "All of that shooting."

"They should not be. I will go to them. I will speak to them."

Wang returned to the church where the sisters had gathered once again and spoke to them kindly. He said that they were good people and had nothing to fear.

In the most polite Chinese fashion he bowed himself out.

Such friendliness brought a vague sense of security. The priests and nuns were in a heightened mood when they went to the sisters' dining room for breakfast. "It was a pleasant meal, as I recall it now," wrote Bishop Galvin. "Anyone seeing us there at breakfast together would never have guessed that we were surrounded by bandits. God in His mercy hides the future from us all; it was well we did not know the terrible day that lay ahead of us."

Suddenly the dining room door flew open and two men with drawn revolvers stood there. One of them, Yuen, took the bishop to an adjoining room while the other kept an eye on the nuns and priests at the table.

Yuen said he had nothing against the Church and that the Columbans had nothing to fear. However, he wanted the priests to come to town with him "to talk things over."

Later the bishop wrote: "I had a suspicion of what that might mean. I did not wish any priest to leave the compound, so I told him it was very inconvenient for me to go, that we had treated them well, that if they had anything to talk over why could they not come to the Mission instead of asking us to go to their headquarters, that we had to protect the church, and that if we went with them everything that we had would be looted."

Just as he made the last point, Father Laffan came to the room to say, "They are breaking up the church."

"You see, what I have told you is true. If we go, they will smash everything in the church."

"No," said Yuen, "I will stop them," and out he went with the bishop and Father Laffan following.

The church was filled with bandits, all looting. They had smashed the statue of Our Lady, a gift of Father Laffan's mother, and it lay about the foot of the altar in a thousand fragments. The statue of the Sacred Heart was broken, too, and the altars stripped of their cloths. The sacristy was a wreck.

Yuen ordered the looters from the church and he and the bishop and Father Laffan returned to the sisters' house. At the door the three were joined by two bandits brandishing revolvers. The old argument was resumed, the one about the priests needing to go to town "to talk things over."

Suddenly Yuen turned to Father Laffan: "What's your name? You will have to go!"

The bishop protested, but the priest said, "It's useless. The fellow behind me with the revolver says I must go, and I'll go."

Father Laffan went into the dining room and asked Father O'Collins to give him absolution. He turned to the sisters and asked that they pray for him.

Upon returning to the front door, where the bishop and the bandits waited, Father Laffan removed his Chinese slippers and while lacing his shoes, looked up at the bishop, smiled, and said, "I'll meet you on the other side of the grave. Write home and tell them about it." As he started to go he whispered, "Whatever I write you, you will know what I *mean*."

The bishop wrote to Father O'Dwyer: "When he had gone about half a dozen paces from the door, he turned again and waved goodbye to me. His face was pale, but he was still smiling.

"To my dying day that awful picture will always be in my mind—the picture of that brave man going out to die and asking me to send a last message to his mother. For, I did not think of you or anyone in the Society, I saw only his mother and she seemed to be before me there with a vividness and a reality which I can neither describe nor analyze.

"So far I had tried to be steady and keep my balance, but now a strange weakness had come over me; I could feel the tears running down my face and there was a choking sensation in my throat. The bandits were all around me, but I didn't see them. I walked up and down the front of the house trying to hold myself in check. After some time I went into the dining room to tell Father O'Collins and the Sisters. I thought I was calm again, but when I began to speak about it, I couldn't go on."

The nuns were steady, but anxiety showed in their faces. "Offer him up to God," said Mother Lelia. "God will take care of him."

Bandits were coming and going in the dining room grabbing whatever struck their fancy. The bishop told Father O'Collins to take the sisters into the adjoining room, while he and Fathers Walsh and Linehan remained outside to do whatever they could.

"Our great fear was, what was to become of the Sisters if we were taken off—one by one—as seemed to be the intention of the bandits. Were we to bring the Sisters with us into captivity, or were we to leave them there in the compound surrounded by the bandits. It was a fearful alternative."

The bishop walked around the compound several times looking for a way of escape. There was none. The front gate was well guarded and at the back gate three brigands were dividing the loot. On either side of the compound were groups of riflemen.

As the bishop rejoined Father Linehan, two bandits approached with drawn revolvers, and one said, "Another man must go."

"One of our men has already gone," said the bishop.

"One is not enough. There is a man here named Linn (Father Linehan's Chinese name.) We want him, too."

"I'll go," said Father Linehan. He was cool, though his face was pale. He showed no trace of nervousness as he went out, followed by the two bandits, very much as if he was going to some ordinary duty of the day.

It was now 8:30 a.m. The bishop returned to the dining room to tell Father Walsh of the latest defeat.

"What are you doing?" he asked the priest.

"There is no hope. I am writing a letter to Doctor O'Dwyer so that he will know about it."

"If they come for another man, I'll go," said the bishop.

"No, you stay with the Sisters as long as you can. I'll go next, if they come for another man. You stay and save the Sisters, if you can."

Father Laffan's houseboy hurried into the room to warn the bishop to change his soutane. He had heard the bandit chief say, "The man wearing the clothes with the red trimmings is the superior. We must have him."

Another band of looters came surging into the dining room.

By now Bishop Galvin had lost all his patience. He no longer tried to speak with kindness: "I asked them what harm the Catholic Church had done them or anyone in China. I said we had come here to teach the people to do good, to tell them about God who had created us all and to help the poor. I put it to them to go to anyone in town and find out if we weren't good men who had always tried to help everyone."

The bandit spokesman said, "Yes, you are good men. And we mean you no harm. But you are in league with the imperialists of Ireland."

"The imperialists of Ireland!" The bishop exploded. "Ireland has never been an imperialistic nation. Ireland has never occupied any country."

"Your soldiers and battleships are here."

"Where?"

"In Hankow and Shanghai."

"You won't find an Irish soldier in all of China."

The looters seemed slightly impressed. The bishop followed up his advantage by asking for the release of the two priests.

The bandit said he could not do that, but would guarantee their safety.

After the looters had taken everything movable from the dining room, one of them, with a revolver, demanded that the bishop open the door to where the nuns were waiting. The bishop went into the room to tell the sisters that they should go upstairs.

In the stack of medical supplies was a bottle of brandy. Mother Lelia pointed to it and asked, "Shall I bring this?"

"Do!"

As the sisters began to come from the room, one by one, the bandit stood there pointing a revolver. "They must be searched," he said.

"Mother Lelia held up her shawl for him to see," wrote the bishop, "while all the time she had the bottle of brandy safely tucked away under her arm. She never turned a hair. It was too funny for words—the Lord save us!—we had no time for fun."

As soon as the sisters had gone upstairs a horde of bandits rushed into the room grabbing left and right at anything and everything. There was a good deal of medicine in the room which they packed up and took away. The parish registers were there, too; they would have given the Reds the names of every Catholic in the locality. By sheer coolness and diplomacy Father O'Collins succeeded in saving the registers.

The room was so crowded with bandits that the bishop wondered if perhaps some had deserted their posts. So he hurried to the back of the compound and found the rear gate unguarded. It was now or never.

The sentry at the door was still a problem. The bishop told him that with all of the looting the women would be frightened and so he would take them to a different building.

The sentry, meaning to be helpful, shouted to the looters on the upstairs veranda to come down at once. They paid no heed, for which Bishop Galvin was thankful.

In the upstairs room the bishop said to the nuns, "Follow me." That they did in good order and without undue haste.

"We passed the sentry without difficulty, for he had the impression that I was taking them to some other room at the back. He thought that the back gate was still guarded. From the Sisters' compound we passed through the door which led to the women's catechumenate. Fathers O'Collins and Walsh brought up the rear."

The bishop told the houseboy, Ma, to go ahead as a scout. The Columbans followed, slipping from one clump of bushes to another, taking advantage of every stand of trees and every fold in the ground. Ma kept twenty yards ahead, feeling his way, constantly looking for bandits.

Ma sought out faint paths and avoided all roads. The people along the way gave all the help they could, suggesting the safest paths.

Some distance out of town the group stopped to rest. The sisters removed their white headdresses for fear they would be too easily seen from a distance.

Just as they started again a bandit came down the road on horseback. On his way to town, he passed within fifteen yards of the group but gave no indication of having seen them.

Across the fields they went at a brisk pace, alternating between a fast walk and a trot. With the Han dike in sight hopes mounted. Suddenly Father O'Collins commanded, "Down! They have seen us." Down flat into the wheat went the houseboy, five nuns, two priests, and a bishop. Peering through the blades they saw six bandits, with rifles slung on shoulders, about a hundred yards away.

When the bandits had passed, the group crossed the dike of the Han and took a rest within a dense clump of trees. Everyone was surprised when Sister Michael produced from the folds of her robes Mother Lelia's bottle of brandy. She even produced the scissors with which to open the bottle. Bishop Galvin wrote, "Every priest and Sister had a sip as it passed around and it gave us new life and courage."

A boatman said, "Are you fleeing? Get in!" and took them across the Han. The group walked three miles downriver and finally found two boats that would take them toward Hanyang.

"It should be borne in mind that we had eaten nothing since early morning and it was now five in the evening so we bought some Chinese bread and some boiled eggs and had a pleasant if simple meal on board, as our boats went downriver.

"No words of mine can convey the glorious spirit of comradeship which bound together that little fugitive band and the fortitude and courage which the Sisters displayed throughout that terrible day. They were simply wonderful. The awful agony which they went through can never be put into words. Nor can any of us ever cease thanking God, for it was He who led them out to safety."

The bishop disembarked in the darkness several miles below Sien Tao Chen. Everyone urged him to continue on to Hanyang but he insisted on returning to the mission compound, saying that from there he would be better able to work for the release of Fathers Laffan and Linehan.

The first thing the bishop did after picking his way through the rubble of the looted compound was to ask a parishioner, Gaw, to serve as a go-between. Another parishioner, Li, said, "I will go with him. If we don't come back, remember our names when you are saying your prayers."

In Hanyang the Columban sisters, the Loretto sisters and the girls at the school had Exposition of the Blessed Sacrament daily. The Columban priests offered their masses for the safe return of their confreres.

Days became weeks and weeks grew to months, and spring unfolded into summer and it turned into fall. Bishop Galvin kept a tenuous contact with the hostages through the efforts of Gaw and Li.

The captives were kept on the move much of the time. They slept in boats, private homes, government buildings, and wayside huts. The Reds kept demanding rifles, something the Columban fathers in Hanyang were unable to provide and certainly the government troops would not. So the missionaries were beaten and threatened with knives and pistols. Each day they expected to be executed.

When government troops attacked the Reds the priests saw this as a chance to escape. As refugees crowded into the house in which they were being held, causing commotion, it seemed possible to slip away unnoticed. When the guards slept the priests made their beds to look as though they were still in them, and even left their shoes next to the beds, which were merely doors taken from their hinges.

Fathers Laffan and Linehan started in the direction they thought might bring them to the camp of the government forces. Guided by stars they plodded southwest as best they could through mud and streams, and across rocky ground. At five in the morning they saw what they thought were government troops, but were really bandits.

The bandits beat the priests, put them in a small boat on Red Lake where they somehow survived in the hot sun without food until their condition was so weakened that they could not possibly attempt an escape. By now both suffered from malaria. The vermin in their clothes was maddening. The captors gave them Red uniforms which they refused to wear. A doctor, brought from a nearby hospital to treat them, made arrangements to get medicine and a change of clothes from the Columbans in Hanyang.

When it became evident to the Reds, after seven months of trying, that they would never get the rifles, they suddenly lost interest in their captives. In late November the bandits put their prisoners in a small boat and told them to row to the *Mantis,* a steamboat, which was waiting to take them aboard.

In that last lap the missionaries nearly lost their lives, for a storm overtook them and they were nearly drowned. They had to postpone getting to the *Mantis* until the following day, and so they rowed back to shore and spent the night in a Chinese house.

The two priests boarded the *Mantis* at nine o'clock one morning and arrived at Hanyang twenty-four hours later. Their captivity had extended from April 25 until December 2.

While the reception was a joyful one, still a shadow fell across it. While helping Fathers Laffan and Linehan catch up with the events of the past seven months, the priests and nuns in Hanyang were the bearers of bad news.

For example, when the priests asked, "How are things in Sien Tao Chen?" they had to be told that the White Spears had taken over. This anti-Communist defense society was about as rigorous as the Reds. Such big-spear-and-knife men talked in loud voices when the Reds were at some distance, but as soon as a bandit appeared they would remove the spearheads from their staves and put the latter over their shoulders to pose as coolies.

With the Communists gone, the White Spears were now restricting travel, acting with arrogance, demanding contributions to their funds, and even helping themselves to private property. To counteract the antireligious campaign of the Reds, the White Spears insisted that everybody must honor Buddha.

During the reception in Hanyang everyone dreaded telling Fathers Laffan and Linehan that their confrere, Father Cornelius Tierney, had been captured on November 13. At dawn when the church bell rang for Mass the Reds had attacked the town of Shang Tang Hsu. At the church door two Communists seized Father Tierney. One of them pinned the priest's arms behind his back and said, "You are our greatest enemy."

When Father John Kerr, seventeen miles away, heard of this he disguised himself as a coolie and set out with his teacher, Yang Mao, to keep in touch with the captured missionary. The two men put up at the home of a Catholic three miles from where Father Tierney was being held captive, and Yang Mao went into town each day to learn the news.

The news was never good. For instance, Father Tierney had been stripped of his clothes, scourged with bamboo, and given a soldier's red coat to wear. His fellow prisoners so admired his spirit that they shared their quilts, tea, and rice with him.

Father Walsh reported to Hanyang: "Pagans especially expressed their indignation openly and fearlessly that such a good man should be made to suffer so. But whatever leniency was extended to others, there was no mercy for a foreigner among these fanatics. They said he had come to China as a forerunner of imperialism."

Yang Mao, disguised as a carpenter, entered the Red camp. He found Father Tierney, dressed in the red coat, sitting dazed in a crowd of Red soldiers listening to their leader harangue them. The priest recognized Yang Mao and surreptitiously gave him a letter written in Latin with a Chinese pen saying that the Reds demanded $10,000 in ransom, that he had twenty Mass intentions not yet fulfilled, and that he had hidden $500 under a stone near the church door.

This is how things stood when Fathers Laffan and Linehan heard the news on the day they returned to Hanyang. For the next three months they, and other Columbans, followed the grim story as Father Kerr sent it back bit by bit. To keep in touch with the ever-shifting situation, Father Kerr lived in the mountains, raking leaves with the villagers as a way of maintaining his disguise.

At one time Father Tierney was released. The ransom had been paid, the Reds said. This was not true. Perhaps they said this in order to "save face."

The Columban had traveled twenty miles when another band of Reds seized him. In groping for something to feel good about the nuns decided that if he could travel so far he must be well recovered from his severe illness, which they had judged to be malaria.

Father Tierney died at 2 p.m. on Saturday, February 28, 1931, and was buried two hours later in a wild mountainous place. This information reached Hanyang in late March, coming from an old pagan woman who had also been held captive by the Reds. She said that a doctor had told her that the cause of death was malaria.

Yang Mao made arrangements with the bandits to recover the body. After much discussion they eventually promised him the remains if he would buy them some fountain pens and some watches.

The dependable Yang hired four men to open the grave. He immediately identified the missionary's features. Since no coffin could be bought in this remote place, the coolies carried the corpse for forty miles atop a broad board.

On foot and in a pouring rain, Fathers Quinlan and Quigley traveled to attend the funeral in Kien Chang. There, on April 1, they buried Father Tierney after a Requiem High Mass.

The Chinese have a saying, "Adversity is needed for virtue." With such an abundance of adversity, virtue must have thrived on the missions in those days.

·9·

Next the Floods

The Columban sisters felt they were taking another step forward in October of 1930, on the Feast of the Little Flower, when Sister Mary Patrick opened a new clinic. The first patient, a boy on crutches, was followed by ten soldiers, six seeking treatment and four coming along just to gawk. Another early arrival was a soldier whose ear had been severed by his officer for being absent without leave. The victim suggested to Sister Mary Patrick that he bring her a bandit's ear and that she graft it to his head. As she tended the wound the young man admitted having considered drowning himself in the Yangtze, but now he thought he might change his mind and become a member of the Catholic Church.

The clinic was not long open when an epidemic of smallpox raged through Hanyang. As soon as the first cases appeared the sisters began a program of vaccinations. In one day Sisters Mary Ignatius and Mary Michael gave vaccinations to 95 people from the neighborhood while Sisters Mary Patrick and Lelia vaccinated 105 women in the catechumenate.

In those days leprosy was not uncommon in China and was still considered practically incurable. In the early stages the features swelled and assumed a peculiar, frowning aspect suggesting the face of a lion. Later face and body were disfigured by loathsome ulcers that gave off a sickening odor. Ulcers sometimes invaded eyes and throat destroying eyeballs and vocal chords. The extremities usually became useless and gradually decayed, the joints falling off one by one.

Sister Mary Patrick urged all lepers to go live in a leprosarium, but she did it with heavy heart, especially after hearing Father Patrick Maguire tell of the trauma he had suffered on his first visit to such a place. He and a brother were no sooner on the grounds than they found themselves surrounded by hundreds of the malformed in various stages of putrefaction.

"Its poor victims do not die and rot; they rot and die," said Father

Maguire. "We tried to speak to them in cheerful tones, but sheer pity broke the words on our lips. We felt like bursting into tears."

One leper who had lost hands and feet and the sight of both eyes hobbled forward to listen, a ghastly figure supported by two comrades whose feet were partially intact. The priest thought the man was dying; he seemed to be vomiting blood, but it was really just the red juice of betel which he was chewing with vigor to sooth himself.

The Columban sisters felt humble when Father Maguire told them how the sisters in the colony worked amid the sight and stench of putrefying bodies. "They astonished us," he said, "They seemed to be in excellent health and spirits. They were in snow-white habits dressing with gentle hands the festering sores. It was their sole employment all day every day."

When one of the Columban sisters expressed her admiration, Father Maguire said, "You can imagine how I felt when the parish priest rode by on a bicycle on his way to anoint some poor soul who was fortunate enough to be dying. The pastor insisted on anointing every case personally, refusing to allow his young curate to take the risk."

In the clinic the sisters came to depend more and more on Lomo, "a real treasure," they called him. The young man, on loan from Father Joseph Crossan, knew enough Latin to read labels on the bottles, and having been a policeman was adept at managing crowds. "Joined to all of this he is gentle and well-mannered," Sister Agnes wrote home.

Time and again they said, "What would we do without him?" and then quite suddenly they found out. Lomo drowned, June 29, 1931, while swimming in a pool. One of the boys who had gone with him returned to the convent, and in a roundabout way told of the accident.

Three nuns hurried to the pool to try to revive Lomo with artificial respiration. They were terribly hampered in their effort by the crowd pressing around them.

"It was stifling hot already," one of them wrote, "so you can imagine what it was like with the rough, half-naked mob yelling and pressing—they were actually walking on us as we knelt. Father Crossan came and anointed Lomo. We gave him a couple of injections, but I felt from the beginning that it was hopeless."

The body was carried to the dispensary where the nuns found it impossible to keep out the crowd. About fifty people jammed the waiting room all arguing and yelling about money—some because they had helped recover the body, and one man who had brought a bowl of dirty water demanded thirty cents for it.

"At last with the help of the police we got rid of them, but then the deceased boy's relatives arrived. His sister threw herself on the ground beside the body; her grief was terrible to witness. Later the poor old father came. He, too, was broken-hearted. Two of us waited until the body had been put into the coffin. The Chinese said he must be put in that night because of the heat. He was buried next day. It is a great consolation to us that he was such a good boy."

At the time the clinic was being started word came from Ireland that Mother Theopane had been elected the new superior general to succeed Mother Finbarr. When Sister Theophane had left China to attend the first general chapter of the congregation, Sister Agnes had been made acting superior of the China foundation.

Now Sister Agnes would be called Mother Agnes. She was amused that she should have such a dignified title for she had long been something of a convent jester. It seemed that amusing things always happened to her, or at least she recognized them when they came along and made capital of them.

For example, she always said that José, the sacristan, looked upon her with professional jealousy. No matter how thoroughly she dusted the altar José would come behind her and blow away imaginary dust. If she trimmed candle wicks, he gave them an extra touch. If she straightened the candles, he gave them a slight readjustment.

He showed a new-found humility, however, when Mother Agnes began teaching him to cook. He told her that if he did not cook things the the right way she should hit him on the head. To demonstrate his feelings he made a fist and gave himself a terrible whack.

One day Mother Agnes caught a thief. When she saw a man carrying a bundle past the kitchen window she thought he might be delivering the laundry and went out to meet him. Upon hearing her voice he ran through the front gate, and Mother Agnes, wearing a sun helmet and with skirts tucked up, gave chase. Through Louga's lane they raced with the nun shouting in Chinese until the thief dropped the bundle. It contained an ironing blanket and ironing sheet.

As she wrote back to Ireland, "I came home feeling quite proud of myself."

The women in the catechumenate went to great lengths to celebrate Mother Agnes's feast day in February of 1931. The *Donja,* as the mother superior was called, enjoyed great popularity. Preparations went on for days as mysterious sounds issued from the *shensien's* (teacher's) room where rehearsals were in progress at every spare moment.

The catechumens presented their show from one until half past three on the Feast of Saint Agnes. When the *Donja* was seated with ceremony, on the best flowered blanket to be found in Hanyang, the performance began. It opened with a little child doing a scarf dance; despite her lightness and delicacy the stage creaked at each movement, for it consisted of bed boards placed across benches.

The play was the thing. Anna, director of the whole program, had cast herself in the roles of magistrate, priest, and doctor. Pedalo, the cook, refused a part in the show, but his wife starred as an old man whose black mustache ran parallel to the earth until in moments of excitement it fell off. Enessa, resplendent in red shirt, played with grand gestures the aristocratic lady who provided a feast for a poor family, a scene that held the audience like no other.

When the curtain fell, at the close of each act, a group of children persisted in rushing under it. At the final curtain, when Mother Agnes asked Rosa to make a brief speech of thanks in her behalf the elderly spinster used the occasion to preach a lengthy sermon.

With the morale high among the 105 women living and studying religion in the catechumenate and with the clinic caring for a steady flow of patients, the Columban sisters could now feel some satisfaction. Yet frustration never really left them, for they saw so much else that needed to be done.

Their hearts grew heavy every time they heard Father Michael Moran speak of the baby girls who were abandoned at his door in Nan Feng. He said, "The mother comes along to the door with the baby she wishes to get rid of, stands there for a while gazing into space in a careless sort of manner, but really to see that there's nobody around. Even among the pagans the abandonment of the baby is regarded as a disgrace to the family. Having ascertained that the coast is clear, she puts the baby on our doorstep, gives a few sharp knocks, and runs away."

The nuns thought that the babies were probably born out of wedlock, but Father Moran said that was not the case. In a poor family more than two infant girls was considered an impossible burden. The abandonment was not hardhearted, he said, because the mother would sometimes return to the rectory to ask how the child was progressing.

What to do with infants who have such a scant hold on life was often an agony for the missionary. Father Moran said, "I ask around the town for a woman who is able and willing to nurse a baby. Such women are hard to find just now. So three of the five infants left with me recently are still on my hands. It is a smart man who knows what to do with them.

"I have given one to each of three girls in our school and also some tins of milk which they mix with hot water to feed the mites. Once I watched the operation. They just lay the baby on the flat of its back and spill in the milk-and-water with a large spoon. Why the mites have not been choked long ago is a mystery to me. If the baby does not swallow at once they just grip its nose with their fingers as in a vise. This makes the baby squeal—and so it opens its mouth and the milk runs down its throat.

"The girls were delighted while the babies were new, but they found that infants cry at night and that one must get up, heat the milk, and go through the elaborate process of feeding them. They gave me to understand that if I can find a few nursing women they will not object."

In every way the Columban sisters were crowded for space. Their convent, the one they had inherited from the Sisters of Loretto, was falling apart. As one of them wrote home: "Even the room upstairs has ceased to keep out the rain and there is a collection of basins night and day collecting the water. One night a sister was driven to putting her basin on top of her mosquito net and she got up at intervals to exchange it for another one. The community room is letting in the rain too. In fact the whole house is, and all things considered, I think it is time we were moving into the new house."

They were just moving into a new convent, in the first week of August of 1931, and had slept there just one night when at five o'clock in the morning the dikes broke on the Yangtze. Refugees began pouring in and the nuns turned their new convent over to some three hundred of them. The catechumenate housed 170 refugees and the embroidery school more than 200. The Columban priests could not house any because only the top story of the buildings in their compound remained above water; in a sampan they entered and left through upper floor windows.

Bishop Galvin wrote home: "In the Columban Sisters' Convent which we converted into a refugee shelter, Father Crossan and I slept on the floor of the bathroom. It was difficult to snatch any sleep. In that house the lamps were never extinguished. The peace and quiet of a hospital ward were entirely absent; women and children tramped up and down the stairs the whole night long. There was a continual babel of voices, intermingled with the moans of the dying. The pitiful wails of sick children were never for a moment stilled.

"The people were dying rapidly, at the rate of four or five per day. Cholera takes about twelve to twenty-four hours to do its deadly work and is so infectious that the body has to be removed and coffined immediately after the patient dies. The coffins were carried out for burial in the early hours of the morning and a wailing crowd of refugees followed them to the door of the compound. Every day for two months, five carpenters were busily engaged making coffins. I could never pass the little shed where they worked without a shudder."

Only the roofs of many houses showed above the water. Human corpses and dead animals floated in what seemed a vast tideless sea. In and around Hankow, twelve thousand people drowned. The water brought destitution to twenty-three million and serious loss to fifty million.

The flood set an all-time record, an achievement for a country notorious through the centuries for its high-water marks. After rising to fifty-three feet above normal in the Hankow-Hanyang areas, the river began to subside.

As the water receded the sisters extended their care over a wider area. They and the Columban priests took quick courses in how to diagnose and treat diseases from Father Francis McDonald, a qualified doctor. Sister Mary Patrick, who had studied nursing in London and Dublin, and Sister Mary Ignatius, a graduate of St. Vincent's Hospital, Dublin, were also instructors.

The sisters began making daily expeditions to Black Hill, an area swarming with refugees. Two boys, carrying baskets of medicines, accompanied them on a trip that was always an adventure.

After walking for twenty minutes they boarded a boat. On this part of the trip they were hailed from junks by half-starved people calling in hoarse voices the full particulars of the sickness on board. To transfer from boat to junk the nuns either walked a shaky plank or took a small sampan. After doing a tightrope walk along the riggings and crawling through a tiny hatch they finally reached the sick and dying in the dark, fetid heart of the junk.

Upon leaving the boat the missionaries walked for another ten minutes around the enclosure of the powder plant. Next they crossed a lake on a bridge one plank wide, a plank so slippery that many Chinese women crossed on hands and knees, but the nuns managed to bring it off with more dignity.

At this point their "beat" began. Extending before them was a long stretch of the bank of the Han, a hill, a long road, and another hill, all crowded with refugees who stood looking in dumb wonder, the way cows look at strangers.

On dry spots people huddled together under straw mats supported by bamboo sticks. To reach the sick inside such huts the nuns crawled on hands and knees. Some patients refused treatment saying they had been tended by the *poosay* (charm worker), but most were grateful for attention. After a quick diagnosis the missionaries reached into their baskets for medicines to treat smallpox, dysentery, beriberi, scarlet fever, influenza, and typhoid.

Sister Mary Patrick wrote home: "You have heard of the many cases of 'cholera.' The Chinese say it is cholera, but the doctors are doubtful. Whatever it is, it is a most virulent disease, and carries the patient off in a day's illness. It killed two of our best Hanyang pupils. One poor woman in St. Joseph's lost her mind with it. Her people took her home and she died shortly."

Whatever it was, it flamed like fire, sweeping from camp to camp.

The missionaries fought back with a series of injections, often inoculating as many as nine hundred people a day. The injections contained a triple antidote against cholera, typhoid, and paratyphoid. This eventually stemmed the ravages of the epidemic, or perhaps it burned itself out.

The miracle is that all of the missionaries survived. While working long hours on two sandwiches a day they came in contact with death in the stench of the huts, but it did not touch them. To add to their burden was the awareness that after the water was gone, famine would linger for months, and the city would be buried in mud, and pestilence would follow.

·10·

Bandits Again

During the flood Mother Agnes wrote to Cahiracon to express delight in the news that three more sisters would soon be on the way. Perhaps she was trying to assure them that adventure awaited them, for she included in the letter two grim sentences. "A few days ago we saw three dead men on the roadside and learned that they were Communists who had been shot the day before. For three whole days the bodies lay there—an example and a warning to passersby."

The shooting might have been a retaliation, judging from something a priest wrote home during the flood. "And the most brutal part of it all is that the Reds everywhere have taken advantage of the disaster. They have commandeered every available boat and have stolen everything that had been salvaged by the homeless flood victims. They are also murdering to an extent hitherto unknown. What monsters they are!"

Soon Red bandits were threatening the Columbans more than ever. At the time the waters were subsiding, in September of 1931, the Japanese seized control of Manchuria, and Chiang Kai-shek moved his troops northward toward the threat, giving Communists the run of central China. They took every advantage of it. Soon missionaries were on the run.

The Columban sisters heard Father Patrick Maguire tell of his escape from Huan Ja San. Expecting the bandits, he had avoided his rectory and spent the night in the village. When Wang, his house boy, scaled the mission wall and hurried to the village to alert his pastor, the priest hid in tall grass until the next morning. At great risk he traveled by boat to Hanyang.

Father John O'Carroll escaped from Yuin Lung Ho to Lay Ja where he hid out for two weeks. His parishioners feared he had been captured by the Reds, and when they heard otherwise they were elated. Realizing that they would reveal his hiding place if they visited him in a body, they began to come one by one.

"When the first man arrived I was sitting in the back room," Father

O'Carroll told the sisters. "He came straight in, all excitement, threw himself on his knees, took hold of my hands, kissed them and wept. I asked him what was wrong. He sobbed, 'You are safe. You escaped. Thank God they did not get you.'

"The next day his wife came. There was a cold north wind. She saw I had practically no clothes and on my feet were a pair of white cotton slippers. She measured the length of my foot and examined my bed, shaking her head. That evening she sent me a change of linens, some warm clothes, and a few days later new slippers, my exact fit."

All over the vicariate priests slipped through the Red net. It was almost as though they led charmed lives. And then, during the worst days of the flood, word reached the convent that Father Hugh Sands had been captured.

The sisters had last seen Father Sands when he stopped at the convent shortly after the rupture of the dikes. He told them at the time that in Hankow, in one night, eight thousand people were drowned. He was hurrying to his mission in Chi Woo Tai, he said, to be there for the Feast of the Assumption. The nuns felt this was taking an undue risk, but Father Sands did not see it that way.

For eight days the missionary traveled by water past millions of refugees. In Chi Woo Tai he found that rafts and boats and anything that would float were the homes of his parishioners. The first thing the people told him was that the Reds, in more than a hundred boats, had landed at a village two miles away.

The exhausted priest went to the upper floor of his presbytery to take a nap, and had no sooner fallen asleep when a boy ran into the room crying, "The Reds are here!" The next moment a bandit burst into the room brandishing a revolver and screaming at the top of his voice.

The prisoner spent the next few days with a convoy of fifty boats, each manned by four Reds. At every village the inhabitants had to give whatever was demanded. One person must contribute forty dollars, another a hundred—each according to his means. It was evident the Reds knew how much each could afford.

In time the convoy reached a camp atop a hill outside of a pretty village. The Reds took possession of it, having driven out the military. His captors were so successful, Father Sands felt, in that they worked for an ideal while the government soldiers worked for pay.

Since this was the first time a white man had been seen in these parts, all of the villagers had to inspect the priest. They examined his clothes, rubbed his hair, and pawed him all over. One examination was not enough; the curious returned each day and brought friends who also found the stranger amusing. Amid giggles they asked a thousand times his name, age, occupation, and home country.

All of this unsought attention came in the ruins of an ancient temple atop a hill. The room, forty-one by twenty-three feet was spacious during the day, but at night it was shared with thirty donkeys, mules, and horses. As the animals milled around, Father Sands tried to sleep on a plank, fourteen inches wide and five feet in length, placed atop several bricks.

Anyone opposing the Reds was immediately executed. The missionary witnessed a dozen such deaths. The one he found most painful to observe was the crucifixion of a man to a tree with the bandit rubbing salt water into the victim's wounds saying, "this is how to treat a spy."

One evening when the Reds feared the military was about to attack, they hurried to their boats. In the confusion Father Sands slipped into a house where an old man led him through several flooded rooms, out through a flooded yard, up a ladder and over a wall. He piloted the missionary atop an old door to a neighboring house where he seated him on a stool set on a table in a flooded room. Within minutes the Reds had found their prisoner. Strangely enough at no time did they make any reference to his attempt to escape.

Back in Hanyang the nuns, despite all of their troubles, prayed daily for Father Sands's safe return. They gathered with eagerness bits and pieces of information about his condition in captivity. Since rural China was something of a gigantic grapevine, word was passed along about the foreign priest, but how much could be believed was something the sisters asked each other again and again.

They had learned by now that to get a message delivered in China, especially in the rural parts, took some doing. They knew that the only sure way to have it reach the recipient was to deliver it yourself.

No matter how carefully the messenger was selected, and no matter with what good intentions he set out, "the way was long." When tired he would ask a friend who was "going near the place" to take the message. The friend also became tired—as the Chinese say, "*Sceeang fa tze*" (he looks for a way out)—and he, too, passed the message to a friend who was "going just beside the place." Eventually the message was distorted, or reached the wrong person, or was never delivered to anyone.

The sisters did put trust in the information brought back by Mah Shien Sin, the teacher who had risked his life so often interviewing the Reds to secure the release of Fathers Laffan and Linehan. When Mah returned to Hanyang he said that the Reds had asked Father Sands to write for guns, but that the priest had convinced them it was a futile request. They demanded that he write for £3,000, but he refused to do that, too. Finally, both sides agreed on £300 and the missionary wrote the letter to Bishop Galvin. Since no answer came the Reds had him write another letter. When Mah arrived at the Red camp he learned that for a reason no one could explain neither letter had been sent.

Mah departed as suddenly as he had arrived, leaving Father Sands to wonder what his own status might be. Almost immediately he was taken on a three-day journey to Doz Lao Dzay, ten miles from Red Lake. Because of the flood, the islands in Red Lake were under water, and so the Soviet headquarters had been shifted from lake to village.

In the village Father Sands found that everybody seemed to be antiforeign, except for a Chinese Red with the improbable name of White. Whenever White took the priest for a walk a taunting mob followed. The mob became so threatening on one occasion that had it not been for two Reds with revolvers the priest might well have been murdered. Thereafter White and the missionary did not take their walks until after dark.

Father Sands lived on the edge of starvation through the fall of 1931. When he seemed sufficiently weakened by hunger and loneliness the Reds said that if he would apostatize they would free him immediately.

"Would you renounce your Communism and join the government army?" he asked.

"Certainly not," they said.

"Then you know how I feel."

This seemed to appeal to his captors. Perhaps that is why they brought in Father Lazzeri, an Italian Franciscan, and allowed the two priests to talk for a few minutes every day. Father Sands decided, however, that the Reds were doing him no favors because the Franciscan was so pessimistic that all he did was to make the day seem darker than it already was.

Father Lazzeri said that he had written a letter for his ransom, a supply of medicines. When the Reds asked Father Sands to write for medicines, he did so.

On November 26 a Red guard came to the Columban and said, "You are free to go. Your ransom is here."

"What about him?" Father Sands asked, pointing to Father Lazzeri.

"No ransom. He stays."

Father Sands looked at the old Franciscan. Without medical attention and better food he would not last another month.

"Let him go instead." Even as he said it, the Columban wondered why he was doing it. As he said later, "I didn't even like the fellow."

Somehow Father Sands got hold of a pencil and writing pad and began slipping out notes, some of which eventually reached Hanyang. He described being crowded into a room with sixty-six other prisoners, men and women, all of the whom were held for ransom. The place was filthy and infested with vermin and rats. "There are," he wrote, "two buckets in two corners of the room, with no screens, and they are the W.C."

Finally, on May 9, 1932, five months after his capture, Father Sands was released.

Back in Hanyang it was evident that he needed medicine and substantial food. The sisters were prepared to provide both. As they nursed him back to health they were aware of one of the notes that he had sent from Red Lake: "Nothing dries more quickly than a tear."

·11·

A Better Season

In the fall of 1932, Chiang Kai-shek's troops began attacking the Reds with a vigor never seen before. The effort was so effective that Communists fell back on all fronts, even in the Red Lake district. Once more people could move about with relative safety.

Even where pockets of bandits remained in control they acted with more civility. For example, when they captured Father Joseph Hogan, three of his teachers and eleven pupils, they soon released the priest not knowing what a foreigner could eat and not wanting him to die on their hands. With a mere carton of cigarettes Father Hogan paid ransom for his friends.

Bishop Galvin wrote home: "Our priests are all in their places, and like other people they are trying to bring order out of the ruins. Everything we have was looted by the Communists; nothing remains but the roof and the walls. Vestments were stolen, altars were destroyed, and even the doors and the windows were torn out and burned by these Communist brigands, the first plank in whose creed seems to be hatred of religion."

Most priests, homesick for their parishes, were pleased to leave Hanyang and return to the country. As Father Frank Murray said: "During the year we were away I used to picture to myself the road that ran in front of the church and wonder if there were any people going to or coming from the town. I used to think of the fields along the road and wonder if there were any people working in them. Or had they all fled? And then as the days and sometimes months passed without any signs of improvement, the thought used to come to my mind that it might be years before we could get back."

And when they returned what a welcome they received!

Father Murray, for example, was surprised to be met by a dozen elders in a boat twenty miles from his destination. They had come to greet him and to escort him home. As the procession came within sight of the village, the church bell began to ring and all of the people hurried down the road to embrace their priest.

"The welcome I received from young and old is indescribable. The old women in particular were almost foolish in their outbursts of joy and welcome. They just clung to me till I thought they would never release me."

On their way back to their districts the missionaries wondered if the Catholics had succumbed to the pressures, physical and economic, put on them by the Reds. They found that their parishioners had stood up under the strain remarkably well.

"The reign of terror," said Father Charles Donnelly, "so far from weakening the appeal of the Catholic Church in this area, seems to have strengthened it. It was an extraordinary reawakening. I opened fifteen schools and they were filled immediately. The rest had to be satisfied with promises of having their needs attended to next year."

Father Leahy spoke of a new rush of conversions in Tsan-Dan-Kow: "Last year, in this parish, sixteen thousand people of their own accord expressed a wish to enter the Catholic Church."

This wish was expressed in a formal manner. The most influential man in each village took the names of those desiring instruction. After copying the names into an elegant book, he also included them in an ornate letter praising the Catholic Church. A deputation of village potentates would arrive carrying the letter and the register of prospective Catholics to the priest.

Father Sands, who had known more than his share of troubles, returned to his district to find a problem different from the one he had left. In a letter he expressed his plight: "Here is a priest with a smattering of the language, fair health, and a little money. Five thousand pagans crowd around him and ask to be made Christians. Many of them are sick, most are hungry, and practically all are poor. If he selects as many as he can deal with, who shall they be? And what will the others say or do?"

Such waves of conversions came periodically to China, almost always in the wake of tragedy. In those days, the twenties and thirties, there was an abundance of tragedy what with the civil war, bandits, Communists, warlords, Japanese, excessive taxes, floods, and pestilence.

As new optimism spread abroad in the land, the Columban sisters responded with a surge of confidence. They knew that they had conducted themselves admirably in escaping the bandits, and they had performed noble work in caring for refugees during the most damaging flood in China's history. It was evident that their clinic was creating good will, and the catechumenate was so crowded that ground had to be broken for a new one. Three more sisters had recently arrived, and four others would be on the way within a year.

By the summer of 1933 everything was going their way, excepting the weather. How fiercely hot it was! An old Chinese parishioner leaned in the convent doorway and said, "If it is hotter than this in Purgatory, I could never stand it."

The teaching sisters could close the catechumenate and go to Kuling for a few weeks to enjoy the coolness of the mountains, but the clinic could not be closed, for illness took no holiday. The worst times were those when the nursing sisters had to visit the homes of severe cases.

In August, for example, when undue exertion was a thing to be avoided, a Chinese woman swallowed opium in an attempt to kill herself. To reach her, Sisters Mary Agnes and Mary Patrick followed a messenger through fetid streets oppressive with humidity. They carried a basket containing mustard, permanganate, and a few other simple remedies. Upon entering a small crowded room the nuns felt there was no air in it left to breathe. All the neighbors began speaking at once, telling what had happened. Poverty and hunger, they said, drove her to it.

Sister Mary Agnes observed later, "I had a notion it was a family quarrel and that the nervous little husband must have been trying to assert himself unduly. She didn't look like a woman who would stand any nonsense."

Sister Mary Patrick turned to the woman sprawled on a pad and forced down her throat some mustard in lukewarm water, enough to upset the equilibrium of a dozen normal people, but it brought no results. Permanganate also went down with no effect.

"She must be wakened up." Said Sister Mary Patrick, "She musn't go to sleep or she will die."

Her companion began slapping and pinching the patient. Despite the seriousness of the moment, Sister Mary Patrick could not help but laugh at the sound from the smacking the poor woman was getting. Sister Mary Agnes asked for a wet towel, and was handed one that had been filthy even before being soaked in muddy water. With it she smacked the unconcious woman with such vigor that the crowd showed signs of concern.

"I think it must have been over an hour," Sister Mary Agnes wrote home, "before the patient came back to her senses enough to resist the treatment. Then we got a couple of able-bodied men to march her up and down the room—or rather to drag her for she wouldn't lift her feet. This commandeering of the onlookers was an inspiration, for soon one could see the crowd thinning, and we got a breath of air which we needed badly.

"When it was all over and the woman was better, the little man sat down on the bed and laughed and laughed hysterically, and so did we. It's just a thing one can't describe, but it was funny.

"We left them and heard no more of the case for some days. Then thinking it would be well to look them up, two of us called again on Sunday afternoon, and asked our patient how she felt. She told us her health was improved but that her whole body was sore, and she pulled up her sleeves and showed us the marks where she had been pinched and battered. I could hardly keep a straight face, but I don't think she ever suspected I was the culprit."

Each Sunday was "open house" at the convent. After Mass dozens of Chinese friends stopped by to say "good morning." The Columbans could point to any one of them and tell a story.

Margaret Mary, for example, was baptized when in danger of death during the cholera. She recovered after the sisters had given her saline injections.

Tommy and his mother came to the convent from the little boat they lived on in the creek. The boy, at sixteen a chronic invalid, found the trip an agony, and yet he looked forward to it each week.

Mr. Ho, a pagan who never missed Mass on Sunday, was a great favorite among the sisters. Crippled by arthritis, he was unable to work for months, but after a course of injections he was fit to work as a watchman, walking the lanes by night shaking a rattle to frighten off thieves.

One Sunday in November of 1933 Bishop Galvin came to the open house. He expressed his delight in the way the sisters were approaching the people.

The bishop said that there were now 21,000 Catholics in the vicariate of Hanyang and that 27,000 pagans were under instruction. Since it was not unusual for 10,000 people to apply to a missionary for instruction it seemed the only way to serve such members would be to instruct them with native catechists. But where to get all of those catechists?

It was evident to the sisters that the bishop was concerned about these new problems. It was also evident that he preferred these new ones to all of those he had been forced to accept in recent years.

·12·

New Good

During the days of many conversions, the mission territory that the Columban fathers administered in Kiangsi Province grew in importance. So much so that on July 21, 1933 the Holy See in Rome saw fit to appoint Dr. Patrick Cleary prefect apostolic of the newly-created vicariate of Nancheng, in Kiangsi.

Before joining the original band of Columbans in 1918, Dr. Cleary had taught theology at Maynooth. He was rector at the seminary in Dalgen before coming to China in 1931 to replace the martyred Father Tierney as ecclesiastical superior of the Columbans in Kiangsi Province.

The tall, slim priest, a scholarly man, was as elegant in manner and in appearance as Bishop Galvin was rough-cut. Some people in Ireland wondered if he had enough tough fiber for work in China, but a friend who knew him well said, "He has more the look of a poet than of a fighter, but watch out!" That observation proved so right when eventually he faced the Japanese military in a dispute over General Doolittle's wounded pilots. More of that later.

The Columban sisters in Hanyang knew that several of them would be asked before long to leave Bishop Galvin's vicariate in Hupeh province and help Monsignor Cleary at Nancheng, in Kiangsi Province, just to the south. So when the new prefect apostolic came to visit their convent in Hanyang they were full of questions.

Monsignor Cleary told the nuns that in three years he had seen vast changes. "Three years ago we were thirty centuries behind the times; it looks as if three years hence we shall be thirty centuries ahead of them."

With amusing hyperbole, Monsignor Cleary described life in his vicariate: "The rickshaw has come to Nancheng, but the horse-drawn vehicle is unknown. We have jumped straight from the wheelbarrow to the motorbus and the aeroplane, Ah, yes, we have bridged thirty centuries overnight."

In most of the main streets soldiers had pulled down enough housefronts so that two motorcars could pass one another comfortably. That is if they blew their horns loud enough and allowed sufficient time for the wheelbarrowmen to trundle out of the way.

"We have no electric light," the monsignor told the nuns, "but we have telephone wires enough for a country. We have no water supply, no plumbing, no hospital, no laundry. We lack a bakery, beef, and mutton. But we import Palmolive soap, Parisian cosmetics, Korean apples, Three Castles cigarettes, and Sunkist oranges. In the modern store, with plate-glass windows, foreign products stand cheek by jowl with the things made in household industries."

When the sisters asked about the status of education in his vicariate, the monsignor said that religion could be taught only outside of school hours. Ever-changing rules and government minutiae annoy every school administrator, he said. "The great consolation, though, is that nobody knows better than a Chinese official how to turn his blind eye and deaf ear when faced with the absurd and impractical. Especially after a glass of wine. As the old Irishwoman said after a good cup of tea, 'Glory be to God, how calm the night has got!' "

The monsignor was a great one for predicting the future. He ended his conversation at the convent by speaking of the China that the sisters might see unfold. What he told them can be guessed from a magazine article he wrote a few weeks later:

"Here is the battle of two civilizations, and I suspect that the older is doomed. China the immovable is moving with lightning rapidity. We are in a hurry and cannot afford to wait; we must overhaul the centuries in a few years.

"We thought that Bolshevism would help and found it a failure. We are sounding the possibilities of Fascism because it is now the fashionable panacea. We are really snobs, and with our half-knowledge we will ape what is Western while we miss the factors that made the West what she is. We hate the West, and when we have absorbed what she has to give us we shall probably hate her the more. Then we shall be a great nation, but we shall have lost our soul."

Although the sisters knew that some of them would soon be leaving for Nancheng, to join with a few newcomers from Ireland, they continued to extend the area of their visitations well outside the walls of Hanyang. Weary after a day of visiting the sick and hard travel, they would return to the convent each evening to tell of what the day had offered. They spoke with frustration about the difficulty of treating opium patients and told with amusement of the young woman who swallowed a hairpin to spite her mother-in-law, and of the girl who swallowed her gold ring when her father scolded her, and of how Mr. Ho accidentally sat in Mrs. Ri's lunch basket, breaking two eggs and not noticeably improving his appearance.

In early February of 1935 Bishop Galvin asked the sisters to be ready to send a few of their number, along with sisters about to leave Ireland, to establish a convent in Nancheng. The preparations culminated at half past five in the evening on Saint Patrick's Day when seven sisters rode in a bus through the West Gate of the walled city of Nancheng. Mother Agnes accompanied Sisters Columban, Gertrude, Monica, Angela, Campion, and Attracta.

One of the sisters wrote in her diary: "The city is beautifully situated in the midst of mountains and lovely scenery. I am afraid some of us misinterpreted the terrible noise of the firecrackers let off to welcome us and thought we had made the acquaintance of bandits early in our career. Monsignor Cleary and some of the priests were waiting for us, to say nothing of the hundreds of Chinese, all of whom escorted us to the convent. The Chinese serenaded us all evening, and crowded round the windows and in the door, and just stared at us while we had dinner. Our first visit, naturally, was to the chapel which is fairly big and very devotional. We were all delighted with it and happy to call it our own."

Mother Agnes said that she would stay only a short time and then would return to Hanyang. Sister Columban would be at the head of the new house. Mother Agnes, by now, an old China hand, took satisfaction in helping the new arrivals learn the ropes. But when it came to the language she felt less than adequate and observed: "I am afraid that I have reached the stage which someone prophesied we would one day reach, that is, to be content with the little we know. God help us, it is a terrible language, and the more you learn the more you realize that you know little about it."

Sister Agnes told the newcomers that "tones" would sooner or later cause them embarrassment, explaining that in Chinese the four tones give four completely different meanings to any sound.

As an example she said, *t'ang* in a high tone means soup, and, in a low, sugar. This can cause complications when giving directions to the cook. He might bring an axe when you thought you asked for a napkin, or having sent him to the kitchen for salt he goes to the village for tobacco. She admitted that while giving religious instruction she had difficulty with *t'ien* which in a high tone means heaven, and, in a low one, field.

Monsignor Cleary said that "face" is something else that the new sisters would have to come to terms with. This force that rules Chinese life above all others is difficult to define, but the monsignor said, he could tell an anecdote that might describe it.

A mother and a daughter were returning to their home one evening, walking along the city wall, when two armed men robbed them. They reported this to the police immediately, and martial law was proclaimed.

Someone must be found. The "face" of the authorities must be saved. But no robber could be located.

The police interviewed the women time and again and at last asked them for the names of anyone they had seen that night. They gave the names of two young men in a missionary's parish. The police at once went to the youths' homes, pulled them from their beds, and hauled them off to jail. There they spent the night only to be released in the morning after paying a fine of two dollars.

They were innocent, of course, but someone had to be punished for the robbery. The police had done their duty. The "face" of the city was saved.

The sisters found Father James Griffin a delightful raconteur. His stories helped the nuns get a better sense of life going on around them in Kiangsi Province, and what an abundance of life there was. On his first visit to the convent he told of an elegant Chinese dinner at which he had learned once again that pride goeth before the fall.

Upon receiving an invitation to the district manager's dinner he still had enough humility so that his mind was "sick at the thought of the endless ritual and my ignorance thereof." Pride entered when the courier arrived at three o'clock to say that the feast was ready and the missionary suddenly realized that he had gained great face because along the way everyone beamed at him and asked if he was attending the grand affair. He became even more pleased with himself when the host rushed forward to greet him. The thirty guests looked down upon "the outer-kingdom-man" until he spoke Chinese and then their icy gaze thawed and they showed signs of warmth and this too brought pride.

Everything went his way until the dining began, said Father Griffin: "I was trying to preserve the niceties of Chinese deportment. Imagine trying to carry from bowl to mouth the slippery contents on two smooth sticks and holding a delicate conversation on international politics at the same time. Can you blame a man who is accomplishing that if his large sleeve catches the tip of the wine bowl and floods the table. Oh horror! Oh catastrophe! But when it happens again five minutes later!!! Oh ye mountains fall upon me!"

With scarcely a transition Father Griffin switched from the story of an elegant dinner party to tell of life in his most remote mountain mission. He spoke of his mission in Bon San where people have a superfluity of fingers and toes. One man has a toe in the center of his foot.

"During my visit I was pleased to observe that the recent Red visit had a good effect on Bon San. It drew back many of those who had lapsed from the Church."

On the way down the mountain the missionary said that he was entertained by two merry coffin makers. "Those young men were the most jovial fellows I have ever met. They gave me tea and showed me specimens of their work. They were amused when I commented that it was a waste of timber to make such thick, heavy coffins. They just laughed and laughed and said that the supply of timber is plentiful and that I need not worry."

With anecdotes Father Michael Moran also helped the sisters learn the ways of Kiangsi Province. The nuns enjoyed stories about his visits to the Eagle's Nest, a village fifteen miles from his rectory.

"The place is well named," said Father Moran. "From an eagle's point of view, the location is ideal. You climb a very high hill, so high that at places you literally pull yourself along by gripping ledges of rock and tufts of brushwood that stick out from the mountain. One of the most inaccessible places imaginable!"

Because the place is so inaccessible, Catholics came there centuries earlier to escape persecution. Their selection was such a good one that no soldier has ever been sighted within miles of the place. As an extra deterrent to outsiders, tigers abound.

Father Moran dreaded sick calls to the Eagle's Nest, for they always came when snow lay deep on the ground, or rain lashed, or the night was exceedingly dark. Nobody seemed to face death up on that cliff in lovely weather.

On New Year's Eve in Kienchang, Father Moran was preparing his church for Mass on the next day, a day for which his parishioners had long prepared. Darkness was just beginning to fall when a man came to the rectory mud-bespattered and three-parts frozen. The day was bitterly cold and recent rains still lay deep on the roads. Through chattering teeth the visitor conveyed the message: A man was dying up at Eagle's Nest. Father Moran's heart became a millstone at the thought of fifteen miles up there and fifteen back on a dark and bitter night.

Father Moran asked the messenger why he had not come earlier. With embarrassing truthfulness the fellow answered that no one had wanted to make the trip and that it had taken the elders a long time to fix on a victim.

The missionary could not but admire the faith of the village that would not let a man die without a priest. So he put on his oversize shoes, trimmed the lantern, and prepared to face fifteen miles of slippery inclines, biting wind, tigers, and tiger traps.

In spite of the oversize shoes Father Moran reached his destination, administered the Last Sacraments to the sick man, ate a snack, and set out for home. It was now pitch dark with the wind howling above in the heights. When the lantern went out it took ten matches to relight it. Within twenty yards the light was out again.

"This lighting and extinguishing process went on at close intervals for about an hour," said Father Moran. "I cheerfully suggested to my guide that we should be half way home by now. He received the remark with less than enthusiasm. We had covered less than a mile! Fourteen to go."

The two men climbed down a steep gradient in darkness so intense that when the lantern went out again they dared not take a step either back or forward. Soon there would be no more matches.

Spend the night on a hill? Those unprincipled tigers would rejoice at such a decision. With wild gestures the guide argued for a return to the hilltop. Father Moran said that he must say Mass in his church on New Year's morning; everybody had looked forward to it for so long.

"The growing shortage of matches had sharpened my inventive faculties," said the missionary. "The openings in and around the lantern, I decided, would have to be sealed, and I must trust to the wind to supply enough oxygen to keep the flame alive. I succeeded in steadying the flame to some degree by unbuttoning the cape of my soutane and wrapping it around the chimney of the lantern. On we crept. The lantern still went out occasionally and it took skillful manoeuvering to keep the cape at the required angle to parry the icy blasts blowing up from the valley."

Once down on the plain the priest needed no light. He could poke along somehow. It meant a little blind walking with occasional lapses into waterlogged rice fields on each side of the path, but this was a minor matter.

Eventually Father Moran reached his church cold and sodden. By the time his congregation began assembling, he was already vested for Mass.

The sisters were scarcely settled in their new convent in Nancheng when the Columban and Lorettine convents in Hanyang were inundated by another flood. In the priests' house the water rose to six feet. Boats plied the streets of Hanyang. Outside the city only the tops of houses were visible. All of the country for miles along the Han valley was one uninterrupted sea. It was even worse than 1931.

Monsignor Cleary came almost daily to the convent in Nancheng to bring news of missionaries in Bishop Galvin's vicariate. He said that the parishes hardest hit were those served by Fathers Patrick O'Connell, John Mackey, Charles Donnely, Francis Murray, William Holland, Robert Staples, and Joseph Grimley.

The anguish of those caught in the flood can be felt in Father Grimley's letter, which the sisters practically memorized:

"On July 8th word came that the bank of the Han river had burst somewhere about one hundred miles from here. When the people heard the news they rushed to the fields to collect what they could of their crops and prepare for a flood. We moved our church and sacristy, goods and cooking utensils to the top of the house, but long before we had finished, in fact, within two hours of the time word came we saw the waters rushing across the plain towards our village. Everybody was bustling and gathering goods and putting them in the church. In an hour the water was knee-deep in my room upstairs. The teachers and a few people and the students found refuge in the loft in the school. The water mounted up and up until it was level with the windows of the church and halfways up the stairs of our house.

"Night came on and the air was filled with the pitiable cries of the people and the rushing of the water about the church. I think I shall never forget the night that followed. Needless to say none of us slept for we were in terror of our lives. We prayed to God all night long to save us from the great danger that threatened us.

"Morning came and the water was still rising. When I looked out the window the scene I beheld was a sorrowful one indeed. The people of the village were sitting on their houses and there was no boat to take them to the church. Boats from other places passed along but they were unable to help for they were filled with people to the very last inch. The situation was really desperate.

"The marooned people shouted to me to pray for them. I was pained to the heart at the sight of their suffering. But there was nothing I could do but pray. I thought of Matt Talbot and all day long I appealed to him and prayed before the Blessed Sacrament which I had reserved upstairs, and the people on the housetops among the village joined with me. If no boat came before night all of them would certainly be lost. But our prayers were heard and just at dark a boat came and brought all of those to the church who had survived the terrible day and the previous night.

"But some of them had sad tales to tell. One family lost a little girl during the night: she slipped off the roof and was drowned. An old blind woman while trying to go to the roof, missed her footing and was carried away, but she got hold of a wooden bed and floated to a tree about fifty yards away. The poor thing climbed up the tree and there she remained the whole night and next day until the boat I mentioned rescued her. There were other cases where whole families were swept away and all were lost."

The flood was still the major topic of conversation when at Christmas of 1935 three of the Hanyang sisters moved to Kiangsi to bring the total number in that convent up to eight.

There was good news too in the conversation. The Kiangsi nuns showed with pride their school with an enrollment of eighty pupils, twenty of whom were boarders. The sisters from Hanyang described in detail the new dispensary and catechumenate, the buildings of which had been dedicated in November.

During 1935 it seemed that the news had been swinging back and forth between good and bad. With the coming of 1936 good news seemed in the ascendance.

Lady Frances Moloney
(Mother Mary Patrick) ca. 1918

Lady Moloney
on horseback

Chinese junks on the Yangtze River

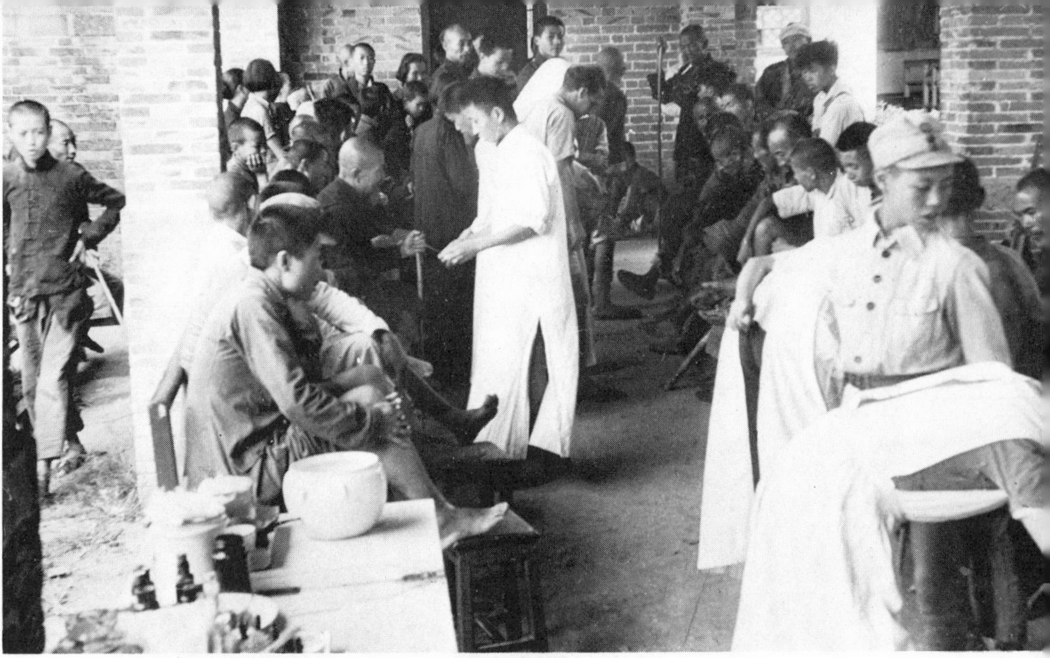

Patients waiting at the sisters' dispensary in Nancheng

Sister Mary Thaddeus and Sister Mary Michael on a sick call along the Yangtze

Sister Mary Kilian and Sister Mary Agnes with Bishop Edward Galvin

Sister Mary Baptist with pupils in Nancheng

Child dressed for
New Year celebrations
outside the convent in Hanyang

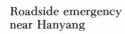

Roadside emergency
near Hanyang

Sister Mary Emmanuel with Russian pupils of the Sancta Sophia School, Shanghai

Sister Mary Thaddeus and Sister Mary Michael visit an island in the Yangtze

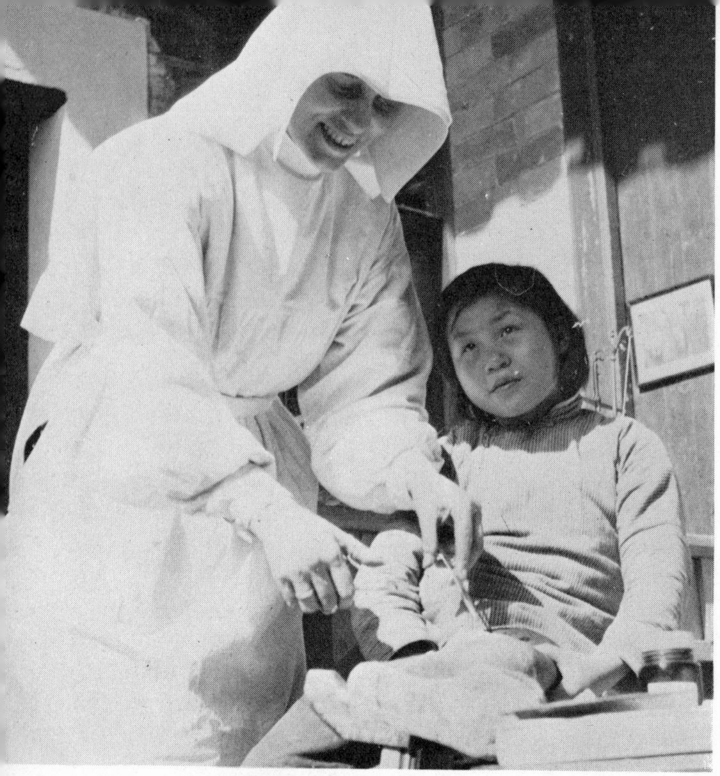

Sister Mary Attracta
with patient in Nancheng

Sister Mary Thomas
with children
in Hong Kong

Sister Mary Malachy with friend in Hanyang

Sister Mary Damian with Hakka women in Fanling, New Territories, Hong Kong

Sister Maureen Byrne in the marketplace, Hong Kong

Sister Mary Roberta visits the squatter areas in Hong Kong

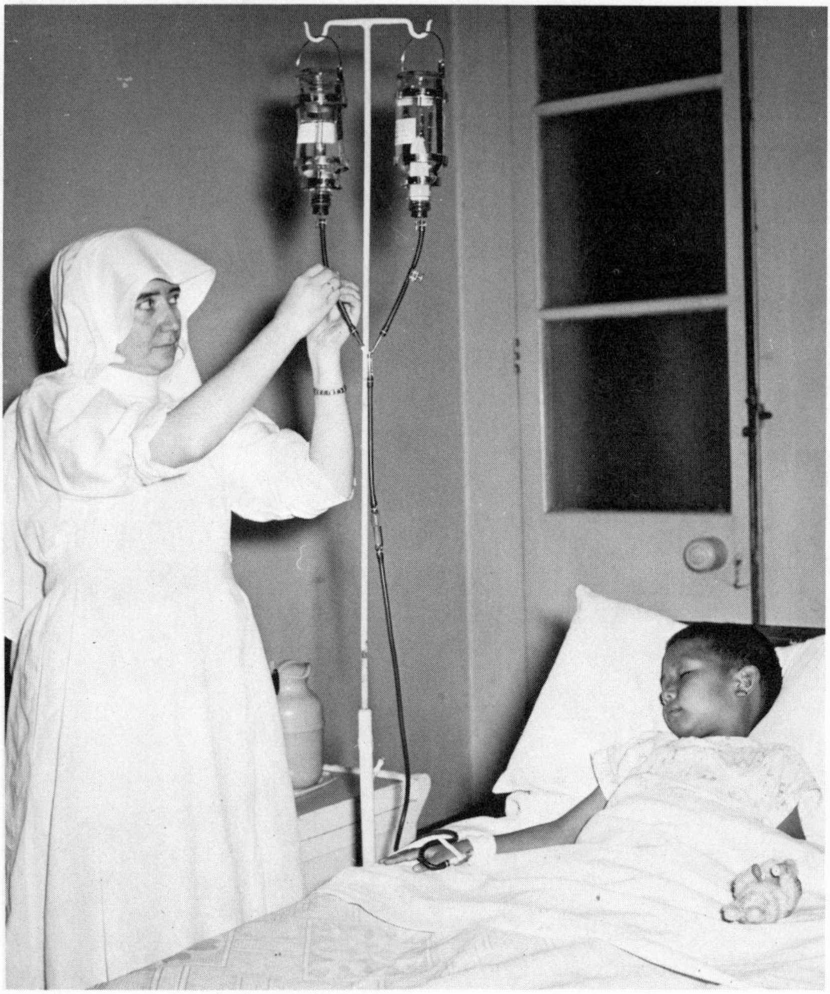

Sister Mary Justin adjusts a "drip" in
Ruttonjee Sanatorium, Hong Kong

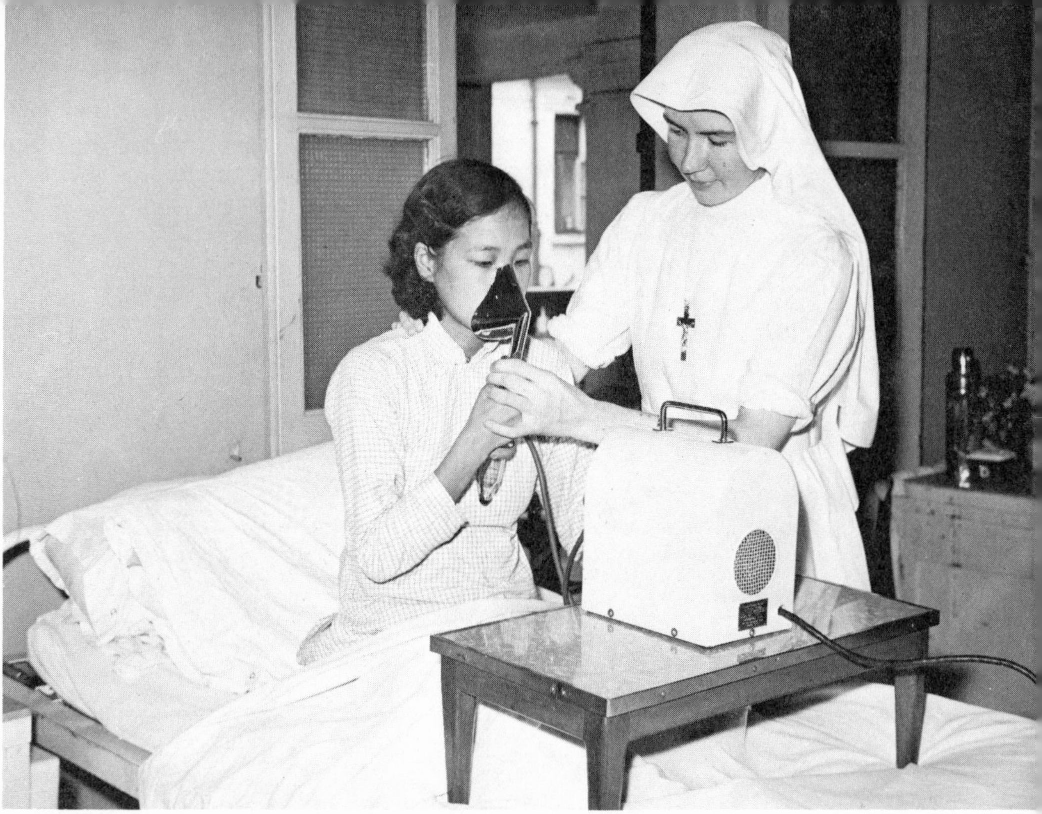

Sister Mary Madeleine with a postoperation patient

Sister Mary Gabriel in the Hong Kong hospital

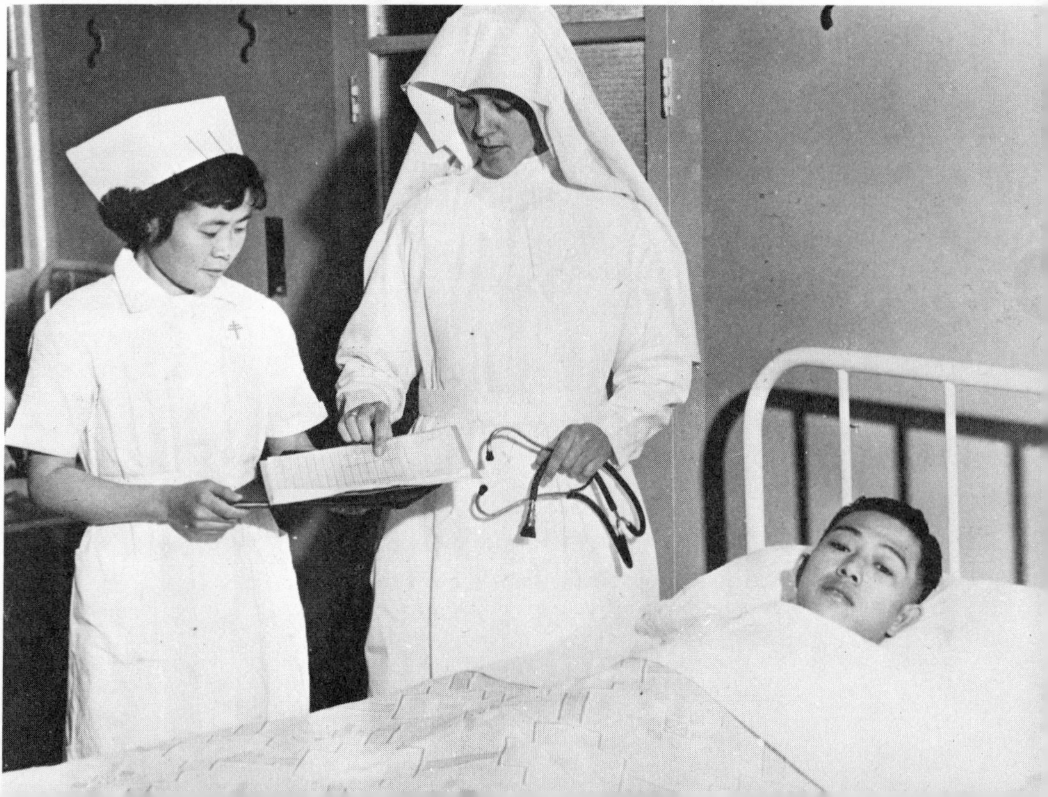

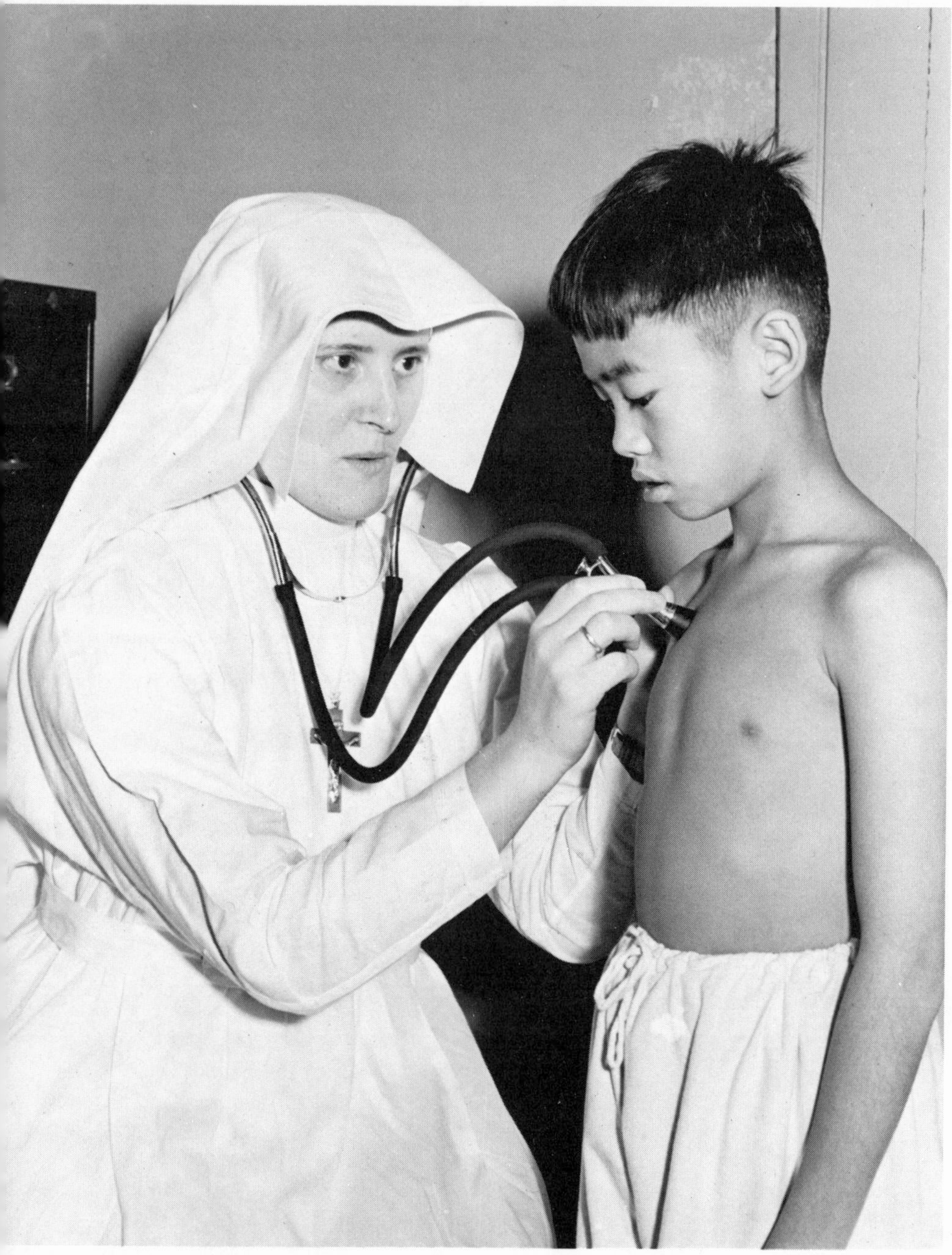

Sister Mary Aquinas, one of the three nuns with M.D.'s on the staff of Ruttonjee Sanatorium

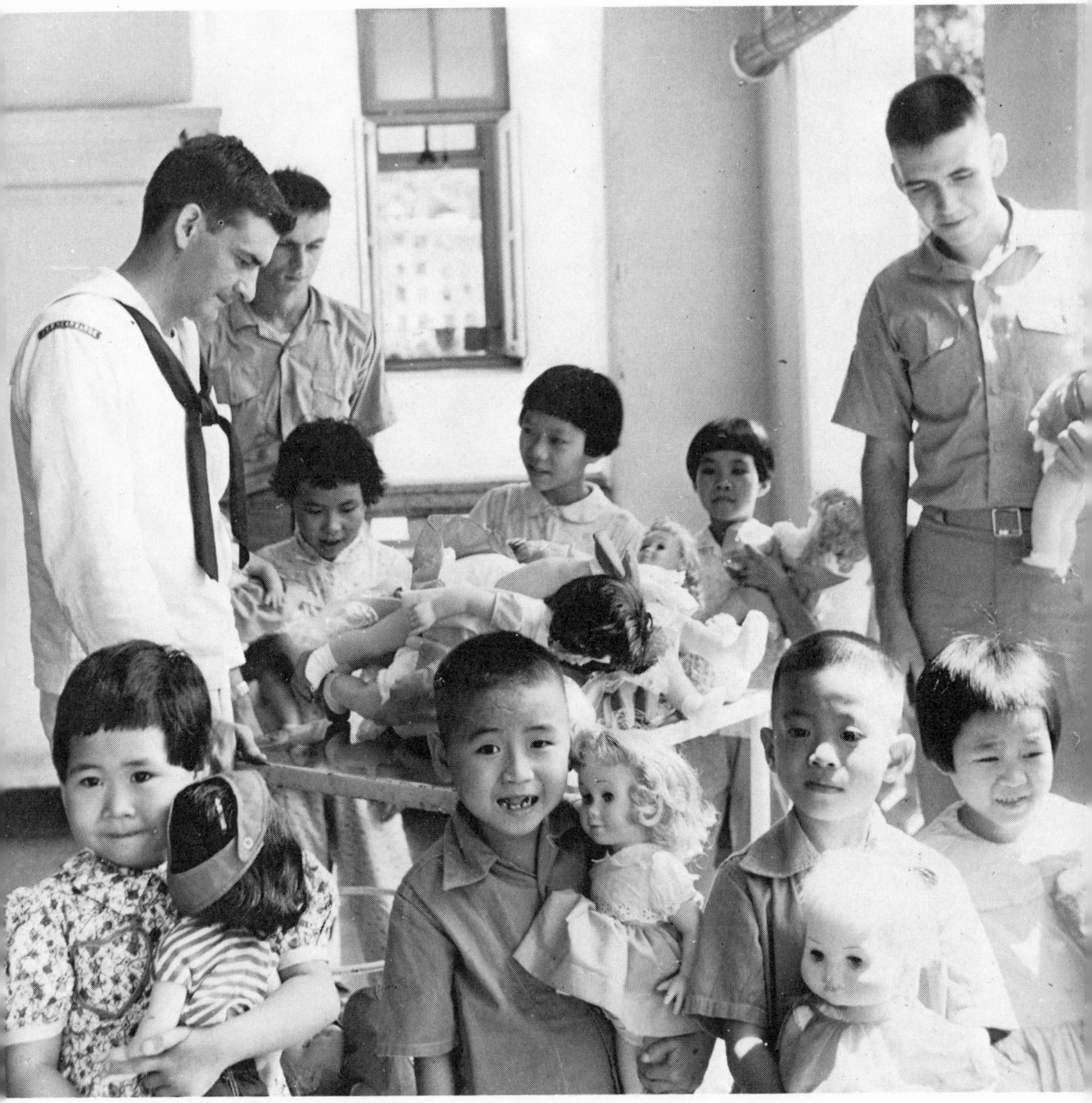

Servicemen from the U.S. Carrier *Kearsarge* distribute toys at Ruttonjee Sanatorium

Sister Mary Gemma visits the Crib with a young girl

·13·

Stubborn Soil

"If you speak to a pagan about the importance of serving God and saving his soul it leaves him quite cold," Bishop Galvin had said to the sisters. "He knows nothing of either. One must make contact with him in a way he can understand and appreciate. He understands and appreciates charity and friendship and sympathy and things that minister to the body."

When Sister Mary Patrick returned to Cahiracon, after nearly a decade in China, she had the satisfaction of knowing that the Columban sisters were doing remarkable work with their "charity and friendship and sympathy and things that minister to the body." Upon returning home to attend the second general chapter of the congregation, she found herself elected superior general to replace Mother Theophane, who had served her six-year term.

It was at that time, in 1936, that Bishop Galvin decided to ask the sisters to accept a difficult assignment. Would they go to Shinti, a place always considered the black spot of the vicariate? The martyred Father Tierney had spent himself establishing catechumenates and schools in Shinti but to little effect. A Chinese priest who had worked there for several years said that he felt any priest stationed in Shinti was wasting time, especially since other districts showed more promise. And yet Bishop Galvin was sending the sisters there "in hope that Shinti will awake from its slumbers."

Bishop Galvin had not forgotten Sientaochen and how the sisters had to flee from the Communists there in 1930. He decided, though, that Shinti was safe enough now. The Reds were still active in other parts of China, so much so that they even kidnapped Chiang Kai-shek and held him briefly, in December of 1936.

On that day Sisters Michael, Aloysius, and Bernadette left Hanyang by riverboat, and after traveling southward on the Yangtze for twenty-four hours reached Shinti. Father Sands met them at the dock so filled with plans that before reaching the convent he had described how they might start a school, a catechumenate, and a dispensary. He was so charged with expectations that within a day of their arrival he would give them a basket and send them off to visit a new mission he was founding a mile out of town.

In such country places nuns were still a rarity and so whenever the Columbans paused even briefly they were surrounded by a curious crowd, pushing, giggling, pointing. The comments were personal: she has leather shoes, there is a bit of gold in her tooth, her nose is long, what do you think that robe cost?

If the sisters asked the distance between two villages the Chinese wanted to know in which direction. If going uphill they gave a higher figure than downhill, for uphill is harder and so seems longer.

In Shinti the sisters worked with well-to-do Chinese for the first time. As one nun wrote home, "Today there was not a single poor person at Mass." Because of the level of education among these parishioners, Father Sands was interested in having the sisters teach English. Educated Chinese were attracted to that, he said.

The sisters were not long in Shinti when one wrote: "The catechumenate opened a few days ago. The pupils come after their morning meal and remain until four o'clock. The school has also opened. Sister Mary Aloysius teaches music and singing."

The dispensary opened, early in 1937, with a brown bag, a tray, and five bowls. Two desks, leaning together for mutual support, formed the treatment table.

Sister Bernadette wrote to Cahiracon: "After a patient is treated he or she likes to keep looking on at the other victims; this results invariably in congestion. However, we are better organized for the last few days. Father Sands's factotum came and told me he would *shang fah tze* (think of a plan). Next day when I arrived he had a table outside, under the roof, at the entrance gate. On the table was a piece of wood with a long nail on which he stuck tickets. The patients waited impatiently in order of their arrival."

In the dispensary waiting room, patients were curious about the religious pictures on the walls. They asked questions and the nuns gave answers. Many said, "When I am cured I will *chin jou* (enter the Church)." Some did, but most did not.

A sister wrote to Mother Mary Patrick: "Considering the conversions all over the vicariate, ours are but as drops in the ocean. Would it be too much to ask the sisters to give a special intention to Shinti in the second Mass they hear each day? We are working as hard as we can, and now we want prayer.

"The bishop writes 'to have patience and go slowly.' Father Sands is very optimistic and says things are better than he had expected.

"Get as many as you can to adopt Shinti—spiritually, I mean: prayer and prayer and more prayer. We look to Cahiracon to awaken Shinti."

Bishop Galvin announced that in the preceding four years the Columbans had instructed and baptized 15,524 adults and that 17,000 others were seeking instruction. But no lines were forming in Shinti.

Although Catholicism had been brought to Shinti years earlier, the sisters felt at the approach of Holy Week that they were making a new beginning. With only one priest and with no trained altar boys, they had little hope of any special ceremonies. But on Palm Sunday Father Sands said, "We must have the ceremonies. We'll manage them somehow or other."

On Monday morning Sister Michael went to measure the tabernacle, the one that would be used on Holy Thursday as part of the Altar of Repose, only to find it badly in need of repair. The lock was broken and the door wedged shut. Father Sands used scissors to pry open the door only to find the bottom of the tabernacle badly damaged. The state of that altar was almost symbolic of the state of the faith in Shinti.

When Sister Michael went to the market to buy some silk to decorate the Altar of Repose, Sister Aloysius sent for a carpenter. The fellow arrived on Tuesday and had hardly removed the tabernacle door from its hinges when he received an urgent call home; there was a row and he had to make the peace. By noon on Wednesday he had the repairs complete and the nuns went to work on the Altar of Repose, having first done the sweeping for the coolie could not be found. As Sister Michael said, "It seems his aunt's husband's first-cousin's husband had died and John had to go to the obsequies."

To the surprise of the nuns the ceremonies went off without a hitch. Sister Michael wrote: "The little boys responded wonderfully to the training and apart from some difficulty in getting into their surplices were good and very decorous. Sister A. was the choir and was at her best. We had all the ceremonies on Good Friday—Adoration of the Cross and Mass of the Presanctified; in the afternoon there were public Stations of the Cross, and the Stabat Mater was sung.

"In the evening we had to try our hand at a triple candle. The trouble was to make it branch out, but we eventually succeeded. We got a tin socket made on the street and stuck it on a pole: it was fine.

"The ceremonies began early on Saturday—the Paschal Fire, reading of the Prophecies, singing of the Litany, and Mass. As generally happened, the server forgot to ring the bell on Holy Thursday during the Gloria, but I got a message up to him on Saturday and he more than made up for the default.

"On Easter morning eight of our catechumens were baptized. It was the most impressive ceremony I ever attended. As soon as the priest entered the church with the catechumens holding on to the stole, the whole congregation stood and chanted the Creed. There was a Missa Cantata followed by Benediction of the Blessed Sacrament. Thank God, a big crowd came to the sacraments."

Eight catechumens were baptized on Easter morning at Shinti, but eighty were baptized on Ascension Thursday in Nancheng. Such statistics reflected the vitality of the two districts. The nuns in Shinti were not confronted with the problem of overcrowding in the schools, but those in Nancheng found it necessary to have more and more benches built for the children. Shinti with all of its well-to-do families was difficult to "wake from its slumbers."

In that summer of 1937 one of the sisters wrote a letter from the hills of Kuling reflecting a new problem that China was facing: "A good many refugees have come this way, and they have terrible tales to tell of the air raids. The Japanese are doing their best to terrorize the Chinese, and things are looking pretty black at present."

She was writing about the start of China's war with Japan which would, in time, become a part of the Second World War. It began on the night of July 7, 1937, with an exchange of shots at the Marco Polo Bridge outside of Peking.

·14·

War Comes to Hanyang

Shortly after the war had begun between Japan and China, the Sisters of Loretto, although not nurses, opened a place for wounded soldiers. They took over the old houses of Pai Ya T'ai where a decade earlier the Christian Brothers had conducted a school for boys, until radicals drove them from it. "Hospital" would be a polite title for that collection of buildings long in need of repair. And yet they did give shelter to thousands of soldiers.

"Then came a heaven-sent blessing," said Father Abraham Shackleton, who wrote of those hectic days in some detail. When directors of the Irish Hospitals' Sweepstakes sent £5,000 to the Red Cross in Hanyang, the Red Cross decided it was fitting that Irish priests and nuns should receive most of the money to care for the wounded.

The Columbans met to plan how best to proceed. They were unanimous in deciding that the so-called hospital at Pai Ya T'ai must be made more comfortable and more sanitary. Clothing must be made for two thousand wounded. So at the Loretto embroidery school and in Saint Mary's catechumenate, sewing machines hummed, and needles flew day and night. Father Joseph Crossan hurried about with a tape measure making plans that included estimates for brick and mortar. From the orphange at Ying Wu Chow came sounds of hammer and saw as beds were built and of the laughter of children enjoying themselves stuffing mattresses with straw.

The Columbans met to plan how best to proceed. They were unanimous catechumenate and the church into something of a hospital. Father Francis McDonald, himself a medical doctor, was in charge. He moved into Father Pigott's house across the street from the convent, and three Chinese women doctors took up quarters above the dispensary. Eight Chinese nurses arrived and four more were promised. A small army of Chinese boys, sent by their pastors, came to do the coolie labor.

Father Shackleton wrote especially about Friday night, December 10, 1937, the night the makeshift hospital opened. He even described the pale new moon of December and the cold stillness of the Hanyang darkness. Suddenly he heard a heavy battering at the gates.

Two young Chinese officers stood shivering outside the mission compound.

"Father, the wounded have arrived. Can they be admitted tonight?"

The Columban led the officers to the convent to consult the sisters. The priest knocked and after a pause the grill slid back.

"Sister, the wounded soldiers have arrived. Two officers are with me. They have come to ask whether their wounded can be admitted tonight."

Sister decided that the question must be referred to reverend mother. Keys rattled and bolts creaked. The three men and Mother Dolores met and agreed that the wounded should not remain another night on a cold riverboat on the Yangtze.

A sister disappeared and soon returned with a formidable bunch of keys—big keys and little keys, keys that opened medicine chests and those that opened the great doors between convent and catechumenate, now known as the hospital.

The place sprang into activity. Lights came on in the buildings. Nuns hurried about to see that all was in readiness. With a quick, heavy throb the power engine suddenly came to life and seemed to share in the excitement.

Stretchers were hurried to the boat where two hundred of the wounded waited. Within a half hour the first batch arrived. They came on stretchers, and in rickshaws. Some hobbled on crutches and some rode the shoulders of coolies.

"They were laughing, they were moaning, they were indifferent," wrote Father Shackleton. "Some lacked an arm, others a leg. It was a pitiful procession of the halt and the maim. It was a nightmare of human suffering.

"A wave of confusion broke over the hospital compound, but Father McDonald, our doctor, and the sisters with gentle firmness took command and quickly restored order. Gradually, the different rooms were filled—classrooms, refectory, dormitories, and even the catechumenate chapel received its number.

"If the walls of that little chapel could speak they would tell the history of a strange evolution from Chinese house in a pagan city to the first cathedral in Hanyang, which had witnessed the final profession of the first St. Columban Sisters in China and the consecration of Bishop Galvin."

Father Shackleton recorded fragments of conversation heard through the night: "Chest shot away . . . machine gun . . . die . . . morning . . . Baptism . . . sufficient instruction . . . conditional . . . saline injection . . . Dakin's solution . . . sterile dressing . . . poor fellow, not more than eighteen . . . bullet holes . . . amputation."

By the time Christmas arrived, two weeks later, the hospital was caring for 210 patients. Although they were pagans the soldiers were pleased to help make lamps, flowers, and bright-colored hangings so that all of the rooms might be filled with color by Christmas Eve.

A sister said: "The little crib in our ward attracted a good many, and it took all of the Chinese language at my disposal to tell our pagan patients the story of Christmas.

"Santa Claus paid a visit to make each a present of a face towel and some cigarettes. In the afternoon we played a few gramophone records in each ward and the patients seemed to appreciate it.

"We had a party and a Christmas tree for the doctors and nurses. Afterward they all came to the convent for Benediction. The doctors and nurses came to us for Midnight Mass. You can see that Christmas was a day of peace and goodwill.

"In regard to keeping order, our soldiers are not bad, at any rate when one of the sisters is around, though they are a bit hilarious at times. A few mouth-organs and games help to pass the time for them.

"We have given out a good many catechisms, and many of them seem well disposed toward the Church. Some of them go to Mass on Sundays and I encourage them. One of the officers has learned to make the sign of the cross, and when Mother Mary Dolores was in the other day sister asked him to make it for her. You should have seen him squaring his shoulders, pulling up his sleeves and striking an attitude!"

After a few weeks some of the soldiers were well enough to leave the hospital. In almost every instance the parting was reluctant.

"I turned into Ward E," a sister recalled, "and what a sight met my eyes. Thirty strong men crying aloud! I spoke a few words to them and turned away. They had known five or six weeks of real happiness and were grateful for it."

It was a mystery to the nuns where the soldiers acquired the gifts to leave with them: goldfish in a bowl, oranges, a dog, two dead chickens, a bottle of perfume.

When a bugle sounded those who could walk, or get along well enough on crutches, moved out of the wards, bowing and thanking the sisters as they went. The bad cases left on sixty stretchers.

When one soldier showed great reluctance to go, a nun pinned a religious medal on his uniform and told him what he must do when in danger at the front: "Believe in God and be sorry for your sins."

As the men neared the door, many of them glanced at a bed in which a young officer had just died. One of the nuns remembered the officer, an amputee, as a man of character: "I visited him several times a day.

He bore all of his sufferings with great patience and died with the names of Jesus and Mary on his lips. Father McDonald said the prayers for the dying and he passed away as the sisters recited the rosary at his side."

By this time eight more Columbans had arrived in China: Sisters Brigid, Kilian, Margaret, Mary Aloysius, Teresa, and Vianney were in Hanyang; Sisters Berchmans and Dolorosa in Nancheng.

With the passing of grey days and cold nights, spring brought days that were sunny and evenings balmy and clear. This was not wholly a blessing, in the early months of 1938, because benign weather meant a return of bombers to Hanyang.

The nights of Holy Saturday and Easter Sunday were especially bad. Although the hospital was crowded, space had to be made for dozens of victims of air raids. On the evenings of bombings it seemed that all roads in Hanyang led to the mission compound. Surgery went on night and day for there were many amputations needed among the critical cases.

Mother Michael feared the sisters might break down; they seemed to be going at top speed all the time. She kept a watchful eye and insisted that they get rest whenever possible.

What may have helped them extend themselves beyond normal endurance was that they were aware of how noble people can be when confronted with tragedy. For example, the refugees living in Father Hogan's hostel in Hanyang went without food for a day or so in order to buy towels for the wounded soldiers in the hospital.

A delegation, saying that they wanted to express their appreciation to the men who had suffered for China, went from ward to ward giving out towels. Sister Mary Laurence, the cook, could stand in the kitchen and follow their progress through the hospital from the rolling waves of cheers that followed them.

Not to be outdone in generosity several soldiers went to Sister Mary Laurence to tell her that all patients in the hospital wished to go on half rations for four days to save enough money to buy presents for the refugees.

"There was great excitement," recalled Mother Michael. "Presents were bought and wrapped in neat parcels, a packet for each man, woman, and child. There were sweets for the children. A delegation started off headed by two men carrying a large flag with an inscription telling what was being done. A few rickshaws carried the baskets of presents. Needless to say as the procession passed through the streets it aroused considerable interest."

The worst air raid came on August 16, 1938. After the "all clear" had sounded and smoke had drifted away, the Columbans could see that the districts behind East Gate and South Gate were being consumed by flames.

"You can imagine our feeling," Mother Michael wrote to Mother Mary Patrick, "for so many of the people there were people we had known and loved. Only a short time before Sisters Attracta and Laurence had baptized thirty-five babies in that neighborhood, all of whom must have perished in their cradles or in their mothers' arms. Our only comfort lay in the fact that the little ones had flown straight to God."

During a lull in the bombing, the sisters made ready for the victims. The rooms on the ground floor of the catechumenate were already filled, but the upper rooms were empty, and there was still some space in the old cathedral.

Before dawn the compound was strewn with the dying and the wounded. Bishop Galvin and the priests arrived and began helping as best they could.

Sisters Bernadette, Attracta, and Teresa assisted the surgeons in the operating room all night. At five o'clock they retired to rest. Mass was at half past six. By eight o'clock the surgeons and sisters were again at work. Father McDonald and two Chinese doctors worked all day without stopping for meals.

What a shock it was, on Saturday morning, August 20, when Bishop Galvin ordered the hospital closed! Everyone was to move across the river to Hankow, a city more easily defended against the Japanese who were on the move along the Yangtze.

Father McDonald hurried to Hankow to find accommodations for his patients. Mother Michael hurriedly wrote a letter to Cahiracon. The very tempo of her sentences reveals the tensions of the times:

"We could get no stretcher bearers. Hanyang is emptied out. There are no coolies or rickshaws. The few hospital boys we had effected the transportation of the sick.

"It was late on Sunday evening when the last of the patients had been transferred. On Sunday morning at about a quarter of seven when the priest was giving us Holy Communion during Mass, bombing began and continued for some time. There was no alarm given. Later in the morning the siren went. During that raid I decided to send at least half the community to Hankow that evening.

"After the patients had all been removed we took the key from the gateman to ensure that no one would return and that there would be no chance of anyone getting in next morning. Hard measures, but it was necessary as we wanted to leave the hospital in some kind of order and to make everything as secure as possible in the house. We were working until all hours of the night."

The next morning there was a Mass at six o'clock. An air raid came just as the service ended. Another came at eleven and a third at three in the afternoon.

Air raids slowed down the preparation for moving. The chapel and sacristy were stripped, shutters were fitted into the windows, and all movable property was taken to the top of the house.

Mother Michael concluded her letter to Cahiracon: "I had hoped so much that we could keep on in our convent, but I think that any attachment I had was severed in that last raid. We felt so helpless.

"As we all came away it was hard to keep back the tears. The Chinese said: 'What shall we do when the sisters have gone!' May God help them all."

The Columbans went to Hankow because it was supposed to be easily defended, but it fell without a shot being fired. The invasion was so quiet that the sisters could scarcely believe that the Japanese were in possession.

Bishop Galvin came to see them in their temporary convent, on Sunday, October 23, 1938, after his meeting with the mayor of Hankow. It was touching, the bishop told the sisters, to hear the young mayor, speaking in perfect English, announce that ammunition had been removed from all fortifications, that nothing was to be defended, and that he himself had been ordered to leave the city.

Two days later the last of the Chinese soldiers retreated from Hankow. That night the city was encircled by flames. One of the nuns wrote to Mother Mary Patrick: "The sky was red in all directions and explosions were heard all through the night. Dear Hanyang was much in our thoughts and prayers. We could see Wuchang ablaze.

"For days fires raged and there were wild rumors. The Protestants sent a man over to Hanyang on Wednesday, but, like the raven from the ark, he did not return. However, after some days the priests got a messenger over who reported that all was well. Our convent and that of the Loretto sisters had not been touched.

"On Wednesday afternoon, Bishop Galvin took Sister Justa and myself to see the kitchens in the German concession. We went by the Bund, and saw Japanese boats steaming up the river. The evening was grey, the boats were grey, and the smoke was grey. There was a weirdness about it all.

"Sister Justa and I saw two groups of armed soldiers sitting near the bank. We asked a man what soldiers they were.

" 'They are Japanese,' he answered. We were passing them by when we saw a priest coming hurriedly towards us.

" 'Get outside the gates at once,' he said. 'There may be trouble. These soldiers are going to have a victory parade.'

"As we turned, the soldiers fell into line for marching and a fusillade of firecrackers was let off by the Chinese as a welcome to the Japanese. Their politeness remains with them even in the hour of defeat."

Thousands of refugees sought shelter in Hankow. When the public buildings were filled, those who could not force their way inside lived in the streets. To keep off starvation two kitchens were erected, one in the German concession and the other in the gardens of the Hong Kong Bank. In each kitchen the sisters divided the work among themselves and several Protestant women missionaries.

Each kitchen had four stoves with the capacity to cook five rounds a day, with each round providing enough rice for a thousand refugees. Twice a day sisters accompanied the truck to distribution points to ration rice and keep some semblance of order.

Suddenly the Japanese ordered the refugees to go to a refugee zone in Wushenmao, an area of Hankow. When the homeless refused to move, German civilians came to the sisters saying, "We can't drive them out, but *you* can lead them out."

The nuns felt like the Pied Piper as they led contingent after contingent across the city on the long trek to Wushenmao. Upon arrival they found that Bishop Galvin and Father Pigott were already there, living in a house lent to them by Methodists missionaries.

One of the Irish sisters remarked that the sight of poor people herded together beneath their bundles reminded her of the Cromwellian ultimatum: "To Hell or to Connaught."

Bishop Galvin was head of the committee for management, a vague title which meant that he was in charge of seeing that the refugees were kept alive. By now he had forty-one thousand on his rice list. At a glance the sisters saw the bishop was not well. He looked so worn, and his deep chronic cough was getting worse. But this was no time to rest for the refugees kept coming from Nanking, Honan, and other parts until the streets seemed like a sluggish river of humanity.

When cholera and diptheria broke out Bishop Galvin asked the sisters to move to the refugee area at once to open an isolation hospital. The request came at noon and at three o'clock Sisters Justa and Nicholas, of Loretto, and Sisters Kilian, Bernadette, and Attracta, of Saint Columban, were sitting atop their bedding in a truck with Brother Colman at the wheel and Father Nicholas Hughes beside him.

The building chosen for an isolation hospital was an old disused police barracks. Ventilation was no problem because not a door nor window remained intact.

Within a few hours sixteen patients had arrived. They were almost beyond help; five were dead by morning. When the cholera was at its worst, the sisters admitted as many as twenty-six patients a day.

Soon there were nine Columbans and four Lorettines working long hours under discouraging conditions. One of them wrote to Mother Mary Patrick: "The children here have no chance. Hanyang is hard enough on them at the best of times, but it is simply wonderful compared with this place. Along with all the other hardships they have had to endure, the children have been suffering from a very bad type of malaria this year and are not able to fight their way back to health now that the winter is setting in."

Since the Japanese had cut off river traffic on the Yangtze and the Han no supplies were reaching Hankow. "Food is scarce but we are not starving. No milk or eggs can be procured, but as we get fresh fish almost daily we are not badly off. For a change we get German sausages."

Early in 1939 the city officials permitted the sisters to return to their convent in Hanyang. At every gate stood a Japanese sentry. Each sister was required to show an identification card with her photograph inside and the Rising Sun on the outside.

As they passed through check points, the soldiers usually laughed, causing a Columban to write home: "On such occasions I remind myself that our Irish soldiers would do the same if a Japanese woman in queer clothes went past them, and I forgive them."

·15·

Away from the Fighting

While a dozen Columbans in Hanyang and Hankow served food to starving refugees and nursed the wounds of soldiers, other Columbans were doing what is normally thought of as missionary work. In Shanghai, Shinti, Nancheng, and Mo-Wong-Tsui, sisters were teaching and visiting the sick. The war was not disrupting their plans, at least not for the moment.

In Shanghai, for example, the outbreak of war between China and Japan was still two months away when a letter of request went out from there to Cahiracon, signed by Father William McGoldrick, the director of the Columbans' Mission in Shanghai. It was really from Bishop Haouisee, S. J., who wished to open a school for the children of Russian exiles. He preferred English-speaking nuns, and wondered if the Columbans might be interested. As an inducement, an Irish woman, a Miss Brennan, was offering to give the sisters a school she had established in Shanghai.

Mother Mary Patrick accepted the offer. Plans to send sisters were well under way before Shanghai became an unsafe city. On August 14, 1937, Chinese bombers sent to destroy Japanese warships in Shanghai harbor missed their targets, killing nearly six hundred people when bombs fell into the heart of the city.

Many Chinese complained that when dealing with the Japanese, Chiang Kai-shek was still using diplomacy instead of arms, preferring to save his forces to fight the Communists. Chiang responded that he feared the enemy from within more than he feared the enemy from without.

Pressure on him was so great, however, that on September 22, 1937, the Nationalists officially recognized the existence of the Communist army. This came only after the Communists had agreed to drop the designations of "Soviet" and "Red Army" in favor of the less abrasive "Border Region Government" and the "Eighth Route Army."

A cablegram arrived at Cahiracon, in December of 1937, saying that everything was in readiness and so please send the sisters right away. Many people in Ireland thought it madness to send sisters to Shanghai with fighting going on in and around the city.

Within a few days, though, four Columban sisters sailed for China. Sisters Emmanuel Sinnot and Carmel Pryer left from Ireland and Sisters Ignatius O'Keeffe and Oliver Piel from the United States where the Columban sisters had established a convent at Silver Creek, New York. In mid-January of 1938 all four sisters arrived in Shanghai, now somewhat tranquil, and within a few days Sancta Sophia school was founded. Sister Dolores Callan and Francis de Sales Hogan arrived later.

The school opened with sixteen pupils, but before 1938 had run its course there were 110 girls of Russian parentage being educated by the Sisters of Saint Columban.

Arranging classes was a problem in the beginning because the children were of different ages and stages of development and spoke various languages. Some of them knew a little English; others none at all. Since the Russian community in Shanghai was a fluctuating one there was an ebb and flow in school attendance. The severity of the Shanghai winter also influenced attendance.

Judging from a letter, the amount of work that the Columbans faced each day was appalling.

"I am taking over Sister Francis de Sales's history class, and another class in French. It was a bit staggering to plunge into the Napoleonic wars and Gladstone's Reform Bill after twenty years! My hands being full with the three French classes, two geography classes, a Scripture class, as well as the games, I have had to drop Russian altogether for the present. By the time school is through there is only time for our spiritual duties, and the pile of exercise-books for correction generally has to wait over for night recreation. It is surprising, really, how much time correcting takes; for most of us it means a pile of about sixty copybooks each, but, thank God, I am able for it, for I have never felt stronger and more vigorous since I entered."

The Russian girls, fine athletes, showed an interest in games—volleyball, baseball, and basketball—especially after they began competing with other schools in the city. This interest was one of the things the sisters used to develop school spirit and raise morale.

In taking kindly to the sisters, the children influenced the attitude of their parents. By the end of the second year, when enrollment had reached 130, Russian prejudice against the Catholic Church had mostly disappeared.

Practically all of the Russian families belonged to the Eastern Orthodox Church. They had the Mass and the Sacraments but did not recognize the authority of the pope and their priests celebrated Mass in the Byzantine Rite instead of the Roman Rite.

Cardinal Tisserant, of the Sacred Congregation of the Eastern Church, wrote to Mother Mary Patrick saying that he wished the sisters in Shanghai would follow the Oriental Rite. This, he felt, would help in creating good will with the Russian Christians. The Holy Father approved of having the sisters change over from the Roman Rite. The change would be gradual, the cardinal said, and would be intended only for sisters working in Shanghai. Should any sister leave the Shanghai school she would immediately revert to the Roman Rite.

A Jesuit, Father Wilcock, began instructing the sisters in a liturgy new to them. One observed: "It is a liturgy rich in beautiful prayers. The Mass takes somewhat longer than the Mass in the Roman Rite; the time varies according to the feast and circumstances."

The sisters were careful to refrain from anything that might be taken for proselytism, all the while explaining that the gulf was not wide between the Catholic and the Orthodox churches.

What probably impressed the Russian parents the most was the quality of the instruction. Sancta Sophia stood among the best schools in Shanghai. Even at the end of the first year the pupils scored well in the Oxford and Cambridge Local Examinations.

Shinti was another mission safe for the time being. There three Columban sisters went on frequent sick calls, but gave most of their time to the dispensary and to the catechumenate.

Father Hugh Sands was generous in his praise of them. He told everyone he met how the nuns worked in the dispensary from nine until noon each day and often attended to a hundred patients a morning. "How they do it is a mystery to me!"

One of the sisters wrote home with pride telling of seventy new catechumens: "They are a motley crowd—from babes in arms to an old grandmother of eighty-three. The girls are quick and intelligent and the young mothers on the whole are good and diligent, but the grannies don't find study too easy. Two of them are blind, three are lame, a few are deaf, a couple of them are over eighty, nearly all are over seventy, so their powers of concentration are limited.

"The poor old dears find it difficult to learn their prayers by heart. Doctrine comes easier to them, especially when we come to the death of our Lord they are very interested."

The sisters of Shinti opened a school—"a very unpretentious affair"—where courses included Christian doctrine, reading, arithmetic, singing, English, and needlework.

In Nancheng life was so tranquil that one of the nuns wrote home saying that the number of students had increased and that if peace continues all through 1939 "there will be one thousand baptisms to record in the vicariate."

The relaxed attitude of the sisters working with Monsignor Cleary in the Vicariate of Nancheng was reflected in the anecdotes they wrote home:

"I must tell you a funny episode that happened today. During the principal Mass in the church, some new Christians were there to make their first Confession. One poor man, who I feel convinced had never before seen the inside of a church, came in quickly, and knelt at the side of the confessional, with his hat on his head. I wondered what was going to happen, when suddenly from the back, up came a Christian and rather violently removed the offending object. Whereupon the poor victim, thinking his hat was being stolen, got up from his knees and dashed after the thief, giving tongue in a most audible manner. The poor priest, who was at the other side of the box, had to get up and intervene, and the affair ended with the penitent, hat under his arm, being shriven."

Excitement of a pleasant sort reached Nancheng in early 1939. Word arrived from Rome that Monsignor Cleary would become the first bishop and vicar apostolic of Nancheng, Kiangsi Province. The date for the consecration was set for April 26, the Feast of the Patronage of Saint Joseph.

Preparations began immediately. Sisters made arrangements for beds and linens for the visitors and priests helped to paint the church and landscape the grounds. Sister Mary Francis sketched a Celtic design for the crosier which priests in Shanghai promised to have made in Zikawei; she also designed the coat of arms with the motto selected by the monsignor: *Christi simus, non nostri* (We belong to Christ, not to ourselves).

Meanwhile the war moved nearer. On April 9, Easter Sunday, the Japanese captured Nanchang, the capital of Kiangsi Province, a hundred miles up river from Nancheng (two towns with only the difference of one vowel between them).

So as not to subject visitors to the increasing dangers of travel, all invitations were cancelled. The date for the ceremony was moved forward to April 16, Low Sunday. Monsignor Cleary hoped the ceremony would be somewhat private, but it turned out otherwise.

Bishop Galvin tried to get a pass that would admit him through military lines between Hanyang and Nancheng, but his effort was in vain. At the last minute a truck loaded with priests from the Vicariate of Kanchow came through the gate in the thick high walls of Nancheng. They joined other missionaries from the area until thirty-five priests had gathered at the presbytery. At half past eight in the morning the procession began to move from the mission compound to the cathedral only to be stopped because the mandarin had not yet taken his place inside the church.

Even after the mandarin was seated the procession had difficulty reaching the cathedral; the combined effort of every policeman in Nancheng was needed to open a corridor through the crush of humanity. The church, although spacious, was too small to contain the crowd that pressed to gain admission. It seemed that every pagan and Christian in the city of 20,000 wanted to witness the solemn ceremony.

Father Michael Moran, who was in the procession, wrote later: "The cathedral was crowded to the doors; everything was aglow in the festive atmosphere. The devotional care of the sisters had made the sanctuary look like a well laid out flower garden. Sanctuaries are, of course, a little bit of heaven on earth."

Bishop O'Shea, C.M., of Kanchow, was the consecrating prelate. Because of the war it was impossible to have the usual two assisting co-consecrating prelates and so the Holy See granted a dispensation, permitting Fathers Patrick Dermody and Luke Teng, a Chinese priest, to assist Bishop O'Shea.

A few days after the ceremony Father Patrick O'Connor arrived at the cathedral. He would, in time, be serving as a war correspondent in the Second World War and in the Korean conflict. Now he was visiting the Columban missionaries to write a series of articles about them for the *Far East* magazine, with editions published in Ireland, the United States, and Australia.

In an ancient automobile, Father O'Connor lurched through one of the gates of Nancheng, having crossed a hundred miles of new road from the provincial capital. He drove past the sentry and came around the corner into a spacious enclosure, continued up a tree-lined driveway and halted beside a large church built of slate-colored brick.

A familiar figure with a familiar stride was walking toward the church. Father O'Connor recognized it as his former rector at the seminary in Ireland.

"It says that this place is named Kienchang," said Father O'Connor in mock puzzlement pointing to his map.

After Bishop Cleary had greeted his old student he got around to explaining that in recent years the name of the town had been changed to Nancheng and to add to the confusion the spelling was almost the same as that of Nanchang, the capital of the province.

One of the first things that the two Columbans did was to visit the graves of three of their colleagues:

Father T. P. Leonard, who had been stabbed to death by bandits in

July of 1929, was buried at a Catholic village on the road between Nanfeng and Nancheng.

Father William O'Flynn, who died of an illness, October 30, 1929, was buried in Nancheng.

Father Cornelius Tierney, who died while a prisoner of the Reds, February 28, 1931, was buried on a green hill near the walls of Nancheng.

Bishop Cleary spoke of how it had been seven years earlier when he arrived in Nancheng to succeed Father Tierney. He inherited the trials of a mission superior trying to bring some order out of chaos in a district plagued by warfare. Red armies ravaged the province; it was several years before Chiang Kai-shek could come to the aid of Kiangsi.

That night Father O'Connor wrote in his magazine article: "The Red terror is still a vivid memory in the hills and valleys of Kiangsi. The people and their priests went through a long period of danger, uncertainty and suffering. As you drive now along the new road leading out of Nanfeng, you pass through hilly, lonely country where six or seven years ago Communism was a grim fact.

"The city itself went through a gruelling siege and was saved from a disastrous surrender only by government aeroplanes that dropped supplies within the beleaguered walls. Going through the hills now you hear of (for instance) a village that once had ninety families, some of them Catholic, and now has only ten. The Reds wiped out the others."

Father O'Connor had scarcely departed, in the summer of 1939, when an epidemic of cholera broke out in Nancheng. The teaching sisters turned nurses and for weeks worked around the clock. Some six hundred people died in the town, eighteen of them inside the mission compound. No Columban, however, suffered from that acute, infectious disease.

At Mo-Wang-Tsui there were also three Columban sisters outside the path of the war, at least momentarily. They had been sent up country at Christmas of 1937 to help Father James Vallely, and had found it a tonic to be away from Hanyang with all of its sick and wounded. The country there was fresh and lovely.

A sister reported with enthusiasm: "It is marvellous what graces are being showered on this place. All the people want to enter the Church, and are coming in by the hundreds because they are convinced of the truth of the Faith.

"A number of women and girls (preceded by coolies carrying cradles—each with its occupant) come to the catechumenate and stay a few weeks at much inconvenience to themselves. We instruct them all day long in the principal mysteries of Faith. They require no persuasion, being convinced already of how wonderful a privilege is the gift of baptism.

"After they have been baptized and received Holy Communion they stay another few days, make their first confession, and return home happy and satisfied. Another batch takes their place and gets the same instruction, with like results.

"Father Vallely's hand must be tired from baptizing these days. He has administered the sacrament to hundreds since we came."

The frustration that the Columbans had felt a decade earlier was gone. Then they had been hindered by illness and an inability to use the language. Now they went about their work with sureness, for it was evident that they were doing something worth doing.

·16·

In Spite of War

When Japanese planes attacked Chungking, May 4, 1939, fire bombs burned to death four thousand people in one night. Never before in the history of warfare had bombs killed so many so fast. This record would not last, however, because four months later Germany would invade Poland and with the start of the Second World War the number of such casualties surpassed all previous bounds.

While keeping informed of such news, Mother Mary Patrick was aware that travel was becoming increasingly dangerous, and yet she was determined to go from Cahiracon in Ireland to the missions in China. Not having been there in more than three years, she felt the need to make an official visitation, especially since everything was so uncertain.

By the time she reached China in early 1940, Japanese armies had occupied all the cities of the coast—Shanghai, Canton, Tientsin, Peking—and all of the cities of the Yangtze valley up to Hanyang.

Chungking, the wartime capital of the Nationalists, was protected from eastern invasion by tortuous mountain passes and the turbulent Yangtze gorges. To reach it with foot soldiers the Japanese would have to stretch their lines of supply too thin, and so from this natural fortress, Chiang Kai-shek directed his armies.

Upon arrival in China, Mother Mary Patrick went directly to Hanyang. During her four weeks there she could not help but compare past with present:

"Many of the Hanyang streets are masses of ruins, and places one remembers as dotted with houses have been transformed into large open spaces, for all of the building material has been carried away."

She was pleased to note, however, how much Catholicism had spread since her departure four years earlier. She saw the enlargement of the cathedral as symbolic; it had been extended to twice the length that she remembered.

During her visit with Bishop Galvin, Mother Mary Patrick reminded him that in this year, 1940, the Columban priests were twenty years in

China. Yes, he said, and the first dozen had been the hardest what with bandits, Reds, floods, pestilence, and an acute shortage of money. How discouraging it had been!

Things changed for the better in 1932 when the Reds were cleared from the vicariate. And yet, the bishop admitted, in a strange way the Communists had helped Christianity: "Calamities are forerunners of waves of grace."

The bishop recalled that when the Columbans had reached Hanyang in 1920 there were about 120 Catholics there, and now, two decades later, there were 6,000. In the whole vicariate the Catholic population had grown from 17,000 to 55,000.

Despite the miseries of war, 1938 and 1939 had been years of exceptional growth. The inhabitants of a hundred pagan villages had been converted. The bishop said, "An entire countryside is in motion toward the Church."

This meant preparing ten thousand people for baptism. Without the help of the Columban sisters, he observed, this would not be possible. Nuns taught in the catechumenates where prospective converts came for instruction.

Mother Mary Patrick showed a special interest in what the bishop referred to as "sisters' parishes." He explained that scarcely had the nuns returned to their convent, in early 1939, having been refugees in Hankow, than he had asked them to consider trying an experiment. He wanted them to start "sisters' parishes" in the country. If they would open schools, visit the sick, and get to know the people in a certain area, it would be a way of preparing the ground for the start of an official parish.

The idea had come to him when he saw how one woman had converted a village. When the woman, a pagan, had complained of ulcers, he had sent her for treatment to the sisters in Hanyang. While there she became interested in Catholicism, and before leaving the clinic had been baptized. No sooner had she returned home than she began to interest friends and neighbors in her religion. Soon the whole village was Catholic.

The bishop suggested that the sisters make their country headquarters at Chwan Kow and that they extend their work beyond as soon as they could find a means of transportation.

The mother general recalled that one sister had written:

"At present there are no rickshaws and no ferrys. Sampans cost dollars so there is no hope of them. But I am confident that God will find a means to get us about."

Soon the sisters were using rowboats to reach an island in a lake. There in thirteen villages every person was pagan.

The islanders were friendly enough and began calling at the convent; some even attended Mass on Sunday. One old man offered to become a Catholic, if he were made bishop.

The sisters, finding the islanders excellent people, admired them so much that one had written to Cahiracon: "We want prayers, and prayers that can move mountains. These people have centuries of paganism behind them and nothing but the grace of God in abundance can shake their belief in it."

The nuns worked hard to open a school. They tried to secure a big, airy house owned by two brothers, but just as they thought all was arranged, one of the brothers changed his mind. Finally, in spite of an abbot in a neighboring pagan temple who worked against them, the sisters succeeded in renting a shack that answered the purpose fairly well.

When the mother general said she would like to visit the new mission on the island in the lake, Sister Mary Thaddeus escorted her there, nearly three hours by rowboat. By now the school—in which sixty-seven adults had gathered to study catechism and learn prayers on the day it opened—was gaining in enrollment at a remarkable rate. Within the year one hundred fifty islanders had joined the Church.

When Father Frank McDonald said the first Mass ever celebrated on the island, the chapel was filled to overflowing. Many pagans stood on the backs of their buffaloes to get a glimpse of what was going on.

Back in Hanyang the sisters took their mother general to visit a parish they had helped found in a crowded part of the city. The story of its founding went back to 1938 when the Columbans were refugees in Hankow:

Sister Mary Teresa and Sister Mary Basil were walking down a Hankow street, in search of a piece of pork, when an excitable woman stopped them to tell of a dying baby. She led the sisters to three hundred people lying on the floor of a loft over a tea shop, all refugees from Hanyang. After registering them for rice rations and bringing straw, blankets, and clothes, the nuns returned each day to nurse the sick.

When the refugees returned to their old neighborhood in Hanyang, the sisters and Father John O'Carroll continued to visit them. When a sizeable number converted to Catholicism, Bishop Galvin built a church for them and dedicated it to Saint Patrick.

It is one more example, observed Sister Mary Patrick, of how God breaks into life in new and startling ways. Little did the two sisters dream when they climbed into the fetid loft to visit a sick baby that they were helping to found a new parish.

In Hanyang, in the spring of 1940, the Columbans were teaching four hundred catechumens in their school and attending the needs of 140 patients each day at the clinic.

The talk during the recreation hour each evening reminded Mother Mary Patrick of the ten years when she was a part of the Hanyang community. For example, a sister said: "Today a child fell from a loft onto a basin. It received a nasty gash on the head. The wound bled profusely until we put in a few stitches. The gratitude of the parents was touching."

Another added: "These people have wonderful powers of recovery. A week ago a man came here whose head had been badly cut with a hatchet. Father McDonald removed a piece of his skull bone and put in at least a dozen stitches. Now the man walks back here every day to have the dressings changed. The wound is healing nicely."

One of Mother Mary Patrick's greatest delights in revisiting Hanyang was meeting such old friends as blind Ineza and her husband, Ai Po. With scarcely a half an eye between them they still went about gathering leaves for fuel.

"Whenever I see that old couple," she said, "I am reminded of the saying that it takes a martyr to live with a saint. Ai Po I believe to be the martyr and Ineza the saint. He waits on her hand and foot and leads her about wherever she wants to go."

Each day little things happened that were touching. An old woman brought the mother general a basket of eggs, saying that the nun had, years ago, saved her husband's life.

In a farewell concert the sisters sang "Killarney," "Vale of Avoca," and "Hills of Donegal," escaping momentarily from the grim realities of China to "The fair hills of Holy Ireland."

By Japanese steamer the mother general traveled to Shanghai. There, while visiting Sancta Sophia, the school for Russian girls taught by the Columbans, she organized a club. She encouraged a group of Russian women to keep open house at the school each Saturday and Sunday from 2:00 to 8:00 p.m. The sisters set aside a room for reading and music and another for games; they served tea Russian style with a samovar of boiling water standing by.

Mother Mary Patrick and Sister Mary Baptist set out from Shanghai to visit the Columbans in Nancheng. The day they chose to leave happened to be the day that Bishop Haouisee visited Sancta Sophia to celebrate the Byzantine Mass and to give the Russian pupils an examination in catechism. The girls were more interested in Sister Mary Baptist's leaving than in the bishop's visit.

When the sisters were ready to depart they set up loud lamentations. Brushing past the bishop, they thrust baskets of flowers upon the departing nuns. Such distress, said the bishop, was *tres touchant*.

On that drizzling Sunday afternoon the mother general felt "a vague uneasiness while setting out on such a journey." However, the depressing day was brightened when Father Nicholas Cody discovered a Chinese lady traveling with her children and her servants and arranged for the two nuns to join the party. The lady, the wife of a bank manager in Foochow, had been educated by the Canossian sisters. During the journey her servants made all arrangements with coolies "thus saving us many dollars and much disputing," as Mother Mary Patrick observed.

The first stage of the trip to Nancheng was southward four hundred miles along the China coast. A customs official on board the steamer alarmed the sisters by warning them that Foochow was a dangerous place subjected to air raids. He advised them to avoid it and to strike out up country by a mountainous route where one met bandits "only occasionally."

Sister Baptist said that bombs were preferable to bandits. So the sisters continued on the journey to Foochow.

After three days on the steamer they disembarked on the island of Santao. A Chinese priest directed them to the Spanish Dominican Sisters of the Holy Rosary, who were, at that time, training a Chinese sisterhood, the Sisters of Merciful Love.

The Spanish nuns were building an attractive convent, one that resembled San Marco in Florence. The sight of it must have reminded the superior general of her days in Florence, where as Lady Frances Moloney she had taken residence while her husband lived out his last days, in 1913, in the hospital of the Blue Nuns in nearby Fiesole.

The chaplain at the convent, also Spanish, celebrated Mass for the visitors at a quarter to six on the following morning. An hour later the two nuns and the Chinese lady took a boat to the mainland, where they hired sedan chairs to carry them on the start of the three-day journey overland to Foochow. The mountain road often demanded such stiff climbing that the nuns walked much of the way, for they could not stand to see how, on slanting trails, the bamboo poles pressed into the thick leathery callouses on the coolies' shoulders.

The scenery was dramatic and wild flowers grew in abundance beside the paths. Mother Mary Patrick wrote: "Huge white roses, millions of them, sprawled over the boulders. There were trees and shrubs with gorgeously-colored leaves and berries and pine trees, alone or in groups.

"Everywhere one saw pagan shrines by the wayside, and, at longer intervals, big temples with their glaring gods. The only sign of Christianity we met with in those mountains was when a Catholic soldier hailed us and showed us his rosary."

The travelers stopped the first night in tiny Loyuan, where Father Pius, O.P., gave them hospitality in the women's quarters of the mission compound. They were off before dawn and at noon reached Tanyang, a town without a Catholic in it. The nuns had a frugal meal at a noisy inn, surrounded by curious Chinese "who seemed keenly interested to discover by what means foreigners are nourished."

At Lienkang the coolies conducted the nuns to the Protestant mission by mistake. Excusing themselves they were escorted to the Catholic mission by a crowd of lively schoolboys who fetched the priest, Father Li, a man of great charm.

"During our short stay here," Mother Mary Patrick wrote, "we could see that he has great control over his boys and girls, whom he teaches himself. His church is the cleanest I have seen since I came to China. We two Sisters were given an immaculately tidy room in the girls' quarters and Mrs. Tao and her children were also accommodated by our host. We had a wait of some four hours for a meal, but when it did arrive it *was* a meal; course after course to which Sister Baptist and I failed to do justice."

The Protestant missionaries came to the Catholic compound the following morning to return the inadvertent call the nuns had made the previous day. A lame Chinese boy, an orphan, went to great trouble to tell the Protestants that they were *chia dih,* on the wrong track.

"We diverted the attention of our visitors from him as speedily and as tactfully as we could," said the mother general.

The last lap of the journey to Foochow was a stiff climb over a mountain. The travelers arrived at Kuantao, at the mouth of the Min river, at four o'clock. A small river steamer was due to leave for Foochow after dark. The sisters boarded immediately; where soon there was scarcely standing room. To make matters worse, rain beat down in torrents on all of the passengers.

It was midnight when the steamer reached Foochow. The nuns went directly to the hospital, but the sisters there had expected them the previous day and had given up hope of their arrival that night and so had retired. The two nuns beat at the heavy gate time and time again but got no response. For two dark, wet and chilly hours they walked the streets of the strange town looking for the Dominican procure.

"Eventually, after praying to St. Terese, we found the Dominican convent and were warmly welcomed by Reverend Mother. We called on the Bishop the next day, who commented on our adventures of the night before, saying, 'You have Irish hearts!' "

The Columbans were much impressed with the splendid orphanage that the Dominican sisters operated in Foochow. The nuns owned a small farm, and so were able to raise enough food to support their 150 girls.

"Every day three or four dying babies are brought to them," said Mother Mary Patrick. "They are baptized in the convent chapel. Most of them wing their way to heaven soon, and the survivors, who all look strong and healthy, are trained to be useful when they grow up."

The bishop of Foochow sent a servant to travel with the sisters as far as Kienningfu. There three Columban sisters met them and conducted them the rest of the way.

In passing through the gate of the mission compound in Nancheng, Mother Mary Patrick was delighted to see the hospital that the sisters had opened recently. Through redesign and renovation an old house had been sufficiently enlarged to hold thirty-five beds.

A German, Dr. Homberger, and a Chinese, Dr. Teng, worked with the sisters and their Chinese helpers. The hospital was rich only in human resources; aside from that it was poorly equipped. As Mother Mary Patrick, with her trained nurse's eye, observed: "Its medicine cupboard has more keys than medicines."

Bishop Cleary told the visiting sisters that seventeen years ago the bishops of China had assembled for the First Chinese National Synod. At that time they expressed the desire to see a Catholic hospital in every vicariate.

During the conversation the mother general recalled that the foreign missionaries were pioneers of scientific medical treatment in China. The government had shown little concern for the health of the people until 1931 when it created the ministry of health. The Protestant missionaries had surpassed the Catholics in medical care when the Columbans arrived thirteen years earlier and she wondered if this was still true.

Bishop Cleary took down a copy of the *China Year Book of 1936*, now five years old, that listed 232 Protestant hospitals and 233 Catholic. The article said that there were one thousand doctors working in hospitals, but that the country's vast population needed forty thousand doctors and nearly a half million nurses.

The bishop observed that practically every missionary had become a medical doctor of sorts; all were by now adept at treating those skin diseases and eye ailments so prevalent throughout China. He recalled an injunction of the Pope of the Missions, Pius XI: "Let the preachers of the gospel remember that they are to approach the natives by the same methods which their Divine Master used during His ministry on earth. Before he preached to the people, Jesus was accustomed to heal the sick."

Mother Mary Patrick and the bishop agreed that the eight sisters in Nancheng were doing remarkable work. During the past year the dispensary had treated 34,538 patients and the hospital had cared for 787. The pupils in the schools numbered nearly 2,000, and the sisters could take credit, the bishop said, for helping many of the fifty seminarians find their vocations.

The conversation between Bishop Cleary and Mother Mary Patrick closed with agreement on some administrative details. For example, Mother Michael and Sister Veronica would disembark at Hong Kong, fly to Namyung just within the Canton border, and from there endure the long bus ride to Nancheng. Mother Columban and Sisters Dolores and Angela would depart for home, reversing that route.

In leaving China, the mother general felt that the morale of all Columbans was higher than it had been a dozen years earlier. For the time being, many of the old frustrations were gone. The thirty-five Columban sisters in the vicariates of Hanyang and Nancheng were having the satisfaction of watching things grow.

They were such old China hands that some had experienced "the call of the East," a homesickness for the Orient that comes after departing it. Mother Mary Patrick spoke of having observed that when a nun returned to Cahiracon she was often surprised to find something inside her tugging toward the Far East.

Father Timothy Leahy told Mother Mary Patrick that "the call of the East" was a mystery that had long haunted him. The scenery of Hupeh Province, he admitted, is completely lacking in charm: flat, monotonous tableland stretching away for miles from the muddy waters of the Han and the Yangtze with thousands of drab Chinese villages, sheltering some forty million pagans, surrounded by hundreds of thousands of unsightly graves. And yet he loved it.

In trying to think through the things that puzzled him, Father Leahy said, "The average missionary is by no means a hero. Except for moments of loneliness his burden seems light. Of course there are windowless houses made of mud; bad food and sleeping on a board. And rats and mosquitoes. And the spasmodic companionship of dysentry and malaria. There are cold winters without a fire and hot summers without a well or icebox. Bandits. Floods. The cumulative effect would not seem to make you say, 'Ah, this is the life for me!' "

Father Leahy and the sisters decided it was not just the life of the religious that made them feel the way they did. They could work as religious in Ireland, the United States, or Australia, and not feel the same. Why should China draw them?

The sisters found their attitude changing toward China the longer they were there. For example, in the beginning they tended to smile at Chinese medicine, feeling that the Western way alone had merit. Now they showed some respect for ancient methods.

Acupuncture was no longer amusing. They observed that when fine needles of silver or gold were inserted properly the result was often helpful. Rheumatism and gout were among the pains treated this way.

They came to have some respect for manipulative surgery. In addition to the painless setting of fractures, the touch of the Chinese surgeon on nerves and nerve-centers was sure and skillful. To have a violent headache allayed by a few touches from the surgeon's hand was not unusual.

Herbal cures, handed down from father to son for generations, were not without value. Some ancient wisdom was there that could not be ignored.

By the time the mother general visited them, the sisters were speaking Chinese well, and several had decided to learn to read and write the language, too. Speaking was difficult enough; reading and writing were more so. Those who pushed on learned that almost all Chinese characters have a phonetic element which gives the sound, and an idea element which gives the meaning. Most of the nuns did not continue their language studies; their rounds of prayer, nursing, and teaching drained all of their energy.

Yes, Mother Mary Patrick departed China feeling good about what she had seen there. As for herself, she must have enjoyed some personal satisfaction, too: The sisterhood she had helped start had found its wings, and here she was, nearing seventy, and bearing up under the hardships of wartime travel in the Orient.

·17·

A Dangerous Time

After leaving Shanghai, Mother Mary Patrick returned to the Philippine Islands, where she had stopped on her way out to China. She had attended Midnight Mass in the Columban sisters' chapel in Lingayen on Christmas Eve 1939. Years later she would recall that the celebrant had been Father John Heneghan, one of the six Columban fathers who would be killed in the Philippines during the Second World War.

The superior general was now returning because Bishop Hayes had requested that the Columban sisters start schools in parishes staffed by Columban priests on Mindanao. The journey to that tropical island would be difficult, missionaries in Manila warned, but she went ahead anyway, traveling by steamboat down the length of the archipelago. Although conditions on Mindanao were primitive in those days, the superior general assured Bishop Hayes that sisters would be on the way as soon as she could find the money to pay their passage from Ireland, little dreaming that Japanese soldiers would capture Mindanao shortly after the arrival of the nuns.

From the Philippines, Mother Mary Patrick sailed to the west coast of the United States. Upon landing in July 1940, she proceeded to the convent of the Columban sisters in Silver Creek, New York. There she described with satisfaction the schools and the hospitals which she had visited since November.

She wrote of her world tour through countries at war: "I can still visualize the shadowy forms of the worshippers at early Mass in the London and Paris churches to which we found our way by flashlight. Paris was not blacked out so completely as London was. In the French capital a delicate shade of peacock blue pervaded the city.

"In the sunny land of Italy we found worshippers on bended knees at the same Holy Mass. Here, as elsewhere, mothers and wives were pleading before the throne of God for the safety of their dear ones."

While resting at Silver Creek, Mother Mary Patrick said that at last

County Clare seemed near, although it was at least three thousand miles away. She little dreamed that the most dramatic part of her thirteen-month journey was still ahead of her; it would come in the final days of the last five hundred miles.

The superior general and her traveling companion, Sister Ellen Muldoon, from Chicago, traveled from Silver Creek to a pier in New York harbor on December 4, 1940. Two members of the Silver Creek community, Sisters Mary Brendan and Mary Vianney, went as far as the pier with them. Only after boarding the British ship, *Western Prince,* did the two nuns bound for Ireland learn that the sailing had been postponed for nearly twenty-four hours.

The next morning, in the darkness before dawn, the Columbans came with caution down an icy gangplank. As they were asking a night watchman to call a taxi, an Irish policeman came along and added his whistle to form a duet. The cab driver, expressing surprise at seeing nuns on the waterfront at that hour, took them to the nearest church, Sacred Heart.

After attending the seven and the eight o'clock Masses, they crossed the street and had breakfast at the convent of the Sisters of Charity. Their hostess, Sister Miriam Patrick, brought to the dining room an elderly Irish lady from County Clare, Mary O'Brien, who wept tears of joy at the sight of someone who knew well the hills of home. As the Columbans prepared to leave for the ship, Mary O'Brien exclaimed, "God stand between you and harm!" an appropriate prayer considering what was ahead.

As they approached the *Western Prince,* the Columbans marveled at the beauty of it: here was a fairy ship, or a gigantic diamond, all aglitter with icicles in the morning light. At the head of the gangplank the captain greeted them and commented on the inadvisability of nuns making a sea voyage in these times. He was aware, in this second winter of the war, that German U-boats freely roamed the North Atlantic and that many ships went down.

"Missionaries, like sailors, must take risks," said the superior general. The captain spoke no more of danger.

The Columbans became friends with Dr. Dorothy Galbraith, herself a missionary. At the table the three women spoke of China with such affection that other passengers began to tease them, calling them the Old China Hands. When Dr. Galbraith and the sisters were assigned the same lifeboat, during ship's drill, they helped each other adjust life jackets, and went together to a class in first aid at which the ship's doctor suggested a method for treating hysteria: knock the hysteric over the head lest the condition become contagious.

The superior general brought out of her luggage religious medals which Sister Gabriel Plunkett, of the Sisters of Charity, had given her in Shanghai, "The Captain accepted one," she later wrote. "One officer assured us that St. Christopher was good enough for him, but I replied that St. Christopher was small fry compared with the Blessed Mother of God. A Catholic stewardess brought up the First Officer who asked for one and immediately pinned it under his lapel."

The nuns made a special effort to be as exacting in their spiritual duties on the high seas, as a community of two, as they would be in a convent at home. So they followed the Ordinary and the Proper of the Mass every day, "uniting ourselves to the Holy Sacrifice all over the world," as Mother Mary Patrick put it.

After saying their prayers on Friday night, December 13, the Columbans retired early. A torpedo struck at a quarter to six the next morning. It passed through the ship which shivered and stood still.

Sister Muldoon, having fallen from her bunk, jumped up and said, "Mother, what was that?"

"It's a torpedo. We have nothing to fear. God and his Blessed Mother are with us."

The nuns hurried into their habits, quickly adjusted lifebelts, and seized cloaks and shawls. The steward arrived, found them waiting, and led them on the run to their appointed place on deck. They were literally thrown into the lifeboat. A Greek and a Russian jumped in just as the first officer commanded, "Let down the boats!" and the captain cried out, "Pull off and good luck!"

Rain, sleet, and an icy spray swept over the passengers in the crowded open boats. The tiny vessels seemed so fragile riding the deep troughs of the high seas. Fifty minutes after the first torpedo, a second struck the *Western Prince*. The ship burst into flames and began slipping slowly into the sea. From that bright flare in the darkness came three long, slow blasts of a foghorn, the captain's way of saying farewell.

"Some of the sailors tried to keep up their hearts by swearing and joking," recalled Mother Mary Patrick. "After a time I ventured to suggest it would be well to say a prayer, for only God could save us. I started the Our Father and many of them joined in. We sang hymns to Our Lady, the 'Ave Maris Stella,' and 'Hail Queen of Heaven.' Afterward some of the men made a point of saying what a comfort it had been to them.

"At twelve noon we said the Angelus. Soon after this we heard them call out: 'Ship ahead!' "

The freighter, not seeing the lifeboats, began to diminish on the horizon. The sailors rowed in pursuit like demons. After what seemed an eternity, a lookout on the freighter, scanning the sea for submarines, sighted the lifeboats.

It took two hours to reach the ship. The danger was far from over; getting everyone aboard was hazardous, for high waves slammed the small boats against the freighter. One lifeboat capsized and its passengers perished. The freighter's captain ordered oil thrown overboard to make the waves less rough.

Sister Ellen Muldoon was young enough to climb the rope ladder with some alacrity. The seventy-year old superior general was assuring everyone that she too could do the same when a voice called down, "Bring the Mother Superior up in the basket!" So the mother superior arose from the sea with only her feet showing over the sides of the basket.

Life on deck was hectic. Some passengers suffered shock. A few had severe wounds. One man had to have his leg amputated.

"We were greeted by a fellow passenger imploring us to say whether we had seen his wife," wrote Mother Mary Patrick. "Alas! this bright young creature, whom we had admired and spoken to on a few occasions, had gone down."

A roll call revealed that six passengers and eleven crewmen had perished. Sadness tempered the joy of being rescued. Some heroic unselfishness came out of all this. Everyone's character was put to a test.

Space was so limited that not everyone could lie down at once, not even on the deck, and so passengers rested in turns. Food was scarce, as might be expected when a crew of thirty-five was suddenly joined by 160 passengers.

"We were wet and chilled to the bone," recalled Mother Mary Patrick. "A kind Negro took us to the stokehole to get warm. Our generous friend, Dr. Galbraith, insisted on my wearing a Chinese robe which she had worn under her mackintosh. No one would have recognized me as a member of St. Columban's sisterhood. Sister Muldoon was attired in an officer's coat."

A fear of submarines haunted the ship, adding mental anguish to physical hardship. Another sub was sighted two days from land but by then a destroyer was escorting the freighter.

Mother Mary Patrick called it "a happy augury" that the ship reached port on December 18, the Feast of Our Lady of Good Hope. Buses carried the survivors to the Grand Central Hotel in Glasgow where they could bathe, eat nourishing food, and sleep between fresh sheets, but not until reporters had deluged them with questions.

Early the next morning the Columbans went searching for a Catholic church. "I had forgotten our appearance," said Mother Mary Patrick. "I leave to your own imagination the collapse of the starched cap, and how I looked with only the veil pinned round my head. And Sister Muldoon was minus a cape."

The Scottish priest viewed the nuns with suspicion, asking what order they belonged to. When they said, the Sisters of St. Columban, he observed that he had seen those sisters in the magazine, *Far East,* and that their habits looked quite different.

Mother Mary Patrick recalled: "He unbent considerably after having heard our story and kindly piloted us to the ship, which we could never have found by ourselves in Glasgow.

"It was a twelve hours' run to the coast of Ireland, and never did our country look so attractive and desirable. A newsboy escorted us to St. Malachy's Church where we made our thanksgiving for our miraculous escape.

"Like two bedraggled seabirds we arrived in Dublin, leaving next day for Cahiracon. We reached our convent at 8 p.m., Friday, December 20. The sisters were all assembled in the hall to welcome us."

·18·

Another Storm Breaks

When the Japanese bombed Pearl Harbor, December 7, 1941, the Columbans sensed that this would make a difference in their lives. Up until now the fight had been between East and East, but with the West entering the war the status of every westerner in the Far East would change, especially those Columbans who were of American or Australian birth. It was inevitable that all non-Orientals would now be held suspect.

Right off the missionaries began to feel isolated. Hardest to bear was the uncertainty: How long will it last?

The *Far East* magazine was reduced to running bare notices: "News has recently been received from Bishop Galvin in Hanyang, and from Bishop Cleary in Nancheng that our missionaries in these two Chinese vicariates are safe and well." In time letters did get back and forth between China and neutral Ireland, but the mail was always uncertain. It depended on passing travelers, chance callers, and the Red Cross.

The Columbans wondered if the Chinese would now turn their whole effort against the Japanese, and so end the war in short order. Up until the time of Pearl Harbor they had been fighting each other more than fighting the common enemy. Chiang Kai-shek summed it up in a sentence: "The Japanese are a disease of the skin; the Communists are a disease of the heart."

A few days after Pearl Harbor, Father Joseph Hogan witnessed a dogfight between Japanese and Chinese pilots in the sky above Hanyang. The Chinese plane, plummeting toward the ground like a stone, suddenly came out of the dive, leveled off and made a perfect landing two hundred yards from Father Hogan.

When the missionary ran to the plane to find it a sieve of bullet holes, the intricacies of the Chinese language became evident.

"*Wo song tsai na li?*" shouted the excited pilot.

In nine cases out of ten this means, "Where have I landed?"

"In Hanyang," answered the priest.

"No," said the pilot with impatience. "That is not what I meant." and he repeated the sentence.

It dawned on Father Hogan that *song,* besides meaning "upon" also means "wounded." The pilot was asking, "Where am I wounded?"

The missionary examined him and found scarcely a scratch.

The pilot hugged himself with glee and did a little dance. And Father Hogan was of a mood to do an Irish jig.

For a time the nuns spent most days as though the war did not exist. They continued doing the things that they had come halfway around the world to do.

For example, one evening when the Angelus was ringing at the convent there came a loud knocking on the compound's outer gate. An old woman, emaciated but respectably dressed, begged the sisters to hurry to her dying son.

Two sisters, gripping their black medicine bags, followed the old lady who with bound feet took short quick steps through the jostling crowd as far as a well-known tea shop in the Street of Gold. The sisters had often passed the establishment and had wished that they might have some contact with the proprietors and with their many patrons.

The low roof of the rather dreary restaurant was supported by wooden pillars from which the paint was peeling. The walls had faded to a uniform greyness. The room was furnished with square tables and stools of lacquered wood. About fifty patrons chatted as they sipped tea from large bowls.

With a quick glance at the surroundings the sisters passed through the restaurant to an apartment at the back. There they found the patient, the proprietor of the tea shop in the Street of Gold, stretched out on the floor of beaten earth. His wife lit an oil lamp revealing a face drawn by suffering and a body thin and wasted. The sisters saw that he had suffered a severe hemorrhage and was of such low debility that he could no longer understand what was said.

As the nuns were leaving the tea shop they were stopped by a patron, a Mr. Lee, who asked news of the sick man. The nurses said that they had made him as comfortable as possible and would return later to continue the treatment.

The following morning the patient's wife came to the convent to say that her husband was much better. The sisters returned with her to the tea room to find that a sizeable crowd had gathered, word having gone out that the "foreign lady doctors" were expected to return. Some parents had brought ailing children to be treated; some patients had an arm or leg of their own that required attention. Mr. Lee said that his nephew had been ailing for months and that he had dispatched messengers to bring the boy up from the country for inspection. To each patient the sisters gave a note of introduction to be presented at the mission dispensary.

As soon as they could free themselves from the crowd they turned their attention to the proprietor of the tea shop. Indeed he was improved and filled with gratitude for the "miracle" they had wrought in his favor.

"In a few days he was out of danger," a sister wrote. "For the Chinese there is no such thing as a period of convalescence after an illness, and in a comparatively short time the good man was back at his business. The sisters, however, continued to bring him tonics."

The proprietor of the tea shop said that he wanted to study the Christian religion. In due course he was baptized, along with his wife, daughter, and widowed mother. Mr. Lee, his nephew, and all members of the family also became Christian.

In Nancheng, for a time, life went on as usual. Now and again something happened to remind the nuns that there was a war on. For example, two Chinese officers stepped from a limousine at the gate of the Columbans' Nancheng hospital; the younger told Sister Catherine Labouré that he would like to "engage a room." He was a cavalryman, about thirty, who wore spurs that flashed in the sunlight and a tunic covered with ribbons.

The young officer suffered from tuberculosis of the throat, a serious condition at any time, but magnified in wartime China with medicines at a premium. Although he was responding to treatment, after two weeks he grew restless and said that he must return to his regiment.

A few weeks later he returned, his throat badly damaged. His attitude had changed; from abrupt and aloof he was now warm and friendly. While undergoing treatment he read books of a religious nature kept on a shelf in the hospital. This time when he decided to leave he spoke with Father Thomas Ellis about Catholicism and took some books with him to study at leisure.

"I was hurrying along to dinner when I noticed a uniformed officer, accompanied by a servant, sitting in the hospital vestibule," said Sister Catherine Labouré. "Something made me look a second time, whereupon the man spoke to me in a muffled voice. Immediately, I recognized our friend. Back again! And, feeling faint, decided to rest for a while in the shade of the hospital. Would I give him a stimulant to help him on his way?"

At a glance the nursing sister saw that the Chinese officer was near death and suggested that he spend the night in the hospital; tomorrow he might feel stronger. She prepared a bed for him in the passageway, for the hospital wards were filled.

The dying man asked to see Father Ellis. The priest spent most of the day with him, instructing him in the Catholic religion. "Toward evening another officer who had heard of the condition of the dying man vacated his room for him," the nursing sister recalled. "Early morning again found Father Ellis at the patient's bedside. The poor fellow suffered greatly during the day, but he was quiet, and the look on his face expressed inner peace. He was baptized early in the morning, with the name of John, and died a short time afterward."

Soon refugees were arriving from the embattled north. The nuns, successful in treating people worn thin with malaria, dysentery, and tropical ulcers, found that in getting patients back on their feet they were creating another problem: What will these people do to keep alive after walking out of the hospital door?

The sisters took the problem to Father Ellis, who was a man of imagination. He said right off that the Columbans must provide light employment for convalescents.

Father Ellis approached Bishop Cleary and a few of the priests, saying: "We have no Mass candles, so let's make our own. We can no longer get catechisms, so let's start printing them. We can no longer buy rosaries, so let's make them. Now here is where you come in—I need all the money you can spare for tools and a printing press."

The first experiments failed: candles turned brown, rosaries had chains thick enough to anchor a battleship, and hot weather turned the ink into unmanageable gobs. Eventually life in the workshop began to run smoothly. The print shop became so well known that orders for print jobs began reaching Nancheng from three provinces.

The war moved closer to Nancheng on April 18, 1942. On that day sixteen specially equipped B-25 bombers, under Lt. Col. (later Lt. Gen.) James H. Doolittle, took off from the carrier *Hornet,* 650 miles east of the Japanese islands, and made a raid on Tokyo. After releasing their bombs they proceeded westward until most of them reached safety in China. Five, however, crashed in the mountains near Nancheng.

Of the crewmen who bailed out one suffered a badly dislocated arm. One of the airmen approached a Chinese family working in the fields and crossed his index fingers to form a cross. The Chinese read the sign correctly and led the Americans to the cathedral of Nancheng. The sisters cared for the injured man until all of the Americans were picked up and flown to the airbase in Kunming. In time other American flyers stopped at the cathedral on their way to safety.

Doolittle himself visited Bishop Cleary and the Columban sisters to thank them for their help. He said that he hoped they would not suffer any retaliation.

The Japanese launched a punitive expedition into Kiangsi Province to make the Irish missionaries and the Chinese pay for giving hospitality to the Americans. Since a Chinese military unit was garrisoned in Nancheng the Japanese air force made frequent bombing runs on the town to soften it up for the assault of ground troops.

The priests painted white crosses on the roofs of all buildings as a way of asking for immunity from air attack. This did little good since the mission was near the west gate, which for some reason seemed to be the center of interest, and stray bombs fell in the compound with uncomfortable frequency.

As the Japanese infantry approached the city, most of the twenty thousand inhabitants fled to the comparative safety of the countryside. Eight hundred terrified men, women, and children crowded into the mission compound.

Living there at the time were Bishop Cleary, four priests, the hospital physician, and seven Sisters of Saint Columban.

The final artillery attack began at half past four on the afternoon of June 11, 1942. When the first shells made that frightening "shusshing" sound as they flew over the compound, Bishop Cleary removed the Blessed Sacrament from the tabernacle and hid it in a better protected place. A shell exploded on the roof of the priests' residence, sending a shower of tiles into the room below. As darkness fell the attack increased in intensity. At nine o'clock when the bishop brought bread and coffee to where the sisters were sheltered the noise from bursting shells and exploding grenades was terrifying.

During the night fifteen shells fell within the compound walls. The church received five hits, and the hospital one.

"Looking back at it now," Mother Mary Michael wrote at the end of the war, "it seems nothing short of the miraculous that we should have come through that night without a single casualty.

"A shell hit the roof of our compound well—less than ten yards from where some sisters were sheltered at the time. On another occasion Sister Francis had taken cover with me under a heavy table. After a time I sent her to a safer place at the other end of the compound. She had barely gone when a shower of shrapnel fell right beside me in the place she had occupied.

"Towards dawn the shelling grew heavier. Then gradually it eased and lessened. At about half past six in the morning Bishop Cleary came over and told us that the Japanese were in."

The Japanese had hardly come through the town gate when an officer stalked into the hospital to berate the sisters for taking care of "American belligerents." Mother Michael said with calmness, "We take care of anyone in need."

The Japanese hit her a blow on the back.

Mother Michael tried to explain that the nuns were Irish, not English, and so were not part of the war.

"You speak English!" the officer said accusingly. "You have a language of your own?"

"Yes, we have a language," said Mother Michael, and immediately the nuns began reciting the rosary in Irish.

"Why do you bow at a certain time," the Japanese asked with suspicion.

"We, too, have manners like the Japanese," Mother Michael said.

Just then Bishop Cleary arrived. He stood up to the assembled soldiers with a fierceness that would have startled everyone back in Ireland who knew him as a scholarly man with the look of a poet.

The bishop said that the hospital would treat anyone in need, Japanese included. Perhaps this saved the Columbans from personal harm, but it did not save the hospital. The Japanese burned it and destroyed all the supplies that they could not take with them.

By now the refugees who had fled Nancheng were a hundred miles to the south at Kwang Chang. They stopped there because Father Con O'Connell, the pastor, was a Columban, and the refugees had come to feel that Columbans were ready to solve all problems.

The young missionary began piling refugees into the boys' school, the girls' school, the catechumenate, the church compound and even into his own house, until everything was overflowing with humanity.

No sooner were the refugees somewhat settled than a woman suddenly took sick and died. It was evident from the dark hue that quickly overspread her body that she had died of the dreaded cholera. With resistance lowered by fatigue, lack of food, and hardships of the flight, the refugees were especially susceptible to disease.

When the cholera epidemic died down, dysentery took its place. The compound swarmed with flies. Medicine was unavailable. Deaths multiplied. Sanitation alone could fight the disease.

Father Bernard Murtagh, hearing of Father O'Connell's plight, hurried across the Min river and the Wuyi Shan mountains to help. One of the priests took care of sanitation while the other nursed the sick and dying.

The Japanese army departed Nancheng on July 8. In the smouldering ruins only eighteen houses stood intact. Fifty neighboring villages had been completely wiped out. Thousands of families had lost all their possessions: their homes, furniture, bed coverings, and padded winter clothing. In hundreds of farms the very plows had been burned or smashed to bits, the pigs and fowl slaughtered.

The Japanese had made the Chinese and the Irish pay a steep price for being kind to the Americans who had bombed Tokyo.

When the refugees heard that the Japanese had departed from Nancheng, they returned to the desolation. What a pitiful procession, those thousands weakened by malaria, malnutrition, ulcers, running sores, and dysentery. And rains fell without ceasing day after day.

Father Edward McManus wrote in his journal: "After fifteen years of China, I thought I knew the Chinese. But my eyes were opened by the capacity for endurance of those poor and sorely-tried people. Not once did I hear a complaint from anyone. Their song was one of joy and thanksgiving to God that their lives had been spared. Their chief worry was for the safety of the bishop, priests and sisters."

Again Father Ellis called on his imagination. The hospital was gone but the school was still there, and so he declared it to be a hospital. Hundreds of patients who would have died along the road were crowded two to a bed and stretched side-by-side on classroom floors. The church housed the less serious cases. Despite such vicissitudes Sisters Catherine and Veronica did heroic work in nursing those who came under their care.

From dawn until dusk Father Ellis and Sisters Baptist and Malachy visited people in what had once been their homes. The missionaries searched the rubble of the city and went into the scarred countryside seeking the helpless. Their reports were painful to read:

"Visited the city from the church to the jail, going into every inhabited spot, finding out the condition of those who were most destitute." The words "inhabited spot" replace the word "house," for people lived in shattered temples, stables, tents of matting, and even under the sky amid smoke-blackened ruins.

At the end of the first month some fifty outlying villages were still unvisited. Each day the Columbans of Nancheng saw more devastation: "The death toll has been terrible. One of us discovered a family of ten of whom only two are left. In another case the father, mother and children had died in two weeks. In a hamlet of four houses the fathers of three families had died. The conditions under which these poor people are living are almost incredible."

Hope brightened the dismal scene on September 30, 1942, the day that Bishop Cleary asked several prominent citizens of Nancheng to come to the cathedral. He said that he was forming a local committee to ascertain how to spend the money offered by the Kannan Committee of International Relief.

The citizens of Nancheng said they hoped Bishop Cleary would serve as chairman of the local committee. He agreed to do so and said that he wanted Mother Michael as his assistant.

At the end of the meeting Mother Michael wrote a no-nonsense report saying the money from International Relief would be used to buy food, coffins, medicine, clothing, bedding, and farm implements.

·19·

Darkness on Nancheng

Bishop Cleary was not satisfied with merely caring for the needs of the moment. He wrote to the Kannan Committee for International Relief: "The problem will not be solved till people are provided with funds to rebuild their homes, restock their farms, and redevelop their little home industries."

As a result of this letter, farmers received loans to buy seed and farm implements. Loans were also made to start small businesses. To get help the borrower had to produce a document signed by two reliable persons guaranteeing repayment. Most of the repayments fell due in December of 1943. About two thirds were repaid at that time, far more than expected considering the poverty.

Perhaps the most successful rehabilitation project was the revival of the spinning industry. Here again Father Ellis was the guiding light. He distributed cotton to the needy who made thread in their homes. After selling the thread at the market he distributed the money to the spinners.

In one shop Father Ellis employed two hundred women to make shoes, cloth, and stockings. Many of the women had lost their husbands in the war; most had two or more children to support.

In speaking of Father Ellis's activities, Father McManus wrote: "He meets all trials and difficulties with a smile, a trust in Divine Providence that nothing can shake."

At Christmas of 1942 the Columbans in Nancheng momentarily forgot the war and its afflictions when caught up in the happiness of seeing James Yang ordained a priest. As one of the sisters explained: "He is our own in a way the other Chinese priests are not since they were educated and trained by the French Vincentians. Father James has been Bishop Cleary's pupil since his early school days, and the Bishop has personally supervised all of his studies right through to the great moment of his ordination."

The cathedral overflowed on December 20, a frosty morning when the charcoal in the firepots smoked enough to make throats tickle and yet the place was strangely quiet. Usually on such festive days the church was filled with the noises of crying children and of a roving congregation. All was tranquil except for a murmur of delight at the sight of the semicircle of priests with outstretched hands standing by the bishop at the moment of the imposition of hands.

A few days later one of the sisters reported: "A Vincentian priest who had been to the border of India arrived here on Christmas Eve, on his way home, with a barrow load of goods. He extracted from the precarious depths two tins of coffee, and what more fragrant offering could he have brought to us in wartime?

"On Christmas night we listened to Christmas greetings from England. We heard the North of Ireland, too, and Ballymena Station, but good old Dublin did not reach us. However, what we did get brought home very near."

Except for that Christmas gift, coffee was just a memory. Some Columbans began rationing their supply as far back as 1939, and by brewing just one cup a day managed to stretch the limited stock until 1942. One of them said, "Perhaps some of them have the makings of a potful locked up in the safe for a very special visitor, but nothing less than a bishop will bring it out into the open."

Indian tea was also a memory. The missionaries began experimenting with local teas only to find them so bitter and unpalatable that they thought teatime was out for the duration. And just then, one of the missionaries at the extreme end of the vicariate discovered an excellent brand of Chinese tea, Anwhei, one that had been in demand for export. Since the export trade was no more, he was able to buy a year's supply for the whole vicariate and so win the unanimous praise of all.

No imported food reached the missions during the war. Shanghai, the usual port of entry, was closed to anything going to or coming from the United States or Europe. In time the Air Transport Command began flying supplies from India across the Himalayas into Kunming, but that was for the military only.

The Yangtze and the Han, in former days full of sails and shipping, now ran idly to the sea. All necessities soared to unprecedented heights. Available food, even at dear cost, was still poor stuff.

A few Columbans, those with iron constitutions, could adopt a native diet completely, but most needed a supplement. Fortunately, several priests in Nancheng vicariate had invested in a few cows, and so there was just about enough milk and butter to go around during the lean years.

Even though the meals grew frugal as the war dragged on, the anecdotes told at each meal were as memorable as ever. For instance there was the story of a *tandze* which made the rounds of the vicariate.

A *tandze* is a girl who is born unwanted. *Tandze* means literally "a jug of wine." Fathers of such children sometimes said, "Friends, we expected a son but it is only a daughter. Let us console ourselves with a jug of wine!"

Nan Dzin, eight years old, was a *tandze*. She was a great admirer of the *sen-fu* (priest), who happened to be Father Tomothy Leahy. She liked his large, baggy pockets from which came peanuts, apples, or tangerines. How it delighted her to see him perform his act: the *sen-fu* would flip a Chinese penny high into the air, slap his palms together as it decended, and lo, the coin vanished. A moment later it reappeared as the *sen-fu* extracted it from Nan Dzin's pocket, or discovered it inside the lining of her multi-colored cap. This always brought howls of delight.

One day Father Leahy could see that the *tandze* had something on her mind. He did not have to ask her about it, for she came to the point at once.

"*Sen-fu,* I want you to save a soul."

She took the priest's hand and led him through the compound gate. Just outside, resting in the shade of the ancient wall, was the "kennel man."

Kennel men were not unusual in China. They were poor, without friends, and were unable to use their limbs. They spent their lives inside a little house, not much larger than a dog's kennel. Such houses, usually crude boxes, could be easily carried by two men from place to place.

A kennel man would appear at a village uninvited. The villagers would feed him scraps of food from their own lean fare, until they felt he had been with them long enough. Then two of their young men would transport him to the next village.

The kennel man outside the mission compound was dying. His mind was still clear, but Nan Dzin, who had been talking to him all morning, discovered that he was failing fast.

"Whether she realized it or not," said Father Leahy, "she was a beautiful example of the old saying, that what you see depends largely on what you are. Several hundred people had passed the kennel man that morning and had looked at him, but had not 'seen' him because they lacked the sympathetic interest that Nan Dzin had."

The little girl had discovered that in his twenty years of wanderings the kennel man had stayed many times in church compounds. From conversations with Catholic teachers he had picked up a considerable amount of Catholic doctrine.

After the priest had spent an hour with the invalid he baptized him. Later that evening the priest and the child went to the little house again. Together they taught the man a simple prayer. When the invalid's mind wandered and he got the aspirations mixed up, Nan Dzin with the tireless energy of a child insisted on putting him right.

The next morning the man died. He could not be buried in his own land, like other Chinese, because he had none. The *sen-fu* and the *tandze* bought a coffin for two dollars and together they found a place to dig the kennel man's grave.

The wear of war began to show in 1943 when deaths in Nancheng suddenly became more numerous. Sister Mary Baptist explained: "The people have no reserve of strength left, and a nourishing diet is beyond the means of all except the wealthy, so that dysentery and malaria have wrought havoc. This year very many babies and young children died in our Catholic families and amongst our catechumens, some because their mothers could not feed them and there are no baby foods to be had nowadays, and others by reason of an epidemic of some kind which took them off in a few days."

Sister Mary Baptist said that going downtown with Sister Catherine Labouré was like taking a walk with a celebrity. "All the reverential bows of well-groomed officers who have recovered from typhoid and dysentery, and the smiles of stout venerable gentlemen who had once bemoaned their woes in some screened-off bed in the men's wards, and all the kind enquiries for her health make one feel that this good land of our adoption is as lovable as any country in the world."

The two nuns walked across town almost daily on their way to and from a prison. There were two prisons in Nancheng, one for short-term and the other for long-term convicts. Those on short terms were allowed to visit the dispensary for treatment, but long-term convicts had to stay behind bars, and so the nuns had to come to them.

When typhoid broke out in the long-term prison Mother Michael pleaded with the local police chief asking that the patients be sent to the hospital. When asked if she could guarantee that no prisoner would escape she admitted that such a guarantee was impossible, and so her appeal was turned down. The nuns continued making their daily trip to prison, a task that further taxed their energies.

Such dedication did not go unappreciated. For instance, at the Chinese New Year the sisters heard the sound of bugles at the compound gate and before they knew it eight men were kowtowing at the convent door. The mandarin had sent them to offer greetings and thanks for the care given at the hospital and at the dispensary.

Sisters Veronica and Catherine Labouré acknowledged the esteem brought by the mandarin's envoys. Mother Michael and Sisters Malachy and Francis served tea. Firecrackers added to the festivity.

Bishop Cleary said at the time, "I think it is true that the status of the Catholic Church was never so good in China as at present. I do not mean legally. I am speaking of the place of the Church in the minds of the people."

Time and again he spoke of the way the Columban sisters were winning the hearts of all they helped. He wrote to Dalgan: "I am delighted to see that Mother General is paying so much attention to the training of doctors and nurses, for their work gets more ready recognition than any other from people of all classes."

The Columbans in Nancheng were stunned when Father Tom Ellis died on March 8, 1945. Bishop Cleary said, "I never saw so many tears shed over the death of anybody." The scholarly bishop felt close to the frail, young priest who was also a scholar.

Tom Ellis had a fine knowledge of the Old Testament, especially of the major prophets, and was studying the New Testament trying to recover his Greek. Just before he died he took up Hebrew hoping to get something out of the unintelligible parts of the psalms. The sisters were amused at the way he might appear at any moment with a volume of Augustine, or Aquinas, or Bossuet, and say, "Listen to this."

His vast fund of knowledge astonished them. He could discuss engines, charcoal burners, the annealing of metals, the tanning of leather, and also sing the latest ditties. Besides getting the poor started at making thread, candles, shoes and cloth, and printing books, he installed an electric plant, learned to smelt brass and aluminum, and investigated the mysteries of electro-plating. All in the heat of a Chinese summer.

The nursing sisters remembered Father Ellis mainly for his compassion. He seemed to search out the most ulcerous, evil-smelling, tuberculous down-and-outs of Nancheng. Whenever he brought in an especially "ripe" pathetic case he would say to the sister in charge, "Here is one of ours." Then he would sit down on the patient's bed, even after a hard day's work, and talk to the poor creature as a friend and father.

Father Ellis felt affection for the unattractive. Such love is a grace from God, not something ordered on demand. Every missionary needs it, for to do good without love demeans both giver and receiver.

During a two-week fall of snow Father Ellis slaved in the hospital with ninety derelicts who were in an appalling condition from frost bite, relapsing fever, and a litany of ailments. At one time he had seven corpses on hand because he could get no one to bury them. He met with the beggars who seemed to rise out of the blizzard at Chinese New Year, and investigated the cases to determine the most needy.

During the winter before his death, while visiting his mountain missions in bitter weather, he gave his coat and shoes to a carrier whom he had to send down to the city. On the way back to Nancheng he found a dead soldier by the path and stopped long enough to bury him.

He was forever attending the "feasts" of the refugees in the compound to put some self-respect into them and show that he was not too grand to share their poor dinners. Bishop Cleary always thought that it was at one of those "feasts" that Father Ellis contracted typhoid. He had no reserve of energy to fight such an illness and so he lasted only a few days.

The bishop wrote home: "We buried him here in Nancheng beside Father Tim Beecher. The funeral was a purely religious one, as rubrical as we could make it. On the occasion of Father Beecher's funeral he remarked: 'I am glad to see there were none of the minor superstitions,' and there were none at his, not even the firecrackers so beloved by the Chinese. To give the priests time to come to Nancheng we kept the coffin in the church for three days, and it would have delighted his heart to see the constant stream of Catholics who came to pray, mostly in tears, for the repose of his soul."

How much longer will it last? the Columbans kept asking. They followed bulletins issued by the minister of war, but found them of little help, for no one trusted official news, and not without cause. Everyone remembered that Chungking had suppressed for a week the story of the capture of Hankow, and then only admitted that "traces of the enemy have appeared in Hankow." It was difficult to take seriously official bulletins that referred to the Japanese as "dwarf bandits"; Japanese attacks as "sneaking about," and Chinese retreats as "major strategic outflanking movements."

The Columbans felt that the people back home might well know more of China's plight than they did. Missionaries reached the point that the only thing about the war that they believed was what they could see with their own eyes at any given moment. All news was reduced to rumor.

·20·

Hanyang's Worst Days

At the time of Pearl Harbor, forty-two foreign priests worked in the vicariate of Hanyang. Thirty-four of these were Irish citizens. Of the remaining eight, five were American, two Australian, and one British. The eight, declared "enemy aliens," were Fathers Gerald O'Collins, Patrick Hennessy, Eugene Spencer, Joseph Spahn, Stanislaus Walczak, Michael Scanlon, Philip Donahue, and Francis McDonald. All eight had to report to Japanese headquarters in Hankow and from there were sent downriver to Shanghai where there were several camps called "civilian assembly areas."

In February 1943 priests of "belligerent nationality" were placed in the French Jesuit compound in the district of Siccawei and in the Vincentian and Franciscan houses within the city. Sisters stayed at the convent of the Religious of the Sacred Heart, on Avenue Joffre.

Japanese officials moved the Columban priests, on April 13, to lay camps. There, while serving as chaplains, the missionaries were permitted to say Mass daily.

On September 15 the five American Columbans learned that they might be sent back to the United States in exchange for Japanese civilians. They accepted the offer since they saw no chance of returning to Hanyang until the war had ended.

Four days later they boarded the *Teia Maru* in Shanghai and sailed the following day down the Whampoo, past the go-downs, and out into the yellow waters of the China Sea. The *Teia Maru* sailed, as did the *Gripsholm* on the way from New York, under full guarantee of safe passage, provided it kept all lights ablaze.

The *Teia Maru* reached Hong Kong, September 23, to take on more passengers. Next day it sailed southwards to the Philippines, where internment camps in Manila and Baguio were releasing some of their inmates. On September 28 she turned around and went westward to Saigon in French Indochina. Upon leaving Saigon, October 2, she sailed for Singapore.

Each mile of the trip taken by the two exchange ships was subject to exact agreement between the countries concerned. Explicit reservations and restrictions now barred the *Teia Maru* from sailing directly to India. So she took a southeasterly course, passing between Sumatra and Java, and after making a wide swing, came north to Mormugao, on the west coast of India.

There on October 15 she found the *Gripsholm* had already arrived.

"Have you any ice cream on board?" was the first question shouted from the *Teia Maru*.

"Plenty," came the answer from the *Gripsholm*.

This brought a cheer.

"And coffee?"

"Plenty"

Another cheer.

Something bright flew from the *Gripsholm* to the *Teia Maru*. Half a dozen hands reached out to catch the orange. Then followed a shower of fruit, a foretaste of the memorable meal awaiting the repatriates.

These were minor but unforgettable incidents in the seventy-two-day voyage, over 20,000 miles that brought 1,236 Americans home from Manchuria, China, French Indochina, and the Philippines.

While the thirty-four Irish priests in China were spared incarceration, their lives were much confined. The question of Ireland's neutrality had been settled in Tokyo, just after Pearl Harbor, but commanders of Japanese forces in the field reluctantly recognized such neutrality. Every priest up-country had to fight out this matter of neutrality with the local commander.

The issue often hung in the balance when a missionary, upon being asked where Ireland was, could produce only an ancient, pre-treaty map showing Ireland as a British possession. The commanders recalled that in school in Japan they had learned that the Irish were under British rule. All of this debate had to be carried on through a Chinese interpreter who only added to the confusion.

Even when the neutrality was recognized local commanders would either restrict movements of priests to the confines of their parishes or send them to live in Hanyang. So it was that Fathers John McNamara, Thomas Tracy, John Mackey, Robert Staples, Aidan McGrath, Charles Donnelly, Michael McCarthy, Thomas O'Rourke, Ulick Burke, and Hugh Sands were removed from their up-country parishes and sent to the central mission residence in Hanyang city.

The Japanese permitted only eleven Irish and four Chinese priests to reside up-country from the summer of 1942 until the winter of 1944. Theirs was a restricted, lonely life. As an example of the fear they lived with it is well to repeat an ancedote that Father Fergus Murphy told the Columban sisters at war's end.

When the Japanese held the road that passed through Father Murphy's parish, bandits still roamed both sides of it. The night an excitable pagan came to the rectory saying that a Catholic had been beaten by bandits and wanted the Last Sacraments, the priest wondered if he could be trusted. Should he risk the trip from Kin Shan to Liao Chia Tsang, fifteen miles away? He had heard of bandits luring a priest out into the country with a false sick call. Under close questioning the messenger seemed to be telling the truth.

The missionary would need a pass to get past the Japanese troops, and that he did not have. The Japanese colonel, friendly enough, had always refused him one. What to do? Father Murphy decided to take a chance and leave his rectory without a word to anyone.

Early in the morning he mounted his tiny pony and found slipping past the first Japanese sentry was easy. Soon, though, he began to feel lost. The messenger had said to take the main road to Sen Gia Chiao, branch off to the northwest, and go five more miles to Liao Chia Tsang.

"I soon found," said Father Murphy, "that the going was not so simple. The war had but recently passed over my road and there were unburied bodies in the villages that I passed through. Not a living soul in sight. I had no way of recognizing Sen Gia Chiao."

After two hours of riding the priest came upon a troop of Japanese cavalrymen. The captain, mounted on a tall sixteen-hand horse, towered above the priest on the tiny pony.

"Where are you going?" asked the officer.

"I am a Catholic priest and I am on my way to see a sick man."

In a wild attempt to distract the officer from asking for a pass, Father Murphy said, "Will you change horses with me?"

It worked. The captain laughed and waved the priest on with a warning that he had better stick to the main road to avoid bandits.

When Father Murphy found the place he thought might be Sen Gia Chiao it was alive with Japanese troops. In skirting the village looking for a Chinese he might question, he finally found one, a water carrier.

"Can you tell me the road to Liao Chia Tsang?"

"Never heard of it."

"Is this Sen Gia Chiao?"

"You passed it three miles back."

Father Murphy rode back three miles hoping to find someone who would give further directions. He found only dead bodies at the place he decided must be Sen Gia Chiao.

After heading his pony in what he guessed to be a northwesterly direction he found himself in mountainous country, bandit country. The missionary tried to reassure himself that bandits operated only at night, but was not easily convinced.

After two more deserted villages Father Murphy saw a man digging a dike. He offered to pay the fellow to guide him to Liao Chia Tsang. The fellow accepted but was exceedingly nervous on the road, walking fast and keeping a watch on the hills. This did not make the Columban feel any more relaxed, and it was with relief that he finally reached the village.

Father Murphy quickly attended the sick man, gulped a cup of tea, and despite protestations made a hasty departure. His chances of avoiding Japanese sentries and bandits were better in daylight than after dark.

Dusk was falling as he approached his mission at Kin Shan. Suddenly he noticed two Japanese sentries standing atop a hill overlooking the road. His hope of passing unobserved was shattered with the cry, "Halt there!"

One Japanese stood on top of the hill pointing the rifle at the Columban and the other ran down the slope with bayonet fixed.

"My heart jumped up and then sank to my boots," Father Murphy later told the sisters in Hanyang. "Visions of being shot or slashed with a bayonet sped through my mind. I dismounted with my knees trembling. I clutched the pony's neck for support."

The Japanese came charging up panting, "Would you have a cigarette?"

A cigarette—not a passport!

"Eagerly the missionary pulled a packet from his pocket. "Here you are. Divide these with your friend on the hill."

The Japanese beamed and the Irishman beamed. Cheerfully bidding the soldier goodnight the priest rode the last half-mile into Kin Shan as darkness fell.

The Columban sisters were also restricted, even in Hanyang, unless they showed the proper pass with photo attached. They found it an ordeal passing surly sentries, with fixed bayonets, whose only expression seemed a gruff grunt.

The last year of the war was the worst time for the sisters of Hanyang because of the constant strain of air raids. When the alarm sounded, five or six times a day, the nuns locked the compound and sought safety in the fields outside the city. Even when the bombers failed to appear, waiting for them was almost as bad as an attack.

One night Hanyang was bombed so heavily that a vast area around the cathedral was reduced to a wilderness of ruins. Inside the cathedral a thousand Chinese huddled in fear.

Bishop Galvin took for granted that the bombardier seeing the Celtic cross had delayed pressing the button until the cathedral compound had cleared his sights. When the Japanese had departed the city, months later, he talked with some men from the B-25 group who had bombed Hankow, Hanyang, and Wuchang.

"We pattern-bombed the area," said the bombardier. "We just laid them over everything. Who could see a cross down there at night!"

A pilot said, "If I didn't see this I would say it was impossible. This island shouldn't be here. The whole area should be flat."

The cathedral across the river in Hankow was not spared. The night that bombers destroyed it, Bishop Massi died with a shell fragment in his heart. This was a great personal loss to Bishop Galvin who visited the old Italian prelate whenever troubled or in doubt.

"It did one good to talk with him," said Bishop Galvin, "for he looked on life with a smile, and no matter how dark things were he saw a silver lining. During these last years, however, when worries came to him thick and fast, that smile was not so evident as it used to be.

"Shortly before his death I called to see him on business and found him worried and discouraged. I tried to console him, and pointed to the work he had done and the merit he had gained during forty years on his mission life in China. 'No, Monsignor,' he said, 'I have accomplished nothing. My hands are empty. All I can hope for now, through the mercy of God, is a small place in Paradise.'

"That was not mock humility. It merely reflected the mind of many a missionary who, looking back, cannot see what he has accomplished because of the immense work still to be done."

The cathedral and residence were in ruins, so the bishop's coffin was taken to the seminary, just outside the city. Since the chapel was too small to contain the crowd, Bishop Galvin said the Requiem Mass at a temporary altar on the veranda. On that bitterly cold December day, in 1944, snow began to fall on Bishop Galvin's vestments, and when he turned to give the Absolution after Mass he noticed that it was falling gently on the coffin.

Four Italian Sisters of Charity and eight nurses were also killed in that air raid. They worked just across the street from the cathedral of Kankow in the Canossa Institute, where for eighty years nuns had cared for the poor, sick, and abandoned. Two severe bombings reduced the hospital, orphanage, schools, and convent to a pile of shattered bricks.

Bishop Galvin said the Requiem Mass amid the rubble. The four coffins were opened just before burial at the request of the Italian sisters.

"It was the most heartrending scene I have ever encountered," wrote the bishop. "Yet the Mother Superior never shed a tear. With hands clenched and with suffering written on her face she looked at the bodies of the four sisters, so terribly shattered. All around her were the ruins of her Institute, the work of eighty years had been destroyed.

"Yet her great faith did not waver. Holding out her hands to the weeping sisters she said, 'Don't cry. It is God's will. Why should we doubt Him?'

"As I stood beside her, she reminded me of the Mother on Calvary. It was inexpressibly sad. Yet it had a magnificence that no words of mine could tell."

Fear of more bombings caused Bishop Galvin to send all the sisters in Hanyang to a seminary thirty miles out of town. The nuns took turns returning to the city for short periods to help bring some order out of chaos. The Columbans opened their buildings as a general hospital and as a refugee center for sisters, brothers, and priests who had fled from Hankow, across the river. The Lorettines opened a maternity hospital and also housed three hundred refugees in their compound. To add to the confusion fifty seminarians and their professors arrived from Hankow seeking refuge.

Hanyang, with fewer industries and fewer Japanese troops within its walls was considered safer than Hankow, and so it soon became the capital and business center of the province. Rumors were rampant saying that the three cities—Hankow, Hanyang, and Wuchang—were scheduled to be wiped out. Tenseness grew so that the day leaflets floated from the sky advising people to flee, thousands formed streams of panic flowing into the country in all directions.

A Japanese observer took up quarters next door to the cathedral in Hanyang to keep an eye on the foreigners. He searched every room in the Columbans' convent. Upon entering one of the sister's cells, the Japanese sergeant came upon a large pair of shoes. Pouncing upon them he cried out with excitement, "Man here!" When told the shoes belonged to one of the sisters he kept repeating, "Man here!" The sister in question stepped forward and held up her foot for inspection. The sergeant grunted in astonishment and departed without a word.

All through the war Bishop Galvin expected that at any moment he and the Irish Columbans would be sent to prison camps. He admitted that this worried him a great deal and later said of such concerns: "It is very foolish to worry about anything; it does not help in the least. Everybody tells you that, yet worrying is one of the most popular indoor pastimes—almost as popular as bridge."

A few days after the Japanese surrendered, Father William Holland died, August 29, 1945. He was one of the "lonely" Columbans who had stayed in remote country after the Japanese had sent most of the missionaries into Hanyang. He and his curate, Father Ivar McGrath, lived in Anlu, as far from Hanyang as it was possible to be and still be within the vicariate. They saw no other priests all through the Second World War.

What started as a cold became complicated with pleurisy and malaria and finally the missionary's heart could not stand the strain. Father McGrath buried his pastor in the mission compound just opposite the front door of the proposed new church. The two priests had often pointed to the spot declaring, with levity, that it would be an ideal final resting place.

Right after the funeral, Father McGrath decided that now that peace had come he ought to visit his out-missions, so neglected during the war. He found, however, that there was really no peace, for Communists and Nationalists were starting to decide what kind of a government China should have.

In breaking the news of the death to William Holland's father in Kilmurry, Bishop Galvin wrote: "These years have been difficult, but the writing of this letter is one of the most difficult and saddest things I have had to do. My heart goes out to you all."

He later said to Sister Thaddeus: "I sometimes think that I should never have started the mission. It is too hard for men."

·21·

New Beginnings

The war had been over for a year when in the summer of 1946 Mother Mary Vianney was elected superior general, a position held by Mother Mary Patrick for a decade. When the new superior general decided in 1947 to make her visitations in the Far East, her society by then had missions in the Philippines, and in Burma and was considering opening a new foundation in Hong Kong.

Mother Mary Vianney arrived on December 19, 1947, in Shanghai on a flight from Hong Kong, accompanied by Mother Mary Annunciata and Sister Catherine Labouré, who had been in Hong Kong to review the medical situation. Plans to continue on to Hanyang were delayed because of bitter cold; one night 150 people froze to death in the streets of Shanghai.

Before the coming of winter, Shanghai had been subjected to such fierce downpours that water penetrated every crack in the convent roof at Sancta Sophia. When a ceiling had collapsed above a bed, a nun was encased in damp debris but escaped unharmed. During vespers the floor beneath the altar in the chapel had caved in requiring the priest to jump clear of the yawning cavity.

Although the weather was severe, the mother general was thankful that the sisters were now spared some of the severities of wartime. Thanks to the Catholic Welfare Society and the Irish Red Cross they received shipments of oatmeal, flour, powdered milk, medicines, and even some toys for the children.

The Russian children were delightful. Pupils from early days, now married, returned with their babies for a visit. They told Mother Mary Vianney that after the war many of the fifty thousand Russian emigrés living in Shanghai began to dream of returning to their homeland. Those who did found only a few churches, with congregations mainly of old people, a reminder that a generation had grown up without hearing of Christianity. Such reports caused many Russians in Shanghai to consider seeking haven in the United States, Canada, or South America.

The 198 pupils at Santa Sophia gathered to give a concert in honor of Mother Mary Vianney. Juniors, under direction of Madame Korda, their Russian teacher, produced two Russian playlets, "with picturesque costumes portraying field flowers, insects, and even a couple of mushrooms, whose awkwardness set in relief the graceful gestures of the dancing flowers and caused considerable enjoyment." The senior girls under direction of Sister Mary Cecilia sang excerpts from Gilbert and Sullivan's *Iolanthe*.

In Hanyang, the superior general visited Bishop Galvin. She spoke of how pleased everyone had been in Cahiracon when word arrived that Hanyang had been raised to the rank of a diocese. The war was still on when the apostolic internuncio, Archbishop Riberi, arrived at the cathedral, April 1, 1945, for the ceremony that made the Most Reverend Edward J. Galvin, former vicar apostolic of Hanyang and titular bishop of Myrna, the first bishop of the diocese of Hanyang. It was evident that Bishop Galvin was pleased for he knew that the Catholic Church does not create a diocese casually, and once created it exists forever; no matter how much the map changes, the name is carried on, as in the case of Myrna, forgotten even in Asia Minor.

The bishop told Mother Mary Vianney that he had just returned from three months of visiting in the country parishes. He had gone out in September to share the problems of the priests and to confirm any Catholics ready for confirmation. Judging from the deep drawn lines in his face, Mother Mary Vianney judged that the trip had been difficult.

Just as the bishop was completing his visitation bandits had swept down on the mountain village of Sung Ho while he and Father James Donohoe were there. The two Columbans had only a few minutes of warning, and, with no transportation available, they walked one hundred miles on blistered feet. Since the bandits were only a half-hour behind them for the first twenty-four hours they had to keep moving; finally, they found brief rest in a heap of straw in an old Chinese shack.

At dusk on December 22, they had arrived at Hwan-Chia-Shan and were greeted by Fathers John McMullan and Daniel Fitzgerald. Bishop Galvin ignored the suggestion that he rest there a few days for he was determined to set off early the next morning so as to be at his cathedral for Christmas Eve. Despite lacerated feet, he walked ten miles to the river to embark on a boat for the remaining twenty miles to Hanyang.

During that three-month trip he had seen things deeply disturbing, the bishop told Mother Mary Vianney. Those bandits springing up everywhere were not the same as those of the pre-war days. These were a part of a pattern, part of a script, created by Communists. The procedure was simple and efficient. The brigands moved into an area, chosen by the Reds, to rob and terrorize the people. Soon the Red Army—disciplined, well-behaved and under strict orders—appeared and established order. The people, of course, were grateful.

Next came "the men in blue," officials and clerks. They interrogated, handed out questionnaires, and somehow set class against class. They had a knack for encouraging bitterness, self-pity, and anger. In this way the revolution moved like volcanic lava across the land.

When Mother Mary Vianney returned to the convent, after her talk with the bishop, she found the nuns more optimistic. With pride they showed her the new Saint Columban's Hospital, the best equipped medical center they had ever owned. It was overcrowded, of course, and many of the cases were serious: adults suffering from typhoid and children from smallpox.

The superior general could not help but compare the suffering Chinese children with the lively Russian pupils who had entertained her in Shanghai.

A nursing sister said: "For the past two years there has been no reliable vaccine. These babies are undernourished from birth and so have scarcely any resistance. Of those that come through alive many are blind or disabled. Sometimes a mother with a sick baby tells us it is the last of seven or eight. We need baby food, cod liver oil, vitamin tablets, anything to help build up and nourish."

It was painful to see a mother hurry from the hospital to return with a photographer. He would take one final picture of the dying child.

Fortunately, amusing things sometimes happened at the hospital. For instance, during *Go Nien,* the Chinese New Year, a young ruffian was admitted with a cut head and various bruises and injuries. When the nun in charge handed him an admission ticket he asked for one "for the other fellow." When the other fellow, the one he had been fighting, was placed in the same ward, the ruffian came over to review the result of his handiwork. He seemed satisfied that his opponent's condition was equal to his own. When Mother Mary Vianney first saw them they were sitting on their beds facing each other, heads swathed in gauze, and chatting confidentially.

Sister Mary Agnes said that the hospital seemed to attract more than its share of the victims of family feuds. Last month three men had been carried in with severe wounds but had soon recovered enough to go for walks in the hospital yard. When the day arrived for them to appear in court, to decide the rights and wrongs of the feud, they hired bamboo beds from the outside and had themselves carried to court by stretcher bearers, wearing long faces all the way.

The procession amused staff and patients. Later in the day the three fellows walked through the hospital gate, smiling with satisfaction for they had won their case.

Mother Mary Vianney accompanied Sister Mary Ignatius and Mary Agnes to the Hanyang jail. As they approached, an armed guard at the gate saluted and shouted, "The sisters have come!"

The inside proved a pleasant surprise; it was like visiting a well-to-do Chinese house with its large living room and high ceiling and polished timber walls covered with ornamental carvings. At small square tables sat the warden and his assistants leisurely smoking pipes and compiling reports.

From this staff living room all down the line a general bustle preceded the visitors as word raced ahead that the sisters had arrived. As usual the chief superintendent welcomed the nuns with a profound bow just before they entered a room with a small barred window through which prisoners might talk with friends.

In the actual prison, a big hall with barred windows high up and out of reach, a dozen cells housed about ten men each. The cells had thick wooden bars and doors securely padlocked. Since there was no furniture the prisoners either squatted on the floor or stretched out wrapped in padded quilts.

The room was bright and airy, too airy for this cold January morning. Sister Mary Ignatius went from cell to cell treating coughs, rheumatism, sciatica, and other ills brought on by draughts and damps. Sister Mary Agnes, looking after the spiritual side, had the prisoners chanting the catechism and prayers so lustily that it reminded Mother Mary Vianney of the chanting at the catechumenate.

Before leaving Hanyang, Mother Mary Vianney, realizing that the time remaining for the sisters' hospital might be brief, decided to take Sisters Mary Martin and Frances for the sanatorium in Hong Kong.

From Hanyang Mother Mary Vianney traveled to Nancheng where the vicariate, like that of Hanyang, had also been raised to the status of a diocese. When she paid a formal visit to Bishop Cleary he started right off telling her about Bishop Galvin's surprise appearance in Nancheng a few months earlier, his first trip back in twenty years.

When in 1927 Ned Galvin had been offered some new mission territory in Kiangsi Province, four hundred miles south of Hanyang, he and Father John McGrath had traveled by riverboat three hundred miles down the Yangtze, crossed Poyang Lake in a small boat, and tramped the last hundred miles over cobblestones to the boundaries of Hanyang vicariate. To get a good look at the five counties offered them, the two Columbans packed their baggage atop a mule, and took as a guide an Italian Vincentian whose French confreres had labored in Kiangsi for a century.

Ned Galvin had described these parts as "pleasant country, not exactly mountainous, but hilly enough to bring back memories of Ireland."

He liked what he saw, during that 1927 trip, and was especially pleased that the mission buildings were solid and servicable. He said that when Columbans were settled here he would return, please God, for a holiday.

First the civil war and then the Japanese invasion delayed the holiday, but then one wet Saturday in May of 1947, the Eve of Pentecost, Bishop Galvin walked unannounced into the mission house in Nancheng.

The sunny days passed quickly as priests of the territory trekked into Nancheng to welcome Bishop Galvin. The conversations ranged widely over floods, bandits, and air raids. The older men spoke of the exciting days when the mission was in its infancy.

Bishop Cleary, in recalling the visit for Mother Mary Vianney, said: "They had many tales to tell of kindnesses received, of unbelievable generosities. Or the talk would turn to college days in Maynooth, or to old comrades dead and gone."

Bishop Galvin left Nancheng to return to Hanyang at the end of June. As he boarded the squat, brown bus he said, "I'm fit for anything now. This has been the happiest month I've spent in China."

Bishop Cleary and the superior general spoke at length about life in Nancheng since the end of the war. Mother Vianney said she had been told that the death rate was still extremely high, still exceeding the birth rate.

"Yes," the bishop said, "the people's powers of resistance to disease suffered seriously during the war. I am happy to say that infant mortality seems to be diminishing. For this we may largely thank the Columban sisters.

"UNRRA and CNRRA kindly placed large supplies of milk and other foods at our disposal. In the hands of the sisters these have yielded excellent results. From the International Relief Committee we have splendid supplies of medicines for our hospital and dispensaries.

"Unfortunately we have not been able to afford to rebuild our hospital. Our quarters still have the appearance of emergency wards. As Sister Nathy said, 'Why call it a hospital, anyway?'

"Prices are unbelievably high. We used to buy six pounds of meat for a Chinese dollar. Today meat costs $5,000 a pound. Of course the rate of exchange for foreign money is very different today, but when every allowance is made, the cost of living is exceedingly high.

"The fact affects our work very seriously as the people have to use every effort to make ends meet and, as they say, have no time to study. It is really surprising that so many of them attend their classes faithfully when their day's work is done."

In Nancheng Mother Mary Vianney heard many stories of the return of banditry. Brigands had flourished in the vicinity before the Second World War as Nationalists and Communists fought each other. Banditry died down somewhat when the Japanese were seen as the common enemy, but as soon as the Japanese surrendered, Nationalists and Communists resumed fighting each other and bandits once more afflicted the countryside. These new ones were usually ex-soldiers who having learned to use weapons were now unwilling to put them aside.

Typical of the new bandit stories that the superior general heard was one that Father Michael Halford told:

When bandits were reported near his parish the people sent out three men armed to the teeth with instructions to determine the nearness of the foe. The men proceeded in single file, their guns at the ready. The trouble started when the second man accidentally shot the first man in the leg. The injured one, thinking he had been the victim of a treacherous attack from the rear, spun around and shot the second man in the shoulder. The third man managed to get both victims home with no information whatever.

The panting messenger came to the church to report that villagers five miles away had killed two pigs and were offering a meal to 193 desperadoes, hoping that they would eat and leave. Since rumor had put the figure at anything from one thousand to ten thousand, a mere 193 seemed almost welcome.

Since a contingent of the Nationalist army was in pursuit, the bandits had to eat and run. Which bridge would they use? If they came by Tafang bridge they would cross six miles downstream, but if they used Wuming bridge they would pass the church door.

Fathers Halford and DesRosiers climbed a hill to see which route was being used. The only living creatures in sight were three men on the summit keeping a lookout. In scrambling up, so there would be no mistaken identification, Father Halford shouted, "the Catholic Church."

The men atop the hill answered, "*Lao Be Sing*."

At this point, Father Halford interrupted the narrative to explain: "*Lao Be Sing* means 'the people.' Literally, 'We of the Hundred Names,' for at one time the roll call of the entire population of China did not exceed a hundred common names.

"Actually it would take a book to explain the different shades of meaning that can be read into *Lao Be Sing*. It means civilians as opposed to the military, and the governed class as opposed to those who do the governing. It means the inarticulate mass of peasant farmers and shrewd shopkeepers who make up the real China.

"Nowadays you read fiery arguments between Democrats and Communists. You hear of violent mutual recriminations between so-called progressives and reactionaries. The *Lao Be Sing* ask only to be allowed to continue the even tenor of their ways unmolested, and to be allowed to earn their daily bowl of rice peacefully in the sweat of their brow. Governments may come and go but *Lao Be Sing* will go on forever."

When Father Halford returned to the narrative, he finally reached the point where the bandits took the Tafang bridge and so did not pass the church. It happened that they ordered a farmer to serve as guide, telling him to show them the way to Ruming bridge, but he ignored the order and led them by way of Tafang.

"His action so incensed the Tafang people," said Father Halford, "that they thought seriously of taking the guide quietly to one side and cutting off his head. His defense was that he had heard that the Tafang people had armed themselves and were ready for the bandits. He thought the best thing to do was to lead the lawless ones into the ambush so that they might be annihilated by the brave men of Tafang. There was no way to refute this argument in Tafang without admitting that when the great chance arrived the brave men had fled ignominiously into the hills."

Father Halford ended his rambling story by announcing. "Three days later the brigands laid down their arms."

When Mother Mary Vianney and Sister Catherine started the journey from Nancheng to Shanghai they little dreamed it would turn into a six-day nightmare. Upon arriving at Fuchow airport, expecting to fly to Shanghai that afternoon, they came upon the sign Closed—Under Repairs. Someone told them that the train service was being reopened at Yintang and so they jounced along for several hours in a truck over a road made almost impassable by a recent thaw.

In Yintang the nuns heard that the train would leave in a couple of hours and so they squeezed into a crowded boxcar. It did not depart until late the next day. Three times it went off the track and on one occasion lost half of its boxcars when one of them became uncoupled. (On the train's return journey the Reds captured it.)

As they approached Shanghai Mother Mary Vianney wondered how it ever got the name, "City-by-the Sea." It is no longer seaside, if indeed it ever was. The crow has to fly a good ten miles across country to get to the ocean; a steamer must churn five hours in from open sea, up through the muddy waters of the Yangtsekiang and of the Whangpoo, the tributary on which Shanghai is built.

Upon reaching Sancta Sophia in Shanghai, the best that Mother Mary Vianney and Sister Catherine could say about their journey was that at least no one had pointed a revolver at them. They were recalling an incident that happened the last time that Mother Mary Michael and Sister Veronica had traveled from Nancheng to Shanghai.

Mother Mary Michael had told the story with much relish: Inside the crowded bus rode three soldiers and one rode the running board and next to the motor rode another. The bus was speeding along through barren, bleak, and lonely country, and most of the passengers were nodding in the noonday heat, when suddenly a shot rang out.

"Immediately, all were wide awake," said Mother Mary Michael. "They found themselves staring into three revolvers held by the soldiers. I shall never forget the expressions on the faces of those people: surprise and dismay changing to fear and terror."

The soldiers searched the passengers and relieved them of their money. One rested his revolver on Mother Mary Michael's shoulder, telling her not to be afraid. The robber riding the running board told the driver to stop, and when he did the fellow reached under the hood and ripped out the distributor.

The four soldiers went around the bus with small bags collecting money. So anxious were the passengers to be rid of them that they helped put money into the bags.

Before departing, the leader stood in the door of the bus to deliver a speech to an attentive audience. He explained that Chinese soldiers had rescued the people from an aggressive enemy and so deserved some practical recognition for their services.

At each pause in his oration, passengers would stand and reply, "Yes, you are right," displaying an interesting example of the use of Chinese politeness.

When the soldier stated that he and his comrades were no common highwaymen, the people bowed, smiled, and said, "Yes, you speak the truth."

When he called attention to the fact that he had not disturbed their baggage, they answered, "Yes, this is true, thank you, thank you!"

At the end of the speech the soldier bowed three times and the passengers thanked him for the courteous way in which he had relieved them of their money. He advised the passengers that it would be safer to stay in the bus until he and his companions were out of sight.

An old man who had lost a large sum of money began to object, but was hushed into silence. Without a mumbling word the Chinese gathered up their little bundles and began walking back to the nearest town. Mother Mary Michael and Sister Veronica stood by the bus and wondered what to do next.

They were surprised when a white-trousered gentleman dropped from the roof and landed beside them. He had been riding up there for lack of room inside. His first remark was as unexpected as his mode of travel.

"To what church do you belong?"

When the nuns responded, he said that he was a Protestant.

"Let us beg God to help us in our difficulty," he said.

"Apart from the three of us, only the driver was left at the bus," said Mother Michael. "We were unwilling to trust him as Sister Veronica had seen the soldiers surreptitiously slipping him a packet of bank notes. Sister Veronica wanted to join the others, but I thought we should stay and wait for help. We decided to pray to Father Ellis who had never turned down a begging hand.

"Soon a man came down the road to advise us that this was a dangerous place and suggested that we walk to the nearest town. We decided to face the ten-mile walk.

"Just then a lorry came along. Passengers were clinging to the tops and sides. The driver stopped to say he would like to take us but there was not an inch of room left. We began with all the eloquence at our command to try to persuade him to find room for us.

"In the middle of our appeal a voice broke in from behind asking if we were Catholic *priests*. It was the driver of another bus speaking. He said he had heard of the Catholic Church and would be glad to give us a lift. His was a military vehicle with only a few officers traveling in it."

This was not the end of the story. It continued on with shots being fired at the bus, a bridge washed out, a hectic train ride, a jeep ride, and a flight in a plane. The final ten miles to the convent in Shanghai were in a U.S. Army truck.

In Shanghai, Mother Mary Vianney spoke with Father Jeremiah Pigott about the new missionary territory the Columban priests had accepted. Through Bishop Deymier, the French Vincentian fathers had petitioned Rome at the end of the war to relieve them of some of the vicariate of Hunchow, in the northern part of the province.

Father Pigott, a veteran of eighteen years in Hanyang, was named superior of the new mountainous mission, about a hundred miles from Shanghai in the maritime province of Chekiang. In this territory, seventy miles wide and fifty deep, lived two million people, of whom thirty-five hundred were Catholic.

It was a case of life coming full circle when the nine Columbans reached Chekiang, for there in 1916 Fathers Edward Galvin, Joseph O'Leary, and Patrick O'Reilly had discussed ways and means of getting Ireland to support a mission to China. And it was a Chekiang missionary, Father John M. Fraser, who in 1911 had inspired men at Maynooth to found the Columbans, and who, while speaking at the seminary at Beardson, in Scotland, had so inspired Father Andrew McArdle that the Scottish priest went to China to develop the very territory the Columbans now inherited.

Although they had been in Chekiang province for only eighteen months, Father Pigott was able to tell Sister Mary Vianney that he had opened a large central catechumenate under the care of the native Chinese sisters, and that the primary school was going well with about sixty children enrolled.

He spoke of how helpful the five Chinese priests on loan from the Archbishop Deymier had been. They not only helped in mission work, he explained; they also assisted the young Columbans in their language study.

"Many of our young men are now in sole charge of parishes," said Father Pigott, "It is amazing how priests, just out of college, have in so short a time developed into hard-headed and successful missionaries."

Father Pigott had his headquarters in Huchow, but it was evident to Mother Mary Vianney that he had fallen in love with the city of Hangchow, the principal city of the vicariate. Of it he said: "The Chinese call it the city of Heaven and foreigners the Venice of the East. Although I have seen neither Heaven nor Venice, I can say it is certainly beautiful."

Hangchow was already old when it yielded to the Mongols under Kublai Khan and when Friars Odoric of Italy and James of Ireland saw it six hundred years ago. At that time it had twelve thousand bridges and Blessed Odoric called it "the greatest city in the whole world."

On Wednesday, March 3, 1948, Mother Mary Vianney sailed from Shanghai on the S.S. *General Gordon* en route to the Philippines where the Columban sisters had been working for nine years. The thing most on her mind, though, was what the future might hold for the Columbans in China. A month earlier Bishop Galvin had written:

"In the provinces north of us, the country districts are entirely in the hands of the Reds. One of our priests, writing recently from Peking, says that there are one thousand priests in that city from Hopeh, Honan, Shantung, Manchuria, Inner Mongolia (where the Belgians took terrible losses), and Shansi, etc. All mission work throughout those provinces has come to a complete stop and losses are terribly heavy. There has been nothing like it in living memory."

·22·

The Approaching Storm

When Mother Mary Vianney departed China, in the spring of 1948, it was clear the Communist forces under Mao would defeat the Nationalists under Chiang Kai-shek. Mao's men had more spirit, were better organized, and more devoted to their cause, while Chiang's were tired and disillusioned after eight years of war.

Before the Japanese invasion, Chiang had been in the ascendancy. His Nationalists, in killing sixty thousand Red Army soldiers in October of 1933, had started Mao's troops on the Long March, a six-thousand-mile trek that began near Foochow, went west as far as Kunming, and then swung northward and eastward at Pao An. The march, really a series of running battles, lasted for more than a year, crossing eighteen mountain ranges and twenty-four rivers.

During the Second World War, Mao bided his time. His policy was to conserve munitions and men to use later in promoting the cause of Communism. On the very day that Japan offered to surrender, August 10, 1945, his men began disarming Japanese soldiers to get weapons. Chiang ordered his soldiers to do the same.

Such confusion resulted that Japanese commanders in China sent messengers daily to General Douglas MacArthur informing him that their garrisons were caught in a conflict between Communists and Nationalists. Who is in charge? they wanted to know. The United States sided with the Nationalists, but the Communists continued seizing arms.

At the same time, Red Workers, supporters of Mao, were seizing factories and driving out the Yellow Workers, supporters of Chiang.

Since the Nationalists at war's end had a four-to-one superiority in both weapons and men, Mao put into practice his theory of warfare that applies when one is short of everything: "The enemy advances, we retreat. The enemy halts, we harass. The enemy tires, we attack. The enemy retreats, we pursue."

Despite the horrors of the civil war, letters out of China in the spring of 1948 were really not so dreary. The sisters wrote with excitement about Cardinal Spellman's visit, about the new foundation in Hong Kong, and included the kind of human interest stories that had filled their correspondence since their arrival in China twenty-two years earlier.

Judging from one letter, the biggest day in the history of Sancta Sophia was the day that Cardinal Spellman, archbishop of New York, paid a visit. He had arrived in Shanghai on May 31, 1948, accompanied by members of the Commission for the Near East who were touring the Philippines, Malaya, Japan, and China.

The day after his arrival, four Columban sisters from the Russian school met the cardinal at a reception at Aurora University. As a courtesy they invited him to visit their school, and to their surprise he accepted, saying he would be there the next day.

Back to school the four nuns hurried and the excitement began. Sister Mary Laurence used a crumpled piece of silk from a theatrical costume to transform a plywood kneeler into a magnificent prie-dieu. Sister Mary Eucharia coached a blushing, nervous young lady in the graces of a curtsy and in the art of delivering an address of welcome. Sister Mary Cecilia said, "I think the higher we go the nicer it is," as she rehearsed the choir in Russian Easter hymns. Sister Joan sent the Girl Guides flying for their trim blue uniforms and green ties. Sisters Benedict, Madeleine Sophie, and Emmanuel impressed good behavior on the little ones by speaking of the "bigness" of the visitor, and did it so well that several of the children told their mothers that a "giant" would visit the school.

When word came that the Cardinal had left Saint Michael's College and was on his way to Sancta Sophia, the Girl Guides, neat in their uniforms, lined the short entrance; a group of pupils in navy and white school uniforms lined the steps of the stairway, and the nuns waited in the entrance hall. Cardinal Spellman came swiftly up the steps and passed into the chapel as the choir burst into the joyous and lovely, "Dostoyno," the Russian welcoming hymn of Our Lady.

One of the sisters wrote: "Then back into the classroom where the whole school was assembled—rows and rows of glowing eager faces, their blonde Russian fairness accented by the brilliant sunlight that poured through the open windows and doors, and set them in relief against the green of the trees in the garden outside. The high sweet notes of the traditional Russian Easter songs (for this was still Russian Paschal season) rang out—and Father Wilcox bent with a word of explanation to His Eminence. Magdalen, a Russian Catholic, stepped forward to read a simple welcome, and was obviously surprised when His Eminence unexpectedly went over to her, and pointing to the sheet of notepaper in her hand said, "You must give me that. I want that."

The cardinal turned from the girl and said, "I want to meet the Sisters, all of the Sisters, and tell me where you are from."

"We're all from Ireland, Your Eminence," said Sister Mary Emmanuel.

"But Ireland is a big place—tell me where in Ireland."

The Columbans introduced themselves: Sister M. Emmanuel, Wexford; Sister M. Eucharia, Kerry; Sister M. Basil, London and Donegal; Sister M. Laurence, Clare; Sister M. Cecilia, Royal Meath; Sister M. Sophie, Cork; Sister M. Joan, Dublin; Sister M. Angela, Tipperary; Sister M. Benedict and Sister M. Anastasia, Limerick; Sister Majella Ryan, Wexford.

Little Aldona Wondracz, came shyly forward, curtsied and said, "A gift for your Em-in-ence," offering a Russian icon on a flower-decked tray.

After speaking a few words to the children, Cardinal Spellman made ready to leave. With all of their hearts the whole school sang, the "Many Years."

Just before stepping into the car the cardinal whispered to Sister M. Emmanuel: "Now, all of the Sisters must have three or four free days, and a few good sleeps."

The weariness must have been showing.

Cardinal Spellman had intended to go directly from Shanghai to Peking, but a wire from Bishop Galvin caused him to fly four hundred miles out of his way. The two men were old friends, having met a quarter-century earlier when Spellman was a young assistant at the cathedral in Boston.

Since only four hours were allotted to the cardinal's visit, there was not time to cross the Han river to Hanyang, and so the reception was held in Hankow. In making arrangements, Bishop Galvin had the cooperation of Archbishop Rosa of Hankow, of Bishop Kowalski of Wuchang, and of the United States' consul-general. The reception began at the cathedral and moved on to the American consulate.

In describing the occasion, Father Gerry O'Collins wrote: "Rarely had I seen the Bishop show such signs of exhaustion and fatigue as he did just prior to the visit of Cardinal Spellman. During the four-hour stay the Bishop traveled with the Cardinal in the same car from the aerodrome through Hankow streets lined by Catholic schoolchildren. The zeal and the exhausted condition of the veteran missionary Bishop did not fail to make a deep impression on the Cardinal, as was shown by the talk he gave in Los Angeles a few weeks later."

Even as the shadow of Communism moved across China north of the Yangtze river in 1948, the Columbans in Hanyang and Nancheng felt they were still held in high regard by the authorities. Perhaps Bishop Cleary was whistling in the dark when he wrote to Dalgan: "The civil authorities everywhere have been not only friendly but helpful, and the people have come to realize that adherence to the Catholic Church is no longer frowned upon as unpatriotic or un-Chinese."

He wrote that on the occasion of the twentieth anniversary of the coming of Columban priests to Nancheng. His diocese now had twenty-seven Irish priests, four Chinese priests, and six Colomban sisters who supervised the hospital, dispensary, orphanage, and girls' school, and three Chinese girls who aspired to be Columbans. As for education, the bishop provided each parish with a primary school, hoped to start two high schools soon, and took pride in a seminary that numbered twenty-four students.

Bishop Cleary was aware that the Reds were uprooting missionaries with thoroughness in some parts of China, but he was living in hope that the Columbans would not be driven from Kiangsi province. His older parishioners were less optimistic than their bishop. They remembered too well when the Red army had moved through the province in 1928 leaving behind a scene of havoc and desolation; thousands of people had fled from the fertile fields to comparative safety in the walled towns of Nanfeng and Nancheng, remaining there until the Reds left on the Long March six years later.

The civil authorities, where Reds had not infiltrated, showed their regard for the Columbans in many ways; for example, when in May of 1948 the Generalissimo granted a general amnesty to prisoners by way of celebrating his reelection, the Columban sisters in Hanyang took for granted that their services were no longer needed at the jail. After a few weeks a messenger delivered a letter from the governor of the prison:

"Since the beginning of its existence, this prison has been well looked after by your Hon. Sister Doctors, who came to visit the prisoners and medicated them. No word in this world can express the gratitude of the public and of the individuals to you.

"Having had no visits from your Hon. Sister Doctors for the last month, the sick prisoners are expecting them anxiously, as people suffering from the dry weather expect cloud and rain. We, therefore, humbly ask you, the Venerable Catholic Mission, whose heart is mercy itself and whose mission is to give life to all, to continue sending your Sister Doctors to medicate our prisoners, in order to relieve the suffering and to manifest your kindness and mercy.

"Sincerely yours, Lo-Gi-Shi; Director of the Prison."

Two nuns hurried to the jail to find that there were indeed sick prisoners, mostly Communists who had been captured in recent fighting.

In attending the ailments they proved that Bishop Clearly had spoken the truth when he had told the Japanese, "We care for anyone who needs our care."

During this time of uncertainty, the Columban sisters were glad of Mother Mary Vianney's decision to staff a sanatorium in Hong Kong. This would enable them to continue their mission to the Chinese, no matter what happened on the mainland.

Sister Mary Dolorosa Ryan remembers the grey day, early in 1948, when she and Sister Catherine Labouré went to the deserted Royal Naval Hospital in Wanchai, a district in teeming Hong Kong. Sister Mary Dolorosa felt overwhelmed by the gloom of the corridors, wards, and especially of the peculiar cement baths built by the Japanese when they occupied the building during the Second World War.

Sister Catherine Labouré, however, did not seem a bit depressed; she vibrated with ideas, seeing possibilities at every turn. Anyone hearing her sing the praises of the old building would not have guessed that the navy had abandoned the place for a better site.

The two Columbans were doing this inspecting because of a suggestion that Father P. Joy, a Jesuit, had made. He had told the Anti-Tuberculosis Association that the Columban sisters should be asked to staff a hospital for victims of tuberculosis.

The disease was rampant in Hong Kong right after the war. It spared neither poor nor rich. A wealthy Parsee, J.H. Ruttonjee, lost a daughter to the disease. In his grief he decided to help others suffering from TB and so he contributed the money needed to establish a sanatorium.

The Columbans moved into the old navy building and began raising funds to pay for all of the changes which would have to be made. Thirty years later Sister Dolores said, "Sister Catherine Labouré, whom the present-day jargon would describe as 'totally committed,' did seem to have the magic touch. With her own brand of Mandarin Chinese, she would charm careful proprietors and blasé clerks so that they ended up as our willing helpers."

What touched the hearts of the wealthy and loosened their purse strings was that the Columbans ministered to the very poor. Even the Hong Kong Jockey Club became one of the major patrons of the hospital.

On a fine sunny afternoon, February 24, 1949, visitors gathered on the front lawn to greet the governor of Hong Kong. All members of the staff, in best white habits and starched uniforms, advanced to meet Sir Alexander Grantham. After the amenities, the governor gave a talk and the Ruttonjee Sanatorium was officially open.

With the opening of this new foundation, several Columbans made a quick study of the history of Hong Kong. They learned that it has been a British crown colony since it was wrested from China in 1842, and that exactly a hundred years later the Japanese occupied it and remained until British rule returned in 1945. As soon as the civil war resumed on the mainland an unparalleled number of refugees began coming across the border into Hong Kong. This sudden influx of the disinherited brought an increase in sickness to the whole area.

The island of Hong Kong, a little eastward of the entrance to Canton, was originally a tiny fishing village. The harbor, extending for seventeen miles, lies between the island and the mainland part of Hong Kong called Kowloon. On the eastern slope of a mountain is a large exclusively Chinese district, Wanchai, and it was here that the Columbans opened Ruttonjee Sanatorium.

"The situation to my mind seems ideal," wrote Sister Mary Bernadette. "So convenient to the market and to town, and yet so much fresh air. We have a different view from every angle—the peak towering behind us and the lovely harbor stretching out before us. I imagine the secular nurses will like being here. It is a real beauty spot, and there are many places they will be able to go to, so they will not find it dull."

During this time of uneasiness right after the Second World War, missionaries in China continued to strive for what missionaries always must—for the patience that never wearies. On one occasion Bishop Galvin had said to the sisters, "Always, in this country, one has to learn to hold his patience in his hands, to look at it and to remind himself that it is necessary to him."

He knew that they had learned, as every missionary does, how easy it is to see people as less than human after watching them live lives less than human. And there were all of those annoying persistences: the smell of stale sweat on the body, the stench of hunger on the breath, the dumb-animal ways.

The tendency is to grow calloused. To flare out. But the Columban sisters had not come all this way for that.

·23·

A Dark Season

On March 4, 1949, Bishop Galvin wrote to a friend in Brooklyn: "The Communists have control of all of the country north of the Yangtze, except these three cities and we think they can take them any time they wish. We have no notion how we will fare when they take them. We know from what happened in the north that they have no love for the Church, to put it mildly. On the other hand, it is the wish of the Holy See that priests and Sisters remain at their posts. I do not want to conceal that there is tension. We would not be human if there wasn't. I have, as you know, three communities of Sisters; one from Kentucky, one from Ireland, and twenty-six Chinese Sisters. When I think of the uncertainties of the future, I can't help being worried about them. Keep us in your prayers every day."

Two months later the bishop felt even greater concern when he saw with what ease the Reds captured Nanking and crossed the Yangtze at several points. When they were within thirty miles of Hanyang he concluded a letter: "The priests and Sisters are quite calm. We shall welcome what God is pleased to send and hold out as long as we can."

Since Hanyang, Hankow, and Wuchang were crowded with Nationalist troops, the sisters expected to be well defended. They learned, however, how wrong they were when six of the soldiers, who had been regulars at the clinic, asked for extra dressings, explaining that they would be crossing over to the south bank that night: "It will be easier to get away from the Reds from there."

Trucks and heavy equipment made such a racket rumbling southward that the Columbans had a difficult time sleeping. At dawn on May 17 they arose to learn that not a soldier or a policeman was left in Hanyang.

During their final visit to the jail that morning the sisters found that guards had fled leaving prisoners in charge. One dangerous fellow—accused of multiple murders—was still behind bars. Let the Reds deal with him, said the other convicts, as they divided the supplies among themselves and took off down the lane.

The citizens, terrified of what lawless bandits might do to an unprotected city, sent a formal invitation asking the Red Army to please hurry. That day Hanyang was like a city of the dead. Anyone who could afford it had fled southward while all others, filled with trepidation, hid inside their houses.

The Red soldiers seemed uneasy as they marched down silent streets with no cheering, no flag waving. They had not expected to have such an easy time of it, and possibly suspected a trap. As soon as they were certain of no opposition, however, they quickly took control of things.

On the first night in town several officers came to the mission compound, saying they wanted to billet troops in the hospital. The palaver lasted for hours. It ended when the officer in charge said to Dr. Chiu, "Do these foreigners know what liberation means?" The Chinese doctor answered, "Oh yes, they are Irish and have just been liberated after seven hundred years." Whether or not this piece of information did the trick, the sisters never knew, but they were relieved to see the officers go elsewhere to seek billets for their soldiers.

Every household had to send workers to help on government projects, or face prison, even execution. Children were let out of school, without examinations, to quarry stones on the hillside.

This approach brought out so many "volunteers" that the airfield was finished in three months instead of the six that had been planned. New roads were constructed, dikes repaired, and barracks built.

Factories turned out millions of uniforms which were becoming the only costume for loyal patriots. Boys and girls dressed so alike that the latter could be distinguished only by their short bobbed hair.

All were supposed to try to be more efficient than the next worker. There were contests for the best nurse, the quickest machinist, the strongest laborer. Life was anything but relaxed.

For indoctrination every school had its Red professors who started straight away with full Marxist theories. "You must learn to hate. Hate the foreign imperialists. Hate your parents, teachers, brothers, and sisters if they are not loyal to the People's Republic."

When the Communists asked for volunteers for the army, boys and girls crowded into the recruiting offices. Sister Ignatius told of a family in Hankow whose two boys, of twenty-one and eighteen, volunteered. When the third presented himself, though, he was told that at age fifteen he was too young.

"Put me down for seventeen, or I will report you as a reactionary," he told the recruiting officer, and so was accepted.

The parents, in a frantic state, went to the headquarters to protest.

They were received coldly and in spite of evidence to the contrary were told that the boy was seventeen and already in the army. Besides, said the bureaucrat, the parents were acting like reactionaries; they should be glad to offer all of their sons to the glorious cause. The parents withdrew; they had already seen the terrible public trials at which children witnessed against their parents, screaming as though possessed and sometimes demanding the execution of their relatives.

In the midst of this tumult the Franciscan Missionaries of the Divine Motherhood, who had lived with the Columban sisters in Hanyang for sixteen months, left for home. They had come to China shortly after the Second World War and had gone to Anlu, but after a couple of weeks they realized that the Communists would not permit them to start their mission work there. While guests of the Columbans they studied the language and helped in the dispensary and in the maternity section of the hospital.

Soon all three American communities departed from Wuchang, across the river from the Columbans' convent. At the time one of the Columbans observed: "The poor Charity Sisters are heartbroken with their million-dollar hospital not yet roofed and all the equipment lying idle. We feel it is an immense privilege to be allowed to stay at our posts, especially as it is the expressed wish of the Holy Father, so whatever way things work out we are happy to be carrying out his wishes, when in these troubled days so many sorrows are piled upon him."

Communist troops continued southward into Bishop Cleary's diocese of Nancheng, taking towns, and villages, one by one. What happened to Father Seamus O'Reilly, at Chuliang, was typical of the experience of other Columbans, and so is worth describing here in some detail. In his parish, as in others, people were running here and there and everywhere as fresh batches of rumors arrived even before the soldiers.

What distressed Father O'Reilly most was the constant barrage of questions that he felt incapable of answering. His parishioners, especially the women, wanted to know if they should go or stay, did he believe they were in danger, what should they do with their goods?

Most of them would run out into the country and then come back only to repeat the trip the next day. The kind of chaos this caused can be guessed from a story about how Sister Malachy asked a little hunchbacked woman to help with some sewing only to be told, "But I didn't bring my needle back from the country yet."

To help some of the women carry their possessions to Chuliang, Father O'Reilly festooned his bike with laundry bags and with five hens and one duck, alive, hanging by their legs from the handlebars and saddle. When the Nationalist troops along the way saw this lively load they gave a rousing cheer.

One morning in May of 1949 the missionary was sitting on the verandah when he heard the brrrp, brrrp of machine guns, the crackle of irregular rifle fire, and the deep heavy thud of mortar shells coming from the direction of Nancheng. He said, "This is it!" and took off on his bike towards a Nationalist post on a hill down the road. There an officer informed him that 300 Reds were less than two miles away.

"Aren't you going to leave?" the officer asked the priest.

"No."

The soldier gave a look of disbelief, shook his head, and walked away.

Back at the church, Father O'Reilly found Swee Bao, the sacristan, and ten women and children waiting for him to tell them what to do. He gathered his little following into the school, a squat, U-shaped building, and barricaded the windows, feeling that this would be safe except for a direct hit of a mortar shell.

At this point, the Nationalist troops moved into the mission compound and soon were firing from all around the school. Of course they drew fire from the Reds, and then the women and children began to scream. When things got too hot for the Nationalists, they withdrew and a strange silence fell over the place.

Father O'Reilly heard shouts and stepped from the school just in time to see three Communists coming through the gate. They began to ply him with questions: How many people are here? What kind of place is this? Who are you? Are you an American?

As they talked the forward elements of the Communist army began to arrive. Troops passed through the town for the rest of the day but the Columban had no more calls until nightfall. He was alone in the house, reading Maurice Walsh's *The Key Above the Door,* when he heard a shouting at the gate. There he found a soldier armed with a rifle.

"What place is this?"

"A Catholic mission."

"Come on," commanded the soldier, gesturing with his rifle.

Father O'Reilly recalled later: "My first thought was that I had left the front door open and I was about to tell him that I wanted to close it when I decided that after all it didn't matter: if I returned everything would be all right; if I didn't, it would make little difference whether I had left the door open or closed."

At a bivouac down the road, the soldier said, "I've got a Yank."

"I'm not a Yank, I'm Irish," said Father O'Reilly, showing his identification card with the word Ireland printed on it.

"I know, you're Dutch," said one of the Chinese.

After questioning their prisoner the soldiers sent him back to his rectory for the night. At half past five the next morning, when he was on his way to church to say Mass about a hundred soldiers marched into the compound. They needed a place to rest, they said, and so Father O'Reilly opened his house to them. Soon all the rooms were crowded. The officers sat in the office and plied the pastor with familiar questions: Have you a radio? Are you an American? What do you think of the Kuomintang? How do you like the Communists?

On the office wall hung a calendar featuring a photograph of O'Connell Street, Dublin, with the statue of Daniel O'Connell in the foreground. When the Chinese officers showed curiosity about the statue, the Irishman said, "That is our liberator." This seemed to please the Communists.

A message arrived from Bishop Cleary saying that Nancheng had changed hands. All is going well, he said; the incoming troops are orderly and disciplined, and there is no looting. They did not go near the cathedral and the sisters saw nothing of them until three soldiers came to the dispensary asking to buy medicine.

Two weeks later some four hundred troops were billeted within the cathedral grounds for a few days. Afterwards Bishop Cleary received assurance that no more would be sent there.

All over the diocese towns and villages changed hands, but missionaries were not harmed and no property destroyed. Restrictions, however, were severe: no one could go anywhere without the proper civilian or military pass.

Father O'Reilly concluded a letter home: "Even when I have troops in the compound we have full ceremonies, including Mass, Benediction, and public prayers. While such conditions last, we have no cause for complaint."

During this time, the spring of 1949, the Columban sisters in Shanghai knew that the days of their school were numbered. Pupils were leaving them as the White Russians fled China in ever increasing numbers. Some of the older Russians could remember fleeing from the Bolsheviks in their mother country thirty years earlier, when they had crossed Siberia to Harbin and Vladivostok and had proceeded on down the coast to Shanghai.

By now the sisters had lost 116 Russian pupils. The 46 remaining Russian children plus other foreign pupils held briefly the enrollment of Sancta Sophia at 96, and then it declined once more.

To add to the distress, Bishop Haouisee died. Having invited the Columban sisters to Shanghai in 1938, he had been their patron ever since.

In August of 1949, *Star of the East*, a magazine published in Ireland by the Columban sisters, made the brief announcement: "Our Russian school, which functioned so successfully in Shanghai for nearly twelve years, was obliged to close down, when the pupils fled at the approach of civil war."

During these years when Mao and Chiang were in a life-and-death struggle, a Columban, Father Patrick O'Connor, was director and editor-in-chief of Hua Ming News Service. Into his headquarters in Shanghai came dispatches written in Chinese, French, English, Latin, German, Italian, and Spanish from more than seventy correspondents, most of them missionaries, scattered throughout China.

After the dispatches were translated, Father O'Connor and his assistant, Father Charles J. McCarthy, a Jesuit from San Francisco, cast the stories into journalistic form and sent them to secular and religious newspapers throughout China. Among the well-known subscribers were Reuter's News Agency, Associated Press, United Press International, *Time*, and *Life*.

Hua Ming reflected aspects of Catholic life—education, culture, social welfare, scientific discovery, medical work—and it also covered epidemics, earthquakes, typhoons, famines, and floods. It was responsible for several notable stories; for example, its survey of the harvest prospects based on reports from missionaries all over China, predicting where there would be abundance and where famine. No other news agency could have published so authoritative an estimate of crop prospects. The Catholic news agency, of course, covered the civil war. The irony is that it started, and grew, and prospered just in time to tell the story of the decline and termination of mission work in China. The fate of the missions was sealed from the day Chiang Kai-shek departed mainland China for Formosa in December of 1949.

In the early spring of 1950, Sisters Senan and Damian left Hanyang with the Sisters of Loretto. Sisters Kilian, Agnes, and Ignatius, three of those remaining, kept Cahiracon informed: "As far as we are concerned the hospital has closed, but it looks as if it will reopen soon under new management. They have put up a new gate surmounted by a huge red star."

From Nancheng letters became vague. It was evident that anyone taking pen in hand was aware that every word would be read by the new government. The most optimistic sentence was: "We are reasonably busy; the dispensary is still open and Sister Mary Attracta has her usual crowd of patients every day."

Bishop Galvin's feelings came through clearly when he wrote to Dalgan in the autumn of 1950:

"Not being a prophet, I shall say nothing of the future. Our numbers are now very much smaller than they used to be. Even those who remain have little or nothing to do. Still, I suppose, they also serve who only stand and wait, and look on patiently, and try to accept what comes. God has His own strange and wise ways; He takes the long view, and He permits things to work themselves out in that wise and wonderful way of His.

"Almost all we had has gone—I mean the material things. But, thank

God, the spiritual edifice is still sound. You and those there in that happy little country will keep us in your prayers."

A flicker of optimism came from Hanyang at Christmas of 1950. Mother Mary Kilian told of the many Masses on Christmas Eve and on Christmas day. "The numbers who attended and approached the Sacraments were very consoling as well as edifying. Thank God for such a brave Profession of Faith."

Sister Kilian well remembers those last days. "It was the feast of the Conversion of St. Paul, January 25, 1951. The hospital was to be signed over to the Chinese Red Cross. Bishop Galvin came to witness the takeover. The three of us picked up our meager baggage and turned our backs on the convent and hospital for what length of time we did not know."

When the last of the Columban sisters left Hanyang and Nancheng in 1951, Bishop Galvin knew that he and Bishop Cleary and the remaining priests would soon be told to go. He was surprised to find himself still there, celebrating his forty years in China in the spring of 1952. He would not be there for his seventieth birthday in November, of that he felt sure.

Through the summer of 1952, two renegade Catholics tried with little success to convince the Catholics of Hanyang that they ought to turn against their bishop. Finally, on September 10, they said that there would be a meeting in the school behind the bishop's house so that the people might make any accusations they wished. No one attended except the two Red officials.

Early in the morning of September 15, just as the bishop was preparing to celebrate Mass, a policeman entered the sacristy and ordered the prelate to come along to police headquarters in Hankow, across the river. The bishop asked if he might say Mass first, it would take only a half-hour, but the policeman said, no, the chief of police was waiting.

An hour later the chief of police read a document that charged the bishop with obstructing the Independent Church movement in China, establishing the reactionary Legion of Mary in his diocese, engaging in anti-patriotic propaganda against the government, destroying the property of the people, and disobeying the laws of the Communist government.

Three policemen escorted the bishop back to Hanyang and went through his personal effects, examing them item by item. One of them said, "You are a criminal under sentence of expulsion from China. You are not to communicate with anyone inside this compound or outside of it."

How long it would be before he would be taken to the border, or to prison, he did not know. Later he wrote of those dreary hours: "I need not tell you how I felt. Indeed I could not do so if I tried. I, who came to Hanyang so many years ago to do my little best there for God and souls, was now leaving it as a criminal. The memories of the past thronged in my mind: the great priests, Brothers, and Sisters, who under almost insuperable difficulties, had worked for God throughout the diocese so zealously and loyally; the high ideals, the grand ideas they had; the mass conversions; the struggle to finance the work; the great hope that in the distant future the diocese of Hanyang would be entirely Catholic! Now, the diocese was almost completely deprived of its priests. It was a mass of ruins and the hopes of other days seemed to have vanished like a dream."

He had such thoughts on his mind when on the morning of September 17, 1952, seven policemen came to his rectory. Three Communist policemen escorted him to the border, a journey of thirty-six hours, during which he had no food and was unable to sleep.

Sister Gabriel wrote from Hong Kong: "Bishop Galvin arrived here last night, September 19. Thin and worn looking, he was more like a beggar than anything else. Fathers John McNamara and Malachy Murphy were at the border to meet him when he crossed over to freedom. We got word as soon as the three of them got to the Catholic Center in Hong Kong and went immediately."

A dozen Columban fathers were still in China along with Bishop Cleary who wondered how long the Reds would abide by the eight-point program that they had posted in Nancheng when taking over that city in May of 1949. Part of the program stated that freedom of religion was guaranteed and that the lives and property of foreigners would be protected. The Communists assured the bishop that they had completely changed their policy since the days, fifteen years earlier, when young Reds had run riot through Kiangsi province.

The bishop took a wait-and-see attitude. He watched the situation deteriorate as the Reds moved from politeness in 1949 to arrogance in 1952. At that time a missionary was being berated in prison for saying that the Communists vacillate. Monsignor Provost of the Quebec Foreign Mission told a Red official that he seemed to say one thing today and something quite different tomorrow. The official replied:

"Truth is what is good for the people—not all the people, but the proletariate whose minds have been washed and trained to understand truth. Sometimes it is good for the people to be told one thing now and a different thing tomorrow. Truth is variable; it is in evolution and demands different things at different times. We can say one thing today and another thing tomorrow, and they will both be true."

With each passing month the Reds treated Bishop Cleary with a little more curtness. This reached a climax on Sunday morning, December

14, 1952, when they hauled him before the People's Court. When neither Father Luke O'Reilly nor Father Seamus O'Reilly was allowed to accompany him to court, the bishop felt that his time in Nancheng had run out.

During the two and a half hours of his trial the bishop had to stand facing the audience, with accusers and judges on the bench behind him. His crimes, they said, consisted in establishing the Legion of Mary, exploiting Chinese workers, giving inferior medicine to the poor and good to the rich, and in interfering with the Reform Movement.

At each accusation a leader in the audience shouted at the top of his voice, "Should Li Pei (Bishop Cleary) be expelled?" The audience howled back, "Yes, he should!"

The chairman of the court, after ordering the prisoner to face the judges, said that the sentence was immediate expulsion and read a four-page document that had been prepared before the start of the trial.

In the rectory that night armed guards paced back and forth at the door of the bishop's bedroom. The missionary wondered if perhaps he might be imprisoned instead of expelled; after all, in Hanchow, where the Columbans had worked only since 1947, four priests had been arrested in June and, six months later, were still in prison.

At one o'clock in the morning the chairman of the Reform Movement and four policemen came to the bedroom to order the bishop to get dressed. After searching his room, and those of the other two priests, they took nothing except a few photographs.

Bishop Cleary was forbidden to speak to the priests that night, but on Monday morning he managed to advise them to apply for exit visas. Later in the morning, under military escort, he walked to the bus station in Nancheng.

One guard, well armed, accompanied the bishop on a roundabout journey that lasted four days. Instead of starting southward toward Hong Kong they went north and spent the first night in Fuchow, the second in Nancheng, and then proceeded westward to stop in Changsha and from there traveled directly southward to Canton. Each night in a Chinese hotel the guard slept against the bedroom door.

After his belongings were searched for one final time Bishop Cleary crossed the border on Friday morning, December 19, 1952, and found himself safe in the British territory of Hong Kong.

Time and again the Sisters of Saint Columban welcomed to Hong Kong missionaries expelled from China. For example, when Fathers John Casey, Patrick Reilly, Patrick Ronan, and Owen O'Kane arrived on November 24, 1953, after seventeen months in prison, Sister Mary Attracta boarded the train to greet them as they came inside the free territory.

She was shocked at the sight of these gaunt hollow-eyed men with shaven heads, looking like survivors of the prison camps of Europe at the end of the Second World War.

Sister Attracta accompanied the priests to the hospital where all was in readiness. After they had a series of tests, a doctor said that they suffered from malnutrition and acute exhaustion but that with rest and food they would recover.

The story that these four Columbans told was typical of those the sisters heard from other missionaries. Upon being arrested in June of 1952 all four priests had been put into one cell, eighteen by sixteen feet, with eleven other prisoners, some of whom had been planted there to persuade the missionaries to confess their "crimes."

Each priest was assigned a small space in the cell and from that space was forbidden to move. Discussions, questions, and the confessing of "crimes" filled morning and afternoon. One basin of wash water for the four priests to share was brought to the cell once each twenty-four hours. Two lean meals a day kept them alive. Time dragged as they spent long hours squatting on the floor.

During the torrid summer the cells crawled with vermin. Every mosquito in China seemed to gather there to feed on the prisoners' unprotected bodies. Even the Chinese, accustomed to the heat, sweated all the time. The stench was so dreadful that guards wore masks over their mouths and nostrils.

All four missionaries agreed that prayer had been their consolation during those agonizing seventeen months. They prayed, their rosaries formed of bits of dried bread dough strung on pieces of thread pulled from prison clothes.

Prisoners without prayer and faith often went mad, said Father Aedan McGrath, himself incarcerated for two years and eight months. He told the sisters about a man in a nearby cell who had called his family all day long: "Mother, Mother! Tommy, Tommy!" He had shouted to the guards at any time of day or night, "Open the gate! Open the gate!"

"Listening to him," said Father McGrath, "sent shivers up my spine, and we all began to get jumpy after a while." Another prisoner's madness took the form of absolute disobedience of all prison regulations. He paid no heed to the guards. "When we got up in the morning he lay down to sleep. When we went to bed he got up and spent the whole night talking to himself for weeks, with the guards cursing him for his obstinacy and we trying to get some rest."

When Father McGrath was expelled on May 2, 1954, and Father Edward MacElroy eleven days later there were no more Columbans in China. Six years earlier there had been 150. When the last Columbans departed there were still 163 foreign missionaries in China, a decline from more than 5,000 at the time the Communists took over five years earlier.

The seventy thousand Catholics that the Columbans left in Hanyang, Nancheng, and Huchow were cared for by a handful of Chinese priests, all under pressure to abandon their religion.

In the summer of 1954 Bishop Galvin returned to Ireland.

·24·

New Growth

The new mission in Hong Kong seemed a gift of providence. There the Columban sisters could continue working with the Chinese people free from the troubles of Communist rule.

In their reconstructed naval hospital, perched on high ground overlooking the harbor, they saw mainly refugees, a million of whom swarmed across the border during the first five years that the Columban sisters were in the British crown colony.

The Columban sisters extended their work beyond the Ruttonjee Sanatorium but at first only on a part-time basis. After working all day at the hospital they would get off duty at half past four, have a hurried meal, and depart for one of the distant dispensaries to give B.C.G. injections to immunize those who had not yet contracted TB. The mobile clinic, donated by American Catholics, was a great help in their work in the leper colony.

When the Columbans began visiting Fanling, at the edge of no-man's-land separating Hong Kong from Red China, Sister Mary Gabriel observed: "We shall be in good company here. Among the police are O'Sullivan and Fitzpatrick from Cork, Reidy from Clare and Greene from Dublin."

Each Saturday two sisters visited a small clinic in Fanling that had been started by CARITAS. They arrived by van at noon, having driven the forty miles from Ruttonjee across the harbor, to treat as many as seventy patients, mostly refugees.

In time the sisters staffed a maternity and child welfare center two miles from Fanling, at Kwu Ling. This was possible because of donations by individual Americans and the help of two charitable organizations, CARITAS and MISEREOR. Fortunately, the Anti-Tuberculosis Association was providing funds for Ruttonjee.

The people there on the China border were grateful to have medical attention so near. When only a bicycle is available for transportation, the hospitals at Kowloon and Hong Kong, forty miles away, seem as distant as the craters of the moon.

In 1956 the Columban sisters staffed a home for men recovering from surgery or undergoing prolonged treatment. The Freni Convalescent Hospital, also financed by the Ruttonjee family, was designed to hold 106 beds. A ten-minute walk from Ruttonjee Sanatorium, it is located on high ground overlooking the fine harbor and with a racecourse so near that during the season the fourth floor of the convalescent home becomes a grandstand.

At Freni the staff is kept to a minimum. Except for the cooks the patients do most of the housework. Sister Mary Justin set it up that way. Right off she began writing directives with such titles as "How to Clean the Recreation Room" and "Daily Duties in the Dining Room." Each Monday patients are assigned new duties so that those who washed rice bowls one week will have less prosaic occupations the next week.

"Poor lads," said Sister Mary Attracta. "They love to go to their homes from time to time and will readily trump up any excuse. Many come with a cock-and-bull story. A youngster said he wanted to visit his mother who is very ill in Canton. He had been away just two days ago, and so I asked that he bring his chart. In clear type was recorded in his history: 'Both parents dead.' "

Since boredom can be destructive during convalescence, keeping up morale is part of the cure. The sisters try to get the patients interested in painting, sewing and carving. "They have their good days and their bad days," said Sister Mary Attracta. "But it is a haven of rest for most of them."

Drug addiction complicates the work done with tubercular Chinese. Almost every night, addicts, exhausted and ill, ask to be readmitted to the sanatorium. Usually they are in such an advanced stage of withdrawal that their sickness could be fatal. Caring for them can be frustrating, for rarely do they cooperate in finishing their course of treatment.

Drugs are smuggled into Hong Kong on dilapidated junks and on sophisticated airplanes. They are brought from the Shan states in Burma, northern Thailand, Laos, and the Yunnan Province of China.

"Given a friendly hearing," said Sister Winifred Moane, "it is amazing how the secretiveness of the addict can develop into complete openness about his illicit operations. When Lee Hop was a patient of mine he smoked opium every day, and he told me quite frankly that there was nothing I could do about it. He would still get his supply—which he did—right under my nose."

Sister Winifred and the addict were close friends by the time he confided in her that hospital life was boring and he would like to continue treatment as an outpatient. Besides, he needed money for his daily fix and could only earn enough in a hurry by peddling opium.

The nun tried to dissuade him from his folly, but there was no holding him. She gave him a letter to the drug addiction center but he never used it.

When the time came for his next injections he failed to show. To get in touch with him, the nursing sister contacted several private agencies but Lee Hop managed to evade her. So she set out with a student nurse to visit his home at Ma Shan, a village near Causeway Bay. The place reeked of opium. Fierce dogs kept the women at bay. Only the children were friendly. They led the sisters to Lee Hop's home. The door was locked.

"In answer to our knocking," said Sister Winifred, "a head appeared at a neighboring window, and we met Contact A. He had never in his life heard of Lee Hop. Finally, he relented a little and escorted us to a Coca Cola stand where there was a telephone.

"We were put through to Lee Hop's wife. Her voice drifted to us as though from another world to which her late husband, she informed us, had departed a month ago.

"Looking around I saw Contact B standing nearby. Quite obviously he was another opium addict. He assured us, rather too eagerly I thought, that Lee Hop had died in hospital a month ago."

As the children escorted the women down the steep hill they gave warning whenever an exceptionally vicious dog needed to be avoided. At the bottom of the hill the little procession came upon one of Lee Hop's customers.

The nun's question caught him unprepared. Yes, he knew where to find Lee Hop. At his peddling site, of course. Yes, he would get a message to him.

"Sure enough," said Sister Winifred, "the following morning Lee Hop was in for his injections. And not a day too soon."

There are an estimated eighty thousand such addicts in Hong Kong's population of four million. In the thousands of squatter's huts clustered on the colony's hillsides one in every twelve adult males is believed to be an addict.

There are happier stories, too. Sister Mary Aquinas likes to tell how the space program of the United States of America brought a day of magic to the children in Ruttonjee Sanatorium. The story begins when a U.S. carrier, the *Kearsarge,* picked up astronauts Shirra and Cooper, as they splashed down at the end of their space excursion.

An additional assignment that the ship's crew had was to improve

East-West relations. To help do this the *Kearsarge* carried in its hold a vast storehouse of excellent toys to be distributed with a reckless magnanimity among impoverished children of the Orient.

When the commanding officer of the carrier telephoned Ruttonjee to ask if the sisters would like toys for their tiny patients, the nun who took the call left no doubt as to the answer. She expected that someone would come bearing a few parcels in the back of a jeep.

In no time at all, two U.S. Shore Patrol wagons loaded with crates stopped at the sanatorium entrance. Several sisters were at the door to welcome a dozen members of the carrier's crew. With military precision the sailors unpacked the crates and stacked toys on top of stretchers, trolleys, wheelchairs, and anything else that might be used for indoor transportation.

"In attendance were some of our hospital's unforgettable characters," said Sister Aquinas. "They included Wat Son, who prowls the compound for twenty-five hours a day with tool kit in hand repairing the day's disasters. And Ng Hay, the miscellaneous odd-job man. And Thomas Shu, the casual painter, whose brush can move only to the sound of a Beethoven symphony. Of course, there was the debonair Won Wei Man, our orderly, whose tailored suits and dashing ties make him the Best Dressed Man of Every Year."

Eventually the convoy of toys was under way. As it rattled down the labyrinthine passages the procession behind it grew, for everyone not involved in some life-saving task joined in.

As the traveling Disneyland rolled into the children's wards there was a hushed pause and then excitement broke all bounds. How could so much animation be shown when most of the patients were bed-and-plaster bound!

Sister Mary Justin gave expert advice on individual tastes. She knew, for instance, that Madame Chan, age five, wanted the blonde doll with freckles and upswept hair instead of the brunette with curls, and that Master Wong, age three, preferred a racing car to a jeep.

The squeals of delight drew so much attention that scarcely anyone noticed how the crewmen from the *Kearsarge* were taking it.

The Columban sisters at Ruttonjee were invited to take over the nursing and administration of a children's orthopedic hospital at Sandy Bay. It had been built a few years earlier by a voluntary organization, the Hong Kong Society for the Relief of Disabled Children and had medical assistance provided by the orthopedic department of Hong Kong University. What it needed was the organization and discipline that sisters would bring.

The first two Columbans sent there were Sister M. Justin and Sister M. Ann, both on the staff of Ruttonjee. They had received special training in orthopedic nursing at the Princess Margaret Rose Hospital in Edinburgh where each had won the Nurse of the Year award in her time.

In passing down the winding wooded road to Sandy Bay, the sisters observed that there was an English air about this route. The road passed through the dignified university quarters and unwound in smooth, flowing curves past the Great Queen Mary Hospital, past undulating graveyards, down to the Pacific shore.

The hospital consisted of two bungalow-style units on high ground with a concrete ramp that led to the sea. In time the Hong Kong government would begin to reclaim the shore and the hospital would lose its nearness to the sea, but this was not a total loss because on the reclaimed land it was able to build two wards and units for physiotherapy and hydrotherapy.

The sisters found that there were a few more than a hundred crippled children at Sandy Bay, ranging in age from six months to fourteen years. They came from overcrowded rooftop cubicles, squatters' huts, tenements, tiny boats, and the streets. Some were there because of serious accidents but most were incapacitated by TB of the bone and joint and by post-poliomyelitis paralysis.

"They had known hunger, malnutrition, and insecurity," said Sister Ann. "They were familiar with suffering and pain. Physically they will never enjoy entire freedom of movement. They came to convalesce from major operations. They learned to accept the disablement and to live with it."

Right off the sisters introduced a policy of trying to make the Children's Home a real home, allowing children to lead as near a normal life as possible. Age groups were kept together for it seemed more normal that way than to divide the patients into medical groups. So the four wards were simply called: Bigger Boys, Bigger Girls, Smaller Boys, Smaller Girls.

"When they got up for the day," Sister Ann said, "we got them to dress in day clothes. It meant an awful lot of scrounging to get day clothes for some of them. But we thought it worth it, seeing how much it meant to them. We got even those who must stay in bed into day clothes."

The primary school gave the patients a sense of purpose and progress. Children in wheelchairs maneuvered into place in the classroom. Crutches rested against the seats. Children in long leg plasters who could not sit leaned against the desks. Legs bound in shining calipers stuck stiffly out from under small desks. The heavy plaster of paris leggings thudded dully on the floor when a pupil walked bravely up to the blackboard.

"Normal children work off surplus energy and tension in noisy play outside school hours," said Sister Ann. "Ours could not. So when they shouted and made a din, we usually let them alone. Distinguished visitors were sometimes shocked to find the children in full cry, but we liked to see it. As for their own visitors, there were no fixed hours because we wanted parents to come as often as possible. If we had fixed hours a father might have to give up a day's work to see his child."

The swimming pool was the gift of the Australian Junior Chamber of Commerce. In the pool a handicapped child came as near as possible to throwing off disablement. Only in the water could he let himself go and tumble about to his heart's content. The pool helped tone muscles that were unused for weeks while the child was in bed. It speeded up recovery by months.

As was said earlier, the Columbans took over Sandy Bay Hospital so that they might give it some organization. By June of 1977 things were going well enough for the sisters to turn over the patients to the Hong Kong Society for the Relief of Disabled Children. Like good missionaries who plant and cultivate, they leave others to reap the harvest.

The Ruttonjee family has kept in touch with the Columbans. In addition to many informal calls each year, the family pays an official visit to the sanitorium and to the men's convalescent home each Christmas, bringing gifts for each of the 350 patients.

These are not purchased haphazardly. Well in advance each patient is consulted; even the children's specifications for toys are carefully noted. Everybody's gift appears as if by magic on the afternoon of Saint Stephen's Day in the hands of the benefactors.

An apostolate of education is something the Columban sisters in Hong Kong had not planned on. Not until two requests came—one from Bishop Hsu and the other from the Maryknoll Sisters—did they feel they had to accept.

In 1970 the bishop of Hong Kong asked the Columbans to staff the school about to be built in the resettlement estate of Sau Mau Ping, explaining that the area of 150,000 lacked a secondary school for girls.

When the sisters accepted this new apostolate the construction began and the school was named Leung Shek Chee, in memory of the grandfather of K.K. Leung, who financed much of the construction. By the time the first group of students graduated in June, 1982, the school's enrollment had passed 1,000.

In 1976 the Maryknoll Sisters asked the Columbans to accept their well-established secondary school for girls in Blue Pool Road. It had an enrollment of 850 and adjacent to it was a primary school for girls with an enrollment of 1,000. The Columbans now operate both.

Sister Isobel Loughery said that although these figures may not loom large when compared with the teeming population of Hong Kong the seeds were worth planting. She quoted Lao Tzu: "A tree as big as a man's embrace springs from a tiny sprout."

The Hong Kong of today is different from the one the sisters were introduced to in 1948. In those days the nuns had to step over rows of street sleepers on their way to early Mass. Almost everyone seemed poorly clad and ill-nourished.

While there are still human miseries, an air of prosperity prevails. After a slow recovery from the paralyzing effects of the war, the crown colony became a metropolis with skyscrapers and all of the hustle and bustle of an important city.

Tuberculosis has almost come under control since the day in 1949 when the governor dedicated the Ruttonjee Sanitorium. The Columban sisters contributed greatly to this change. Under the leadership of Sisters Dolorosa, Aquinas, and Gabriel the staff of Ruttonjee cooperated with the Medical Research Council of Britain. Their research into the effects of certain drugs on tuberculosis has helped in the international fight against that disease.

In summing up, Sister Gabriel said: "The sisters' vocation is the whole world where eventually they hope the scourge of tuberculosis will be eradicated. In Hong Kong their influence is widespread; they are present in medical schools teaching future doctors and in nursing schools training nurses.

"They were pioneers in the clinical management of all types of tuberculosis—tubercular meningitis, tubercular spines. Now they are reaching out to drug addicts for tuberculosis is prevalent among them. They are also interested in the apostolate of the dying—the dying tubercular, the dying cancer patient, and abandoned drug addicts."

As a symbol of appreciation, Hong Kong University conferred on Sister Aquinas an honorary Doctorate of Social Sciences in 1978. A year later she was honored by Queen Elizabeth with the Order of the British Empire.

·25·

A New Season

When Mao Tse-tung died in September of 1976, Father Hugh Sands, by then in his eighties, became a focus of journalistic attention in Ireland. Newspapermen and broadcasters sought him out at Magheramore, in County Wicklow, where he was serving as chaplain at the motherhouse of the Columban sisters. The reporters asked him to recall the Christmas afternoon that Mao had visited him in his cell.

By Christmas of 1931 Father Sands had been a prisoner of the Reds for several months. That summer and fall he had traveled many miles with his captors for wherever they went they took him along. On December 22 the Columban was in a village beside the Red Lake when a ten-year-old boy came to his cell carrying a white rabbit. The boy offered the rabbit as a gift.

"I was half starved," Father Sands told the reporters, "so how was I going to feed a rabbit when I hadn't enough for myself. I thanked him for his good intention and he bowed and went out."

The boy returned next day with a rabbit under each arm and offered the priest the two of them. Again Father Sands refused.

The next day, Christmas Eve, the boy brought a big orange. He peeled it carefully and divided it in two.

"I never tasted anything so wonderful!" the old missionary recalled. After the boy had left someone told the priest that Mao Tse-tung was the child's father.

Mao himself came to the cell on Christmas afternoon.

"What are you doing in China?" he asked.

Father Sands explained that he was a Catholic missionary trying to spread the Christian faith.

"Wasting your time. We're not interested," said Mao. "Confucius used to say, '*Wei dzi sin yen dzi si?*' " (We scarcely know the things of this world how are we to know the things of another one?)

After a long pause Mao asked, "Where are you from?"

"Ireland."

"Oh, England."

"Certainly not. Ireland is an independent country. It has its own language, its own stamps and its own currency."

"Nonsense," said Mao. "Empires do not allow independent countries on their doorsteps. Especially not small countries."

Father Sands decided that here was an occasion when politics and religion were topics to avoid. He began describing the frightful mistakes he had made while learning the Chinese language. He told how he had asked his houseboy to go down and sweep the church and dust the altar. The phonetics he used were correct, but the accent was all wrong. So what he actually said was: 'Go down and burn the church and curse the altar."

Mao laughed, admitting that he had found English equally difficult.

"We can't for instance, distinguish between the consonants L, M, N, and R. I can't see any difference between 'lend me your knife,' and 'lend me your wife.' "

The conversation continued in such a light vein throughout Christmas afternoon. At dusk Mao bowed out.

After Mao's death, Father Sands and other "China watchers" among the Columbans noticed changes taking place in the People's Republic. Father Edward MacElroy, the last Columban expelled from China, used Hong Kong as his "window." There he read Chinese newspapers and magazines, listened to the government-controlled radio broadcasts, interviewed refugees, and talked with Chinese who had made brief visits to the homeland.

Father MacElroy believed that Chairman Mao, although officially in charge, was probably senile toward the end of his life and that the real power was in the hands of the radicals headed by Mao's wife, Chiang-Ching, and her colleagues, Wang Hung-Win, Yao Wen-Yuan, and Chang Chun-Chao. The Gang of Four. They had grabbed power during the Great Cultural Revolution which began in 1965. Their revolution within a revolution ended when members of the Gang of Four were arrested in October of 1976, a month after Mao's death.

Mao had concocted the Great Cultural Revolution because he found much dissatisfaction within China. The old spirit needed to be rekindled in the young, he decided: "You learn to swim by swimming; you learn revolution by revolting."

He presided at the first rally of the Red Guards, August 18, 1965, attended by a million students. So that more young people would have time to work with the Red Guards, schools were closed temporarily the following spring. The youths were told to purify Communist society and force it back into the orthodox Marxist-Leninist-Maoist line.

The Red Guards were their own worst enemies. They became so arrogant that the army had to quell their barbarity and hooliganism. Their arrogance flared out in the late 1960s when young people all over the world seemed determined to save society by destroying it.

The Little Red Book made its appearance during the Cultural Revolution. More than eight hundred million people were expected to meditate on the sayings of Mao for about twenty minutes each morning and evening. The "cult" of Mao required that this activity be performed in front of a statue or a picture of the Chairman. This went on for several years.

Some teachings of the Little Red Book caused friction between Mao and Chou En-Lai. For instance, should ideology hold preference over pragmatism? The conflict between "Redness" and "Expertness" is what the Little Red Book called it. The radicals, headed by Chairman Mao, claimed "Redness" should have preference; the moderates, headed by Chou En-lai, claimed that "Expertness" is the more important. Such disagreements disappeared with the death of Mao and the arrest of the Gang of Four.

In trying to assess Mao's worth as a national figure, Father MacElroy quoted from the October 7, 1977 issue of the *Far East Economic Review:* "Espousing a policy of self-reliance, he hauled China painfully through a series of drastic social experiments which did indeed bear some useful fruits. The Mandarin attitude of the bureaucracy was challenged and to some extent broken down. A semblance of self-sufficiency in food production was achieved. Political enslavement to the Kremlin was averted. Education took on a new orientation toward practical results. Medical services were spread more widely throughout the country, and production units were encouraged to mount their own welfare schemes. . . . These achievements, however, were bought at an enormous cost."

Father MacElroy observed: "The whole country is in the process of writing off a sizeable portion of its recent past. It is taking a new look on the problems that confront it." One of its most important new plans, he said, is called the Four Modernizations, an attempt to modernize agriculture, industry, technology, and defense.

What happened to religion in China during the time of Mao?

To understand the answer, one must begin with the Three Autonomies, a government proclamation issued in 1951 saying that churches in China should be self-propagating, self-supporting, and self-governing. In other words, churches should be completely cut off from the outside.

In promoting this policy, the official press often criticized the Pope, depicting him and missionaries as agents of foreign imperialists, saying that a new theological system should be created so that the Church might better promote the political aspirations of the people.

Pope Pius XII condemned this attitude, in December 1954, warning that China was in danger of establishing a national church. By then practically all foreign missionaries had been expelled, and many Chinese bishops and priests were in prison for having resisted the Three Autonomies.

To sell its ideas, the Communist government organized conferences for Catholic clergymen all over China; some of the conferences lasted as long as three months. To reform the minds of the prelates, leading Red officials worked long and hard. While Catholics were being lectured, so were Protestants and Muslims. Similar conferences were held for university professors, writers, lawyers, economists, and so on.

While such conferences were in vogue, in 1957–58, Mao started his Hundred Flowers experiment. He encouraged people to speak their minds freely: "Let a hundred flowers bloom; let diverse schools of thought contend." To show his goodwill he released some political prisoners. A new freedom seemed abroad in the land. When criticism became too open, however, the Chairman changed his mind. Those who had spoken too freely were arrested and severely punished.

The Red government formed the Patriotic Association of Chinese Catholics in July 1957. Within a year the association elected two bishops and notified Rome by telegram. The Holy See replied by telegram refusing to recognize the appointment and warning that any bishop performing the ceremony or any priest receiving consecration would be automatically excommunicated. The two bishops were consecrated in April 1958.

Sixty such consecrations took place during the next quarter-century. The ceremonies were in Latin with pre-Vatican II liturgy, for all church services in China follow traditional forms. Prayer books are still published with the old morning and evening prayers; practically the only change is in the Litany of the Saints where the invocation to pray for the Holy Father is replaced by "let us pray for our superior."

No bishop from China attended the Second Vatican Council. The dissidents were not invited, and the Chinese government would not permit the others to leave the country.

When the Red Guards went on the rampage, in the late 1960s, the Patriotic Association of Chinese Catholics came under attack. It disappeared from public life. The few churches that were open were desecrated and closed, and for nearly ten years no word came out of China as to what was happening to religion there.

As part of the general liberalization that followed the death of Mao and the arrest of the Gang of Four, some churches were reopened. Many priests and lay Catholics who had been imprisoned for a quarter-century were released. The priests were not allowed, however, to perform a religious ministry.

Protestant churches, united in 1953 under the name Chinese Christian Three-Self Patriotic Movement, are also ruled by the Communist government. In recent years the Protestants were permitted to reopen churches in eleven cities.

Concerning all of this confusion, one China watcher, Father L. La-Dany, S.J., said early in 1981: "The present situation seems ambiguous. . . . Some think the ambiguity deliberate. A semblance of freedom is being created as a sort of sorting out who is who, who joins the government-run organizations and who will not join. Others think that now, when so many things are changing in China, the leadership is sounding new ways of solving the insoluble religious question."

Cardinal Etchegarary of Marseilles looked into the ambiguous confusion when he spent seventeen days in China in 1980. After talking with officials of church and state he summed up his impression in a sentence: "The motives for hope are stronger than the motives for doubt."

What has happened to the Columbans in the three decades since they were expelled from China?

The main missions of the sisters are in Hong Kong, Korea, the Philippines, Chile, and Peru; and those of the priests are in Korea, the Philippines, Fiji, Japan, Chile, and Peru. Both sisters and priests were expelled from Burma in the late 1970s when the government there began purging itself of "foreign influence."

Practically all of the Columbans whose names were mentioned at the beginning of this story are dead. Mother Mary Patrick died August 15, 1959, and Mother Finbarr, January 19, 1977. Both rest in the cemetery at the motherhouse at Maheramore, County Wicklow. Bishop Galvin died February 23, 1956; Bishop Cleary October 23, 1970 and Father Blowick, June 19, 1972. They are buried in the community cemetery at St. Columban's Seminary, Navan, County Meath.

Since the Columbans, both sisters and priests, were founded shortly after the First World War to work in China—and only China was considered at the time—being expelled from there must have been a traumatic experience. Now, with hindsight available, how do they feel about those early hopes?

This question came up when the Columban fathers celebrated their golden anniversary in 1968. Somebody asked, "If Fathers Galvin and Blowick had foreseen the catastrophe in China, would they have stopped in their tracks?"

Bishop Cleary, then 81, considered this for a few moments before answering: "Probably not. The harvest that was garnered was immense. The good seed remains in the ground for a second spring."

Praise for Jane Mayer's

DARK MONEY

"Amazing. . . . The most important political book of the year." —*St. Louis Post-Dispatch*

"*Dark Money* emerges as an impressively reported and well-documented work. . . . The importance of *Dark Money* [flows] from its scope and perspective. . . . It is not easy to uncover the inner workings of an essentially secretive political establishment. Mayer has come as close to doing it as anyone is likely to come anytime soon. . . . She makes a formidable argument."
—*The New York Times Book Review*

"[A] comprehensive history. . . . Stunning." —*Salon*

"Deeply researched and studded with detail . . . it seems destined to rattle the Koch executive offices in Wichita as other investigations have not."
—*The Washington Post*

"Bombshells explode in the pages of *Dark Money*, Jane Mayer's indispensable new history." —*The Guardian*

"*Dark Money* is almost too good for its own good."
—*Los Angeles Review of Books*

"An extraordinarily well-documented account of the influential, interlocking organizations with innocuous names created by the Koch brothers."

—*Pittsburgh Post-Gazette*

"Mayer is telling the epic story of America in our time. It is a triumph of investigative reporting, perhaps not surprising for a journalist who has won most of the awards her profession has to offer. . . . She's given the world a full accounting of what had been a shadowy and largely unseen force. . . . Remarkable."

—*The New York Review of Books*

"With such turmoil on the right wing of American politics, reading *Dark Money* is like reading the first chapter of what may be a great political page-turner."

—*Chicago Tribune*

"For those who care about the future of democracy in America, *Dark Money* is a must read."

—*The Post and Courier* (Charleston, SC)

Jane Mayer

DARK MONEY

Jane Mayer is a staff writer for *The New Yorker* and the author of three previous bestselling and critically acclaimed narrative nonfiction books. She coauthored *Landslide: The Unmaking of the President, 1984–1988*, with Doyle McManus, and *Strange Justice: The Selling of Clarence Thomas*, with Jill Abramson, which was a finalist for the National Book Award. Her book *The Dark Side: The Inside Story of How the War on Terror Turned into a War on American Ideals*, for which she was awarded a Guggenheim Fellowship, was named one of *The New York Times*'s Top 10 Books of the Year and was a finalist for the National Book Award and the National Book Critics Circle Award, among numerous other accolades. For her reporting at *The New Yorker*, Mayer has been awarded the John Chancellor Award, the George Polk Award, the Toner Prize for Excellence in Political Reporting, and the I. F. Stone Medal for Journalistic Independence presented by the Nieman Foundation at Harvard. Mayer lives in Washington, D.C.

www.jane-mayer.com

ALSO BY JANE MAYER

The Dark Side: The Inside Story of How the War on Terror Turned into a War on American Ideals

Strange Justice: The Selling of Clarence Thomas
(with Jill Abramson)

Landslide: The Unmaking of the President, 1984–1988
(with Doyle McManus)

DARK MONEY

The Hidden History of the Billionaires Behind the Rise of the Radical Right

Jane Mayer

ANCHOR BOOKS
A DIVISION OF PENGUIN RANDOM HOUSE LLC
NEW YORK

FIRST ANCHOR BOOKS EDITION, JANUARY 2017

 Published in the United States by Anchor Books, a division of Penguin Random House LLC, New York, and distributed in Canada by Random House of Canada, a division of Penguin Random House Canada Limited, Toronto. Originally published in hardcover in the United States by Doubleday, a division of Penguin Random House LLC, New York, in 2016.

The Cataloging-in-Publication Data for the Doubleday edition is available from the Library of Congress.

Anchor Books Trade Paperback ISBN: 978-0-307-94790-1
eBook ISBN: 978-0-385-53560-1

Author photograph © Stephen Voss
Maps by Mapping Specialists, Ltd.
Book design by Maria Carella

www.anchorbooks.com

Printed in the United States of America
10

FOR BILL HAMILTON:

Everyone needs an editor,
but not everyone is lucky enough to marry one.
Thank you for always being there with just the right words.

We must make our choice. We may have democracy,
or we may have wealth concentrated in the hands of a few,
but we can't have both.

—Louis Brandeis

CONTENTS

PART THREE:
PRIVATIZING POLITICS: TOTAL COMBAT, 2011–2014

PREFACE TO THE ANCHOR BOOKS EDITION (2017)

ELECTION NIGHT 2016 WAS A STUNNING POLITICAL UPSET auguring a new political order in almost every respect. Donald Trump, a billionaire businessman with no experience in elected office, running on a promise to upend the status quo, defeated Hillary Clinton, the designated heir to Barack Obama's Democratic presidency. Trump's triumph defied the predictions of almost every pundit and pollster. It rocked the political establishments in both parties and sent shock waves around the globe. Markets trembled before recovering their equilibrium. The political world seemed to shift on its axis, spinning toward an unknown and unpredictable future. Although Trump ran as a self-proclaimed outsider against what he portrayed as entrenched and corrupt political elites, there was an unexpectedly familiar representative of this moneyed class at his victory party in Manhattan. Standing with a jubilant smile amid the throng of revelers at the Hilton hotel in midtown Manhattan was David Koch.

During the presidential primaries, Trump had mocked his Republican rivals as "puppets" for flocking to the secretive fund-raising sessions sponsored by David Koch and his brother Charles, co-owners of the second-largest private company in the United States, the Kansas-based energy and manufacturing conglomerate Koch Industries. Affronted, the Koch brothers, whose political spending had made their name almost shorthand for special-interest clout, withheld their financial support from Trump. As a result, the story line adopted by many in the media was that the Koch brothers in particular, and big political donors in general, were no longer a major factor in American politics. Trump had after all defeated far bigger-spending rivals, including Clinton.

It might be nice to think the era of big money in American politics is over, but a closer look reveals a far more complicated and far less reassuring reality.

Trump had indeed campaigned by attacking the big donors, corporate lobbyists, and political action committees that have come to dominate American politics as "very corrupt." In doing so, he fed into a national, bipartisan outpouring of disgust at the growing extent to which campaigns have become little more than relentless pursuits of obscene amounts of cash. To the surprise of many, Trump and Bernie Sanders, the left-wing insurgent who challenged Clinton in the Democratic primaries, seemed to transform big political money from an advantage into a liability. Trump nicknamed Clinton "Crooked Hillary," claiming that she was "100% owned by her donors." By Election Day, the public's trust in her was in tatters.

Improbably, Trump, a New York businessman who had global financial interests and who spent some $66 million of his own fortune to get elected, ran against Wall Street. He successfully positioned himself as pristine because he was a billionaire in his own right, rather than one beholden to other billionaires. In a tweet less than a month before the election, Trump promised, "I will Make Our Government Honest Again—believe me. But first I'm going to have to #DrainTheSwamp." His DrainTheSwamp hashtag became a rallying cry for supporters riled by the growing economic inequality in the country and intent on ending corruption in Washington, which they blamed for putting the interests of the rich and powerful over their own.

Yet as Ann Ravel, a Democratic member of the Federal Election Commission who had championed reform of political money for years, observed just days after Trump's election, instead "the alligators are multiplying."

Despite having been elected as a populist outsider, Trump

put together a transition team that was crawling with the kinds of corporate insiders he vowed to disempower. Especially prominent among them were lobbyists and political operatives who had financial ties to the Kochs. This was perhaps unexpected, because the Kochs had continued to express their distaste for Trump throughout the campaign. Charles Koch called himself a libertarian. He supported open immigration and free trade, both of which benefited his vast multinational corporation. He had denounced Trump's plans to bar Muslim immigrants as "monstrous" and "frightening."

Yet there were signs of a rapprochement. The chair of Trump's transition team, Vice President elect Mike Pence, had been Charles Koch's first choice for the presidency in 2012 and a major recipient of Koch campaign contributions. David Koch had personally donated $300,000 to Pence's campaigns in the four years before Trump chose Pence as his running mate. Pence, who in the past had shared the Kochs' enthusiasm for privatizing Social Security and denying the reality of climate change, had been a featured guest at a fund-raiser that David Koch hosted for about seventy of the Republican Party's biggest political donors at his Palm Beach, Florida, mansion in the spring of 2016. He had also been slated to speak at the Kochs' donor summit in August 2016 but canceled after joining the Republican ticket. Meanwhile, Pence's senior adviser in the sensitive task of managing Trump's transition to power was Marc Short, who just a few months earlier had actually run the Kochs' secretive donor club, Freedom Partners. This was the same elite group whose meetings Trump had ridiculed during the campaign.

The Kochs' influence was also evident in the transition team members that Trump picked in the areas of energy and the environment, which were crucial to Koch Industries' bottom line. For policy and personnel advice regarding the Department of Energy, an early chart of the transition team showed that Trump chose Michael McKenna, the president of the lobbying firm MWR Strategies, whose clients included Koch Industries. McKenna also had ties to the American Energy Alliance, a tax-exempt nonprofit that advocated for corporate-friendly energy policies, to which the Kochs' donor group, Freedom Partners, had given $1.5 million in 2012. The group, which didn't disclose its revenue sources, was a textbook example of the way secret spending by billion-dollar private interests aimed to manipulate public opinion.

Another lobbyist for Koch Industries, Michael Catanzaro, a partner at the lobbying firm CGCN Group, headed "energy independence" for Trump's transition team and was mentioned as a possible White House energy czar. Meanwhile, Harold Hamm, a charter member of the Kochs' donor circle, who became a billionaire by founding Continental Resources, an Oklahoma-based shale-oil company known for its enormously lucrative "fracking" operation, was reportedly advising Trump on energy issues and under consideration for a cabinet post, possibly energy secretary.

To the alarm of the scientific community, Trump chose Myron Ebell, an outspoken climate change skeptic, to head his transition team for the Environmental Protection Agency (EPA). Ebell too had Koch money ties. He worked at a Washington think tank, the Competitive Enterprise Institute. It didn't disclose its funding sources, but in the past, it had been bankrolled by fossil fuel interests, including the Kochs. His stridently antiregulatory views meshed perfectly with theirs. The Kochs had long been at war with the EPA, which had ranked Koch Industries one of only three companies in America that was simultaneously a top ten polluter of air, water, and climate. Joining Ebell on the transition team was David Schnare, a self-described "free-market environmentalist" who had accused the EPA of having "blood on its hands." Schnare worked for a think tank affiliated with the State Policy Network, which was also funded in part by the Kochs. He was reviled in environmental circles for hounding the climate scientist Michael

Mann with onerous public records requests until the Virginia Supreme Court ordered him to desist in 2014. The Union of Concerned Scientists had described these actions against climate scientists as "harassment."

Thus, less than a week after having been elected on a wave of populist anger, Trump appeared set to fulfill many of the special interests' fondest dreams, including the deregulatory schemes of the Kochs. He promised to "get rid of" the EPA in "almost every form" and to withdraw from the 2015 international climate accord in Paris, and against the overwhelming scientific evidence to the contrary, he called climate change "a hoax." The Trump transition had a self-imposed ethics code barring lobbyists from shaping the rules and staffing the departments in which they had financial interests, but in the early stages, at least, these commonsense strictures appeared to have been sidestepped.

Experts in government ethics were aghast. "If you have people on the transition team with deep financial ties to the industries to be regulated, it raises questions about whether they are serving the public interest or their own interests," warned Norman Eisen, who devised the Obama administration's conflict-of-interest rules. "Let's face it, in the Beltway nexus of corporations and dark money, lobbyists are the delivery mechanism for special-interest influence." Peter Wehner, who served in the administrations of Ronald Reagan and both presidents Bush, told the *New York Times,* "This whole idea that he was an outsider and going to destroy the political establishment and drain the swamp were the lines of a con man, and guess what—he is being exposed as just that."

The Kochs' influence reached greater heights with Trump's nomination of Mike Pompeo, a Republican congressman from Kansas, to direct the CIA. Pompeo was the single largest recipient of Koch campaign funds in Congress. The Kochs had also been investors, and partners, in Pompeo's business ventures prior to his entry into politics. In fact, as Burdett Loomis, a University of Kansas professor of political science, noted, the future CIA director's nickname was "the congressman from Koch." Helping to guide the transition team in these fateful choices was Rebekah Mercer, the daughter of Robert Mercer, the wealthy New York hedge fund manager who "out-Koched the Kochs" in 2014, as Bloomberg News put it, giving more money to their political club than even they had.

Clearly the reports of the Kochs' political 'death' in 2016 were exaggerated. While they had refrained from backing a presidential candidate, the tentacles of the "Kochtopus," as their sprawling political machine was known, were already encircling the Trump administration before it had even officially taken power.

Many had counted the Kochs out after their refusal to back a presidential candidate. Their initial 2015 plan called for their donor group to spend an astounding budget of $889 million in order to purchase the presidency. But they sat out the primaries, as they had in the past, and then found their plan rudely upended when Trump emerged as the nominee. He was the only major Republican presidential candidate whom they opposed. Sidelined, they continued to withhold their support.

But while the media fixated on the extraordinary presidential race, the Kochs and their network of right-wing political patrons quietly spent more money than ever on the three-pronged influence-buying approach they had mastered during the previous forty years. They combined corporate lobbying, politically tinged nonprofit spending, and "down ballot" campaign contributions in state and local races, where their money bought a bigger bang for the buck.

Far from shutting their wallets, they simply downgraded their budget to $750 million and directed several hundred million dollars of it to races beneath the presidential level. Few noticed, but in 2016 Koch Industries and Freedom Partners poured huge sums into at least nineteen Senate, forty-two House, and four gubernatorial races as well as countless lesser ones all over the country.

They also mobilized what a 2016 study by two Harvard University scholars, Theda Skocpol and Alexander Hertel-Fernandez, described as an unprecedented and unparalleled permanent, private political machine. In fact, amazingly, in 2016 the Kochs' private network of political groups had a bigger payroll than the Republican National Committee. The Koch network had 1,600 paid staffers in thirty-five states and boasted that its operation covered 80 percent of the population. This marked a huge escalation from just a few years earlier. As recently as 2012, the Kochs' primary political advocacy group, Americans for Prosperity, had a paid staff of only 450.

The Kochs ran their political operation centrally like a private business, with divisions devoted to various constituency groups, such as Hispanics, veterans, and young voters. One of their top people explained that their aim during the 2016 election had been to target five million voters in eight states with key Senate races. In the past, labor unions probably provided the closest parallel to this kind of private political organizing, but they of course represented the dues of millions of members. In comparison, the Koch network was sponsored by just four hundred or so of the richest people in the country. It was for this reason that the Harvard scholars who studied it said that the Koch network was "like nothing we've ever seen."

Irrespective of Trump, the Kochs and their fellow megadonors succeeded in their chief political objective in 2016, which was to keep both houses of Congress under conservative Republican control, ensuring that they could continue to advance their corporate agenda. They succeeded in their secondary goal too, which was to further crush the Democratic Party by continuing the nationwide sweep of state legislatures and local offices that they had begun in 2010. By controlling statehouses, they could dominate not just legislation but also the gerrymandering of congressional districts, in hopes of securing their grip on the House of Representatives for years to come.

Many of the races they backed were too minor to merit press attention. In Texas alone, they supported candidates in seventy-four different races, reaching all the way down to a county court commissioner. Thanks in no small part to huge quantities of targeted money spent by the Kochs and their allied donors, the Democratic Party lost both houses of Congress, fourteen governorships, and thirty state legislatures, comprising more than nine hundred seats, during Obama's presidency. By the time the votes were tallied in the 2016 election, Republicans controlled thirty-two state legislatures, while Democrats controlled only thirteen. Five others were split. This imbalance posed a huge problem for Democrats not only in the present but for the future, because state legislatures serve as incubators for rising leaders.

The Kochs might have disavowed Trump, but in several important respects he was their natural heir and the unintended consequence of the extraordinary political movement they had underwritten since the 1970s. For forty years, they had vilified the very idea of government. They had propagated that message through the countless think tanks, academic programs, front groups, ad campaigns, legal organizations, lobbyists, and candidates they supported. It was hard not to believe that this had helped set the table for the takeover of the world's most powerful country by a man who made his inexperience and antipathy toward governing among his top selling points.

Charles Koch's mentor, the quasi-anarchist Robert LeFevre, had taught the Kochs that "government is a disease masquerading as its own cure." Their extreme opposition to the expansions of the federal government that had taken place during the Progressive Era, the New Deal era, the Great Society, and Obama's presidency had helped to convince voters that Washington was corrupt and broken and that, when it came to governing, knowing nothing was preferable to expertise. Charles Koch had referred to himself as a "radical," and in Trump he got the radical solution he had helped to spawn.

The Kochs had also primed America for Trump by pouring gasoline on the fires lit by the antitax Tea Party movement starting in 2009. Charles Koch decried Trump's toxic rhetoric in 2016, and David Koch complained to the *Financial Times* that "you'd think we could have more influence" after spending hundreds of millions of dollars on American politics. But in fact, the influence of the Kochs and their fellow big donors was manifest in Trump's use of incendiary and irresponsibly divisive rhetoric. Only a few years ago, it was they who were sponsoring the hate.

In the 1960s, Charles Koch had funded the all-white private Freedom School in Colorado, whose head had told the *New York Times* that the admittance of black students might present housing problems because some students were segregationists. That was long ago, and his views, like those of many others, could well have changed. But in a 2011 interview with the *Weekly Standard,* David Koch echoed specious claims, made by the conservative gadfly Dinesh D'Souza, that Obama was somehow African rather than American in his outlook. He claimed that Obama, who was born in America and abandoned by his Kenyan father as a toddler, nonetheless derived his "radical" views from his African heritage.

The effort to attack Obama, not as a legitimate and democratically elected American political opponent, but as an alien threat to the country's survival, was very much in evidence at a summit that the Kochs' political organization Americans for Prosperity hosted in Austin, Texas, during the summer of 2010. Between Tea Party training sessions, operatives working for the Kochs gave an award to a blogger who had described Obama as the "cokehead-in-chief" and asserted that he suffered from "demonic possession (aka schizophrenia, etc.)." The Kochs and other members of the Republican donor class might have disowned the vile language of the 2016 campaign, but six years earlier they were honoring it with trophies.

The same incendiary style characterized the big donors' fight against the Affordable Care Act. Rather than respectfully debating Obama's health-care plan as a policy issue, the Kochs and their allied donors poured cash into a dark-money group called the Center to Protect Patient Rights, which mounted a guerrilla war of fearmongering and vitriol. Television ads sponsored by the group featured the false claim that Obama's plan was "a government takeover" of health care, which PolitiFact named "the Lie of the Year" in 2010. Meanwhile, a spin-off of Americans for Prosperity organized anti-Obamacare rallies at which protesters unfurled banners depicting corpses from Dachau, implying that Obama's policies would result in mass murder. Koch operatives also purposefully sabotaged the democratic process by planting screaming protesters in town hall meetings at which congressmen met with constituents that year. In short, during the Obama years, the Kochs radicalized and organized an unruly movement of malcontents, over which by 2016 they had lost control. "We are partly responsible," one former employee in the Kochs' political operation admitted to *Politico* a month before Trump was elected. "We invested a lot in training and arming a grassroots army that was not controllable."

In other ways too, the Kochs and their allied big donors became victims of their own success in 2016. They inadvertently laid the groundwork for Trump's rise by too thoroughly capturing the Republican Party with their cash. Their narrowly self-serving policy priorities were at odds with those of the vast majority of voters. Yet virtually every Republican presidential candidate other than Trump pledged fealty to the donors' wish lists as they jockeyed for their support. The candidates promised to cut taxes for those in the highest brackets, preserve Wall Street loopholes, tolerate the off-shoring of manufacturing jobs and profits, and downgrade or privatize middle-class entitlement programs, including Social Security. Free trade was barely debated. These positions faithfully reflected the agenda of the wealthy donors, but studies showed that they were increasingly out of step with the broad base of not just Democratic but also Republican voters, many of whom had been left behind economically and socially for decades, particularly acutely since the 2008 financial crash. Trump, who could afford to forgo the billionaires' backing and ignore their policy priorities, saw the opening and seized it.

Whether Trump would fulfill his supporters' hopes and break free from the self-serving elites whose money had captured the Republican Party prior to his unorthodox election remained to be seen. The early signs were not promising. Not only was Trump's early transition team swarming with corporate lobbyists, including those who had worked for the Kochs, but Trump's inaugural committee featured several members of the Kochs' billion-dollar donor club, too. Neither Diane Hendricks, a building supply company owner whose $3.6 billion fortune made her the wealthiest woman in Wisconsin, nor billionaire Sheldon Adelson, founding chairman and chief executive of the Las Vegas Sands Corporation casino empire, signaled a break from politics as usual.

Inaugurals had long been underwritten by rich donors, so perhaps reading too much into this was unfair. But Trump's tax proposals, to the extent that they could be gleaned, were if anything even more of a bait and switch. While he had garnered blue-collar support by promising to stick it to the elites who "are getting away with murder," his proposals, according to economic experts, threatened instead to enshrine a permanent aristocracy in America. He appeared poised to repeal the estate tax, presenting a windfall to heirs of estates worth $10.9 million or more. There had been fewer than five thousand estates of this size in 2015. He also had plans to abolish the gift tax, which put the brakes on inherited wealth. Capital gains taxes and income taxes for top earners were headed toward the chopping block, too. Charles and David Koch, who together were worth some $84.5 billion, stood to benefit to an extent that dwarfed earlier administrations, as did many other billionaires. As the headline on Yahoo Finance proclaimed on the day after the election, "Trump's Win Is a 'Grand Slam' for Wall Street Banks."

The fact of the matter was that while Trump might have been elected by those he described as "the forgotten" men, he would have to deal with a Republican Party that had been shaped substantially by the billionaires of the radical Right. He would have to work with a vice president once funded by the Kochs and a Congress dominated by members who owed their political careers to the Kochs. Further, he would have to face a private political machine organized in practically every state, ready to attack any deviation from their agenda. No one could predict what Trump would do. Nor could they predict how much longer the Kochs, by then in their eighties, would stay active. But one thing was certain. The Kochs' dark money, which they had directed their successors to keep spending long after they had passed away, would continue to exert disproportionate influence over American politics for years to come.

November 2016
Washington, D.C.

Dark Money

INTRODUCTION

The Investors

ON JANUARY 20, 2009, THE EYES OF THE COUNTRY WERE ON Washington, where over a million cheering celebrants crowded the National Mall to witness the inauguration of the first African-American president. So many supporters streamed in from all across the nation that for twenty-four hours they nearly doubled Washington's population. Inaugurations are always moving celebrations of the most basic democratic process, the peaceful transfer of power, but this one was especially euphoric. The country's most famous and iconic musicians, from the Queen of Soul, Aretha Franklin, to the cellist Yo-Yo Ma, gave soaring performances to mark the occasion. Celebrities and dignitaries pulled strings to get seats. Excitement was so feverish that the Democratic political consultant James Carville was predicting a long-term political realignment in which the Democrats "will remain in power for the next forty years."

But on the other side of the country during the last weekend in January 2009, another kind of gathering was under way, of a group of activists who aimed to do all they could to nullify the results of the recent election. In Indian Wells, a California desert town on the outskirts of Palm Springs, one polished sports utility vehicle after the next cruised down the long, palm-lined drive of the Renaissance Esmeralda Resort and Spa. Stepping out onto the curb, as bellboys darted for the luggage, were some of America's most ardent conservatives, many of whom represented the nation's most powerfully entrenched business interests. It would be hard to conjure a richer tableau of the good life than the one greeting them. Overhead, the sky was a brilliant azure. In the distance, the foothills of the Santa Rosa Mountains rose steeply from the Coachella Valley, creating a stunning backdrop of ever-changing hues. Velvety green lawns stretched as far as the eye could see, meandering toward a neighboring thirty-six-hole golf course. Swimming pools, one with a man-made sandy beach, were surrounded by chaises and intimate, curtained pavilions. As dusk fell, countless tea lights and tiki torches magically lit the walkways and flower beds.

But inside the hotel's dining room, the mood was grim, as if these luxuries merely highlighted how much the group gathered there had to lose. The guests meeting at the resort that weekend included many of the biggest winners during the eight years of George W. Bush's presidency. There were billionaire businessmen, heirs to some of America's greatest dynastic fortunes, right-wing media moguls, conservative elected officials, and savvy political operatives who had made handsome livings helping their patrons win and hold power. There were also eloquent writers and publicists, whose work at think tanks, advocacy groups, and countless publications was quietly subsidized by corporate interests. The guests of honor, though, were the potential political donors—or "investors," as they referred to themselves—whose checkbooks would be sorely needed for the project at hand.

The group had been summoned that weekend not by the leader of a recognized opposition party but rather by a private citizen, Charles Koch. In his seventies, he was white-haired but youthfully fit and very much in charge of Koch Industries, a conglomerate headquartered in Wichita, Kansas. The company had grown spectacularly since its founder, Charles's father, Fred, had died in 1967, and he and his brother David took charge, buying out their two other brothers. Charles and David—often referred to as the Koch brothers—owned virtually all of what had become under their leadership the second-largest private company in America. They owned four thousand miles of pipelines, oil refineries in Alaska, Texas, and Minnesota, the Georgia-Pacific lumber and paper company, coal, and chemicals, and they were huge traders in commodity futures, among other businesses. The company's consistent profitability had made the two brothers the sixth- and seventh-wealthiest men in the world. Each was worth an estimated $14 billion in 2009. Charles, the elder brother, was a man of unusual drive, accustomed to getting his way. What he wanted that weekend was to enlist his fellow conservatives in a daunting task: stopping the Obama administration from implementing Democratic policies that the American public had voted for but that he regarded as catastrophic.

Given the size of their fortunes, Charles and David Koch automatically had extraordinary influence. But for many years, they had magnified their reach further by joining forces with a small and intensely ideological group of like-minded political allies, many of whose personal fortunes were also unfathomably large. This faction hoped to use their wealth to advance a strain of conservative libertarian politics that was so far out on the political fringe as recently as 1980, when David Koch ran for vice president of the United States on the Libertarian Party ticket, it received only 1 percent of the American vote. At the time, the conservative icon William F. Buckley Jr. dismissed their views as "Anarcho-Totalitarianism."

The Kochs failed at the ballot box in 1980, but instead of accepting America's verdict, they set out to change how it voted. They used their fortune to impose their minority views on the majority by other means. In the years since they were trounced at the polls, they poured hundreds of millions of dollars into a stealthy effort to move their political views from the fringe to the center of American political life. With the same foresight and perseverance with which they invested in their businesses, they funded and built a daunting national political machine. As far back as 1976, Charles Koch, who was trained as an engineer, began planning a movement that could sweep the country. As a former member of the John Birch Society, he had a radical goal. In 1978, he declared, "Our *movement* must destroy the prevalent statist paradigm."

To this end, the Kochs waged a long and remarkable battle of ideas. They subsidized networks of seemingly unconnected think tanks and academic programs and spawned advocacy groups to make their arguments in the national political debate. They hired lobbyists to push their interests in Congress and operatives to create synthetic grassroots groups to give their movement political momentum on the ground. In addition, they financed legal groups and judicial junkets to press their cases in the courts. Eventually, they added to this a private political machine that rivaled, and threatened to subsume, the Republican Party. Much of this activism was cloaked in secrecy and presented as philanthropy, leaving almost no money trail that the public could trace. But cumulatively it formed, as one of their operatives boasted in 2015, a "*fully integrated network*."

The Kochs were unusually single-minded, but they were not alone. They were among a small, rarefied group of hugely wealthy, archconservative families that for decades poured money, often with little public disclosure, into influencing how Americans thought and voted. Their efforts began in earnest during the second half of the twentieth century. In addition to the Kochs, this group included Richard Mellon Scaife, an heir to the Mellon banking and Gulf Oil fortunes; Harry and Lynde Bradley, midwesterners enriched by defense contracts; John M. Olin, a chemical and munitions company titan; the Coors brewing family of Colorado; and the DeVos family of Michigan, founders of the Amway marketing empire. Each was different, but together they formed a new generation of philanthropists, bent on using billions of dollars from their private foundations to alter the direction of American politics.

When these donors began their quest to remake America along the lines of their beliefs, their ideas were, if anything, considered marginal. They challenged the widely accepted post–World War II consensus that an activist government was a force for public good. Instead, they argued for "limited government," drastically lower personal and corporate taxes, minimal social services for the needy, and much less oversight of industry, particularly in the environmental arena. They said they were driven by principle, but their positions dovetailed seamlessly with their personal financial interests.

By Ronald Reagan's presidency, their views had begun to gain more traction. For the most part, they were still seen as defining the extreme edge of the right wing, but both the Republican Party and much of the country were trending their way. Conventional wisdom often attributed the rightward march to a public backlash against liberal spending programs. But an additional explanation, less examined, was the impact of this small circle of billionaire donors.

Of course rich patrons on both sides of the ideological spectrum had long wielded disproportionate power in American politics. George Soros, a billionaire investor who underwrote liberal organizations and candidates, was often singled out for criticism by conservatives. But the Kochs in particular set a new standard. As Charles Lewis, the founder of the Center for Public Integrity, a nonpartisan watchdog group, put it, "The Kochs are on a whole different level. There's no one else who has spent this much money. The sheer dimension of it is what sets them apart. They have a pattern of lawbreaking, political manipulation, and obfuscation. I've been in Washington since

Watergate, and I've never seen anything like it. They are the Standard Oil of our times."

By the time Barack Obama was elected president, the billionaire brothers' operation had become more sophisticated. By persuading an expanding, handpicked list of other wealthy conservatives to "invest" with them, they had in effect, created a private political bank. It was this group of donors that gathered at the Renaissance. Most, like the Kochs, were businessmen with vast personal fortunes that placed them not just in the top 1 percent of the nation's wealthiest citizens but in a more rarefied group, the top 0.1 percent or higher. By most standards, they were extraordinarily successful. But for this cohort, Obama's election represented a galling setback.

During the previous eight years of Republican rule, this conservative corporate elite had consolidated its power, amassing enormous sway over the U.S. government's regulatory and tax laws. Some in this group faulted President Bush for not having been conservative enough. But having molded policy to serve their interests during the Bush years, many members of this caste had accumulated phenomenal wealth and regarded the newly elected Democratic president as a direct threat to all they had gained. Participants feared they were seeing not just the passing of eight years of Republican dominance but the end of a political order, one that they believed had immeasurably benefited both the country and themselves.

In the 2008 election, Republicans had been defeated up and down the ballot. Democrats had not only recaptured the White House but held majorities in both houses of Congress. The 2008 election hadn't just been a disappointment. It was a complete rout. "They'd just gotten blown out. The question was whether they could survive at all," recalled Bill Burton, former deputy press secretary to President Obama. John Podesta, the liberal political activist who later became Obama's senior adviser, recalled that in the early days after the election "there was a sense of triumphalism, that Bush had crapped out, that he'd be Hoover and Obama would be Franklin Roosevelt and dominate. There was a feeling that the pendulum had swung and a new progressive era had begun. Bush's poll ratings were below those of Nixon! There had been a complete failure of his economic and foreign policy ideas. There was a sense of 'How can we blow it?'"

Exacerbating conservatives' sense of political peril, the economy was in the most vertiginous free fall since the Great Depression of the 1930s. The day that Obama was inaugurated, the stock market had plummeted on fresh doubts about the viability of the nation's banks, with the Standard & Poor's 500 stock index shedding more than 5 percent of its value and the Dow Jones Industrial Average plunging by 4 percent. The continuing economic collapse had laid waste not just to some conservatives' portfolios but also to their belief system. The notion that markets are infallible, a fundamental tenet of libertarian conservatism, looked like a folly. Free-market advocates saw their entire ideological movement in peril. Even some Republicans had become doubters. The retired general Colin Powell, for instance, a veteran of both Bush administrations, argued that "Americans are looking for more government in their life, not less." *Time* magazine captured the zeitgeist by emblazoning a Republican elephant on its cover under the headline "Endangered Species."

Charles Koch himself described Obama's election in almost apocalyptic terms, sending an impassioned newsletter to his company's seventy thousand employees earlier that January declaring that America faced "the greatest loss of liberty and prosperity since the 1930s." Fearing a liberal resurgence of federal spending, he told his employees that more government programs and regulation were exactly the wrong approach to the deepening recession. "It is markets, not government, that can provide the strongest engine for growth, lifting us out of these troubling times," he insisted.

Obama's inaugural address lived up to his worst dreams. The freshly sworn-in president all but declared war on the notion that markets work best when government regulates them least. "Without a watchful eye, the market can spin out of control," Obama warned. Then, sounding almost as if he were taking aim directly at corporate plutocrats like those gathered in Indian Wells, Obama declared that "the nation cannot prosper long when it favors only the prosperous."

It was against this threatening political backdrop that Charles Koch mustered what a fellow conservative, Craig Shirley, described as "the mercantile Right" to take back, and if possible take over, American politics. Obama's election added urgency to the mission, but the gathering in Indian Wells was not a first for the Kochs. Charles and his brother David had been quietly sponsoring similar sessions for conservative donors twice a year since 2003. The enterprise started small but exploded as antagonism toward Obama built among the 0.01 percent on the right.

While they largely hid their ambitious enterprise from the public, avoiding all but the minimum legally required financial disclosures, the Kochs portrayed their political philanthropy inside their circle as a matter of noblesse oblige. "If not us, who? If not now, when?" Charles Koch asked in the invitation to one such donor summit, paraphrasing the call to arms of the ancient Hebrew scholar Rabbi Hillel. "It was obvious we were headed for disaster," Koch later told the conservative writer Matthew Continetti, explaining his plan. The idea was to gather other free-market enthusiasts and organize them as a pressure group. The first seminar in 2003 attracted only fifteen people.

One former insider in the Kochs' realm, who declined to be named because he feared retribution, described the early donor summits as a clever means devised by Charles Koch to enlist others to pay for political fights that helped his company's bottom line. The seminars were, in essence, an extension of the company's corporate lobbying. They were staffed and organized by Koch employees and largely treated as a corporate project. Of particular importance to the Kochs, he said, was drumming up support from other business leaders for their environmental fights. The Kochs vehemently opposed the government taking any action on climate change that would hurt their fossil fuel profits. But suddenly in January 2009, these narrow concerns were overshadowed. Obama's election stirred such deep and widespread fear among the conservative business elite that the conference was swarmed, becoming a hub of political resistance. The planners were all but overwhelmed. "Suddenly they were leading the parade!" he said. "No one anticipated that."

By 2009, the Kochs had indeed succeeded in expanding their political conference from a wonky free-market swap fest to the point where it was beginning to attract an impressive array of influential figures. Wealthy businessmen thronged to rub shoulders with famous and powerful speakers, like the Supreme Court justices Antonin Scalia and Clarence Thomas. Congressmen, senators, governors, and media celebrities came too. "Getting an invitation means you've arrived," one operative who still works for the Kochs explained. "People want to be in the room."

The amount of money raised at the summits was also increasingly eye-catching. Earlier businessmen had certainly spent outsized sums in hopes of manipulating American politics, but the numbers at the Koch seminars far outstripped those in the past. As *The Washington Post*'s Dan Balz observed,

"When W. Clement Stone, an insurance magnate and philanthropist, gave $2 million to Richard M. Nixon's 1972 campaign, it caused public outrage and contributed to a movement that produced the post-Watergate reforms in campaign financing." Accounting for inflation, Balz estimated that Stone's $2 million might be worth about $11 million in today's dollars. In contrast, for the 2016 election, the political war chest accumulated by the Kochs and their small circle of friends was projected to be $889 million, completely dwarfing the scale of money that was considered deeply corrupt during the Watergate days.

The clout of the participants at the retreats served to burnish the Kochs' reputations, conferring a new aura of respectability on their extreme libertarian political views, which many had dismissed in the past as far outside the mainstream. "We're not a bunch of radicals running around and saying strange things," David Koch proudly told Continetti. "Many of these people are very successful, and occupy very important, respected positions in their communities!"

Exactly who attended the January 2009 summit, the first of the Obama era, and what transpired inside the resort can only be partly pieced together because the guest list, like many other aspects of the Kochs' political and business affairs, was shrouded in secrecy. As one Republican campaign consultant who has worked for the Kochs in the past said of the family's political activities, "To call them under the radar is an understatement. They are underground!"

Participants at the summits, for instance, were routinely admonished to destroy all copies of any paperwork. "Be mindful of the security and confidentiality of your meeting notes and materials," the invitation to one such gathering warned. Guests were told to say nothing to the news media and to post nothing about the meetings online. Elaborate security steps were taken to keep both the names of the participants and the meetings' agendas from public scrutiny. When signing up to attend the conferences, participants were warned to make all arrangements through the Kochs' staff, rather than trusting the employees at the resort, whose backgrounds were nonetheless investigated by the Kochs' security detail. In an effort to detect intruders and impostors, name tags were required at all functions, and smartphones, iPads, cameras, and other recording gear were confiscated prior to sessions. In order to foil eavesdroppers during one such gathering, audio technicians planted white-noise-emitting loudspeakers around the perimeters, aimed outward toward any uninvited press and public. It went without saying that breaches of this secrecy would result in excommunication from future meetings. When a breach did occur, the Kochs launched an intense weeklong internal investigation to identify and plug the leak. The donations raised at the summits were not publicly disclosed, nor were the names of the donors, although the planners' hope was that the money would have a decisive impact on the nation's affairs. "There is anonymity that we can protect," Kevin Gentry, vice president for special projects at Koch Industries and vice president of the Charles G. Koch Charitable Foundation, reassured the donors at one summit while soliciting their cash, according to a recording that later leaked out.

In case anyone misunderstood the seriousness of the enterprise, Charles Koch emphasized in one invitation that "fun in the sun" was not "our ultimate goal." Golf games and gondola rides were fine for after hours, but breakfast discussions would start bright and early. He reminded the invitees, "This is a gathering of *doers*."

No fewer than eighteen billionaires would be among the "doers" joining the Kochs' clandestine opposition movement during the first term of Obama's presidency. Ignoring the mere millionaires in attendance, many of whose fortunes were estimated to be worth hundreds of millions of dollars, the combined fortunes of the eighteen known billionaire participants alone as of 2015 topped $214 billion. In fact more billionaires participated anonymously in the Koch planning sessions during the first term of the Obama presidency than existed in 1982, when *Forbes* began listing the four hundred richest Americans.

The participants at the Koch seminars reflected the broader growth in economic inequality in the country, which had reached the level of the Gilded Age in the 1890s. The gap between the top 1 percent of earners in America and everyone else had grown so wide by 2007 that the top 1 percent of the population owned 35 percent of the nation's private assets and was pocketing almost a quarter of all earnings, up from just 9 percent twenty-five years earlier. Liberal critics, like the *New York Times* columnist Paul Krugman, a Nobel Prize–winning economist, worried that the country was in danger of being transformed from a democracy into a plutocracy, or worse, an oligarchy like Russia, where a handful of extraordinarily powerful businessmen bent the government into catering to them at the expense of everyone else. "We are on the road not just to a highly unequal society, but to a society of an oligarchy. A society of inherited wealth," Krugman warned. "When you have a few people who are so wealthy that they can effectively buy the political system, the political system is going to tend to serve their interests."

The term "oligarchy" was provocative and might have seemed an exaggeration to those accustomed to thinking of oligarchs as despotic rulers who were incompatible with democracies like the United States. But Jeffrey Winters, a professor at Northwestern University specializing in the comparative study of oligarchies, was one of a growing number of voices who were beginning to argue that America was a "civil oligarchy" in which a tiny and extremely wealthy slice of the population was able to use its vastly superior economic position to promote a brand of politics that served first and foremost itself. The oligarchs in America didn't rule directly, he argued, but instead used their fortunes to produce political results that favored their interests. As the left-leaning Columbia University professor Joseph Stiglitz, a Nobel Prize–winning economist, put it, "Wealth begets power, which begets more wealth."

For years, American economists had tended to downplay the importance of economic inequality in the country, arguing that its growth was simply the inevitable result of huge and unavoidable shifts in the global economy. Over time, they suggested, extreme inequality would naturally stabilize, and a rising tide would lift all boats. What mattered most, free-market advocates argued, was not equality of results but rather equality of opportunity. As the conservative Nobel Prize–winning economist Milton Friedman wrote, "A society that puts equality—in the sense of equality of outcome—ahead of freedom will end up with neither equality nor freedom . . . On the other hand, a society that puts freedom first will, as a happy by-product, end up with both greater freedom and greater equality."

In the new millennium, however, this consensus was beginning to fray. A growing number of academics studying the nexus of politics and wealth regarded the accelerating inequality in America as a threat not only to the economy but to democracy. Thomas Piketty, an economist at the Paris School of Economics, warned in his zeitgeist-shifting book, *Capital in the Twenty-First Century,* that without aggressive government intervention economic inequality in the United States and elsewhere was likely to rise inexorably, to the point where the small portion of the population that currently held a growing slice of the world's wealth would in the foreseeable future own not just a quarter, or a third, but perhaps half of the globe's wealth, or more. He predicted that the fortunes of those with great wealth, and their inheritors, would increase at a faster rate of return than the rate at which wages would grow, creating what he called "patrimonial capitalism." This dynamic, he predicted, would widen the growing chasm between the haves and the have-nots to levels mimicking the aristocracies of old Europe and banana republics.

Some argued that an elite minority was also driving extreme political partisanship as its interests and agenda lost touch with the economic realities faced by the rest of the population. Mike Lofgren, a Republican who spent thirty years observing how wealthy interests gamed the policy-making apparatus in Washington, where he was a staff member on the Senate Budget Committee, decried what he called the "secession" of the rich in which they "disconnect themselves from the civic life of the nation and from any concern about its well-being except as a place to extract loot." America, as Jacob Hacker and Paul Pierson described it, had become a "winner-take-all" country in which economic inequality perpetuated itself by pressing its political advantage. If so, the Koch seminars provided a group portrait of the winners' circle.

Only one full guest list of attendants at any of the Koch summits has surfaced publicly. It was for a session in June 2010. Like Mrs. Astor's famous 400, which defined the top bracket of New York society in the late nineteenth century on the basis of those who could fit into the Astors' ballroom, the Kochs' donor list provides another portrait of a fortunate social subset. They were mostly businessmen; very few were women. Fewer still were nonwhite. And while some had made their own fortunes, many others were intent on preserving vast legacies they had inherited. While those attracted to the Kochs' meetings were uniformly conservative, they were not the predictable cartoon villains of conspiracy theories but spanned a wide range of views and often disagreed among themselves about social and international issues. The glue that bound them together, however, was antipathy toward government regulation and taxation, particularly as it impinged on their own accumulation of wealth. Unsurprisingly, given the shift in the way great fortunes were made by the end of the twentieth century, instead of railroad magnates and steel barons who had ruled in the Astors' day, the largest number of participants came from the finance sector.

Among the better-known financiers who participated or sent representatives to Koch donor summits during Obama's first term were Steven A. Cohen, Paul Singer, and Stephen Schwarzman. All might have been principled philosophical conservatives, with no ulterior motives, but all also had personal reasons to fear a more assertive federal government, as was expected from Obama.

Cohen's spectacularly successful hedge fund, SAC Capital Advisors, was at the time the focus of an intense criminal investigation into insider trading. Prosecutors described his firm, which was based in Stamford, Connecticut, as "a veritable magnet of market cheaters." *Forbes* valued Cohen's fortune at one point at $10.3 billion, making his checkbook a formidable political weapon.

Paul Singer, whose fortune *Forbes* estimated at $1.9 billion, ran the hugely lucrative hedge fund Elliott Management. Dubbed a vulture fund by critics, it was controversial for buying distressed debt in economically failing countries at a discount and then taking aggressive legal action to force the strapped nations, which had expected their loans to be forgiven, to instead pay him back at a profit. Although Singer insisted that he didn't buy debt from the poorest of the poor nations, his methods, while highly lucrative, brought public scorn and government scrutiny. Even New York's tabloid newspapers chimed in. After Singer supported the campaign of the former New York mayor Rudolph Giuliani, a July 2007 *New York Post* story was headlined "Rudy's 'Vulture' $$ Man" with the subhead "Profits Off Poor." Singer described himself as a Goldwater free-enterprise conservative, and he contributed gene
to promoting free-market ideology, but at the same ti
firm reportedly sought unusual government help in squ

several desperately impoverished governments, a contradiction that applied to many participants in the Koch donor network.

Stephen Schwarzman, who was in general less of a political activist than Singer, might have first become involved in the Kochs' political enterprise out of happenstance. In 2000, he paid $37 million for the palatial triplex that had previously belonged to John D. Rockefeller Jr. at 740 Park Avenue, the same Manhattan co-op building in which David Koch bought an apartment three years later. By the time Obama was elected, Schwarzman had become something of a poster boy for Wall Street excess. As Chrystia Freeland writes in her book *Plutocrats,* the June 21, 2007, initial public offering of stock in Blackstone, his phenomenally successful private equity company, "marked the date when America's plutocracy had its coming-out party." By the end of the day, Schwarzman had made $677 million from selling shares, and he retained additional shares then valued at $7.8 billion.

Schwarzman's stunning payday made a huge and not entirely favorable impression in Washington. Soon after, Democrats began criticizing the carried-interest tax loophole and other accounting gimmicks that helped financiers amass so much wealth. In the wake of the 2008 market crash, as Obama and the Democrats began talking increasingly about Wall Street reforms, financiers like Schwarzman, Cohen, and Singer who flocked to the Koch seminars had much to lose.

The hedge fund run by another of the Kochs' major investors, Robert Mercer, an eccentric computer scientist who made a fortune using sophisticated mathematical algorithms to trade stocks, also seemed a possible government target. Democrats in Congress were considering imposing a tax on stock trading, which the firm he co-chaired, Renaissance Technologies, did in massive quantities. Although those familiar with his thinking maintained that his political activism was separate from his pecuniary interests, Mercer had additional business reasons to be antigovernment. The IRS was investigating whether his firm improperly avoided paying billions of dollars in taxes, a charge the firm denied. Employment laws, too, would prove an embarrassing headache to him; three domestic servants soon sued him for refusing to pay overtime and maintained that he had docked their wages unfairly for infractions such as failing to replace shampoo bottles from his bathrooms when they were less than one-third full. The tabloid news stories about the case invariably mentioned that Mercer had previously brought a suit of his own, suing a toy-train manufacturer for overbilling him by $2 million for an elaborate electric train set he had installed in his Long Island, New York, mansion. With a pay package of $125 million in 2011, Mercer was ranked by *Forbes* as the sixteenth-highest-paid hedge fund manager that year.

Other financiers active in the Koch group had additional legal problems. Ken Langone, the billionaire co-founder of Home Depot, was enmeshed in a prolonged legal fight over his decision as chairman of the compensation committee of the New York Stock Exchange to pay his friend Dick Grasso, the head of the exchange, $139.5 million. The sum was so scandalously large that it forced Grasso to resign. Angry at his critics, Langone reportedly felt that "if it wasn't for us fat cats and the endowments we fund, every university in the country would be fucked."

Another Koch seminar goer from the financial sector, Richard Strong, founder of the mutual fund Strong Capital Management, was banned from the financial industry for life in a settlement following an investigation by the former New York attorney general Eliot Spitzer into his improperly timing trades to benefit his friends and family. Strong paid a $60 million fine and publicly apologized. His company paid an additional $115 million in related penalties. But after Strong sold his company's assets to Wells Fargo, the Associated Press reported that he would be "an even wealthier man."

Many participants in the Koch summits were brilliant leaders not only in business but also in tax avoidance. For instance, the Colorado oil and entertainment billionaire Philip Anschutz, a founder of Qwest Communications, whom *Fortune* magazine dubbed America's "greediest executive" in 2002, was fighting an uphill battle on a tax matter that practically required an accounting degree to explain. Anschutz, a conservative Christian who bankrolled movies with biblical themes, had attempted to avoid paying capital gains taxes in a 2000–2001 transaction by using what are called prepaid variable forward contracts. These contracts allow wealthy shareholders such as Anschutz, whose fortune *Forbes* estimated at $11.8 billion as of 2015, to promise to give shares to investment firms at a later date, in exchange for cash up front. Because the stock does not immediately change hands, capital gains taxes are not paid. According to *The New York Times,* Anschutz raised $375 million in 2000–2001 by promising shares in his oil and natural gas companies through the firm Donaldson, Lufkin & Jenrette.

Eventually, the court sided against Anschutz on something of a technicality. The former *Times* reporter David Cay Johnston wrote that in essence the court had ruled that "prepaids done slightly differently than the Anschutz transactions will survive. But why should they?" he asked. "Why should anyone get to enjoy cash from gains now without paying taxes?" Johnston concluded, "The awful truth is that America has two income tax systems, separate and unequal. One system is for the superrich, like Anschutz and his wife, Nancy, who are allowed to delay and avoid taxes on investment gains, among other tax tricks. The other system is for the less than fabulously wealthy."

Some donor families had clearly committed tax crimes. Richard DeVos, co-founder of Amway, the Michigan-based worldwide multilevel marketing empire, had pleaded guilty to a criminal scheme in which he had defrauded the Canadian government of $22 million in customs duties in 1982. DeVos later claimed it had been a misunderstanding, but the record showed the company had engaged in an elaborate, deliberate hoax in an effort to hoodwink Canadian authorities. He and his co-founder, Jay Van Andel, were forced to pay a $20 million fine. The fine didn't make much of a dent in DeVos's fortune, which *Forbes* estimated at $5.7 billion. By 2009, DeVos's son Dick and daughter-in-law Betsy were major donors on the Koch list and facing a record $5.2 million civil fine of their own for violating Ohio's campaign-finance laws.

Energy magnates were also heavily represented in the Koch network. Many of this group too had significant government regulatory and environmental issues. The "extractive" industries, oil, gas, and mining, tend to be run by some of the most outspoken opponents of government regulation in the country, yet all rely considerably on government permits, regulations, and tax laws to aid their profits and frequently to give them access to public lands. Executives from at least twelve oil and gas companies, in addition to the Kochs, were participants in the group. Collectively, they had a huge interest in staving off any government action on climate change and weakening environmental safeguards. One prominent member of this group was Corbin Robertson Jr., whose family had built a billion-dollar oil company, Quintana Resources Capital. Robertson had bet big on coal—so big he reportedly owned what *Forbes* called the "largest private hoard in the nation—21 billion tons of reserves." Investigative reports linked Robertson to several political front groups fighting efforts by the Environmental Protection Agency (EPA) to control pollution emitted by coal-burning utilities. Almost comically, one such front group was called Plants Need CO_2.

Another coal magnate active in the Kochs' donor network was Richard Gilliam, head of the Virginia mining concern Cumberland Resources. The dire stakes surrounding the sinking coal industry's regulatory fights were evident in the 2010 sale of Cumberland for nearly $1 billion to Massey Energy, just weeks before a tragic explosion in Massey's Upper Big Branch mine killed twenty-nine miners, becoming the worst coal mine disaster in forty years. A government investigation into Massey found it negligent on multiple safety fronts, and a federal grand jury indicted its CEO, Don Blankenship, for conspiring to violate and impede federal mine safety standards, making him the first coal baron to face criminal charges. Later, Massey was bought for $7.1 billion by Alpha Natural Resources, whose CEO, Kevin Crutchfield, was yet another member of the Koch network.

Several spectacularly successful leaders of hydraulic fracturing, who had their own set of government grievances, were also on the Kochs' list. The revolutionary method of extracting gas from shale revived the American energy business but alarmed environmentalists. Among the "frackers" in the group were J. Larry Nichols, co-founder of the huge Oklahoma-based concern Devon Energy, and Harold Hamm, whose company, Continental Resources, was the biggest operator in North Dakota's booming Bakken Shale. As Hamm, a sharecropper's son, took his place as the thirty-seventh-richest person in America with a fortune that *Forbes* estimated at $8.2 billion as of 2015, and campaigned to preserve tax loopholes for oil producers, his company gained notoriety for a growing record of environmental and workplace safety violations.

One shared characteristic of many of the donors in the Kochs' network was private ownership of their businesses, placing them in a low-profile category that *Fortune* once dubbed "the invisible rich." Private ownership gave these magnates far more managerial latitude and limited public disclosures, shielding them from stockholder scrutiny. Many of the donors had nonetheless attracted unwanted legal scrutiny by the government.

It was, in fact, striking how many members of the Koch network had serious past or ongoing legal problems. Sheldon Adelson, founding chairman and chief executive of the Las

Vegas Sands Corporation, the world's largest gambling company, whose fortune *Forbes* estimated at $31.4 billion, was facing a bribery investigation by the Justice Department into whether his company had violated the Foreign Corrupt Practices Act in securing licenses to operate casinos in Macao.

The Kochs had looming worries about the Foreign Corrupt Practices Act, too. As Bloomberg News later revealed, the company's record of illicit payments in Algeria, Egypt, India, Morocco, Nigeria, and Saudi Arabia was spilling out in a French court. Further, in the summer of 2008, just a few months before Obama was elected, federal officials had questioned the company about sales to Iran, in violation of the U.S. trade ban against the state for sponsoring terrorism.

Meanwhile, another donor, Oliver Grace Jr., a relation of the family that founded the William R. Grace Company, was at the center of a stock-backdating scandal that resulted in his being ousted from the board of Take-Two, the company behind the ultraviolent *Grand Theft Auto* video games.

The legal problems of Richard Farmer, the chairman of the Cincinnati-based Cintas Corporation, the nation's largest uniform supply company, included an employee's gruesome death. Just before the new and presumably less business-friendly Obama administration took office, Cintas reached a record $2.76 million settlement with the Occupational Safety and Health Administration (OSHA) in six safety citations including one involving a worker who had burned to death in an industrial dryer. The employee, a Hispanic immigrant, had become caught on a conveyor belt leading into the heat source. Prior to the fatal accident, OSHA had cited Cintas for over 170 safety violations since 2003, including 70 that regulators warned could cause "death or serious physical harm." As Obama took office, the company was still fighting against paying a damage claim to the employee's widow and arguing that his death had been his own fault. Farmer, too, ranked among the Koch group's billionaire donors, with a fortune that *Forbes* estimated at $2 billion.

Given the participants' unanimous espousal of antigovernment, free-market self-reliance, the network also included a surprising number of major government contractors, such as Stephen Bechtel Jr., whose personal fortune *Forbes* estimated at $2.8 billion. Bechtel was a director and retired chairman of the huge and internationally powerful engineering firm Bechtel Corporation, founded by his grandfather, run by his father, and, after he retired, by his son and grandson. Paternalistic and family-owned, Bechtel was the sixth-largest private company in the country, and it owed almost its entire existence to government patronage. It had built the Hoover Dam, among other spectacular public projects, and had storied access to the innermost national security circles. Between 2000 and 2009 alone, it had received $39.2 billion in U.S. government contracts. This included $680 million to rebuild Iraq following the U.S. invasion.

Like so many of the other companies owned by the Koch donors, Bechtel had government legal problems. In 2007, a report by the special inspector general for Iraq reconstruction accused Bechtel of shoddy work. And in 2008, the company paid a $352 million fine to settle unrelated charges of substandard work in Boston's notorious "Big Dig" tunnel project. The company was facing congressional reproach too for cost overruns in the multibillion-dollar cleanup of the Hanford nuclear facility in Washington State.

Antagonism toward the government ran so high within the Koch network that one donor angrily objected to federal interference not just in his business but on behalf of his own safety as well. Thomas Stewart, who built his father's Seattle-based food business into the behemoth Services Group of America, reportedly loved flying in his helicopter and corporate jet. But when a former company pilot refused to take his aeronautic advice because it violated Federal Aviation Administration regulations, according to an interview with the pilot in the *Seattle Post-Intelligencer,* Stewart "rose out of his chair, and screamed, 'I can do any fucking thing I want!'"

The highlight of the Koch summit in 2009 was an uninhibited debate about what conservatives should do next in the face of their electoral defeat. As the donors and other guests dined in the hotel's banquet room, like Roman senators attending a gladiator duel in the Forum, they watched a passionate argument unfold that encapsulated the stark choice ahead. Sitting on one side of a stage, facing the participants, was the Texas senator John Cornyn, the head of the National Republican Senatorial Committee and a former justice on the Texas Supreme Court. Tall, with a high pink forehead, puffy cotton-white hair, and a taste for dark pin-striped suits, his image conveyed his role as a pillar of the establishment wing of the Republican Party. Cornyn was rated as the second-most conservative Republican in the Senate, according to the nonpartisan *National Journal.* But he also was, as one former aide put it, "very much a constitutionalist" who believed it was occasionally necessary in politics to compromise.

Poised on the other side of the moderator was the South Carolina senator Jim DeMint, a conservative provocateur who defined the outermost antiestablishment fringe of the Republican Party and who in the words of one admirer was "the leader of the Huns." Fifty-seven at the time, he was five months older than Cornyn, but his dark hair, lean build, and more casual, aw-shucks style made him appear years younger. Before his election to Congress, DeMint had run an advertising agency in South Carolina. He understood how to sell, and what he was pitching that night was an approach to politics that according to the historian Sean Wilentz would have been recognizable to DeMint's forebears from the Palmetto State as akin to the radical nullification of federal power advocated in the 1820s by the slavery defender John C. Calhoun.

The two Republican senators had been at loggerheads for some time. That night they gave opposing opening statements. Cornyn spoke in favor of the Republican Party fighting its way back to victory by broadening its appeal to a wider swath of voters, including moderates. "He understands that Republicans in Texas and in Maine aren't necessarily exactly alike," the former aide explained. "He believes in making the party a big tent. You can't win unless you get more votes."

In contrast, DeMint portrayed compromise as surrender. He had little patience for the slow-moving process of constitutional government. He regarded many of his Senate colleagues as timid and self-serving. The federal government posed such a dire threat to the dynamism of the American economy, in his view, that anything less than all-out war on regulations and spending was a cop-out. DeMint was the face of a new kind of extremism, and he spoke that evening in favor of purifying, rather than diluting, the Republican Party. He argued that he would rather have "thirty Republicans who believed in something than a majority who believed in nothing," a line that was a mantra for him and that brought cheers and applause from the gathered onlookers. Rather than compromising their principles and working with the new administration, DeMint argued, Republicans needed to take a firm stand against Obama, waging a campaign of massive resistance and obstruction, regardless of the 2008 election outcome.

As the participants continued to cheer him on, in his folksy, southern way, DeMint tore into Cornyn over one issue in particular. He accused Cornyn of turning his back on conservative free-market principles and capitulating to the worst kind of big government spending, with his vote earlier that fall in favor of the Treasury Department's massive bailout of failing banks. The September 15, 2008, failure of Lehman Brothers, one of the nation's largest investment banks, had triggered a stunning run on financial institutions and the beginning of a generalized panic. The Federal Reserve chairman, Ben Bernanke, warned congressional leaders that "it is a matter of days before there is a meltdown in the global financial system." In hopes of staving off economic disaster, Bush's Treasury Department begged Congress to approve the massive $700 billion emergency bailout known as the Troubled Asset Relief Program, or TARP.

Both Obama and the Republican presidential nominee, John McCain, supported the emergency measure in the run-up to the 2008 election. But ever since, outraged opposition to the bailouts had built both from the public and from anti-government, free-market conservatives like DeMint. Having expected a gentlemanly debate over the future of the Republican Party, Cornyn suddenly found himself on the defensive as the donors jeered and the moderator, Stephen Moore, a free-market gadfly and contributor to *The Wall Street Journal*'s editorial page, egged them on. The room started to explode. Rebuking Cornyn, one donor, Randy Kendrick, said, "You just keep electing RINOs!"—invoking the slur that Moore was said to have coined for squishy moderates who were, in his phrase, "Republicans in Name Only."

Sitting silently at a table in the front row through all of this were Charles Koch and his wife, Liz. No one came to Cornyn's defense. It was widely assumed that the Kochs, as hard-core free-market enthusiasts, had opposed the huge government bailouts of the private sector. Later, many reporters assumed this too, ascribing the Kochs' opposition to Obama as stemming from their principled disagreement over issues such as the TARP bailouts. But none of this was true. Had people checked the record carefully, they would have found it quite revealing. At first, the Kochs' political organization, Americans for Prosperity (AFP), had in fact taken what appeared to be a principled libertarian position against the bailouts. But the organization quickly and quietly reversed sides when the bottom began to fall out of the stock market, threatening the Kochs' vast investment portfolio. The market began to collapse on Monday, September 29, when, in the face of heavy opposition from conservatives, the House unexpectedly failed to pass the federal rescue plan. By the end of the day, the Dow Jones Industrial Average had fallen 777 points, losing 6.98 percent of its value. It was the stock market's largest one-day point drop ever.

Although some conservative groups and politicians such as DeMint still opposed the bailout, the market panic was enough to change many minds. Among those who flipped during the next forty-eight hours were the Kochs. Two days after the unexpected House vote, as the measure was about to be considered by the Senate, a list of conservative groups now supporting the bailouts was circulated behind the scenes to Republican legislators, in hopes of persuading them to vote for the bailouts. Among the groups now listed as supporters was Americans for Prosperity. Soon after, the Senate passed TARP with overwhelming bipartisan support, including that of John Cornyn. A source familiar with the Kochs' thinking says that Americans for Prosperity's flip-flop mirrored their own.

But if the Kochs' personal interest in protecting their portfolio had trumped their free-market principles, they weren't about to mention it in front of a roomful of fired-up libertarians whose cash they wanted to combat Obama. So, although they could have changed the dynamic in the room instantly by speaking up, no one defended Cornyn or the idea of acting responsibly within the bounds of traditional, reasonable political opposition.

Instead, the sentiment among the donors as the first Koch seminar of the Obama era came to an end was, as one witness put it, "like a bunch of gorillas beating their chests." After hearing both sides out, the assembled guests chose the path of extremism.

The Kochs had already concluded that they would need

to resort to extraordinary political measures to achieve their goals. A few days before the January 2009 donor seminar, Charles and David Koch had privately weighed their options with their longtime political strategist in a meeting inside the black-glass fortress that served as Koch Industries' corporate headquarters in Wichita, Kansas.

As they later revealed in an interview with Bill Wilson and Roy Wenzl in *The Wichita Eagle,* after hearing Obama's inauguration address, they agreed with their political adviser, Richard Fink, that America was on the road to ruin. Fink reportedly told the billionaire brothers, whose wealth, when combined, put at their disposal the single largest fortune in the world, that if they wanted to beat back the progressive tide that Obama's election represented, it would take "the fight of their lives."

"If we're going to do this, we should do it right, or not at all," Fink said, according to the Wichita newspaper account. "But if we don't do it right, or we don't do it at all, we will be insignificant and we will just waste a lot of time, and I would rather play golf."

If the Kochs decided that they did want "to do it right," however, as Fink put it, they should be prepared, he warned, because "it is going to get very, very ugly."

Advisers to Obama later acknowledged that he had no inkling of what he was up against. He had campaigned as a post-partisan politician who had idealistically taken issue with those who he said "like to slice and dice our country into red states and blue states." He insisted, "We are one people," the United States of America. His vision, like his own blended racial and geographic heredity, was of reconciliation, not division. Echoing these themes in his first inaugural address, Obama had chided "cynics," who, he said, "fail to understand . . . that the ground has shifted beneath them—that the stale political arguments that have consumed us for so long no longer apply."

The sentiment was laudable but, alas, wishful thinking.

Had the newly sworn-in president looked down at the ground directly beneath his polished shoes as he delivered these optimistic words, he might have been wise to take note. The red-and-blue carpet on which he was standing, which had been custom made in accordance with a government contract, had been manufactured by Invista, a subsidiary of Koch Industries. In American politics, the Kochs and all they stood for were not so easy to escape.

Part One

Weaponizing Philanthropy

The War of Ideas, 1970–2008

CHAPTER ONE

Radicals: A Koch Family History

ODDLY ENOUGH, THE FIERCELY LIBERTARIAN KOCH FAMILY owed part of its fortune to two of history's most infamous dictators, Joseph Stalin and Adolf Hitler. The family patriarch, Fred Chase Koch, founder of the family oil business, developed lucrative business relationships with both of their regimes in the 1930s.

According to family lore, Fred Koch was the son of a Dutch printer and publisher who settled in the small town of Quanah, Texas, just south of the Oklahoma border, where he owned a weekly newspaper and print shop. Quanah, which was named for the last American Comanche chief, Quanah Parker, still retained its frontier aura when Fred was born there in 1900. Bright and eager to get out from under his overbearing old-world father, Fred once ran away to live with the Comanches as a boy. Later, he crossed the country for college, transferring from Rice in Texas to attend the Massachusetts Institute of Technology. There, he earned a degree in chemical engineering and joined the boxing team. Early photographs show him as a tall, formally dressed young man with glasses, a tuft of unruly curls, and a self-confident, defiant expression.

In 1927, Fred, who was an inveterate tinkerer, invented an improved process for extracting gasoline from crude oil. But as he would later tell his sons bitterly and often, America's major oil companies regarded him as a business threat and shut him out of the industry, suing him and his customers in 1929 for patent infringement. Koch regarded the monopolistic patents invoked by the major oil companies as anticompetitive and unfair. The fight appears to be an early version of the Kochs' later opposition to "corporate cronyism" in which they contend that the government and big business collaborate unfairly. In Fred Koch's eye, he was an outsider fighting a corrupt system.

Koch fought back in the courts for more than fifteen years, finally winning a $1.5 million settlement. He correctly suspected that his opponents bribed at least one presiding judge, an incompetent lush who left the case in the hands of a crooked clerk. "The fact that the judge was bribed completely altered their view of justice," one longtime family employee suggests. "They believe justice can be bought, and the rules are for chumps." Meanwhile, crippled by lawsuits in America during this period, Koch took his innovative refining method abroad.

He had already helped build a refinery in Great Britain after World War I with Charles de Ganahl, a mentor. At the time, the Russians supplied England with fuel, which led to the Russians seeking his expertise as they set up their own oil refineries after the Bolshevik Revolution.

At first, according to family lore, Koch tore up the telegram from the Soviet Union asking for his help. He said he didn't want to work for Communists and didn't trust them to pay him. But after securing an agreement to get paid in advance, he overcame his philosophical reservations. In 1930, his company, then called Winkler-Koch, began training Russian engineers and helping Stalin's regime set up fifteen modern oil refineries under the first of Stalin's five-year plans. The program was a success, forming the backbone of the future Russian petroleum industry. The oil trade brought crucial hard currency into the Soviet Union, enabling it to modernize other industries. Koch was reportedly paid $500,000, a princely sum during America's Great Depression. But by 1932, facing growing domestic demand, Soviet officials decided it would be more advantageous to copy the technology and build future refineries themselves. Fred Koch continued to provide technical assistance to the Soviets as they constructed one hundred plants, according to one report, but the advisory work was less profitable.

What happened next has been excised from the official corporate history of Koch Industries. After mentioning the company's work in the Soviet Union, the bulk of which ended in 1932, the corporate history skips ahead to 1940, when it says Fred Koch decided to found a new company, Wood River Oil & Refining. Charles Koch is equally vague in his book *The Science of Success*. He notes only that his father's company "enjoyed its first real financial success during the early years of the Great Depression" by "building plants abroad, especially in the Soviet Union."

A controversial chapter is missing. After leaving the U.S.S.R., Fred Koch turned to Adolf Hitler's Third Reich. Hitler became chancellor in 1933, and soon after, his government oversaw and funded massive industrial expansion, including the buildup of Germany's capacity to manufacture fuel for its growing military ambitions. During the 1930s, Fred Koch traveled frequently to Germany on oil business. Archival records document that in 1934 Winkler-Koch Engineering of Wichita, Kansas, as Fred's firm was then known, provided the engineering plans and began overseeing the construction of a massive oil refinery owned by a company on the Elbe River in Hamburg.

The refinery was a highly unusual venture for Koch to get involved with at that moment in Germany. Its top executive was a notorious American Nazi sympathizer named William Rhodes Davis whose extensive business dealings with Hitler would eventually end in accusations by a federal prosecutor that he was an "agent of influence" for the Nazi regime. In 1933, Davis proposed the purchase and conversion of an existing German oil storage facility in Hamburg, owned by a company called Europäische Tanklager A.G., or Eurotank, into a massive refinery. At the time, Hitler's military aims, and his need for more fuel, were already well-known. Davis's plan was to ship crude petroleum to Germany, refine it, and then sell it to the German military. The president of the American bank with which Davis dealt refused to have anything to do with the deal, because it was seen as supporting the Nazi military buildup, but others extended the credit. After lining up the American financing, Davis needed the Third Reich's backing. To gain it, he first had to convince German industrialists of his support for Hitler. In his effort to ingratiate himself, Davis opened an early meeting with Hermann Schmitz, the chairman of I.G. Farben—the powerful and well-connected chemical company that soon after produced the lethal gas for the concentration camps' death chambers—by saluting him with a Nazi "Heil Hitler." When these efforts didn't produce the green light he sought, Davis sent messages directly to Hitler, eventually securing a meeting in which the führer walked in and ordered his henchmen to approve the deal. On Hitler's orders, the Third Reich's economic ministers supported Davis's construction of the refinery. In his biography of Davis, Dale Harrington draws on eyewitness accounts to describe Hitler as declaring to his skeptical henchmen, "Gentlemen, I have reviewed Mr. Davis's proposition and it sounds feasible, and I want the bank to finance it." Harrington writes that during the next few years Davis met at least half a dozen more times with Hitler and on one occasion asked him to personally autograph a copy of *Mein Kampf* for his wife. According to Harrington, by the end of 1933 Davis was "deeply committed to Nazism" and exhibited a noticeable "dislike for Jews."

In 1934, Davis turned to Fred Koch's company, Winkler-Koch, for help in executing his German business plan. Under Fred Koch's direction, the refinery was finished by 1935. With the capacity to process a thousand tons of crude oil a day, the third-largest refinery in the Third Reich was created by the collaboration between Davis and Koch. Significantly, it was also one of the few refineries in Germany, according to Harrington, that could "produce the high-octane gasoline needed to fuel fighter planes. Naturally," he writes, "Eurotank would do most of its business with the German military." Thus, he concludes, the American venture became "a key component of the Nazi war machine."

Historians expert in German industrial history concur. The development of the German fuel industry "was hugely, hugely important" to Hitler's military ambitions, according to the Northwestern University professor Peter Hayes. "Hitler set out to create 'autarchy,' or economic self-sufficiency," he explained. "Gottfried Feder, the German official in charge of the program, reasoned that even though Germany would have to import crude oil, it would be able to save foreign exchange by refining the products itself."

In the run-up to the war, Davis profited richly from the arrangement, engaging in elaborate scams to keep the crude oil imports flowing into Germany despite Britain's blockade. When World War II began, the high-octane fuel was used in bombing raids by German pilots. Like Davis, the Koch family benefited from the venture. Raymond Stokes, director of the Centre for Business History at the University of Glasgow in Scotland and co-author of a history of the German oil industry during the Nazi years, *Faktor Öl* (The oil factor), which documents the company's role, says, "Winkler-Koch benefited directly from this project, which was designed to help enable the fuel policy of the Third Reich."

Fred Koch often traveled to Germany during these years, and according to family lore he was supposed to have been on the fatal May 1937 transatlantic flight of the *Hindenburg,* but at the last minute he got delayed. In late 1938, as World War II approached and Hitler's aims were unmistakable, he wrote admiringly about fascism in Germany, and elsewhere, drawing an invidious comparison with America under Franklin Roosevelt's New Deal. "Although nobody agrees with me, I am of the opinion that the only sound countries in the world are Germany, Italy, and Japan, simply because they are all working and working hard," he wrote in a letter to a friend. Koch added, "The laboring people in those countries are proportion-ately much better off than they are any place else in the world. When you contrast the state of mind of Germany today with what it was in 1925 you begin to think that perhaps this course of idleness, feeding at the public trough, dependence on government, etc., with which we are afflicted is not permanent and can be overcome."

When the United States entered World War II in 1941, family members say that Fred Koch tried to enlist in the U.S. military. Instead, the government directed him to use his chemical engineering prowess to help refine high-octane fuel for the American warplanes. Meanwhile, in an ironic turn, the Hamburg refinery that Winkler-Koch built became an important target of Allied bombing raids. On June 18, 1944, American B-17s finally destroyed it. The human toll of the bombing raids on Hamburg was almost unimaginable. In all, some forty-two thousand civilians were killed during the long and intense Allied campaign against Hamburg's crucial industrial targets.

Fred Koch's willingness to work with the Soviets and the Nazis was a major factor in creating the Koch family's early fortune. By the time he met his future wife, Mary Robinson, at a polo match in 1932, the oilman's work for Stalin had put him well on his way to becoming exceedingly wealthy.

Robinson, a twenty-four-year-old graduate of Wellesley College, was tall, slender, and beautiful, with blond hair, blue eyes, and an expression of amusement often captured in family photographs. The daughter of a prominent physician from Kansas City, Missouri, she had grown up in a more cosmopolitan milieu. Koch, who was seven years older than she, was so smitten he married her a month after they met.

Soon, the couple commissioned the most fashionable architect in the area to build an imposing Gothic-style stone mansion on a large compound on the outskirts of Wichita, Kansas, where Winkler-Koch was based. Reflecting their rising social status, the estate was baronial despite the flat and empty prairie surrounding it, with stables, a polo ring, a kennel for hunting dogs, a swimming pool and wading pool, a circular drive, and stone-terraced gardens. Some of the best craftsmen in the country created decorative flourishes such as wrought-iron railings and a stone fireplace carved with a whimsical snowflake motif. Within a few years, the Kochs also purchased the sprawling Spring Creek Ranch near Reece, Kansas, where Fred, who loved science and genetics, bred and raised cattle. Family photographs show the couple looking glamorous and patrician, hosting picnics and pool parties, and riding on horseback, dressed in jodhpurs and polo gear, surrounded by packs of jolly friends.

In the first eight years of their marriage, the couple had four sons: Frederick, known by the family as Freddie, was born in 1933, Charles was born in 1935, and twins, David and William, were born in 1940. With their father frequently traveling and their mother preoccupied with social and cultural pursuits, the boys were largely entrusted to a series of nannies and housekeepers.

It is unclear what Fred Koch's views of Hitler were during the 1930s, beyond his preference for the country's work ethic in comparison with the nascent welfare state in America. But he was enamored enough of the German way of life and thinking that he employed a German governess for his first two sons, Freddie and Charles. At the time, Freddie was a small boy, and Charles still in diapers. The nanny's iron rule terrified the little boys, according to a family acquaintance. In addition to being overbearing, she was a fervent Nazi sympathizer, who frequently touted Hitler's virtues. Dressed in a starched white uniform and pointed nurse's hat, she arrived with a stash of gruesome German children's books, including the Victorian classic *Der Struwwelpeter,* that featured sadistic consequences for misbehavior ranging from cutting off one child's thumbs to burning another to death. The acquaintance recalled that the nurse had a commensurately harsh and dictatorial approach to child rearing. She enforced a rigid toilet-training regimen requiring the boys to produce morning bowel movements precisely on schedule or be force-fed castor oil and subjected to enemas.

The despised governess ruled the nursery largely unchallenged for several years. In 1938, the two boys were left for months while their parents toured Japan, Burma, India, and the Philippines. Even when she was home, Mary Koch characteristically deferred to her husband, declining to intervene. "My father was fairly tough with my mother," Bill Koch later told *Vanity Fair*. "My mother was afraid of my father." Meanwhile, Fred Koch was often gone for months at a time, in Germany and elsewhere.

It wasn't until 1940, the year the twins were born, when Freddie was seven and Charles five, that back in Wichita the German governess finally left the Koch family, apparently at her own initiative. Her reason for giving notice was that she was so overcome with joy when Hitler invaded France she felt she had to go back to the fatherland in order to join the führer in celebration. What if any effect this early experience with authority had on Charles is impossible to know, but it's interesting that his lifetime preoccupation would become crusading against authoritarianism while running a business over which he exerted absolute control.

Fred Koch was himself a tough and demanding disciplinarian. John Damgard, David's childhood friend, who became president of the Futures Industry Association, recalled that he was "a real John Wayne type." Koch emphasized rugged pursuits, taking his sons big-game hunting in Africa and filling the basement billiard room with what one cousin remembered as a frightening collection of exotic stuffed animal heads, including lions and bears and others with horns and tusks, glinting glassy-eyed from the walls. In the summer, the boys could hear their friends splashing in the pool at the country club across the street, but instead of allowing the boys to join them, their father required them to dig up dandelions by the time they were five, and later to dig ditches and shovel manure at the family ranch. Fred Koch cared about his boys but was determined to keep them from becoming what he called "country-club bums," like some of the other offspring of the oil moguls with whom he was acquainted. "By instilling a work ethic in me at an early age, my father did me a big favor, although it didn't seem like a favor back then," Charles has written. "By the time I was eight, he made sure work occupied most of my spare time."

All four sons later professed admiration and affection for their father, but their fond recollections gloss over a dark streak. Fred Koch's rule was absolute, and his idea of punishment was corporal. He did not just spank the boys for their transgressions. Sometimes he hit them with a belt or worse. One family member remembers seeing him take a tree branch, strip it down, and "whip the twins like dogs." They had marred the stone patio in some way that enraged him. "He was a hard man to love," adds the family member, who declines to be identified. A second family member too remembers the belt beatings. Fred Koch "wasn't around much," he said, but when his sons misbehaved, they "really got it."

Sibling rivalry in the family, which reached epic levels in adulthood, was always intense. Family photographs and films show the brothers fenced in outdoor playpens, grabbing each other's toys, making each other cry, and boxing at early ages with gloves almost as big as their heads. Before long, Charles, the second born, emerged as the domineering leader of the pack. Fiercely competitive, driven, and self-confident, he appeared a paragon of handsome, blond athleticism. One family member recalls that Charles's favorite game was king of the hill. "It hasn't changed," another family member said.

Charles rarely lost, but when he did, he took it badly. When his younger brother Bill defeated him once in a boxing match, according to family lore, Charles refused to ever box again.

It became clear early that Freddie was different from the others, and not of his rough-hewn father's type. He was bookish and oriented toward his artistic mother, preferring to disappear into his room to read while the twins played ball with Charles, who liked to give commands. (Freddie did, however, hold his own against Charles on at least one occasion, punching him so hard in the face he broke his brother's nose.) Charles later told *Fame* magazine, "Father wanted to make all his boys into men and Freddie couldn't relate to that regime." Charles added, "Dad didn't understand and so he was hard on Freddie. He didn't understand that Freddie wasn't a lazy kid—he was just different."

The father was hard on the other boys too. David liked reading and became obsessed for a while with the Wizard of Oz books, which of course are set in Kansas, but his father preferred that he do chores. Increasingly, David attached himself to his elder brother Charles, becoming his sidekick and accomplice, willing to drop everything at his brother's command. "I was closer to David because he was better at everything [than the others]," Charles told *Fame,* bluntly.

Mary Koch recalled that as a result, "Billy always felt that Charles and David were leaving him out." She said that he "had no confidence or self-esteem." The only redhead among the pack, Bill had an explosive temper that resulted in memorable tantrums, including one in which he picked up a priceless antique vase and hurled it to the floor, shattering it. Fred Koch's response was more spanking.

Clayton Coppin, a former associate professor and research historian based at George Mason University, was one of the rare outsiders to the Koch family with firsthand knowledge of its inner workings. In 1993, Koch Industries commissioned him to write a confidential corporate history. For the next six years, Coppin had nearly unlimited access to the private archives in the company's headquarters in Wichita, along with the private papers of Fred and Mary Koch. He also had carte blanche to interview their business associates. After he completed the history in 1999, the company laid Coppin off. Subsequently, in 2002, Bill Koch hired him for a second confidential research project, this time on his brother Charles's political activities. In interviews, Coppin described what he learned about the family while researching the first report and shared a copy of the second report, a lengthy three-part 2003 study titled "Stealth: The History of Charles Koch's Political Activities."

According to Coppin, who read many of Fred Koch's private letters, in 1946, when Freddie was thirteen, his father confided to a family friend that there was a child-rearing crisis at home with which he needed help. Freddie had undergone some kind of emotional turmoil while being forced to labor at the family ranch that summer. The family friend recommended a consultation with Portia Hamilton, a clinical psychologist in New York who specialized in child development, with whom Fred began to correspond. Hamilton met with the family and wrote up an evaluation. The psychologist recommended that the boys be separated and that Mary Koch, who was already busy with social life and travel, further distance herself from them in order to make them more "manly." Psychological theories during that period attributed homosexuality to "over mothering."

As a result, Freddie was sent to Hackley, a prep school in Tarrytown, New York, where he could follow his cultural interests, attending the opera in Manhattan and acting in school productions. Later, he came to feel that Hackley rescued him.

In order to keep him from picking on his brothers, the Kochs sent Charles away to school as well, in his case, at the age of eleven. The school they chose for him was the Southern Arizona School for Boys, renowned for its strictness. His mother made clear that it was done for his younger brother Billy's sake, which only heightened resentments between the boys.

"I pleaded with them not to send me away," Charles told *Fortune* in 1997. Charles did poorly at the boarding school, but instead of yielding to his pleas to come home, the Kochs sent him to an even more rigid boarding school, the Fountain Valley School in Colorado. "I hated all that," Charles recalled. At one point, his parents finally "took pity" on him, he said, and let him attend public high school in Wichita, which he loved, but "I got into trouble," he recalled, so they packed him off to the Culver Military Academy in Indiana, which also emphasized discipline. There, Charles did better academically but repeatedly got into trouble. Eventually, Culver expelled him for drinking on a train (although he was eventually readmitted, enabling him to earn his diploma). "I have a little bit of a rebel, and free spirit in me," Charles later acknowledged. As punishment, Charles's father banished him to live with his relatives in Texas. "Father put the fear of God in him," David later recalled. "He said, 'If you don't make it, you'll be worthless. You've disappointed me.' Father was a severe taskmaster."

In his confidential report for Bill Koch, Coppin wrote, "Charles spent little of the next fifteen years at home, only coming there for an occasional holiday." After he was exiled by the family, "the first thing Charles did when he came home on vacation was to beat up" his younger brother Bill.

Young Bill grew alarmingly depressed. He was socially withdrawn and preoccupied with his sense of inferiority to his twin, David, and his older brother Charles. Soon the twins too were sent to boarding school. Bill, interestingly, chose to follow Charles's footsteps to Culver Military Academy, while David chose the eastern prep school Deerfield Academy. "There was a lot of strife between the boys. Charles was in constant rebellion against authority. It was a miserable childhood," Coppin said in an interview.

Yet later, as a parent, Charles partially repeated the pattern. When his own son, Chase, then thirteen, played a half-hearted tennis match, Charles had an employee pick him up and deliver him to a baking, reeking feedlot on one of the family ranches where he was forced to work seven days a week, twelve hours a day. Charles proudly recounted the story with a grin, telling *The Wichita Eagle,* "I think he thought he'd have a job here in Wichita and could go out with his friends at night." Chase became an exceptionally good tennis player but later had another, more serious problem. While driving as a high school student in Wichita, he ran a red light and fatally injured a twelve-year-old boy. He pleaded guilty to a misdemeanor charge of vehicular manslaughter and was sentenced to eighteen months of probation and a hundred hours of community service and was required to pay for the boy's funeral. After college, Chase, like his father, joined the family company.

Meanwhile, in an online blog, Charles's other child, Elizabeth, a Princeton graduate, described her own efforts to prove herself to her father. Of a visit home, she wrote, "As soon as we arrived I felt an overwhelming urge to prostrate myself on the floor and eat dirt in order to illustrate how grateful I am for everything they've done for me, that I'm not the spoiled monster they warned me I'd become if I wasn't careful." She described "chasing" her father around the house, trying to impress him with her interest in economics, and "staring down that dark well of nothing you do will ever be good enough you privileged waste of flesh."

A generation before, stern admonitions against becoming spoiled had emanated from Fred Koch to his offspring as well. Even as he laid plans to leave huge inheritances to his sons, he wrote a prophetic letter to them in 1936. In it, he warned,

> When you are 21, you will receive what now seems like a large sum of money. It will be yours to do what you will. It may be a blessing or a curse. You can use it as

> a valuable tool for accomplishment or you can squander it foolishly. If you choose to let this money destroy your initiative and independence, then it will be a curse to you and my action in giving it to you will have been a mistake. I should regret very much to have you miss the glorious feeling of accomplishment and I know you are not going to let me down. Remember that often adversity is a blessing in disguise and certainly the greatest character builder. Be kind and generous to one another and to your mother.

Charles Koch keeps a framed copy of this letter in his office, but as *Fortune* observed, given the brothers' future protracted legal fights against each other, "Never did such good advice fall on such deaf ears."

David Koch recalled that his father tried to indoctrinate the boys politically, too. "He was constantly speaking to us children about what was wrong with government," he told Brian Doherty, an editor of the Koch-funded libertarian magazine *Reason* and the author of *Radicals for Capitalism*, a 2007 history of the libertarian movement with which the Kochs cooperated. "It's something I grew up with—a fundamental point of view that big government was bad, and imposition of government controls on our lives and economic fortunes was not good."

Fred Koch's political views were apparently shaped by his traumatic exposure to the Soviet Union. Over time, Stalin brutally purged several of Koch's Soviet acquaintances, giving him a firsthand glimpse into the murderous nature of the Communist regime. Koch was also apparently shaken by a steely government minder assigned to him while he worked in the Soviet Union, who threatened that the Communists would soon conquer the United States. Koch was deeply affected by the experience and later, after his business deals were completed, said he regretted his collaboration. He kept photographs in the company headquarters in Wichita aimed at documenting how the refineries he had built had later been destroyed. "As the Soviets became a stronger military power, Fred felt a certain amount of guilt at having helped build them up. I think it bothered him a lot," suggests Gus diZerega, a Wichita acquaintance of the family's.

In 1958, Fred Koch became one of eleven original members of the John Birch Society, the archconservative group best known for spreading far-fetched conspiracy theories about secret Communist plots to subvert America. He attended the founding meeting held by the candy manufacturer Robert Welch in Indianapolis. The organization drew like-minded businessmen from all over the country, including Harry Bradley, the chairman of the Allen-Bradley company in Milwaukee, who later financed the right-wing Bradley Foundation. Members considered many prominent Americans, including President Dwight D. Eisenhower, Communist agents. (The conservative historian Russell Kirk, part of an effort to purge the lunatic fringe from the movement, famously retorted, "Ike isn't a Communist; he's a golfer.")

In a 1960 self-published broadside, *A Business Man Looks at Communism,* Koch claimed that "the Communists have infiltrated both the Democrat [*sic*] and Republican Parties." Protestant churches, public schools, universities, labor unions, the armed services, the State Department, the World Bank, the United Nations, and modern art, in his view, were all Communist tools. He wrote admiringly of Benito Mussolini's suppression of Communists in Italy and disparagingly of the American civil rights movement. The Birchers agitated to impeach Chief Justice Earl Warren after the Supreme Court voted to desegregate the public schools in the case *Brown v. Board of Education,* which had originated in Topeka, in the Kochs' home state of Kansas. "The colored man looms large in the Communist plan to take over America," Fred Koch claimed in his pamphlet.

Welfare in his view was a secret plot to attract rural blacks to cities, where he predicted that they would foment "a vicious race war." In a 1963 speech, Koch claimed that Communists would "infiltrate the highest offices of government in the U.S. until the President is a Communist, unknown to the rest of us."

Blazing a trail that would later be followed by his sons, Koch tapped his fortune to subsidize his political activism. He underwrote the distribution of what he claimed were over two and a half million copies of his book, as well as a speaking tour. According to the Associated Press, during one speech in 1961 he told the members of a Kansas Women's Republican club that if they were afraid of becoming too "controversial" by joining his fight against Communism, they should remember that "you won't be very controversial lying in a ditch with a bullet in your brain." Such rants brought Koch to the attention of the FBI, which filed a report describing his rhetoric as "utterly absurd."

The John Birch Society's views were primitive, but its marketing was quite sophisticated. Welch, the candy manufacturer who founded the group, urged organizers to implement a modern sales plan, advertising heavily and pushing pamphlets door-to-door. The movement flourished in Wichita, where Fred Koch frequently attended local John Birch Society meetings and was a generous benefactor.

Ironically, the organization modeled itself on the Communist Party. Stealth and subterfuge were endemic. Membership was kept secret. Fighting "dirty" was justified internally, as necessary to combat the imputed treacherousness of the enemy. Welch "explicitly sought to use the same methods" he attributed to the Communists, "manipulation, deceit, and even dishonesty," recalled diZerega, who attended Birch Society meetings in Wichita in his youth. One ploy the group used, he said, was to set up phony front groups "pretending to be other than what they were." An alphabet soup of secretly connected organizations sprang up, with acronyms like TRAIN

(To Restore American Independence Now) and TACT (Truth About Civil Turmoil). Another tactic was to wrap the group's radical vision in mundane and unthreatening slogans that sound familiar today, such as "less government, more responsibility." One of Welch's favorite tropes, decrying "collectivism," would cause some head-scratching more than fifty years later when it was echoed by Charles Koch in a 2014 diatribe in *The Wall Street Journal* denouncing his Democratic critics as "collectivists."

Welch was "a very intelligent, sharp man, quite an intellectual," Fred Koch's wife, Mary, later told her hometown newspaper *The Wichita Eagle*. The family's admiration for the John Birch Society, however, proved somewhat embarrassing on November 22, 1963, when President John F. Kennedy was assassinated. As Lee Fang recounts in his book, *The Machine: A Field Guide to the Resurgent Right,* when President Kennedy arrived in Dallas that morning, he was confronted by a hate-stoked, full-page newspaper ad paid for by several Texas members of the John Birch Society, accusing him of treasonously promoting "the spirit of Moscow." At the time, Kennedy had moved from trying to ignore the Birchers to realizing he needed to confront their increasingly pernicious fearmongering, which he denounced as "crusades of suspicion" and "extremism."

In a hasty turnabout, soon after the assassination Fred Koch took out full-page ads in *The New York Times* and *The Washington Post* mourning JFK. The ads advanced the conspiracy theory that JFK's assassin, Lee Harvey Oswald, had acted as part of a Communist plot. The Communists wouldn't "rest on this success," the ads warned. In the corner was a tear-out order form, directing the public to sign up for John Birch Society mailings. In response, the columnist Drew Pearson slammed Koch's "gimmick" and exposed him as a hypocrite for having profited himself from Soviet Communism by building up the U.S.S.R.'s oil industry.

Fred Koch continued to be active in extremist politics.

He provided substantial support for Barry Goldwater's right-wing bid for the Republican nomination in 1964. Goldwater, too, opposed the Civil Rights Act and the Supreme Court's landmark desegregation decision, *Brown v. Board of Education*. Instead of winning, the Far Right helped ensure the Republican Party's humiliating defeat by Lyndon Johnson that year. In 1968, Fred Koch went further right still. Before the emergence of George Wallace, he called for the Birch Society member Ezra Taft Benson to run for the presidency with the South Carolina senator Strom Thurmond on a platform calling for racial segregation and the abolition of all income taxes.

David and Charles absorbed their father's conservative politics and joined the John Birch Society too, but they did not share all of his views. According to diZerega, who befriended Charles in the mid-1960s after meeting him while browsing in a John Birch Society bookstore in Wichita, Charles didn't accept all of the group's conspiracy theories. He recalls that Charles, who was several years older, steered him away from the Communist conspiracy books and toward the collection of antigovernment economic writers whose work he found especially exciting. "This is the good stuff," he recalls Charles telling him. The founder of the John Birch Society, Welch, was a board member of the Foundation for Economic Education, which spread a version of laissez-faire economics so extreme "it bordered on anarchism," as Rick Perlstein writes in his history of Goldwater's ascent, *Before the Storm*. Unlike his father's conspiracies, these were the theories that captivated Charles.

The postcollege years were a restless period in Charles's life. In 1961, when he was twenty-six, his father, whose health was failing, persuaded him despite his doubts to return to Wichita to help run the family business. After graduating with a bachelor of science in engineering and master's degrees in nuclear and chemical engineering from MIT, where his father was on the board of trustees, Charles had been enjoying his freedom working in Boston as a business consultant. Convinced that his father would sell the company otherwise, Charles reluctantly returned to Wichita to help but found himself intellectually hungry back in his hometown. In his telling, he was almost feverishly bent on finding some overarching system of political theory to bridge his father's emotional anti-Communism with his own more analytical approach to the world. He also wanted to merge his thinking about business and his interests in engineering and mathematics. "I spent the next two years almost like a hermit, surrounded by books," he told *The Wall Street Journal* in 1997. Visitors to his apartment recall him littering almost every surface with abstruse economic and political texts. He later explained that having learned that "there are certain laws that govern the natural world," he was trying to discover "if the same isn't true for the societal world."

Contributing to Charles's intellectual ferment at this time were his father's dinner table diatribes against taxation. Fred saw taxes in America darkly, as incipient socialism. Early on, the Internal Revenue Service had sued his company for underpayment of taxes, requiring a large additional payment as well as penalties and legal fees. He remained vehemently opposed to estate taxes, and told Charles that he feared the U.S. government would tax him so heavily it might force him to sell the family business, diminishing his sons' inheritances. To minimize future taxes, Fred Koch took advantage of elaborate estate planning. Among other strategies, he set up a "charitable lead trust" that enabled him to pass on his estate to his sons without inheritance taxes, so long as the sons donated the accruing interest on the principal to charity for twenty years. To maximize their self-interest, in other words, the Koch boys were compelled to be charitable. Tax avoidance was thus the original impetus for the Koch brothers' extraordinary philanthropy. As David Koch later explained, "So for 20 years, I had to give away all that income, and I sort of got into it."

Fred Koch's estate plan treated each son equally, but according to Coppin, to ensure that his offspring would continue to obey him, he arranged to pass his fortune on to them in two stages, with the second half passing on only after his death. The first distribution gave all four boys equal ownership of Koch Engineering, the smaller of his two companies. The later distribution thus hung over his sons' heads, subject to their father's whim.

Charles's embrace of the John Birch Society, according to Coppin, was in part designed to please the old man. According to diZerega, whom Charles invited to participate in an informal discussion group at the Koch mansion during this period, "It was pretty clear that Charles thought some of the Birch Society was bullshit." He recalls that "Charles was bright as hell." And in fact, in 1968, the year after his father died, Charles resigned from the organization over its support for the Vietnam War, which he opposed.

A related fringe group, though, became seminal to Charles Koch's political evolution during this period, the Freedom School, which was led by a radical thinker with a checkered past named Robert LeFevre. LeFevre opened the Freedom School in Colorado Springs in 1957 and from the start there were close ties to the John Birch Society. In 1964, Robert Love, a major figure in the Wichita branch of the John Birch Society, introduced Charles to the school, which offered one- and two-week immersion courses in "the philosophy of freedom and free enterprise." Robert Welch, the John Birch Society's founder, also visited. But LeFevre's preoccupations were slightly different. He was almost as adamantly opposed to America's government as he was to Communism.

LeFevre favored the abolition of the state but didn't like the label "anarchist," so he called himself instead an "autarchist." LeFevre liked to say that "government is a disease masquerading as its own cure." Doherty, the historian of the libertarian movement, related that "LeFevre was an anarchist figure who won Charles's heart" and that the school was "a tiny world of people who thought the New Deal was a horrible mistake." An FBI file on the Freedom School shows that by 1966 Charles Koch was not only a major financial supporter of the school but also an executive and trustee.

LeFevre, who looked like a jolly, white-haired Santa, had reportedly been indicted earlier for mail fraud in connection with his role in a cultlike right-wing self-actualization movement called the Mighty "I AM" that worked audiences into frenzies as they chanted in response to Franklin and Eleanor Roosevelt's names, "Annihilate them!" As the journalist Mark Ames recounts, LeFevre escaped prosecution by becoming a witness for the state, but he continued on a wayward path, claiming to have supernatural powers and struggling through bankruptcy and an infatuation with a fourteen-year-old girl. Later, at the height of Senator Joe McCarthy's anti-Communist crusades, LeFevre became an FBI informant, accusing Hollywood figures of Communist sympathies and leading a drive to purge the Girl Scouts of Reds. A stint writing editorials for the archconservative *Gazette-Telegraph* in Colorado Springs enabled him to drum up funds to launch the Freedom School on a rustic, five-hundred-acre campus nearby. There, he assumed the title of dean.

The school taught a revisionist version of American history in which the robber barons were heroes, not villains, and the Gilded Age was the country's golden era. Taxes were denigrated as a form of theft, and the Progressive movement, Roosevelt's New Deal, and Lyndon Johnson's War on Poverty, in the school's view, were ruinous turns toward socialism. The weak and poor, the school taught, should be cared for by private charity, not government. The school had a revisionist position on the Civil War, too. It shouldn't have been fought; instead, the South should have been allowed to secede. Slavery was a lesser evil than military conscription, the school argued, because human beings should be allowed to sell themselves into slavery if they wished. Like Charles Koch during this period, the school tried to meld its version of history, economics, and philosophy into one theoretical framework, which it called "Phronhistery."

A group of Illinois teachers sent to a session at the school in 1959 by a local chamber of commerce returned so shocked that they notified the FBI and published a letter denouncing the school for advocating "no government, no police department, no fire department, no public schools, no health or zoning laws, not even national defense." They noted that "this of course is anarchy." They also described the school as proposing that the Bill of Rights be reduced to "just a single one: the right to own property."

In 1965, *The New York Times* ran a feature describing the school as a bastion of "ultraconservatism" and mentioning that among the prized alumni whose lives had been transformed by its teachings was Charles Koch. He had obtained a second graduate degree from MIT in chemical engineering, the *Times* reported, after realizing that his previous degree in nuclear engineering would have required him to work closely with the government. At the time, according to the paper, the school was so implacably opposed to the U.S. government it was proposing that the Constitution be scrapped in favor of one that limited the government's authority to impose "compulsory taxation." The *Times* described LeFevre as also opposing Medicare and antipoverty programs and hinted that the school opposed government-sponsored integration, too. LeFevre told the paper that black students, of which the school had none, might pose a problem because, the *Times* wrote, "some of his students are segregationists."

Charles Koch was so enthusiastic about the Freedom School he talked his three brothers into attending sessions. But Freddie, the outlier in the family, who had spent more time than the others studying history and literature, disparaged the curriculum as bilge. He said that LeFevre reminded him of the con artists in Sinclair Lewis's novels. Charles was so incensed by his brother's apostasy, Frederick told people later, he threatened to "deck" him if he didn't toe the line.

DiZerega says that Charles arranged for him to attend a session at the school, too, and, he believes, paid his tuition. At the time, the only other faculty member he recalls besides LeFevre was James J. Martin, an anarchist historian who later won a reputation as a notorious Holocaust denier for his "revisionist" work with the Institute for Historical Review, in which he described claims of Nazi genocide in World War II as "invented." "It was a stew pot of ideas," recalled diZerega, who later became a liberal academic, "but if you grew up with more money than God, and felt weird about it, this version of history, where the robber barons were heroes, would certainly make you feel a lot better about it."

At the Freedom School, Charles became particularly enamored of the work of two laissez-faire economists, the Austrian theorist Ludwig von Mises and his star pupil, Friedrich Hayek, an Austrian exile, who visited the Freedom School. Hayek's book *The Road to Serfdom* had become an improbable best seller in 1944, after *Reader's Digest* published a condensed version. It offered a withering critique of "collectivism" and argued that centralized government planning, in which liberals were then engaged, would lead, inexorably, to dictatorship. In many respects, Hayek was a throwback, romanticizing a lost golden age of idealized unfettered capitalism that arguably never existed for much of the population. But Hayek's views were more nuanced than many American adherents understood. As Angus Burgin describes in *The Great Persuasion,* many reactionary Americans knew only the distorted translation of Hayek's work that had appeared in *Reader's Digest.* The conservative publication omitted Hayek's politically inconvenient support for a minimum standard of living for the poor, environmental and workplace safety regulations, and price controls to prevent monopolies from taking undue profits.

Hayek's ideas arrived in America during the post-Depression years, when conservative businessmen were scrambling to salvage the credibility of the laissez-faire ideology that had been popular before the 1929 market crash. Since then, Keynesian economics had taken its place. Hayek's genius was to recast the discredited ideology in an appealing new way. As Kim Phillips-Fein writes in her book *Invisible Hands: The Making of the Conservative Movement from the New Deal to Reagan,* rather than describing the free market as just an economic model, Hayek touted it as the key to all human freedom. He vilified government as coercive, and glorified capitalists as standard-bearers for liberty. Naturally, his ideas appealed to American businessmen like Charles Koch and the other backers of the Freedom School, whose self-interest Hayek now cast as beneficial to all of society.

Charles's funding of the Freedom School was his first step toward what would become a lifelong, tax-deductible sponsorship of libertarianism in America. His hope was to use his wealth to inject his fringe views into the mainstream by turning the Freedom School into an accredited graduate school and then a four-year undergraduate program specializing in libertarian philosophy, to be called Rampart College. A 1966 brochure features a photograph of LeFevre with Charles, shovel in hand, breaking ground for the new institution. Martin was hired to head Rampart's history department. But, as Ames recounts, the venture soon fell victim to mismanagement, leaving a trail of disgruntled backers. Eventually, the school moved to the South, where for a number of years it was sustained by the anti-union textile tycoon Roger Milliken. By the time LeFevre died in 1986, the Kochs had largely distanced themselves from him, perhaps sensing that he was a political liability. But Charles wrote a warm letter to LeFevre in 1973. He also gave a speech in the 1990s crediting the Freedom School with profoundly influencing him. It was, he said, "where I began developing a passionate commitment to liberty as the form of social organization most in harmony with reality and man's nature, because it's where I was first exposed in-depth to thinkers such as Mises and Hayek." He added, "In short, market principles have changed my life and guide everything I do."

As Charles grew increasingly ideologically driven, his brothers David and Bill, as he had, earned engineering degrees at their father's alma mater, MIT. In contrast, Frederick, who no longer went by the name Freddie, attended Harvard and later, after serving in the U.S. Navy, studied playwriting at the Yale School of Drama. He evinced no interest in joining the family company, preferring to write and produce plays and to collect art, antiques, antiquarian books, and spectacularly lavish historic houses.

The private life of the younger Frederick, who remained single, became the focus of a vicious blackmail attempt by the other brothers, according to a sworn deposition given by Bill Koch in 1982. In his deposition, Bill described an emotionally wrenching confrontation in the mid-1960s in which he, Charles, and David tried to force their older brother Frederick, who they believed was gay, to relinquish his claim to a share of the family company, or else they threatened to expose his private life to their father.

According to Bill's account, the brothers' blackmail scheme began after Charles and a friend talked the manager of the Greenwich Village building in which Frederick lived into letting them into his apartment without his permission when he was not home. Evidently, once inside, they snooped around and discovered personal information that they regarded as compromising. Frederick returned to find the uninvited twosome in his apartment. Soon after, according to Bill's deposition, Charles called his younger brothers to discuss whether Frederick should be allowed to continue as an officer of the family company. Bill admitted in cross-examination that he, along with his brothers, had regarded the situation as potentially embarrassing to the family enterprise, and so they had entrusted Charles to work out a plan to confront Frederick. According to the deposition, Charles then arranged a meeting in Boston of the directors of Koch Engineering, the part of the enterprise that the four boys had inherited together by this point and whose board they formed. In reality, as Bill described it, the meeting was a trap. Instead of addressing corporate business, it was a kangaroo court aimed at putting Frederick's personal life on trial. Chairs were arranged so that Frederick was on one side, facing his three brothers. According to the deposition, Charles then led an inquisition in which he accused Frederick of being gay and argued that his behavior was inappropriate for the family company. If Frederick refused to turn over his shares to his brothers, he was told, they would expose him to their father. If their father learned, they warned, it would likely impair his fragile health and also result in Frederick's disinheritance.

The subject of Frederick's private life had never been openly discussed in the family. Mary Koch referred to her eldest son, with whom she was close, as "artistic," and the senior Fred Koch evidently avoided the subject. One family member says homosexuality was so taboo in the family during those years, "it would have meant excommunication."

According to Bill's deposition, Frederick tried to defend himself in the face of his brothers' accusations, arguing that he had a right to speak. But Charles cut him off, telling him to "shut up," insisting that he had no say in the matter. At that point, Frederick stood up, said he wanted no more of the discussion, and walked out. Bill swore that he had tried to intercede on Frederick's behalf in the end, feeling bad for him. Because of this, he claimed, Charles had angrily reprimanded him after Frederick left, saying the three brothers had to stand together. Under cross-examination Bill recounted that afterward he had apologized to Frederick, who had thanked him for trying to defend him, however belatedly. The subject, though, remained almost too painful to talk about.

The full story of this confrontation never surfaced because Bill's deposition is sealed. But in 1997 *Fortune* carried a fleeting reference to "a homosexual blackmail attempt by Charles against Freddie to get his stock at a cheap price." The magazine noted that Charles "vigorously denied" it. Years later, Frederick also briefly alluded to it, telling the biographer Daniel Schulman that "Charles' 'homosexual blackmail' to get control of my shares did not succeed for the simple reason that I am not homosexual." For reasons that remain disputed, Frederick's inheritance was nonetheless handled differently than that of the other boys. He took more money up front, and was left out of a final distribution.

In the midst of this filial rancor, in 1967, Fred Koch died of a heart attack. Charles, then thirty-two years old, became chairman and CEO of the family business, which the sons renamed Koch Industries, in honor of their father. At the time, the company's principal business was refining oil, operating pipelines, and cattle ranching. Its annual revenues were estimated at $177 million, making it a substantial company but slight in comparison with the behemoth it would become.

Fred Koch's fears of confiscatory taxes turned out to be overblown. When he died, he was described as the wealthiest man in Kansas, and his will made his sons extraordinarily rich. Charles Koch has often lauded the virtuous habits it takes to succeed, publishing a book on the subject in 2007 called *The Science of Success*. He has been less forthcoming about his inheritance. His brother David, in contrast, has made less pretense of being self-made. He joked about his good fortune in a 2003 speech to alumni at Deerfield Academy, the Massachusetts prep school from which he graduated and where, after pledging $25 million, he was made the school's sole "lifetime trustee." He said, "You might ask: How does David Koch happen to have the wealth to be so generous? Well, let me tell you a story. It all started when I was a little boy. One day, my father gave me an apple. I soon sold it for five dollars and bought two apples and sold them for ten. Then I bought four apples and sold them for twenty. Well, this went on day after day, week after week, month after month, year after year, until my father died and left me three hundred million dollars!"

Fred Koch also left his sons the building blocks with which they could construct one of the most lucrative corporate empires in the world. The crown jewel, according to one former Koch Industries insider, was the Pine Bend Refinery, then called the Great Northern Oil Company, in Rosemount, Minnesota, not far from Minneapolis. In 1959, Fred Koch bought a one-third interest in the concern.

In 1969, two years after Charles Koch took the company's helm, Koch Industries acquired the majority share in the refinery. Charles later described the purchase as "one of the most significant events in the evolution of our company."

Pine Bend was a gold mine because it was uniquely well situated geographically to buy inexpensive, heavy, "garbage" crude oil from Canada. After refining the cheap muck, the company could sell it at the same price as other gasoline. Because the heavy crude oil was so cheap, Pine Bend's profit margin was superior to that of most other refineries. And because of a host of environmental regulations, it became increasingly difficult for rivals to build new refineries in the area to compete.

By 2015, Pine Bend was processing some 350,000 barrels of Canadian crude a day, and according to David Sassoon of the Reuters-affiliated *InsideClimate News,* Koch Industries was the world's largest exporter of oil out of Canada. In 2012, he wrote, "This single Koch refinery is now responsible for an estimated 25 percent of the 1.2 million barrels of oil the U.S. imports each day from Canada's tar sands territories." The Kochs' good fortune, however, was the globe's misfortune, because crude oil derived from Canada's dirty tar sands requires far greater amounts of energy to produce and so is especially harmful to the environment.

In 1970, a year after Koch Industries completed the Pine Bend deal, the twins joined their elder brother at Koch Industries, with David working out of New York and Bill near Boston. Charles characteristically assumed control, and it was not long before the long-standing sibling rivalries flared anew. Bill, according to court records, felt slighted and resented Charles's insistence on plowing almost all of the earnings back into the company, skimping on pay for his brothers. "Here I am one of the wealthiest men in America and I had to borrow money to buy a house," he complained. A political independent, Bill also complained that "Charles was giving as much to the Libertarians as he was paying out in dividends. Pretty soon we would get the reputation that the company and the Kochs were crazy."

In 1980, Bill, with assistance from Fred, attempted to wrest control of the company from Charles, who ran it with "an iron hand," according to Bruce Bartlett, a former associate. The attempted coup fizzled when Charles and David caught on and swung the board their way and, in retaliation, fired Bill.

Lawsuits were filed, with Bill and Frederick on one side and Charles and David on the other, re-creating the sibling rivalries of their childhood. In 1983, Charles and David bought out their brothers' shares in the company for about $1.1 billion. The settlement reportedly left Charles and David owning over 80 percent of Koch Industries' stock, evenly split between the two of them. But the fraternal litigation continued for seventeen more years. Among other accusations, Bill and Frederick alleged that Charles and David had cheated them by undervaluing the company. The Pine Bend Refinery in particular became the focus of contention, with Bill and Frederick arguing that Charles and David had hidden its true worth from them—an accusation Charles and David denied. As the acrimony built, the brothers hired rival legal teams and rival private investigators, who reportedly literally rummaged through the family garbage of the opposing brothers.

In 1990, the brothers walked past one another with stony expressions at their mother's funeral. Frederick, however, was absent. A confidant claimed later that Charles, who lived in Wichita, where their mother had died, hadn't given him early enough notice about the funeral arrangements for him to be able to attend. There had been an ice storm in Chicago, which complicated his travel arrangements. In the end, Frederick was only able to arrive in Kansas in time to attend a reception after the service. "He was heartbroken," the confidant said.

Bill, too, nearly missed the funeral. He was given such short notice he had to charter a private plane to make it in time and then was seated not with the immediate family but with cousins. In addition, both he and Frederick believed they were excluded from a private memorial at their father's ranch, arranged and attended by Charles and David.

Then, when Mary Koch's will was opened, it included a provision denying any inheritance from her $10 million estate to any son who was engaged in litigation against any other within six weeks of her death. Frederick and Bill, who were in the midst of suing their other two brothers, suspected their mother, who had suffered from dementia, had been unduly influenced during her fading days into adding this provision to her will. Again they sued, but lost, appealed, and lost again.

Eventually, Frederick, who lived alone, spent much of his life abroad, buying and restoring spectacular historic estates in France, Austria, England, New York, and Pennsylvania and filling them with art, antiques, and literary manuscripts, many of which he donated to museums and rare book libraries. Unlike his brothers, Frederick preferred to keep most of his donations anonymous, explaining to friends that his father had taught them to be modest and that taking credit for charity was vulgar. He refused to speak to Charles for the rest of his life.

Bill founded his own carbon-heavy energy company,

Oxbow, becoming a billionaire in his own right, according to *Forbes*. He lived lavishly, spending an estimated $65 million to win yachting's America's Cup in 1992. Like his brothers, he was a major Republican donor and became embroiled in tumultuous legal fights against environmentalists, opposing a proposed wind farm in the waters off his Cape Cod summer compound, because it would interfere with his view. He, too, barely spoke to Charles for decades but gradually underwent a rapprochement with his twin, David.

With Charles as the undisputed chairman and CEO, Koch Industries expanded rapidly. Roger Altman, who heads the investment-banking firm Evercore, described the company's performance as "beyond phenomenal." He added, "I'd love to know how they do it." Much of the credit went to Charles, who won a reputation as a brilliant, detail-oriented, metrics-driven manager. He was such a tough negotiator, one associate joked, that "in a fifty-fifty deal, he takes the hyphen."

As the company grew, Charles remained in Wichita, working ten-hour days, six days a week. When he proposed to his future wife, Liz, he did so reportedly over the phone, and she could hear him flipping through his busy date book in search of an open day for the wedding. In preparation, he required her to study free-market economics.

David, meanwhile, resided in New York City, where he became an executive vice president of the company and the CEO of its Chemical Technology Group. A financial expert who knows Koch Industries confided, "Charles *is* the company. Charles runs it." David, described by associates as "affable" and "a bit of a lunk," enjoyed for years the life of a wealthy bachelor. He rented a yacht in the South of France and bought a waterfront home in Southampton, where he threw parties that the Web site New York Social Diary likened to an "East Coast version of Hugh Hefner's soirées." David was known for his laugh, which has been described as a "window-shattering honk." To one longtime family insider, however, he often seemed "a bit lost" and "socially awkward. People don't really register with him that much," she said. In 1991, he was badly injured in a plane crash in Los Angeles. He was the sole passenger in first class to survive. As he was recovering, a routine physical exam led to the discovery of prostate cancer. He received treatment and reconsidered his life. He got married, settled down, and started a family. As he told *Upstart Business Journal,* "When you're the only one who survived in the front of the plane and everyone else died—yeah, you think, 'My God, the good Lord spared me for some greater purpose.' My joke is that I've been busy ever since, doing all the good work I can think of, so He can have confidence in me."

When they are not at their vacation houses in Southampton, Palm Beach, and Aspen, he and his wife, Julia Flesher, a former fashion assistant, live in a nine-thousand-square-foot duplex at 740 Park Avenue with their three children. The wealthiest resident of New York, David has become a huge benefactor of the arts and medicine, donating millions of dollars to Lincoln Center, the Metropolitan Museum of Art, and the American Museum of Natural History, among other institutions. But according to *Park Avenue,* a documentary by the Academy Award winner Alex Gibney, he has been less generous with the household help. A former doorman described Koch as "the cheapest person" in the building. "We would load up his trucks—two vans usually—every weekend for the Hamptons. In and out, in and out, heavy bags. We would never get a tip from Mr. Koch. We would never get a smile from Mr. Koch." For Christmas, which the doorman had anticipated would make up for the year's travails, Koch merely gave him a $50 check. When the documentary aired on the Public Broadcasting Service in 2012, David Koch was so incensed he resigned from the board of New York's public television station, WNET, reneging on a promise to make a major donation. A spokeswoman at Koch Industries declined to comment on whether the documentary was his reason for punishing the station, but Koch bluntly told one friend about the film, "It's going to cost them $10 million."

"They live, and always have, in a rarefied bubble," said the longtime family insider, explaining the Kochs' outrage at being subjected to critical scrutiny. "They move in a world with people like them, or who want to be. They know no poor people at all. They're not the kind of people who feel obligated to get to know the help."

As their fortunes grew, Charles and David Koch became the primary underwriters of hard-line libertarian politics in America. Though David's manner is more cosmopolitan, and more sociable, than that of Charles, Doherty, the libertarian chronicler who has interviewed both brothers, couldn't think of a single issue on which the brothers disagreed. Charles's aim, he said, was to tear the government out "at the root."

Having read the family's private letters and conducted interviews with the Kochs and their intimates as few other outsiders could, Clayton Coppin, the researcher hired first by the company and later by Bill Koch, saw Charles Koch's strong political views in the context of his family upbringing. In "Stealth," his unpublished 2003 report on Charles's political development, Coppin suggests that Charles harbored a hatred of the government so intense it could only be truly understood as an extension of his childhood conflicts with authority.

From his earliest years, he writes, Charles's goal was to achieve total control. "He did not escape his father's authority until his father died," he notes. After that, Charles went to great lengths to ensure that neither his brothers nor anyone else could challenge his personal control of the family company. Later clashes with unionized workers at the Pine Bend Refinery and with the expanding regulatory state strengthened his resolve. "Only the governments and the courts remained as sources of authority," Coppin writes, and if enacted, Charles's "libertarian policies would eliminate these."

Had Charles wanted merely to promote free-market economic theories, he could have supported several established organizations, but instead he was attracted to fringe groups that bordered on anarchism. Coppin suggests, "He was driven by some deeper urge to smash the one thing left in the world that could discipline him: the government."

Drawing on a cache of private documents, some of which remain in the possession of Bill Koch, Coppin was able to trace Charles's political evolution as he moved away from the intellectual fringe of his old mentor, LeFevre, in favor of gaining hands-on power. In response to libertarian thinkers who argued that ideas, not practical politics, were the best instruments of change, Charles wrote a revealing 1978 article in the *Libertarian Review,* arguing that outsiders like themselves needed to organize. "Ideas do not spread by themselves; they spread only through people. Which means we need a *movement,*" he wrote. His language was militant, demanding that "our movement must destroy the prevalent statist paradigm."

In Coppin's view, it was already clear by this point, at the end of the 1970s, that Charles "was not going to be satisfied with being the Engels or even the Marx of the libertarian revolution. He wanted to be the Lenin."

Around the same time, an obscure conference subsidized by Charles Koch laid out much of the road map for the Kochs' future attempted takeover of American politics. In 1976, with a contribution of some $65,000 from Charles Koch, the Center for Libertarian Studies in New York City was launched and soon held a conference featuring several leading lights of the libertarian movement. Among those delivering papers on how the fringe movement could obtain genuine power was Charles Koch. The papers are striking in their radicalism, their disdain for the public, and their belief in the necessity of political subterfuge. Speakers proposed that libertarians hide their true antigovernment extremism by banishing the word "anarchism," because it reminded too many people of "terrorists." To attract a bigger following, some suggested, they needed to organize synthetic "grassroots" groups and issue meaningless titles to volunteers, without yielding any real control.

Charles Koch's contribution was a paper that methodically analyzed the strengths and weaknesses of a group he knew intimately, the John Birch Society, as a model for their future enterprise. His assessment was clear-eyed and businesslike. He pointed out that despite the fringe group's shortcomings, it boasted 90,000 members, 240 paid staffers, and a $7 million annual budget. While these numbers were impressive, he faulted the John Birch Society's obsession with conspiracies, as well as the unchecked cult of personality that Welch had built up. He noted that Welch's ownership of the organization's stock had centralized control in his hands, making him impervious to constructive criticism. (Interestingly, Charles would go on to issue stock in his own nonprofit think tank, the Cato Institute, in much the same way.) But he also found much to admire. In particular, he argued in favor of copying the John Birch Society's secrecy.

"In order to avoid undesirable criticism, how the organization is controlled and directed should not be widely advertised," Charles wrote, arguing for stealth in his future plans to influence American politics.

He also wrote that to fund their future political enterprise, they should, like the John Birch Society, make use of "all modern sales and motivational techniques to raise money and attract donors . . . including meeting in a home or other place the prospect enjoys being." The Kochs' donor summits would follow this marketing approach, transforming fund-raising into exclusive, invitation-only social events held in luxurious settings.

Charles cautioned his fellow radicals that to win, they

would need to cultivate credible leaders and a positive image, unlike the John Birch Society, requiring them to "work with, rather than combat, the people in the media and arts." The brothers followed this plan too. David became a lavish supporter of the arts in New York and appeared regularly in the society pages. Charles, meanwhile, kept a lower profile but assiduously invited sympathetic members of the media to his donor summits, such as the talk radio host Glenn Beck, the *Washington Post* columnist Charles Krauthammer, and the *National Review* columnist Ramesh Ponnuru. Two of the top donors in the Koch network owned their own news outlets. The oil tycoon Philip Anschutz owned the *Washington Examiner* and *The Weekly Standard,* and the mutual fund magnate Foster Friess was the largest shareholder of *The Daily Caller.* The Kochs seriously considered buying the Tribune Company in 2013, too.

As for gaining adherents, Charles suggested, their best bet was to focus on "attracting youth" because "this is the only group that is open to a radically different social philosophy." He would act on this belief in years to come by funneling millions of dollars into educational indoctrination, with free-market curricula and even video games promoting his ideology pitched to prospects as young as grade school.

In support of building their own youth movement, another speaker, the libertarian historian Leonard Liggio, cited the success of the Nazi model. In his paper titled "National Socialist Political Strategy: Social Change in a Modern Industrial Society with an Authoritarian Tradition," Liggio, who was affiliated with the Koch-funded Institute for Humane Studies (IHS) from 1974 until 1998, described the Nazis' successful creation of a youth movement as key to their capture of the state. Like the Nazis, he suggested, libertarians should organize university students to create group identity.

George Pearson, a former member of the John Birch Society in Wichita, who served as Charles Koch's political lieutenant during these years, expanded on this strategy in his own eye-opening paper. He suggested that libertarians needed to mobilize youthful cadres by influencing academia in new ways. Traditional gifts to universities, he warned, didn't guarantee enough ideological control. Instead, he advocated funding private institutes within prestigious universities, where influence over hiring decisions and other forms of control could be exerted by donors while hiding the radicalism of their aims.

As Coppin summarized Pearson's arguments, "It would be necessary to use ambiguous and misleading names, obscure the true agenda, and conceal the means of control. This is the method that Charles Koch would soon practice in his charitable giving, and later in his political actions."

Soon after the 1976 conference, Charles plunged into Libertarian Party politics. He became not just the group's financial angel but also the author of its plank on energy policy, which called for the abolition of all government controls. The brothers took an even more audacious step into electoral politics in 1979, when Charles, who preferred to operate behind the scenes, persuaded David, then thirty-nine, to run for public office. The brothers were by then backing the Libertarian Party's presidential candidate, Ed Clark, who was running against Ronald Reagan from the right. They opposed all limits on campaign donations, so they found a legal way around them. They contrived to make David the vice presidential running mate, and thus according to campaign-finance law he could lavish as much of his personal fortune as he wished on the campaign rather than being limited by the $1,000 donation cap.

"David Koch ran in '80 to go against the campaign-finance rules. By being a candidate, he could give as much as he wanted," the conservative activist Grover Norquist later acknowledged. "It was a trick," suggests Bartlett, the economist who formerly worked at a Koch-funded think tank. David

Koch had no political experience and was little known, which initially caused consternation. But at the Libertarian Party convention, when he pledged to spend half a million dollars on his campaign, whoops of joy reportedly rose from stunned party members. The ticket's slogan was "The Libertarian Party has only one source of funds: You." The populist language was misleading. In fact, its primary source of funds was David Koch, who spent more than $2 million on the effort, just short of 60 percent of the campaign's entire budget.

In hindsight, it seems that David Koch's 1980 campaign served as a bridge between LeFevre's radical pedagogy and the Tea Party movement. Indeed the Libertarian Party's standard-bearer that year, Clark, told *The Nation* that libertarians were getting ready to stage "a very big tea party," because people were "sick to death" of taxes. The party's platform, meanwhile, was almost an exact replica of the Freedom School's radical curriculum. It called for the repeal of all campaign-finance laws and the abolition of the Federal Election Commission (FEC). It also favored the abolition of all government health-care programs, including Medicaid and Medicare. It attacked Social Security as "virtually bankrupt" and called for its abolition, too. The Libertarians also opposed all income and corporate taxes, including capital gains taxes, and called for an end to the prosecution of tax evaders. Their platform called for the abolition too of the Securities and Exchange Commission, the Environmental Protection Agency, the FBI, and the CIA, among other government agencies. It demanded the abolition of "any laws" impeding employment—by which it meant minimum wage and child labor laws. And it targeted public schools for abolition too, along with what it termed the "compulsory" education of children. The Libertarians also wanted to get rid of the Food and Drug Administration, the Occupational Safety and Health Administration, seat belt laws, and all forms of welfare for the poor. The platform was, in short, an effort to repeal virtually every major political reform passed during the twentieth century. In the view of the Kochs and other members of the Libertarian Party, government should be reduced to a skeletal function: the protection of individual and property rights.

That November, the Libertarian ticket received only 1 percent of the vote. Its stance against war and the military draft, and in favor of legalizing drugs and prostitution, won it some support among young rebels. But as a market experiment, libertarianism proved a massive flop. The brothers realized that their brand of politics didn't sell at the ballot box. Charles Koch became openly scornful of conventional politics. "It tends to be a nasty, corrupting business," he told a reporter at the time. "I'm interested in advancing libertarian ideas."

According to Doherty's history, the Kochs came to regard elected politicians as merely "actors playing out a script." Instead of wasting more time, a confidant of the Kochs' told Doherty, the brothers now wanted to "supply the themes and words for the scripts." In order to alter the direction of America, they realized they would have to "influence the areas where policy ideas percolate from: academia and think tanks."

After the 1980 election, Charles and David Koch receded from the public arena. "They weren't really on my radar," recalls Richard Viguerie, whose hugely successful right-wing direct-mail company won him the nickname the "Founding Funder of the Right." But during the next three decades, they contributed well over $100 million, much of it undisclosed, to dozens of seemingly independent organizations aimed at advancing their radical ideas. Their front groups demonized the American government, casting it as the enemy rather than the democratic representative of its citizens. They defined liberty as its absence, and the unfettered accumulation of enormous private wealth as America's purpose. Cumulatively, the many-tentacled ideological machine they built came to be known as the Kochtopus.

The Kochs were not alone. As they sought ways to steer

American politics hard to the right without having to win the popular vote, they got valuable reinforcement from a small cadre of like-minded wealthy conservative families who were harnessing their own corporate fortunes toward the same end. Philanthropy, with its guarantees of anonymity, became their chosen instrument. But their goal was patently political: to undo not just Lyndon Johnson's Great Society and Franklin Roosevelt's New Deal but Teddy Roosevelt's Progressive Era, too.

In taking on this daunting task, they were in many cases refighting battles that had been lost by their fathers. Complacent liberals, and many Republicans also, assumed by the 1970s that the political pendulum in America had shifted permanently away from archconservative groups like the John Birch Society. Robust government was almost universally accepted as a necessary instrument for social and economic betterment. Redistributive taxes and spending were largely uncontroversial. Even Richard Nixon had proclaimed in 1971, "I am now a Keynesian in economics."

Not everyone in the Grand Old Party, however, agreed. A small but deep-pocketed reactionary rear guard was already hard at work, devising plans to fight moderation and win the battle for the radical Right in an ingenious new way.

CHAPTER TWO

The Hidden Hand: Richard Mellon Scaife

FOR MANY YEARS, IN THE FOYER OF RICHARD MELLON SCAIFE'S Pittsburgh mansion stood a prized possession, a brass elephant on a mahogany stand. Visitors could be forgiven for mistaking it for the usual Republican mascot, because Scaife's forebears, who founded the Mellon banking, Alcoa aluminum, and Gulf Oil empire, were a financial mainstay of the Republican Party in Pennsylvania for more than a century. But the elephant in question was instead an homage to Hannibal, the fabled military strategist who daringly scaled the Alps on elephant back to launch a surprise attack on the Roman Empire. It served as the inspiration for a private organization that Scaife founded in 1964. This little-heralded group was just the first small step in what would become an improbably successful effort by one of the richest men in the country, along with a few other extraordinarily wealthy conservative benefactors, to cast themselves as field generals, in Hannibal's mold, in a strategic war of ideas aimed at sacking American politics.

For decades, Scaife was described as a recluse, mysterious even to the recipients of his largesse. Over a fifty-year period, he personally spent what he estimated to be upward of $1 billion from his family fortune on philanthropy, once the sum was adjusted for inflation. Most of it, some $620 million, he reckoned, was aimed at influencing American public affairs. In 1999, *The Washington Post* called him "the leading financial supporter of the movement that reshaped American politics in the last quarter of the 20th century." When he died on July 4, 2014, *The New York Times* carried a lengthy obituary, along with his photograph. Yet he gave almost no interviews or speeches on his motives and aims. He rarely spoke with those who ran the institutions he funded and was estranged from many former friends and family members, including two former wives and his two grown children. When Karen Rothmyer, a reporter for the *Columbia Journalism Review,* tried to ambush him into an interview in 1981, he warned her, "You fucking Communist cunt, get out of here!" In 2009, however, five years before he was diagnosed with inoperable cancer, Scaife penned a previously private, still-unpublished memoir, "A Richly Conservative Life," that serves as a secret tell-all about the building of the modern conservative movement.

In his memoir, Scaife describes how he and a handful of other influential conservatives who shared the view that American civilization faced an existential threat from progressivism began meeting during the Cold War years, at first informally, to plot against the country's liberal drift. At one such session, someone suggested that the threadbare cliché comparing America's ostensible downfall to that of ancient Rome was inadequate. The group decided that a better analogy was to the fall of Carthage, in North Africa. Carthage ostensibly fell when its wealthy elites failed to adequately back their military leader, Hannibal, as he reached the gates of Rome. The passivity of the ruling class allowed the enemy to triumph, burying the noble Carthaginian culture forever. Out of this discussion was born the League to Save Carthage, an informal network of influential, die-hard American conservatives determined, as Scaife writes, "that America must not go the way of Carthage, that we must win the struggles of our time."

In 1964, when this group incorporated itself formally as the Carthage Foundation, many conservatives felt like the remnants of a lost civilization. Their standard-bearer, the Republican presidential nominee, Barry Goldwater, had been badly defeated at the polls. The Democratic victor, Lyndon Johnson, meanwhile, was forging ahead with liberal civil rights legislation and ambitious Great Society antipoverty programs, radically expanding the reach of government and challenging the old order. Liberal dominance over arts and letters was so uniform during these postwar years that the cultural critic Lionel Trilling had declared with self-satisfaction, "Nowadays there are no conservative or reactionary ideas in general circulation." M. Stanton Evans, a leading intellectual on the right, captured conservatives' sense of marginalization in his 1965 book, *The Liberal Establishment: Who Runs America . . . and How*. He declared that "the chief point about the Liberal Establishment is that it is in control." In response, right-wing activists like Evans, who had studied with Ludwig von Mises, militated for a "counter-establishment." Yet they lacked the wherewithal with which to build it.

Stepping into this void and up to this challenge was, as the engraved brass plate beneath his elephant proclaimed, "Field Marshall Richard Mellon Scaife, the Carthaginian hero of the half century, 1950–2000." The plaque praised Scaife's "Audacity, Fidelity and Persistence." Christopher Ruddy, a conservative reporter and publisher who worked closely with Scaife for many years, sharing some of his political adventures, believes that Scaife was the progenitor of a new form of hard-hitting political philanthropy. "He's the originator" of the current model, says Ruddy. "I don't know anyone who did what he did before. He's a bit like Santa Claus."

In his early years, few would have expected Scaife to exert major influence on politics, or much else. Certainly he was born into extraordinary wealth. In 1957, *Fortune* ranked his mother, Sarah Mellon Scaife, and three other members of the Mellon family among the eight wealthiest people in America. But Scaife wasn't notably distinguished in any other way. Until his mid-thirties, he had no real career or accomplishments. Even by his own estimation, his life was dissolute. In his memoir, he writes that one of his favorite authors was John O'Hara because no one has better captured the decadence and the disappointment that were rife in his own upper-crust circle. "How beautifully he summed up Pennsylvanians of a certain class," Scaife writes, "their country club values, the wrecks they made of their lives on too much money and alcohol."

Scaife's great-grandfather Judge Thomas Mellon, the founder of the family fortune, had worried about the corrupting influence that inherited wealth might have on future heirs. The son of an Irish farmer who settled in Pennsylvania during the first half of the nineteenth century, Mellon proved an uncannily good businessman. He leveraged real estate investments into a thriving loan business that became Pittsburgh's stately Mellon Bank. During the Gilded Age, the family acquired huge stakes in a number of burgeoning industrial corporations, including Gulf Oil and Alcoa. Surveying his great fortune, however, in 1885, Mellon fretted that "the normal condition of man is hard work, self-denial, acquisition and accumulation; as soon as his descendants are freed from the necessity of exertion they begin to degenerate sooner or later in body and mind."

By the time his great-grandson Richard Mellon Scaife was born in Pittsburgh in 1932, some of the patriarch's darkest fears had been realized. Sarah Mellon Scaife, the mother of the boy who was known to his family as Dickie, by all accounts struggled to fight a losing battle with alcoholism. She was "a gutter drunk," according to her daughter, the late Cordelia Scaife May. "So was Dick," Cordelia said of her brother. "So was I."

If they were born with silver spoons, they were also born with chips on their shoulders. In his memoir, Scaife describes himself as fundamentally "anti-establishment," which may seem puzzling given his heritage, but his place within the Mellon dynasty was tinged with resentment. His mother had married a handsome and well-connected local patrician, Alan Scaife, who rode well to the hounds and had attended all the most elite schools but whose forebears had run the family metalworking company into the ground. As a result, Richard

Scaife's uncle R. K. Mellon, who like his mother had inherited a large part of the vast Mellon fortune, treated the Scaife family with scorn. "My father—he was suckin' hind tit," Scaife told Burton Hersh, who wrote a biography of the family in 1978. In his memoir, Scaife writes that his uncle, who was his closest Mellon relative and whom he and his sister dubbed Uncle Piggy, "treated my father like an errand-boy." Alan Scaife was given ceremonial titles in the various Mellon business concerns but no real power, other than to oversee his wife's enormous inheritance.

Alan Scaife briefly cut a dashing figure during World War II, when he enlisted in the Office of Strategic Services (OSS), the forerunner of the Central Intelligence Agency (CIA), as an army major. But while his tailor-made uniforms made a memorable impression, this was less true of his job performance. Richard Helms, who later became director of the CIA, recalled Scaife, who had been a colleague, as "a lightweight."

The family brush with the spy service, however, ignited Richard Scaife's lifelong infatuation with intelligence intrigue, conspiracy theories, and international affairs. Scaife writes that it also gave rise to his strongly anti-Communist views. In his memoir, he recalls his father admonishing the family while on furlough from the war that the scourge of Communism loomed large, not just abroad, but at home in America. "My political conservatism which eventually unmasked me as the villain behind the 'vast right-wing conspiracy' of Hillary Clinton's imagination—but only her imagination," he writes, began "before I had reached my twelfth birthday" over a lunch with his father at New York's Colony Club in 1944. Alan Scaife warned the family that wealthy capitalists like themselves were under attack. He invoked images of labor riots and class warfare. "He was concerned for the security of the country and gave us the feeling around the table that our entire future was at stake," Scaife writes. A local newspaper editor, William

Block of the *Pittsburgh Post-Gazette,* had similar recollections. He remembered Alan Scaife as overwrought during the 1940s about what he regarded as the growing threat that leftists posed to the rich. "Alan Scaife was terribly worried about inherited wealth," he later recalled.

The family's preoccupation with preserving its wealth was shared by previous generations. Scaife was heir not just to one of the country's greatest industrial fortunes but also to a distinctly reactionary political outlook rooted in the age of the robber barons. His great-uncle the Pittsburgh banker Andrew Mellon, who served as Treasury secretary under Presidents Warren Harding, Calvin Coolidge, and Herbert Hoover, was a leading figure in the counterrevolution against the Progressive movement, and in particular he was an implacable foe of the income tax.

Before Congress instituted the federal income tax in 1913, following the passage of the Sixteenth Amendment to the Constitution, America's tax burden fell disproportionately on the poor. High taxes were levied on widely consumed products such as alcohol and tobacco. Urban property was taxed at a higher rate than farms and estates. "From top to bottom, American society before the income tax was a picture of inequality, and taxes made it worse," writes Isaac William Martin, a professor of sociology at the University of California in San Diego.

In his history, *Rich People's Movements: Grassroots Campaigns to Untax the One Percent,* Martin notes that the passage of the income tax in 1913 was regarded as calamitous by many wealthy citizens, setting off a century-long tug-of-war in which they fought repeatedly to repeal or roll back progressive forms of taxation. Over the next century, wealthy conservatives developed many sophisticated and appealing ways to wrap their antitax views in public-spirited rationales. As they waged this battle, they rarely mentioned self-interest, but they consistently opposed high taxes that fell most heavily on themselves. And no figure was more instrumental in leading the early opposition than Andrew Mellon.

When Congress instituted the federal income tax, Mellon was one of the wealthiest men in America, with interests in dozens of monopolistic conglomerates then called "trusts." His Union Trust bank reportedly financed almost half the investments in Pittsburgh. In his view, the economic inequality that such arrangements produced was not only inevitable; it was the just reward for excellence and virtue. In an effort to win popular support for this outlook, he wrote a mass-market book called *Taxation: The People's Business,* in which he argued counterintuitively that cutting taxes on the rich would boost tax payments, not lower them, and so was a matter of broad public interest, not narrow private gain. Sixty years later, Jude Wanniski, the father of "supply-side economics," would pay homage to Mellon as his inspiration. At the time, though, Mellon's antitax book sold poorly, despite bulk purchases by business leaders.

Once in public office, Mellon helped define the 1920s as an era during which business succeeded in rolling back many of the Progressive Era's reforms. In 1921, capital gains taxes were cut, and the stock market boomed. After repeated efforts during his dozen-year tenure at Treasury, in 1926 Mellon finally succeeded in getting a bill passed that "cut the tax rates on the richest Americans more deeply than any other tax law in history," according to Martin. Mellon promised greater growth and prosperity. When instead the stock market crashed in 1929 after a frenzy of speculation, his legacy was tarnished. Not only did his economic theories look self-serving and irresponsible, but it surfaced that Mellon himself had been secretly providing tax credits and subsidies to some of the country's biggest businesses, including many in which the Mellon family had major investments. Eventually, Mellon was charged and acquitted of income tax fraud. He was required, though, to pay back taxes, which was a humiliation and indignity for the patrician family.

Three years after the 1929 stock market crash, against this backdrop of class conflict and financial chicanery, Richard Mellon Scaife was born. His family, and later he himself, would continue to portray their embrace of low taxes and limited government as matters of high principle, as Andrew Mellon had. But his parents' elaborate estate planning in order to minimize their own tax bills suggests that they had more than an abstract interest in the subject.

Scaife's parents created the largest of the family's tax-exempt, charitable foundations, the Sarah Scaife Foundation, in December 1941, days after the Japanese attack on Pearl Harbor. It appears to have been timed to shelter the family's wealth from anticipated tax increases. Scaife writes, "I don't know what my parents' specific motives were," but he notes that because of the impending war "there was talk . . . of a top income tax rate of above 90 percent." Roosevelt and the labor unions argued that the wealthy should shoulder a greater share of the cost of the war buildup, to provide an "equality of sacrifice." Despite their hawkish views on national defense, the family nonetheless took steps to avoid paying its share for the military buildup. As Scaife writes matter-of-factly in his memoir, "The rich inevitably are going to organize their wealth to avoid government confiscation. They'll do whatever the law allows to use their money as they see fit, out of reach of the tax collector."

Meanwhile, the Scaifes lived large. They commissioned a hulking Cotswold-style stone country house on 725 acres in Ligonier, Pennsylvania, next to Rolling Rock Farms, the Mellon family's 9,000-acre ancestral estate. They called their place Penguin Court, for the pet penguins that Sarah Scaife found amusing to let waddle the grounds. (Rookeries were built in the shape of igloos and filled daily with slabs of ice.) The weekend house was so vast that by Scaife's reckoning he had four rooms to himself as a boy. Rather than counting sheep, like less well-off insomniacs, he writes, "When I can't sleep, I try to recount the rooms, which numbered fifty or sixty."

The lavish lifestyle didn't protect Scaife, however, from suffering a terrible head injury in a riding accident at the age of nine. The fall fractured his skull, knocking him unconscious for eight to ten hours and requiring metal clips to be implanted in his head. As a result, he had to be tutored at home for more than a year and avoid vigorous athletics all his life. The injury also barred him from military service. But as he lay at home in his sickbed, he followed current events closely, mapping the troop movements during World War II and developing a lifelong passion for newspapers, which he read avidly as a boy and later would own.

The family's insulation from workaday life also couldn't protect the Scaife children from being jeered during the Depression and war years by passersby who catcalled at the sight of them being chauffeured, by themselves in the backs of limousines, as gas was rationed for others. Scaife recalls that by the time he was about ten, he realized that "compared to most people, the Scaifes were different. We were very wealthy." He says that in his youth he feared people would dislike him because of it. But he writes that unlike most liberals, as he grew older, he came to feel entitled to his good fortune. "Some of my friends—most I'd say—feel a sense of guilt about having money. I do not, and never have." As he describes it, "An inheritance comes to the person but also to his community and country. It can do powerful good." He notes, "I've felt good about being able to put dollars to work in the battle of ideas."

Scaife recalled his childhood as happy. He liked the governess who raised him, admired his father, and adored his mother. But his sister, Cordelia, who was four years older, saw their upbringing differently. She described the family as excelling principally in "making each other totally miserable." The only substance that appears to have been in nearly as great supply as money in the Scaife household was alcohol. By the time he was sent off to Deerfield Academy at the age of fourteen (the same prep school attended eight years later by David Koch), Scaife was already a drinker. Caught drinking off campus with some local girls in his senior year, in violation of Deerfield's rules, he almost didn't graduate. Scaife recalls that his parents hastily donated funds for a new dormitory for the school in order to assure his diploma. Years later, he would nonetheless, help fund the social critic Charles Murray, a leading proponent of the theory that a superior work ethic and moral codes account for much of the success among the affluent.

Despite having barely squeaked through prep school, Scaife was accepted at his father's college, Yale, from which he was soon expelled following several drunken benders. A reputation as a frat boy bully was cemented by an episode in which an empty beer keg was rolled down a flight of stairs, injuring a classmate. (Scaife writes that he was falsely accused of launching the keg, which was actually jettisoned by his friends.) After getting arrested off campus in another drunken escapade, he belittled the dean who was adjudicating his case, hastening his expulsion. Nonetheless, the following year, Scaife was given the chance to repeat his freshman year at Yale. But after spending time at the movies rather than in class, he soon flunked out, this time for good. Yet with the help of his father, who was chairman of the board, he graduated from the University of Pittsburgh and soon went on to enter the family business, Gulf Oil.

His behavior, however, didn't much improve. At the age of twenty-three, after drinking and in a hurry to visit his fiancée, Frances Gilmore, on a rainy night, he caused a near-fatal car accident that left him with a shattered knee and an expensive legal settlement with the family whose car he had rear-ended. Alcoholism and freakish tragedy continued to dog his adult life. One friend committed suicide in front of him. Another, his sister's husband, died of a gunshot wound under mysterious circumstances. His brother-in-law's death was ruled an accident or suicide but caused a scandal and a lasting rift between the siblings because Cordelia suspected that somehow her brother had been involved. In 2005, facing fatal illness, Cordelia, too, took her own life, asphyxiating herself with a plastic bag. She left an estate valued at $825 million.

Before these later tragedies unfolded, though, in 1958, Scaife's father died suddenly. Scaife was only twenty-six. He recalled that it "was a watershed year for me." His father bequeathed him the failing family metal company, which he soon sold for a dollar, and a powerless seat on the Mellon Bank board, which his disdainful uncle chaired. More important, Scaife was put in charge of his mother's finances, giving him responsibility for investing hundreds of millions of dollars. "The first priority had to be to look after Mother's affairs, as Dad had done," he writes. "At the age of fifty-four Sarah Scaife was a woman of wealth, but no experience managing it . . . so an unavoidable role for me became simply that of investor. Just taking care of it all."

Soon after his father died, his mother set up two charitable trusts of $50 million each. The beneficiaries were Scaife and his sister. Like the Koch family, the Scaifes designed the trusts so that all net income had to be donated to nonprofit charities for the next twenty years. After that, the $50 million principal could pass to each of the Scaife offspring free from inheritance taxes. In other words, two decades of philanthropy was the price for a tax-free inheritance. As Scaife wrote of the setup, "Isn't it grand how tax law gets written?"

Scaife notes that his mother thought it a good deal because in 1961 she created a second pair of similar trusts for her children, this time with $25 million for each beneficiary. This time the terms of the trust required Scaife and his sister to donate the net interest to charity over just ten years. And in 1963, his mother set aside another $100 million more in trusts, this time for her grandchildren, called the Sarah Scaife Grandchildren's

Trust. The net interest, again, had to be donated, this time over twenty-one years. Because Cordelia had no children, control of the entire $100 million in the Grandchildren's Trust reverted to Scaife, who by then had a small son and a daughter. So for the next twenty-one years, until 1984, he thus directed virtually all of the charitable donations stemming from the interest on all three trusts, which cumulatively held assets of $250 million. Both the assets and the amount of annual interest they spun off were remarkably large sums in those years.

Scaife, in his memoir, describes the method by which his mother was able to pass on her fortune to him tax-free as "a socially useful tax shelter." He writes, "It enabled a donor to set aside a lump sum for heirs free of inheritance tax or gift tax, but only after an interval of public benefit. To me, that's a good deal for both sides."

A consequence, however, was that the tax code turned many extraordinarily wealthy families, intent upon preserving their fortunes, into major forces in America's civic sector. In order to shelter themselves from taxes, they were required to invent a public philanthropic role. In the instance of both the Kochs and the Scaifes, the tax law ended up spurring the funding of the modern conservative movement.

Motivated in part by tax concerns, Scaife's role as a philanthropist grew. An immediate question, however, was how to disperse the constantly accumulating piles of interest from the trusts, which needed to be distributed to charity in order to satisfy the tax laws. One attractive solution for enormously wealthy families like the Scaifes and the Kochs was to donate to their own private philanthropic foundations. By doing so, they could get the tax deductions and still keep control of how the charitable funds were spent.

Private foundations have very few legal restrictions. They are required to donate at least 5 percent of their assets every year to public charities—referred to as "nonprofit" organizations. In exchange, the donors are granted deductions, enabling them to reduce their income taxes dramatically. This arrangement enables the wealthy to simultaneously receive generous tax subsidies and use their foundations to impact society as they please. In addition, the process often confers an aura of generosity and public-spiritedness on the donors, acting as a salve against class resentment.

Because of all these advantages, private philanthropic foundations proliferated among the ultra-wealthy during the last century. Today, they are commonplace, and rarely controversial, but Americans across the political spectrum once regarded the whole idea of private foundations with enormous suspicion. These aggregations of private wealth, intruding into the public arena, were seen as a form of unelected and unaccountable plutocratic power.

The practice began in the Gilded Age with John D. Rockefeller, whose philanthropic adviser Rev. Frederick Gates warned him with alarm, "Your fortune is rolling up, rolling up like an avalanche! You must keep up with it! You must distribute it faster than it grows!" In response, in 1909 Rockefeller sought legal permission from Congress to obtain a federal charter to set up a general-purpose private foundation whose broad mission was to prevent and relieve suffering and promote knowledge and progress. Critics, including the former president Theodore Roosevelt, assailed the idea, declaring, "No amount of charity in spending such fortunes can compensate in any way for the misconduct in acquiring them." At the time, a parade of notable Americans testified in Congress against the creation of private foundations, including the Reverend John Haynes Holmes, who denounced them as "repugnant to the whole idea of a democratic society." Frank Walsh, chairman of the U.S. Commission on Industrial Relations, in 1915, suggested that "huge philanthropic trusts, known as foundations, appear to be a menace to the welfare of society." Rob

Reich, a professor of political science at Stanford University and co-director of the Stanford Center for Philanthropy and Civil Society, explains that private foundations, which "represent virtually by definition plutocratic voices," were "troubling because they were considered deeply and fundamentally antidemocratic . . . an entity that would undermine political equality, affect public policies, and could exist in perpetuity."

Unable to gain congressional approval, Rockefeller got the New York state legislature to approve his plan. Legally, however, the Rockefeller Foundation, the granddaddy of all private foundations, was at first limited to promoting only education, science, and religion. Over time, however, the number of private foundations grew along with the kaleidoscope of issues into which they delved. By 1930, there were approximately two hundred private foundations, according to Reich. By 1950, the number had grown to two thousand, and by 1985 there were thirty thousand. In 2013, there were over a hundred thousand private foundations in the United States with assets of over $800 billion. These peculiarly American organizations, run with little transparency or accountability to either voters or consumers yet publicly subsidized by tax breaks, have grown into 800-billion-pound Goliaths in the public policy realm. Richard Posner, the iconoclastic libertarian legal scholar, has called perpetual charitable foundations a "completely irresponsible institution, answerable to nobody," and suggested that "the puzzle in economics is why these foundations are not total scandals."

When the robber barons first began donating to charities, their gifts were not tax deductible. With the implementation of the federal income tax in 1913, however, the wealthy soon convinced Congress that unless they were granted a special tax break, philanthropists might no longer donate their fortunes for public purposes. So in 1917 donors were granted unlimited charitable deductions. The rationale was that despite their wealth they deserved the public subsidy, so long as their gifts profited the public, rather than their own private interests. Conservatives who opposed the use of the tax code for all kinds of other social engineering nonetheless fully embraced the loophole in this instance.

Scaife had already set up his own small foundation by the time his father died in 1958. A family lawyer had explained to him when he turned twenty-one and received the first "booster shot," as he put it, of his inheritance that charitable foundations provided good tax shelters. Called the Allegheny Foundation, his early foundation was focused on local community improvement projects. In 1964, he added the Carthage Foundation, named for his political club. It focused on national security issues at first.

After his mother died in 1965, he and his sister shared control of the much larger Sarah Scaife Foundation. But their different priorities soon created irreconcilable fights. Before long, the siblings were at such odds they ceased speaking to each other for most of the rest of their lives. Cordelia Scaife's priorities, like their mother's, were art, conservation, education, science, and population control (Sarah Scaife had been a friend of Margaret Sanger's and was a staunch supporter of Planned Parenthood). Scaife too was a supporter of Planned Parenthood over the years, but his interests tilted more toward what he terms in his memoir "public affairs." By 1973, he had succeeded in reorienting the Sarah Scaife Foundation's grant making almost entirely to his own causes. "The result," he writes, "was very considerable grant-making power," enabling him to "advance ideas that I believe are good for America." Spurred by tax avoidance, Scaife became not only one of the country's richest citizens but also one of its biggest philanthropists. "This was the beginning of the legend of Richard Mellon Scaife as the dark spirit behind right-wing causes," he writes archly in his memoir.

The looming question, though, was how all this money could best be spent. Scaife, who was an early admirer of William F. Buckley Jr.'s, came into his full inheritance just as intellectuals on the right were incubating the idea that they needed to build their own establishment to counter that of the liberals. A leading voice of this cause was a member of Scaife's League to Save Carthage—Lewis Powell, the future Supreme Court justice who was then an eminent corporate lawyer from Richmond, Virginia. And at just that moment, Powell was in search of deep-pocketed donors to bankroll the project.

Powell was the author of a brilliant battle plan detailing how conservative business interests could reclaim American politics. In the spirit of Hannibal, it called for a devastating surprise attack on the bloated and self-satisfied establishment, which regarded itself as nonpartisan but which the conservatives regarded as liberal. Carrying out this attack would be an alternative opinion elite that would look like the existing one, except that it would be privately funded by avowedly partisan donors intent on implementing a pro-business—and, critics would say, self-serving—political agenda.

Powell's ties to corporate conservatives were manifold. In addition to a thriving corporate law practice, he held seats on the boards of over a dozen of the largest companies in the country, including the cigarette maker Philip Morris. So in the spring of 1971, Powell, who was then sixty-three, had watched with growing agitation as student radicals, antiwar demonstrators, black power militants, and much of the liberal intellectual elite turned against what they saw as the depravity of corporate America. Powell believed American capitalism was facing a crisis. All summer long, he clipped magazine and newspaper articles documenting the political threat. He was particularly preoccupied with Ralph Nader, the young Harvard Law School graduate whom Daniel Patrick Moynihan, then assistant secretary of labor, had hired to investigate auto safety hazards. Nader's 1965 exposé on General Motors, *Unsafe at Any Speed,* accused the auto industry of putting profits ahead of safety, triggering the American consumer movement and undermining Americans' faith in business. Powell was a personal friend of General Motors' corporate counsel and regarded this and other anticorporate developments with almost apocalyptic alarm.

That summer, two months before Powell was nominated by Richard Nixon to the Supreme Court, his neighbor Eugene Sydnor Jr., a close friend and director of the U.S. Chamber of Commerce, who shared Powell's political upset, commissioned Powell to write a special memorandum for the business league. In August, Powell delivered a seething memo that was nothing less than a counterrevolutionary call to arms for corporate America, warning the business community that its very survival was at stake if it didn't get politically organized and fight back. The five-thousand-word memo was marked "confidential" and titled "Attack on American Free Enterprise System." A virtual anti–*Communist Manifesto,* it laid out a blueprint for a conservative takeover. As Kim Phillips-Fein describes it in her history, *Invisible Hands,* Powell's memo transformed corporate America into a "vanguard."

Also heeding the battle cry were the heirs to some of America's greatest corporate fortunes, including Scaife, who were poised to enlist their private foundations as the conservative movement's banks. Foundations had several advantages for both the donors and the recipients of this largesse. Unlike most businesses, few people controlled them, so they could move quickly on controversial projects. And they provided the donors with tax breaks while conferring the aura of a high-minded cause. Reflecting on this period, James Piereson, a scholar at the Manhattan Institute who became a crucial figure in several conservative foundations, said, "We didn't have anything when we started in the late 1970s. We had no institutions at all in the mainstream of American political life." He debunked what he called the liberal misconception that corporations directly funded most of the far-right movement, arguing, "What we did was way too controversial for corporations." Instead, he said, in the beginning "there were only a small number of foundations," including the Earhart Foundation, based on an oil fortune, the Smith Richardson Foundation, derived from the cough and cold medicine dynasty, and, most importantly, the various Scaife family foundations.

The late 1960s and the early 1970s were in fact a daunting time for corporate America and for those living off great corporate fortunes. The business community was reeling from the birth of the environmental and consumer movements, which spawned a host of tough new government regulations. Following the 1962 publication of Rachel Carson's *Silent Spring,* exposing the devastating environmental fallout from irresponsible chemical practices, Congress passed the Clean Air Act, the Clean Water Act, the Toxic Substances Control Act, and other laws creating the modern regulatory state. In 1970, with strong bipartisan support, President Nixon signed legislation creating both the Environmental Protection Agency and the Occupational Safety and Health Administration, giving the government new powers with which to police business. The standards decreed by the Clean Air Act were notably tough. In developing regulations, the EPA was directed to weigh only one concern—public health. Costs to industry were explicitly deemed irrelevant. Meanwhile, as opposition grew to the Vietnam War, protesters turned angrily against companies they accused of fueling the conflict, such as Dow Chemical, the producer of napalm, which became the target of more than two hundred demonstrations in the 1970s. New Left leaders, like Staughton Lynd, urged the antiwar movement not to waste time on Washington but instead, as he wrote in 1969, to "lay siege to corporations." Polls showed that Americans' respect for business was plummeting.

As scientists linked smoking to cancer, the tobacco industry was under particularly pointed attack, which might have heightened Powell's alarmism. As a director at Philip Morris from 1964 until he joined the Supreme Court, Powell was an unabashed defender of tobacco, signing off on a series of annual reports lashing out at critics. The company's 1967 annual report, for instance, declared, "We deplore the lack of objectivity in so important a controversy . . . Unfortunately the positive benefits of smoking which are so widely acknowledged are largely ignored by many reports linking cigarettes and health, and little attention is paid to the scientific reports which are favorable to smoking." Powell took umbrage at the refusal by the Federal Communications Commission to grant the tobacco companies "equal time" to respond to their critics on television and argued that the companies' First Amendment rights were being infringed. Powell's legal argument failed in the courts, increasing his sense of corporate embattlement. Jeffrey Clements, in *Corporations Are Not People,* suggests Powell's defense of the tobacco companies was a harbinger of the corporate rights movement and a big part of what led him to push in his memo for conservatives to empower more pro-business courts.

Exacerbating corporate America's woes, the economy was buckling from "stagflation," the unusual combination of high inflation and high unemployment. There were oil shocks and gas lines as well. And after generations of redistributive progressive income and inheritance taxes, the economic elite was losing its lead. Income in America during the mid-1970s was as equally distributed as at any time in the country's history.

"No thoughtful person can question that the American economic system is under broad attack," Powell declared in his memo. What distinguished his jeremiad from many other conservative screeds was his argument that the greatest threat was posed not by a few "extremists of the left," but rather by "perfectly respectable elements of society." The real enemies, he suggested, were "the college campus, the pulpit, the media, the intellectual and literary journals, the arts and sciences," and "politicians."

Powell called on corporate America to fight back. He urged America's capitalists to wage "guerilla warfare" against those seeking to "insidiously" undermine them. Conservatives must capture public opinion, he argued, by exerting influence over the institutions that shape it, which he identified as academia, the media, the churches, and the courts. He argued that conservatives should control the political debate at its source by demanding "balance" in textbooks, television shows, and news coverage. Donors, he argued, should demand a say in university hiring and curriculum and "press vigorously in all political arenas." The key to victory, he predicted, was "careful long-range planning and implementation," backed by a "scale of financing available only through joint effort."

Powell was not alone. A number of activists on the right issued similar calls to arms, including Irving Kristol, the godfather of neoconservatism. A former Trotskyite, Kristol had become a columnist on the conservative editorial page of *The Wall Street Journal,* where he counseled business leaders to be more wily about public relations, arguing that they needed to downplay their "single-minded pursuit of self-interest" and instead tout moral values like family and faith. The Nixon White House aide Patrick Buchanan similarly argued in 1973 that in order to become a permanent political majority, conservatives needed to persuade corporate America and pro-Republican foundations to fund a think tank that would act as a "tax-exempt refuge," a "talent bank," and a "communications center." But it was Powell's memo that electrified the Right, prompting a new breed of wealthy ultraconservatives to weaponize their philanthropic giving in order to fight a multifront war of influence over American political thought.

During this period, Scaife, like many conservatives, was growing disillusioned with more conventional political spending. Goldwater's defeat was a huge personal disappointment. Afterward, Scaife got involved in one more campaign in a big way, donating almost $1 million in $3,000 checks to 330 different front groups associated with Nixon's 1972 reelection campaign. The small increments of cash were designed to evade federal contribution limits.

But when Nixon was implicated in the Watergate scandal, Scaife turned against him and against the idea of funding candidates. Scaife, who by then had bought a local newspaper, the *Tribune-Review,* in Greensburg, outside Pittsburgh, published a scalding editorial demanding Nixon's impeachment in 1974. Soon after, he refused to even take the president's phone calls. "He was never a big candidate person since," says Christopher Ruddy.

Frustrated by the electoral process, Scaife, like Charles and David Koch, sought to finance political victory through more indirect means. Though he continued to donate money to political campaigns and action committees, he began to invest far more in conservative institutions and ideas. His private foundations emerged as a leading source of funds for political and policy entrepreneurship. Think tanks, in particular, became what Piereson called "the artillery" in the conservative movement's war of ideas. In his memoir, Scaife estimates that he helped bankroll at least 133 of the conservative movement's 300 most important institutions.

In 1975, the Scaife Family Charitable Trust donated $195,000 to a new conservative think tank in Washington, the Heritage Foundation. For the next ten years, Scaife became its largest backer, donating $10 million more. By 1998, these donations had reached a total of some $23 million, which meant that Scaife accounted for a vastly disproportionate share of the think tank's overall funding. Previously, Scaife had been the largest donor to the American Enterprise Institute (AEI), the older, rival conservative think tank in Washington, but Heritage had a new model that won him over. In contrast to the research centers of the past, it was purposefully political, priding itself on creating, selling, and injecting deeply conservative ideas into the American mainstream.

In fact, the Heritage Foundation was born out of two congressional aides' frustration with the more conventional think tank model. One of them, Edwin Feulner Jr., was a Wharton School graduate and Hayek acolyte, with a flair for fund-raising. The other, Paul Weyrich, was a brilliant and fiercely conservative working-class Catholic press aide from Wisconsin, who described himself openly as a "radical" who was "working to overturn the present power structure." The duo had become exasperated by AEI's refusal to weigh in on legislative fights until after they were settled, a cautious approach reflecting the older think tank's fear of losing its nonprofit status. Instead, they wanted to create a new sort of action-oriented think tank that would actively lobby members of Congress before decisions were made, take sides in fights, and in every way not just "think" but "do."

Lewis Powell's memo awoke the financial angels their project needed. The first of these was Joseph Coors, a scion of the archconservative Colorado-based Coors brewery family. After reading Powell's memo, he was so "stirred" up he sent a letter to his senator the Colorado Republican Gordon Allott, offering "to invest in conservative causes." Weyrich, who worked for Allott, saw Coors's letter and pounced. He urged the magnate, who seemed to be offering unlimited funds with no strings attached, to come to Washington immediately. "I do believe I've never met a man as politically naive as Joe Coors," he reportedly said with a chuckle afterward. But Coors was enthralled. Weyrich had talked of being "engaged in a war to preserve the freedom this country was built on. Think of what we need as combat intelligence," he told Coors.

Coors immediately enlisted. Like the Kochs and Scaife, he and his brothers had inherited a lucrative private family business along with their parents' reactionary views. A supporter of the John Birch Society, Joe Coors regarded organized labor, the civil rights movement, federal social programs, and the counterculture of the 1960s as existential threats to the way of life that had enabled him and his forebears to succeed. The Coors Brewing Company, founded in 1873 by Adolph Coors, a Prussian immigrant, was famously hostile to unions and had repeated run-ins with the Colorado Civil Rights Commission, which accused the company of discriminating against minority employees. Convinced that radical leftists had overrun the country, Joe Coors, the youngest grandson of the founder, became the center of controversy when as a regent at the University of Colorado he had tried to bar left-wing speakers, faculty, and students on campus. His attempt to require faculty to take a pro-American loyalty oath was defeated by the other regents. Enraged that his own son had become a hippie at the school, he railed during a commencement address against "pleasure-minded parasites . . . living off the state dole." By the time he connected with Weyrich, he already believed that the Right needed new and more militant national institutions of the kind Weyrich described.

Before long, Coors became the first donor to the fledgling conservative think tank that Weyrich and Feulner were launching, the forerunner of the Heritage Foundation, then called the Analysis and Research Association. On top of his initial contribution of $250,000, Coors promised $300,000 more for a headquarters building. Soon he was reveling in his new status as a national figure and jetting back and forth from Golden, Colorado, to Washington. Backed by the first of many multimillionaire political ideologues, the Heritage Foundation opened for business in 1973.

Scaife's money soon followed, on an even bigger scale. A popular saying at the time was "Coors gives six-packs; Scaife gives cases."

Independent research institutes had existed since at least the turn of the century in the United States, but as John Judis writes in *The Paradox of American Democracy*, 'the earlier think tanks strove to promote the general public interest, not narrow private or partisan ones. In the tradition of the Progressive movement, they professed to be driven by social science, not ideology. Among the best known was the Brookings Institution, founded in 1916 by the St. Louis businessman Robert Brookings, who defined its mission as "free from any political or pecuniary interest." To assure an ethic of "disinterestedness," Brookings, who was himself a Republican, mandated that scholars of many viewpoints populate its board.

The same ideals animated the Rockefeller, Ford, and Russell Sage Foundations, as well as most of academia and the elite news organizations of the era, like *The New York Times,* which strove to deliver the facts free from partisan bias. Because the self-perception of these institutions was that they were engaged in a modern, even scientific pursuit of the truth, they did not regard themselves as liberal, although frequently the answers they brought to social problems involved government solutions.

In the 1970s, with funding from a handful of hugely wealthy donors like Scaife, as well as some major corporate support, a whole new form of "think tank" emerged that was more engaged in selling predetermined ideology to politicians and the public than undertaking scholarly research. Eric Wanner, the former president of the Russell Sage Foundation, summed it up, saying, "The AEIs and the Heritages of the world represent the inversion of the progressive faith that social science should shape social policy."

According to one account, it was Hayek who spawned

the idea of the think tank as disguised political weapon. As Adam Curtis, a documentary filmmaker with the BBC, tells the story, around 1950, after reading the *Reader's Digest* version of Hayek's *Road to Serfdom,* an eccentric British libertarian named Antony Fisher, an Eton and Cambridge graduate who believed socialism and Communism were overtaking the democratic West, sought Hayek's advice about what could be done. Should he run for office? Hayek, who was then teaching at the London School of Economics, told him that for people of their beliefs getting into politics was futile. Politicians were prisoners of conventional wisdom, in Hayek's view. They would have to change how politicians thought if they wanted to implement what were then considered outlandish free-market ideas. To do that would require an ambitious and somewhat disingenuous public relations campaign. The best way to do this, Hayek told Fisher, who took notes, was to start "a scholarly institute" that would wage a "battle of ideas." If Fisher succeeded, Hayek told him, he would change the course of history.

To succeed, however, required some deception about the think tank's true aims. Fisher's partner in the venture, Oliver Smedley, wrote to Fisher saying that they needed to be "cagey" and disguise their organization as neutral and nonpartisan. Choosing a suitably anodyne name, they founded the grandfather of libertarian think tanks in London, calling it the Institute of Economic Affairs. Smedley wrote that it was "imperative that we should give no indication in our literature that we are working to educate the public along certain lines which might be interpreted as having a political bias. In other words, if we said openly that we were re-teaching the economics of the free market, it might enable our enemies to question the charitableness of our motives."

Fisher would go on to found another 150 or so free-market think tanks around the world, including the Manhattan Institute in New York, to which both Scaife and other conservative philanthropists would become major contributors. The Sarah

Scaife Foundation in fact for many years was the Manhattan Institute's single largest contributor. The donations paid off, from Scaife's viewpoint, when they helped launch the careers of the conservative social critic Murray and the supply-side economics guru George Gilder, whose arguments against welfare programs and taxes had huge impacts on ordinary Americans.

Fisher's early collaborator in founding the Manhattan Institute was William Casey, the Wall Street financier and future director of the CIA. The early think tank was not a spy operation, but it was funded by wealthy men who had no objections to using pretexts and disinformation in the service of what they regarded as a noble cause. In fact, Scaife during this period was simultaneously funding a CIA front group. In his memoir, he acknowledges that in the early 1970s he owned a London-based news organization called Forum World Features that was in reality a CIA-run propaganda operation. He had taken it over from Jock Whitney, the publisher of the *New York Herald Tribune*, who was a friend of his father's in the OSS.

An element of subterfuge was also discernible in Weyrich's early planning. His papers include correspondence that make his political organizations sound like clandestine corporate front groups. One associate writes, "As you well know, business people have been notoriously apathetic in the political field. This is primarily, I feel, due to the businessman's fear of his involvement with respect to his business and possible repercussions from the federal government. The organization we propose would screen him and provide him a vehicle which would in effect do his political work for him at a price."

Earlier attempts by American tycoons to hide behind nonprofit front groups had proven both legally and politically toxic. In the 1930s, Democrats gleefully unmasked the Du Pont family's funding for the American Liberty League, an ostensibly independent organization that opposed FDR's

New Deal, ridiculing it as the "American Cellophane League" because "it's a DuPont product and you can see right through it." In 1950, Congress investigated the group that became AEI, denouncing it as a "'big business' pressure organization" that should register as a lobbying shop and get barred from offering its donors tax deductions. In 1964, top AEI personnel took leaves of absence to form the brain trust for Goldwater's 1964 presidential campaign. The Internal Revenue Service nonetheless threatened the think tank's tax-exempt status. It was this searing experience that prompted AEI and other conservative groups of this period to avoid the appearance of being too partisan or of acting as corporate shills.

But in the 1970s, such concerns became outmoded. Powell and others in the newly aggressive corporate vanguard inverted from a negative into a positive the accusation that conservative organizations were slanted by successfully redefining existing establishment organizations like Brookings and *The New York Times* as equally biased but on the liberal side. They argued that a "market" of ideas was necessary that would give equal balance to all views. In effect, they reduced the older organizations that prided themselves on their above-the-fray public-service-oriented neutrality to mere combatants in a polarized war.

Disoriented, Brookings and the *Times* rushed to add conservatives to their ranks in hopes of demonstrating their nonpartisanship. Brookings hurriedly made a Republican its president, while the *Times* in 1973 added Nixon's former speechwriter Bill Safire to its op-ed page as a columnist. In 1976, after the Scaife-funded Institute for Contemporary Studies issued a report accusing the media of liberal bias, the *Times* forced out the editorial page editor John Oakes for having an antibusiness tone. The Ford Foundation, meanwhile, which had funded much of the early bipartisan environmental movement, as well as the public interest law movement, donated the first installment of $300,000 in grants to AEI in 1972 in an attempt to fight criticism that it was liberal. "That was quite the heist you pulled on the Ford Foundation, congratulations!" a friend exclaimed in a note to a top AEI official.

The upshot was that by the end of the 1970s conservative nonprofits had achieved power that was almost unthinkable when the League to Save Carthage first formed. Enormously wealthy right-wing donors had transformed themselves from the ridiculed, self-serving "economic royalists" of FDR's day into the respected "other side" of a two-sided debate.

The new, hyper-partisan think tanks had impact far beyond Washington. They introduced doubt into areas of settled academic and scientific scholarship, undermined genuinely unbiased experts, and gave politicians a menu of conflicting statistics and arguments from which to choose. The benefit was a far more pluralistic intellectual climate, beyond liberal orthodoxy. The hazard, however, was that partisan shills would create "balance" based on fraudulent research and deceive the public about pressing issues in which their sponsors had financial interests.

Some insiders, like Steve Clemons, a political analyst who worked for the Nixon Center among other think tanks, described the new think tanks as "a Faustian bargain." He worried that the money corrupted the research. "Funders increasingly expect policy achievements that contribute to their bottom line," he admitted in a confessional essay. "We've become money launderers for monies that have real specific policy agendas behind them. No one is willing to say anything about it; it's one of the big taboo subjects."

In an effort to prove their intellectual integrity, all of the new think tanks could cite occasional instances where they parted positions with some of their donors, but far more typical was the example of John M. Olin, a chemical and munitions company magnate whose foundation was a top sponsor of the American Enterprise Institute. Letters from Olin show that he grew increasingly agitated over what he regarded as the think tank's lassitude after he had earmarked a donation demanding that AEI militate against raising the estate tax during the Nixon years. In a note to the think tank's president, Olin railed about the tax as "socialism out and out" and complained that if the think tank didn't speak out soon, "my estate would be practically liquidated upon my death."

David Brock, a conservative apostate who became a liberal activist, described the Heritage Foundation, where he was a young fellow, as almost completely under the thumb of its wealthy sponsors. In his tell-all book *Blinded by the Right,* he writes, "I saw how right-wing ideology was manufactured and controlled by a small group of powerful foundations" like Smith Richardson, Adolph Coors, Lynde and Harry Bradley, and John M. Olin. Scaife in his estimation was "by far the most important"; indeed, Brock describes him as "the most important single figure in building the modern conservative movement and spreading its ideas into the political realm."

How intellectually engaged Scaife personally was—rather than delegating authority to key advisers such as his longtime aides, Richard Larry and Larry's fellow ex-marine R. Daniel McMichael—remains something of a mystery. The recipients of Scaife's largesse, such as David Abshire, head of the Center for Strategic and International Studies, and Edwin Meese III, Reagan's former attorney general and a fellow at the Heritage Foundation, invariably praised his acumen. It was Meese who described Scaife as "the unseen hand" who brought "balance and sound principles back to the public arena" and "quietly helped to lay the brick and mortar for an entire movement." Yet one former aide to Scaife, James Shuman, told *The Washington Post* that had Scaife not inherited a huge fortune, "I don't think he had the intellectual capacity to do very much."

In his memoir, Scaife recounts his life story with some wit and charm, suggesting he could be quick and entertaining, if lacking in self-awareness. Yet one of the few public speeches he gave, at a Heritage Foundation rally celebrating Republicans' takeover of the House and Senate in 1994, was less than reassuring about his clarity of mind. Scaife meandered somewhat incoherently as he declared, "With political victory, the ideological conflicts that have swirled about this nation for half a century now show clear signs of breaking into naked ideological warfare in which the very foundations of our republic are threatened and that we had better take heed."

Scaife's rambling remarks were made in the same year that he returned to drinking after a life in and out of rehab programs. In 1987, his second wife, Margaret "Ritchie" Battle, took him with her to the Betty Ford Center. He stayed sober, associates said, for several years. His life, however, remained flamboyantly turbulent. After he met Ritchie—who was married, as was he—in 1979, the couple carried on a soap-opera-worthy affair. Scaife claimed he consummated it after Ritchie, a glamorous and memorably feisty southerner, appeared in his office in an irresistible white angora sweater. "We did what comes naturally," he told *Vanity Fair*. She retorted, "Never owned an angora sweater. I'm allergic to things like that!" While they were courting, Ritchie reportedly kicked Scaife in the testicles so hard he had to be taken to a hospital emergency room. Meanwhile, he and his first wife wrangled for almost ten years over the divorce settlement as he fought to keep her from taking a share of some Gulf Oil stock he'd belatedly come into. At one point, in order to evade a subpoena, Ritchie was carried out of Scaife's house rolled in a carpet, like Cleopatra, by his servants.

His family life was in tatters. According to Scaife's son, David, Ritchie and Scaife visited him during this period at prep school—Deerfield again—bringing alcohol and marijuana, which Scaife smoked with his son. In 1991, he married Ritchie, who continued to live in her own house around the corner. Their wedding reception scandalized Pittsburgh's upper crust with its blazing double-entendre lawn sign spelling out "Ritchie loves Dick."

That scandal paled, however, in comparison with the couple's spectacular breakup. After hiring a private detective who trailed Scaife to a roadside motel where rooms rented by the hour, and after documenting trysts between Scaife and a tall, blond woman named Tammy Vasco who had an arrest record for prostitution, Ritchie herself was arrested for "defiant trespass" at her husband's house, for peeping into his windows and crawling in after spying servants setting a romantic, candlelit dinner table for two. The charges were dismissed, but the scorned wife soon came to blows with Scaife's housekeeper over custody of the couple's yellow Labrador retriever, Beauregard. After Ritchie succeeded in absconding with the dog, Scaife posted a sign in his front yard reading, "Wife and dog missing—reward for dog."

These skirmishes were a minor prelude to the epic fight over their divorce settlement. Over the advice of his lawyer, Scaife had declined to insist upon a prenuptial agreement with Ritchie, a mistake he regretted bitterly in his memoir. Scaife maintained he hadn't meant to humiliate his former wife, explaining that he just believed in having "an open marriage." It was an issue, he joked, "that Bill Clinton and I have in common." Tammy Vasco, meanwhile, stayed in Scaife's life through his final days, accompanying him on trips to his houses in Nantucket and Pebble Beach, California, to the chagrin of his household staff and the disdain of Pittsburgh society. A friend of Scaife's said that despite her arrest record for prostitution, he kept a photograph of Vasco by his bedside as he lay dying of cancer.

All of which calls into question how in 1990 the Scaife Foundation could justify pressing the Heritage Foundation, of which it was the largest funder, to focus more on conservative social and moral issues and in particular family values. Heritage's president, Ed Feulner, quickly complied with his donor's request, hiring William J. Bennett. Soon after, Bennett, an outspoken social conservative who had been the secretary of education under Ronald Reagan and the director of National Drug Control Policy under George H. W. Bush, was appointed Heritage's new distinguished fellow in cultural policy studies. Lee Edwards, who wrote Heritage's official history, confirms that the Scaife Foundation "had particularly in mind the disintegration of the family, an issue which became a major Heritage concern." Bennett also served as a Scaife Foundation director.

Equally hard to fathom is how Scaife rationalized his foundations' funding of an obsessive investigation of President Clinton's marital infidelities during the 1990s that came to be known as the Arkansas Project. Hiring private detectives to dig up dirt from anti-Clinton sources, the project funneled smutty half-truths to *The American Spectator* magazine, which was also funded by Scaife's family foundations. Scaife's foundations also poured money into lawsuits against Clinton, all of which helped whip up the political frenzy that led to the Clinton impeachment hearings.

Scaife, meanwhile, succumbed to a far-fetched conspiracy theory positing that the death of the Clinton White House aide Vincent Foster, which police had ruled a suicide, was actually a murder and, as he put it at one point, "the Rosetta Stone to the Clinton Administration." Scaife even insisted in an interview that Clinton "can order people done away with at will . . . God there must be 60 people [associated with Clinton] who have died mysteriously."

Scaife's extraordinary self-financed and largely tax-deductible vendetta against Clinton demonstrated the impact that a single wealthy extremist could have on national affairs, and served as something of a dress rehearsal for the Kochs' later war against Obama. Presidents might surround themselves with Secret Service agents and phalanxes of lawyers and operatives, but Scaife proved how hard it was to defend against unlimited, untraceable spending by an opponent hiding behind nonprofit front groups.

Eventually, however, the Arkansas Project got so out of hand that Scaife found himself ensnared in a serious legal mess, subpoenaed to testify before a grand jury about possible charges of tampering with a federal witness. One of the two pilots he kept on his staff flew him down to Arkansas in his private DC-9 to testify. No charges were brought. Enraged, however, Scaife cut off *The American Spectator* from his foundation's funding and turned against his longtime aide Richard Larry, who had led the anti-Clinton charge. Soon after, Larry resigned.

Then, in a stunning turnaround in 2008, Scaife met with Hillary Clinton, who had fingered him as the ringleader of what she called a "vast right-wing conspiracy" to torment the Clintons. Conservative political pundit Byron York declared, "Hell has officially frozen over." After a pleasant editorial board chat, Scaife came out and wrote an opinion piece in his own paper declaring that his view of her as a Democratic presidential contender had changed and was now "very favorable indeed." The rapprochement testified both to Hillary Clinton's political skills and to Scaife's almost childlike impressionability. Repeatedly in his memoir, he changes his political views after meeting antagonists in person, whether the liberal Kennedy family member Sargent Shriver or the Democratic congressman Jack Murtha. "Like many billionaires, he lived in a bubble," concluded his friend Ruddy (whose relations with the Clintons also thawed). Contrary information rarely penetrated it. Instead, Scaife's family fortune enabled him to build a political bulwark reinforcing his ideology and imposing it on the rest of the country.

In Wichita, meanwhile, where he was rapidly expanding his family's company and searching for more effective means than electoral politics with which he could spread libertarianism, Charles Koch, too, was galvanized by Lewis Powell. In

1974, Charles gave a speech to a group of businessmen gathered at a hotel in Dallas, quoting Powell. "As the Powell Memorandum points out," Koch warned the group, "business and the enterprise system are in trouble, and the hour is late."

Koch urged his fellow business leaders to "undertake radical new efforts to overcome the prevalent anti-capitalist mentality." He declared that "the development of a well-financed cadre of sound proponents of the free enterprise philosophy is the most critical need facing us today." Opponents of "socialistic" regulations, he said, should "leverage" their power by investing in "pro-capitalist research and educational programs." That way, he argued, their efforts would have a "multiplier effect."

Charles's anger at the government by this point was more than merely philosophical. Koch Industries had just become the target of federal regulators. One month earlier, the government had charged the company with violating federal oil price controls. By 1975, the government had also cited a subsidiary of Koch Industries for overcharging $10 million for propane gas. More serious government allegations against the company were to come.

Not long after echoing Powell's call to arms, Charles too set up a think tank, transforming his private foundation into the Cato Institute. The name paid homage to the nom de plume used by the authors of a series of pro-liberty letters during the American Colonial period. Its start-up funding, according to one account, dwarfed even Scaife's early contributions to the Heritage Foundation, with Charles giving an estimated $10 to $20 million of tax-deductible donations to the nation's first libertarian think tank during its first three years.

According to Ed Crane, a young, rakish California financier who shared Koch's enthusiasm for libertarianism but lacked his checkbook, the idea for the think tank was his. After the Libertarian Party candidate was predictably crushed in his 1976 presidential quest, Crane, who had been instrumental in the campaign, was ready to go back to the private sector.

Instead, Charles, whom he'd met during the campaign, took him aside and asked what it would take to keep him in the libertarian movement. "I said my bank account is empty," Crane later recalled. "He said, 'How much do you need?'" "A libertarian think tank along the model of Brookings or AEI might be nice," Crane answered. To which, he said, Charles instantly replied, "I'll give it to you."

Crane became Cato's president, but early employees at Cato described Charles as single-handedly exerting absolute iron control. David Gordon, a libertarian activist who worked at Cato in the early days, told *Washingtonian* magazine, "Ed Crane would always call Wichita and run everything by Charles. It was quite clear that Koch was in charge." Another early Cato employee, Ronald Hamowy, added, "Whatever Charles said, went." Despite Crane's antipathy toward government, by 1977 Cato was based in Washington, D.C. It soon hired a slew of scholars whom the mainstream media respectfully quoted as nonpartisan experts.

Fundamentally, though, Cato was devoted to espousing Charles Koch's vision: that government's only legitimate role was to "serve as a night watchman, to protect individuals and property from outside threat, including fraud. That is the maximum," as he told the Wichita Rotary Club in the 1970s. The Kochs consistently depicted Cato and other ideological projects their philanthropy supported as nonpartisan and disinterested. But from the start, the Kochs' ideology and business interests dovetailed so seamlessly it was difficult to distinguish one from the other. Lower taxes, looser regulations, and fewer government programs for the poor and the middle class all corresponded to the Kochs' accumulation of wealth and power.

It's impossible to know exactly how much money private foundations and trusts, funded by a handful of extraordinarily wealthy families, poured into the right-wing think tanks beginning in the 1970s or how effective it was. Their grants were soon mixed with those from corporate donors, who cautiously followed the families' bold lead. Unlike other forms of paid political influence, much of this money was never revealed. Gifts to nonprofit groups could be concealed from the public. The new think tanks thus became fast-growing, sub-rosa corporate arsenals. In fact, after Watergate the conservative think tanks pitched themselves to businesses as the safest way to influence policy without scandal. By the early 1980s, a list of the Heritage Foundation's sponsors found in the private papers of one of its early supporters, Clare Boothe Luce, is crammed with Fortune 500 companies. Amoco, Amway, Boeing, Chase Manhattan Bank, Chevron, Dow Chemical, Exxon, General Electric, General Motors, Mesa Petroleum, Mobil Oil, Pfizer, Philip Morris, Procter & Gamble, R. J. Reynolds, Searle, Sears, Roebuck, SmithKline Beckman, Union Carbide, and Union Pacific were all by then paying the think tank's bills—while the think tank was promoting their agendas.

James Piereson, the scholar and key figure in conservative philanthropy, has suggested at a minimum "that the think tanks and conservative foundations made conservative ideas respectable." Before the surge in spending, he said, conservatives were seen as "cranks" on America's political fringe.

One measure of the movement's impact was that starting in 1973, and for successive decades afterward, the public's trust in government continually sank. If there was a single unified message pushed by those financing the conservative movement, it was that government rather than business was America's problem. By the early 1980s, the reversal in public opinion was so significant that Americans' distrust of government for the first time surpassed their distrust of business.

Another early sign that the investment was yielding real results on the national scale was the Republican wave that swept the 1978 midterm elections. That year, Republicans gained three Senate seats, fifteen House seats, and six governorships. In Georgia, in a development that would have unforeseen future repercussions, Newt Gingrich was elected to Congress. External events such as the energy crisis and "stagflation" of course played into the election results, too. But the new conservative think tanks and other right-wing political organizations fanned the discontent and shaped the dominant narrative.

Aiding the conservative resurgence was a newly organized and shockingly aggressive independent campaign offensive funded by donors on the right, run by the National Conservative Political Action Committee, or NCPAC, which introduced a whole new level of privately financed attack ads to American campaigns.

Growing conservative clout was apparent in Congress, too. The labor movement, which had expected ambitious gains under Jimmy Carter's presidency, instead soon suffered a series of devastating setbacks dealt by the ascendant business caucus backed by the expanding network of think tanks and outside lobby groups. Weyrich's hand was key here, too. He cemented the movement's influence in Congress by creating the Republican Study Committee, a caucus that united outside activists and conservative elected officials. For years, Heritage Foundation personnel were the only outsiders allowed to regularly caucus with Republican members of Congress because of this hybrid organization. "We are basically a conduit to and from the Heritage Foundation to and from conservative members of the House," its director, Don Eberly, said in 1983.

Weyrich, with Scaife's financial backing, launched several other ingenious political organizations during this period. One was the American Legislative Exchange Council (ALEC), a group aimed at waging conservative fights in every state legislature in the country. From 1973 until 1983, the Scaife and Mellon family trusts donated half a million dollars to ALEC, constituting most of its budget. "ALEC is well on its way to fulfilling the dream of those who started the organization," a Weyrich aide wrote to Scaife's top adviser in 1976, "thanks wholly to your confidence and the tremendous generosity of the Scaife Family Charitable Trusts." When one ALEC administrator complained that Scaife's foundation had too much influence over the organization's agenda, a Scaife employee retorted that they operated on "the Golden Rule—whoever has the gold rules."

Weyrich, meanwhile, dramatically enlarged the conservative groundswell by co-founding with Jerry Falwell the Moral Majority, which brought social and religious conservatives into the pro-corporate fold. Weyrich was particularly adept at capitalizing on white anger over desegregation.

The results of these efforts became visible in 1980. At the top of the ticket, Reagan, a movement conservative, overwhelmingly defeated Carter. Conservatives, whose obituaries had been written by the liberal elite just a few years before, were stunningly resurgent. The upset reverberated at every level, including the Senate, where four liberal marquee names, George McGovern, Frank Church, John Culver, and Birch Bayh, were all defeated.

Scaife, like the Kochs, hadn't initially backed Reagan's candidacy in 1980. In the primary, Scaife preferred John Connally. It barely mattered, though. By creating their own private idea factory, extreme donors had found a way to dominate American politics outside the parties. Once elected, Reagan embraced the Heritage Foundation's phone-book-sized policy playbook, *Mandate for Leadership*, and distributed a copy of it to every member of Congress. His administration soon delivered an impressive number of items on its wish list. Heritage had laid out 1,270 specific policy proposals. According to Feulner, the Reagan administration adopted 61 percent of them.

Andrew Mellon himself would have been pleased with the succession of hefty tax cuts that Reagan pushed through Congress. He slashed corporate and individual tax rates, particularly helping the wealthy. Between 1981 and 1986, the top income tax rate was cut from 70 percent to 28 percent. Meanwhile, taxes on the bottom four-fifths of earners rose. Economic inequality, which had flatlined, began to climb.

The fossil fuel industry's fondest wishes were also fulfilled. Following proposals set forth by the Heritage Foundation, as soon as Reagan entered the White House, he abolished the economic controls on oil and gas that Nixon had imposed in order to address the energy crisis. These were among the regulations that Charles Koch had so bitterly opposed. He also cut taxes on oil profits. Koch Industries' profits, predictably, skyrocketed. *Forbes* noted that Koch, though little known, "may well be the most profitable private business in the U.S."

The new conservative nonprofits were thriving, too. By 1985, the Heritage Foundation's budget equaled that of Brookings and AEI combined. Scaife, who by then had donated $10 million to the think tank, was contributing at a rate of $1 million a year. He had gone far to turn Lewis Powell's dream into a reality. But one key part of Powell's agenda remained unfinished. Conservative foundations might have financed a parallel intellectual establishment of their own, but the League to Save Carthage still hadn't conquered America's colleges and universities. The Ivy League was no more hospitable to Scaife and his ilk than it had been the day he was expelled. Scaife claimed he was thankful to have been spared the liberal indoctrination. "I was lucky. Higher education did not push me left, and I've never regretted it," he wrote in his memoir. "I'd say the main reason that rich people feel guilty is that the schools *teach* them they should."

That was about to change.

CHAPTER THREE

Beachheads: John M. Olin and the Bradley Brothers

IF THERE WAS A SINGLE EVENT THAT GALVANIZED CONSERVATIVE donors to try to wrest control of higher education in America, it might have been the uprising at Cornell University on April 20, 1969. That afternoon, during parents' weekend at the Ithaca, New York, campus, some eighty black students marched in formation out of the student union, which they had seized, with their clenched fists held high in black power salutes. To the shock of the genteel Ivy League community, several were brandishing guns. At the head of the formation was a student who called himself the "Minister of Defense" for Cornell's Afro-American Society. Strapped across his chest, Pancho Villa–style, was a sash-like bandolier studded with bullet cartridges. Gripped nonchalantly in his right hand, with its butt resting on his hip, was a glistening rifle. Chin held high and sporting an Afro, goatee, and eyeglasses reminiscent of Malcolm X, he was the face of a drama so infamous it was regarded for years by conservatives such as the journalist David Horowitz as "the most disgraceful occurrence in the history of American higher education."

John M. Olin, a multimillionaire industrialist, wasn't there at Cornell, which was his alma mater, that weekend. He was traveling abroad. But as a former Cornell trustee, he could not have gone long without seeing the iconic photograph of the armed protesters. What came to be known as "the Picture" quickly ricocheted around the world, eventually going on to win that year's Pulitzer Prize.

Traveling almost as fast was the news that Cornell's administrators had quickly capitulated to the demands of the black militants, rather than risk a bloody confrontation. Under duress, the university's president had promised to accelerate plans to establish an independent black studies program at Cornell, as well as to investigate the burning of a cross outside a building in which several black female students lived. And to the deep consternation of many conservative faculty members and students on campus, the president also agreed to grant full amnesty to the protesters, some of whom were facing previous disciplinary proceedings following an earlier uprising in which they had reportedly flung books from the shelves of Cornell's libraries, denouncing the works as "not relevant" to the black experience.

By all accounts, the confrontation was especially distressing to Olin. Cornell's library was one of four buildings on the Cornell campus bearing his family's name. Both he and his father had graduated from the school and had been proud and generous donors. Almost worse than the behavior of the protesters, from his standpoint, was the behavior of Cornell's president, James Perkins, a committed liberal who had gone out of his way to open the university's doors to inner-city minority students and now seemed to be bending the curriculum and lowering disciplinary standards to placate them.

"The catastrophe at Cornell inspired Olin to take his philanthropy in a bold, new direction," according to John J. Miller, whose authorized biography, *A Gift of Freedom,* provides a treasure trove of original research on Olin's life and legacy. Olin "saw very clearly that students at Cornell, like those at most major universities, were hostile to businessmen and to business enterprise, and indeed had begun to question the ideals of the nation itself," an Olin Foundation memo recounts.

As a result, according to Miller, instead of continuing to direct the bulk of his charitable contributions to hospitals, museums, and other standard patrician causes, as he had in the early years after he set up the John M. Olin Foundation in 1953, Olin embarked on a radical new course. He began to fund an ambitious offensive to reorient the political slant of American higher education to the right. His foundation aimed at the country's most elite schools, the Ivy League and its peers, cognizant that these schools were the incubators of those who would hold future power. If these young cadres could be trained to think more like him, then he and other donors could help secure the country's political future. It was an attempted takeover, but instead of waging it with bandoliers and rifles, he chose money as his weapon.

By the time the John M. Olin Foundation spent itself out of existence in 2005, as called for in its founder's will, it had spent about half of its total assets of $370 million bankrolling the promotion of free-market ideology and other conservative ideas on the country's campuses. In doing so, it molded and credentialed a whole new generation of conservative graduates and professors. "These efforts have been instrumental in challenging the campus left—or more specifically, the problem of radical activists' gaining control of America's colleges and universities," Miller concluded in a 2003 pamphlet published by the Philanthropy Roundtable, an organization run for conservative philanthropists.

"These guys, individually and collectively, created a new philanthropic form, which was movement philanthropy," said Rob Stein, a progressive political strategist, speaking of the Olin Foundation and a handful of other private foundations that funded the creation of a conservative counter-intelligentsia during this period. "What they started is the most potent machinery ever assembled in a democracy to promote a set of beliefs and to control the reins of government." Stein was so impressed that he went on to try to build a liberal version of the model. Each side would argue that the other had more money and more influence, depending on how broadly they defined the rival camp. But beginning in the 1970s, the Left felt hard-pressed to match the far-ranging propagation of ideology pioneered by a few enterprising donors on the right.

There is little doubt that the Cornell uprising radicalized Olin's philanthropy, but the official account citing this as the key to his thinking is incomplete. The protest took place in 1969, and Olin didn't begin to transform his foundation into an ideological instrument aimed at "saving the free enterprise system," as his lawyer put it, until four years later, in the spring of 1973. On closer inspection, it appears that there were additional factors involved that shed less flattering light on his motivations.

By 1973, the Olin Corporation was embroiled in multiple, serious controversies over its environmental practices, undermining its reputation, threatening its revenues, and ensnarling the company in expensive litigation. Founded by Olin's father, Franklin, in 1892, the company had begun in East Alton, Illinois, as a manufacturer of blasting powder for coal miners but expanded into making small arms and ammunition. Like the Koch sons, Olin followed closely in his father's path. After attending prep school, he entered his father's alma mater, Cornell, where he struggled until he was allowed to conduct chemical research relating to his family's company. He graduated in 1913 with a degree in chemistry. He then returned to Illinois to join the family business.

Although Olin regarded himself as self-made and disapproved of the New Deal–era government social programs, beliefs that fueled his later financing of free-market ideology, the federal government was one of the greatest contributors to his company's growth and his personal wealth. As Miller's biography details, the firm's huge government arms contracts in World Wars I and II dramatically improved its bottom line. Revenues quintupled during World War I and exploded during World War II. Olin complained about the government's interference and inefficiency, but his company reaped $40 million in profits during World War II alone. By 1953, it was being celebrated by *Fortune* as one of the few great family-owned corporations.

In 1954, the company went public and merged with the Mathieson Chemical Corporation, doubling in size, diversifying its operations, and eventually changing its name to the Olin Corporation. The conglomeration, whose revenues were half a billion dollars a year by then, made everything from pharmaceuticals in its Squibb division to cigarette paper. It manufactured Winchester rifles and, later, the hydrazine rocket fuel that powered Neil Armstrong's 1969 lunar landing. Meanwhile, Olin's national profile was growing. By 1957, *Fortune* ranked John M. Olin and his brother Spencer, who had taken over the company from their father, as the thirty-first wealthiest Americans, with fortunes estimated at over $75 million. Honors proliferated along with Olin's great wealth. Following his retirement as the company's executive committee chairman in 1963, he devoted himself to serving on the boards of several prestigious universities, including Cornell, and to his passion for the outdoors. He had appeared on the cover of *Sports Illustrated* with his wife in 1958, carrying shotguns and dressed in natty tweeds amid picturesque tall grass, for a profile highlighting his role as a hunter, and a breeder of champion dogs. Known as a conservationist, he was a director of the World Wildlife Fund.

So it must have been a rude blow to him personally, as well as to the prestige and bottom line of his company, when in 1973 the Environmental Protection Agency singled out the Olin Corporation as one of its first targets, soon after Richard Nixon signed the agency into existence. Suddenly under tougher scrutiny, the company that Olin had built was an outlaw, facing charges of egregious pollution practices in several states at once.

In Alabama, the Olin Corporation became embroiled over its production of DDT. Rachel Carson, in her book *Silent Spring,* had identified the pesticide as a deadly contaminant to the biological food chain. The Olin Corporation had been producing 20 percent of the DDT used in the United States. Soon it was fighting a vigorous but losing battle with federal officials against new pollution standards tightening the chemical's production and use, which the company said would make it impossible to keep its plant open. In addition, three conservation groups, the Environmental Defense Fund, the National Audubon Society, and the National Wildlife Federation, were all suing the company to enjoin it from releasing effluents laced with DDT into a national wildlife preserve near Olin's Alabama plant. In 1972, the federal government banned the use of DDT altogether, forcing Olin to shut its production down.

The company's extensive use of mercury in its production of chlorine and other products had also become a huge problem. In the summer of 1970, according to a front-page story in *The New York Times,* the U.S. Interior Department charged the Olin Corporation with dumping 26.6 pounds of mercury a day into the Niagara River in upstate New York. Mercury was by then a known human health hazard. Scientists had documented its damage to the human brain and reproductive and nervous systems. Subsequently, the Justice Department also charged the Olin Corporation with falsifying records, showing that the company had dumped sixty-six thousand tons of chemical waste, including mercury, into a landfill in Niagara Falls, New York. The Hooker Chemicals and Plastics Corporation was simultaneously charged with dumping toxic chemicals at the same site, as well as the nearby "Love Canal," which became an international symbol of toxic pollution. Eventually, the Olin Corporation and three of its former corporate officers were convicted of falsifying records in the dumping case, after which the presiding judge imposed the maximum available fine of $70,000 on the company.

In the tiny Appalachian town of Saltville, Virginia, meanwhile, in the far southwestern corner of the state, the Olin Corporation was facing an environmental crisis of such major proportions that it threatened to end not only Olin's industrial operations there but also the entire town's way of life for years to come. The Olin Corporation's pollution was so extensive and intractable that the company faced the prospect of tens if not hundreds of millions of dollars in cleanup costs, with no end in sight.

For decades, Saltville had been a prototypical company town, owned and run in an almost feudal fashion by its only large employer, the Olin Corporation. The company owned ten thousand acres in the ruggedly beautiful mountainous gap, as well as 450 modest clapboard houses that it rented to the town's 2,199 residents. It also owned the local grocery stores, the water system, the sewerage system, and the only school, which many workers left after no more than sixth or seventh grade. The company prided itself on paternalistic flourishes like a swimming pool and a small stadium for residents. When employees got sick, the company paid for the doctors. The mayor and virtually everyone else in Saltville worked in the chemical plant, which Olin acquired in its merger with the Mathieson Chemical Corporation in 1954. The town's vast natural salt deposits made it a perfect place to produce chlorine and salt ash, and for years it was the picture of American industrial prosperity, at least for its owners. But for the employees, there was an ominous, unaddressed issue. Olin's chlorine production process used huge quantities of mercury, which the plant leaked into the public waterways on a daily basis. From 1951 to 1970, the company estimated its factory spilled about a hundred pounds of mercury every day. Most of it emptied directly into the North Fork of the Holston River, which ran picturesquely along the town's edge. An open sediment pond, meanwhile, into which the company dumped its mercury waste, contained an astounding fifty-three thousand pounds of the toxic substance.

"They all knew the dangers back then. They had some

really good scientists and chemists. But you didn't have the regulations," says Harry Haynes, who runs a small history museum in Saltville and whose father used to work at the Olin plant. "We all played with the mercury as children," he recalls. "Daddy brought it home from the chemical plant. You'd drop it on the floor, and it would explode into a zillion little bits, and then sweep it together and it would clump back together again." The company issued gas masks to workers because of the pervasive chemical vapors, but, another resident recalled, "no one wore them."

In 1972, however, the world recoiled at photographs of birth defects resulting from severe mercury contamination at Minamata Bay in Japan. Scientists definitively linked the birth defects—as well as other health horrors including cerebral palsy, mental retardation, blindness, deafness, coma, and death—to consumption of seafood that had been contaminated by mercury waste in local fishing areas. After having been dumped in the water, the mercury had broken down into a soluble form toxic to aquatic life and to those ingesting it. The nightmare at Minamata drew concern about the effects of mercury pollution elsewhere, including at the Olin plant in Saltville. Testing conducted by the state soon revealed high levels of mercury in the sediment in the North Fork of the Holston River, which ran from Saltville on down to Tennessee, where it flowed into the Cherokee Lake recreation area, a favorite fishing destination. Dangerous levels of mercury were discovered in the fish for eighty miles south of the Olin plant, according to one report.

In response to the rising concerns in Saltville, in 1970 Virginia passed strict new standards that the company said it couldn't meet. As a result, Olin said, it would cease operations in Saltville by the end of 1972. The company actually had several other reasons for shutting the plant. It was unable to compete with more efficient western salt ash manufacturers. Also, it was under pressure from the United Mine Workers union, which had succeeded after bitter battles in representing the employees. In all likelihood, the factory was doomed not just for environmental reasons.

Yet the story line blaming environmental activists for its problems proved irresistible. *Life* magazine produced an elegiac photo essay called "End of a Company Town," and *The Wall Street Journal* lamented the crushing new regulatory burden on corporate America. The Olin Corporation, meanwhile, demolished its factory and sold most of its Saltville real estate back to local residents but found no takers for its mercury waste "muck" pond. It tried removing a foot or so of topsoil around it, and it tried building a ditch along the river to divert the toxic runoff, but these efforts were hopelessly deficient. Soon after, the EPA designated Saltville one of the country's first "Superfund" sites.

"It's a ghost town. It was extremely polluted and still is," says Shirley "Sissy" Bailey, who grew up near Saltville and still lives there. "To this day, that muck pond is still there, and you can still see clumps of mercury along the river. The drinking water is so full of lead and mercury it isn't fit for a dog to drink." She says she "lived" the history, ran as a kid on riverbanks so poisoned no grass grew. The air often smelled of chlorine and other chemicals. "The Olin Company was dirty and treated the people bad, not like people," she says. "Most of the workers were poorly educated, and they led them around like sheep. A lot of people got sick, and there were more birth defects in Saltville than in other parts of the state," she asserts, although there has been no study proving this or establishing any causal correlation.

"Common sense should have made companies take responsibility, but until the 1970s there were no regulations on this. The EPA became a form of accountability," says Stephen Lester, the Harvard-educated science director for the Center for Health, Environment, and Justice in Falls Church, Virginia, a nonprofit environmental group that provided technical assistance to Bailey in a later mercury contamination fight in Saltville. "Of course that imposes costs and affects the bottom line, so it wasn't popular with the company." The cost of cleaning up Saltville, in fact, was projected to be upward of $35 million.

Former officials at the Olin Foundation, when asked about the company's ignominious environmental record, downplay any link to the nonprofit's pro-corporate, antiregulatory ideology. "It is possible that Mr. Olin was influenced to some degree by litigation and regulations against the company," says James Piereson, the conservative scholar, who was executive director and trustee of the Olin Foundation from 1985 to 2005. "But that would be one factor among many others; and he was no longer running the company on a day to day basis by this time." He added, "There were a lot of cross currents in the air: the Cold War, détente, Watergate, inflation, a stock market crash, war in the Middle East, Vietnam, environmentalism, feminism." William Voegeli, who was program officer at the Olin Foundation from 1988 to 2003, says, "The Olin family had very little to do during these years with either the John Olin Foundation or the Olin Corporation." He added, "I never heard one word, during my years at the foundation, about how its grants might affect the Olin Company (whose stock constituted less than one percent of our endowment), or the finances of the Olin family. Whatever else can be said of our conservative agenda, it was disinterested."

It was, however, against a backdrop of serious clashes with the increasingly robust regulatory state that John Olin directed his lawyer to enlist his fortune in the battle to defend corporate America. As he put it, "My greatest ambition now is to see free enterprise re-established in this country. Business and the public must be awakened to the creeping stranglehold that socialism has gained here since World War II."

At first, the foundation funneled money into the same conservative think tanks that Scaife and Coors were supporting, the Heritage Foundation, the American Enterprise Institute, and the Hoover Institution, the conservative think tank located on Stanford University's campus. But soon John Olin's focus diverged. Perhaps because of his upset over Cornell, his foundation became uniquely centered on transforming academia. As he wrote in a private letter to the president of Cornell, he regarded the campus as overrun by scholars "with definite left-wing attitudes and convictions." Olin noted, "It matters little to me whether the economic development is classified as Marxism, Keynesianism, or whatnot." He said he regarded "liberalism" and "socialism" as "synonymous." All of these academic trends, he asserted, needed "very serious study and correction."

To get his bearings, Olin's labor lawyer, Frank O'Connell, contacted a handful of other private conservative foundations. He sought advice from colleagues at the Koch and Scaife Foundations, as well as a few others on the right such as the Earhart Foundation and the Smith Richardson Foundation, which was funded by the Vicks VapoRub fortune. George Pearson, who was running the Charles G. Koch Foundation at that point, guided O'Connell, assigning him a free-market reading list that included Hayek's essay "The Intellectuals and Socialism." Hayek's point was emphatic: to conquer politics, one must first conquer the intellectuals. O'Connell recalled, "It was like a home-study course."

The fledgling right-wing foundations were also studying their establishment counterparts during this period, particularly the giant Ford Foundation. By the late 1960s, Ford was pioneering what its head, McGeorge Bundy, a former dean at Harvard and national security adviser to the Kennedy and Johnson administrations, called "advocacy philanthropy." Ford was, for instance, pouring money into the environmental movement, funding the Environmental Defense Fund and the Natural Resources Defense Council. By supporting public interest litigation, it showed conservatives how philanthropy could achieve large-scale change through the courts while bypassing the democratic electoral process, just as the early critics of private foundations had feared.

In 1977, Olin raised his foundation's stature by choosing William Simon as its president. Simon was a social acquaintance of Olin's from East Hampton, Long Island, where they both had beach houses, and Olin described Simon's thinking as "almost identical with mine." While Olin kept a low profile, however, Simon loved the spotlight, the hotter the better. As Voegeli recalled, Simon was like Alice Longworth's description of her father, Theodore Roosevelt. "He wanted to be the bride at every wedding, and the corpse at every funeral."

Simon had been energy czar and later Treasury secretary under Presidents Nixon and Ford and was a famously intemperate critic of those he considered "stupid." This large category included liberals, radicals, and moderate members of his own Republican Party. Like Olin, he was incensed by the expansion of the regulatory state. He especially detested environmentalists and other self-appointed guardians of the public interest, describing them as the "New Despots." In his 1978 manifesto, *A Time for Truth,* he wrote, "Since the 60's, the vast bulk of regulatory legislation passed by congress . . . [has] been largely initiated by a powerful new lobby that goes by the name of the Public Interest movement." Simon disparaged these "college-educated idealists" who claimed to be working for "the well being of 'consumers,' the 'environment,' 'minorities,'" and other nonmaterial causes, accusing them of wanting to "expand the police powers of the state over American producers." He challenged their purity. Noting that they claimed to care little for money, he accused them of being driven by another kind of self-interest. Quoting his colleague Irving Kristol, the neoconservative intellectual, he charged that these usurpers wanted "the power to shape our civilization." That power, he argued, should belong exclusively to "the free market."

Simon's hatred and suspicion of the liberal elite approached Nixonian levels in his 1980 sequel manifesto, *A Time for Action*. He claimed that a "secret system" of academics, media figures, bureaucrats, and public interest advocates ran the country. Picking up where Lewis Powell had left off in his memo nine years earlier, Simon warned that unless businessmen fought back, "Our freedom is in dire peril."

Simon's foreboding, like that of Olin, is somewhat hard to fathom given that both men had reached pinnacles of American power and wealth. They were both millionaires many times over, with more properties, possessions, titles, honors, and accomplishments than they could easily count. Both men were born into privilege. Like Scaife, Simon was chauffeured to grade school, and his family was so wealthy he likened his parents to the carefree and careless characters in F. Scott Fitzgerald's fiction. Nonetheless, he regarded himself proudly as self-made. His father evidently lost his mother's fortune, motivating Simon to make his own. On Wall Street, he became a hugely successful partner at Salomon Brothers, where he was an early leader in the lucrative new craze for leveraged buyouts. But what neither Olin nor Simon had was influence over the next generation. "We are careening with frightening speed towards collectivism," Simon warned.

Only an ideological battle could save the country, in Simon's view. "What we need is a counter-intelligentsia . . . [It] can be organized to challenge our ruling 'new class'—opinion makers," Simon wrote. "Ideas are weapons—indeed the only weapons with which other ideas can be fought." He argued, "Capitalism has no duty to subsidize its enemies." Private and corporate foundations, he said, must cease "the mindless subsidizing of colleges and universities whose departments of politics, economics and history are hostile to capitalism."

Instead, they "must take pains to funnel desperately needed funds to scholars, social scientists and writers who understand the relationship between political and economic liberty," as he put it. "They must be given grants, grants, and more grants in exchange for books, books, and more books."

Under Simon's guidance, the Olin Foundation tried to fund the new "counter-intelligentsia." At first, it tried supporting little-known colleges where conservative ideas—and money—were welcome. But Simon and his associates soon realized that this was a losing strategy. If the Olin Foundation wanted impact, it needed to infiltrate prestigious schools, especially the Ivy League.

The man who put his mark on the Olin Foundation more than its namesake, or even Simon, was its executive director, Michael Joyce, a fierce former liberal who had become a neoconservative acolyte of Kristol's. A friend of Joyce's said that he believed philanthropy was about power and that those with great fortunes needed political capos like him to tell them how to wield it. Joyce was a brawler who wanted to take on America's liberal establishment, not just supplement it in some milquetoast way. In the words of Ralph Benko, a libertarian blogger for *Forbes,* "Joyce was a true radical. He was inspired by Antonio Gramsci. He wanted to effect radical transformation." In Miller's view, Joyce was "an intellectual among activists, and an activist among intellectuals. He understood how the world of ideas influenced the real world." Joyce was characteristically more blunt. "My style," he said, "was the style of the toddler and the adolescent: fight, fight, fight, rest, get up, fight, fight, fight. No one ever accused me of being pleasant. I made a difference. It was acknowledged by friend and foe."

Joining Joyce was Piereson, a thoughtful, soft-spoken neoconservative whose path to the Olin Foundation had also run through Irving Kristol. Piereson had befriended the Kristol family at the University of Pennsylvania, where he taught government and political theory alongside Irving's son, Bill.

Both had felt marginalized by their more liberal peers. Having closely observed America's academic intelligentsia, Piereson concluded that the foundation needed to "penetrate" the most elite institutions, "because they were emulated by other colleges and universities of lesser stature." As Hillel Fradkin, who also worked at the Olin Foundation, put it, "The only way you're going to change the debate in this country is by looking to those schools. Giving money to conservative outposts won't get much done."

What emerged was a strategy they called the "beachhead" theory. The aim, as Piereson later described it in an essay offering advice to fellow conservative philanthropists, was to establish conservative cells, or "beachheads," at "the most influential schools in order to gain the greatest leverage." The formula required subtlety, indirection, and perhaps even some misdirection.

The key, Piereson explained, was to fund the conservative intelligentsia in such a way that it would not "raise questions about academic integrity." Instead of trying to earmark a chair or dictate a faculty appointment, both of which he noted were bound to "generate fierce controversy," he suggested that conservative donors look for like-minded faculty members whose influence could be enlarged by outside funding. In time, such a professor could administer an expanded program. But Piereson warned that it was "essential for the integrity and reputation of the programs that they be defined not by ideological points of view." To overtly acknowledge "pre-ordained conclusions" would doom a program. Instead of saying the program was designed to "demonstrate the falsity of Marxism" or to promote "free-enterprise," he advised that it was better to "define programs in terms of fields of study, [like the] John M. Olin Fellowships in Military History." He wrote, "Often a program can be given a philosophical or principled identity by giving it the name of an important historical figure, such as the James

Madison Program [in] American Ideals and Institutions at Princeton University."

(Indeed, after years of trial and error, the Olin Foundation funded Princeton's Madison Program with $525,000 in start-up grants in 2000. Run by Robert George, an outspoken social and religious conservative, the program serves as the beau ideal of the "beachhead" theory. As a friend of George's described him to *The Nation* in 2006, he is "a savvy right-wing operative, boring from within the liberal infrastructure.")

Piereson warned conservative philanthropists that taking the liberal out of liberal arts education would require patience and cunning. As a former academic himself, he knew how politically charged a frontal assault would be. Rather than openly trying to overhaul academia overnight, he suggested, "perhaps we should think instead about challenging it by adding new voices." As he put it, "This may well be the best means of changing the college culture, for a few powerful voices of criticism may at some point bring the entire ideological house of cards crashing down upon itself."

If the Olin Foundation was less than transparent about its mission, it was not for the first time. Between 1958 and 1966, it secretly served as a bank for the Central Intelligence Agency. During these eight years, the CIA laundered $1.95 million through the foundation. Olin, according to Miller, regarded his undercover role as just part of his patriotic duty. Many of the government funds went to anti-Communist intellectuals and publications. But in 1967, the press exposed the covert propaganda operation, triggering a political furor and causing the CIA to fold the program. The CIA money at the Olin Foundation, which was not publicized at the time, disappeared as quietly as it had arrived. The idea of using the private foundation to fund ideologically aligned intellectuals, however, persisted.

Soon the Olin Foundation was investing in William F. Buckley Jr., whose television show, *Firing Line,* the foundation supported. It was also funding Allan Bloom, author of the best-selling slam from the right at American higher education, *The Closing of the American Mind* (in which Bloom also lashed out at rock music as a "nonstop, commercially prepackaged masturbation fantasy"). The foundation also supported Dinesh D'Souza, author of *Illiberal Education,* which blasted "political correctness," castigating rules requiring sensitivity to women and minorities as the overreaching of liberal thought police. In addition, the Olin Foundation funded professors at leading schools all over the country, including Harvard's Harvey C. Mansfield and Samuel P. Huntington. It donated $3.3 million to Mansfield's Program on Constitutional Government at Harvard, which emphasized a conservative interpretation of American government, and the foundation donated $8.4 million to Huntington's John M. Olin Institute for Strategic Studies, which inculcated a hawkish approach to foreign policy and national security.

Through these carefully curated programs, the foundation trained the next generation of conservatives, whom Joyce likened to "a wine collection" that would grow more valuable as its members aged, increasing in stature and power. The foundation kept track of those who passed through Huntington's Olin program, proudly noting that many went into public service and academia. Between 1990 and 2001, fifty-six of the eighty-eight Olin fellows at the Harvard program continued on to teach at the University of Chicago, Cornell, Dartmouth, Georgetown, Harvard, MIT, Penn, and Yale. Many others became public figures in government, think tanks, and the media. In all, by the time it closed its doors in 2005, the Olin Foundation had supported eleven separate programs at Harvard, burnishing the foundation's name and ideas and proving that even the best-endowed American university would allow an outside, ideological group to build "beachheads," so long as the project was properly packaged and funded.

On top of these programs, the foundation doled out $8 million to more than a hundred John M. Olin faculty fellows. These funds enabled scores of young academics to take the time needed to research and write in order to further their careers. The roster of recipients includes John Yoo, the legal scholar who went on to become the author of the George W. Bush administration's controversial "torture memo" legalizing the American government's brutalization of terror suspects.

Without the rigorous peer-reviewed standards required by prestigious academic publications, the Olin Foundation was able to inject into the mainstream a number of works whose scholarship was debatable at best. For example, Olin Foundation funds enabled John R. Lott Jr., then an Olin fellow at the University of Chicago, to write his influential book *More Guns, Less Crime.* In the work, Lott argued that more guns actually reduce crime and that the legalization of concealed weapons would make citizens safer. Politicians advocating weaker gun control laws frequently cited Lott's findings. But according to Adam Winkler, the author of *Gunfight,* Lott's scholarship was suspect. Winkler wrote that "Lott's claimed source for this information was 'national surveys,'" which under questioning he revised to just one survey that he and research assistants had conducted. When asked to provide the data, Winkler recounts, Lott said he had lost it in a computer crash. Asked for any evidence of the survey, writes Winkler, "Lott said he had no such evidence." (Proving that the recipients of Olin funds weren't ideologically monolithic, Winkler, too, had received funds from the foundation.)

Another Olin-funded book that made headlines and ended in accusations of intellectual dishonesty was David Brock's *Real Anita Hill,* to which the foundation gave a small research stipend. In the book, Brock defended the Supreme Court justice Clarence Thomas by accusing Hill of fabricating her sworn testimony against him during his Senate confirmation hearings. Later, though, Brock recanted, admitting that he had been wrong. He apologized for the book and said that he had been deceived by conservative sources who had misled him.

Still, the combined impact of the Olin grantees was "a triumph," according to Miller. Writing as a conservative in 2003, he enthused that "a small handful of foundations have essentially provided the conservative movement with its venture capital." He noted that in contrast to the days when Lionel Trilling had declared conservatism over, "conservative ideas are in broad circulation, and many believe they are now ascendant." He added, "If the conservative intellectual movement were a NASCAR race, and if the scholars and organizations who compose it were drivers zipping around a race track, virtually all of their vehicles would sport an Olin bumper sticker."

In time, the Olin Foundation's success in minting right-leaning thinkers drew the envy of the Left. "On the right, they understood that books matter," says Steve Wasserman, now the editor at large at Yale University Press, who was dismayed by the failure of wealthy liberal donors to match the intellectual investments being made by conservatives. "I remember meeting at a restaurant in California with some of the most savvy Democratic supporters, Margery Tabankin, Stanley Sheinbaum and Danny Goldberg. We wanted to figure out how to fund books on the Left. But they said that for most donors books weren't sexy, preferring to give money to candidates and causes. The Democrats were hostage to star personalities and electoral politics."

The Olin Foundation's most significant beachheads, however, were established in America's law schools, where it bankrolled a new approach to jurisprudence known as Law and Economics. Powell, in his memo, had argued that "the judiciary may be the most important instrument for social, economic and political change." The Olin Foundation agreed. As the courts expanded consumer, labor, and environmental rights and demanded racial and sexual equality and greater workplace safety, conservatives in business were desperate to find more legal leverage. Law and Economics became their tool.

As a discipline, Law and Economics was seen at first as a fringe theory embraced largely by libertarian mavericks until the Olin Foundation spent $68 million underwriting its growth. Like an academic Johnny Appleseed, the Olin Foundation underwrote 83 percent of the costs for all Law and Economics programs in American law schools between the years of 1985 and 1989. Overall, it scattered more than $10 million to Harvard, $7 million to Yale and Chicago, and over $2 million to Columbia, Cornell, Georgetown, and the University of Virginia. Miller writes, "John Olin, in fact, was prouder of Law and Economics than any other program he supported."

Following Piereson's cautious playbook, the program's title conveyed no ideology. Law and Economics stresses the need to analyze laws, including government regulations, not just for their fairness but also for their economic impact. Its proponents describe it in apolitical terms as bringing "efficiency" and "clarity" to the law, rather than relying on fuzzy, hard-to-quantify concepts like social justice.

Piereson, however, admitted that the beauty of the program was that it was a stealth political attack and that the country's best law schools didn't grasp this and therefore didn't block the ideological punch it packed. "I saw it as a way into the law schools—I probably shouldn't confess that," he told *The New York Times* in 2005. "Economic analysis tends to have conservatizing effects." In a later interview with the political scientist Steven M. Teles, he added that he would have preferred to fund a conservative constitutional law program, but had the foundation tried such a direct political challenge, it probably would have been barred entry to America's best law schools. "If you said to a dean that you wanted to fund conservative constitutional law, he would reject the idea out of hand. But if you said you wanted to support Law and Economics, he would be much more open to the idea," he confided. "Law and Economics is neutral, but it has a philosophical thrust in the direction of free markets and limited government. That is, like many disciplines, it seems neutral, but it isn't in fact."

The Olin Foundation's route into the country's best law schools was circuitous. The foundation began by financially supporting an early leading figure in Law and Economics, the libertarian Henry Manne, an acolyte of the Chicago school of free-market economics. Brilliant, impolitic, and an ideological purist, Manne "was considered a marginal, even eccentric character in the legal academy," according to Teles, when the Olin Foundation first started funding him in the early 1970s. To the frustration of the foundation, though, he didn't teach at high-prestige schools. In 1985, however, the foundation seized a golden opportunity to establish a beachhead at the pinnacle of legal prestige. That year, Harvard Law School was riven by controversy. Leftist professors were urging students to "sabotage" corporate law firms from within. Conservative professors and alumni were scandalized. The ruckus attracted national press coverage in *The New Yorker* and elsewhere. Among the many outraged Harvard Law School alumni was one of the Olin Foundation's trustees, George Gillespie. Sensing an opening, he contacted a conservative Harvard Law School professor, Phil Areeda, whom he had been in school with, and offered the foundation's help. The Olin Foundation took the initiative, and Harvard took the cash. Out of this ideological pact came the John M. Olin Center for Law, Economics, and Business at Harvard Law School, on which the foundation ultimately spent $18 million. The donation was the biggest in Olin's history. Harvard's president at the time, Derek Bok, was reportedly delighted at the new source of funding and the opportunity to soothe the disgruntled alumni.

After Harvard approved Law and Economics, other schools soon followed. By 1990, nearly eighty law schools taught the subject. Olin fellows in Law and Economics, meanwhile, began to beat a path to the top of the legal profession, winning Supreme Court clerkships at a rate of approximately one each year, starting in 1985. Many of the adherents were outstanding lawyers and not all were conservative, but they were changing the prevailing legal culture. By 1986, Bruce Ackerman, then a professor at Columbia Law School, called Law and Economics "the most important thing in legal education since the birth of Harvard Law School." Teles, in his 2008 book, *The Rise of the Conservative Legal Movement,* described Law and Economics as "the most successful intellectual movement in the law of the past thirty years, having rapidly moved from insurgency to hegemony."

As Law and Economics spread, underwritten at each step by the Olin Foundation and other conservative backers including the Kochs and Scaife, liberal critics grew alarmed. The Alliance for Justice, a liberal nonprofit in Washington, published a critical report in 1993 warning that "a small wealthy group" was trying to "fundamentally alter the way that justice is dispensed in our society." It revealed that the Olin Foundation was paying students thousands of dollars to take classes in Law and Economics at Georgetown Law School and to attend workshops on the subject at Columbia Law School. Despite this ethically dubious situation, only one law school, at the University of California in Los Angeles, turned the Olin funds away, arguing that by plying students with grant money, the foundation was "taking advantage of students' financial need to indoctrinate them with a particular ideology."

More controversial still were Law and Economics seminars that the Olin Foundation funded for judges. The seminars were initiated by Henry Manne, who had become dean of the George Mason University School of Law in Virginia, which he was trying to transform into a hub of libertarian jurisprudence.

The seminars treated judges to two-week-long, all-expenses-paid immersion training in Law and Economics usually in luxurious settings like the Ocean Reef Club in Key Largo, Florida. They soon became popular free vacations for the judges, a cross between Maoist cultural reeducation camps and Club Med. After a few hours of learning why environmental and labor laws were anathema, or why, as Manne argued, insider-trading laws did more harm than good, the judges broke for golf, swimming, and delightful dinners with their hosts. Within a few years, 660 judges had gone on these junkets, some, like the U.S. Court of Appeals judge and unconfirmed Supreme Court nominee Douglas Ginsburg, many times. By one count, 40 percent of the federal judiciary participated, including the future Supreme Court justices Ruth Bader Ginsburg and Clarence Thomas.

A variety of major corporations eagerly joined Olin and other conservative foundations in footing the bills. A study by the nonpartisan Center for Public Integrity found that between 2008 and 2012 close to 185 federal judges attended judicial seminars sponsored by conservative interests, several of which had cases before the courts. The lead underwriters were the Charles Koch Foundation, the Searle Freedom Trust, ExxonMobil, Shell Oil, the pharmaceutical giant Pfizer, and State Farm, the insurance company. Topics ranged from "The Moral Foundations of Capitalism" to "Terrorism, Climate, and Central Planning: Challenges to Liberty and the Rule of Law."

Simultaneously, the Olin Foundation provided crucial start-up funds for the Federalist Society, a powerful organization for conservative law students founded in 1982. With $5.5 million from the Olin Foundation, as well as large donations from foundations tied to Scaife, the Kochs, and other conservative legacies, the Federalist Society grew from a pipe dream shared by three ragtag law students into a powerful professional network of forty-two thousand right-leaning lawyers, with 150 law school campus chapters and about seventy-five lawyers' groups nationally. All of the conservative justices on the Supreme Court are members, as are the former vice president Dick Cheney, the former attorneys general Edwin Meese and John Ashcroft, and numerous members of the federal bench. Its executive director, Eugene B. Meyer, son of a founding editor of *National Review*, acknowledged that without Olin funding "it possibly wouldn't exist at all." Looking back, the Olin Foundation's staff described it as "one of the best investments" the foundation ever made.

John M. Olin died in 1982 at the age of eighty-nine, but after his death his foundation became even more robust. He left it about $50 million in his estate and another $50 million in a trust for his widow, which came to the foundation in 1993 after she died. The funds were well invested, growing to some $370 million in all before the foundation spent it down and closed its doors in 2005. Olin had directed his foundation to shut down during the lifetime of the trustees for fear that it would fall into the hands of liberals, as he believed the Ford Foundation had tragically done.

William Simon remained the head of the Olin Foundation until his own death in 2000. He also continued to amass a stupendous fortune of his own during the 1980s, using controversial financial maneuvers. By the late 1980s, *Forbes* estimated Simon's wealth at $300 million.

Around the same time, the Olin Foundation made a key $25,000 investment of its own in an unknown writer named Charles Murray, funding a grant at the Manhattan Institute that would support a book he was writing that attacked liberal welfare policies. The backstory to *Losing Ground*, Murray's book, was a primer on the growing and interlocking influence of conservative nonprofits. At thirty-nine, Murray was an unknown academic, toiling thanklessly at a Washington Beltway firm evaluating U.S. government social programs.

Frustrated and just scraping by, he was about to try writing a thriller novel in order to make ends meet when his application for a job at the Heritage Foundation caught the eye of the conservative philanthropy world. Soon, he was the beneficiary of its growing network. Heritage placed an antiwelfare piece by Murray on the op-ed page of *The Wall Street Journal.* This sparked a grant from the Olin Foundation that enabled him to work full-time on what became his pathbreaking 1984 book, *Losing Ground,* even though he hadn't previously considered turning his research into a book. "It was a classic case of philanthropic entrepreneurship," Murray says. The hidden force behind Murray was Joyce, the Olin Foundation's enfant terrible. "Mike Joyce was one of the most influential obscure people of the last century," says Murray.

Losing Ground, which was written in a tone of sorrow rather than anger, blamed government programs for creating a culture of dependence among the poor. Critics said it overlooked macroeconomic issues over which the poor had no control, and academics and journalists were split, with several challenging Murray's scholarship. Nonetheless, with ample funding from Olin and other conservative foundations, Murray succeeded in shifting the debate over America's poor from society's shortcomings to their own.

Despite Reagan's professed antipathy toward big government, his administration steered cautiously away from Murray's controversial libertarianism, preferring to criticize welfare cheaters rather than the whole idea of government-run antipoverty programs. But to the dismay of liberals, Bill Clinton, a "New Democrat," later embraced his ideas, calling Murray's analysis "essentially right" and incorporating many of his prescriptions, including work requirements and the end to aid as an entitlement, in his 1996 welfare reform bill. "It took ten years," Murray has said, "for *Losing Ground* to go from being controversial to conventional wisdom."

The Olin Foundation also backed what came to be known

as the Collegiate Network, privately financing a string of right-wing newspapers on America's college campuses. Among them was *The Dartmouth Review,* which infamously published an editorial in Ebonics proclaiming, "Now we be comin' to Dart-mut' and be up over our 'fros in studies, but we still be not graduatin' Phi Beta Kappa." The paper hosted a feast of lobster and champagne to mock a student fast against global hunger, sledgehammered shantytowns erected by students protesting apartheid in South Africa, and published a transcript of a secretly taped meeting of students belonging to Dartmouth's gay student association. *The Dartmouth Review* became an incubator for right-wing media figures like D'Souza and the future conservative radio host Laura Ingraham. Its counterpart at Vassar, meanwhile, gave starts in journalism to the ABC correspondent Jonathan Karl and Marc Thiessen, an online columnist at *The Washington Post* best known for his defense of the Bush administration's use of torture.

As the Olin Foundation spent itself out of existence, Michael Joyce jumped to a new and far more powerful private foundation, started by another conservative family. In 1985, a corporate merger in Milwaukee created a spectacular windfall, boosting a previously sleepy local charity, the Lynde and Harry Bradley Foundation, overnight into a nonprofit juggernaut. Its assets rocketed from $14 million to over $290 million, making it one of the twenty largest foundations in the country. Swimming in cash, the foundation's small, unpaid staff, which had mostly focused on conventional local do-gooding until then, sought out Joyce, telling him, "We've got money, and we want to do what you did at Olin. We want to become Olin West." Almost on the spot, Joyce moved to Milwaukee to run the Bradley Foundation himself. He left Piereson behind to cope with Simon's famously short temper and the twenty-year plan to spend the Olin Foundation out of business.

At the Bradley Foundation, Joyce had a freer hand. "He basically invented the field of modern conservative philanthropy," according to Piereson. During the next fifteen years, the Bradley Foundation would give away $280 million to his favorite conservative causes. It was small in comparison with older research foundations like the Ford Foundation, but unlike Ford, under Joyce's direction Bradley regarded itself as a righteous combatant in an ideological war, giving it a single-minded focus. At least two-thirds of its grants, according to one analysis, financed conservative intellectual activity. It paid for some six hundred graduate and postgraduate fellowships, right-wing think tanks, conservative journals, activists fighting Communism abroad, and its own publishing house, Encounter Books. Continuing the strategic emphasis on prestigious schools, the foundation gave both Harvard and Yale $5.5 million during its first decade under Joyce's management. It was an activist force on the secondary-school level, too. The Bradley Foundation virtually drove the early national "school choice" movement, waging an all-out assault on teachers' unions and traditional public schools. In an effort to "wean" Americans from government, the foundation militated for parents to be able to use public funds to send their children to private and parochial schools.

When Joyce took over the Bradley Foundation, he continued to fund many of the same academic organizations he had at Olin, including half of the same colleges and universities. "Typically, it was not just the same university but the same department, and in some cases, the same scholar," Bruce Murphy wrote in *Milwaukee Magazine,* charging that this led to a kind of "intellectual cronyism." The anointed scholars were good ideological warriors but "rarely great scholars," he wrote. For instance, Joyce stuck with Murray in the face of growing controversy over his 1994 book, *The Bell Curve,* which correlated race and low IQ scores to argue that blacks were less likely than whites to join the "cognitive elite," and was loudly and convincingly discredited. The Manhattan Institute fired Murray over the controversial project. "They didn't want the grief," says Murray. But Joyce reportedly kept an estimated $1 million in grants flowing to Murray, who decamped to the American Enterprise Institute. "I knew from Mike Joyce my fellowship was portable," Murray says. But the controversy stirred by the book clouded the Bradley Foundation's reputation. Joyce, who was accused of racism, said he received death threats. He felt so threatened he demanded enhanced security. The book, he acknowledged, left "an indelible imprint on us."

Joyce stepped down from Bradley in 2001 amid rumors of alcoholism and erratic and self-destructive behavior. "Demons were rumored," recalls a friend. According to one well-informed source, Joyce's drinking, which had escalated from three-beer lunches to complete benders, reached a crisis when he presided as the master of ceremonies at a formal Washington event in a state of scandalous, public inebriation. Afterward, the Bradley Foundation's board gave Joyce the choice of going into a rehab program or resigning. Realizing he had lost the board's respect, he resigned. After that, the few remaining years of his life were a lonely, powerless downward spiral.

Nonetheless, Joyce's achievements transcended his personal problems. When he retired, Joyce was showered with accolades from the Right. *National Review* described him as "the chief operating officer of the conservative movement." It added, "Wherever you looked in the battle of ideas, a light dusting would have turned up his fingerprints." The tribute concluded, "Over the period of his Bradley service, it's difficult to recall a single, serious thrust against incumbent liberalism that did not begin or end with Mike Joyce."

What received no attention, however, was that the small-government conservatism that the Bradley Foundation promoted was fueled by federal funds. The Bradley Foundation very deliberately cast itself as a foe of big government. In 1999, Joyce wrote a confidential memo to the foundation's board arguing that to win, conservatives needed to "package for public consumption . . . dramatic stories" depicting citizens as "plucky Davids fighting gallantly against the massive, statist, bureaucratic Goliath." But the foundation owed much of its existence to that Goliath—in the form of taxpayer-funded defense spending.

The event that multiplied the Bradley Foundation's assets by a factor of twenty almost overnight, transforming it into a major political force, was the 1985 business takeover in which Rockwell International, then America's largest defense contractor, bought the Allen-Bradley company, a Milwaukee electronics manufacturer, for $1.65 billion in cash. The deal created an instant windfall for the Bradley family's private foundation, which held a stake in the company. Its assets leaped from $14 million to some $290 million.

When it bought the Allen-Bradley company, two-thirds of Rockwell's revenues, and half of its profits, came from U.S. government contracts. Rockwell had become, in fact, a poster child for wasteful government spending. The *Los Angeles Times* called it a "symbol of a military industrial complex gone berserk." Rockwell's coffers were bulging with cash, but its reputation had taken a hit from its role as the main contractor producing the B-1 bomber, an aircraft so maligned it earned the nickname the Flying Edsel. President Carter had canceled the program as a waste of money, but after Rockwell waged a strenuous lobbying campaign, President Reagan had brought it back to life. As part of his administration's huge defense buildup, Reagan also authorized the manufacture of the MX missile system, another multibillion-dollar defense program that was widely criticized as unnecessary, for which Rockwell was the largest contractor. Thus, by 1984, thanks to profligate government spending, Rockwell had one of the strongest balance sheets in the business, with $1.3 billion in cash piling up on its ledgers. Business analysts warned that the company needed to diversify in order to become less reliant on federal contracts. It was this dubious set of circumstances that sent the company on the shopping spree that ended in its purchase of Allen-Bradley and the phenomenal enrichment of the Bradley Foundation.

In its early days especially, Allen-Bradley had relied heavily on government defense contracts, too, to pull it through. Founded in 1903 by two enterprising high school dropouts, brothers Lynde and Harry Bradley, along with investor Stanton Allen, it grew from making rheostats to many other kinds of industrial controls, particularly for the radio, machine tool, and auto industries. The business had "teetered on the edge of solvency" until the United States entered World War I, according to a history by the Milwaukee historian John Gurda that was commissioned and published by the Bradley Foundation. But thanks to government defense contracts, which accounted for 70 percent of the company's business, orders increased tenfold over six years, and the company was, according to Gurda, "launched." World War II proved even more of a boon. Gurda describes its impact on the company as "staggering." By 1944, government war work accounted for nearly 80 percent of the company's orders. Its business volume more than tripled during World War II.

Even more than the Olin Corporation, Allen-Bradley sponsored an amazing array of generous if paternalistic fringe benefits for its workers, including its own jazz orchestra, led by a full-time music director, which serenaded lunch crowds. There were badminton courts on its roof deck, overseen by an athletic director, and an employee reading room, too. The Bradley brothers, who erected an iconic four-faced, Florentine-style clock tower that soared seventeen stories above the plant on the South Side of Milwaukee, regarded themselves as benevolent civic leaders, overseeing a family of employees. They were therefore bitterly wounded when their employees, who saw the situation differently, unionized and then went out on strike in 1939.

The elder brother, Lynde, died not long after, but the younger brother, Harry, who lived until 1965, became avidly right-wing. Like Fred Koch, he was a vigorous supporter of the John Birch Society, frequently hosting its founder, Robert Welch, as a speaker at company sales meetings. Bradley also was a devoted follower of Dr. Frederick Schwarz, a melodramatically anti-Communist physician from Australia who had converted to Christianity from Judaism, and who stumped across the heartland for his Christian Anti-Communism Crusade preaching that "Karl Marx was a Jew," and "like most Jews he was short and ugly and lazy and slovenly and had no desire to go out and work for a living" but also possessed "a superior, evil intelligence like most Jews." Schwarz, too, was a regular visitor to the company and a favorite among Bradley's causes. Bradley was also a keen supporter of the Manion Forum, whose followers believed that social spending in America was part of a secret Russian plot to bankrupt the United States. Despite the lifesaving financial boost that federal spending had provided to his own company, Bradley reportedly regarded the growing federal government in America and world Communism as "the two major threats" to human "freedom."

The company's embrace of the free market, however, didn't preclude price-fixing. In 1961, Harry Bradley's successor and confidant of many years, Fred Loock, was convicted of price-fixing with twenty-nine other electrical equipment firms. He narrowly escaped incarceration, according to the authorized history. Both the company and its chief executive paid substantial fines.

The company's relations with federal authorities worsened further in the 1960s as the Allen-Bradley company, not unlike the Olin Corporation, found itself in the crosshairs of new laws driven by more demanding societal expectations. In 1966, a federal judge sided with a group of female employees who sued the company for paying them lower wages than male employees operating the same machinery. Then, in 1968, federal authorities targeted the company for racially discriminatory hiring policies. In response, the company agreed to institute an affirmative action plan. Meanwhile, unionized employees at the plant went on strike, causing an eleven-day work stoppage. The combination of antitrust, race, gender, and labor disputes at the company provided fertile ground for the politics of backlash building in the executive suite.

The Bradley Foundation, meanwhile, also became increasingly politicized. Originally, the foundation's purpose was to help aid needy employees and the residents of Milwaukee, as well as prevent cruelty to animals. Harry Bradley and his wife were animal lovers, doting on a pet poodle, Dufy, who was named for the modern artist and who had a penthouse dog run. After Joyce took over the foundation in 1985, however, a new mission statement was drafted, directing its grants to the support of "limited, competent government," "a dynamic marketplace," and "vigorous defense."

The Bradley brothers had hoped to keep the company in the private hands of the family, and the jobs in the community, in perpetuity. Their will was explicit about this. Their heirs, however, with the help of the Milwaukee law firm Foley & Lardner, managed to sell the company to Rockwell nonetheless, cashing in handsomely. One of the law firm's partners, Michael Grebe, subsequently became chairman and CEO of the newly enriched foundation.

What remained of Allen-Bradley, however, did less well. Its sad slide traced the fall of American manufacturing during the end of the twentieth century and the hollowing out of decent blue-collar jobs. In 2010, Rockwell Automation, which is what was left of the company in Milwaukee twenty-five years after it was sold, outsourced the last of the plant's remaining manufacturing jobs to low-wage areas, largely in Latin America and Asia. Robert Granum, president of Local

1111 of the United Electrical, Radio, and Machine Workers of America, the union that represented the last laid-off workers, told the *Milwaukee Business Journal* that Rockwell's decision would "deprive future generations of working people of the opportunity to have decent family-supporting jobs."

Allen-Bradley's distinctive Florentine clock tower still rose above Milwaukee's South Side. But by then Milwaukee was described as "the most polarized part of the most polarized state in a polarized nation." The industrial base had collapsed, the manufacturing jobs disappeared, and many of the white immigrants who had worked at Allen-Bradley had long since moved to the suburbs, leaving Milwaukee close to 40 percent black, with the second-highest black poverty rate in the country and with an unemployment rate that was nearly four times higher for blacks than for whites.

The Bradley Foundation, meanwhile, had become central to the conservative movement. Thanks to smart investments, its assets ballooned, enabling it to finance a movement that ascribed poverty to dependency on government handouts, not to the trade, labor, and industrial policies that had resulted in American jobs, such as those at Allen-Bradley, getting shipped overseas. By 2012, the Bradley Foundation's assets had reached more than $630 million, enabling it to dole out more than $32 million in grants during that year alone. The funds continued to finance welfare reform initiatives that required the poor to find jobs, as well as attacks on public schools. The foundation also continued to support conservative beachheads in thirty-five different elite colleges and universities including Harvard, Princeton, and Stanford.

The foundation's annual Bradley Prizes had by then become the glittering Academy Awards ceremony for conservatives, a night at Washington's Kennedy Center on the banks of the Potomac filled with evening gowns, tuxedos, overlong acceptance speeches, live musical fanfares, and up to four annual $250,000 prizes given to a Who's Who of the movement.

Over the years, winners have included the newspaper columnist George Will, who subsequently became a trustee of the foundation. Also honored with the award were the founders of the Federalist Society as well as Princeton's Robert George; Bill Kristol, the neoconservative editor of *The Weekly Standard;* the Harvard professor Harvey Mansfield; the Fox News president, Roger Ailes; and the Heritage Foundation's stalwarts Ed Meese and Ed Feulner. Almost all of the recipients had played major roles in tugging the American political debate to the right. And almost all had also been supported over the years by a tiny constellation of private foundations filled with tax-deductible gifts from a handful of wealthy reactionaries whose identities and stories very few Americans knew but whose "overarching purpose," as Joyce said, "was to use philanthropy to support a war of ideas."

CHAPTER FOUR

The Koch Method: Free-Market Mayhem

FOR TWENTY-ONE YEARS, WHILE THE KOCHS WERE FINANCING an ideological war aimed at freeing American business from the grip of government, Donald Carlson was cleaning up the dregs their industry left behind. Stitched to the jacket he wore to work at Koch Refining Company, the booming Pine Bend Refinery in Rosemount, Minnesota, was the name Bull. His colleagues called him this because of his brawn and his willingness to shoulder the tasks no one else wanted to touch. "He wasn't always the greatest guy or dad, but he got up every morning and went to work. He stepped up to the plate every day," recalls his widow, Doreen Carlson. "If a job was too hard, they gave it to him."

Beginning in 1974, when he was hired, Carlson worked twelve- and sometimes sixteen-hour shifts at the refinery. Its profitability had proven the Kochs' purchase of Pine Bend prophetic. It had become the largest refinery north of Louisiana with the capacity to process 330,000 barrels of crude a day, a quarter of what Canada exported to the United States. It provided over half of the gas used in Minnesota and 40 percent of that used by Wisconsin. Carlson's job was demanding, but he enjoyed it. He cleaned out huge tanks that contained leaded gasoline, scraping them down by hand. He took samples from storage tanks whose vapors escaped with such force they sometimes blew his helmet off. He hoisted heavy loads and vacuumed up fuel spills deep enough to cause burns to his legs. Like many of the one thousand employees at the refinery, Carlson was often exposed to toxic substances. "He was practically swimming in those tanks," his wife recalled. But Carlson never thought twice about the hazards. "I was a young guy," he explained later. "They didn't tell me anything, I didn't know anything."

In particular, Carlson said, no one warned him about benzene, a colorless liquid chemical compound refined from crude oil. In 1928, two Italian doctors first detected a connection between it and cancer. Afterward, numerous scientific studies linked chronic benzene exposure to greatly increased risks of leukemia. Four federal agencies—the National Institutes of Health (NIH), the Food and Drug Administration, the Environmental Protection Agency, and the Centers for Disease Control—have all declared benzene a human carcinogen. Asked under oath if he'd been warned about the harm it posed to his hemoglobin, Carlson replied, "I didn't even know what hemoglobin was."

In 1995, Carlson became too sick to work any longer at the refinery. When he obtained his company medical records, he and his wife were shocked by what they read. In the late 1970s, OSHA had issued regulations requiring companies whose workers were exposed to benzene to offer annual blood tests, and to retest, and notify workers if any abnormalities were found. Companies were also required to refer employees with abnormal results to medical specialists. Koch Refining Company had offered the annual blood tests as legally required, and Carlson had dutifully taken advantage of the regular screening. But what he discovered was that even though his tests had shown increasingly serious, abnormal blood cell counts beginning in 1990, as well as in 1992 and 1993, the company had not mentioned it to him until 1994.

Charles Koch had disparaged government regulations as "socialistic." From his standpoint, the regulatory state that had grown out of the Progressive Era was an illegitimate encroachment on free enterprise and a roadblock to initiative and profitability. But while such theories might appeal to the company's owners, the reality was quite different for many of their tens of thousands of employees.

Carlson continued working for another year but grew weaker, needing transfusions of three to five pints of blood a week. Finally, in the summer of 1995, he grew too sick to work at all. At that point, his wife recalls, "they let him go. Six-months' pay is what they gave him. It was basically his accumulated sick pay." Carlson argued that his illness was job related, but Koch Refining denied this claim, refusing to pay him workers' compensation, which would have covered his medical bills and continued dependency benefits for his wife and their teenage daughter. "The doctor couldn't believe he was never put on workmen's comp," she added. "We were just naive. We didn't think people would let you die. We thought, 'They help you, don't they?'"

In February 1997, twenty-three years after he joined Koch Industries, Donald Carlson died of leukemia. He was fifty-three. He and his wife had been married thirty-one years. "Almost the worst part," she said, was that "he died thinking he'd let us down financially." She added, "My husband was the sort of man who truly believed that if you worked hard and did a good job, you would be rewarded."

Furious at the company, Doreen waged a one-woman battle to get Koch Industries to acknowledge some responsibility for her husband's death and apologize. "I'm looking for some accountability," she told Tom Meersman, a reporter for the Minneapolis *Star Tribune*. For three years, Carlson pressed her legal claim. The company offered her some money but refused to call it compensation for a work-related death. It resisted until minutes before the case was about to be heard by a judge. And when it did finally agree to her terms, it did so only if there was no written agreement. "They never admitted it. They avoided court. There was no written record. They just gave me those little crumbs," she recalled.

More than a dozen years later, Carlson took the opportunity to speak out. "I don't think you could write what I think of Koch. You're just collateral damage. It's just money for them, and they never have enough." Pressed about whether it was fair to pin the blame on the Kochs themselves, rather than on lower-level executives she dealt with, she retorted, "Charles Koch owns the refinery." She went on, "And they want less regulations? Can you imagine? What they want is things that benefit them. They never cut into their profits. I hear they're backing a lot of people politically, and I bet it's all about getting rid of regulations," she said. "But those regulations are for safety. It's not to make your workers rich; it's so they don't die."

Carlson's case was just one of many targeting Koch Industries' corporate conduct in the decades after Charles took over the company. The company was expanding at a breathtaking rate into a global conglomerate with vast chemical, manufacturing, energy, trading, and refining interests. But growing at an equally astonishing pace were its legal conflicts. Rather than making peace with the government overseers who frustrated his libertarian ideals, Charles declared war. As he portrayed it, his defiance was a stand for high principle. In 1978, for instance, he wrote an impassioned call to arms to other businessmen in the *Libertarian Review,* arguing, "We should *not* cave in the moment a regulator sets foot on our doorstep . . . Do not cooperate voluntarily; instead, resist wherever and to whatever extent you legally can. And do so in the name of *justice*."

It's difficult to disentangle Charles's philosophical opposition to regulations from his financial interest in avoiding them. As he described it, he was trying to "unceasingly advance the cause of liberty" in the face of "arrogant, intrusive, totalitarian laws." Critics such as Thomas Frank, the author of *What's the Matter with Kansas?* who grew up in Kansas watching the

Kochs, saw it quite differently. "Libertarianism is supposed to be all about principles, but what it's really about is political expedience. It's basically a corporate front, masked as a philosophy." What is indisputable is that whatever the motivations were, in the quarter century between 1980 and 2005, under Charles Koch's leadership, his company developed a stunning record of corporate malfeasance.

In April 1996, for instance, as Bull Carlson was dying of leukemia in Minnesota, Sally Barnes-Soliz, a Koch Industries environmental technician, knocked on the door of government regulators in Corpus Christi, Texas, where the Kochs owned and operated another refinery, and blew the whistle on the company for lying about illegal quantities of benzene that it was leaking into the air. Environmental regulations, even more than those dealing with workplace safety, proved to be constant obstacles for Koch Industries, as the problems at the refinery in Corpus Christi exemplified.

Barnes-Soliz later told *Bloomberg Markets* magazine, "The refinery was just hemorrhaging benzene into the atmosphere." Rather than comply with a new 1995 federal regulation requiring reductions in such emissions, Koch Industries had tried to conceal its output in a report that it was required to file with the Texas Natural Resource Conservation Commission. Internally, a Koch lawyer conceded that the company's self-reporting was "misleading and inaccurate," so the company had then called in Barnes-Soliz to provide a more accurate account.

She had been working with Koch Industries for five years and loved the job because she felt she was contributing directly to the health and safety of employees and the public. As directed, she carefully re-tabulated the refinery's benzene emissions and found the company had released fifteen times more than the legal limit. Her bosses were unhappy with her findings. She had a bachelor's degree in science and environmental health and a master's of science in industrial hygiene, so she knew what she was doing, but nonetheless she redid the math many times. But she kept getting the same unwelcome results. "There were a lot of meetings to try and get me to change the number. It was hard, but I held firm to my convictions," she recounted to *Bloomberg Markets*. She was thus shaken when she saw the subsequent report submitted by Koch to the Texas authorities. It falsified the benzene emissions to 1/149th of the amount she had calculated.

"When I saw they had actually falsified that document, I had no recourse but to notify the authorities," she told *Bloomberg Markets,* which described the episode as part of a pattern of outlaw behavior by Koch Industries. On her lunch break, she drove to the state regulators' office and reported the fraud.

Defenders of Koch Industries have suggested that the whistle-blower was merely a disgruntled employee, looking for a pretext to save her job. But Koch Industries in Corpus Christi was hit with a ninety-seven-count indictment on September 28, 2000, charging it with covering up the discharge of ninety-one metric tons of benzene. The company faced the potential of $352 million in fines, and four Koch employees faced potentially long prison sentences and fines of $1.75 million each. The company fought back hard in the courts, trying to withhold hundreds of internal e-mails about its emissions, but the presiding judge rejected its argument that these were trade secrets, castigating its lawyer as a "front man" who was trying to "impede" regulators from discovering the "extent of its noncompliance." During the course of the wrangling, the company revealed that it would have cost $7 million to comply with the emission standards. High though the cost might seem, it was dwarfed by the refinery's profits. Prosecutors testified that the Kochs' Corpus Christi refinery earned $176 million in profits during 1995 alone.

Eventually, Koch Industries pleaded guilty to one felony charge of "concealment of information" about its benzene emissions and paid $10 million in fines, and made another $10 million payment for projects to improve the environment in Corpus Christi. A spokeswoman for the company stressed afterward that the charges against the individual Koch managers had been dropped, and she argued, "The government's case ultimately collapsed." David Uhlmann, the career prosecutor who headed the environmental crimes section of the Justice Department at the time, however, said that to the contrary Koch Industries pleaded guilty to "an orchestrated scheme to conceal benzene emissions—a known carcinogen"—from regulators and the community. He calls the suit "one of the most significant cases ever brought under the Clean Air Act." He notes, "Environmental crimes are almost always motivated by economics and arrogance, and in the Koch case there was a healthy dose of both."

An eye-opening sideline was the company's treatment of Barnes-Soliz. For her whistle-blowing, she said she was quarantined to an empty office with no responsibilities and no e-mail access. Eventually, she quit and sued the company for harassment, and in 1999 Koch paid her an undisclosed amount in a sealed settlement.

Around the same time, another would-be whistle-blower, Carnell Green, who was a low-level employee at Koch Industries in Louisiana, said that the company threatened to arrest him if he didn't recant. According to two statements that Green gave in 1998 and 1999 to a private investigator who was working for Bill Koch, Green was a pipeline technician and gas meter serviceman for Koch Industries when he ran afoul of the management. He had worked for the company from 1976 until 1996, during which time he said that he was told to sweep mercury spills from the thirty-six gas meters that he monitored out the door and onto the ground. He said that he was also told to dispose of the old meters, which contained about a quart of mercury each, in dumpsters and to pour additional containers of mercury down the sink, as he witnessed his supervisor doing. Green said the mercury was so pervasive that when he got home, balls of it would roll off his clothes and out of his shoes.

After attending a class on hazardous materials in 1996, though, Green said that he sent a report to his supervisors alerting them that mercury posed a serious health hazard and should be disposed of more carefully. Green said his supervisors told him not to talk about it. Soon after, Green said, a man who identified himself as "FBI Special Agent Moorman" came to interrogate him and accused him of lying about the mercury. He said the official threatened to arrest him and put him in jail if he did not retract his allegations against the company and also warned him that if he told anyone else, including outside authorities, about the mercury, he would be fired. Green said his immediate supervisor then presented him with a prepared statement to sign, saying there was no mercury at the Koch facilities. Fearing that he would otherwise be imprisoned, Green signed it.

Worried about his health, Green said that he nonetheless filed a complaint with OSHA. Koch Industries subsequently fired him, he said, for "making false statements."

In his statement, Green added that he later learned that Special Agent Moorman worked not for the FBI but "for Koch Security in Wichita Kansas." At the time, Larry M. Moorman was an investigator in Koch Industries' legal department. Moorman later became the director of corporate security for Koch Industries.

According to the private investigator, Richard "Jim" Elroy, soil samples were later taken from one of the locations that Green identified as having been polluted with mercury by Koch Industries and sent to an independent laboratory for testing. The soil samples, according to Elroy's report, were so highly contaminated with mercury that the lab refused to send them back through the U.S. mail and demanded payment for specialized disposal of hazmat substances. But by then, Green had lost his job. "Green was just a nice, working-class black guy from Louisiana, trying the best he could to make a living," said Elroy, who took Green's statement while working on behalf of Bill Koch in his litigation against his brothers Charles and David at the time. "Koch just runs over these people and then discards them as trash," Elroy said. Asked about Green's allegations, neither Moorman nor the spokesman for Koch Industries responded.

But as allegations concerning pollution mounted nationally, federal prosecutors began to piece together an enormous case against the company for violating the Clean Water Act. In 1995, the Justice Department sued Koch for lying about leaking millions of gallons of oil from its pipelines and storage facilities in six different states. Federal investigators documented over three hundred oil spills during the previous five years, including one 100,000-gallon crude oil spill that left a twelve-mile-long slick in the bay off Corpus Christi, not far from where the Koch refinery was located.

Angela O'Connell, the lead federal prosecutor in the case against Koch Industries, later described it as unlike any other oil company she had ever dealt with, noting that over her twenty-five-year career at the Justice Department she dealt with most of them. "They're always operating outside of the system," she told Daniel Schulman, who provides a vivid account of the company's serial lawbreaking in *Sons of Wichita*. Leaks and spills, she noted, are endemic in the oil business, but she maintained that while other companies would sit down with regulators and admit their failings, Koch Industries "repeatedly lied . . . to avoid penalties."

As O'Connell compiled the massive multistate case against Koch Industries, she developed an uneasy sense that she was being spied on. She thought her trash was being searched, and her phone bugged, but she could never prove it. She was rattled badly enough by the situation that from that point on she monitored everything she said and did, to make sure it couldn't be used against her.

Documents show that beginning in 1983 Koch Industries hired a former employee of the U.S. Secret Service, David Nicastro, to assist its security operations. By 1994, Nicastro had his own small investigative firm in Texas, Secure Source, and "for the next four or five years," he confirmed, "I worked on different projects" for the Kochs, including the litigation between the brothers. In court papers, he described his role as conducting "numerous investigations" for Koch Industries and what he called its "entities." Joining Nicastro was Charles Dickey, a former FBI agent.

In looking back many years later, O'Connell said she regarded the Kochs as "dangerous" and still felt uncomfortable talking about them. Dropping her voice, as if they might be listening, she recalled, "They tried to attack my reputation." She recounted that as she was working on the case against the company, it obtained a meeting with the head of the Environmental Protection Agency at the time, Carol Browner, at which company representatives accused O'Connell of acting overzealously, in an unsuccessful effort to have her removed from the case. "They lie about everything, and they get away with it because they're a private company," she says. "They obstructed every step of discovery. It was always, 'I didn't do it,' 'It's not our oil,' 'It's not our pipes.' You can't believe anything they say. They definitely don't play the game the way other companies do," she says.

On January 13, 2000, O'Connell's division at the Justice Department prevailed. Koch Industries agreed to pay a $30 million fine, which was the biggest in history at that point, for violations of the Clean Water Act. The EPA issued a press release accusing Koch Industries of "egregious violations" and trumpeting that the huge fine proved that "those who try to profit from polluting our environment will pay the price." But

O'Connell, who retired from the Justice Department in 2004, was still haunted by the damage from the oil leaks a decade later. "The thing is, oil sinks to the bottom and poisons the fish. If people eat it, they get really, really sick," she said. "People die."

While a few legal violations could be understood as misfortunate accidents, Koch Industries' pattern of pollution was striking not just for its egregiousness but also for its willfulness. As the company was settling the oil spill case that O'Connell brought, its Pine Bend Refinery in Rosemount, Minnesota, pleaded guilty to still more violations of the Clean Water Act. The refinery paid an $8 million fine for dumping a million gallons of ammonia-contaminated wastewater onto the ground, along with negligently spilling some 600,000 gallons of fuel into a protected natural wetland and the nearby Mississippi River. Earlier the refinery had already paid a $6.9 million fine to the Minnesota Pollution Control Agency to settle charges stemming from the same violations. In this pollution case, like that in Corpus Christi, government authorities accused Koch of trying to cover up its offenses, in this instance by surreptitiously dumping extra pollutants on weekends and late at night in order to evade monitoring, and later falsifying the records. A former employee, Thomas Holton, who had worked at the Pine Bend Refinery, told the Minnesota *Star Tribune,* "There were times when . . . yeah, we lied. We did do that. And I won't cover that up."

These misdeeds paled, however, in comparison with what befell two teenagers in the rural town of Lively, Texas, some fifty miles southeast of Dallas, on August 24, 1996. That afternoon, Danielle Smalley, a newly minted high school graduate, was at home in the family trailer, packing her things for college. A friend, Jason Stone, was over, to talk about the farewell party they were planning for her that night. Smalley's father, Danny, a mechanic, was home too, watching sports on television. A faint but increasingly nauseating gassy smell was the only sign that something was amiss. After they could find no source, Danielle and Jason decided to drive to a neighbor's house to report a possible gas leak. The family had no phone of their own. Borrowing Danny Smalley's truck, they set out, but the truck stalled a few hundred yards away. When Danielle, who was at the wheel, tried to restart it, the ignition lit an invisible cloud of butane gas that was leaking from a corroded, underground Koch pipeline that ran not far from the house, setting off a monstrous blast. A towering fireball utterly consumed the truck. Danielle and Jason burned to death.

Koch Industries offered Danny Smalley, Danielle's father, money to drop the wrongful death lawsuit he subsequently brought against the company. Like Doreen Carlson, however, the surviving family member wanted more than cash.

The pretrial maneuvering was fierce, with Koch Industries reportedly hiring a fleet of top-flight lawyers and a private investigator to tail Smalley. Smalley's lead lawyer, Ted Lyon, meanwhile, suspected his law office was being bugged. He hired a security firm to inspect, which discovered that tiny transmitters had been planted in his office. "I'm not saying the Kochs did it," the lawyer later said. "I just thought it was very interesting that it happened during the period we were litigating the case."

As the two sides prepared for trial, a chilling picture of corporate negligence emerged. An investigation by the National Transportation Safety Board found that Koch Pipeline Company, the unit in charge, knew that the pipeline was corroded and had neither made all of the necessary repairs nor told the forty or so families living near the explosion site how to handle an emergency. An expert witness for the Smalleys described the pipeline as "Swiss cheese." The explosion, according to the witness, Edward Ziegler, a certified oil industry safety expert, resulted from "a total failure of a company to follow the regulations, keep their pipeline safe and operate it as the regulations require."

For three years, the company had in fact stopped using the old pipeline in favor of a newer one. But the company decided to revive the older pipeline when it realized it could make an additional $7 million annually by patching it and using it to carry liquid butane. Bill Caffey, an executive vice president at Koch Industries, admitted in a deposition, "Koch Industries is definitely responsible for the death of Danielle Smalley," but he stressed that he had believed that the pipeline was safe when he authorized its use. He praised Charles Koch as admirably focused on complying with safety and other regulations but acknowledged there were financial pressures. "We were to work on reducing wasteful spending," he explained. A former employee, Kenoth Whitstine, testified in a deposition that when he brought concerns to his boss at the company about another corroding pipeline, which he feared could cause a fatal accident if ruptured, he was told that it would be cheaper to pay off damages from a lawsuit than make the repairs.

Finally getting the chance he had waited for, Danny Smalley took the stand as the last witness in the trial and delivered an enraged soliloquy denouncing the Kochs as caring only about money. As he later told *60 Minutes,* "They said, 'We're sorry, Mr. Smalley, that your child lost her life and Jason lost his life.' Sorry doesn't get it. They're not sorry. The only thing they looked at was the bottom dollar. How much money would they lose if they shut the pipeline down. They didn't care, all they wanted was the money."

If the Kochs' cavalier safety practices were a gamble, they lost when the jury rendered its verdict. On October 21, 1999, it found Koch Industries guilty not just of negligence but of malice, too, because it had known about the extreme hazard its decaying pipeline had posed. In his suit, Danny Smalley had asked for $100 million in damages from the company, a staggering sum. The jury, however, imposed a fine almost three times larger, demanding Koch Industries pay him $296 million. At the time, it was the largest wrongful death award on record.

As they reeled from the verdict, the brothers also faced a growing political crisis. The U.S. Senate had opened an investigation into allegations that the company stole tens of millions of dollars' worth of oil from wells on Native Americans' tribal land. After a yearlong investigation in 1989, it released a scathing report accusing Koch Oil of "a widespread and sophisticated scheme to steal crude oil from Indians and others through fraudulent mis-measuring."

The Senate investigation had penetrated Koch Industries' well-guarded secrecy, compelling Charles Koch to be deposed at the company headquarters in Wichita. One committee official recalled him as "quietly enraged" by the government intrusion. Under oath, Charles admitted that the company had improperly taken approximately $31 million worth of crude oil over a three-year period from Indian lands but argued that it had been accidental. He told investigators that oil measurement is "a very uncertain art." The committee, however, produced evidence showing that none of the other companies buying oil from Indian land at the time had substantial problems with measurements. In fact, the other companies, most of which were far better known, had secretly turned Koch in, because they regarded it as cheating.

The Senate investigation was marked by what was becoming a familiar pattern: those challenging the Kochs began to feel that someone was trying to watch and possibly intimidate them. Richard "Jim" Elroy, who later became a private eye himself, was at the time an FBI agent detailed to the Senate investigation. His specialty had been investigating corruption in Oklahoma, and he had handled a number of tough cases, including some involving organized crime. But he soon faced a situation that he said he had never before encountered even when investigating the Mafia: he became certain that he was being followed.

One day, Elroy stopped his car, jumped out, and confronted the driver who had been tailing him, dragging him out of his car at gunpoint, flashing his FBI identification, and warning him, "Tell your boss the next time he tries this, you'll be in a body bag." Elroy recounted that the driver explained, "I'm a private investigator who works with Koch Industries." The company's legal affairs head reportedly denied hiring private investigators to spy on Elroy. But other Senate investigators had unsettling experiences as well. According to the Senate report, another investigator discovered that a Koch employee tried to get dirt on him from his former wife.

The committee's chief counsel, Kenneth Ballen, who had previously worked as a prosecutor against organized crime in New Jersey, believed that one of his assistants was paid to get dirt on him. Luckily, Ballen said, there wasn't any. "It wasn't like politics; it was like investigating organized crime," Ballen recalled. Charles Koch, he maintains, "is a scary guy to take on. Most people back off, rather than tangling with them," Ballen observed. "These people have amassed an amazing amount of unaccountable power."

Another young lawyer working on the Senate investigation, Wick Sollers, who later became a managing partner at the blue-chip law firm King & Spalding, also found the experience disturbing. Sollers was an assistant U.S. attorney in Baltimore when the Senate committee recruited him. "The company was unhappy with the investigation," he noted. "They sent various people to try to stop us—emissaries, lawyers—as well as a senator to try to stop the investigation." The senator in question was the Oklahoma Republican Don Nickles, a social and fiscal conservative who received many campaign contributions from Koch Industries over the years and whose lobbying firm was later hired by the company.

Sollers said that several staff members believed that someone was going through their garbage. "We don't know who sent them," Sollers said carefully, "but someone hired private investigators to dig up anything they could." Later, after he left the Senate for King & Spalding, he recalled that an anonymous package was sent to his mentor at the firm, filled with news clippings and court documents meant to sully his reputation. Some of the documents trumpeted the Kochs' innocence. "I've not experienced anything like this in any other part of my practice," he said. "Someone was trying to intimidate and silence the Kochs' critics. I'm not political, but it was troubling."

Christopher Tucker, a witness against the Kochs who testified to committee investigators, also experienced unusual harassment. After accusing Koch Industries of cheating in its oil measurements, he was smeared in newspaper stories as a perjurer, denounced in a letter by four senators, and tipped off by his landlady's daughter that men in business suits had taken away his garbage. The basis of the complaint against him was that a professional credential he had cited on his résumé wasn't finalized until shortly after he testified. In this instance, when pressed, the company acknowledged initiating the senators' letter against him. "It's very intimidating," Tucker told the reporter Robert Parry. "You have a company with lots of money. They've got more money than many small countries do."

The Senate Select Committee on Indian Affairs nonetheless released a remarkably damning report on Koch Industries. Afterward, Elroy, who was still an FBI agent, wrote a memo to the U.S. attorney in Oklahoma City referring a potential criminal case against the company, alleging that it stole oil. Before sending the memo, however, Elroy warned Bill Koch that these developments could result in his brothers going to jail. "Then lock 'em up!" Elroy recalled Bill saying. "I did not want my family, my legacy, my father's legacy, to be based on organized crime," Bill told one news outlet.

The level of enmity between the brothers had only grown.

Soon after Charles and David bought the other two brothers out in 1983 for a total of some $800 million, Bill became convinced that he had been cheated out of his fair share of the family fortune, because he thought his brothers had deliberately undervalued the company. In retaliation, Bill had launched a barrage of litigation against Charles and David, and even at one point against their mother. But soon Bill Koch again felt outmaneuvered.

After weighing the committee's charges against Koch Industries for eighteen months, the Oklahoma City grand jury cleared the company in a decision that was clouded by the kind of intrigue that would characterize the Kochs' later political involvement. *The Nation* obtained internal company records showing that in the face of potential criminal charges the Kochs had launched an emergency strategy aimed at buying political leverage. In Oklahoma, where the grand jury was meeting, they made donations to key politicians, including Senator Nickles. Around the same time, Nickles recommended the appointment of a new U.S. attorney in Oklahoma City to oversee the grand jury investigation. In making his recommendation, Senator Nickles passed over the head of the criminal division in the office and chose a protégé, Timothy Leonard, a former Republican state senator with no experience in criminal law whose family had financial interests in oil wells receiving Koch royalties. There were calls for his recusal, but President George H. W. Bush's Justice Department granted his request for a waiver.

Nancy Jones, the assistant U.S. attorney in the office who was handling the Oklahoma grand jury investigation of Koch Industries, parsed her words carefully when asked later if political pressure had ended the probe. "You can say this," she said, after a notably long pause. "The man who was passed over to be U.S. attorney was a liberal Democrat from out of state, and the one they appointed was a Republican with no federal, criminal, or trial experience." Elroy, the former FBI agent, was less circumspect. In his opinion, "Nickles put the kibosh on the prosecution there. He got involved in the appointment of the U.S. attorney. He was getting a tremendous amount of support from Koch. He was their man. He was the best senator money could buy."

Nickles summarily dismissed allegations of political interference, saying he was "not even aware that the U.S. Attorney's office was involved in a criminal investigation of Koch." He added that he had "never had a conversation" with Leonard, the U.S. attorney, "about it." Leonard also denied any impropriety.

But Arizona's Democratic senator, Dennis DeConcini, a former prosecutor who had chaired the Select Committee on Indian Affairs, said at the time, "I was surprised and disappointed. Our evidence was so strong. Our investigation was some of the finest work the Senate has ever done. There was an overwhelming case against Koch."

The federal criminal investigation had also been stymied by the mysterious disappearance of key Koch Industries documents. Jones had tried to assemble the record corroborating the Senate testimony so that it wasn't reliant on witnesses whose testimony might be dismissed as the word of disgruntled employees. But when she subpoenaed documents from the company, she was told that many had simply vanished. Discouraged, she eventually gave up and resigned. Elroy also departed. He retired from the FBI and went to work for Bill Koch as a full-time private investigator, ensuring that both sides of the family had their own personal detectives. Bill Koch also retained the services of a former Israeli intelligence officer. "You have to have intelligence," Bill explained when asked about this. "But there are legal ways, and illegal ways to do it."

With his hopes fading of seeing his brothers criminally prosecuted, Bill Koch pressed an alternative legal strategy that stirred even greater problems for Koch Industries. In his own display of the family's relentlessness, he filed a whistle-blower lawsuit against Koch Industries under the False Claims Act, accusing the company of stealing oil from government lands. A Civil War–era statute allows citizens to bring such *qui tam* suits in instances where they can prove that private contractors have defrauded the government. It was essentially the same case as the one that the Oklahoma grand jury had rejected, but the level of proof required in civil cases is lower.

As the civil case wended its way forward, Elroy went to work, gathering more evidence against Koch Industries. He crisscrossed the country, interviewing five hundred potential witnesses. In a fraternal version of the comic *Spy vs. Spy*, Bill Koch's investigators became convinced that Charles and David had private eyes intercepting their communications. Bill's team resorted to buying a $5,000 secure phone. Suspecting that Bill's lawyer's office had been infiltrated, his team also planted a salacious fake memo on a desk as bait, which his investigator, Elroy, claims the other side soon asked about. "They had a mole who was getting into the lawyer's office," maintains Elroy. "He worked on another floor in the same building, and they were paying him to get into the legal department."

Elroy's suspicions were not baseless. A Republican political operative who signed a confidentiality agreement, and so asked not to have his name disclosed, admits that Charles and David Koch hired him, through a law firm, to trek across the country for months, scouring for anything he could find in the way of damaging personal, business, or legal information on their brother Bill. He recalled, "It was to find anything that would cause trouble, that could be used like a sharp stick to poke in his eye."

The results of one such espionage operation still reside in a padlocked rental storage locker just off a busy highway on the Eastern Shore of Maryland. Inside the locker, boxes of old files document a remarkable effort by private investigators to compile dirt on Bill Koch. The files contain the confidential work records of a now-defunct private investigative firm called Beckett Brown International. Handwritten notes scrawled on the documents reveal that in 1998 the detective firm was hired to find out if Bill Koch was behind a spate of anti-Koch television advertisements that had begun airing. The ads, which were made by a group calling itself Citizens for a Clean America, showed the Koch brothers stuffing money into their pockets while they polluted the environment. The investigation did in fact point to Bill Koch being behind the group. But it appears that the methods used to unmask him were easily as questionable as his ploy.

The files show that the detective firm set up "D lines," which is slang for an operation that digs through garbage containers. They also surreptitiously obtained private telephone records, including those belonging to the advertising executive in Richmond, Virginia, whose small firm had produced one of the anti-Koch commercials. The executive, Barbara Fultz, says that she had no idea any of the Kochs were involved. She thought that she was making an ad for a good-government group. When she heard fifteen years later that investigators had somehow obtained her personal phone records, which still sat in a pile of old files in a locked storage unit on Maryland's Eastern Shore, many with handwritten notes scrawled about whom she was calling, Fultz said, "That blows my mind."

"I definitely did not give my phone records to anyone," said Fultz, a grandmother who is now retired. Fultz remembered that many years earlier the Richmond police had called her at two in the morning to tell her that the door to her office suite was ajar, which struck her as strange. She wondered if this is how her phone records were obtained. "It's frightening that someone would go into my space looking through my records without me knowing. I'm not political," she said, "but it makes me sad that the awesome freedom we have in the U.S.A. can be undermined by sneaky, power-hungry, unethical people."

In late 1999, at the same moment that Danny Smalley's wrongful death case went to trial in Texas, Bill Koch's whistle-blowing lawsuit alleging that Koch Industries engaged in a "deliberate pattern of fraud" simultaneously went on trial in Tulsa, Oklahoma. Elroy and other investigators working for Bill Koch had produced a devastating list of witnesses. Under oath, one former Koch employee after the next described stealing oil for the company. "I had to do what they said to do or I wouldn't have a job," one former employee, L. B. Perry, told the jury. In rebuttal, Koch Industries produced its own witnesses, who defended the company's practices as commonplace and legal and debunked its accusers as liars and disgruntled employees. But the turning point in the trial was reached when Phil Dubose, a Louisianan who had worked for Koch Industries for twenty-seven years before being laid off in 1994, took the stand.

Dubose had started as a "gauger," one of the grunts who measure crude oil as it's bought from suppliers, and had worked his way up to a senior management post supervising the company's transport of oil up and down the Eastern Seaboard. He oversaw four thousand miles of pipeline, 186 trucks, and a full marine division of barges. Dubose took the stand and testified about what he and other employees called "the Koch Method." As he later described it, "They were just mis-measuring crude oil from the Indian reservations as they did all over the U.S. If you bought crude, you'd shorten the gauge. They'd show you how. They had meters in the field. They'd recalibrate them, so if it showed a barrel, they'd say it was just three-quarters of a barrel when they were buying it. You did it in different ways. You cheated. If we sold a barge with fifteen hundred barrels, you'd say it was two thousand. It all involved weights and measurements, and they had their thumb on the scale. That was the Koch Method."

Bill Koch's investigators said they had stumbled across Dubose blindly, going down a list of former Koch employees. Not long before they knocked on Dubose's door, he had suffered a family tragedy and become more religious. When they arrived to ask him questions about Koch Industries, Dubose said he'd try to answer as best he could. As he began talking, in his Louisiana drawl, they knew they had struck another kind of gusher—an invaluable witness.

Dubose contended, "The Kochs never did play by the rules. They had their own playing field. They just didn't abide by anything. Not the EPA or anything else. They constantly polluted. If they got fined, it didn't matter, because they made so much money doing it. We never reported things like busted pipeline out in the field. Otherwise, we'd get fined. When we spilled oil, we never reported the real amount. We were told to do that, to keep our costs down. The Kochs expected us to lie and try to cover it up," he said.

Dubose maintained that the pressure to keep costs low was intense and, he believed, sprang from the top, infusing every level of the company. "If your books were short for more than a month or two, you'd be looking for a job," he said. Perhaps because he had been laid off without explanation, he was bitter, but he made an indelible impression. "They got that money dishonestly," he asserted. "They made it off the girls and the boys in the trenches, through their deceit. You don't have to be a genius like Bill Gates to make money the way they did," he concluded. "They just did it by breaking the rules all over the country."

Before the trial ended, Charles Koch himself took the stand, while his wife as well as David and David's wife, Julia, all watched. He denied defrauding the government and argued that if oil producers believed his company cheated, they would have sold their oil to the Kochs' competitors instead.

Evidently, the jury wasn't convinced. On December 23, 1999, it found Koch Industries guilty of making 24,587 false claims to the government. The company faced a potential fine of more than $200 million. As an additional insult, it would have to pay up to a quarter of the penalty to Bill Koch, who triumphantly declared to the press, "This shows they are the biggest crooks in the oil industry."

"It was the first time they were defeated," said Dubose, looking back. "We won because they didn't have a weapon as big as the one we used." Asked to what he was referring, he answered, "The truth."

In the end, Koch Industries settled Bill Koch's whistle-blower suit for $25 million. While most of the fines went to the federal government, the company paid over $7 million to Bill, along with his legal fees. As part of what came to be known in the family as the "global settlement," by mid-2001 the warring brothers finally also agreed to a cease-fire. Charles, David, and Bill signed a pact promising no further litigation and agreeing to a binding non-disparagement clause that imposed hefty escalating financial penalties for violations. On at least one occasion when Bill spoke too freely about his brothers, the general counsel for Koch Industries warned him that he was risking a fine. The pact bought an uneasy peace. But the damage to the company's image, and to the family's reputation, was already profound.

The Koch Industries' spokeswoman Melissa Cohlmia has said that the Kochs' serious legal losses were a learning experience and that as a result the company stepped up its corporate compliance efforts. After the 1990s, the company's overall environmental record did improve some, although in 2010 the company was still rated as one of the top ten air polluters in the United States by the Political Economy Research Institute at the University of Massachusetts Amherst. In 2012, the Environmental Protection Agency's database revealed Koch Industries to be the number one producer of toxic waste in the country. Producing 950 million pounds of toxic waste, it topped the list of 8,000 companies required by law to account for their handling of 650 toxic and carcinogenic chemicals spun off by industrial processes.

Charles Koch has acknowledged that he miscalculated earlier, writing in his 2007 book, *The Science of Success,* "We were caught unprepared by the rapid increase in regulation." As he explained it, "While business was becoming increasingly regulated, we kept thinking and acting as if we lived in a pure market economy."

From Charles's standpoint, the problem wasn't so much Koch Industries' conduct as the legal regime in which it operated. He seemed to be arguing that in the "pure market economy" that he favored, no such regulations would exist. As the Kochs took stock, it was clear that America was far from the laissez-faire utopia they idealized in the Freedom School. Having had their company fined hundreds of millions of dollars, labeled crooked by the U.S. Senate, and barely escaping federal criminal prosecution, the Kochs retooled. They sold off many of their most troublesome pipelines, paring their holdings down to four thousand miles, and they moved heavily into the finance sector, trading commodities and derivatives, where regulations and oversight were weaker. They diversified rapidly, acquiring DuPont's synthetic textile division, Invista, for $4.1 billion in 2004, which made them the world's producers of Lycra and other well-known brands such as StainMaster carpet. A year later, in 2005, they bought out Georgia-Pacific, the huge wood-products company, for $21 billion, which made them among the world's biggest manufacturers of plywood, laminates, and ubiquitous paper products like Dixie cups, Brawny paper towels, and Quilted Northern toilet paper. It also made them a major producer of formaldehyde, whose classification as a human carcinogen Koch Industries quietly fought, despite David Koch's public philanthropic support for cancer research.

The clash between Koch Industries' corporate interests

and David Koch's philanthropic work surfaced publicly in 2009. While David Koch sat on the advisory board of the National Cancer Institute (NCI), and the National Institutes of Health was concluding that formaldehyde should be treated as a "known human carcinogen," a top executive at Georgia-Pacific protested the government's findings. Traylor Champion, the company's vice president of environmental affairs, sent a formal letter of protest to federal health authorities stating that the company "strongly disagrees" with the NIH's conclusion that formaldehyde should be treated as "a known human carcinogen." David Koch neither recused himself from the NCI's advisory board nor divested himself of his company's stock while the carcinogenic properties of formaldehyde were evaluated.

When questions were raised, Koch, who had undergone rounds of advanced treatment for prostate cancer, was incensed that anyone could question his integrity. But James Huff, deputy director at the National Institute of Environmental Health Sciences, a division of the NIH, said it was "disgusting" for Koch to be serving on the advisory board. "It's just not good public health," he said. "Vested interests should not be on the board. Those boards are very important. They're very influential as to whether NCI goes into formaldehyde or not. Billions and billions are involved in formaldehyde." Harold Varmus, a former director of the National Cancer Institute, who knew Koch as a donor to scientific institutions, noted that many philanthropists had large business interests but admitted that he was "surprised" to learn of the company's stance on formaldehyde.

The Kochs' corporate interests clashed with their philosophical positions on other issues as well, including their opposition to government-supported "crony capitalism." Koch Industries took full advantage of a panoply of federal subsidies, ranging from artificially low grazing fees on the 40 percent of their 500,000 acres of cattle ranches that used federal lands, to a deal with the Bush administration in 2002 to sell eight million barrels of crude oil to fill the Strategic Petroleum Reserve, a federal supply set aside as a hedge against market disruptions. "Can you think of any more anti-free-market tool than the Strategic Petroleum Reserve?" asked a former Koch executive. "Energy doesn't operate in a free market," he pointed out.

Koch Industries' practices belied its owners' virtuous talk in other ways, too. According to an investigative report by *Bloomberg Markets,* Koch Industries was "involved in improper payments to win business in Africa, India and the Middle East" and had "sold millions of dollars of petrochemical equipment to Iran, a country the U.S. identifies as a sponsor of global terrorism." The report suggested that the Kochs' Iranian deals flouted a trade ban put in place against the outlaw state by President Clinton in 1995. Koch Industries acknowledged that it had helped Iran build what became the largest methanol plant in the world in the midst of the trade embargo but insisted that the deal had been structured in a strictly legal way, by relying on foreign subsidiaries. The company subsequently fired the employee who exposed the controversial practices.

Yet as Charles and David continued to plow 90 percent of their company's profits back into their business—a strategy they often noted would be impossible if they were required to pay quarterly dividends to public shareholders—its revenues grew phenomenally. In 1960, it grossed a healthy $70 million, but by 2006 it was grossing an astounding $90 billion. "It is beyond spectacular," one Wall Street investment banker, Roger Altman of Evercore, observed. "It's just gigantically successful. It is in *everything.*"

CHAPTER FIVE

The Kochtopus: Free-Market Machine

AFTER SUFFERING HUMILIATING LOSSES IN THE COURTS AND Congress, the Kochs began to retool their approach not just to business but also to politics. They began to engage far more strategically, funneling money into the pursuit of power in a whole new way. More than anyone else, the man behind the Kochs' political transformation was Richard Fink, nicknamed the Pirate by detractors within their sphere for the handsome living he made on their payroll.

Fink was famous for flying to Wichita in the late 1970s as a twenty-seven-year-old graduate student, wearing a garish blue tie, a checkered shirt, and a brand-new white-piped black polyester suit, to beg for money from Charles. "What a jackass I looked like," he later admitted. After growing up in Maplewood, New Jersey, in a family that he joked made *The Sopranos* look like a home movie, Fink had become a devotee of Austrian free-market theory. He hoped Charles would fund a program in it at Rutgers in New Jersey, where he was teaching part-time while pursuing a graduate degree at NYU. Courses in Austrian economics were as rare as Viennese waltzes in most colleges at that time. But soon after Fink made the pitch, Charles pledged $150,000 for the program. When Fink later asked Charles why he'd thrown so much money at a long-haired, bearded graduate student in a shiny disco suit, Charles had supposedly quipped, "I like polyester. It's petroleum based."

By the late 1980s, Fink had supplanted Cato's Ed Crane as Charles Koch's main political lieutenant. Unlike Crane, who was interested in libertarian ideas but regarded it as "creepy when you have to deal with politicians," Fink was fascinated by the nuts and bolts of power. After studying the Kochs' political problems for six months, he drew up a practical blueprint, ostensibly inspired by Hayek's model of production, that impressed Charles by going beyond where his own 1976 paper on the subject had left off. Called "The Structure of Social Change," it approached the manufacture of political change like any other product. As Fink later described it in a talk, it laid out a three-phase takeover of American politics. The first phase required an "investment" in intellectuals whose ideas would serve as the "raw products." The second required an investment in think tanks that would turn the ideas into marketable policies. And the third phase required the subsidization of "citizens" groups that would, along with "special interests," pressure elected officials to implement the policies. It was in essence a libertarian production line, waiting only to be bought, assembled, and switched on.

Fink's plan was tailor-made for Charles Koch, who deeply admired Hayek and approached both business and politics with the systematic mind-set of an engineer. While some might find it disturbing to regard the democratic process as a factory, Charles soon adopted the approach as his own. As he told Brian Doherty, the libertarian writer, "To bring about social change requires a strategy that is vertically and horizontally integrated." It must span, he said, from "idea creation to policy development to education to grassroots organizations to lobbying to political action." Before long, libertarian wags had dubbed the Kochs' publicity-shy, multiarmed assembly line the Kochtopus, a name that stuck.

In contrast to their idealistic but amateurish approach during the old Libertarian Party days, with Fink's help the Kochs' methods became decidedly more pragmatic. Facing serious threats to their business, they began playing the Washington political game as aggressively as any other corporation, if not more so. After the public relations fiasco of the Senate hearings into Indian oil theft, for instance, Koch Industries crossed ideological lines to hire Robert Strauss, the former chairman of the Democratic National Committee, who was by then Washington's premier lobbyist. The company soon opened an office in the capital, which grew into a formidable in-house lobbying operation. Fink explained that it had been necessary for the company to establish a presence in Washington because it had felt "so brutalized by the process" and lacked "corporate defense" capabilities.

The Kochs had previously disdained conventional politics, but now they became major Republican donors. "It was the investigation that got them to the Republican Party," notes Kenneth Ballen, the former counsel to the Senate's investigative committee. Before that, he points out, "Charles had been so far right he was off in the ether. They thought Reagan was a sellout. But they were worried about their business. It was about power." Doherty saw the Kochs' embrace of the Republican Party in much the same way. He credits the Kochs with being by far the largest funders of libertarian ideas but notes they also became "direct funders of Republican politicians for all the same reasons other businesses are. It confuses a lot of people in the libertarian world, who think of them as sellouts," he conceded.

Their investment quickly transformed the brothers' political status. By 1996, they had grown into major players in the Republican Party. David Koch went from dismissing Bob Dole, the senator from Kansas, the home of Koch Industries, as just another "Establishment" politician "with no moral principles," in the early 1980s, to becoming the vice-chair of Dole's 1996 presidential campaign against Bill Clinton. No longer an outsider, the Koch family became Dole's third-largest financial backer. David Koch in fact hosted a birthday party for Dole, at which the candidate raised $150,000.

Dole reportedly helped the Kochs, too. Critics said he

did them a legislative favor designed to indemnify companies like theirs that had been charged with regulatory violations from having to pay huge federal legal fines. But the proposed legislative fix died when a sudden outbreak of salmonella in hamburgers scared Congress from weakening such penalties. Had it passed, though, it would have nullified tens of millions of dollars in fines that had been levied on Koch Industries. According to *The Washington Post,* Koch Industries did succeed in getting Dole's help on another matter, an exemption from a new real estate depreciation schedule, a favor that saved the company millions of dollars. As Dole conceded decades later, after he retired from politics, "I've always believed when people give big money, they—maybe silently—expect something in return."

The Kochs' affinity for hardball in politics, as in business, soon stirred controversy. In 1997, they became the focus of yet another Senate investigation. That year, the Clintons were in the headlines for campaign-finance scandals ranging from virtually renting the Lincoln Bedroom to big donors to taking contributions from a dubious Democratic bundler who later pleaded guilty to raising some of the money from China. The bundler, Johnny Chung, had infamously said, "I see the White House is like a subway. You have to put in coins to open the gates." In retaliation, the Democrats in the Senate, who were in the minority, conducted their own much less noticed probe, which soon led to the two little-known brothers from Wichita.

The Democrats produced a scathing report exposing what they called an "audacious" scheme by undisclosed big donors to illegally buy elections in the final moments of the 1996 campaign. It was undertaken by a suspicious shell corporation called Triad Management Services that had paid more than $3 million for unusually harsh attack ads against Democratic candidates in twenty-nine races. More than half of the advertising money came from an obscure nonprofit group whose real source of funds was a mystery, the Economic Education

Trust. The Senate committee's investigators believed that "the 'trust' was in fact financed in whole or in part by Charles and David Koch of Wichita, Kansas." The trust was a front group, according to the Senate report, designed to conceal the real donors' identities, in violation of campaign-finance laws.

The brothers, who had long opposed restrictions on their political spending, were suspected of having secretly paid for the attack ads, most of which aired in states where Koch Industries did business. In Kansas, where Triad Management was especially active, the funds were suspected of having tipped the outcome in four close races. The conservative Republican Sam Brownback's race for the U.S. Senate received a special boost, which included a barrage of phone calls informing voters that his opponent, Jill Docking, was a Jew. The shady victories in Kansas had national impact, helping Republicans retain control of the House of Representatives, despite President Clinton's reelection.

The Kochs, when asked by reporters if they had given the money, refused to comment. Charles Koch also failed to respond to an inquiry from the Senate investigators. In 1998, however, *The Wall Street Journal* finally confirmed a link, noting that a consultant on the Kochs' payroll had been involved in the scheme. Republicans argued that they were simply trying to balance the score against spending by labor unions, but in 1998 business outspent labor by a ratio of twelve to one. In the end, the Federal Election Commission ruled that the Triad scheme was illegal and fined its president and founder, Carolyn Malenick. Other participants, however, were never identified.

Charles Lewis, who heads the Investigative Reporting Workshop at American University and who founded the Center for Public Integrity, a nonpartisan watchdog group, describes the Triad scandal of 1996 as a "historic" moment in American politics. There had of course been many bigger campaign scandals before then. But Triad was a new model. He said it was the first time a major corporation used a tax-exempt nonprofit as a front group or, as he put it, "a cutout to secretly influence elections in a threatening way." He said the Kochs showed that "you could dump a million dollars on someone's head by using cutouts." After reporting on political corruption in Washington for years, Lewis concluded that "Koch Industries was the poster child of a company run amok."

What made the Koch family's growing financial role in American politics extraordinary was not just its willingness to flout the rules but also the way that in accordance with Fink's plan it merged all forms of political spending—campaign, lobbying, and philanthropic—into one investment aimed at paying huge future dividends to the donors. Lewis's Investigative Reporting Workshop spent a year in 2013 culling through the Kochs' financial records and concluded that their operation was "unprecedented in size, scope, and funding" and also in the way that it was "mutually reinforcing to the direct financial and political interests" of Koch Industries.

In 1992, David Koch likened the brothers' multipronged political strategy to that of venture capitalists with diversified portfolios. "My overall concept is to minimize the role of government and to maximize the role of the private economy and to maximize personal freedoms," he told the *National Journal*. "By supporting all of these different [nonprofit] organizations I am trying to support different approaches to achieve those objectives. It's almost like an investor investing in a whole variety of companies. He achieves diversity and balance. And he hedges his bets."

What resulted from this approach was a complicated flowchart enabling the Kochs to use their fortune to influence public policy from an astounding number of different directions at once. At the top, the funds all came from the same source—the Kochs. And in the end, the contributions all served the same pro-business, limited-government goals. But they funneled the money simultaneously through three different kinds of channels. They made political contributions to party committees and candidates, such as Dole. Their business made contributions through its political action committee and exerted influence by lobbying. And they founded numerous nonprofit groups, which they filled with tax-deductible contributions from their private foundations. Other wealthy activists made political contributions, and other companies lobbied. But the Kochs' strategic and largely covert philanthropic spending became their great force magnifier.

By 1990, enterprising conservative and libertarian activists were wearing a path to Wichita, where they, like Fink before them, would pitch their proposals to Charles Koch in hopes of his patronage. Typical was the experience in 1991 of two former Reagan administration lawyers, Clint Bolick, a former aide to Clarence Thomas, and William "Chip" Mellor III, in search of seed money for a new kind of aggressive, right-wing public interest law firm that would litigate against government regulations in favor of "economic liberty." Mellor recalled thinking, "Who else would give us enough money to be serious?" According to Mellor, after lower-level aides initially turned down the proposal, Charles Koch himself committed $1.5 million on the spot, but with strings attached, keeping him in control. As Mellor recalled, "He said, 'Here's what I'm going to do. I'll give you up to $500,000 a year for three years, each year, but you have to come back each year and demonstrate that you've met these milestones that you've set out to accomplish and I will evaluate it on a yearly basis, and there's no guarantees.'" The legal group, the Institute for Justice, went on to bring numerous successful cases against government regulations, including campaign-finance laws, several of which reached the Supreme Court.

"In recent years," a prescient news story noted in 1992, "money from Wichita has gushed into the coffers of virtually every Washington think tank and public interest group dedicated to free-market economics and the libertarian credo of minuscule government regulation." In 1990 alone, the article noted, the three main private foundations controlled by Charles and David Koch disbursed $4 million to such ostensibly nonpartisan but politically motivated groups.

Few outside the rarefied world of far-right, laissez-faire economics noticed, but the Kochs' multidimensional political spending kept growing. Between 1998 and 2008, for instance, Charles Koch's private fund, the Charles G. Koch Charitable Foundation, made more than $48 million in tax-deductible grants, primarily to groups promoting his political views. The Claude R. Lambe Charitable Foundation, which was controlled by Charles and his wife, Liz, along with two company employees and an accountant, similarly made more than $28 million in tax-deductible grants. David Koch's fund, the David H. Koch Charitable Foundation, made more than $120 million in tax-deductible grants—many to cultural and scientific projects rather than political. Meanwhile, during those years Koch Industries spent more than $50 million on lobbying. Separately, the company's political action committee, KochPAC, donated some $8 million to political campaigns, more than 80 percent of it to Republicans. In addition, the Kochs and other family members spent millions more on personal campaign contributions.

Only the Kochs know precisely how much they spent on this sprawling political enterprise, because the public record remains incomplete. By dispersing much of the money through a labyrinth of nonprofit groups, the Kochs made the full extent of their political "investment" difficult if not impossible for the public to detect. In 2008 alone, public tax records indicate that the three main Koch family foundations gave money to thirty-four different political and policy organizations, three of which they founded and several of which they directed.

There were some legal boundaries. By law, tax-exempt charities, which the IRS designates as 501(c)(3)s, must refrain from involvement in lobbying and electoral politics and serve the public rather than their donors' interests. But such laws are rarely enforced and are subject to flexible interpretation.

Critics began to complain that the Kochs' approach to philanthropy subverted the purpose of tax-exempt charitable giving. A 2004 report by the National Committee for Responsive Philanthropy, a watchdog group, found the Kochs' philanthropy self-serving. "These foundations give money to nonprofit organizations that do research and advocacy on issues that impact the profit margin of Koch Industries," it charged.

But the Kochs defended the millions they gave to groups fighting environmental regulations and supporting lower taxes on industry and the rich as public-spirited. Several longtime associates questioned this. Gus diZerega, the former family friend, suggested that the Kochs' youthful ardor for libertarianism had largely devolved into a rationale for corporate self-interest. "Perhaps he has confused making money with freedom," he said of Charles. One conservative who worked closely with the Kochs but declined to be identified in order not to inflame the relationship went so far as to call their tax-exempt giving "a shell game." He contended they merely saw philanthropy as preferable to paying taxes. "People say, 'Wow—they're so generous!'" he marveled. "It's just the best available option for them. If they didn't give it to their causes, they would have to give it to the government. At least this way they control how it's spent." He noted that by blending their corporate and charitable work, "they draw some pretty fine lines. It's really another form of lobbying." But he conceded, "They've built a pretty amazing machine."

From the start, the Kochs exerted unusually tight personal control over their philanthropic endeavors. "If we're going to give a lot of money, we'll make darn sure they spend it in a way that goes along with our intent," David Koch has acknowledged. "And if they make a wrong turn and start doing things we don't agree with," he told Doherty, "we withdraw funding."

An early example of Charles Koch flexing his muscles took place at the Cato Institute in 1981, when he fired one of the think tank's five original stockholders. Ironically, although Charles had criticized Robert Welch for turning the John Birch Society into a cult of personality by flaunting his ownership of the organization's stock, Charles had set Cato up in the same way, as a nonprofit with stockholders, who picked the board of directors. The arrangement was rare in the nonprofit world. But as Charles had observed of the John Birch Society, it guaranteed the directors an unusual measure of continuing control.

The director whom Charles fired at Cato was a major figure in libertarian circles, Murray Rothbard, a radical Upper West Side Jewish intellectual whose work Charles had subsidized in happier days. Rothbard called the putsch "iniquitous," "high-handed," and "illegal." He went on to claim that Charles had "confiscated the shares which I had naively left in Koch's Wichita office for 'safekeeping,' an act clearly in violation of our agreement as well as contrary to every tenet of libertarian principle."

Some suspected that Rothbard, an Austrian economic school purist, was fired for criticizing Koch, whom he had accused of watering down unpopular libertarian positions in order to get more votes for his brother's 1980 candidacy. The platform, for instance, had pulled back from advocating the complete abolition of all income taxes. It also called for shrinking rather than abolishing the military. The controversy set off alarms in the hothouse libertarian community, marking Charles in the eyes of those who took Rothbard's side as ruthless and rapacious, more interested in power than in principle.

Charles's drive for control was the focus later of testimony that Rothbard gave in one of the many rounds of fights between the four Koch brothers over their patrimony. A memo summarizing Rothbard's prospective testimony quoted him saying that Charles "cannot tolerate dissent" and will "go to any end to acquire/retain control over the nonprofit foundations with which he is associated." Rothbard accused Charles of dictating everything from the office decor to the design of Cato's stationery. Further, he alleged that while Charles wanted "absolute control" of the nonprofits with which he was associated, he was intent on "being able to spend other people's money." This criticism would later be reprised in connection with the Koch seminars, which some saw as Charles's means of creating a political slush fund filled with other people's money but under his own control. Rothbard also accused Charles of using nonprofit organizations to "acquire access to, and respect from, influential people in government."

In the mid-1980s, as called for in the first phase of Fink's plan, the Kochs also began to establish an academic beachhead of their own. Their particular focus was on George Mason University, a little-known campus of Virginia's prestigious higher-education system, located in the Washington suburbs. In 1977, *The Washington Post* described the school as toiling in "the wilderness of obscurity." By 1981, Fink had moved his Austrian economics program there from Rutgers, eventually naming it the Mercatus Center. The think tank was entirely funded by outside donations, largely from the Kochs, but it was located in the midst of the public university's campus, so it touted itself, somewhat misleadingly, as "the world's premier university source for market-oriented ideas—bridging the gap between academic ideas and real-world problems."

Financial records show that the Koch family foundations donated some $30 million to the school, much of it going to the Mercatus Center. *The Washington Post* described Mercatus as a "staunchly anti-regulatory center funded largely by Koch Industries Inc." This, however, raised questions about whether the Mercatus Center was in fact an independent intellectual center or an extension of the Kochs' lobbying operation. Clayton Coppin, who taught history at George Mason and compiled the confidential study of Charles's political activities for

Bill Koch, describes Mercatus outright in his report as "a lobbying group disguised as a disinterested academic program." The arrangement, he points out, had financial advantages for the Kochs, because it enabled Charles "to have a tax deduction for financing a group, which for all practical purposes is a lobbying group for his corporate interest."

Sharing a building with the Mercatus Center was the heavily Koch-funded Institute for Humane Studies, chaired by Charles Koch. The IHS was founded by F. A. "Baldy" Harper, a free-market fundamentalist who had been a trustee at the Freedom School, where he had written essays for *The Freeman*, calling taxes "theft," welfare "immoral," and labor unions "slavery" and opposing court-ordered remedies to racial segregation. Charles Koch had eulogized Harper glowingly, saying, "Of all the teachers of liberty, none was as well-beloved as Baldy, for it was he who taught the teachers and, in teaching, taught them humility and gentleness."

The aim of the IHS was to cultivate and subsidize a farm team of the next generation's libertarian scholars. Anxious at one point that the war of ideas was proceeding too slowly, Charles reportedly demanded better metrics with which to monitor students' political views. To the dismay of some faculty members, applicants' essays had to be run through computers in order to count the number of times they mentioned the free-market icons Ayn Rand and Milton Friedman. Students were tested at the beginning and the end of each week for ideological improvement. The institute also housed the Charles G. Koch summer internship program, a paid fellowship placing students who shared the Kochs' views in like-minded nonprofit groups, where they could join the libertarian network.

George Mason's economics department, meanwhile, became a hotbed of controversial theories that began to transform Americans' tax bills, serving as an incubator for the supply-side tax cuts in the Reagan administration that hugely advantaged the rich. Paul Craig Roberts, an adjunct professor at

GMU, drafted a precursor to the first supply-side tax cut bill of the Reagan era, which was introduced by his former boss Congressman Jack Kemp. While these tax cuts starved the government, George Mason also belittled its role philosophically. A star on its faculty was James Buchanan, the founder of "public choice" theory, who often described his approach as "politics without romance" because he categorized elected officials and public servants as just another greedy, self-aggrandizing private interest group, a view popular with antigovernment libertarians. In 1986, Buchanan was awarded a Nobel Prize in economics. Liberal economists were aghast. Robert Lekachman, for instance, lambasted Buchanan for reducing "all human behavior to simple self-interest." The prize nonetheless was an indisputable achievement, helping to put the school, and libertarianism, on the map.

Julian Sanchez, a fellow at the Cato Institute, soon exalted George Mason as a "libertarian mecca," saying, "It may well be the most heavily libertarian-staffed institution of higher education in the country." Liberals, however, regarded the Kochs' singular influence over the school with suspicion. "It's ground zero for deregulation policy in Washington," said Rob Stein, the Democratic political strategist who studied how the right wing spent money. Noting the Kochs' unusually large role, he said, "George Mason is a public university and receives public funds. Virginia is hosting an institution that the Kochs practically control."

The many hats that Rich Fink wore only underscored critics' concerns. As he grew in importance to Charles Koch, Fink relinquished his formal role at the Mercatus Center, handing its stewardship off to a protégé, and joined Koch Industries as its head of lobbying but remained on the university's prestigious Board of Visitors. He also was at one point the president of the Charles G. Koch Charitable Foundation, the president of the Claude R. Lambe Charitable Foundation, a director of the Fred C. and Mary R. Koch Foundation, and an integral member of several of the Kochs' political groups. The fungibility of his roles hinted at the fine line between nonprofit and for-profit pursuits within the Kochs' enterprise.

As Fink's star rose, Crane's fell. Crane still ran the Cato Institute, but in 1992 Charles Koch resigned from the libertarian think tank's board, although David remained a trustee. Associates suspected that Crane, who didn't take orders gladly, had not demonstrated sufficient fealty to his patron. Crane had privately ridiculed Charles's management philosophy, which Charles trademarked under the name Market-Based Management, or MBM, and later distilled into his book *The Science of Success*. In essence, Charles believed that businesses' corporate culture should replicate the competitiveness of the free market. Employees at almost every level of his company were compensated on the basis of the value they created, competing with each other for bonuses, which constituted large portions of their annual pay. Charles described MBM as a "holistic system" containing "five dimensions: vision, virtue and talents, knowledge processes, decision rights and incentives." Some company employees privately mocked the cutthroat culture that MBM fostered as "Making the Brothers Money." *Forbes*, too, lampooned Charles a bit, in its review of his book, describing him as an "autodidact" who had "almost a Marxist faith in 'fixed laws' that 'govern human well-being'" and whose "system for grading employees" was "especially obtuse."

Despite the mixed reviews, Charles insisted that personnel in all corners of his enterprise adhere to his system, setting aside regular time to practice and review the techniques. "It became exactly the kind of bureaucracy that libertarians detest," noted one former employee, before adding, "He's the billionaire, not me, so who knows?" Market-Based Management embraced the notion that employees at every level, even the bottom, might have superior ideas to those at the top. Theoretically, it was an egalitarian approach, yet how open Charles really was to those like Crane who challenged his top-down authority is debatable. Many found him remarkably humble for one of the wealthiest men in the world, noting that he lunched regularly in the company cafeteria alongside his employees. But in a 1999 speech, Charles likened his fixed beliefs to those of Martin Luther, the founder of Protestantism. "In that, I echo Martin Luther," he said of his own free-market views. "Here I stand. I can do no other." The comparison was revealing.

In any case, Crane was less than reverent when Charles tried to impose his management system on the Cato Institute. From his large office in Cato's strikingly modern, light-filled Washington headquarters, Crane later made clear that he regarded Charles as a serious thinker and an exemplary businessman, but he couldn't help but poke fun at MBM. "He thinks he's a genius. He's the emperor, and he's convinced he's wearing clothes," Crane said with a snicker. Fink, by contrast, was much more solicitous of Charles's ideas. "Richie exploited MBM to the hilt," a Cato official said of Fink. "He took over with a shiv" in Crane's back. "He's well named."

With Cato and the Institute for Humane Studies, the Kochs checked off the first item on Fink's shopping list for social change—institutions that could hatch scholarly ideas in line with their own thinking. The Mercatus Center checked off the second item, a more practical organization aimed at promoting these ideas into action. Its location, just across the Potomac from the Capitol, was a bonus, enabling its fellows to testify regularly as independent experts at congressional hearings. By 2004, *The Wall Street Journal* dubbed it "the most important think tank you've never heard of" and noted that fourteen of the twenty-three regulations that President George W. Bush placed on a "hit list" had been suggested by Mercatus scholars. Eight of those were environmental protections. Fink told the paper that the Kochs have "other means of fighting [their] battles" and that the Mercatus Center does not actively promote the company's private interests. But Thomas McGarity, a law professor at the University of Texas who specialized in environmental issues, argued that "Koch has been constantly in trouble with the EPA, and Mercatus has constantly hammered on the agency." One environmental lawyer who clashed repeatedly with the Mercatus Center dismissed it as a lobbying shop dressed up as a nonprofit, calling it "a means of laundering economic aims." The lawyer explained the strategy: "You take corporate money and give it to a neutral-sounding think tank," which "hires people with pedigrees and academic degrees who put out credible-seeming studies. But they all coincide perfectly with the economic interests of their funders."

In 1997, for instance, the EPA moved to reduce surface ozone, a form of air pollution caused, in part, by emissions from oil refineries. Susan Dudley, an economist who became a top official at the Mercatus Center, came up with a novel criticism of the proposed rule. The EPA, she argued, had not taken into account that by blocking the sun, smog cut down on cases of skin cancer. She claimed that if pollution were controlled, it would cause up to eleven thousand additional cases of skin cancer each year.

In 1999, the District of Columbia Circuit Court embraced Dudley's pro-smog argument. Evaluating the EPA rule, the court found that the EPA had "explicitly disregarded" the "possible health benefits of ozone." In another part of the opinion, the court also ruled, 2–1, that the EPA had overstepped its authority.

Afterward, the Constitutional Accountability Center, a watchdog group, revealed that the judges in the majority had previously attended one of the all-expenses-paid legal seminars for judges that were heavily funded by the Kochs' foundations. This one had taken place on a Montana ranch run by a group that the Kochs helped subsidize called the Foundation for Research on Economics and the Environment. The judges claimed that their decision was unaffected by the junket. Their embrace of the Mercatus Center's novel argument, however, soon proved embarrassing. The Supreme Court overruled their position unanimously, noting that the Clean Air Act's standards are absolute and not subject to cost-benefit analysis. Although their side lost in the end, the case illustrated that the Kochs' ideological pipeline was humming.

The most fateful Mercatus Center hire might have been Wendy Gramm, an economist and director at the giant Texas energy company Enron who was the wife of Senator Phil Gramm, the powerful Texas Republican. In the mid-1990s, she became the head of Mercatus's Regulatory Studies Program. There, she pushed Congress to support what came to be known as the Enron Loophole, exempting the type of energy derivatives from which Enron profited from regulatory oversight. Both Enron and Koch Industries, which also was a major trader of derivatives, lobbied desperately for the loophole. Koch claimed there was no need for government policing because corporations' concern for their reputations would cause them to self-regulate.

Some experts foresaw danger. In 1998, Brooksley Born, chair of the Commodity Futures Trading Commission, warned that the lucrative but risky derivatives market needed more government oversight. But Senator Gramm, who chaired the Senate Banking Committee, ignored such warnings, crafting a deregulatory bill made to order for Enron and Koch, called the Commodity Futures Modernization Act. Despite Born's warning, the Clinton administration embraced the exemptions too, swayed by Wall Street pressure.

In 2001, Enron collapsed in a heap of bogus financial statements and fraudulent accounting practices. But Wendy Gramm had pocketed up to $1.8 million from Enron the year after arguing for the loophole. And it emerged that before going under, Enron had made substantial campaign contributions to Senator Gramm, while its chairman, Kenneth Lay, had given money to the Mercatus Center.

By the end of 2002, the Gramms had gone into semiretirement, but at the Mercatus Center the zeal to exempt enormously risky markets, including energy derivatives favored by Koch Industries, lived on. The consequences wouldn't become fully visible until the economic crash of 2008. By then, George Mason University was both the largest single recipient of Koch funds for higher education and the largest research university in Virginia.

George Mason was the Kochs' largest libertarian academic project but far from the only one. By 2015, according to an internal list, the Charles Koch Foundation was subsidizing pro-business, antiregulatory, and antitax programs in 307 different institutions of higher education in America and had plans to expand into 18 more. The schools ranged from cash-hungry West Virginia University to Brown University, where the Kochs, in the tradition of the Olin Foundation, established an Ivy League "beachhead."

At Brown, which is often thought of as the most liberal of the Ivy schools, Charles Koch's foundation gave $147,154 in 2009 to the Political Theory Project, a freshman seminar in free-market classics taught by a libertarian, Professor John Tomasi. "After a whole semester of Hayek, it's hard to shake them off that perspective over the next four years," Tomasi confided "slyly," according to a conservative publication. Charles Koch's foundation gave additional funds to Brown to support faculty research and postdoctoral candidates in such topics as why bank deregulation is good for the poor.

At West Virginia University, the Charles Koch Foundation's donation of $965,000 to create the Center for Free Enterprise came with some strings attached. The foundation required the school to give it a say over the professors it funded, in violation of traditional standards of academic independence. The Kochs' investment had an outsized impact in the small, poor state where coal, in which the Kochs had a financial interest, ruled. One of the WVU professors approved for funding,

Russell Sobel, edited a 2007 book called *Unleashing Capitalism: Why Prosperity Stops at the West Virginia Border and How to Fix It,* arguing that mine safety and clean water regulations only hurt workers. "Are workers really better off being safer but making less income?" it asked. Soon, Sobel was briefing West Virginia's governor and cabinet, as well as a joint session of the Senate and the House Finance Committees. The state Republican Party chairman declared Sobel's antiregulatory book the blueprint for its party platform.

In 2014, a sparsely regulated West Virginia company, Freedom Industries, spilled ten thousand gallons of a mysterious, foul-smelling chemical into the drinking water of Charleston, the state's largest city, triggering panic in 300,000 residents, whom authorities ordered away from their taps. It was just another in a seemingly endless history of tragic industrial disasters afflicting West Virginia. By then, though, Sobel was long gone. He was listed as a visiting scholar at the Citadel in South Carolina, and an expert at the Mercatus Center at George Mason University.

Defenders of the Kochs' growing academic influence, like John Hardin, director of university relations at the Charles Koch Foundation, argued that their grants were bringing ideological diversity and debate to campuses. "We support professors who add to the variety of ideas available on college campuses. And in every case the school maintains control over its staffing and teaching decisions," he wrote in *The Wall Street Journal.*

But in the eyes of critics, the Kochs had not so much enriched as corrupted academia, sponsoring courses that would otherwise fail to meet the standards of legitimate scholarship. John David, an economics professor at West Virginia University Tech who witnessed the school's transformation, wrote in a scathing newspaper column that it had become clear that "entire academic areas at universities can be bought just like politicians. The difference is that universities are supposed to permit open dialogue and exchange of ideas and not be places for the indoctrination of innocent students with dictated propaganda prescribed by outside special interests."

The first two steps of Fink's plan were now complete. Yet the Koch brothers concluded that these steps were still not enough to effect change. Free-market absolutism was still a sideshow in American politics. They needed the third and final phase of Fink's plan—a mechanism to deliver their ideas to the street and to mobilize the public's support behind them. "Even great ideas are useless if they remain trapped in the ivory tower," Charles noted in a 1999 speech. David put it differently. "What we needed was a sales force."

Part Two

Secret Sponsors

Covert Operations, 2009–2010

Total liberty for wolves is death to the lambs.

—Isaiah Berlin

CHAPTER SIX

Boots on the Ground

IN HIS 1976 BLUEPRINT FOR THE CREATION OF A LIBERTARIAN movement, Charles Koch had emphasized the need to use "all modern sales and motivational techniques." Less than a decade later, in 1984, he set out to launch a private political sales force. On paper, it was yet another Koch-funded conservative nonprofit group fighting for less government. It called itself Citizens for a Sound Economy (CSE). From the outside, it looked like an authentic political group, created by a groundswell of concerned citizens, much like Ralph Nader's Public Interest Research Groups, which had sprung up all over the country.

According to the nonpartisan Center for Public Integrity, however, it was in fact a new kind of weapon in the arsenal of several of America's biggest businesses—a fake populist movement secretly manufactured by corporate sponsors—not grass roots, but "Astroturf," as such synthetic groups came to be known. Unlike corporate lobbying or campaign spending, contributions to Citizens for a Sound Economy could be kept hidden because it classified itself as a nonprofit "educational" group (as well as having its own charitable foundation and political action committee). By far the largest of the new group's shadowy sponsors were the Kochs, who provided it with at least $7.9 million between 1986 and 1993.

The idea of employing a deceptive front group to mask corporate self-interest was not original, even within the Koch family. The same ruse had been used not just by the du Pont family and others during the New Deal years but also by a group to which Fred Koch belonged in the 1950s. He was an early and active member of the Wichita-based DeMille Foundation for Political Freedom, an antilabor union group that was a forerunner of the National Right to Work Legal Defense Foundation. In a revealing private letter, one of its staff members explained the group's "Astroturf" strategy. In reality, he said, big-business industrialists would run the group, serving as its "anonymous quarterbacks," and "call the turns." But he said they needed to sell the "yarn" that the group was "composed of housewives, farmers, small businessmen, professional people, wage earners—not big business industrialists." Otherwise, he admitted, the movement was "almost certainly doomed to failure."

Fred Koch's sons used the same playbook at Citizens for a Sound Economy. Libertarianism remained a lonely crusade, but CSE used corporate treasuries to market its spread and give it the aura of a mass movement. Its mission, according to one early participant, Matt Kibbe, "was to take these heavy ideas and translate them for mass America." Kibbe explained, "We read the same literature Obama did about nonviolent revolutions—Saul Alinsky, Gandhi, Martin Luther King. We studied the idea of the Boston Tea Party as an example of nonviolent social change. We learned we needed boots on the ground to sell ideas, not candidates."

Within a few years, the group had mobilized fifty paid field workers, in twenty-six states, to rally voters behind the Kochs' agenda of lower taxes, less regulation, and less government spending. CSE, for instance, pushed to abolish progressive taxes in favor of a flat tax and to "privatize" many government programs, including Social Security. "Ideas don't happen on their own," noted Kibbe. "Throughout history, ideas need patrons."

Although the Kochs were the founders and early funders of the group, it soon served as a front for dozens of the country's largest corporations. Its head denied that it was a rent-a-movement. But private records obtained by *The Washington*

Post showed that a procession of large companies ranging from Exxon to Microsoft had made contributions to the organization after which it had mobilized public support for their agendas. Many of the companies were embroiled in fights against the government. Microsoft, for instance, was trying to stave off an antitrust suit. It reportedly made a contribution to the foundation set up by Citizens for a Sound Economy that was aimed at reducing the Justice Department's antitrust work.

The group's unorthodox practices occasionally stirred controversy. In 1990, the organization created a spin-off, Citizens for the Environment, which called acid rain and other environmental problems "myths." When the *Pittsburgh Post-Gazette* investigated the matter, it discovered that the spin-off group had "no citizen membership of its own."

One insider said the main organization's membership claims were deceptive as well. "They always said they had 250,000 members," he later recalled, but when he asked if that meant they carried cards or paid dues, he was told no, it just meant they'd contributed money at one point, no matter how long ago or how small an amount. "It was intellectually dishonest," he maintains.

By the time Bill Clinton became president, Citizens for a Sound Economy had become a prototype for the kinds of corporate-backed opposition campaigns that would proliferate after Obama was elected. In 1993, it waged a successful assault on Clinton's proposed tax on energy, which would have taxed fossil fuel use but exempted renewable energy sources. In a show of force, without revealing its corporate sponsors, CSE ran advertisements, staged media events, and targeted political opponents. It also mobilized noisy, grassroots-seeming antitax rallies outside the Capitol—which NPR described as "designed to strike fear into the hearts of wavering Democrats."

Dan Glickman, one of the Democrats who supported the energy tax and who formerly represented the Kochs' hometown of Wichita, believes that secret money they funneled against him ended his eighteen-year congressional career. "I can't prove it, but I think I was probably their victim," he said. Having come from Wichita, he had friends in common with the Kochs who vouched for their ideological sincerity, yet to him it seemed obvious that sincere though they may be, "Their political theory is nothing more than a rationalization for self-interest."

Fink later gave credence to Glickman's suspicions. After the election, he admitted that their campaign to defeat the energy tax had been motivated by their bottom line. "Our belief is that the tax, over time, may have destroyed our business," he told *The Wichita Eagle*.

CSE's success in helping to kill Clinton's energy tax emboldened the group. Next, it went after his proposed tax increase on high earners. According to *The Wall Street Journal*, however, CSE's ads were deeply misleading, focusing on owners of car washes and other mom-and-pop small businesses, implying that the tax was aimed at the middle class when in fact it would affect only the wealthiest 4 percent. It was the kind of exaggerated scare tactic that would become a Koch trademark during the Obama years. The secret corporate donors, though, were ecstatic about Citizens for a Sound Economy. "They can fly under the radar screen . . . There are no limits, no restrictions and no disclosure," one exulted.

But at the end of 2003, internal rivalries caused Citizens for a Sound Economy to split apart. "The split was about control," recalled Dick Armey, the former Republican House majority leader from Texas who chaired the organization after leaving Congress. "I never totally understood it, and I'm not sure I understand it now." He believed the Kochs wanted to use the group "to push their business interests; they wanted CSE to lobby on those issues," he said. Others have suggested it was Armey who was pushing the interests of his law firm's clients, a charge Armey denies. There was another factor, too, behind the split, Armey suggested. "I saw it as a power grab by Richard Fink. He was trying to get a greater place in the sun to maintain his standing and his good living with the Koch family."

Armey didn't know the Kochs well, but he had talked with Charles before joining the organization and found him "a little peculiar. Charles seemed half-mysterious," he said. "He was half-secretive. He'd speak in cryptic tones. You'd have to think, 'What does he mean?' He'd talk about this business of trying to 'save the country' and all that." It seemed to Armey that Charles had conflicting aims. "Charles wanted to be more in control, but he also wanted to be more behind the scenes. I don't get it." Another veteran of Citizens for a Sound Economy concluded that while the Kochs loved liberty as an abstraction, "they were very controlling, very top-down. You can't build an organization *with* them. *They* run it."

Armey went on to start another conservative free-market group, FreedomWorks, with a few other renegades from the organization. It was at this moment, in 2003, that the Kochs inaugurated the first of their twice-a-year donor summits, which, according to one insider, were originally designed as a means of off-loading the costs of Koch Industries' environmental and regulatory fights onto others. The first conference was a fairly dismal affair, with fewer than twenty participants, mostly from Charles's social circle. The lectures were painfully dull, according to one insider.

Meanwhile, David Koch and Richard Fink created a new nonprofit advocacy group out of the remaining shards of Citizens for a Sound Economy. They called their new organization Americans for Prosperity. Like CSE, it would be accused by critics of using the guise of nonprofit status to work, behind a screen of anonymity, on behalf of the Kochs' corporate and political interests. Like Citizens for a Sound Economy, the new group had several different divisions, with different tax statuses. One wing of the new organization was the Americans for Prosperity Foundation, whose board members included both David Koch and Richard Fink. The foundation was a 501(c)(3) educational organization, so donations to it could be written off as tax-deductible charitable gifts. But while it could "educate" the public, it could not participate in electoral politics. The other division was an advocacy organization, just called Americans for Prosperity. Under the tax code, it was a 501(c)(4) "social welfare" group, which meant that it could participate in electoral politics so long as this was not its "primary" activity. Donations to this side of the organization could also be made in secret but were not tax deductible.

To run this more political side of the operation, the Kochs hired Tim Phillips, a political veteran who had worked with Ralph Reed, the former head of the Christian Coalition. Reed was regarded as the religious Right's savviest political operative. He and Phillips had co-founded Century Strategies, a dynamo of a campaign-consulting firm that became notorious for its close and lucrative business ties to Jack Abramoff, a lobbyist who went to prison for defrauding millions of dollars from Native American casino owners, among other clients. Phillips was not charged in connection with the scandal but had helped create a religious-sounding organization that in fact handled casino cash for Abramoff.

Phillips was part of a tough, hardball-playing group, far from the wonky, intellectual mists of Charles Koch's early libertarian musings. Both Reed and Abramoff were early protégés of Grover Norquist, the influential Washington-based antitax activist famous for proclaiming his hope of shrinking government to the size where he could "drown it in the bathtub." Norquist had confided once that he regarded Reed and Abramoff as his two greatest students. "Grover told me Ralph was his Trotsky, and Abramoff was his Stalin," recalls Bruce Bartlett, the conservative economist.

Phillips had grown up poor in South Carolina in a family of Democrats so ardent that his father, who worked in the textile mills before becoming a bus driver, was named Franklin Delano Roosevelt and his grandfather had worked in Roosevelt's WPA. But in what Phillips recalled as one of the most "traumatic" moments of his adolescence, he was mesmerized one evening in 1980 by Ronald Reagan while watching the television news. He told his father, "I'm gonna be for that guy." Shocked, his father turned off the television, called his mother into the room, and warned him sternly that the Republicans "are for the rich man, Son. Come on, are you kidding me?"

Phillips retorted, "Well maybe I want to be rich one day." His parents were so dismayed, he recalled, "You'd have thought I'd said, you know, I'm moving to the Soviet Union, I'm gonna become, you know, a Godless communist atheist or whatever."

A Southern Baptist, Phillips enrolled in Liberty University, Jerry Falwell's evangelical school in Lynchburg, Virginia. But after one semester, he ran out of money and dropped out. From that point on, he was helped by one conservative group after the next, taking internships with free housing until he was hired as an operative on a Republican congressional campaign in Virginia. By 1997, he had founded Century Strategies with Reed. Together, they helped turn out evangelical voters in 2004 to reelect George Bush. The Christian Right drew criticism that year for motivating social conservatives by fanning fears about gay rights. In 2005, David Koch and Art Pope, the North Carolina dime store magnate and regular at the Koch seminars, drafted him to run Americans for Prosperity. "I was intrigued by the idea of being able to build a movement based on economic issues, the way that Christian Right folks had built a movement based on social issues," he recalled, explaining why he took the job.

Phillips's online biography described him as an expert in "grasstops" and "grassroots" political organizing. The Kochs' choice of Phillips, a hardened professional, signaled a tough new phase for the Kochtopus. Norquist, famous for praising "throat slitters" in politics, approvingly called Phillips "a grownup who can make things happen."

Phase three of Fink's plan could now begin in earnest.

CHAPTER SEVEN

Tea Time

ACCORDING TO MOST CONVENTIONAL WISDOM, THE TEA PARTY movement sprang to life in America spontaneously, unsullied by vested financial interests. As with most creation myths, however, the reality is quite another story.

The often-told tale was that the remarkable awakening of antigovernment rage that spread across the country in 2009 was triggered by an unplanned outburst on live television from Rick Santelli, a former futures trader, who was a regular on-air contributor to the CNBC business news network. The date of Santelli's tirade was notably early in Obama's presidency, February 19, 2009, less than one month after Obama was sworn in as president. At the time, Obama enjoyed approval ratings of over 60 percent. A year later, a congressman championing Obama's health-care proposal would be spat on, and two years later his party would lose control of the House of Representatives, effectively ending his ability to enact "change you can believe in," as promised in his campaign. Arguably, the precipitous downhill slide began that day.

Pundits, opponents, and disillusioned supporters would blame Obama for squandering the promise of his administration. Certainly he and his administration made their share of mistakes. But it is hard to think of another president who had to face the kind of guerrilla warfare waged against him almost as soon as he took office. A small number of people with massive resources orchestrated, manipulated, and exploited the economic unrest for their own purposes. They used tax-deductible donations to fund a movement to slash taxes on the rich and cut regulations on their own businesses. While they paid focus groups and seasoned operatives to frame these self-serving policies as matters of dire public interest, they hid their roles behind laws meant to protect the anonymity of philanthropists, leaving more folksy figures like Santelli to carry the message.

What came to be known as Santelli's "rant" started slowly and built as he held forth from the floor of the Chicago Mercantile Exchange. The immediate provocation was the previous guest. Minutes before Santelli appeared, Wilbur Ross Jr. had denounced a proposal Obama had floated the previous day to provide emergency help in restructuring mortgages for millions of homeowners facing foreclosure. Ross, a personal friend of David Koch's, wasn't a disinterested policy analyst. His private equity company, WL Ross & Co., a so-called vulture fund, was heavily involved in servicing mortgages.

Santelli, who tended in general toward tough-guy, free-market pronouncements, excitedly agreed with Ross that the government shouldn't help. "Mr. Ross has nailed it!" he began. He denounced Obama's plan as Cuban-style statism. Stressed homeowners in his view were "losers" who deserved their fate. He objected to the government playing a redistributive role, casting his argument in moral terms. By helping to bail out homeowners who made bad financial bets, he argued, the government was "promoting bad behavior." Critics would later point out that his indignation had not been similarly stirred by the Bush administration's bailouts of the country's largest banks, about which he had grumblingly conceded, "I agree, something needs to be done." Yet when Obama proposed help for the overextended underclasses, Santelli looked into the camera and shrieked, "This is America! How many of you people want to pay your neighbor's mortgage that has an extra bathroom, and can't pay their bills? Raise their hand. President Obama, are you listening?"

As his fellow traders whistled and cheered, he went on to say, "We're thinking of having a Chicago Tea Party in July. All you capitalists that want to show up to Lake Michigan, I'm gonna start organizing." From the start, the analogy was inapt. As Michael Grunwald, author of *The New New Deal,* a richly reported book about Obama's stimulus plan, observed, "The Boston Tea Party was a protest against an unelected leader who raised taxes, while Obama was an elected leader who had just cut them."

Nonetheless, Santelli's spontaneous invocation of the Boston Tea Party, according to most accounts, was what launched the movement. For instance, the Kochs' political adviser, Richard Fink, said, "It was the guy in Chicago, yelling on the stock exchange floor," that started it. He added, "Our programs had nothing to do with it."

In April 2009, as the Tea Party movement was gathering force, Melissa Cohlmia, a spokesperson for Koch Industries, also denied that the Kochs had any direct links to the unrest, issuing a statement saying, "No funding has been provided by Koch companies, the Koch foundations, or Charles Koch or David Koch specifically to support the tea parties." A year later, David Koch continued to insist in *New York* magazine, "I've never been to a tea-party event. No one representing the tea party has ever even approached me." When asked by a sympathetic interviewer for *The Daily Beast,* Elaine Lafferty, if *The New Yorker*'s report on the Kochs' involvement was true, he responded, "Oh, *please.*"

Such denials helped shape the early narrative of the Tea Party movement as an amateur uprising by ordinary citizens, "a new strain of populism metastasizing before our eyes," as Mark Lilla wrote in *The New York Review of Books.* Its members were described as nonpartisan everymen, incensed by the "Democrats and Republicans, national debt and other assorted peeves," as National Public Radio reported.

These reports of spontaneous political combustion weren't entirely wrong. But they were far from the whole story. To begin with, the Tea Party was not "a new strain" in American politics. The scale was unusual, but history had shown that similar reactionary forces had attacked virtually every Democratic president since Franklin Roosevelt. Earlier business-funded right-wing movements, from the Liberty League to the John Birch Society to Scaife's Arkansas Project, all had cast Democratic presidents as traitors, usurpers, and threats to the Constitution. The undeniable element of racial resentment that tinged many Tea Party rallies was also an old and disgracefully enduring story in American politics. Nor could the Tea Party accurately be described as nonpartisan. As a *New York Times* poll later showed, over three-quarters of its supporters identified as Republican. The bulk of the remainder felt the Republican Party was not Republican *enough*. Finally, although many of its supporters were likely political neophytes, from the start the ostensibly anti-elitist rebellion was funded, stirred, and organized by experienced political elites. On closer inspection, as the Harvard political scientist Theda Skocpol and the Ph.D. student Vanessa Williamson observed in their 2012 book, *The Tea Party and the Remaking of Republican Conservatism*, the Tea Party movement was a "mass rebellion . . . funded by corporate billionaires, like the Koch brothers, led by over-the-hill former GOP kingpins like Dick Armey, and ceaselessly promoted by millionaire media celebrities like Glenn Beck and Sean Hannity."

Behind the street theater were some of the country's wealthiest businessmen who had painstakingly been trying to build up the "counter-establishment" since the 1970s and now saw the public's unrest as an amazing opportunity to at long last mobilize popular support for their own agendas. As Bruce Bartlett, the economist, put it, "The problem with the whole libertarian movement is that it's been all chiefs and no Indians. There weren't any actual people, like voters, who gave a crap about it. So the problem for the Kochs has been trying to create an actual movement." With the emergence of the Tea Party, he said, "everyone suddenly sees that for the first time there are Indians out there—people who can provide real ideological power." The Kochs, he said, immediately began "trying to shape and control and channel the populist uprising into their own policies."

In fact they and a handful of other wealthy allies had made repeated efforts to foment antigovernment rebellions well before Santelli's rant, often invoking the image of the Boston Tea Party. The history stretched back decades, to Charles Koch's blueprint for a libertarian revolution in the late 1970s and Richard Fink's three-part plan, "The Structure of Social Change," in the 1980s. By the 1990s, nonprofit "grassroots" advocacy groups funded by the Kochs and a few close associates had begun explicitly pushing the antitax Tea Party theme. But the early efforts, as Bartlett suggested, got little traction.

In 1991, Citizens for a Sound Economy promoted what was advertised as a massive "re-enactment of the Boston Tea Party" in Raleigh, North Carolina, to protest tax increases. Among those present, the press corps nearly outnumbered the clutch of protesters in Revolutionary War, Uncle Sam, and Santa Claus costumes. The following year, Citizens for a Sound Economy was involved in another plan to stage a Tea Party protest. This one was secretly funded by tobacco companies to fight cigarette taxes and was canceled after its covert funding was exposed. By 2007, Citizens for a Sound Economy had split up. The Kochs' new organization, Americans for Prosperity, tried to stage another Tea Party protest against taxes, this time in Texas. It too was a dud. Nonetheless, by the time Obama was elected and the economy was melting down, the rudiments of a political machine were in place, along with a network of paid operatives expert in creating colonially garbed "Astroturf" groups to fake the appearance of public support.

What Obama was up against was a new form of permanent campaign. It was waged not by politicians but by people whose wealth gave them the ability to fund their own private field operations with which they could undermine the outcome of the election. So-called outside money—that spent by individuals and groups outside of the campaigns themselves—exploded during the Obama years. Much attention was paid to the portion of this spending that was directed at elections. Less attention was paid to the equally unrivaled role that outside money played in influencing the way the country was governed. Most of this spending was never disclosed. But as the Kochs' political lieutenant, Fink, boasted to *The Wichita Eagle* in 2012, "I think that's actually one of the things that happened at the Obama administration, is that every rock they overturned, they saw people who were against it, and it turned out to be us."

A trial run of this non-electoral outside spending actually began in the summer of 2008. Karl Rove, the operative whom George W. Bush called "the architect" of his 2004 reelection, had long dreamed of creating a conservative political machine outside the traditional political parties' control that could be funded by virtually unlimited private fortunes. His hope was to draft conservative donors of all stripes into creating a self-financed militia that could be called into action without the transparency, legal restrictions, or accountability that circumscribed conventional campaigns. And that summer, the Kochs had participated briefly in a version of this project, according to the *Politico* reporter Kenneth Vogel. Their representatives met clandestinely with political operatives working for other hugely wealthy donors, such as the Las Vegas casino magnate Sheldon Adelson. The ideal, one participant said, was "a never-ending campaign." After the disappointment of Obama's victory, though, the group disbanded. The Kochs, among others, regrouped.

The lesson learned, as one donor, the late Texas billionaire Harold Simmons, put it, was that next time they needed to spend even more. Simmons, who made a fortune in leveraged buyouts, had put almost $3 million into a group running television ads trying to tie Obama to the 1960s radical Bill Ayers during the 2008 campaign. "If we had run more ads, we could have killed Obama," he lamented.

When Obama took office, the stock market was down nearly six thousand points, and unemployment was shooting up toward 7 percent. As the former senator Tom Daschle later recalled, "There was a growing sense of calamity." Obama expected bipartisan support at a moment that seemed like an economic version of the September 11, 2001, crisis. He had proclaimed in his 2004 keynote address to the Democratic National Convention, "There is not a liberal America and a conservative America. There is the United States of America!" Or so he thought.

Obama's billionaire opponents wasted no time indulging him in a honeymoon. Forty-eight hours after Obama was sworn in, Americans for Prosperity started attacking his first major piece of legislation, a massive $800 billion Keynesian-inspired boost in public spending and tax cuts meant to stimulate the economy, the American Recovery and Reinvestment Act. The Kochs' advocacy group began organizing "Porkulus" rallies around the country, deriding public spending as corrupt "pork." The term was coined by Rush Limbaugh. It's reasonable to assume that the Kochs were too busy to follow such minutiae, but a former member of their inner circle asserts that Americans for Prosperity did "nothing more, and nothing less than they wanted it to do." Poorly attended at first, the "Porkulus" rallies became dress rehearsals for the Tea Party.

Americans for Prosperity soon launched a "No Stimulus" effort that sponsored anti-Obama media events featuring the star of the Koch seminar that January, South Carolina's senator Jim DeMint. The group also hosted a Web site, aired television advertisements, and pushed a petition that it claimed collected 500,000 signatures aimed at stopping Congress from passing Obama's stimulus bill. "We cannot spend our way to prosperity," it proclaimed. As the bill took shape, the group sent a sharply worded letter to Republicans in Congress, demanding that they vote no on the spending bill, regardless of any compromises or modifications that the new administration might offer.

The attacks reflected Charles Koch's revisionist belief that government interference in the economy was what had caused the last Great Depression. "Bankers, brokers and businessmen," he argued, had been falsely blamed. The true culprits were Herbert Hoover and Franklin Roosevelt, both of whom he regarded as dangerous liberals. In his view, the economic policies of Warren Harding and Calvin Coolidge—the latter had famously declared, "The chief business of the American people is business"—had been unfairly maligned. Charles argued that the New Deal only "prolonged and deepened the decline." Shortly after Obama was elected, Charles sent out a newsletter with this "History Lesson" to his seventy thousand or so employees, essentially reprising the robber barons' revisionism that he had been taught at the Freedom School. He also mobilized the Kochtopus, the sprawling network of some thirty-four public policy and political organizations his fortune supported by 2008. During the Bush years, it had been relatively quiescent.

Think tanks funded by the Kochs and their allied network of donors, such as the Cato Institute, the Heritage Foundation, and the Hoover Institution at Stanford University—where six attendees at the Kochs' annual seminars served in official capacities—began cranking out research papers, press releases, and op-ed columns opposing Obama's stimulus plan. Much of the research was later challenged by less biased experts. The Mercatus Center at George Mason University, for instance, released a report claiming that stimulus funds were directed disproportionately at Democratic districts. Eventually, the author was forced to correct the report but not before Rush Limbaugh, citing the paper, had labeled Obama's program "a slush fund" and Fox News and other conservative outlets had echoed the sentiment.

The paid advocates formed a national echo chamber. Phil Kerpen, the vice president for policy at Americans for Prosperity, was a contributor to the Fox News Web site. Another officer at Americans for Prosperity, Walter Williams, the John M. Olin Distinguished Professor of Economics at George Mason University, was a frequent guest host on Limbaugh's radio show, which claimed to have an audience of twenty million listeners.

Some conservatives have insisted that the Tea Party movement owed nothing to wealthy donors, citing the example of Keli Carender, an ostensibly lone Seattle activist whose "Porkulus" protest preceded Santelli's rant by a week. Carender, however, borrowed the term "porkulus" from Limbaugh. The company that syndicated Limbaugh's show, Premiere Networks, meanwhile, was getting paid a handsome $2 million or so a year by the Heritage Foundation to push the think tank's line on issues, tying the message back to the same ultrarich funding pool.

The steady stream of exposés accusing the fledgling Obama administration of malfeasance fanned public anger and provided useful ammunition for congressional Republicans, who in truth needed all the help they could get. The conventional wisdom at the beginning of the Obama presidency was that the 2008 election had been such a wipeout for Republicans that their only hope of staying relevant was to cut deals with Obama, who was seen as far too popular to oppose. But those who expected compromise—which included the president and his top aides—hadn't noticed the growing extremism in the Grand Old Party.

Even before the new congressional session began, Eric Cantor, a lawyer from Richmond, Virginia, who was about to become the new minority whip in the House, told a handful of trusted allies in a private planning meeting in his Washington condo, "We're not here to cut deals and get crumbs and stay in the minority for another forty years." Instead, he argued, the

Republicans needed to fight. They needed to unite in opposition to virtually anything Obama proposed in order to deny him a single bipartisan victory. The group, which included his deputy, Kevin McCarthy, called itself the Young Guns. The strategy of obstruction that they adopted won the Republicans the nickname the Party of No.

At their first official leadership retreat in January 2009, the model that the House Republicans chose to emulate was the Taliban. The Texas congressman Pete Sessions, the new leader of the Republican House campaign committee, held up Afghanistan's infamous Islamic extremists as providing an example of how they could wage "asymmetric warfare." The country might be in an economic crisis, but governing, he told his colleagues, was not the reason they had been elected. As he flashed through a slide presentation at the Annapolis Inn, he asked his colleagues, "If the Purpose of the Majority is to Govern . . . What is Our Purpose?" His answer was simple: "The Purpose of the Minority is to become the Majority." That one goal, he said, was "the entire Conference's mission."

John Boehner, the new minority leader, wasn't himself part of the Young Guns, but it was increasingly clear that if he didn't yield to them, they might depose him. As power shifted from the parties to outside money, much of which came from donors more extreme than the electorate at large, moderates had to fear primary challenges and internal coups from their right flank.

Steve LaTourette, a longtime Republican moderate congressman from Ohio who was a close friend of Boehner's, explained, "In the past, it was rare that someone would run against an incumbent in their own party. But the money that these outside groups have is what gives these people liquid courage to run against an incumbent." He described the outside donors as "a bunch of rich people who you can count on maybe two hands who have an inordinate impact. One or two might have been the guy in high school with the pocket protector picking his nose, but now he's inherited $40 million and has his chance to be a player. Once they were able to infuse massive amounts of money, they got a disproportionate amount of influence. It's not one man one vote anymore," he said with a sigh. "It's all about the money. It's not a function of anything else."

LaTourette was astonished, he said, when he went to the first meeting of the Republican caucus after Obama was elected. "When the question came up, about why we lost, these folks were saying, 'It's because we weren't conservative enough.' Well, I looked at the numbers, and we lost 58 percent of the independents!" Yet moderates like himself were getting frozen out. He became so frustrated he eventually retired, becoming a lobbyist and starting an organization aimed at battling the forces of extremism in his party. "I left," he said, "because I was sick of it. I couldn't take it anymore. I was there eighteen years. I understood it was a contact sport, but whether it was transportation or student loans, there were things you'd do without thinking. Now you can't get anything done. Some people don't want the government to do anything," he concluded.

The Republican leadership, according to an anecdote related by Grunwald, told GOP members of the House that as one of them, Jerry Lewis, a member of the House Appropriations Committee, put it, "We can't play." David Obey, the Democratic chairman of the House Appropriations Committee, was incensed at the lack of cooperation. "What they said right from the get-go," he said, was that "it doesn't matter what the hell you do, we ain't going to help you. We're going to stand on the sidelines and bitch."

The Republicans of course saw it differently. They accused Obama of being too partisan and took umbrage when he flaunted his election mandate and reminded Cantor during one tense session, "I won." In Lewis's view, the Democrats were arrogant, intolerant, and overbearing.

Obama nonetheless continued to seek bipartisan support.

His experience with what Hillary Clinton labeled the "vast right-wing conspiracy" was limited. He had vaulted in only five years from the Illinois State Senate to the White House. He turned out to be unrealistically confident that he could transcend partisan rancor as he had while editing the *Harvard Law Review*. So when he received an invitation from Boehner and the others in the House Republican caucus to come up to Capitol Hill to consult with them about the stimulus package, Obama accepted, with much fanfare.

On January 27, he climbed into his armored limousine for his first presidential motorcade to the Hill. Meeting exclusively with Republicans was unusual, as was a president coming to their turf to lobby. But the administration had promised to discard narrow partisan division. In fact Obama's economic advisers thought they had tailored the stimulus plan for Republican support by deriving one-third of it from tax cuts. Liberals were dismayed by the compromise, warning that government spending would do more to revive the economy than tax cuts and that the overall stimulus spending numbers were too small to really jump-start the economy. Despite these concessions, Obama's meeting on the Hill nonetheless turned out to be a demeaning disaster. Shortly before he arrived to pitch his plan, news leaked that the Republican leadership in the House was already instructing its caucus to vote against it. Obama was left to speak to a roomful of firmly closed minds. Afterward, he was left facing the gathered press corps looking lame and empty-handed.

"It was stunning," David Axelrod, Obama's longtime political adviser, later admitted. "Our feeling was, we were dealing with a potential disaster of epic proportions that demanded cooperation. If anything was a signal of what the next two years would be like, it was that."

The next morning, readers of *The New York Times* and *The Wall Street Journal* opened their papers to see a full-page ad paid for by the Cato Institute, the think tank that Charles

Koch had founded and on whose board David Koch sat. The ad directly challenged Obama's credibility. It quoted Obama saying, "There is no disagreement that we need action by our government, a recovery plan that will help jump start the economy." In large, boldface letters, the ad copy retorted, "With all due respect, Mr. President, that is not true." The statement was signed by 203 individuals, many of whose careers had been subsidized by the largesse of the Kochs, the Bradley Foundation, the John M. Olin Foundation, and other right-wing family fortunes.

Bill Burton, the deputy press secretary for Obama in the White House, looks back at the level of obstruction in the administration's first month as a complete shock. "They turned on Obama so early," he later recalled ruefully. "Not only did we not have the answers yet, we barely knew where to sit down. The chairs in the White House were still spinning from the people who had left them." Looking back, Burton shook his head at the administration's naïveté. "No one at the time saw it coming."

Specifically, he said, "We didn't really see the force, the outside money, until after he was elected. Then the first thing he had to do, the only thing he could do, was spend trillions and trillions of dollars, passing the stimulus bill first, and that led to Stimulus Two, and TARP, and the auto bailouts. The right-wing plutocrats really fed off of that. They tapped into this anger about spending." He admits, "No one saw the Kochs or the Dick Armeys out there."

Within two months of Obama taking office, he recalled, the political environment had been transformed. "In January, we were working with the Republicans on an economic recovery package grounded firmly in centrist thinking," he recalls. "The mainstream economic view was that the size of the calamity required massive economic spending. We asked the Republicans for their ideas. We were getting cooperation. Letters from all sorts of members of Congress were coming in with their heartfelt ideas. One high-ranking member of the House Republicans even suggested high-speed rail! But by early February, it started to shift. They were no longer sending letters. They were all expressing doubt about any kind of spending at all." Senator DeMint, who was headlining the Kochs' No Stimulus campaign, began a floor speech by proclaiming, "I like President Obama very much." He then went on to call the stimulus bill "a trillion-dollar socialist experiment" that was "the worst piece of economic legislation Congress has considered in a hundred years." As Burton put it, "DeMint was saying 'One-Term President' within six weeks of Obama taking office."

On February 17, Obama signed the Recovery Act into law. It had squeaked through Congress with only three Republican votes in the Senate and none in the House. Five years later, a survey of leading American economists chosen for their ideological diversity and eminence in the field, taken by the Initiative on Global Markets, a project run by the University of Chicago, found nearly unanimous consensus that the Recovery Act had achieved its goal of reducing unemployment. Only one of the thirty-seven economists surveyed disagreed. The free-market orthodoxy that dominated the Republican Party in Washington had completely veered from rational, professional expertise, yet the extremists nearly prevailed. As it was, Obama's opponents forced the administration to adopt a smaller stimulus package than many economists thought necessary, undercutting the recovery. One month into his presidency, extreme opponents, fueled by outside money, had already wounded Obama. The day after signing the stimulus bill, Obama announced the $75 billion homeowner rescue plan.

The next morning, Santelli delivered his rant, and within moments it went viral. Matt Drudge, the conservative news aggregator, linked to it under one of his Web site's rotating red siren emblems, promoting it to the site's three million daily readers as a pulsating political emergency.

Within hours, another Web site called TaxDayTeaParty.com appeared on the Internet, spreading the rebellion under the Tea Party label. Its domain name was registered by Eric Odom, a young member of the Libertarian Party of Illinois who lived in Chicago. Odom had been working until recently for an organization called the Sam Adams Alliance, whose chief executive had long and close ties to the Kochs. The strange story of the Sam Adams Alliance was yet another demonstration of the way that years of private funding by a few wealthy ideologues had created an underground political infrastructure.

The Chicago-based tax-exempt organization was named for the original 1773 Boston Tea Party activist Sam Adams. While the group's title evoked the Founding Fathers, its chief executive officer was a Wisconsin investor named Eric O'Keefe who had been involved with the Kochs since his days as a young volunteer in David Koch's Libertarian Party campaign for vice president. O'Keefe eventually became the national director of the Libertarian Party. By 1983, however, like the Kochs, he had moved on to promoting free-market fundamentalism through other means, often joining forces with the brothers through their donor seminars and other ventures. Influenced as a child by *The Wall Street Journal* and the Conservative Book Club, O'Keefe, as *The Washington Post* wrote, "had money. He grew up with some and made a lot more as an investor, allowing him to devote decades to a series of ambitious political crusades, nearly all of them failures."

The founder of the Sam Adams Alliance, according to one account, was a balding, publicity-shy Brooklyn-born real estate tycoon named Howard Rich. Known to friend and foe as Howie, Rich had also been involved in numerous far-flung political ventures with the Kochs. Impressed early by the writings of Hayek and Milton Friedman, he became a tireless supporter of long-shot libertarian causes while amassing a fortune buying apartment buildings in Manhattan, Texas, and North Carolina. Both O'Keefe and Rich served on the Cato Institute's board of directors with David Koch. They had years' worth of ties, as well as ups and downs, with Charles Koch as well. Relations were good enough that the Institute for Humane Studies at George Mason University, whose board Charles Koch chaired, placed some of its thirty or so chosen Charles G. Koch fellows in summer internships with the Sam Adams Alliance.

For decades this small, wealthy, and intense circle had been trying to advance their fervently held libertarian ideas, almost always working in secret, cloaked behind layers of shell groups, so that their role couldn't be detected. Rich in particular rivaled Houdini for sleights of hand, having obscured his role behind a positively dizzying number of name-changing, shape-shifting, interlocking organizations. He almost invariably declined to talk to the press or debate opponents. Until the Tea Party, however, the results had been disappointing. "My 32 years of engagement has been a long and expensive lesson in frustration," his frequent political partner, O'Keefe, admitted.

Among this group's earlier political efforts was a stealth attempt in the early 1990s to get voters to approve ballot measures imposing congressional term limits. Experts suggested that term limits would hurt Democrats, who had more congressional incumbents at the time, and also strengthen the power of outsiders with money, like themselves. As was true of the later Tea Party movement, the supporters of term limits described their movement as a grassroots outpouring fueled by populist outrage at entrenched power. In California, the Kochs were rumored to be behind a 1992 referendum on whether to impose them, but a spokesman denied they had any direct role. But after the referendum succeeded, the *Los Angeles Times* discovered that the true organizers and much of its funding traced back to a secretive group run by Howie Rich and Eric

O'Keefe, U.S. Term Limits. There were ties to the Kochs, too. Fink admitted when confronted by the paper that they had in fact provided "seed money."

Similarly, in Washington State a congressional term-limits ballot initiative nearly passed in 1991 until *The New York Times* exposed what Murray Rothbard, the irreverent libertarian theorist who had split with the Kochs, called "the Kochian deep pockets behind the 'grassroots' movement." The paper discovered that what supporters billed as "a prairie fire of populism" was in fact the product of a Washington-based group calling itself Citizens for Congressional Reform, which was started with hundreds of thousands of dollars from David Koch. "I ignited the spark, and the fire is raging on its own," he claimed once his role was exposed. Fanning the flames, however, was his checkbook. His group contributed nearly three-quarters of the campaign's budget, paying for professional signature gatherers to collect enough names to get the issue on the ballot.

Eventually, the Supreme Court ruled that federal term limits were unconstitutional. This finished off the movement at the congressional level for good, though not its backers' penchant for ersatz populism.

The patrons of libertarianism kept on trying to buy at least the aura of public support. In 2004, one of the first ventures of the Kochs' newly formed advocacy group, Americans for Prosperity, was a radical antitax measure called the Taxpayer Bill of Rights. The measure placed drastic restrictions on state legislators, requiring all tax increases to first be approved by public referenda. The group chose Kansas as its first battleground for the Taxpayers Bill of Rights just as the Kochs were fighting a proposed tax increase in their home state. Despite an outcry about shadowy spending, AFP spent a record amount of money on television ads, and the tax increase was defeated.

Two years later, in 2006, a group created and run by Rich

called Americans for Limited Government spent some $8 million promoting a variety of other ballot drives, including one that demanded that owners get compensated for the impact of land-use laws on their property. Supporters again claimed to have widespread grassroots support. But an investigation by the Center for Public Integrity revealed that in fact just three donors, none of them disclosed, accounted for 99 percent of the organization's funding. Despite the heavy spending, the fringe antigovernment measures were voted down almost everywhere.

Soon afterward, the State of Illinois suspended Rich's group of its charitable license after it failed to supply required financial statements, and in 2006 the group shut down its Chicago headquarters. At this point, Americans for Limited Government moved to Fairfax, Virginia, where several other nonprofit organizations run by Rich were based. Back in Chicago, meanwhile, a new tax-exempt group sprang up at its former address, calling itself the Sam Adams Alliance.

Eric O'Keefe, who had served on the board of Americans for Limited Government, was now the chairman and chief executive officer of the new organization. "We're not going to be shut up," he had vowed when previously investigated in Wisconsin for campaign-finance violations. Tax records showed that some 88 percent of the Sam Adams Alliance's funding that year came from a single gift of $3.7 million from a mysterious undisclosed donor.

In the summer of 2008, as Barack Obama grew closer to capturing the presidency, Eric Odom at the Sam Adams Alliance started experimenting with some of the online communications methods that would later help to organize the Tea Party movement. He tested out the use of Twitter to trigger a right-wing flash mob in the House of Representatives in Washington. He and a friend, Rob Bluey, a twenty-eight-year-old blogger who described himself as "a card-carrying member of the vast right-wing conspiracy," created something they called the DontGo movement. They sent out Twitter messages demanding that the Democratic leadership in the House schedule a vote on legalizing offshore oil and gas drilling, or else Republicans would refuse to go home for the summer recess.

The Twitter experiment worked remarkably well. That August, conservative congressmen, oil lobbyists, and other supporters of offshore drilling poured into the House, creating a wild and seemingly spontaneous protest. They chanted, "Don't go!" and "Drill here! Drill now!" They didn't succeed in lifting the restriction on offshore drilling, but one leader of the revolt, the Arizona congressman John Shadegg, a conservative Republican, exulted that the protest was "the 2008 version of the Boston Tea Party."

Six months later, immediately after Santelli's rant, Eric Odom reactivated the "DontGo" list. He fired off a call to action to the same ten thousand hard-core conservative insiders whose contact information he and Bluey had compiled. Odom also formed what he called the Nationwide Tea Party Coalition with other activists, including operatives from Dick Armey's group, FreedomWorks, and the Kochs' group, Americans for Prosperity. AFP quickly registered a Web site called TaxPayerTeaParty.com and used its network of fifty-some staffers to plan rallies across the country.

As the operatives linked forces online, they set a date for the first national Tea Party protests, February 27. That day, more than a dozen protests were held in cities across the country. The organizers claimed 30,000 participants, but the crowds in many places were still sparse. But on April 15, when there was a second series of "Tax Day" Tea Party rallies across the country, the numbers had increased tenfold, to 300,000.

The Heritage Foundation, the Cato Institute, and Americans for Prosperity provided speakers, talking points, press releases, transportation, and other logistical support. Lee Fang, a blogger for the progressive Web site *ThinkProgress*, was among the first to question whether the movement was organic or synthetic "Astroturf." He noted that Americans for Prosperity was suddenly planning protests "coast to coast," while FreedomWorks seemed to have taken over a local rally in Florida. Not everyone liked the top-down control of the protests. "Americans for Prosperity annoyed some of the Tea Partiers," recalls the libertarian blogger Ralph Benko. "These people drove up, opened the door, put T-shirts on them, then took pictures and sent them to Charles [Koch] saying, 'See? We're doing great things with your money.'"

Thomas Frank, author of *What's the Matter with Kansas?*, had stopped by to see an early Tea Party rally in Lafayette Square, across from the White House, in February 2009. "It was very much a put-up job," he concluded. "All the usual suspects were there, like FreedomWorks, 'Joe the Plumber,' and *The American Spectator* magazine. There were also some people who had Revolutionary War costumes and 'Don't Tread on Me' flags, actual activists, and a few ordinary people," he said. "But it was very well organized by the conservative groups. Back then, it was really obvious that it was put on, and they'd set it up. But then it caught on." Frank argues that "the Tea Party wasn't subverted," as some have suggested. "It was *born* subverted." Still, he said, "it's a major accomplishment for sponsors like the Kochs that they've turned corporate self-interest into a movement among people on the streets."

While the Kochs were continuing to profess no involvement, Peggy Venable, a spunky veteran of the Reagan administration who had been on their payroll as a political operative in Texas since 1994, becoming the head of the Texas chapter of Americans for Prosperity, gushed about her role in the movement. "I was a member of the Tea Party before it was cool!" she said during a conversation at a Koch-sponsored political event called Defending the American Dream, in Austin. As the Tea Party movement took off, she described how Americans for Prosperity had helped to "educate" the activists on policy details. She said they had given the supporters what she called "next-step training" after their rallies so that their political energy could be channeled "more effectively." The organization also supplied the angry protesters with lists of elected officials to target. Venable, who spoke without first checking with the Kochs' public relations representatives, happily said of the brothers, "They're certainly our people. David's the chairman of our board. I've certainly met with them, and I'm very appreciative of what they do." She added, "We love what the Tea Parties are doing, because that's how we're going to take back America!"

Venable honored several Tea Party "citizen leaders" at the summit. The Texas branch of Americans for Prosperity gave its Blogger of the Year Award to a young woman named Sibyl West. Writing on her Web site, West described Obama as the "cokehead in chief" and speculated that the president was exhibiting symptoms of "demonic possession (aka schizophrenia, etc.)."

During a catered lunch at the summit, Venable introduced Ted Cruz, a former solicitor general of Texas and future senator, who told the crowd that Obama was "the most radical president ever to occupy the Oval Office" and had hidden from voters a secret agenda—"the government taking over our economy and our lives." Countering Obama, Cruz proclaimed, was "the epic fight of our generation!" As the crowd rose to its feet and cheered, he quoted the defiant words of a Texan at the Alamo: "Victory, or death!"

No organization played a bigger early role than FreedomWorks, the estranged sibling of Americans for Prosperity, which was funded by donations from companies like Philip Morris and from billionaires like Richard Mellon Scaife. "I'd argue that when the Tea Party took off, FreedomWorks had as much to do with making it an effective movement as anyone," said Armey.

In looking back, Armey gave particular credit to a young aide named Brendan Steinhauser, the group's director of state and federal campaigns, who created a Web site immediately after Santelli's rant that provided all kinds of practical advice to supporters. It counseled them on how to plan rallies and what issues to protest, with Obama's stimulus spending high on the target list. He also suggested slogans and signs and sponsored a daily conference call with over fifty Tea Party activists around the country to coordinate their efforts. Soon FreedomWorks was providing a professional support team of nine for the operation. Armey recalled that Steinhauser "spent hours and hours on the phone with people who'd found the FreedomWorks Web site. The other guys at FreedomWorks were laughing at him" in the beginning, he said. But Armey described how Steinhauser organized the inchoate anger into a mass political movement. "He told them what to do. He gave them training. If it hadn't been for FreedomWorks, the Tea Party movement would never have taken off," Armey later said.

The fact that Armey was himself a Washington insider belied the notion that the Tea Party movement was anti-elitist. Armey had spent eighteen years in Congress and was reportedly paid $750,000 a year as a lobbyist at the law firm DLA Piper, which represented corporate clients such as the pharmaceutical giant Bristol-Myers Squibb. But billionaire backers were useful. They gave the nascent Tea Party movement organization and political direction, without which it might have frittered away like the Occupy movement. The protesters in turn gave the billionaire donors something they'd had trouble buying—the numbers needed to lend their agenda the air of legitimacy. As Armey put it, "We'd been doing this lonely work for years. From our point of view, it was like the cavalry coming."

FreedomWorks, it was later revealed, also had some hired help. The tax-exempt organization quietly cemented a deal with Glenn Beck, the incendiary right-wing Fox News television host who at the time was a Tea Party superstar. For an annual payment that eventually topped $1 million, Beck read "embedded content" written by the FreedomWorks staff. They told him what to say on the air, and he blended the promotional material seamlessly into his monologue, making it sound as if it were his own opinion. The arrangement was described on FreedomWorks' tax disclosures as "advertising services."

"We thought it would be a useful tool if it was done in moderation, but then they started doing it by leaps and bounds," Armey recalled about the arrangement. "They were keeping it secret from their activists and supporters," he alleged. "They were creating an illusion that they were so important this icon, this hero of the movement, was bragging about them. Instead of earning the media, they were paying for it."

Beck, whose views were shaped by W. Cleon Skousen, the fringe theorist whose political paranoia had inspired the John Birch Society, reached a daily audience of some two million, disseminating the ideas of early conservative extremists like Fred Koch on a whole new scale. Frank Luntz describes the impact as historic. "That rant from Santelli woke up the upper middle class and the investor class, and then Glenn Beck woke up everyone else. Glenn Beck's show is what created the Tea Party movement," he said, adding, "It started on Tax Day 2009, and it exploded at town hall meetings in July. You can create a mass movement within three months."

Another factor was Obama's aversion to confrontation and hot rhetoric, which resulted in largely milquetoast messaging about Wall Street. Unlike Franklin Roosevelt, who blamed the "money changers" for the Great Depression in his first inaugural address, Obama's public utterances were muted. In a matter of weeks, critics argued that he had ceded the mantle of populism to his Tea Party opponents. "In an atmosphere primed for a populist backlash, he allowed the right wing to define the terms," John Judis observed in the liberal *New Republic* magazine.

Despite Steinhauser's efforts to police the Tea Party's signs for racism and other expressions of hate, within two months of Obama taking office, the streets and parks were filling with rallies at which white protesters carried placards reading, "Impeach Now!" and "Obama Bin Lyin'." Obama's face was plastered on posters making him look like the Joker from the Dark Knight films, his skin turned chalk white, his mouth stretched almost to his ears, and his eye sockets blackened, with a zombielike dead gaze, over the word "Socialism." A for-profit Internet activism company, ResistNet, featured a video titled "Obama = Hitler" on its Web site. One protester at a February 27 rally, who said he was with the group, carried a sign calling Congress slave owners and taxpayers "the Nigger." Obama's image was also photoshopped to look like a primitive African witch doctor, with a bone stuck through his nose.

Fink, the Kochs' political lieutenant, professed to be discomfited by the racism. But David Koch echoed the specious claims that Obama was somehow African in his outlook, even though he was born in America, abandoned by his Kenyan father as a toddler, raised mainly in Hawaii by his American mother, and had never set foot on the African continent until he was an adult. In a revealing later interview with the conservative pundit Matthew Continetti, David nonetheless disparaged Obama as "the most radical president we've ever had as a nation" and opined that the president's radicalism derived from his African heritage. "His father was a hard core economic socialist in Kenya," he said. "Obama didn't really interact with his father face-to-face very much, but was apparently from what I read a great admirer of his father's points of view. So he had sort of antibusiness, anti–free enterprise influences affecting him almost all his life. It just shows you what a person with a silver tongue can achieve."

Bill Burton, who is biracial himself, believes that "you can't understand Obama's relationship with the right wing without taking into account his race. It's something no one wants to talk about, but really you can't deny the racial factor. They treated him in a way they never would have if he'd been white. The level of disrespect was just dialed up to eleven."

By the end of Obama's second month in office, *Newsweek* ran a tongue-in-cheek cover story asserting, "We are all socialists now," and even the lofty *New York Times* picked up the right wing's framing of Obama as outside the American mainstream. In a presidential interview, the paper asked whether he was a socialist. Obama was apparently so stunned he had to contact the *Times* afterward to fully answer. "It was hard for me to believe that you were entirely serious about that socialist question," he said, noting that it was under his predecessor, George Bush, a Republican, not "under me that we began buying a bunch of shares of banks. And it wasn't on my watch that we passed a massive new entitlement, prescription drug plan, without a source of funding."

As Obama was put on the defensive about the economy, another line of attack was stealthily attracting the attention of many of the same wealthy financial backers. At the Kochs' secretive January summit in Palm Springs, one of the group's largest donors, Randy Kendrick, posed a question. Her shoulder-length cascades of frosted hair and flashy jewelry made her an unlikely-looking rabble-rouser, but Kendrick was an outspoken lawyer who had abandoned the women's movement decades earlier for the Goldwater Institute, a far-right libertarian think tank in Phoenix, where she was on the board of directors. She and her husband, Ken, the co-owner and managing general partner of the Arizona Diamondbacks baseball team, had the kind of fortune that made people take note.

Earl "Ken" Kendrick, who hailed from West Virginia, had made many millions on Datatel, a company he founded that provided computer software to colleges and universities. He subsequently bought into the Woodforest National Bank in Texas, a private bank that was in 2010 forced to refund $32 million and pay a $1 million civil fine to settle charges of usurious overdraft fees. Hard-core economic and social conservatives—except for the state subsidies that paid for the Diamondbacks stadium and brought public transit to the field—the Kendricks were horrified by the election of Obama. They were charter members of the Kochs' donor network, having written at least one seven-figure check. Their generosity had been a two-way street. They had supported institutions that the Kochs favored, such as the Institute for Humane Studies and the Mercatus Center at George Mason University. The Kochs had meanwhile supported the "Freedom Center" at the University of Arizona that they founded, where the Kendrick Professor of Philosophy taught "freedom" to college students.

Now Randy Kendrick wanted to know what the group planned to do to stop Obama from overhauling America's health-care system. She had read the former Democratic senator Tom Daschle's 2008 book, *Critical: What We Can Do About the Health-Care Crisis,* and was alarmed. She warned that Daschle, who favored universal health-care coverage, likely reflected Obama's thinking. Daschle was expected to become Obama's secretary of health and human services. If the new administration adopted a plan of the kind Daschle was floating, she said it would kill business, hurt patients, and lead to the biggest socialist government takeover in their lifetimes. She was adamant. Obama had to be stopped. What was the plan?

Kendrick spoke with passion. Her interest in the issue was both political and personal. She argued that the choice of private health care had saved her from spending the rest of her life confined to a wheelchair after a leg injury. She had initially been told that because she suffered from a rare disorder, she couldn't risk surgery. But a specialist at the renowned Cleveland Clinic had found a successful treatment. She survived the surgery and was now an active mother of teenage twins.

"Randy was convinced that if America had government health care like Canada or Great Britain, she would be dead," a friend who asked not to be identified confided.

It was a powerful testimonial, and the donors at the Koch seminar were deeply moved. But the Obama administration had never proposed government health care like that in Canada or Great Britain. Reached later, after the implementation of Obama's Affordable Care Act, Donald Jacobsen, professor of molecular medicine at the Cleveland Clinic Lerner College of Medicine, who cared for Kendrick, recalled her as a generous donor but dismissed as nonsense her argument that Obama's health-care plan ever threatened treatment of the kind that she received. "I can assure you that 'Obamacare' did not diminish our research efforts in any way," he said. "However, the sequestration efforts of the right-wing conservatives and their Tea Party colleagues have hampered progress in medical research. The National Institutes of Health is suffering greatly, and it is very difficult for all investigators to obtain funding. You can't blame the Affordable Care Act, but you certainly can blame the Republicans."

Nonetheless, when Kendrick finished her emotional pitch, there was an awkward silence from the Kochs, according to two sources familiar with the meeting. The Kochs of course opposed the expansion of any government social program, including any potential universal health-care plan. But the sources said they hadn't focused much on the issue. They had assumed the health-care industry would fight its own battles, in its own interest, so they hadn't thought they'd need to step in. Instead, the Obama administration had cut deals with much of the health-care industry, winning much of its support. "They were unprepared on the issue," said one of the sources.

Despite their later reputation for orchestrating opposition to Obamacare, it was actually Kendrick, not the Kochs, who first led the way. She and a handful of other multimillionaires had recently helped fund an unsuccessful effort to prevent Arizona from "coercing" citizens into buying government-run, or any other kind of, health-care coverage. But Kendrick was not giving up. She was strong-minded and accustomed to getting her way. When she appeared every few weeks at the think tank, a former colleague recalled, "they would often line up and hand her a bouquet of flowers, like a queen."

After the defeat in Arizona, Kendrick vowed to take her fight national. "Who do I have to give money to?" she asked Sean Noble, a Republican political operative in Arizona who had become her de facto personal political consultant. Kendrick demanded to know, "What organizations are doing this?" according to an account written by Eliana Johnson for *National Review.*

At Kendrick's request, Noble surveyed the field and found virtually no organization set up in early 2009 to take aim at Obama on the issue. Or at least none that was a 501(c)(4), the IRS code for a tax-exempt "social welfare" group that can participate in politics so long as it's not the group's primary focus. Unlike conventional political organizations, such nonprofits can hide the identities of their donors from the public, reporting them only to the IRS. Noble knew these so-called dark-money groups were especially appealing to wealthy individuals who wanted to influence politics without public attention, like the members of the Koch network.

Noble had attended Koch seminars with his former boss, John Shadegg, a staunchly conservative Republican congressman from Arizona whose father, Stephen, had been Barry Goldwater's campaign manager and alter ego. For over a decade, Noble had worked for Shadegg, eventually becoming chief of staff of the congressman's Arizona office. In 2008, however, Noble decided to go out on his own, opening a political consulting firm, Noble Associates, at his home in Phoenix. Kendrick, who had been a major supporter of Shadegg, was a prized client. She and Noble had worked closely for years. He hadn't been invited to the January Koch meeting where she held forth, but she called him afterward for help. As he set up his business, her interest in launching a crusade against health-care reform, and her entrée into the Koch network, presented a lucrative opportunity.

Noble wasn't a first-string player in Washington's political big league, but he was respected and had a superabundance of charm. Fit and blond, with just enough gray around his temples to add gravitas to his cherubic features, he was unassuming and fun; even his political opponents found him hard to dislike. Noble described himself as a "Reagan Baby" who was raised in the tiny town of Show Low, Arizona—named by cardplayers—where as a boy he started the day listening to the national anthem on the radio with a hand over his heart. His mother, a homemaker, and father, a dentist, were Mormons and believed America was the promised land. In their household, Barry Goldwater was a hero, and Jimmy Carter a villain. When Carter was elected in 1976, Noble's mother warned that the Soviet Union would take over the world. By the time he was in college, Noble was working for conservative candidates, eventually connecting with Shadegg. Along the way, he got married, had five children, and became a Mormon bishop in his Phoenix ward. Antiabortion and libertarian, he voted for Ron Paul in 1988. In many ways, he was a perfect fit for the Koch network, except for one thing. Noble, who contributed almost compulsively to a personal online blog called *Noble Thinking,* was chatty. Taking on Obama's health-care plan with private money would require stealth.

On April 16, 2009, Noble and Kendrick began putting their plan in place when the Center to Protect Patient Rights (CPPR) was incorporated in Maryland. Physically, the organization existed only as a locked, metal mailbox, number 72465, inside the Boulder Hills post office at the edge of a desert road north of Phoenix. Later records would show Noble was its executive director. The effort was surrounded in such secrecy that when Noble was asked in a 2013 deposition who hired him, he declined to answer, citing confidentiality agreements, as ProPublica, the nonprofit investigative reporting concern, later reported.

Responding to the lawyer's question, he said, "I can't tell you who I do work for."

"Wait a minute," the lawyer interjected. "I asked how your salary got set, and you're telling me that you had a discussion with some people in 2009 and you're refusing to tell me who?"

"I am," Noble answered.

The identities of the donors remained opaque, but one thing clear from tax records was that Noble's sponsors had an astounding amount of money. By June, the Center to Protect Patient Rights had accumulated some $3 million in donations. By the end of 2009, the sum reached $13 million. More than $10 million of that was quickly passed on to other tax-exempt groups, including Americans for Prosperity, which soon took a lead in attacking Obama's health-care plan. By the end of 2010, the sum sloshing through the post office box belonging to the Center to Protect Patient Rights would reach nearly $62 million, much of it raised through the Kochs' donor network.

The first tangible sign of this underground funding stream was a television ad called "Survivor." It featured a Canadian woman named Shona Holmes who said, "I survived a brain tumor," but claimed that if she had been forced to wait for treatment from Canada's government health service, "I'd be dead." Instead, she said, she had received lifesaving treatment in Arizona. Fact-checkers later revealed that her dramatic story was highly dubious and that in fact the reason the Canadian health authorities hadn't expedited her treatment was that she actually had a benign cyst on her pituitary gland. Nonetheless, the Americans for Prosperity Foundation, the charitable wing of the tax-exempt organization chaired by David Koch, spent $1 million airing the ad in the summer of 2009.

The message was made by Larry McCarthy, a veteran Washington media consultant best known for creating the racially charged Willie Horton ad, which featured the crimes of a convicted African-American murderer on a weekend furlough from prison in Massachusetts. It helped sink the presidential campaign of Michael Dukakis in 1988 by making him look soft on crime. McCarthy was infamous for using manipulative emotional messages, especially fear. As Peter Hart, the Democratic pollster, said of McCarthy, whom he had worked against, and occasionally with, over the years, "If you want an assassination, you hire one of the best marksmen in history." That spring, flush with cash, Noble signed McCarthy up.

The Center to Protect Patient Rights wasn't flying blind. At Noble's instigation, that spring the organization had also quietly paid Frank Luntz, the Republican pollster and pitchman, to conduct market testing on the best ways to attack Obama's health-care proposal. Luntz's political science professor at Penn had been James Piereson, who later ran the Olin Foundation. Luntz had studied the building of the conservative movement and become something like a translator, interpreting elite opinion for the masses. "The think tanks became the creators of the ideas, and I became the explainer of the thoughts," he said. "Mostly what I do is listen and I process." He admitted that as communicators "these guys were impossible." In playing this role, Luntz was one of a long succession of "policy entrepreneurs" who served to popularize the agenda of wealthy backers by "framing" their issues in more broadly appealing language.

Luntz used polls, focus groups, and "instant response dial sessions" to perfect the language of health-care attacks and then tested the lines on average Americans in St. Louis, Missouri. Out of these sessions, Luntz compiled a seminal twenty-eight-page confidential memo in April warning that there was no groundswell of public opposition to Obama's health-care plan at that point; in fact, there was a groundswell of public support. By far the most effective approach to turning the public against the program, Luntz advised, was to label it a "government takeover." He wrote, "Takeovers are like coups. They both lead to dictators and a loss of freedom."

"I did create the phrase 'government takeover' of health care. And I believe it," Luntz maintained, noting too that "it gave the Republicans the weapon they needed to defeat Obama in 2010." But most experts found the pitch patently misleading because the Obama administration was proposing that Americans buy private health insurance from for-profit companies, not the government. In fact, progressives were incensed that rather than backing a "public option" for those who preferred a government insurance program, the Obama plan included a government mandate that individuals purchase health-care coverage, a conservative idea hatched by the Heritage Foundation to stave off nationalized health care. Luntz's phrase was so false that it was chosen as "the Lie of the Year" by the nonpartisan fact-checking group PolitiFact. Yet while a rear guard of administration officials tried lamely to correct the record, Luntz's deceptive message stuck, agitating increasingly fearful and angry voters, many of whom flocked to Tea Party protests.

Noble's strategy was carefully targeted. He aimed the attack ads especially at the states of members of the Senate Finance Committee, which was writing the health-care bill and whose support would be needed to vote it out of the committee. The Obama White House had delegated a tremendous amount of authority to the committee's chairman, the Montana Democrat Max Baucus, whom it was entrusting to win bipartisan support. Baucus, in turn, was trying fitfully to win the support of the committee's leading Republican, the Iowa senator Chuck Grassley. Noble studied the committee and singled out members who might be especially susceptible to pressure, along with a few other key swing votes, narrowing his list down to those from Louisiana, Nebraska, Maine, Iowa, and

Montana. With enough pressure, he believed he could even unnerve both Grassley and Baucus.

At the time, few thought that Obama's health-care plan could be derailed. Conservative opposition was focused more on other issues. Noble needed to generate "grassroots" pressure on the potentially persuadable senators, but constituents weren't yet engaged. The stakes grew as the Senate approached its summer recess. "We knew we had to make that summer absolute hell," he told *National Review*. For help, he turned to an old friend in Arizona, Doug Goodyear, whose controversial public relations firm, DCI Group, had truly professionalized the modern use of phony "Astroturf" campaigns on behalf of big-money interests, starting with the industry that really set the standard for deceptive advertising, tobacco.

Goodyear, the firm's managing partner and chief executive, had founded DCI Group in 1996 with two Republican campaign operatives while he was handling outside public relations for the huge tobacco company R. J. Reynolds. The work had shown the trio that ordinary campaign tools could succeed at marketing even the most toxic products. The key, according to an internal 1990 memo the tobacco industry was forced to disclose in a later legal settlement, was to disguise the company's financial interest as a matter of great principle. Instead of pitching cigarette sales, it would create fake "smokers' rights" groups who would agitate against smoking restrictions as a fundamental matter of liberty. Or, as the memo written by Tim Hyde—one of the three founding partners of DCI Group and at the time R. J. Reynolds's director of national field operations—put it, the company needed to "create a movement" that would "build broad coalitions around the issue-cluster of freedom, choice, and privacy." The company, Hyde wrote, "should proceed along two tracks." One was the "intellectual track within the DC–New York corridor," which could influence elite opinion with op-ed pieces, lawsuits, and expert think tank studies. The other was "a grassroots organizational and largely local track," which would use front groups to simulate the appearance of popular political support.

Noble knew that by 2009 DCI Group was unsurpassed at these dark arts. The firm had deep ties to the Republican Party and had worked for powerful interests ranging from ExxonMobil and the Teamsters to the military junta in Myanmar. Goodyear was especially versed in corporate lobbying disguised as hidden-hand "Astroturf" campaigns. But the firm had numerous other talents. While working for ExxonMobil, it had mocked Al Gore's environmental jeremiad, *An Inconvenient Truth,* by secretly launching a cartoon spoof that went viral called "Al Gore's Penguin Army." Only later were DCI's fingerprints discovered on the fake indie film. Unlike lobbying firms, which have to disclose some information, public relations firms exerting political pressure can hide the money trail.

Soon Noble's Center to Protect Patient Rights was dispersing millions of dollars to other nonprofit groups, some of which appeared to be shell organizations fronting for DCI Group. In June, the Center to Protect Patient Rights sent $1.8 million to a confusingly similar-sounding organization called the Coalition to Protect Patient Rights, which was set up that month in Virginia by an accountant who worked for DCI Group. The Virginia organization soon passed most of the funds on to DCI Group. Pretty soon, a former head of the American Medical Association named Donald Palmisano appeared on the national media circuit to take swipes at Obama's health-care proposal on behalf of the newly created coalition. He admitted that donors, whom he declined to name and who were not in the medical field, had recruited him to speak for the group, which called itself a "doctor-led coalition."

The same DCI Group accountant's name appeared on paperwork filed by another Washington-area nonprofit, a tiny organization calling itself the Institute for Liberty. It soon received a $1.5 million grant from Noble's Center to Protect

Patient Rights. Four hundred thousand dollars of these funds were channeled back to DCI Group for "consulting." The previous year, the Institute for Liberty's entire budget had been $52,000. Suddenly it was so awash in cash that the group's president, Andrew Langer, told *The Washington Post*, "This year has been really serendipitous for us." He said a donor, whom he declined to name, had earmarked the funds for a five-state advertising blitz targeting Obama's health-care plan. Although *The Washington Post* wrote about the surprisingly large ad campaign, it failed to trace the money back to its true source. On air, the ads' only sponsorship information was completely misleading. There was a line that said, "Paid for by Keeping Small Business Healthy."

Americans for Prosperity, meanwhile, threw itself headlong into the fight, spinning off a group called Patients United Now, which, according to Tim Phillips, organized more than three hundred rallies against the health-care legislation. At one rally, an effigy of a Democratic congressman was hanged; at another, protesters unfurled a banner depicting corpses from Dachau, implying that Obama's health-care plan was akin to the Nazis' state-ordered murders.

The Bradley Foundation also pitched in. While the tax-exempt foundation did not directly support Tea Party groups, its president, Michael Grebe, said the foundation supported "public education programs run by Americans for Prosperity and FreedomWorks, both of which are very active in the Tea Party."

Although Grebe openly described the Kochs' group, Americans for Prosperity, as "very active" in the Tea Party, Fink was still claiming otherwise. "We never funded the tea party," he still maintained. "We met for 20 or 30 years advancing free-market ideas in universities, think tanks and citizen groups. I am hopeful those ideas filtered down and were a part of the cause of the Tea Party taking off."

By the time of the Kochs' second donor summit of 2009,

titled "Understanding and Addressing Threats to American Free Enterprise and Prosperity," which took place in Aspen, Colorado, at the end of June, Noble had earned his place as an insider. Not only had he been invited; he had been officially put on contract as a Koch political consultant. The Kochs felt they needed extra help, a former insider said, because Obama's election had sparked such vitriol on the right that they were almost overwhelmed by the number of wealthy donors eager to join them. "Suddenly they were raising big money! They were in a hot spot. They were almost hyperventilating," he said.

This time, instead of having to interrupt the proceedings, Randy Kendrick was a scheduled speaker on a health-care panel. And this time, the pitch she made to the others, according to one eyewitness, "set the place on fire." Before the donors dispersed, many more millions were pledged to stop Obama's top legislative priority.

That summer, traditional town hall meetings held by Democratic congressmen and senators returning to their districts and states exploded in acrimony. The anger appeared entirely spontaneous. But the investigative reporter Lee Fang discovered that a volunteer with FreedomWorks was circulating a memo instructing Tea Partiers on how to disrupt the meetings. Bob MacGuffie, who ran a Web site called Right Principles.com, advised opponents of Obama's policies to "pack the hall . . . spread out" to make their numbers seem more significant, and to "rock-the-boat early in the Rep's presentation . . . to yell out and challenge the Rep's statements early . . . to rattle him, get him off his prepared script and agenda . . . stand up and shout and sit right back down." While MacGuffie was quickly dismissed as a lone amateur, some of the outside agitation was professional, paid for by the Koch network. Noble later admitted, "We packed these town halls with people who were just screaming about this thing."

After a military veteran assailed the Washington Democratic congressman Brian Baird for ostensibly defiling the

Constitution by supporting Obama's universal health-care plan, Baird decided to retire from politics, citing the intolerably toxic atmosphere. In Philadelphia, Senator Arlen Specter, a moderate Republican, and the secretary of health and human services, Kathleen Sebelius, were drowned out by hundreds of booing detractors at an event as they tried to explain the health-care legislation. Members of Congress all over the country, in districts as far apart as Tampa, Florida, and Long Island, New York, found themselves ambushed by screaming citizens, some mistakenly believing specious rumors about Obama's plans to create government "death panels" to euthanize senior citizens.

The raucous rallies proved pivotal in eroding Obama's agenda. Grover Norquist, the antitax activist who held a weekly meeting for conservative leaders in Washington, including representatives from Americans for Prosperity, described the summer's pandemonium as a turning point. The Republican leadership in Congress, he said, "couldn't have done it without August, when people went out on the streets. It discouraged deal makers, like Grassley"—Republicans who might otherwise have worked constructively with Obama. Moreover, the appearance of growing public opposition to Obama affected corporate donors on K Street, the center of Washington's lobbying industry. "K Street is a $3 billion weather vane," Norquist said. "When Obama was strong, the Chamber of Commerce said, 'We can work with the Obama administration.' But that changed when thousands of people went into the street and 'terrorized' congressmen. August is what changed it."

As Obama and his family vacationed in Martha's Vineyard during the congressional recess that month, Grassley, who was under bombardment from anti-health-care ads paid for by the Koch network, made clear he would not provide bipartisan support. Baucus, whose state Noble's campaign was also heavily targeting, dithered and delayed. The death of Senator Edward Kennedy, the liberal Democratic senator who had been the greatest champion of universal health care, cast health-care reform under a further cloud. A special election was set for January to fill what was assumed to be his reliably Democratic Senate seat.

Jim Margolis, the Democratic political consultant and advertising expert who had created many of Obama's 2008 campaign spots, watched with growing dismay. He had been advising both the White House and Democrats in Congress on the health-care issue and had begun with high hopes. "I thought on health care you'd get a modest amount of support from thoughtful Republicans," he said. "In March and April, Max Baucus was reaching out to Olympia Snowe and Chuck Grassley. The moderate Republicans were making some of the right sounds. But the progress was slow. Then, over the August recess, it really explodes. It would be interesting to know what the funding streams were like," he mused. "My suspicion is that the outside forces were kicking into high gear as we moved into the summer." Axelrod later acknowledged that he "wasn't really tracking" the right-wing money during this period and only belatedly came to realize that there was a set of "right-wing oligarchs" that "found Obama threatening," because he "believes in using government to solve problems. It was the Gilded Age all over again."

The press, ever alert to a colorful political drama, exaggerated the size of the grassroots groundswell. When fewer than sixty-five thousand Tea Party supporters flocked to the National Mall in Washington on September 12 for Glenn Beck and FreedomWorks' "9/12" rally, carrying signs like one reading, "Bury Obamacare with Kennedy," it was treated as if the entire center of gravity in American politics had shifted.

To be sure, the numbers on the far right had grown. Membership in the Liberty League, the anti–New Deal corollary to the Tea Party during the 1930s, has been estimated at 75,000, while membership in the John Birch Society in the 1960s has been estimated at 100,000 core members. Overall, at its height, 5 percent of Americans approved of the John Birch

Society. The Tea Party movement, in contrast, was estimated by *The New York Times* to have won the support of 18 percent of the population at its zenith, but at its core, according to the researcher Devin Burghart, were some 330,000 activists who had signed up with six national organizational networks. If the estimates were correct, the actual number of hard-core Tea Party activists was not, by historical standards, all that large. But the professionalization of the underground infrastructure, the growth of sympathetic and in some cases subsidized media outlets, and the concentrated money pushing the message from the fringe to center stage were truly consequential.

On October 3, as the first anniversary of Obama's election approached, David Koch came to the Washington area to attend a triumphant Defending the American Dream Summit, sponsored by Americans for Prosperity. Obama's poll numbers were falling fast. Only one Republican senator, Olympia Snowe of Maine, was working with the administration on health care, and she would eventually peel off. Aides said Obama was deeply disappointed. By obstructing every initiative, including his most ambitious domestic program, the Republicans had undermined his greatest appeal, his promise to be a bridge builder beyond old partisan divisions.

Mitch McConnell, the Republican minority leader in the Senate, held the Republican caucus in line partly by noting that Tea Party forces were ready and waiting to launch primary challenges against any who strayed. The outside groups funded by outside money thus provided crucial leverage. The plan worked so well that by the fall pundits who had fallen over themselves to praise Obama a year before were writing about his political ineptitude.

In a speech to a filled ballroom at the Crystal Gateway Marriott in Arlington, Virginia, on that October day, Koch said, "Five years ago, my brother Charles and I provided the funds to start the Americans for Prosperity, and it's beyond my wildest dreams how AFP has grown into this enormous organization." He went on, "Days like today bring to reality the vision of our board of directors when we founded this organization, five years ago." Rubbing his hands together somewhat awkwardly, he added, "We envisioned a mass movement, a state-based one, but national in scope, of hundreds of thousands of American citizens from all walks of life standing up and fighting for the economic freedoms that made our nation the most prosperous society in history . . . Thankfully, the stirrings from California to Virginia, and from Texas to Michigan, show that more and more of our fellow-citizens are beginning to see the same truths as we do."

As he stood at the lectern beaming, delegates from the various chapters of Americans for Prosperity reported in, one by one, describing how they had organized "dozens of tea parties" in their regions as they stood beside oversized vertical signs marking their states. Strobe lights crisscrossed the auditorium as excitement surged. It was hard not to notice that twenty-nine years after David Koch left the national political stage in utter defeat, he had succeeded in financing something that looked a lot like a presidential nominating convention, with himself as the winner.

CHAPTER EIGHT

The Fossils

IN THE FINAL MONTHS BEFORE THE 2008 PRESIDENTIAL ELEC-tion, Michael Mann, a tenured meteorology and geosciences professor at Penn State University who had become a leading figure in climate change research, told his wife that he would be happy whichever candidate won. Both the Republican and the Democratic presidential nominees had spoken about the importance of addressing global warming, which Mann regarded as the paramount issue of the day. But what he didn't fully foresee was that the same forces stirring the Tea Party would expertly channel the public outrage at government against scientific experts like himself.

Mann had started out unconvinced by the science of climate change, but in 1999 he and two co-authors had published a study tracking the previous thousand years of temperatures in the Northern Hemisphere. It included a simple, easy-to-grasp graph showing that the earth's temperature had hovered in a more or less straight line for nine hundred years but then shot sharply upward, like the blade of a hockey stick, in the twentieth century. What came to be known as the hockey stick graph was so powerfully persuasive it gained iconic status within the climate debate. By 2008, Mann, like most experts, had long since concluded that the scientific evidence was overwhelming that human beings were endangering the earth's climate by burning too much oil, gas, and coal. The carbon dioxide and other gases these fuels released were trapping the earth's heat, with devastating effects.

As even the Pentagon, a cautious bastion of technological

nonpartisanship, concluded, "the danger from climate change is real, urgent, and severe." An official U.S. National Security Strategy report declared the situation a growing national security threat, arguing, "The change wrought by a warming planet will lead to new conflicts over refugees and resources; new suffering from drought and famine; catastrophic natural disasters; and the degradation of land across the globe." The report unambiguously predicted that if nothing were done, "climate change and pandemic disease" would directly threaten "the health and safety of the American people."

The American Association for the Advancement of Science, the world's largest and most prestigious scientific society, was equally if not more adamant. It warned that "we face risks of abrupt, unpredictable and potentially irreversible changes" with potentially "massively disruptive consequences."

Mann wasn't particularly political. Middle-aged, friendly, and balding, with a dark goatee shadowing his round face, he was a quintessential science nerd who had majored in applied math and physics at the University of California, Berkeley, got advanced degrees in geology and geophysics at Yale, and for many years didn't think scientists had much of a role to play in public policy. When Obama won, he recalls, "I shared the widespread view that we would see some action on the climate front."

Certainly this assumption seemed reasonable. On the night that Obama clinched the Democratic nomination, he spoke passionately about climate change, vowing that Americans would look back knowing that "this was the moment when the rise of the oceans began to slow and our planet began to heal." Once in office, he pledged to pass a "cap and trade" bill forcing the fossil fuel industry to pay for its pollution, as other industries did, rather than treating it as someone else's problem. Cap and trade was a market-based solution, originally backed by Republicans, requiring permits for carbon emissions. The theory was that it would give the industry a financial incentive to stop polluting. It had worked surprisingly well in previous years to reduce industrial emissions that caused acid rain. By choosing a tested, moderate, bipartisan approach, the Obama administration and many environmentalists assumed a deal would be winnable.

"What we didn't take into account," Mann later noted, "was the ferociousness of the moneyed interests and the politicians doing their bidding. We are talking about a direct challenge to the most powerful industry that has ever existed on the face of the earth. There's no depth to which they're unwilling to sink to challenge anything threatening their interests even if it's science and the scientists involved in it."

Mann contended that "the fossil fuel industry is an oligarchy." Some might dispute that American oil, gas, and coal magnates met the dictionary definition of a small, privileged group that effectively rules over the majority. But it was indisputable that they funded and helped orchestrate a series of vitriolic personal attacks that would threaten Mann's livelihood, derail climate legislation, and alter the course of the Obama presidency.

If there was a single ultra-wealthy interest group that hoped to see Obama fail as he took office, it was the fossil fuel industry. And if there was one test of its members' concentrated financial power over the machinery of American democracy, it was this minority's ability to stave off government action on climate change as science and the rest of the world were moving in the opposite direction. While Obama's health-care bill was useful in riling up Tea Party protesters, his environmental and energy policies were the real target of many of the multimillionaires and billionaires in the Koch circle. For most of the world's population the costs of inaction on climate change were far greater than those of action. But for the fossil fuel industry, as Mann put it, "it's like the switch from whale oil in the nineteenth century. They're fighting to maintain the status quo, no matter how dumb."

Coal, oil, and gas magnates formed the nucleus of the Koch donor network. Guest lists for the summits read like a Who's Who of America's most successful and most conservative fossil fuel barons, the majority of whom were private, independent operators of privately owned companies. They were men who had either made or inherited enormous fortunes in "extractive" energy without having to answer to public shareholders or much of anyone else. Among the group, for instance, was Corbin "Corby" Robertson Jr., the grandson of one of Texas's most legendary oil barons, Hugh Roy Cullen. Robertson, a former captain of the football team at the University of Texas, from which he graduated in 1969, had taken a bold, unorthodox risk with his inherited oil fortune. He had bet almost all of it on coal, reportedly accumulating by 2003 the single largest private cache of coal reserves in America. He owned, by one count, twenty-one billion tons of coal reserves—enough to fuel the entire country for twenty years. Only the U.S. government reportedly owned more coal than his private, Houston-based company, Quintana Resources Capital.

Other donors in the network included Harold Hamm and Larry Nichols, two of the most successful pioneers in "fracking," the environmentally controversial process by which water and chemicals are injected underground into rock formations to extract oil and natural gas. Hamm, the founder of Continental Resources, was a self-made billionaire wildcatter whom the *National Journal* likened to John D. Rockefeller. While his nearly billion-dollar divorce settlement and amazing rise from being born the youngest of thirteen children in a family of sharecroppers made tabloid history, business journals were more focused on his company, which almost overnight had become the face of fracking in North Dakota's Bakken Shale.

Joining him in the network, on the opposite end of the

social scale, was Larry Nichols, head of Devon Energy and later chairman of the American Petroleum Institute, the foremost trade association for the oil industry. A graduate of Princeton and a former Supreme Court clerk, Nichols had urged his family's Oklahoma energy company to buy Mitchell Energy after he noticed that its natural gas output was climbing because of fracking. Nichols combined the process with his own company's expertise in horizontal drilling to "unleash what became known as the unconventional gas revolution," as the energy industry historian Daniel Yergin wrote in *The Quest*. The Kochs, too, had investments in the chemicals, pipelines, and other aspects of fracking.

The donor network also boasted spectacularly successful oilmen like Philip Anschutz, heir to a western oil-drilling fortune, who himself discovered a fabled oil field on the Wyoming-Utah border in the 1980s, after which he diversified into ranches, railroads, and communications. The network included many smaller operators too. There were oilmen from Wyoming, Oklahoma, Texas, and Colorado and coal magnates from Virginia, West Virginia, Kentucky, and Ohio. The largest distributor of propane canisters in the country was also involved. Participating, too, were many of those whose businesses provided ancillary support to America's energy sector. In addition to the Kochs there were numerous other owners of pipelines, drilling equipment, and oil service companies, including the legendary Bechtel family, which made billions building refineries and pipelines in Saudi Arabia, Venezuela, and elsewhere.

Most of the actual donors in this group preferred to keep low profiles, letting the politicians speak for them. They were expert in casting the group's reservations about government regulation in lofty philosophical terms. The politicians called them "job creators" and patriots, responsible for American energy independence. Clearly, though, there were few Americans for whom government caps on carbon posed a more direct financial threat.

The problem for this group was that by 2008 the arithmetic of climate change presented an almost unimaginable challenge. If the world were to stay within the range of carbon emissions that scientists deemed reasonable in order for atmospheric temperatures to remain tolerable through the mid-century, 80 percent of the fossil fuel industry's reserves would have to stay unused in the ground. In other words, scientists estimated that the fossil fuel industry owned roughly five times more oil, gas, and coal than the planet could safely burn. If the government interfered with the "free market" in order to protect the planet, the potential losses for these companies were catastrophic. If, however, the carbon from these reserves were burned wantonly without the government applying any brakes, scientists predicted an intolerable rise in atmospheric temperatures, triggering potentially irreversible global damage to life on earth.

As early as 1997, one member of the Koch group sounded the alarm about the coming regulatory threat. That year Lew Ward, the retiring chairman of the Independent Petroleum Association of America, the trade group of independent oil and gas producers, delivered a jeremiad as his swan song. Ward, who was himself an Oklahoma oilman, began by proudly ticking off the various tax loopholes he helped pass during his tenure. "We've been fortunate the past couple of years to have a Republican Congress," he noted. But he warned that the various policy "skirmishes" the industry had survived recently were nothing but "a dress rehearsal for the real show . . . the possible 'Carbon Tax' that could help pay the costs of reducing greenhouse gas emissions." Ward perceived accurately that the climate change issue was coming and argued that if the "radical environmentalist 'off-oil' agenda" succeeded, "we can look down the road a little way and see an industry under siege." He vowed, "We are not going to let that happen. You can take that to the bank!"

Ward's swagger was well-grounded. The oil industry had held parochial but powerful sway over American politics for years. As early as 1913, the oil industry used its clout to win a special tax loophole, the "oil depletion allowance." On the theory that oil exploration was risky and costly, it enabled the industry to deduct so much income when it hit gushers that many oil companies evaded income taxes altogether. After the loophole was scandalously enlarged in 1926, liberals, stymied by the oil patch's defenders in Congress, tried unsuccessfully for five decades before they were finally able to close it.

No American politician's rise to power in the last century was more fueled by oil than that of Lyndon Johnson. As Robert Caro recounts in *The Path to Power,* starting in 1940 Johnson rose from a neophyte congressman to the Democratic Party's consummate power broker by handing out campaign contributions from his enormously wealthy backers in the Texas oil fields and defending their interests.

Although the oil industry benefited enormously from the federal government in the form of favorable tax treatment, huge government contracts, and aid in building pipelines, as well as other handouts, it became a bastion of antigovernment conservatism. In fact, as its wealth grew, the Texas oil patch was the source not only of an astounding amount of campaign lucre but also of a particularly extreme strain of right-wing politics. In his book about the state's oil fortunes, *The Big Rich,* Bryan Burrough speculates that what animated many of the magnates was "the deep-tissue insecurity of the nouveau riche" who were hell-bent on keeping all they had just gained.

If there was a progenitor of Texas's modern-day ultraconservative oil faction, it was Corby Robertson's grandfather Hugh Roy Cullen, who helped make Quintana a billion-dollar enterprise. With roots in the fallen gentry of the Confederacy, he belonged to a band of oilmen that loathed northern liberals, denigrated FDR's administration as the "Jew Deal," and formed a third party whose plank called for "the restoration of the supremacy of the white race." Cullen's political ambitions expanded with his fortune, and in 1952—half a century before the Kochs became giant political spenders—he was the single biggest donor in American politics and a key supporter of Senator Joseph McCarthy's anti-Communist crusade. But at the time, his brand of radically right-wing, oil-fueled politics was doomed to be marginalized. Burrough explains that "to succeed in politics Cullen needed a support organization of some kind, but building one was something he was unwilling or incapable of doing." Half a century later, however, with the "Kochtopus" in place, Cullen's grandson and fellow oilmen would fare far better.

Opposition to curbs on carbon had long been building in the industry. The concept that the earth was warming, and mankind was causing it, first broke into the mainstream media in 1988 when the climate modeler James Hansen, director of NASA's Goddard Institute for Space Studies, testified before a Senate committee about it, amid a nationwide heat wave. *The New York Times* played his dramatic findings on its front page. During his presidency, George H. W. Bush, like most political leaders of both parties at the time, accepted the science without dispute. He vowed to protect the environment, promising to fight "the Greenhouse Effect with the White House Effect" and sending his secretary of state, James Baker, to the first international summit of climate scientists, the Intergovernmental Panel on Climate Change. Although Bush was a Republican, he was not an outlier in his party. For decades, the environmental movement had enjoyed bipartisan support.

As public opinion mounted in favor of climate action, however, the fossil fuel industry organized and financed a stealthy state-of-the-art counteroffensive. Despite the agreement of both parties' presidential candidates in 2008 that something needed to be done to stave off climate change, powerful outside interests had been working overtime to erode that consensus. The conservative infrastructure necessary to wage a war of ideas was already in place. All it took to focus the attack on climate science was money. And beneath the surface, it was pouring in.

Kert Davies, the director of research at Greenpeace, the liberal environmental group, spent months trying to trace the funds flowing into a web of nonprofit organizations and talking heads, all denying the reality of global warming as if working from the same script. What he discovered was that from 2005 to 2008, a single source, the Kochs, poured almost $25 million into dozens of different organizations fighting climate reform. The sum was staggering. His research showed that Charles and David had outspent what was then the world's largest public oil company, ExxonMobil, by a factor of three. In a 2010 report, Greenpeace crowned Koch Industries, a company few had ever heard of at the time, the "kingpin of climate science denial."

The first peer-reviewed academic study on the topic added further detail. Robert Brulle, a Drexel University professor of sociology and environmental science, discovered that between 2003 and 2010 over half a billion dollars was spent on what he described as a massive "campaign to manipulate and mislead the public about the threat posed by climate change." The study examined the tax records of more than a hundred nonprofit organizations engaged in challenging the prevailing science on global warming. What it found was, in essence, a corporate lobbying campaign disguised as a tax-exempt, philanthropic endeavor. Some 140 conservative foundations funded the campaign, Brulle found. During the seven-year period he studied, these foundations distributed $558 million in the form of 5,299 grants to ninety-one different nonprofit organizations. The money went to think tanks, advocacy groups, trade associations, other foundations, and academic and legal programs. Cumulatively, this private network waged a permanent campaign to undermine Americans' faith in climate science and to defeat any effort to regulate carbon emissions.

The cast of conservative organizations identified by Brulle was familiar to anyone who had followed the funding of the modern conservative movement. Among those he pinpointed as the largest bankrollers of climate change denial were foundations affiliated with the Koch and Scaife families, both of whose fortunes derived partly from oil. Also heavily involved were the Bradley Foundation and several others associated with hugely wealthy families participating in the Koch donor summits, such as foundations run by the DeVos family, Art Pope, the retail magnate from North Carolina, and John Templeton Jr., a doctor and heir to the fortune of his father, John Templeton Sr., an American mutual fund pioneer who eventually renounced his U.S. citizenship in favor of living in the Bahamas, reportedly saving $100 million on taxes. Brulle found that as the money was dispersed, three-quarters of the funds from these and other sources financing what he called the "climate change counter-movement" were untraceable.

"Powerful funders are supporting the campaign to deny scientific findings about global warming and raise public doubts about the roots and remedies of this massive global threat. At the very least," he argued, "American voters deserve to know who is behind these efforts."

Instead, by the time Obama took office some of the biggest bankrollers of the war against climate science had, if anything, gone further underground. Rather than funding the campaign directly, a growing number of private conservative foundations and donors had begun directing their contributions through an organization called DonorsTrust that in essence became a screen for the right wing, behind which fingerprints disappeared from the cash. Housed in a humdrum brick building in Alexandria, Virginia, DonorsTrust and its affiliate, Donors Capital Fund, were memorably described by *Mother Jones*'s

Andy Kroll as "the dark-money ATM of the conservative movement."

Founded in 1999 by Whitney Ball, an ardent libertarian from West Virginia who had overseen development of the Koch-founded Cato Institute, DonorsTrust boasted one key advantage for wealthy conservatives. It made their contributions appear to be going to Ball's bland-sounding "donor-advised fund," rather than to the far more controversial conservative groups she distributed it to afterward. The mechanism thus erased the donors' names from the money trail. Meanwhile, the donors retained the same if not bigger charitable tax deductions. As the DonorsTrust Web site advertised, "You wish to keep your charitable giving private, especially gifts funding sensitive or controversial issues. Set up a DonorsTrust account and ask that your gifts remain anonymous. Know that any contributions to your DonorsTrust account that have to be reported to the IRS will not become public information. Unlike with private foundations, gifts from your account will remain as anonymous as you request."

Between 1999 and 2015, DonorsTrust redistributed some $750 million from the pooled contributions to myriad conservative causes under its own name. Ordinarily, under the law, in exchange for their tax breaks, private foundations such as the Charles G. Koch Foundation were required to publicly disclose the charitable groups to whom they made their grants. It was one way to assure that these public service organizations were in fact serving the public. But donor-advised funds defeated this minimum transparency. Ball argued that the mechanism wasn't suspicious, or even unusual, and that liberals too had their own donor-advised fund, the Tides Foundation. DonorsTrust, the conservative answer to the Tides Foundation, however, soon had four times the funds and a far more strategic board. Its directors consisted of top officials of several of the most important institutions in the conservative movement, including the

American Enterprise Institute, the Heritage Foundation, and the Institute for Justice, the libertarian legal center whose start-up funds had been supplied by Charles Koch. They functioned as a central committee, coordinating grant making.

What Brulle noticed as he studied the money behind climate change denial was that as criticism of those blocking reform increased around 2007, tens of millions of dollars of contributions from fossil fuel interests like Koch and ExxonMobil seemed to have disappeared from the public fight. Meanwhile, a growing and commensurate amount of anonymous money from DonorsTrust started funding the climate change countermovement. In 2003, for instance, Brulle found that DonorsTrust money was the source of only 3 percent of the 140 groups whose financial records he studied. By 2010, it had grown to 24 percent. The circumstantial evidence suggested that the fossil fuel interests bankrolling climate change denial were deliberately hiding their hands, but Brulle couldn't prove it. "We just have this great big unknown out there about where all the money is coming from," he said.

Relations between the Kochs and DonorsTrust were close. Disclosures showed that the Kochs' foundations made sizable gifts to DonorsTrust, which in turn dispersed large amounts of cash to their favorite nonprofit groups. In 2010, for instance, the single largest grant that it made to any organization was a $7.4 million gift to the Americans for Prosperity Foundation, whose chairman was David Koch. These funds accounted for about 40 percent of the AFP Foundation's funding that year, belying the notion that it was a genuine grassroots organization. AFP, meanwhile, not only took a lead role in organizing the Tea Party rebellion but also spearheaded a national drive to block action on climate change, aiming in every way possible to merge the two movements.

What much of the stealth funding bought was the dissemination of scientific doubt. The fossil fuel industry thus followed the same deceptive playbook that had been developed by the public relations firm Hill & Knowlton on behalf of the tobacco companies in the 1960s, in order to fabricate uncertainty about the science linking smoking to cancer. As the firm's memo had notoriously put it, "Doubt is our product." To add credibility to their side, the tobacco companies funded a network of official-sounding institutes and smokers' rights groups. This strategy soon characterized the global warming denial movement, too.

There was in fact some uncertainty about global warming, as there is about virtually every scientific hypothesis. Probability, rather than absolute certainty, is the nature of the scientific method. But as Dr. James Baker, former head of the National Oceanic and Atmospheric Administration, said in 2005, "There's a better scientific consensus on this than on any issue I know—except maybe Newton's second law of dynamics."

Nonetheless, in 1998, the American Petroleum Institute, along with several top oil industry executives and conservative think tank officials, colluded on a secret plan to spend $2 million to confuse the press and the public about this growing scientific consensus. The plan called for recruiting skeptical scientists and training them in public relations so that they could act as spokesmen, thereby adding legitimacy and cover to the industry's agenda.

According to *The Republican War on Science,* the plan was the brainchild of William O'Keefe, a former chief operating officer at the American Petroleum Institute and a lobbyist for ExxonMobil who became president of the George C. Marshall Institute, a conservative think tank in Virginia. O'Keefe continued to lobby for ExxonMobil while heading the research center. Described by *Newsweek* as a "central cog in the denial machine," the think tank specialized in providing contrarian scientific defenses for dubious clients. Funded by the Scaife, Olin, and Bradley Foundations, among others, it had begun as a center for Cold War hawks vouching for President Reagan's "Star Wars" missile shield, but expanded into debunking other scientific findings that could be construed as liberal or anti-corporate. Money from threatened corporate interests, meanwhile, frequently funded the research.

Leading the charge against climate science were two elderly, retired physicists affiliated with the George C. Marshall Institute who had previously defended the tobacco industry, Fred Seitz and Fred Singer. As Naomi Oreskes and Erik Conway write in *Merchants of Doubt,* the two Freds had been eminent physicists in their day, but neither had any expertise in either the environment or health, "yet, for years the press quoted these men as experts." What they were in fact expert in was converting a torrent of unseen funding into "fighting facts, and merchandising doubt," according to Oreskes and Conway.

But for the fossil fuel industry, winning over public opinion was no easy feat. As the new millennium dawned, the general public was broadly in favor of environmental regulations. As late as 2003, over 75 percent of *Republicans* supported strict environmental regulations, according to polls. For help on their public relations campaign, in 2002 the opponents of carbon regulations hired Frank Luntz, who warned that "the environment is probably the issue on which Republicans in general—and President Bush in particular—is most vulnerable." To win, he argued, global warming deniers had to portray themselves as "preserving and protecting" the environment. In his confidential memo "Winning the Global Warming Debate," which eventually leaked to the public, Luntz stressed as his number one point that opponents of carbon regulations "absolutely" must "not raise economic arguments first." In other words, telling the truth about their financial interests was a recipe for losing.

The key, he went on, was to question the science. "You need to continue to make the lack of scientific certainty a primary issue in the debate," he advised. So long as "voters believe there is no consensus about global warming within the scientific community," he said, regulations could be forestalled.

The Koch family poses for a Christmas card, circa 1950s. Left to right: Charles, David, Fred, Mary, Bill, Frederick. (Wichita State University Libraries, Special Collections and University Archives)

The Winkler-Koch unit at the Eurotank oil refinery in Hamburg was completed in 1935. (The United States Strategic Bombing Survey)

David Koch, left, the running mate of Libertarian presidential candidate Ed Clark, center, with Clark's wife, Alicia Garcia Cobos de Clark, at a fund-raising rally and telethon in Los Angeles in 1980 (Randy Rasmussen / Associated Press)

Charles Koch with Liz Koch, his wife, at Koch Headquarters in Wichita in 2012 (Bo Rader / *The Wichita Eagle* / Associated Press)

Richard Mellon Scaife, age twenty-three, at a cocktail party in 1955 (Margaret Bourke-White / The LIFE Picture Collection / Getty Images)

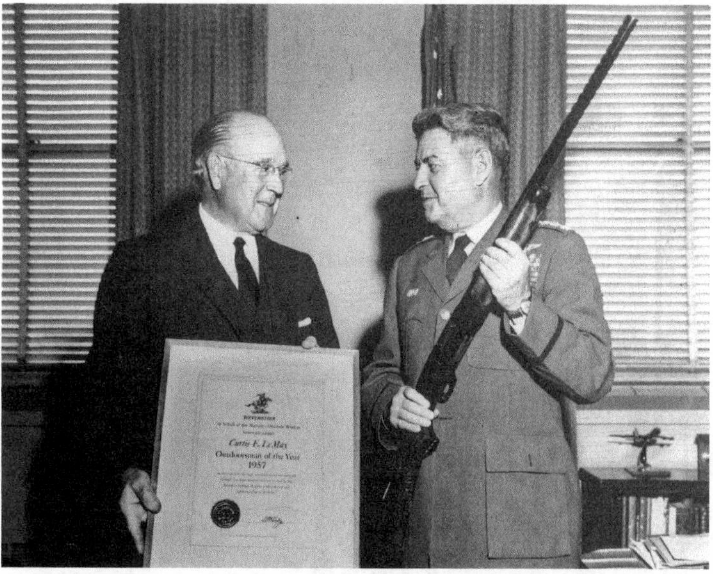

John M. Olin, left, presents the 1957 Outdoorsman of the Year award to General Curtis E. LeMay. (*The Denver Post* / Getty Images)

Michael Mann in Iceland in 2016 (Courtesy of Michael Mann)

Sheldon Adelson, chairman and CEO of the Las Vegas Sands Corporation, at the opening of his casino resort in Macau in 2012 (Kin Cheung / Associated Press)

Robert Mercer at the World Science Festival Gala in New York City in 2014 (Andrew Toth / Getty Images Entertainment / Getty Images)

James Arthur "Art" Pope, then budget director for North Carolina governor Pat McCrory, in his office in Raleigh in 2014 (Ted Richardson / *The Washington Post* / Getty Images)

Philip Anschutz, co-founder of Qwest Communications and founder of The Anschutz Corporation, in 2008 (Lucy Nicholson / Reuters)

Corbin Robertson Jr., owner of the country's largest private cache of coal (Steve Campbell / *Houston Chronicle*)

Language that "worked," he advised, included phrases like "we must not rush to judgment" and "we should not commit America to any international document that handcuffs us." Later, Luntz would switch sides and publicly admit that global warming was a real peril. But in the view of Michael Mann, whose scientific work soon became the target of climate change deniers, Luntz's 2002 memo served as a virtual hunting license. "It basically said you have to discredit the scientists and create fake groups. It doesn't say 'engage in character assassination,' but it was leaning in that direction."

On cue, organizations funded and directed by the Kochs tore into global warming science and the experts behind it. The Cato Institute, the libertarian think tank that Charles Koch founded, put out a steady stream of reports like *Apocalypse Not: Science, Economics, and Environmentalism* and *Climate of Fear: Why We Shouldn't Worry About Global Warming.* A grant from the Charles G. Koch Charitable Foundation, along with funds from ExxonMobil and the American Petroleum Institute, also helped pay for a non-peer-reviewed study claiming that polar bears, who were mascots of the global warming debate, were not endangered by climate change. It quickly drew criticism from experts in the field like the National Wildlife Federation, which predicted that by 2050 two-thirds of the polar bear population would disappear because their habitat was melting. Nonetheless, the conclusions of the oil-financed study were echoed throughout the network of Koch-funded groups. "There are more polar bears today than there have ever been," Ed Crane, the head of Cato, insisted. He argued that "global warming theories just give the government more control of the economy."

It was the authors of the revisionist polar bear study who also took one of the first shots at Michael Mann's iconic hockey stick study, publishing a takedown in 2003. The credentials of the critics, Sallie Baliunas and Wei-Hock "Willie" Soon, looked impressive. Soon was identified as a scientist at the Harvard-Smithsonian Center for Astrophysics. But it later emerged that he had a doctoral degree in aerospace engineering, not climate science, and had only a part-time, unpaid affiliation with the Smithsonian Institution. Without disclosing it, he had accepted more than $1.2 million from the fossil fuel industry from 2005 to 2015, including at least $230,000 from the Charles G. Koch Charitable Foundation. It was later revealed that some of the payments for his papers were marked as "deliverables" by the fossil fuel companies.

Soon's attack on Mann was so controversial that the editor and several other staffers sympathetic to Mann resigned in protest against *Climate Research*, the small journal that published it. Yet from that moment on, Mann, who was at the time an assistant professor in the Department of Environmental Sciences at the University of Virginia, had a target on his back.

As the scientific consensus grew in support of global warming, the industry's efforts to fight it became increasingly aggressive. The presidential candidacy of the environmental activist Al Gore in 2000 posed an obvious threat to the fossil fuel industry. That election cycle, Koch Industries and its employees disbursed over $800,000 in support of his opponent George W. Bush and other Republicans. Koch Industries' political action committee was spending more on federal campaigns than any other oil and gas company, including ExxonMobil. The company's expenditures on Washington lobbying expanded more than twenty-fold from 2004 to 2008, reaching $20 million. The Kochs' corporate self-interest had by then thoroughly trumped their youthful disdain for engaging in conventional politics.

Political contributions from oil, gas, and coal companies became increasingly polarized during this period. In 1990, the oil and gas industry's political giving was skewed 60 percent in favor of Republicans and 40 percent in favor of Democrats. By the middle of the Bush years, 80 percent of the industry's giving went to Republicans. Giving from coal-mining firms was even more lopsided, with 90 percent going to Republicans, according to the Center for Responsive Politics.

The investment soon paid off. As the Harvard political scientist Theda Skocpol writes in a study of climate change denial, the Republican Party, particularly in the U.S. Congress, soon swung sharply to the right on climate issues. Partisan differences remained small among the general public but grew into a gaping chasm among elected officials.

Conservative opponents of carbon regulations, like James Inhofe, a Republican senator from Oklahoma who received serial campaign donations from Koch Industries PAC, turned the rhetoric up to a boiling point. Global warming, he proclaimed, was "the greatest hoax ever perpetrated on the American people." Inhofe's spokesman, Marc Morano, had a reputation as a professional "pit bull," as Mann later put it, derived from his earlier role promoting the claims of the Swift Boat Veterans for Truth, a group that had smeared John Kerry's military record during his 2004 presidential campaign. At the time, Morano was working for a conservative news outlet that was funded in part by the Scaife, Bradley, and Olin Foundations.

By 2006, Morano had moved on to "swiftboating" scientists. "You've got to name names and you've got to go after individuals," he explained in an interview with the documentary filmmaker Robert Kenner. He seemed to relish making political disagreements personal, taunting and inflaming opponents with a grin in televised showdowns. Morano denounced James Hansen as a "wannabe Unabomber" and Mann as a "charlatan." He said of the scapegoating, "We had a lot of fun with it."

Morano charged that Mann was part of what he called "the 'climate con,'" which he described as "a lavishly funded climate machine that is lobbying for laws and uses every bit of data or new study to proclaim 'it's worse than we thought' or 'we must act now.'" Morano's background was in political science, which he studied at George Mason University, not climate science. "I'm not a scientist but I play one on TV," he joked. Nonetheless, he asserted authoritatively that "man-made global warming fears are a grand political narrative, not science."

The George W. Bush years, meanwhile, proved a bonanza for the fossil fuel industry, which had thrown its weight behind his election. The coal industry in particular had played a major role in delivering West Virginia's five electoral votes to Bush in 2000, sealing a victory that would have gone to Al Gore had he carried the formerly Democratic state instead. "State political veterans and top White House staffers concur that it was basically a coal-fired victory," *The Wall Street Journal* wrote. The industry was lavishly rewarded. Vice President Dick Cheney, a former CEO of the oil-field equipment and services company Halliburton, personally took charge of energy policy. Bush had vowed during the campaign to act on climate change by limiting greenhouse gas emissions, but once in office Cheney countermanded him. In what Cheney's biographer Barton Gellman describes as a "case study in managing an errant boss," Cheney shifted the administration's position to arguing that the science on global warming was "inconclusive," requiring "more scientific inquiry."

The 2005 energy bill, which Hillary Clinton dubbed at the time the "Dick Cheney Lobbyist Energy Bill," offered enormous subsidies and tax breaks for fossil-fuel-intensive companies. The Bush administration weakened regulations, for instance, on coal-fired power plants. Taking a position that was eventually overturned by the courts, it exempted mercury emissions from regulation under the Clean Air Act, reversing the position taken by the Clinton administration. Fracking got a boost too. Cheney used his influence to exempt it from regulation under the Safe Drinking Water Act, over objections from the Environmental Protection Agency. The fracking industry boomed. Within five years, Devon Energy, Larry Nichols's company, would rank as the fourth-largest producer of natural gas in the United States. Harold Hamm would become a multibillionaire. Cheney's former company Halliburton also became a major player in the fracking industry, illustrating that free-market advocates greatly benefited from government favors.

In all, the Bush energy act contained some $6 billion in oil and gas subsidies and $9 billion in coal subsidies. The Kochs routinely cast themselves as libertarians who deplored government taxes, regulations, and subsidies, but records show they took full advantage of the special tax credits and subsidies available to the oil, ethanol, and pipeline business, among other areas of commerce in which they were engaged. In many cases, their lobbyists fought hard to protect these perks. In addition, their companies benefited from nearly $100 million in government contracts in the decade after 2000, according to a study by Media Matters, a liberal watchdog group.

When Barack Obama took office, the fossil fuel industry was not only eager to preserve its perks but also more militant in its opposition to climate change science than ever. Skocpol notes that 2007 had been a turning point in the fight. That year, Al Gore was awarded both a Nobel Peace Prize and featured in an Academy Award–winning documentary film, *An Inconvenient Truth.* The film featured Mann's hockey stick graph. Gore's acclaim and Mann's simple chart helped raise concern about global warming to a new peak, with 41 percent of the American public saying it worried them "a great deal."

"At this critical juncture—when Americans in general might have been persuaded of the urgency of dealing with global warming," Skocpol notes, opponents fought back with new vigor. The whole ideological assembly line that Richard

Fink and Charles Koch had envisioned decades earlier, including the entire conservative media sphere, was enlisted in the fight. Fox Television and conservative talk radio hosts gave saturation coverage to the issue, portraying climate scientists as swindlers pushing a radical, partisan, and anti-American agenda. Allied think tanks pumped out books and position papers, whose authors testified in Congress and appeared on a whirlwind tour of talk shows. "Climate denial got disseminated deliberately and rapidly from think tank tomes to the daily media fare of about thirty to forty percent of the U.S. populace," Skocpol estimates.

Climate contrarians also recruited conservative evangelical Christian leaders, who distrusted government in general and had impressive political and communications clout. One by-product of this pact was an organization in the Washington suburbs called the Cornwall Alliance, which released a hit film in evangelical circles called *Resisting the Green Dragon* that equated environmentalism with worship of a false god. It described global warming as "one of the greatest deceptions of our day." Climate change became such a hot-button issue for Christian fundamentalists that Richard Cizik, a vice president of the National Association of Evangelicals, who was considered among the most powerful leaders in the movement, was forced to resign in late 2008 after publicly endorsing climate change science.

Before long, public opinion polls showed that concern about climate change among all but hard-core liberals had collapsed. As the 2008 presidential campaign played out, the issue grew increasingly polarized. Just before the election, with the economy in tumult, John McCain, the Republican presidential candidate, reiterated that the climate problem was real. He also said that green jobs would lead the way to economic recovery. But his choice of Sarah Palin as his running mate, one of whose mantras was "Drill, Baby, Drill," indicated just how influential the voice of climate extremism was becoming within the Republican Party.

As Obama took office, America derived over 85 percent of its total energy from oil, gas, and coal. The business was enormous, with profits and influence to match.

Conventional wisdom nonetheless held that Obama's election portended well for environmentalists. Mann, too, was optimistic, but he worried about what he regarded as a "troubling complacency" among his colleagues. He knew that the Obama administration posed two huge threats to the fossil fuel industry, and he doubted the industry would just roll over. The first threat was Obama's Environmental Protection Agency. Lisa Jackson, the EPA administrator, announced that she intended to treat greenhouse gas emissions as hazardous pollutants, regulating them for the first time under the Clean Air Act. It was an authority that the Supreme Court had upheld in 2007. But no previous administration had tried to take on the industry so frontally. The second was the Democrats' plan to introduce the long-incubating cap-and-trade bill to limit greenhouse gas emissions.

Even before Obama was inaugurated, Americans for Prosperity had begun taking aim at the cap-and-trade idea, circulating a pledge requiring elected officials to oppose new spending to fight climate change. Koch Industries, meanwhile, began lobbying against government mandates to reduce carbon emissions. Then, soon after Obama was inaugurated, an odd television ad popped up around the country that seemed strangely off message. While most Americans were transfixed by the unfolding economic disaster that was preoccupying the Obama administration in its first few months, out of nowhere, it seemed, was a discordant television spot about a spoiled slacker named Carlton.

"Hey there," said a louche-looking young man, plucking away at a plate of canapés. "I'm Carlton, the wealthy eco-hypocrite. I inherited my money and attended fancy schools. I own three homes and five cars, but always talk with my rich friends about saving the planet. And I want Congress to spend billions on programs in the name of global warming and green energy, even if it causes massive unemployment, higher energy bills, and digs people like you even deeper into the recession. Who knows? Maybe I'll even make money off of it!"

"Carlton" was, in fact, the creation of Americans for Prosperity, the nonprofit "social welfare" group founded and heavily funded by David Koch, who of course had inherited hundreds of millions of dollars, attended Deerfield Academy, owned *four* homes (a ski lodge in Aspen; a Belle Epoque mansion, Villa el Sarmiento, in Palm Beach; a sprawling beach house in the Hamptons; and an eighteen-room duplex at 740 Park Avenue in Manhattan), and drove, among other cars, a Land Rover and a Ferrari.

By creating "Carlton" as a decoy, the Kochs and their allies evidently hoped to convince the public that government action on climate change posed a threat to "people like you" or ordinary Americans' pocketbooks. But it of course posed a far greater threat to their own. With ownership of refineries, pipelines, a coal subsidiary (the C. Reiss Coal Company), coal-fired power plants, fertilizer, petroleum coke manufacturing, timber, and leases on over a million acres of untapped Canadian oil sands, Koch Industries alone routinely released some 24 million tons of carbon dioxide into the atmosphere a year. Any financial penalty that the government placed on carbon pollution would threaten both their immediate profit margins and the long-term value of the enormous investments they had in still-untapped fossil fuel reserves.

The Kochs themselves said little about their views on climate change at the time.

But in one interview, David Koch suggested that if real,

it would prove a boon. "The Earth will be able to support enormously more people because a far greater land area will be available to produce food," he argued. Charles's thinking was reflected in the company's in-house newsletter, which featured an article titled "Blowing Smoke." "Why are such unproven or false claims promoted?" it asked. Rather than fighting global warming, the newsletter suggested, mankind would be better off adapting to it. "Since we can't control Mother Nature, let's figure out how to get along with her changes," it advised. A similar line was subtly argued in the David H. Koch Hall of Human Origins at the Smithsonian's National Museum of Natural History in Washington, which opened in March 2010. The message of the exhibition, funded by his fortune, was that the human race had evolved for the better in response to previous environmental challenges and would adapt in the face of climate change, too. An interactive game suggested that if the climate on earth became intolerable, people might build "underground cities" and develop "short, compact bodies" or "curved spines" so that "moving around in tight spaces will be no problem."

Soon the climate issue was creeping into Tea Party rallies, too. As protesters erupted in generalized rage in the spring and summer of 2009, Americans for Prosperity, FreedomWorks, and the other secretly funded Tea Party groups succeeded to a remarkable extent in channeling the populist anger into the climate fight. At the first big "Tax Day" Tea Party rallies on April 15, 2009, while most protesters were flaying Obama's bank bailouts and stimulus plan, the staff of Americans for Prosperity handed out free T-shirts and signs protesting what would ordinarily seem to be an arcane issue for most people in the streets, the cap-and-trade bill. "The Obama budget proposes the largest excise tax in history," the advocacy group's talking points stressed.

To dramatize the issue, offshoots of Americans for Prosperity sent "Carbon Cops," who pranced into Tea Party rallies pretending to be overreaching emissaries from the EPA, warning that backyard barbecues, churches, and lawn mowers were about to be shut down because of new, stricter interpretations of the Clean Air Act. The advocacy group also launched what it called the Cost of Hot Air Tour to mock the cap-and-trade proposal. It featured a seventy-foot-tall bright red hot-air balloon on whose side was emblazoned a slogan reducing the argument against the cap-and-trade proposal to six scary words. Cap and trade, it said, means "higher taxes, lost jobs, less freedom." Americans for Prosperity sent the balloon to so many states in 2009 that the group's president, Tim Phillips, later admitted, "I rode more hot-air balloons in that year-and-a-half period than I ever want to ride again. I do not like hot-air balloons."

The public campaign was accompanied by a darker covert one. Tom Perriello, a freshman Democratic congressman from Charlottesville, Virginia, who favored the cap-and-trade bill, discovered this in the summer of 2009 when constituents started bombarding his office with angry missives. Reams of faxes arrived from voters, many representing local chapters of ordinarily supportive liberal groups like the NAACP and the American Association of University Women. Under official letterheads, they argued passionately that the cap-and-trade legislation would raise electric bills, hurting the poor. But an effort by the congressman's staff to reach the angry constituents revealed that the letters were forgeries, sent on behalf of a coal industry trade group by Bonner and Associates, a Washington-based public relations firm.

After the fraud was exposed, the firm fired an employee. But it wasn't an isolated incident. Perriello, like many other elected officials that summer, also found himself heckled during town hall meetings. One such heckler called him a "traitor" for supporting the cap-and-trade bill, while another videotaped the showdown. Later one of the disruptive members of the audience admitted to the investigative reporter Lee Fang that he had been put up to it by the Virginia director of Americans for Prosperity. Similar outbursts took place all over the country that summer. Mike Castle, a moderate Republican congressman from Delaware, was accosted by voters demanding to know how he could even consider voting for such a "hoax," according to Eric Pooley's account in *The Climate War*. The U.S. Chamber of Commerce, the American Petroleum Institute, and other industry representatives, it turned out, had created a "grassroots" group called Energy Citizens that joined Tea Party organizations in packing the town halls with protesters.

Fanning the flames were the right-wing radio hosts. "It's not about saving the planet," Rush Limbaugh told his audience. "It's not about anything, folks, other than raising taxes and redistributing wealth." Glenn Beck warned listeners it would lead to water rationing. "This is about controlling every part of your life, even taking a shower!" Torquing up the fear, Republicans in Congress quoted from a study by the Heritage Foundation that predicted it would add thousands of dollars to Americans' energy bills and lead to devastating unemployment. The nonpartisan Congressional Budget Office put out an authoritative study contradicting this, demonstrating that the average cost to Americans would be the same as buying a postage stamp a day. But John Boehner, the Republican minority leader in the House, dismissed the real numbers, suggesting anyone who believed them could "go ask the unicorns."

Despite the inflammatory atmosphere, the House passed a bill to cap and trade carbon dioxide emissions on June 26, 2009. The process wasn't pretty. It took an extraordinary push from its sponsors, Congressmen Henry Waxman of California and Ed Markey of Massachusetts, and an epic amount of horse-trading between environmentalists and the affected industries. Many environmentalists thought the final product was so flawed that it wasn't worth the trouble. But for those looking for Congress to reach the kind of moderate compromises Obama had been elected to deliver, it was a first step.

Rather than causing elation, though, the victory was clouded by trepidation. Supporters, particularly Democrats from conservative, fossil-fuel-heavy states like Perriello and Rick Boucher of Virginia, feared there would be a steep price to pay. As the threat to the industry grew, so would its determination to stop them.

That fall, television ads began appearing in states like Montana, where the Democratic senator Max Baucus was already under attack from members of the Koch network on the health-care issue. "There is no scientific evidence that CO_2 is a pollutant. In fact higher CO_2 levels than we have today would help the Earth's ecosystems," the ads said, urging viewers to tell Baucus not to vote for the cap-and-trade bill, which would "cost us jobs." The sponsor for the ad was a group curiously called CO_2 Is Green. Quietly funding it, according to Steven Mufson, the energy reporter for *The Washington Post,* was Corbin Robertson, owner of the country's largest private cache of coal.

Robertson's fingerprints were detectable behind another anti-climate-change front group, too, the Coalition for Responsible Regulation. As soon as Obama's EPA took steps to regulate greenhouse gases, the previously unknown group took legal action to stop it. The group's private e-mails surfaced later, revealing how it successfully egged on Texas's bureaucrats to join the lawsuit, despite the state's own climatologist's belief that man-made global warming posed a real danger and that the EPA's scientific findings were solid. Neither Robertson's name nor that of his company appeared in the papers incorporating the organization. But its address and its top officers were the same as those of Robertson's company, Quintana.

Following hard on the summer's raucous Tea Party protests, things got uglier in Washington as well. As Obama addressed a joint session of Congress laying out his health-care proposal in September 2009, his speech was interrupted by Joe Wilson, a Republican congressman from South Carolina, shouting, "You lie!" from the well of the House. Congress rebuked Wilson for his extraordinary breach of decorum, but within a month, climate skeptics were echoing Wilson's belligerence. One posted a report titled "UN Climate Reports: They Lie!"

The opposition grew as the Obama administration got ready to head to Copenhagen in December 2009 for its first international climate summit. World leaders expected the United States would finally commit to serious reform. Previously, the United States had declined to join other developed nations in agreeing to limit greenhouse gas emissions under the Kyoto Protocol. Given Obama's position, time seemed to be running out for the fossil fuel forces and their free-market allies. Then, on November 17, 2009, an anonymous commenter on a contrarian Web site declared, "A miracle has happened."

With lethal timing, an unidentified saboteur had hacked expertly into the University of East Anglia's Web site and uploaded thousands of internal e-mails detailing the private communications of the scientists working in its famed Climatic Research Unit. The climatologists at the British university had been in constant communication with those in America, and now all of their unguarded professional doubts, along with their unguarded and sometimes contemptuous asides about their opponents, stretching all the way back to 1996, were visible for the entire world to read.

Chris Horner, a conservative climate contrarian working at the Competitive Enterprise Institute, another pro-corporate think tank subsidized by oil and other fossil fuel fortunes, including the Kochs', declared, "The blue dress moment may have arrived." But instead of using Monica Lewinsky's telltale garment to impeach Bill Clinton, they would use the words of the world's leading climate scientists to impeach the climate change movement. If edited down and taken out of context, their exchanges could be made to appear to suggest a willingness to falsify data in order to buttress the idea that global warming was real.

Dubbing the alleged scandal Climategate, they went into overdrive. The web of organizations, funded in part by the Kochs, pounced on the hacked e-mails. Cato scholars were particularly energetic in promoting the story. In the two weeks after the e-mails went public, one Cato scholar alone gave more than twenty media interviews trumpeting the alleged scandal. The story soon spread from obviously slanted venues to the pages of *The New York Times* and *The Washington Post,* adding mainstream credence. Tim Phillips, the president of Americans for Prosperity, jumped on the hacked e-mails, describing them to a gathering of conservative bloggers at the Heritage Foundation as "a crucial tipping point" and adding, "If we win the science argument, I think it's game, set, and match for them."

Eventually, seven independent inquiries exonerated the climate scientists, finding nothing in the e-mails to discredit their work or the larger consensus on global warming. In the meantime, though, Michael Mann's life, along with the environmental movement, was plunged into turmoil.

Mann was among the scientists most roiled by the mysterious hacking incident. Four words in the purloined e-mails were seized upon as evidence that he was a fraud. In describing his research, his colleagues had praised his use of a "trick" that had helped him "hide the decline." Mann's detractors leaped to the conclusion that these words proved that his research was just a "trick" to fool the public and that he had deliberately hidden an actual "decline" in twentieth-century temperatures in order to fake evidence of global warming.

The facts, when fully understood, were very different. It was a British colleague, not Mann, who had written the ostensibly damning words, and when examined in context, they were utterly mundane. The "trick" referred to was just a clever technique Mann had devised in order to provide a backup data set. The "decline" in question was a reference to a decline in available information from certain kinds of tree rings after 1961, which had made it hard to have a consistent set of data. Another scientist, not Mann, had found an alternative source of data to compensate for this problem, which was what was meant by "hide the decline." The only genuinely negative disclosure from the e-mails was that Mann and the other climatologists had agreed among themselves to withhold, rather than share, their research with some of their critics, whom they disparaged. Given the harassment they had been subjected to, their reasoning was understandable, but it violated the customary transparency expected within the scientific community. Other than that, the "Climategate" scandal was, in other words, not one.

It took no time, nevertheless, for the hacked e-mails to spur a witch hunt. Within days, Inhofe and other Republicans in Congress who were recipients of Koch campaign donations demanded an investigation into Mann. They sent threatening letters to Penn State, where he was by then a tenured professor. Later, Virginia's attorney general, Ken Cuccinelli, a graduate of the George Mason School of Law, would also subpoena Mann's former employer, the University of Virginia, demanding all records relating to his decade-old academic research, regardless of libertarians' professed concerns about government intrusion. Eventually, Virginia's Supreme Court dismissed its own attorney general's case "with prejudice," finding he had misread the law.

By New Year's Eve 2009, Mann was feeling under attack from all sides. Conservative talk radio hosts lambasted him regularly. Contrarian Web sites were lit up with blog posts detailing his iniquity. A self-described former CIA officer contacted colleagues in Mann's department offering a $10,000 reward to any who would provide dirt on him, "confidentiality assured." Soon after, Mann asserts, a think tank called the

National Center for Public Policy Research led a campaign to get Mann's National Science Foundation grants revoked. As Mann recounts in his book *The Hockey Stick and the Climate Wars,* two conservative nonprofit law firms, the Southeastern Legal Foundation and the Landmark Legal Foundation, brought legal actions aimed at him. The think tank and the two law firms were funded by combinations of the same small constellation of family fortunes through their private charitable foundations. Omnipresent were Bradley, Olin, and Scaife.

Charles Koch's foundation also was engaged in piling on. It helped subsidize the Landmark Legal Foundation. The Kochs evidently admired Landmark's president, Mark Levin, a longtime associate of the former attorney general Edwin Meese III. In 2010, Americans for Prosperity hired Levin to promote it on his nationally syndicated talk radio show, thereby copying the deal that FreedomWorks had struck with Glenn Beck. Levin was a curious choice of spokesman for the buttoned-down, erudite Koch brothers. His style was incendiary, even rude. He later called Kenneth Vogel, the *Politico* reporter who broke the news of the deal with Americans for Prosperity, "a vicious S.O.B." and told a female caller, "I don't know why your husband doesn't put a gun to his temple. Get the Hell out of here!" His attacks on Obama's policies were similarly heated, particularly regarding climate change. He said Mann "and the other advocates of man-made global warming" did not "know how to conduct a correct statistical analysis" and accused "enviro-statists" of inventing global warming in order to justify a tyrannical government takeover. Their "pursuit," he claimed, "after all, is power, not truth."

An especially grave attack on Mann's livelihood was launched, meanwhile, by yet another group, the Commonwealth Foundation for Public Policy Alternatives in Harrisburg, Pennsylvania. The self-described think tank belonged to a national web of similar conservative organizations known as the State Policy Network. Much of Commonwealth's financial support came through DonorsTrust and Donors Capital Fund, making it impossible to identify the individual backers. But because it was based in Scaife's home state, Commonwealth had particularly deep ties to his family foundations. Michael Gleba, the chair of Commonwealth's board of directors, was also the president of the Sarah Scaife Foundation and treasurer of Scaife's Carthage Foundation and a trustee of both. This arrangement gave Commonwealth unusual clout, particularly over Pennsylvania's state legislature.

The Pennsylvania think tank waged a campaign to get Mann fired and successfully lobbied Republican allies in the legislature to threaten to withhold Penn State's funding until the university took "appropriate action" against Mann. With the public university's finances held hostage, it agreed to investigate Mann. Meanwhile, the think tank ran a campaign of attack ads against him in the university's daily newspaper, as well as helping to organize an anti-Mann campus protest.

"It was nerve-racking to be under that pressure at Penn State," recalls Mann. "There were these nebulous accusations based on stolen e-mails. Ordinarily, it would have been clear there were no grounds for investigation. But it was promoted by the Commonwealth Foundation, which seems to almost have a stranglehold on Republicans in the state legislature. I knew I had done nothing wrong, but there was this uncertain future hanging over me. There was so much political pressure being brought to bear on Penn State I wasn't sure if they'd cave."

In the meantime, death threats began appearing in Mann's in-box. "I tried to shield my family as much as I could," he says. But this became impossible when one day he opened a suspicious-looking letter without thinking, only to have it release a cloud of white powder into his office. Fearing anthrax, he called the campus police. Soon the FBI quarantined his office behind crime tape, disrupting the whole department.

The powder turned out to be harmless, but, Mann recalls, "it was a spectacle. There was a point where I had the hotline number for the chief of police on our fridge, in case my wife saw anything unusual. It felt like there was a very calibrated campaign of vilification to the extent where the crazies might go after us."

It was particularly disturbing to Mann that there appeared to be overlap between hard-core climate change deniers and Second Amendment enthusiasts, whipped up, he came to believe, by "cynical special interests." Mann says, "The disaffected, the people who have trouble putting dinner on the table, were being misled into believing that action on climate change meant that 'They' want to take away your freedom and probably your guns, too. There was a very skillful campaign to indoctrinate them," he said. "We've seen Second Amendment enthusiasts take action against abortion doctors. There's an attempt to paint us as villains in the same way."

He was not alone in receiving death threats. Several climatologists, he said, including Phil Jones, director of the hacked Climatic Research Unit in Great Britain, felt compelled to hire personal bodyguards. "Luckily," Mann relates, both the Penn State investigations—which the legislature required to be done a second time in greater depth—and another one by the inspector general of the National Science Foundation, essentially the highest scientific body in the United States, exonerated Mann. "It lasted two years. It came out well. But two years is a long time," he says. "I never imagined I'd be at the center of some contentious debate. It's not why you study what I did. What worries me," he adds, "is that this circus-like atmosphere may have scared off many young scientists. It actually has a chilling effect. It prevents scientists from participating in the public discourse, because they fear they, or their department head, will be threatened."

By the time Mann's scientific research was upheld, underscoring his integrity as well as the genuine danger posed by climate change, it hardly mattered. By then, the percentage of Americans who believed the world was warming had dropped a precipitous fourteen points from 2008. Almost half of those polled by Gallup in 2010—48 percent—believed that fears of global warming were "generally exaggerated," the highest numbers since the polling firm first posed the question more than a decade before. Watching from afar, Mann could see no cause for the United States to move in the opposite direction from science other than money. "In the scientific community, the degree of confidence in climate change is rising," he said. "In the public, it's either steady or falling. There's a divergence. That wedge is what the industry has bought."

Although the cap-and-trade bill moved to the Senate, it was already dead. At first, Lindsey Graham, the independent-minded Republican from South Carolina, took a courageous leadership role in the fight, offering to co-sponsor the legislation with the Democrat John Kerry and the Independent Joe Lieberman after declaring, to the surprise and delight of environmentalists, "I have come to conclude that greenhouse gases and carbon pollution" are "not a good thing."

Graham, however, feared pressure from his right flank. He warned the Democrats that they had to move fast, before Fox News caught wind of the process. As he feared, in April 2010, Fox News attacked him for backing a "gas tax." A vitriolic Tea Party activist immediately held a press conference in his home state denouncing him as "gay," and a political front group called American Solutions launched a negative campaign against him for his climate stance in South Carolina. American Solutions, it later turned out, was funded by huge fossil fuel and other corporate interests, many of whom were in the Koch fold. Among them were Larry Nichols of Devon Energy,

Dick Farmer of Cintas, Stan Hubbard of Hubbard Broadcasting, and Sheldon Adelson, chairman of the Las Vegas Sands Corporation. Within days of the drubbing, Graham withdrew from the process. Harry Reid, the Democratic majority leader from Nevada, dealt the final blow to the cap-and-trade bill. Facing a tough reelection himself and worried about making Democrats walk the plank for the bill, he refused after Graham backed out to bring the legislation to the Senate floor for a vote.

Opponents of climate change reform got their wish. "Gridlock is the greatest friend a global warming skeptic has, because that's all you really want," Morano later acknowledged. "There's no legislation we're championing. We're the negative force. We are just trying to stop stuff."

Asked why the climate legislation failed, Al Gore told *The New Yorker*'s Ryan Lizza, "The influence of special interests is now at an extremely unhealthy level. It's at a point," he said, "where it's virtually impossible for participants in the current political system to enact any significant change without first seeking and gaining permission from the largest commercial interests who are most affected by the proposed change."

As the first legislation aimed at addressing climate change sputtered out, the Massey mine in West Virginia collapsed in a methane explosion, killing twenty-nine miners. Soon after, a leak from the Deepwater Horizon oil rig in the Gulf of Mexico triggered the largest accidental oil spill in history, killing and causing birth defects in record numbers of marine animals. A grand jury would charge the owner of the Upper Big Branch mine with criminally conspiring to evade safety regulations, while a federal judge would find the oil rig's principal owner, British Petroleum, guilty of gross negligence and reckless conduct.

Meanwhile, the amount of carbon dioxide in the atmosphere was already above the level that scientists said risked causing runaway global warming. Obama acknowledged at this point that he knew “the votes may not be there right now,” but, he vowed, “I intend to find them in the coming months.” The conservative money machine, however, was already far ahead of him on an audacious new plan to try to ensure that he would never succeed.

CHAPTER NINE

Money Is Speech: The Long Road to *Citizens United*

ON MAY 17, 2010, A BLACK-TIE AUDIENCE AT THE METROPOLITAN Opera House in New York City applauded as a tall, jovial-looking billionaire loped to the stage. It was the seventieth annual spring gala of American Ballet Theatre, and David Koch was being honored for his generosity as a member of the board of trustees. A longtime admirer of classical ballet, he had recently donated $2.5 million toward the company's upcoming season and had given many millions before that. As Koch received a token award, he was flanked by two of the gala's co-chairs, the socialite Blaine Trump, in a peach-colored gown, and the political scion Caroline Kennedy Schlossberg, in emerald green. Kennedy's mother, Jacqueline Kennedy Onassis, had been a patron of the ballet and, coincidentally, the previous owner of a Fifth Avenue apartment that Koch had bought in 1995 and then sold eleven years later for $32 million, having found it too small.

The gala marked the official arrival of Koch as one of New York's most prominent philanthropists. At the age of seventy, he was recognized for an impressive history of giving. In 2008, he donated $100 million to modernize Lincoln Center's New York State Theatre building, which now bore his name. He had given $20 million to the American Museum of Natural History, whose dinosaur wing was named for him. That spring, after noticing the decrepit state of the fountains outside the Metropolitan Museum of Art, he pledged at least $10 million for their renovation. He was a trustee of the museum, perhaps the most coveted social prize in the city, and served on the board of Memorial Sloan Kettering Cancer Center, where, after he donated more than $40 million, an endowed chair and a research center were named for him.

One dignitary was conspicuously absent from the gala: the event's third honorary co-chair, Michelle Obama. Her office said that a scheduling conflict had prevented her from attending. In New York philanthropic circles, though, David Koch was a celebrity in his own right. With the help of a bevy of public relations advisers, he had sculpted an impressive public image. One associate said Koch had confided that he gave away approximately 40 percent of his income each year, which he estimated at about $1 billion. This of course left him with an annual income of some $600 million and considerably helped ease his tax burden, but he enjoyed the role, a family member said, in part because it bought him respectability. There was another side to his spending, however, that was then still largely secret. While David was happy to put his name on some of the country's most esteemed and beloved cultural and scientific institutions and to take a public bow at the ballet, his family's prodigious political spending was a much more private affair.

It would in fact take years before the faint outlines of the Kochs' massive political machinations began to surface through required public tax filings, and the full story may never be known. But a decision by the Supreme Court four months earlier in a case that began over a dispute about a right-wing attack on Hillary Clinton had already launched the family's covert spending into a new, more electorally ambitious phase. At the moment that David Koch took the stage in New York, operatives working for his brother and himself were quietly converting thirty years' worth of ideological institution building into a machine that would resemble, and rival, those of the two major political parties. Rather than representing broad-based support, however, theirs was financed by a tiny fraction of the wealthiest families in America, who could now, should they wish, spend their entire fortunes influencing the country's politics.

On January 21, 2010, the Court announced its 5–4 decision in the *Citizens United* case, overturning a century of restrictions banning corporations and unions from spending all they wanted to elect candidates. The Court held that so long as businesses and unions didn't just hand their money to the candidates, which could be corrupt, but instead gave it to outside groups that were supporting or opposing the candidates and were technically independent of the campaigns, they could spend unlimited amounts to promote whatever candidates they chose. To reach the verdict, the Court accepted the argument that corporations had the same rights to free speech as citizens.

The ruling paved the way for a related decision by an appeals court in a case called *SpeechNow*, which soon after overturned limits on how much money individuals could give to outside groups too. Previously, contributions to political action committees, or PACs, had been capped at $5,000 per person per year. But now the court found that there could be no donation limits so long as there was no coordination with the candidates' campaigns. Soon, the groups set up to take the unlimited contributions were dubbed super PACs for their augmented new powers.

In both cases, the courts embraced the argument that independent spending, as opposed to direct contributions to the candidates, wouldn't result in corruption. From the start, critics like Richard Posner, a brilliant and iconoclastic conservative federal judge, declared the Court had reasoned "naively," pointing out that it was "difficult to see what practical difference there is between super PAC donations and direct campaign donations, from a corruption standpoint." The immediate impact, as the *New Yorker* writer Jeffrey Toobin summarized it, was that "it gave rich people more or less free rein to spend as much as they want in support of their favored candidates."

Among the few remaining restraints that the majority of

the Court endorsed was the long-standing expectation that any spending in a political campaign should be visible to the public. Justice Anthony Kennedy, who wrote the majority opinion, predicted that "with the advent of the Internet, prompt disclosure of expenditures" would be easier than ever. This, he suggested, would prevent corruption because "citizens can see whether elected officials are 'in the pocket' of so-called moneyed interests."

The assumption soon proved wrong. Instead, as critics had warned, more and more of the money flooding into elections was spent by secretive nonprofit organizations that claimed the right to conceal their donors' identities. Rich activists such as Scaife and the Kochs had already paved the way to weaponize philanthropy. Now they and other allied donors gave what came to be called dark money to nonprofit "social welfare" groups that claimed the right to spend on elections without disclosing their donors. As a result, the American political system became awash in unlimited, untraceable cash.

In striking down the existing campaign-finance laws, the courts eviscerated a century of reform. After a series of campaign scandals involving secret donations from the newly rich industrial barons in the late nineteenth and early twentieth centuries, Progressives had passed laws limiting spending in order to protect the democratic process from corruption. The laws were meant to safeguard political equality at a time of growing economic inequality. Reformers had seen the concentration of wealth in the hands of oil, steel, finance, and railroad magnates as threatening the democratic equilibrium. The Republican William McKinley's elections in 1896 and 1900, for instance, were infamously lubricated by donations raised by the political organizer Mark Hanna from big corporations like Rockefeller's Standard Oil. In a growing backlash to the corruption, at President Theodore Roosevelt's behest, Congress passed the Tillman Act in 1907, which banned corporate contributions to federal candidates and political committees. Later scandals resulted in further restrictions limiting spending by unions and the size of individual contributions, and requiring public disclosure. By overturning many of these restrictions, the *Citizens United* decision was in many respects a return to the Gilded Age.

Justice John Paul Stevens, a moderate Republican when first appointed but long part of the court's liberal wing, described the decision as "a radical departure from what has been settled First Amendment law." In a lengthy dissent, he argued that the Constitution's framers had enshrined the right of free speech for "individual Americans, not corporations," and that to act otherwise was "a rejection of the common sense of the American people who have recognized the need to prevent corporations from undermining self-government since the founding, and who have fought against the distinctive corrupting potential of corporate electioneering since the days of Theodore Roosevelt." Memorably, Stevens added, "While American democracy is imperfect, few outside the majority of this Court would have thought its flaws included a dearth of corporate money in politics."

Most analyses attributed the about-face on these vital rules guaranteeing fair elections to the increasingly assertive conservatism of Chief Justice John Roberts's Court. Clearly, this was the decisive factor. But there was a backstory, too.

For almost four decades, a tiny coterie of ultrarich activists who wished to influence American politics by spending more than the laws would allow had been chafing at the legal restraints. One family had been particularly tireless in the struggle, the DeVos clan of Michigan. The family, whose members became stalwarts in the Kochs' donor network, had made a multibillion-dollar fortune from a remarkable American business success, the Amway direct-marketing empire.

Founded in 1959 by two boyhood friends, Richard DeVos Sr. and Jay Van Andel, in Ada, Michigan, a suburb of Grand Rapids, it sold household products door-to-door while preaching the gospel of wealth with cultlike fervor. Over time, the private company grew into a marketing behemoth, generating revenues of nearly $11 billion a year by 2011.

The DeVoses were devout members of the Dutch Reformed Church, a renegade branch of Calvinism brought to America by Dutch immigrants, many of whom settled around Lake Michigan. By the 1970s, the church had become a vibrant and, some would say, vitriolic center of the Christian Right. Members crusaded against abortion, homosexuality, feminism, and modern science that conflicted with their teachings. Extreme free-market economic theories rejecting government intervention and venerating hard work and success in the Calvinist tradition were also embraced by many followers. Within this community of extreme views, no family was more extreme or more active than the DeVoses. They were less well-known outside Michigan than some of the other founding families of the conservative movement, but few played a bigger role as its bankrollers. Among the many causes they supported was the Koch donor network. Although their views on social issues were considerably more reactionary than those of the Kochs, they ardently shared the brothers' antipathy toward regulations and taxes.

Amway in fact was structured to avoid federal taxes. DeVos and Van Andel achieved this by defining the door-to-door salesmen who sold their beauty, cleaning, and dietary products as "independent business owners" rather than employees. This enabled the company's owners to skip Social Security contributions and other employee benefits, greatly enhancing their bottom line. It resulted, however, in numerous legal skirmishes with the Internal Revenue Service and the Federal Trade Commission (FTC). In a charge that was later dropped, the government alleged that the company was little more than a pyramid scheme built upon misleading promises of riches to prospective distributors, many of whom bought its products in bulk, found themselves unable to sell them, and so were forced to cover their debts by recruiting additional distributors.

The gray zone in which the company operated made its cultivation of political influence important. In 1975, after Grand Rapids's Republican congressman Gerald R. Ford became president, the usefulness of political clout became particularly apparent. While the Federal Trade Commission investigation was ongoing, DeVos and Van Andel obtained a lengthy meeting with Ford in the Oval Office. Two of Ford's top aides, soon after, became investors in a new venture founded by DeVos and Van Andel. After news of their involvement surfaced, the White House aides dropped out, but Amway later hired one of them as a Washington lobbyist. Meanwhile, perhaps coincidentally, the FTC investigation into whether Amway was an illegal pyramid scheme fizzled, resulting only in the company having its knuckles rapped for misleading advertising about how much its distributors could earn.

The company's political activism was so unusually intense that one FTC attorney at the time told *Forbes*, "They're not a business, but some sort of quasi-religious sociopolitical organization." Indeed as Kim Phillips-Fein writes in *Invisible Hands*, "Amway was much more than a simple direct-marketing firm. It was an organization devoted with missionary zeal to the very idea of free enterprise."

There were legal limits, however, to how much the DeVoses could spend on elections. In 1974, after the Watergate scandal, Congress set new contribution limits and established the public financing of presidential campaigns. Opponents struggled to find ways around the new rules. In 1976, they partly succeeded when the Supreme Court, judging a case brought by a Republican Senate candidate, William F. Buckley Jr.'s brother James, struck down limits on "independent expenditures."

This opened what became an ever-expanding opportunity for big donors.

In 1980, Richard DeVos and Jay Van Andel led the way in "independent expenditures," becoming the top spenders on behalf of Ronald Reagan's presidential candidacy. By 1981, their titles reflected their growing clout. Richard DeVos was the finance chair of the Republican National Committee (RNC), while Jay Van Andel headed the U.S. Chamber of Commerce. In Washington, the pair cut a swath, hosting lavish parties on the Amway yacht, which was docked on the Potomac River, attended by Republican big shots and dignitaries from the dozen countries in which Amway operated. DeVos, the son of a poor Dutch immigrant, appeared as if dressed by a Hollywood costume department, flashing a pinkie ring and driving a Rolls-Royce.

The flood of money from Amway's founders failed, though, to quash an investigation by the Canadian government into a tax-fraud scheme in which both DeVos and Van Andel were criminally charged in 1982. The scandal exploded when Kitty McKinsey and Paul Magnusson, then reporters for the *Detroit Free Press,* shocked readers accustomed to DeVos and Van Andel's professions of patriotism and religiosity with an exposé tracing an elaborate, thirteen-year-long tax scam directly to the bosses' offices. At its highest levels, they revealed, Amway had secretly authorized a scheme creating dummy invoices to deceive Canadian customs officials into accepting falsely low valuations on products the company imported into Canada. Amway had thus fraudulently lowered its tax bills by $26.4 million from 1965 until 1978.

Amway denounced the news reports and threatened to file a $500 million libel suit against the *Free Press.* But the next year, the company released a terse statement announcing that it had pleaded guilty to defrauding the Canadian government and would pay a $20 million fine. In exchange, the plea agreement called for criminal charges to be dropped against four of the company's top executives, including DeVos and Van Andel. In 1989, Amway paid an additional $38 million to settle a related civil suit.

DeVos was soon dethroned as the RNC's finance chair. His standing hadn't been helped by his reference to the brutal 1982 economic recession as a welcome "cleansing process" or by his insistence that he'd never seen an unemployed person who wanted to work. Top donors were also put off by his attempts to transform RNC meetings into patriotic pep rallies akin to those run for Amway salesmen. DeVos would call wealthy contributors to the stage and ask, "Why are you proud to be an American?" A longtime Republican activist told *The Washington Post,* "We were losing contributions and that was the last straw."

The DeVos family nonetheless remained huge financiers of the Republican Party and the growing conservative movement, as well as sponsoring efforts to undo campaign-finance laws. Starting in 1970, they began to direct at least $200 million into virtually every branch of the New Right's infrastructure, from think tanks like the Heritage Foundation to academic organizations such as the Intercollegiate Studies Institute, which funded conservative publications on college campuses. "There's not a Republican president or presidential candidate in the last fifty years who hasn't known the DeVoses," Saul Anuzis, a former chairman of the Michigan Republican Party, said.

The DeVoses were also deeply involved in the secretive Council for National Policy, described by *The New York Times* as "a little-known club of a few hundred of the most powerful conservatives in the country," which it said "met behind closed doors in undisclosed locations for a confidential conference" three times a year. Membership lists were secret, but among the names tied to the organization were Jerry Falwell, Phyllis Schlafly, Pat Robertson, and Wayne LaPierre of the National Rifle Association (NRA). There was overlap with a number of other participants in the Koch seminars, too, including Foster Friess, the multimillionaire founder of a Wyoming mutual fund, Friess Associates, who had collaborated politically with the Kochs at least since the 1996 election, when they both channeled money into Triad Management to surreptitiously fund attack ads. Charles Koch accepted an award from the Council for National Policy but was not a member of the group. It was, in Richard DeVos's phrase, a place that brought together "the doers with the donors."

If anything, the DeVos family's brushes with the law merely emboldened them. During the 1994 midterm elections, Amway gave $2.5 million to the Republican Party, which was the largest known soft money donation from a corporation in the country's history. In 1996, clean-government groups criticized the family for skirting campaign contribution limits by also donating $1.3 million to the San Diego tourist bureau to help air the Republican National Convention there that year.

By then, Richard DeVos Sr. had bought the NBA's Orlando Magic and had passed the management of Amway on to his son Richard junior, who was known as Dick. The younger DeVos shared his father's political and religious views. But he was a pragmatist when it came to business, expanding the zealously free-market company deeply into China. By 2006, fully a third of Amway's revenue came from the Communist state.

The DeVos family's stature and wealth were magnified by Dick's marriage to the other royal family of Michigan's Dutch Reformed community, Betsy Prince. Her father, Edgar Prince, had founded an auto parts manufacturing company that sold for $1.35 billion in cash in 1996. Her brother Erik Prince, meanwhile, founded the global security firm Blackwater, which the reporter Jeremy Scahill described as "the world's most powerful mercenary army."

Betsy DeVos, who eventually became the chairwoman of Michigan's Republican Party, was said to be every bit as politically ambitious as her husband, if not more so. With her support, in 2002 Dick DeVos ceased managing Amway in order to devote more time to his political career. The results, though, were dismal. The DeVos family spent over $2 million in 2000 on a Michigan school voucher referendum that was defeated by 68 percent of the voters. The family then spent $35 million in 2006 on Dick DeVos's unsuccessful bid to become the state's governor.

In their zeal to implement their conservative vision, few issues were more central to the DeVos family's mission than eradicating restraints on political spending. For years, the family funded legal challenges to various campaign-finance laws. Ground zero in this fight was the James Madison Center for Free Speech, of which Betsy DeVos became a founding board member in 1997. The nonprofit organization's sole goal was to end all legal restrictions on money in politics. Its honorary chairman was Senator Mitch McConnell, a savvy and prodigious fund-raiser.

Conservatives cast their opposition to campaign-finance restrictions as a principled defense of free speech, but McConnell, who was one of the cause's biggest champions, had occasionally revealed a more partisan motive. As a Republican running for office in Kentucky in the 1970s, when it was almost solidly Democratic, he once admitted "a spending edge is the only thing that gives a Republican a chance to compete." He had once opened a college class by writing on the blackboard the three ingredients that he felt were necessary to build a political party: "Money, money, money." In a Senate debate on proposed campaign-finance restrictions, McConnell reportedly told colleagues, "If we stop this thing, we can control the institution for the next twenty years."

The James Madison Center aimed to make this dream a reality by taking the fight to the courts. In addition to the DeVos family, early donors included several of the most powerful groups on the right, such as the Christian Coalition and the NRA. But the driving force behind the organization was a single-minded lawyer from Terre Haute, Indiana, James

Bopp Jr., who was general counsel to the anti-abortion National Right to Life Committee. Bopp also became the Madison Center's general counsel.

In fact, Bopp's law firm and the James Madison Center had the same office address and phone number, and although Bopp listed himself as an outside contractor to the center, virtually every dollar from donors went to his firm. By designating itself a nonprofit charitable group, though, the Madison Center enabled the DeVos Family Foundation and other supporters to take tax deductions for subsidizing long-shot lawsuits that might never have been attempted otherwise. "The relationship between this organization and Bopp's law firm is such that there really is no charity," observed Marcus Owens, a Washington lawyer who formerly oversaw tax-exempt groups for the Internal Revenue Service. "I've never heard of this sort of captive charity/foundation funding of a particular law firm before."

In 1997, the same year that she helped found the Madison Center, Betsy DeVos explained her opposition to campaign-finance restrictions. At the time, there was a national outcry against the way both the Democratic and the Republican Parties had evaded contribution limits in the 1996 presidential campaign by paying for what they claimed were "issue" ads rather than campaign ads, with unlimited funds that came to be known as soft money. There was a bipartisan Senate push for reform. But in a guest column in the Capitol Hill newspaper *Roll Call,* DeVos defended the unlimited contributions.

"Soft money," she wrote, was just "hard-earned American dollars that Big Brother has yet to find a way to control. That is all it is, nothing more." She added, "I know a little something about soft money, as my family is the largest single contributor of soft money to the national Republican Party." She said, "I have decided, however, to stop taking offense at the suggestion that we are buying influence. Now I simply concede the point. They are right. We do expect some things in return. We expect to foster a conservative governing philosophy consisting of limited government and respect for traditional American virtues. We expect a return on our investment; we expect a good and honest government. Furthermore, we expect the Republican Party to use the money to promote these policies, and yes, to win elections. People like us," she concluded archly, "must surely be stopped."

Most of the big donors fighting the campaign-finance restrictions were conservatives, but a few extraordinarily rich liberal Democrats belonged to this rarefied club, too. In 2004, Democratic-aligned outside groups spent $185 million—more than twice what the Republican outside groups spent—in a failed effort to defeat George W. Bush's reelection. Of this, $85 million came from just fourteen Democratic donors. Leading the pack was the New York hedge fund magnate George Soros, an opponent of the U.S. invasion of Iraq who regarded President Bush as such a scourge that he vowed he would spend his entire $7 billion fortune to defeat him, if the result could be guaranteed. With the help of Democratic operatives, Soros funneled more than $27 million into the outside spending vehicle of choice that year, known as 527 groups. It was the same year that Republicans used the same mechanism to fund the "Swift Boat" attacks on John Kerry. Prior to *Citizens United,* such schemes were legally dubious at best. The Federal Election Commission ruled that the gargantuan outside spending schemes violated campaign-finance laws and imposed hefty fines on both the Democratic and the Republican perpetrators. Afterward, Soros remained active in ideological philanthropy, spending hundreds of millions to support a network of human rights and civil liberties groups, but he largely withdrew from spectacular campaign contributions.

If the DeVoses expected a "return on our investment" in the Madison Center, as Betsy had put it, they got one in the Supreme Court's *Citizens United* decision. It "was really Jim

[Bopp]'s brainchild," Richard L. Hasen, an expert on election law at Loyola Law School in Los Angeles told *The New York Times*. "He has manufactured these cases to present certain questions to the Supreme Court in a certain order and achieve a certain result," said Hasen. "He is a litigation machine."

Bopp agreed. "We had a 10-year plan to take all this down," he told the *Times*. "And if we do it right, I think we can pretty well dismantle the entire regulatory regime that is called campaign finance law."

Such a statement would have seemed ludicrous just a few years earlier, and in fact, in the beginning, no one took Bopp seriously. With his shaggy gray Beatles haircut and his dogmatic legal style, not to mention his extreme views, he was literally laughed at by one federal judge. At the time, he was arguing that a hyperbolic film attacking Hillary Clinton, who was running for president, deserved the same First Amendment protection as newscasts aired by CBS's *60 Minutes*. The film, a screed called *Hillary: The Movie,* had been produced by Citizens United, an old right-wing group with a history of making vicious campaign ads. The question, as the Supreme Court interpreted it, was whether *Hillary: The Movie* was a protected form of speech or a corporate political donation by its backers, which could be regulated as a campaign donation.

Case by case, financed by wealthy donors who treated the cause as a tax-deductible charity, Bopp had battered away at the foundation of modern campaign-finance law. He had succeeded in part by using the liberals' language of civil rights and free speech against their own practices. The tactic was intentional. Clint Bolick, a pioneer in the conservative legal movement whose group, the Institute for Justice, had received start-up funds from Charles Koch, had argued that the Right needed to combat the Left by asserting appealing "counter-rights" of its own. Thus *Citizens United* was cast as the right of corporations to exercise their free speech. As conservatives had hoped, the argument disarmed and divided the Left, even attracting the support of traditionally liberal champions of the First Amendment.

While polls consistently showed that large majorities of the American public—both Republicans and Democrats—favored strict spending limits, the key challenges that led to dismantling the laws were initiated by an extraordinarily rich minority: the Kochs and their clique of ultra-wealthy conservative activists.

A close look at the *SpeechNow* case, for instance, the lower-court decision following quickly on the heels of *Citizens United,* leads right back to the same people. There was no organization called SpeechNow until several libertarian activists invented it solely for the purpose of challenging the spending limits. The suit was the brainchild of Eric O'Keefe, among others, the Wisconsin investor who had been a libertarian ally of the Kochs since working in David's 1980 vice presidential campaign, which called for the end of campaign spending limits.

Leading the suit was Bradley Smith, a bright and radically antiregulatory lawyer who co-founded the conservative Center for Competitive Politics. He was a proponent of zero public disclosure of political spending and didn't disclose his funders, but IRS records showed that in 2009 his center enjoyed support from several conservative foundations, including the Bradley Foundation. Smith's career illustrated the way that the fortunes of conservative philanthropists cultivated and nurtured talent like his. He had been a scholar at Charles Koch's Institute for Humane Studies before becoming the most outspoken foe of finance restrictions ever to chair the Federal Election Commission, the federal agency charged with policing campaign spending. His patrons for this key post were Mitch McConnell and the Cato Institute. As he acknowledged, "I would not have been an FEC commissioner if not for Cato's efforts to promote me on the Hill."

Also essential to the *SpeechNow* suit was the Institute for

Justice, the group founded with Charles Koch's seed money. The litigation, meanwhile, was underwritten heavily by Fred Young, a libertarian retiree in Wisconsin who made tens of millions of dollars by selling his father's firm, Young Radiator Company, after outsourcing the jobs of unionized workers to non-union states. Young served on the boards of the Koch-backed Reason Foundation and Cato Institute and was yet another regular attendee at the Kochs' donor summits.

In 2010, Young took full advantage of the newfound freedom to spend. He contributed 80 percent of the money spent that year by SpeechNow.org's super PAC, all of which paid for television ads targeting Wisconsin's Democratic senator Russ Feingold. Feingold was a particularly symbolic target. He had been the Senate's premier supporter of strict campaign spending laws. Standing on principle, he urged outside groups not to spend on his behalf. That fall, he went down to defeat.

In the view of defenders, *Citizens United* and its progeny did not represent the black-and-white contrast of progressives' nightmares so much as it clarified gray areas. But this alone was extremely important. By flashing a bright green light, the Supreme Court sent a message to the wealthy and their political operatives that when it came to raising and spending money, they now could act with impunity. Both the legal fog and the political stigma lifted.

Soon, the sums pledged at the Koch donor summits began to soar from the $13 million that Sean Noble raised in June 2009 to nearly $900 million at a single fund-raising session in the years that followed. "This Supreme Court decision essentially gave a Good Housekeeping seal of approval," acknowledged Steven Law, president of American Crossroads, the conservative super PAC formed by the Republican political operative Karl Rove soon after the *Citizens United* decision.

Critics, though, including Obama, saw the change as far more consequential. In his 2010 State of the Union address, Obama made headlines by denouncing the Court's decision, saying that it "reversed a century of law that I believe will open the floodgates for special interests—including foreign corporations—to spend without limit in our elections." In response, the associate Supreme Court justice Samuel Alito Jr., who attended the address, was seen shaking his head and mouthing the words "not true."

Another consequence was that the *Citizens United* decision shifted the balance of power from parties built on broad consensus to individuals who were wealthy and zealous enough to spend millions of dollars from their own funds. By definition, this empowered a tiny, atypical minority of the population.

"It unshackled the big money," David Axelrod contends. "*Citizens United* unleashed constant negativity, not just toward the president, but toward government generally. Presidents before have been under siege, but now there is no longer the presumption that they are acting in the public interest. There's a pernicious drumbeat." After the ruling, he said, "we felt under siege."

CHAPTER TEN

The Shellacking: Dark Money's Midterm Debut, 2010

AS DONORS GATHERED IN PALM SPRINGS AT THE END OF JANUary for the first Koch summit of 2010, the desert air was full of optimism. "It was just a week or two after the special election in Boston," one participant recalled. "Feeling was running pretty high."

A torrent of contributions from undisclosed donors had helped deliver the surprise election of Scott Brown in Massachusetts earlier that month, making him the first Republican elected to the Senate from the liberal state in thirty-eight years. Organizing much of the cash from behind the scenes had been Sean Noble, who was by then on the payroll of the Kochs. Early on, when many others dismissed Brown as a hopeless long shot, Noble had decided that the payoff would be so rich that backing him was worth the gamble. Brown's victory was calamitous for Obama. By filling the seat that had long been held by Ted Kennedy, the legendary Democrat who had died in August, Brown transformed the balance of power in Congress. The Democrats still held the majority in the Senate, but their loss of one seat crippled their power in one key way. Just as Obama was desperately trying to pass a final version of his health-care bill, it deprived the Democrats of the sixty-vote minimum necessary to overcome a Republican filibuster. The Democrats were left without the numbers necessary to bring the bill to a new vote. Brown's triumph appeared to be the Affordable Care Act's downfall.

Brown hadn't won without a lot of help. The numbers told part of the story. Although Brown was a low-profile Republican state senator best known for posing nude for *Cosmopoli-*

tan magazine, he had unexpectedly outspent his Democratic opponent, Martha Coakley, by roughly $8.7 million to $5.1 million during the six weeks after the primaries. An unusual amount of this, almost $3 million, had come from shadowy out-of-state nonprofit groups funded by undisclosed donors. Two of the most active of these dark-money groups, the American Future Fund and Americans for Job Security, had received large infusions of cash from the mysterious "social welfare" group that Noble had registered the spring before, based at an Arizona post office box. For months, the post office box otherwise known as the Center to Protect Patient Rights had been filling with fistfuls of secret cash from Randy Kendrick and other members of the Koch network in an uphill battle to stop the passage of the Affordable Care Act. Noble had redirected much of this money into the front groups spending against Coakley in the Massachusetts special election. The hope was that if Republicans could turn one Senate seat, they could block the health-care bill and mortally wound Obama. So when the plan worked, Brown's win electrified the donors. Many felt that they had personally turned the tide on Obamacare. "We thought we had it won!" the seminar participant recalled.

Obama had been so flummoxed by Brown's election that at a White House senior staff meeting the next morning he had beseeched his staff accusingly, demanding to know, "What's my narrative? I don't have a narrative!" His administration's momentum had been buried in outside money.

Lifting the donors' spirits further was the Supreme Court's *Citizens United* ruling, which had been handed down on January 21, two days after Scott Brown's victory in Massachusetts, and shortly before the Kochs' summit. Brown's race now seemed a promising dress rehearsal for even more outside money, which the Court had ennobled as free speech. So as the self-described "investors" came together to plan for the 2010 midterm elections, they were in a buoyant mood.

Sean Noble, looking dashing with a tan, had been elevated by then from merely moderating a panel at the June 2009 summit six months earlier to now speaking on one. His congressional staff job and unpaid student loans were remnants of the past. As the Web site of his political consulting firm proclaimed ebulliently, "It's not what you know but who you know."

The panel discussion was titled "The Opportunity of 2010: Understanding Voter Attitudes and the Electoral Map." Noble spoke optimistically about the health-care fight, which he believed had awakened a national rebellion. Joining him on the dais were three other men, each representing aspects of the underground political operation that would rout the Democrats in the year ahead.

The best known of the panelists was Ed Gillespie, a top national political tactician who had become the chairman of the Republican National Committee in 2003 at the age of forty-one. Gillespie had made a fortune in lobbying, estimated at as much as $19 million. He was a former Democrat, and the firm he co-founded, Quinn Gillespie & Associates, was bipartisan, more concerned with making deals than political purity. Its clients ranged from Enron, the huge energy company that went scandalously bust, to a health-care group promoting individual insurance mandates akin to those that Obama's opponents called treasonous. The son of an Irish immigrant, Gillespie, according to Capitol lore, had started out parking cars and worked his way up to the top of Washington's booming influence-peddling industry by dint of his easy affability and quick political instincts.

As soon as the Court handed down its *Citizens United* decision, Gillespie grasped its promise. Within weeks, he set out to Texas with his fellow Bush White House alumnus Karl Rove to pitch deep-pocketed oilmen at the Dallas Petroleum Club on a plan to fund a new kind of shadow political machine. Instead of giving just to the Republican Party or its candidates and having the size of their donations limited, the high rollers could now legally funnel limitless amounts of cash to "outside" organizations that Rove and Gillespie were about to create, the two operatives explained. These new groups would act as the privatized auxiliary force Rove had been dreaming of for years. Rove told the moneymen, "People call us a vast right-wing conspiracy, but we're really a half-assed right-wing conspiracy. Now," he emphasized, "it's time to get serious."

Even before the *Citizens United* decision, Gillespie had been busy. While many other conservatives were despondent during the early months of the Obama administration, when the president's approval ratings were stratospherically high, Gillespie had come up with an ingenious plan to exploit the only opening he could see. With Obama dominating Washington, Gillespie looked to the states. He knew that 2011 was a year in which many state legislatures would redraw the boundaries of their congressional districts based on a new census, a process that only took place once a decade. So he put together an ambitious strategy aimed at a Republican takeover of governorships and legislatures all across the country. Capturing them would enable Republicans to redraw their states' congressional districts in order to favor their candidates. While the mechanics of state legislative races were abstruse and deadly dull to most people, to Gillespie they were the key to a Republican comeback.

"It was all conceived sitting in Ed's office in Alexandria, Virginia . . . it was entirely his vision," Gillespie's associate Chris Jankowski later told *Politico*. "It seems like an obvious strategy now, but you have to turn back the clock to realize how demoralized we all were . . . He was saying, 'Here's something smart we can do.'"

Gillespie called the plan "REDMAP," an acronym for the Redistricting Majority Project. To implement it, he took over the Republican State Leadership Committee (RSLC), a nonprofit group that had previously functioned as a catchall bank account for corporations interested in influencing state laws. All he needed was enough money to put REDMAP into action. By the end of 2010, with the help of million-dollar donations from the tobacco companies Altria and Reynolds, as well as huge donations from Walmart, the pharmaceutical industry, and rich private donors like those at the Koch summit, the RSLC would have $30 million, three times its Democratic counterpart. "It was three yards and a cloud of dust," Gillespie later recalled of his scramble for money. "It was a constant working, and working, and working," especially at honeypots like the Koch summit.

Joining the panel with Noble and Gillespie was a short, balding figure with a seemingly inexhaustible command of political minutiae. With his North Carolina drawl and his glasses slipping down his nose, he might be mistaken for a southern shop clerk. But James Arthur "Art" Pope was actually a shop *owner,* in fact the multimillionaire chairman and CEO of Variety Wholesalers, a family-owned discount-store conglomerate with hundreds of outlets stretching up and down the mid-Atlantic and the South. Pope was also a charter member of the Koch network. A longtime friend and ally, he shared Charles's passion for free-market philosophy and credited a summer program he attended at the Cato Institute with exposing him to conservative icons like Hayek and Ayn Rand. After graduating from the Duke School of Law in 1981 and taking over his family's private company, he began to transform the Pope family foundation, which had assets of nearly $150 million, into a remarkable political force.

In the previous decade, Pope and his family and the family foundation had spent more than $40 million in efforts to push American politics to the right. In addition to regularly attending the Kochs' secret planning summits, he served on the board of the Kochs' main public advocacy group, Americans for Prosperity, as he had on its predecessor, Citizens for a Sound Economy, and had joined forces with the brothers on numerous other political enterprises. Tax records showed that Pope had given money to at least twenty-seven of the groups supported by the Kochs, including organizations opposing environmental regulations, tax increases, unions, and campaign spending limits. Pope, like the DeVos family, was a supporter of the James Madison Center for Free Speech. Indeed, Pope's role in his home state of North Carolina was in many respects a state-sized version of the Kochs' role nationally. While he wasn't well-known outside the state, his growing influence at home had led the Raleigh *News & Observer* to begin calling him "the Knight of the Right."

What Pope brought to the panel that weekend was the chance for donors to help him turn North Carolina into a laboratory for REDMAP. Historically, North Carolina had been a pivotal swing state. It was both the face of the New South and the stomping ground of Jesse Helms's race-baiting National Congressional Club. But Obama had carried it narrowly in 2008 and remained popular in 2010. Democrats also dominated the state legislature; the Republicans hadn't controlled both houses of the North Carolina General Assembly for more than a hundred years. "Not since General Sherman," the joke went. Winning a legislative majority in 2010 wouldn't be easy. But no one was better situated than Pope to make it happen. He both was a master of arcane election law and had a fortune that few individuals could match. But like the Kochs and the DeVoses, he had had little luck over the years persuading voters to follow his lead. While he had served in the state legislature in North Carolina, he had been soundly defeated when he ran for lieutenant governor in 1992, his one bid for statewide office. "He was a terrible candidate," recalled Bob Geary, a political reporter for the *Indy Week,* an alternative newspaper in Durham, who covered the race. "I've never seen him smile. He was very introverted and pedantic." With the precision he was known for, Pope admitted, "I'm not a charismatic stump speaker."

Flipping the state would require political artistry and some guile. For this, the panel turned to its fourth member, Jim Ellis. The Kochs were notoriously picky about who received coveted invitations to their summits but didn't seem to mind that he was under indictment at the time for violating campaign-finance regulations. Ellis, an old friend of Noble's, was there to make predictions about the outcome of the 2010 races, but he had other specialties too.

Ellis had a history of creating fake movements in support of unpopular corporations and causes. In the 1990s, he had headed a company called Ramhurst, which documents revealed to be a covert public relations arm of R. J. Reynolds, the giant tobacco company. Under his guidance, Ramhurst organized deceptively homegrown-looking "smokers' rights" protests against proposed regulations and taxes on tobacco. In 1994 alone, R. J. Reynolds funneled $2.6 million to Ramhurst to deploy operatives who mobilized what they called "partisans" to stage protests against the Clinton health-care proposal, which would have imposed a stiff tax on cigarette sales. Anti-health-care rallies that year echoed with cries of "Go back to Russia!"

If the outbursts bore a striking resemblance to those against Obama's health-care proposal fifteen years later, it may be because the same political operatives were involved in both. Two of Ellis's former top aides at Ramhurst, Doug Goodyear and Tom Synhorst, went on in 1996 to form DCI Group, the public relations firm that was helping Noble foment Tea Party protests against the Affordable Care Act.

Ellis, meanwhile, had moved into the heart of Washington's Republican money stream. He became what some news reports described as the "right-hand man" to Tom DeLay, the powerful House Republican leader from Texas who was infamous for his "K Street operation," which serviced corporate lobbyists while shaking them down for campaign contributions. DeLay made him executive director of his political action committee. The duo's high-handed approach resulted in both men getting indicted for campaign-finance violations in 2005. In time, DeLay's conviction was overturned, but Ellis was less lucky. In 2012, he pleaded guilty to a single felony count and paid a fine. Undaunted, he airbrushed DeLay's name from his corporate résumé and kept on. Asked about his career in manufacturing protests for pay, Ellis sounded untroubled. "The grass roots was designed to give people the right to exercise their voice," he said with a shrug. As he addressed the big donors on the "opportunity of 2010," Ellis's legal status was uncertain, but his acquaintance with politics' seamier side was beyond doubt.

The donors left Palm Springs optimistic about 2010, inspired by Noble and the other members of his panel, but their elation over killing Obamacare soon proved premature. "The assumption in Washington and everywhere else was that when they got Scott Brown, it was the death knell for health care," Axelrod recalled. "The guy who wouldn't accept that was Obama. He said, 'We're going to do this underground and find a path.'"

The Democrats eventually came up with a plan to get the bill through. The House would approve the version that had already passed the Senate with sixty votes in December. Then the Senate would use a parliamentary maneuver that would require only fifty-one votes to add modifications—circumventing the threat of a Republican filibuster. Despite widespread skepticism, by mid-March the tenacious House Speaker, Nancy Pelosi, was on the verge of success.

As passage looked increasingly likely, Tea Party protests grew ever more ugly. Behind them, invisible to the public, was the Kochs' money. Tim Phillips, the head of Americans for Prosperity, popped up as the organizer of a March 16 "Kill the Bill" protest on Capitol Hill, at which he accused the Democrats of "trying to cram this 2,000-page bill down the throat of the American people!" At a second Capitol Hill rally a few days later, protesters spat on a passing Democratic congressman; mocked Barney Frank, a gay representative from Massachusetts, in lisping catcalls as a "faggot"; and shouted racist epithets at three black congressmen, John Lewis, Emanuel Cleaver, and Jim Clyburn.

Nonetheless, on March 21, amid mounting excitement, the House's scoreboard registered 216 votes for Obama's Affordable Care Act, the exact number needed to pass the legislation. Spontaneous chants of "Yes we can!" and "Yes we did!" on the House floor evoked election-night euphoria. That night, Obama and his staff held a rare celebration on the Truman Balcony of the White House, but the president suspected political payback wasn't going to wait long. As he raised a champagne flute to his political director, Patrick Gaspard, he cracked, "You know they're gonna kick our asses over this."

Downtown, in the Washington office space that Sean Noble shared with several other Koch operatives, Obama's premonitions proved correct. Shortly after the House passed the Affordable Care Act, Noble and his partners studied the vote numbers closely. The glimmer of a new plan formed. They agreed that what they had to do now was to take the political organization they had built to fight the health-care plan and use it to take over the legislative body that had just given Obama his greatest victory.

"We made a deliberate recommendation that you gotta focus on the House," Noble later told *National Review*. "That's where this bill passed. Pelosi broke so many arms of Democrats that had no business voting for that bill. Obamacare clearly was the watershed moment that provided the juice to deliver the majority back to the Republicans in the House."

Few knew it, but for all intents and purposes a midterm election like no other had begun. Noble spent most of April on the road, talking with Charles Koch, Rich Fink, Randy Kendrick, and others in the network to plan the operational details.

David Koch was more of an afterthought, or as one participant put it, he was very much the younger brother. Charles, who was methodical and deliberate, pressed the planners closely. The Koch network had grown so big that it took weeks just to touch base with its many donors. All across the country, millionaire by millionaire, Noble made his pitch. They've had their vote, the argument went. Now it's time for some accountability.

Fund-raising for Noble's group, the Center to Protect Patient Rights, quadrupled by the end of 2010, to $61.8 million. As with all such "social welfare" groups, under the tax code the sources of its funding didn't have to be publicly disclosed. The same held true for another mysterious Koch-tied group, something called the TC4 Trust, which raised an additional $42.7 million that year. About a third of this was steered back into the Center to Protect Patient Rights through a method disguised on disclosure forms. This brought Sean Noble's kitty up to almost $75 million. Flush with cash, the Kochs finally had a political operation commensurate with their wealth.

Previously, they had given relatively small amounts to 501(c)(4) "social welfare" groups. Before *Citizens United,* these nonprofit corporations, like for-profit corporations, had been restricted from spending money for or against candidates in elections. Some skirted the law by running what they claimed were issue ads. But legal danger hovered. After *Citizens United,* though, the Kochtopus essentially sprouted a second set of tentacles. The first cluster was the think tanks, academic programs, legal centers, and issue advocacy organizations that Fink had described as the ideological production line. These ventures were defined for legal purposes as charities and were still prohibited from participating in politics. Donations to them were tax deductible. Added to this in 2010 was a second cluster, a dizzying maze of "social welfare" groups that disbursed hidden money into the midterm elections.

When Congress created the legal framework for "social welfare" groups almost a century earlier, it never anticipated that they would become a means by which the rich would hide their political spending. In fact, to qualify as tax-exempt, such groups had to certify that they would be "operated exclusively for the promotion of social welfare." The IRS later loosened the guidelines, though, allowing them to engage marginally in politics, so long as this wasn't their "primary" purpose. Lawyers soon stretched the loophole to absurd lengths. They argued, for instance, that if a group spent 49 percent of its funds on politics, it complied with the law because it still wasn't "primarily" engaged in politics. They also argued that one such group could claim no political spending if it gave to another such group, even if the latter spent the funds on politics. Experts likened the setup to Russian nesting dolls. For example, at the end of 2010, the Center to Protect Patient Rights reported on its tax return that it spent no money on politics. Yet it granted $103 million to other conservative groups, most of which were actively engaged in the midterm elections.

The Kochs were part of a national explosion of dark money. In 2006, only 2 percent of "outside" political spending came from "social welfare" groups that hid their donors. In 2010, this number rose to 40 percent, masking hundreds of millions of dollars. Campaign-finance reformers were apoplectic but powerless. "The political players who are soliciting these funds and are benefiting from the expenditure of these funds will know where the money came from," argued Paul S. Ryan, senior counsel at the liberal Campaign Legal Center. "The only ones in the dark will be American voters."

Managing all of this new, dark money was a challenge. In April, as campaign professionals were trying to figure out how to take maximum advantage of the *Citizens United* decision, Gillespie invited Republican operatives to what he described in an e-mail as "an informal discussion of the 2010 landscape." The unusual meeting was to take place in Karl Rove's living room on Weaver Terrace, a well-off enclave of Northwest Washington. Some joked that they attended the first meeting of what came to be known as the Weaver Terrace Group simply so they could tell friends they had been inside the home of the storied political guru. What transpired was a war council in which the twenty assembled chieftains coordinated their plans of action and divided up their territory. Kenneth Vogel, in *Big Money,* describes it as "the birthplace of a new Republican Party—one steered by just a handful of unelected operatives who answered only to the richest activists who funded them."

Two organizations soon emerged as virtual private banks run by these operatives. The first, American Crossroads and its 501(c)(4) wing, Crossroads GPS, was initiated by Rove. For funds, it drew heavily on his network of Texas tycoons. The second was Noble's Center to Protect Patient Rights, which began to fill with donations from the Koch donor summits. Working closely with both was the U.S. Chamber of Commerce, which spent millions of dollars more in undisclosed contributions from businesses, much of it aimed at defeating Obama's health-care act. The chamber sent top officials to both the Weaver Terrace meetings and the Koch donor summits.

Each of the players' roles was carefully differentiated. Noble focused on House races, leaving the Senate to Rove's group. In accordance with his REDMAP strategy, Gillespie continued to concentrate on governorships and state legislatures. To hide their hands, the operatives steered the funds to a plethora of obscure, smaller groups. This also helped satisfy the legal requirement that no single public welfare group spend more than half of its funds on elections. Soon, to the unschooled eye, a rash of spontaneous attacks on Democrats appeared to be breaking out all across the country. In reality, the effort was so centrally coordinated, as one participant put it, "there wasn't one race in which there were multiple groups airing ads at the same time."

As Noble explained his methodology later to Eliana Johnson, Washington editor for the conservative publication *National Review,* he started by producing an Excel spreadsheet. It listed 64 Democratic congressmen "in order of the likelihood of their defeat." By the end of June, he said, the list of targets grew to 88, and by August, 105. He assigned each congressional district a "win potential" of between 1 and 5, and each candidate a score of 1 to 40, "based on the voting record of each member and the composition of the district, among other things." Eventually, he said, he sorted the 105 targeted candidates into "three tiers, based on the likelihood of a GOP victory."

He then disbursed the Koch network's money in accordance with what he regarded as each candidate's odds of winning. Rather than disclose that his organization was paying for the ads, he directed the money through an array of different front groups. For instance, Noble explained to *National Review* that he chose a group called the 60 Plus Association, which was a right-wing version of the senior citizens' lobby AARP, to air attack ads on Democrats in "Arizona's First Congressional District, Florida's Second and Twenty-Fourth, Indiana's Second, Minnesota's Eighth, New York's Twentieth, Ohio's Sixteenth, Pennsylvania's Third, and Wisconsin's Third and Eighth Congressional Districts." Meanwhile, he said, he used another group, Americans for Job Security, the same "business league" he had deployed in the Scott Brown race, to air ads in "New York's Twenty-Fourth, North Carolina's Second and Eighth, Ohio's Eighteenth, and Virginia's Ninth Congressional Districts." He chose the other shadow group that he had used in the Brown race, the Iowa-based American Future Fund, to air attack ads in Alabama's Second, Colorado's Seventh, New Mexico's First, and Washington's Second Congressional Districts.

The American Future Fund, like Noble's own nonprofit group, was a 501(c)(4) "social welfare" group, meaning it could hide the identity of its donors and was not supposed to be primarily engaged in electoral politics. Its stated mission was "to provide Americans with a conservative and free market viewpoint." In reality, though, it appeared to be little more than a front group acting as a screen for conservative political money. Efforts to track down its office led only to a post office box in Iowa. Founded in 2008 by a Republican operative in the state, it received seed money from one of the country's largest ethanol producers, Bruce Rastetter, but tax records showed that 87 percent of its funds in 2009 and approximately half its funds in 2010 came from just one source: Sean Noble's Center to Protect Patient Rights.

Similarly, Americans for Job Security, a 501(c)(6) "business league," or "trade association," was also entitled under the tax code to hide its funders, who were classified as "members." The organization had a physical office in Alexandria, Virginia, but the premises were almost empty. It had only one employee, a twenty-five-year-old Republican campaign aide who was acquainted with Sean Noble. Founded in 1997 with a million-dollar donation from the insurance industry, the organization had been accused of being nothing more than "a sham front group" by Public Citizen, a liberal group that favored tighter campaign-finance regulations. State officials in Alaska, where Americans for Job Security had waged an earlier campaign, concluded that the group "has no purpose other than to cover various money trails all over the country." The state charged the organization with violating Alaska's fair election rules. The group paid a $20,000 settlement but admitted no guilt. But in 2010, with Noble's help, its business was booming. Noble's center would steer this group $4.8 million that year.

In addition, Noble directed millions of dollars into other races through those and other groups, including the antitax activist Grover Norquist's organization, Americans for Tax Reform; Howard Rich's group, Americans for Limited Government; and the Kochs' flagship organization, Americans for

Prosperity. The budget for Americans for Prosperity soared accordingly. In 2004, the budget for the Kochs' flagship group and its foundation was $2 million. By 2008, it had grown to $15.2 million. And in 2010, it reached $40 million, engorged with funds from the Center to Protect Patient Rights.

In June, Noble tested out the system, using Americans for Prosperity to launch an assault on Tom Perriello, the freshman Democratic congressman from Charlottesville, Virginia, who had defied the fossil fuel interests over the cap-and-trade bill. Noble wanted to start unusually early in order to widen the field of Democrats he could weaken. In an exuberant moment, Perriello had called the climate change fight "a gift," proclaiming, "For the first time in a generation, we have the chance to redefine our energy economy." Instead, it was he who got redefined that summer by a barrage of negative ads paid for not by his opponent but by unrecognizable outsiders.

Perriello was an outspoken liberal in a swing district, so an obvious target. But soon mystery money was tarring Rick Boucher, too, a conservative Democratic congressman whose rural Virginia district encompassed Saltville, the factory town that the Olin Corporation had turned into a toxic waste dump. Boucher had represented the district for twenty-eight years in the House and eight more before that in the state senate. A Virginia lawyer and strong ally of business interests, he had been crucial to passage of the cap-and-trade bill in the House, drafting much of the measure and then winning support for it from a number of huge energy firms, including Duke Energy. He had given away so many goodies to the coal industry while negotiating the bill that many environmentalists had been disgusted. Nonetheless, the fact that he had supported the bill at all had angered conservative extremists, including several Virginia coal barons active in funding the Koch network. He was exactly the kind of centrist that big, polarized political money was rendering extinct.

"The Koch brothers went after me literally 24-7," recalled

Boucher, who after his defeat that November became a partner at the law firm Sidley Austin. By Election Day, he recalled, he was reeling from $2 million spent against him by Americans for Prosperity and other conservative outside groups. "This is Appalachia!" he said. "It's a cheap media market. That would have been like $10 million most other places." He said his Republican opponent, Morgan Griffith, "actually didn't raise and spend much, but he didn't have to, because the Koch groups carried his water."

Griffith's only issue was his opposition to addressing climate change and other environmental problems, according to Boucher. Griffith's victory left Saltville—where the EPA had forced the Olin Corporation to take responsibility for remediating a river that was still too toxic to fish—represented by a congressman who painted the EPA as the district's greatest foe.

In Boucher's view, the polluters had triumphed by overturning the campaign-finance laws. "There was a huge change after *Citizens United*," he contends. "When anyone could spend any amount of money without revealing who they were, by hiding behind amorphous-named organizations, the floodgates opened. The Supreme Court made a huge mistake. There is no accountability. Zero."

To shape the midterm message, Noble turned back to the pollster Frank Luntz for market testing. The Center to Protect Patient Rights paid for polls in a hundred congressional districts, often multiple times. The help did not come cheap. Records later showed that CPPR spent over $10 million in 2010 on "communications and surveys."

After conducting focus groups, Luntz suggested that opponents needed to avoid direct attacks on Obama, who was still popular, and instead tie Democratic candidates to Nancy Pelosi, the Speaker of the House. "She was totally toxic," one insider on the project said. "People saw her as so San Francisco, so out of touch. Their verbatims"—unedited comments—"about her were hilarious."

To make the anticipated attack ads, Noble again chose Larry McCarthy, the veteran media consultant who was known for his ability to distill a complicated subject into a simple, potent, and usually negative symbol. McCarthy had a reputation for being a particularly shrewd consumer of *O*, or opposition research on the rival candidates he was targeting. He often honed his ads using polls, focus groups, micro-targeting data, and "perception analyzers"—meters that evaluated viewers' split-second reactions to demo tapes.

McCarthy was an old hand at making disreputable ads for "outside" groups that wanted to be seen as unrelated to the candidates for reasons of legal and political hygiene. By saying the ads were "independent expenditures," candidates got deniability. The Willie Horton ad, for instance, had been paid for by an "outside" group run by the right-wing operative who founded Citizens United, Floyd Brown. It was the same group that later made the film attacking Hillary Clinton and that gave its name to the corporate speech test case. "Larry is not just one of the best ad-makers these days," Brown attested. "He's one of the best advertising minds this *century*. You go into a studio with Larry, and you're watching art. It's beautiful," he said, laughing. "From *my* standpoint, it's beautiful."

Geoff Garin, a Democratic pollster who had occasionally worked in the past with McCarthy but who was far more accustomed to being on the other side, was less effusive. He described McCarthy as a "serial offender" who had played "a pretty big part in lowering the bar on what is acceptable in American politics."

Shortly before the Kochs held their second summit of the year, a June get-together at the St. Regis Resort in Aspen, they got a break that enormously increased their network's financial clout when House Democrats passed a bill, backed by President Obama, to eliminate the so-called carried-interest loophole. The idea of eliminating the special tax break enjoyed by private equity and hedge fund managers struck fear in the finance industry. Obama had won the support of a surprisingly large share of New York's finance titans in 2008, but his stance on the tax—which would never make it through the Senate—enraged many of its heaviest hitters. Stephen Schwarzman, the chairman and CEO of the enormously lucrative private equity firm the Blackstone Group, whose personal fortune *Forbes* then estimated at $6.5 billion, would call the administration's efforts to close the loophole "a war," claiming it was "like when Hitler invaded Poland in 1939."

Schwarzman later apologized for the remark, but in truth the relationship between Obama and Wall Street had begun deteriorating almost as soon as he took office. Financiers resented being blamed for the collapse of the economy in 2008, they took extreme umbrage when Obama had chastised them as "fat cats," and they claimed that his administration was run by college professors who knew nothing about business. But Schwarzman and a number of other financiers regarded this as a new level of affront and flocked to the June Koch summit with their checkbooks in hand, determined to prevent his reelection.

Ironically, it was probably Schwarzman's own excesses that had brought the carried-interest loophole to critics' attention. In 2006, when he decided to transform Blackstone from a private partnership into a public company, he had been required to disclose his earnings for the first time. The numbers stunned both Wall Street and Washington. He made $398.3 million in 2006, which was nine times more than the CEO of Goldman Sachs. On top of this, his shares in Blackstone were valued at more than $7 billion. A 2008 *New Yorker* profile by James B. Stewart quotes a friend of Schwarzman's saying, "You have no idea what an impression this made on Wall Street. You have all these guys who have spent their entire lives working just as hard to make twenty million. Sure, that's a lot of money, but then Schwarzman turns around and, seemingly overnight, has eight billion."

Beyond this, Stewart wrote, Schwarzman "made himself an easy target for critics of Wall Street greed and conspicuous consumption" with "an expanding collection of trophy residences that are lavish even by the current standards of Wall Street." A 2007 *Wall Street Journal* profile also described how, at one of Schwarzman's five houses, an "11,000-square-foot home in Palm Beach, Fla., he complained to Jean-Pierre Zeugin, his executive chef and estate manager, that an employee wasn't wearing the proper black shoes with his uniform . . . [H]e found the squeak of the rubber soles distracting." His own mother told the paper that money is "what drives him. Money is the measuring stick."

Schwarzman's most serious self-inflicted wound, though, was the $3 million sixtieth birthday party he threw for himself in February 2007, at which he paid pop stars Rod Stewart and Patti LaBelle to serenade him. The media sensation stirred by the billionaire bacchanal led directly to congressional calls to close the carried-interest loophole.

The loophole was in essence an accounting trick that enabled hedge fund and private equity managers to categorize huge portions of their income as "interest," which was taxed at the 15 percent rate then applied to long-term capital gains. This was less than half the income tax rate paid by other top-bracket wage earners. Critics called the loophole a gigantic subsidy to millionaires and billionaires at the expense of ordinary taxpayers. The Economic Policy Institute, a progressive think tank, estimated that the hedge fund loophole cost the government over $6 billion a year—the cost of providing health care to three million children. Of that total, it said, almost $2 billion a year from the tax break went to just twenty-five individuals.

Congressional critics had been trying to close the loophole

since at least 2007, but while the Democratic House had passed reform bills three times, the measures always died in the Senate, the victim of both Republican and Democratic protectors, beholden to Wall Street.

With the issue back in play in the summer of 2010, the financiers were again mobilizing. As Clifford Asness, who ran a hedge fund in Greenwich, Connecticut, had declared in a call to arms when Obama first started speaking critically of hedge fund "speculators" and "fat cats," "Hedge funds really need a community organizer."

Organizers were waiting for Schwarzman and others at the June Koch summit, the theme of which was "Understanding and Addressing Threats to American Free Enterprise and Prosperity." The financiers represented a different strain of the Republican Party from the Kochs. Few were fanatically ideological. Most were simply concerned with protecting their continued accumulation of wealth. But when their resources were combined with the idea machinery built by the conservative movement's early funders, along with the ideological zealotry of the Kochs and other antigovernment radicals, the result was a raging river of cash capable of carrying the whole Republican Party to the right.

Another hedge fund manager who attended the Aspen session was the former Obama bundler Ken Griffin, founder and CEO of the Chicago-based hedge fund Citadel, whose shift from a Democratic bundler for Obama to the Republican side was part of what came to be known as the "Hedge Fund Switch." Other billionaire financiers at the event included the Home Depot founder turned investment banker Ken Langone and the Massachusetts-based private equity investor John Childs. Childs was the second-in-command at Thomas H. Lee Partners when it made $900 million in two years in a leveraged buyout deal for the beverage company Snapple. His own company, J. W. Childs Associates, had ups and downs, but he had been a consistently huge investor in conservative politics, once described as "the closest thing the Republican Party has to an automatic teller machine in Massachusetts." In the 2010 election cycle, Childs would go on to spend $907,000 on federal elections.

The hedge fund manager Paul Singer, chairman of the Manhattan Institute and a major contributor to the Republican Party, didn't attend, but his close aide Annie Dickerson appeared on his behalf. Singer's company, Elliott Management, had a unique niche in the financial world. It bought the distressed debt of bankrupt companies and countries and then demanded to be paid in full or, if necessary, took them to court. Critics had called the tactic immoral particularly when applied to impoverished countries, castigating him as a "vulture capitalist" who profited off poverty, but Singer had accumulated a fortune estimated at $900 million from the practice. Singer, who described himself as a Goldwater free-enterprise conservative, was a supporter of gay rights but a harsh critic of the Obama administration's proposed financial regulatory reforms. Furious with the Democrats, he hosted his own fund-raiser in Manhattan for Republican candidates opposing Dodd-Frank and other financial reforms that summer. He also attended a similar meeting at the $14 million home of another disgruntled hedge fund donor, Steve Cohen of SAC Capital. According to later reports, this small and intensely wealthy circle of billionaire moguls soon "pumped at least $10 million" into groups boosting Republicans in the midterms, often without any public trace.

The concentration of wealth at the Koch summit by this point was extraordinary. Of the two hundred or so participants meeting secretly with the Kochs in Aspen that June, at least eleven were on *Forbes*'s list of the four hundred wealthiest Americans. The combined assets of this group alone, assessed in accordance with the magazine's estimates of their wealth at the time, amounted to $129.1 billion.

Hoping to inspire their generosity, Noble previewed a

sample television ad for the donors, slamming Obamacare, as well as touting the Republicans' chances of winning, on a panel titled "Mobilizing Citizens for November." "Is there a chance this fall to elect leaders who are more strongly committed to freedom and prosperity?" the brochure for the discussion asked. "This session will further assess the landscape and offer a plan to educate voters on the importance of economic freedom."

Joining Noble on the panel was Tim Phillips, the president of Americans for Prosperity, who unveiled his group's plan to spend an unheard-of $45 million on a few targeted midterm races.

In the evening, conference goers were treated to a rousing dinner speech from the Fox News host Glenn Beck titled, in homage to Hayek, "Is America on the Road to Serfdom?" Finally, topping off the night was a "cocktails and dessert reception," hosted by DonorsTrust. Whitney Ball, the head of the organization that offered donors a politically safe way to give big and anonymously, later explained her attendance at the event succinctly: It's a "target-rich environment."

On the final day, the donors engaged in auction-like bids over lunch, one-upping each other with their seven-figure pledges amid laughter and applause. Charles and David Koch themselves reportedly pledged $12 million. By the end of the meal, the Koch-backed nonprofits could count on $25 million more in the kitty.

By July, Democratic strategists began to feel a strange undertow, as if an offshore tsunami were gathering force. One operative put together a chart compiling the pledged midterm expenditures by ten Republican-aligned independent groups and was appalled to discover that this slice of the total spending alone would likely reach at least $200 million. Americans for Prosperity had pledged to spend $45 million. Karl Rove's group American Crossroads had pledged $52 million. The

U.S. Chamber of Commerce had committed to spend $75 million. Countless other groups, including an unknown number of dark-money organizations loaded with secret funds, were lined up to spend millions and millions more. A Democratic operative who saw the chart, which was passed around like samizdat within the party, admitted that it was "one hell of a wake-up call."

The numbers caught the Obama administration off guard. The former White House aide Anita Dunn admits, "It was clear that *Citizens United* was going to open the floodgates and it would be bad for the Democrats. But it exploded in 2010. The amount spent in those midterms probably surprised everyone."

As late as May, Axelrod had barely known who the Kochs were. When a reporter asked what he knew about them, he seemed unsure. Later, the Koch public relations team would suggest that press coverage of them was initiated by the White House. In truth, Obama's political team was almost clueless. Only after Noble's team, working undercover, began launching attacks on Democrats all across the country did some in the White House start to sense something odd. As Axelrod recalls, "We began to wonder, where is all this money coming from?"

In Iowa, the American Future Fund began airing an ad created by Larry McCarthy that Geoff Garin, the Democratic pollster, described as perhaps "the most egregious of the year." The ad accused the then congressman Bruce Braley, an Iowa Democrat and a lawyer, of supporting a proposed Islamic community center in lower Manhattan, which it misleadingly called a "mosque at Ground Zero." As footage of the destroyed World Trade Center rolled, a narrator said, "For centuries, Muslims built mosques where they won military victories." Now it said a mosque celebrating 9/11 was to be built on the very spot "where Islamic terrorists killed three thousand Americans"; it was, the narrator suggested, as if the Japanese were to build a triumphal monument at Pearl Harbor. The ad then accused Braley of supporting the mosque.

In fact, Braley had taken no position on the issue. No surprise for a congressman from Iowa. But an unidentified video cameraman had ambushed him at the Iowa State Fair and asked him about it.

Braley replied that he regarded the matter as a local zoning issue for New Yorkers to decide. Soon afterward, he says, the attack ad "dropped on me like the house in 'The Wizard of Oz.'" Braley, who won his seat by a margin of 30 percent in 2008, barely held on in 2010. The American Future Fund's effort against Braley was the most expensive campaign that year by an independent group.

After the election, Braley accused McCarthy, the ad maker, of "profiting from Citizens United in the lowest way." As for those who hired McCarthy, he said, they "are laughing all the way to the bank. It's a good investment for them . . . They're the winners. The losers are the American people, and the truth."

In North Carolina, Congressman Bob Etheridge, a seven-term Democrat, fared worse. He was the target of ads made by McCarthy for another of Noble's front groups, Americans for Job Security. That summer, Etheridge was walking on Capitol Hill when he too found himself the victim of a video ambush. Two young men in suits approached him. One thrust a video camera in his face while the other demanded to know, "Do you fully support the Obama agenda?" Taken aback, Etheridge asked, "Who are you?" When he got no answer, he asked again. Growing irate, he repeated the question five times, until finally he pushed the camera away and gripped his inquisitor.

"Please let go of my arm, Congressman," the inquisitor pleaded as the camera kept recording.

"Who are you?" Etheridge repeated.

Finally, the interviewer stammered, "I'm just a student, sir."

"From?" Etheridge asked.

"The Streets," came the answer.

Within days, a video of the confrontation, edited to make Etheridge seem unhinged, was posted on the conservative Web site *Big Government* under the headline "Congressman Attacks Student." It went viral. Soon afterward, McCarthy inserted the video into an attack ad titled "Who Are You?" in which people purporting to be from Etheridge's district answered, "We're your constituents," and then accused Etheridge—inaccurately—of wanting to cut Medicare. As per Luntz's instructions, Nancy Pelosi figured prominently in the ads as well. The spot that dealt the deathblow to Etheridge, finally, was one that accused him, like Braley, of supporting the "Ground Zero Mosque."

The local television station WRAL-TV in Raleigh, which covered the campaign, noted that Americans for Job Security had spent $360,000 on media against Etheridge, but at the time no one was able to figure out who was behind the group.

After a seventeen-day recount, Etheridge lost in November in a stunning upset to a Tea Party sympathizer, Renee Ellmers, who was a nurse running with the support of Sarah Palin. The next day, the National Republican Congressional Committee (NRCC), which had previously denied any role, acknowledged that it had been behind the ambush video. How the video made its way into the "independent" ad was never revealed, but the NRCC, too, was one of McCarthy's clients.

It was not a coincidence that Braley, Etheridge, Perriello, and other Democrats were all ambushed that year by unidentified videographers. In 2010, Americans for Prosperity and several other conservative groups encouraged members to provoke Democratic candidates into on-camera outbursts. Some gave instructions on how to do it. In time, the practice spread to liberal groups too. The Internet had exponentially increased the power of viral videos, particularly those capturing compromising behavior.

Aiding the effort, several of the wealthiest members of the Koch network launched media ventures during this period, widening the exposure for partisan attacks. Foster Friess, the Wyoming mutual fund magnate, for instance, committed to spend $3 million to found *The Daily Caller* in 2010 after a single luncheon conversation about it with Tucker Carlson, its prospective editor in chief. The online news venture described itself as a conservative version of *The Huffington Post*. In fact, it functioned more as an outlet for opposition research paid for by the donor class. Charles Koch's foundation would later also back the news site. (After *The New Yorker* published my investigative article on the Kochs, "Covert Operations," that August, *The Daily Caller* was the chosen receptacle for the retaliatory opposition research on me, although, after it proved false, the Web site decided not to run it.)

Only in 2011 did it surface that in New York, at least, the "Ground Zero mosque" controversy had been stirred up for political gain in part by money from Robert Mercer, the co-CEO of the $15 billion Long Island hedge fund Renaissance Technologies. To aid a conservative candidate in New York, Mercer gave $1 million. It helped pay for ads attacking supporters of the "Ground Zero mosque." A former computer programmer who had a reputation as a brilliant mathematician and an eccentric loner, Mercer was a relative newcomer to the Koch summits. But he was immediately impressed by the organization. He had long held the government in low regard and shared the Kochs' antipathy toward government regulations. In addition to fanning flames around the "mosque" issue, in 2010 Mercer reportedly gave over $300,000 to a super PAC trying to defeat a Democratic congressman from Oregon, Pete DeFazio, who had proposed taxing stock trades. Renaissance, a so-called quant fund, traded stocks in accordance with computer algorithms at enormously high volumes, so the proposed tax would have bitten into the firm's legendary profits.

Someone familiar with Mercer's thinking maintained that the proposed tax on stock trades was not behind his involvement in the race; rather, Mercer shared deep skepticism about global warming with the Republican candidate, Arthur Robinson. Instead of openly debating these issues, though, Mercer, who declined to speak about his motivations, paid for ads that manipulated voters' fears about terrorism and Medicare.

As the congressional races grew nasty, Gillespie's Republican State Leadership Committee began to channel dark money into one local state legislature race after another. There were furtive, well-coordinated projects to take over the statehouses in Wisconsin, Michigan, Ohio, and elsewhere. North Carolina in particular was living up to its promise as a perfect testing ground for the REDMAP strategy. Art Pope's outsized role there, meanwhile, was also providing an instructive demonstration of how much influence one extraordinarily wealthy activist could have over a single state in the post–*Citizens United* era.

Many of the details remained shrouded from public view. But that fall, in the remote western corner of North Carolina, John Snow, a retired Democratic judge who had represented the district in the state senate for three terms, found himself subjected to one political attack after another. Snow, who often voted with the Republicans, was considered one of the most conservative Democrats in the general assembly, and his record reflected the views of his constituents. His Republican opponent, Jim Davis—an orthodontist loosely allied with the Tea Party—had minimal political experience, and Snow, a former college football star, was expected to be reelected easily. Yet somehow Davis seemed to have almost unlimited money with which to assail Snow.

Snow recalls, "I voted to help build a pier with an aquarium on the coast, as did every other member of the North Carolina House and Senate who voted." But a television attack ad presented the "luxury pier" as Snow's wasteful scheme. "We've lost jobs," an actress said in the ad. "John Snow's solution for our economy? 'Go fish!'" A mass mailing, decorated with a cartoon pig, denounced the pier as one of Snow's "pork projects."

In all, Snow says, he was the target of two dozen mass mailings, one of them reminiscent of the Willie Horton ad. It featured a photograph of a menacing-looking African-American convict who, it said, "thanks to arrogant state senator John Snow," could "soon be let off death row." Snow, in fact, supported the death penalty and had prosecuted murder cases. But in 2009, Snow had helped pass a new state law, the Racial Justice Act, that enabled judges to reconsider a death sentence if a convict could prove that the jury's verdict had been tainted by racism. The law was an attempt to address the overwhelming racial disparity in capital sentences.

"The attacks just went on and on," Snow later recalled. "My opponents used fear tactics. I'm a moderate, but they tried to make me look liberal." On election night, he lost by an agonizingly slim margin—fewer than two hundred votes.

After the election, the North Carolina Free Enterprise Foundation, a nonpartisan, pro-business organization, revealed that two seemingly independent outside political groups had spent several hundred thousand dollars on ads against Snow—a huge amount for a local race in a poor, backwoods district. Pope was instrumental in funding both groups, Civitas Action and Real Jobs NC. In fact, Pope gave $200,000 in seed money in 2010 to start Real Jobs NC, which was responsible for the "Go fish!" ad and the mass mailing that attacked Snow's "pork projects."

Real Jobs NC was also the recipient of a whopping $1.25 million from Ed Gillespie's Republican State Leadership Committee. But as the investigative news outfit ProPublica explained, Gillespie's group distributed its contributions in a way designed to hide its involvement from voters. Instead of putting its own name on the ads, it created new, local-sounding nonprofit groups that lacked the word "Republican." As a social welfare organization, it claimed to be nonpolitical, yet its funds were used to attack twenty different Democrats around the state and no Republicans.

Bob Phillips, the head of the North Carolina chapter of Common Cause, an organization that promotes stricter controls on political money, watched the unfolding drama closely and concluded that the *Citizens United* decision was an even bigger "game changer" at the local level than at the national. He said it enabled a single donor, particularly one with access to major corporate funds like Pope or the Kochs, to play a significant and even decisive role. "We didn't have that before 2010," Phillips says. "*Citizens United* opened up the door. Now a candidate can literally be outspent by independent groups. We saw it in North Carolina, and a lot of the money was traced back to Art Pope."

In fact, misleading attack ads sponsored by the same unknown outside groups popped up in local races all over the state. In Fayetteville, Margaret Dickson, a sixty-one-year-old pro-business Democrat who was seeking reelection to the North Carolina state senate, was depicted as a clone of Nancy Pelosi, even though her record was considerably more conservative. Another ad, funded by her opponent, made her look like "a hooker," she said, showing a doppelgänger applying lipstick and taking piles of greenbacks and suggesting she was prostituting her state job for money. Pope later said he was appalled by the ad, but Americans for Prosperity, on whose board he sat, promoted her opponent. "Those ads hurt me," she said later. "I've been through this four times before, but the tone of this campaign was much uglier, and much more personal, than anything I've seen." On election night, Dickson fell about a thousand votes short of victory in her district, which has a population of more than 150,000.

Chris Heagarty, a Democratic lawyer who ran for a legislative seat that fall in Raleigh, had previously directed an election-reform group and was not naive about political money.

Yet even he was caught off guard by the intensity of the effort marshaled against him. Real Jobs NC and Civitas Action spent some $70,000 on ads portraying him as fiscally profligate, while Americans for Prosperity spent heavily on behalf of his opponent. One ad accused him of having voted "to raise taxes over a billion dollars," even though he had not yet served in the legislature. He said, "If you put all of the Pope groups together, they and the North Carolina GOP spent more to defeat me than the guy who actually won." He fell silent, then added, "For an individual to have so much power is frightening. The government of North Carolina is for sale."

Pope, who regarded himself as an underdog in a historically Democratic state and an honest reformer, took umbrage at such talk. "People throw around terms like 'so-and-so tried to buy the election,'" he said in an interview. But in his view, that evoked bribery, and "that's illegal, corrupt, and something I've fought hard against in North Carolina." He said the money he spent simply helped "educate" citizens so that they could "make informed decisions. It's the core of the First Amendment!" Asked whether those with more cash might drown out less wealthy voices, he said, "I really have more faith in North Carolina voters than that." Martin Nesbitt Jr., the Democratic leader in the North Carolina Senate, wasn't convinced. Of Pope's 2010 spending, he said, "It wasn't an education; it was an onslaught. What he's doing is buying elections."

Other critics accused Pope of using tax-deductible philanthropic pursuits to promote aggressively pro-business, anti-tax policies that helped his company. Scholars who worked at a think tank funded by his family foundations, for instance, opposed any raise in the minimum wage, and in fact any minimum wage laws at all. At the same time, many employees at Pope's discount stores were paid the minimum wage. "I am careful to comply with the law," Pope argued, "and I keep my personal activities separate from my philanthropic, public-policy, grassroots and independent expenditure efforts."

He protested caricatures that portrayed him as greedy and self-serving, saying he deeply cared about the people of North Carolina but believed they were better served by private enterprise than government social programs. He therefore believed in cutting personal and corporate income taxes, abolishing estate taxes, and cutting state spending. Friends explained that Pope believed it was the role of charities, to which he contributed, not the government, to look after the poor and disadvantaged.

The Pope fortune was highly dependent on low-income patrons. In 1930, Pope's grandfather established five small dime stores in North Carolina that he sold to the next generation. Pope's father was a tough and thrifty merchant who expanded the family business into an empire spanning thirteen states. Pope then worked his way up in the company, becoming CEO. Variety Wholesalers owned several chains, including Roses, Maxway, Super 10, and Bargain Town. The company favored a specific demographic: neighborhoods with median incomes of less than $40,000 a year, and populations that were at least 25 percent African-American.

Despite the controversy it stirred, the triumph of Pope and "outside" money in North Carolina in 2010 was sweeping. Of twenty-two local legislative races targeted by Pope, his family, and their organizations, the Republicans won eighteen. As Gillespie and he had hoped, this placed both chambers of the general assembly firmly under Republican majorities for the first time since 1870.

According to the Institute for Southern Studies, three-quarters of the spending by independent groups in North Carolina's 2010 state races came from accounts linked to Pope. The total amount that Pope and his family and groups backed by him spent—$2.2 million—was not that much by national standards but was enough to exert crucial influence within the confines of one state.

The pattern did in fact repeat itself all across the nation.

"The Obama team has done some amazing things, those guys are really something, but the Democrats plain got skunked on the state houses," the former Republican congressman Tom Reynolds, the chairman of REDMAP, later told *Politico*. Gillespie's deputy, Chris Jankowski, later admitted, "At first I was a little panicked, they weren't out there really competing. I thought I was going to get hit by a sucker punch." But then, he said, "I realized what was happening and it was like, how much can we run up the score?"

In the final month before the midterm elections, Obama's political advisers realized there was almost nothing they could do to prevent disaster. "We lost all hope in October," one White House aide later admitted. "We didn't feel much of anything. We just had to let the ship hit the iceberg."

In a last-ditch effort, Obama tried to warn voters that Republicans were trying to steal the elections with secret, special-interest cash. He began speaking out on the campaign about how *Citizens United* had allowed "a flood of deceptive attack ads sponsored by special interests using front groups with misleading names." He even made a barely veiled reference to the Kochs, suggesting that big companies were hiding behind "groups with harmless-sounding names like Americans for Prosperity." Obama said, "They don't have to say who, exactly, Americans for Prosperity are. You don't know if it's a foreign-controlled corporation"—or even, he added, "a big oil company."

In the final days before the election, the Democratic Party aired a national ad accusing "Bush cronies," Ed Gillespie and Karl Rove, and "shills for big business" of "stealing our democracy." The spot depicted an old woman getting mugged. The image, though, was hackneyed, and the message simplistic. It was almost impossible to explain to the public in sound bites the connections between the sea of dark money, the donors' financial interests, the assault on Obama's policies, and their lives. The conventional wisdom among professional political consultants was that Americans either didn't get it or just didn't care.

It's likely given historical trends and an unemployment rate topping 9.5 percent that a Republican wave in 2010 was inevitable, but the unmatched money from a handful of ultrarich conservatives helped turn the likely win into a rout. Noble had made so much progress that by the final weeks in the campaign he was aiming beyond his third-tier candidates at congressmen no one had ever believed were vulnerable. After noticing how little money Jim Oberstar, a Democratic congressman from Duluth, Minnesota, had raised, Noble bought local television time and aired an ad thrown together by McCarthy casting Oberstar as a disco-era relic who cared more about himself than about his constituents. Oberstar, to almost everyone's surprise, became another notch on Noble's belt.

On November 2, 2010, the Democrats suffered massive defeats, losing control of the House of Representatives. Just two short years after he soared to power amid predictions of a lasting realignment, Obama's party, and his hopes of prevailing on any ambitious legislation, were crushed. Republicans gained sixty-three seats in the House, putting them firmly in control of the lower body. It was the largest such turnover since 1948. Pelosi, the first female Speaker and Luntz's favorite target, was exiled to minority status after only four years. The Ohio Republican John Boehner, the new Speaker, now had a caucus bursting with Tea Party enthusiasts who had ridden to power by attacking government in general and Obama in particular. Several had won primaries against moderates. Many owed their victories to donors expecting radically conservative change. Compromise wasn't in their interest.

The Democrats' setbacks were huge at almost every level. Republicans picked up half a dozen Senate seats. At the state level, the Democratic losses were even more staggering. Across the country, Republicans gained 675 legislative seats. They won control of both the legislature and the governor's office in twenty-one states; the Democrats had similar one-party rule in only eleven. The map looked red, with small islands of blue.

As a consequence of their gains, Republicans now had four times as many districts to gerrymander as the Democrats. By creating reliably safe seats, they could build a firewall protecting the Republican control of Congress for the next decade.

Clearly, REDMAP's payoff for a relatively modest investment was impressive. For the Republicans, as Glenn Thrush of *Politico* observed, it became "the gift that keeps on giving." Newly Republican states like Michigan, Wisconsin, Ohio, and North Carolina soon became breeding grounds for attacks on Obama's core agenda. They undermined his policies on health care, abortion, gay rights, voting rights, immigration, the environment, guns, and labor.

"It feels bad," Obama admitted at a press conference the day after the election. What hurt especially, he said, was having to make condolence calls to Democrats who had gone out on a limb to defend him and his policies, such as Ohio's governor, Ted Strickland. "The toughest thing in the last couple of days is seeing really terrific public servants not being able to serve more," he said. "There's not only sadness about seeing them go, but there's also a lot of questioning on my part in terms of could I have done something differently, or something more."

Waxing professorial, he suggested, "This is something that I think every president needs to go through," but then he paused and joked wanly, "Now, I'm not suggesting for every future president that they take a shellacking like I did last night."

One of the biggest, though least-known, winners of the evening was Sean Noble. When he had worked as a congressional aide on Capitol Hill, he had earned a salary of $87,000 a year. In contrast, by 2011 he was wealthy enough to make two major real estate purchases in addition to the two houses that he and his wife owned in Phoenix. He spent $665,000 on a Capitol Hill row house and an undisclosed amount on "a 5,700-square-foot, eight-bedroom house in Hurricane, Utah," Bloomberg News reported. And best of all, the record spending on the 2012 election was just around the corner.

Part Three

Privatizing Politics

Total Combat, 2011–2014

There's class warfare all right.
But it's my class, the rich class, that's making war,
and we're winning.

—*Warren Buffett*

CHAPTER ELEVEN

The Spoils: Plundering Congress

THE OFFICIAL OPENING OF THE 112TH CONGRESS TOOK PLACE on January 5, 2011, when Nancy Pelosi, the Speaker of the House, handed off an oversized ceremonial gavel to her successor, John Boehner. But a new era of ultraconservative billionaire influence had already begun. Before the public swearing-in ceremony got under way, David Koch, whose donor network had spent at least $130.7 million on winning a Republican majority, was in the new Speaker-to-be's ornate office, chatting amiably with his staff. "The People's House" was under new management and, critics would suggest, new ownership.

While Koch was a very public presence in the Capitol, his political adjutant, Tim Phillips, the president of Americans for Prosperity, was deep in the inner sanctum of the congressional committee that mattered most to the bottom line of Koch Industries. Phillips's most important destination that day was the House Energy and Commerce Committee, which under the new Republican majority had now increased its power to block President Obama's environmental agenda in Congress. The committee could bury progress on climate change and harass the Environmental Protection Agency for the foreseeable future.

David Koch's public appearance that day signified a remarkable transformation. The Kochs had come far from their days as Libertarian losers. As the *Los Angeles Times* noted a month later, "Charles and David Koch no longer sit outside Washington's political establishment, isolated by uncompromising conservatism." Instead, their "uncompromising conservatism" now dominated one of Congress's two legislative chambers, as well as one of the country's two major political parties. As the paper's headline put it, "Koch Brothers Now at Heart of GOP Power."

That afternoon, after Boehner was sworn in, Koch donned a herringbone tweed overcoat and a camel-colored cashmere muffler and strode out across the Capitol grounds toward Independence Avenue to celebrate. Before he could get far, though, he was stopped by Lee Fang, the dogged liberal blogger for *ThinkProgress* who had been chronicling the Kochs' rise to power for months. After Fang introduced himself, he and a videographer stuck a microphone in the billionaire's face and asked, "Mr. Koch, are you proud of the Tea Party movement, and what they've achieved in the past few years?"

"Yeah," Koch said, looking a little befuddled. Phillips, who was at his side, tried to cut the questioning off. "Hey, David, Lee here is a good blogger on the LEFT," he warned his boss with a nervous smile. But Koch, who had impaired hearing in his left ear, either didn't grasp the warning or didn't care, because he kept talking. "There are some extremists there," he acknowledged, "but the rank and file are just normal people like us. And I admire them. It's probably the best grassroots uprising since 1776 in my opinion!"

Phillips by this point was trying to drown out the interview without appearing rude on camera, insistently repeating, "Lee—Lee—I'm very disappointed in you—Lee—you're better than this—Lee, *LEE*—THE INTERVIEW IS OVER!"

Fang soldiered on nonetheless, asking Koch what he wanted from the new Congress under Speaker Boehner. "Well," Koch answered, with growing animation, licking his lips as he habitually did, "cut the hell out of spending, balance the budget, reduce regulations, and uh, support business!"

Later, in a round of image-repairing interviews, the Kochs would portray themselves as disinterested do-gooders and misunderstood social liberals who championed bipartisan issues such as criminal justice reform. But when put on the spot and stripped of public relations help, David Koch made his priorities clear. He regarded his self-interest and the public interest as synonymous.

In *Plutocrats: The Rise of the New Global Super Rich and the Fall of Everyone Else,* the journalist Chrystia Freeland describes how those with massive financial resources almost universally use them to secure policies beneficial to their interests, often at the expense of the less well-off. In the United States, a number of studies have shown that in recent years this tendency has distorted politics in very specific ways. In a study he conducted for the nonpartisan Sunlight Foundation, the political scientist Lee Drutman found that increasingly concentrated wealth in America resulted in more polarization and extremism, especially on the right. Very rich benefactors in the Republican Party were far more opposed to taxes and regulations than the rest of the country. "The more Republicans depend upon 1% of the 1% donors, the more conservative they tend to be," he discovered.

The 112th Congress soon unfolded as a case study of what David Frum, an adviser to the former president George W. Bush, described as the growing and in his view destructive influence of the Republican Party's "radical rich." The "radicalization of the party's donor base," he observed, "propelled the party to advocate policies that were more extreme than anything seen since Barry Goldwater's 1964 presidential campaign." It also "led Republicans in Congress to try tactics they would never have dared use before."

Hard data supported this. Harvard's Theda Skocpol found that the House "took the biggest leap to the far right" since political scientists began recording quantitative measurements of legislators' positions. There was no better example than the Kochs' newly won influence over the House Energy and Commerce Committee.

In the previous Congress, the panel had been chaired by Henry Waxman, the liberal Democrat from California who had quarterbacked the House's successful passage of the cap-and-trade bill, only to see it die in the Senate. Now the new Republican leadership stocked the committee with oil industry advocates, many of whom owed huge campaign debts to the Kochs. Koch Industries PAC was the single largest oil and gas industry donor to members of the panel, outspending even ExxonMobil. It had donated to twenty-two of the committee's thirty-one Republican members and five of its Democratic members, too. In addition, five out of the six Republican freshmen on the committee had received "outside" support from Americans for Prosperity.

Meanwhile, many of the new committee members had signed an unusual pledge swearing fealty to the Kochs' agenda. They promised to vote against any kind of carbon tax unless it was offset by comparable spending cuts—an unlikely scenario. The "No Climate Tax" pledge was invented by Americans for Prosperity in 2008 when the Supreme Court cleared the way for the EPA to regulate greenhouse gases, as it did other pollutants. The Kochs' pledge was modeled on the enormously successful one that the antitax crusader Grover Norquist had used to intimidate Republican lawmakers from raising taxes, but in this instance it served not a cause so much as a company.

By the start of the legislative session in 2011, fully 156 members of Congress had signed the Kochs' "No Climate Tax" pledge. Many returning members of the House Energy and Commerce Committee had already taken the pledge, and of the twelve new Republicans on the panel nine were signatories, including five of the six freshmen.

A prime example of the symbiotic relationship between the Kochs and the committee was Morgan Griffith, who had defeated Rick Boucher in the district that represented Saltville, Virginia, and was among the wave of new appointees to the

Energy and Commerce Committee who were openly indebted to the Kochs for their seats. Americans for Prosperity's operatives were guests of honor at a victory rally soon after the election, at which Griffith gushed, "I'm just thankful that you all helped me in so many ways."

The Kochs' investment soon paid off. Once in office, Griffith became an outspoken skeptic of mainstream climate science, drawing national ridicule for lecturing scientific experts, as they testified in Congress, that they needed to consider the possibility that Mesopotamia and the Vikings owed their success to global warming and that melting ice caps on Mars showed that humans were not its cause on Earth.

Congressman Griffith also became a lead player in the House Republicans' "war on the EPA," demanding that the agency be "reined in." Within a month after he took office, he and other House Republicans gutted the EPA's budget by a punishing 27 percent. The Senate objected but eventually agreed to cut 16 percent from the agency that had halted the flow of mercury into Saltville's streams. By then, the 1980 Superfund law that had charged polluters like the Olin Corporation for the cleanup costs had expired, and the $3.8 billion that had accumulated in the fund had run out. Nearly half of America's population lived within ten miles of a toxic waste site, according to one study, but in towns like Saltville, taxpayers rather than corporations were left to clean up the mess.

Koch Industries could breathe a bit freer, but the same couldn't be said of those living near its plants. On just one short street, South Penn Road in the blue-collar town of Crossett, Arkansas, eleven of the fifteen households had been stricken with cancer. Many residents were convinced their plight was caused by chemical waste dumped by the nearby Georgia-Pacific paper mill, owned by Koch Industries. The air stank so badly that young and old residents stayed indoors, breathing from respirators. The company denied responsibility and pointed out that the cancer claims had earlier been "rejected in a class action suit." But David Bouie, a black minister who lived on the street, was trying desperately to get the EPA involved. "All along our street here we have case after case of cancer," he told the liberal investigative filmmaker Robert Greenwald. "We have a problem in this community, for this many people to be sick or dead. Why is the cancer rate so high? Does the paper mill have anything to do with it?" Two years earlier, *USA Today* had published a devastating investigative report based on EPA air pollution data that pinpointed a school in Crossett as among the most toxic 1 percent in the country and identified the Georgia-Pacific plant as a major cause. Lisa Jackson, the EPA's administrator, vowed action, but the congressional budget cuts were huge constraints on doing anything.

The numbers regarding Koch Industries' pollution were incontrovertible. In 2012, according to the EPA's Toxic Release Inventory database, which documents the toxic and carcinogenic output of eight thousand American companies, Koch Industries was the number one producer of toxic waste in the United States. It generated 950 million pounds of hazardous materials that year. Of this total output, it released 56.8 million pounds into the air, water, and soil, making it the country's fifth-largest polluter. The company was also among the largest emitters of greenhouse gases in America, spewing over twenty-four million tons of carbon dioxide a year into the atmosphere by 2011, according to the EPA, as much as is typically emitted by five million cars.

Company officials didn't dispute the statistics but argued that they merely reflected the size of its operations and the kinds of products it made. They stressed that they had achieved a record of compliance that compared favorably with other manufacturers of their ilk. As Steve Tatum, president of Koch Minerals, put it, "The investment banks, they don't pollute very much, because they don't make anything. We make stuff."

Another defender on the committee was Mike Pompeo,

a freshman Republican from Koch Industries' hometown of Wichita, Kansas, who was so closely entwined with the billionaire brothers that he became known as the "congressman from Koch." The Kochs had once invested an undisclosed amount of money in an aerospace company that Pompeo founded. By the time he ran for office, the Kochs were no longer investors in his business but had become major backers of his candidacy. Their corporate PAC and Americans for Prosperity also weighed in on his behalf. After his election, Pompeo turned to the company for his chief of staff, choosing Mark Chenoweth, a lawyer who had worked for Koch Industries' lobbying team. Within weeks, Pompeo was championing two of Koch Industries' legislative priorities—opposition to Obama's plans to create a public EPA registry of greenhouse gas polluters and a digital database of consumer complaints about unsafe products. Without publicly accessible data, of course, it would be extremely difficult to track any company's toxic output. (Ultimately, the Kochs lost the battle, and the database was created.)

Koch Industries' lobbying disclosures showed that the company spent over $8 million lobbying Congress in 2011, much of it on environmental issues. The best measure of its new congressional clout might have been the "naked belly crawl," as the political reporter Robert Draper termed it, performed by the Michigan congressman Fred Upton in hopes of snaring the Energy and Commerce Committee's chairmanship. Prior to 2010, Upton had been known as an environmental moderate. In fact, in 2009, before the Tea Partiers and their patrons took charge, he had said, "Climate change is a serious problem that necessitates serious solutions," adding, "I strongly believe that everything must be on the table as we seek to reduce carbon emissions." In 2010, however, Upton, like many Republican moderates, faced a potentially career-killing primary challenge from the right. Upton survived, but others who accepted the growing scientific consensus on climate change, such as Robert Inglis of South Carolina, were defeated, serving as cautionary warnings to the rest. Inglis became convinced of the reality of global warming on a congressional trip to Antarctica during which scientists showed him polar ice samples containing rising amounts of carbon dioxide following the Industrial Revolution. He was a Christian conservative, but he couldn't in good conscience deny the reality. In the deep red state of South Carolina, his scientific awakening proved his political downfall. "It hurts to be tossed out," he conceded afterward. "But I violated the Republican orthodoxy."

In contrast, Upton became a born-again doubter. By 2010, he had renounced his previous climate apostasy and co-authored an op-ed piece in *The Wall Street Journal* with Tim Phillips, the president of Americans for Prosperity, in which they called the EPA's plans to regulate carbon emissions "an unconstitutional power grab that will kill millions of jobs unless Congress steps in." Upton also joined lawsuits ginned up by Americans for Prosperity aimed at stopping the EPA. The belly crawl paid off. As the new session of Congress began, Upton secured the chairmanship, promising to drag the EPA administrator, Lisa Jackson, to testify before his committee so often, he bragged, that she would need her own congressional parking space.

Soon after, Republicans in the House were proposing measures that Representative Norm Dicks, a Democrat from Washington, called "a wish list for polluters." In addition to halting action on global warming, they tried to prevent the protection of any new endangered species, permit uranium mining adjacent to the Grand Canyon, deregulate mountaintop mining, and prevent coal ash from being designated a form of air pollution. In an effort to subvert the EPA's core mission, they also proposed legislation requiring it to consider the costs of its regulations, without regard to the scientific and health benefits, which the editorial page of the *Los Angeles Times* said "rips the heart out of the 40-year-old Clean Air Act."

Two months into their tenure, Republicans on the House Energy and Commerce Committee also led a crusade against alternative, renewable energy programs. They successfully branded the government's stimulus support for Solyndra, a California manufacturer of solar panels, and other clean energy firms an Obama scandal. In fact, the loan guarantee program in the Energy Department that extended the controversial financing to the company began under the Bush administration. Contrary to the partisan hype, it actually returned a profit to taxpayers. Moreover, while Solyndra's investors were portrayed as Obama supporters, among its biggest backers were members of the conservative Walton family, the founders of Walmart. A huge investor in another solar company that went bust after taking the same Energy Department loans was the venture capitalist Dixon Doll, a major contributor to the Kochs' donor network. But as the House held hearings and various conservative front groups whipped up outrage about "crony capitalism," the facts were buried in favor of a narrative that helped the fossil fuel industry.

Congressman Upton insisted that he hadn't changed his position on environmental issues. But Jeremy Symons, then a senior vice president of the nonpartisan National Wildlife Federation, said that the transformation was "like night and day." He continued, "In the past the committee majority viewed the Clean Air Act as an effective way to protect the public. Now the committee treats the Clean Air Act and the EPA as if they are the enemy. Voters didn't ask for this pro-polluter agenda, but the Koch brothers spent their money well and their presence can be felt."

At the end of 2011, only twenty of the sixty-five Republican members of Congress who responded to a survey were willing to say that they believed climate change was causing the planet to warm. Tim Phillips gladly took credit for the dramatic spike in expressed skepticism. "If you look at where the situation was three years ago and where it is today, there's been a dramatic turnaround," he told the *National Journal.* "Most of these candidates have figured out that the science has become political," he said. "We've made great headway. What it means for candidates on the Republican side is, if you . . . buy into green energy or you play footsie on this issue, you do so at your political peril. The vast majority of people who are involved in the [Republican] nominating process—the conventions and the primaries—are suspect of the science. And that's our influence. Groups like Americans for Prosperity have done it."

Fred Koch, the family patriarch, had a saying, according to a former associate, which was that "the whale that spouts is the one that gets harpooned." As he had warned, the downside to the brothers' increasing visibility was growing public scrutiny. As the donors gathered for their January summit outside Palm Springs at the beginning of 2011, protesters swarmed the hitherto-secret meeting for the first time. Greenpeace, the theatrical environmental group, flew its 135-foot-long "airship" over the resort. Its Day-Glo green blimp was emblazoned with huge blowups of Charles and David's faces along with the words "Koch Brothers: Dirty Money."

The Koch network was no longer a secret. A squadron of local police in riot gear cordoned off the long, winding driveway to the Rancho Mirage resort, which was in virtual lockdown, while a ragtag assortment of protesters out front waved signs proclaiming, "Koch Kills!" and "Uncloak the Kochs!" Some twenty-five arrests were made, and the Kochs' private security guards, wearing gold-colored *K*s in their lapels, threatened to add one more when they caught the *Politico* reporter Kenneth Vogel in the resort's café. Unless he left the premises immediately, they warned, they would make a "citizen's arrest," forcing him to spend "a night in the Riverside County Jail."

Inside the fortified resort, some of America's most celebrated corporate chieftains huddled with Charles Koch, including the DeVos family of Amway, Ken Langone of Home Depot, and Tully Friedman, the private equity tycoon who was also chairman of the American Enterprise Institute. Like besieged royalty, David Koch and his wife, Julia, in dark sunglasses, made a brief appearance from one of the hotel's balconies, from which they grimly surveyed the street theater below.

The heavy-handed security reflected a more combative stance on the part of the Kochs toward the backlash that their outsized role in the public arena was stirring. Confidants described the brothers as obsessed with leaks and stung by the critical press coverage. They seemed surprised and resentful that their growing political influence had resulted in heightened scrutiny. They were accustomed to thinking of themselves as private citizens, and public-spirited ones at that. A golf partner said David "spumed and sputtered" about *The New Yorker* and other publications that had scrutinized the brothers, blaming the media for spurring death threats and forcing his family to hire personal bodyguards.

The Kochs also spoke darkly and inaccurately about the Obama White House conspiring with reporters to smear them. "They somehow thought that they could run tens of millions of dollars in ads, but fly under the radar screen, and that nobody was going to find out," a conservative source familiar with the Kochs told *Politico*. "So they're scrambling now because they weren't nearly as prepared as they should have been."

To handle the growing number of critics, particularly in the press, they brought in a new team of public relations advisers specializing in aggressive tactics. Michael Goldfarb, for instance, a Republican political operative whom the company hired at this point to improve its image, was described by *The New York Times* as "a conservative provocateur" who used "a blowtorch as his pen." Goldfarb had worked for Sarah Palin's vice presidential campaign, where he described his job as "attack the press." Later, he founded an online publication called *The Washington Free Beacon* that practiced what its editor called "combat journalism" against "liberal gasbags." Its motto was "Do unto them." In a profile, one conservative journalist told *The New Republic,* "I mean no disrespect, and I like him personally, but he is the single shadiest person on the right."

Joining Goldfarb was Philip Ellender, co-president of Koch Companies Public Sector, who oversaw the company's lobbying and public relations operations in Washington and who had a reputation, as *Politico* described it, for using "tactics that have helped cement the view that the Kochs play rough." Ellender oversaw a crisis communication project that included frequent polling to assess damage to the company's public image. To fight back, he launched a pugnacious corporate Web site called KochFacts that waged ad hominem attacks, questioning the professionalism and integrity of reporters whose work the company found unflattering, ranging from *The New York Times* to *Politico.* Brass-knuckle tactics were nothing new for the Koch brothers, but they were now deploying them against legitimate news reporters.

I got a taste of these tactics on the afternoon of January 3, 2011, when an e-mail popped onto my screen from David Remnick, the editor of *The New Yorker,* where I had been a staff writer since 1994. Remnick is a brilliant and busy editor who doesn't bother his writers unnecessarily. When he gets in touch, there's usually a good reason.

In his e-mail, Remnick explained that ten minutes earlier he'd received a baffling inquiry about me from Keith Kelly, the reporter who covered the media industry for the *New York Post.* Unsure how to respond, Remnick forwarded it and asked, "Can you help me out on this stuff?" He added courteously, "Sorry to bother you with this."

"Hi," Kelly's inquiry began, breezily. "We're hearing that a right-wing blogger may be preparing to let fly some pretty serious claims against Jane Mayer. On the one hand, it may be seen as payback for her bringdown of the Koch Brothers in August 2010."

His reference was to a ten-thousand-word article I had

written for *The New Yorker* five months earlier, titled "Covert Operations," with the reading line "The billionaire brothers who are waging a war against Obama." The story revealed in depth for the first time how the publicity-shy Koch brothers had stealthily leveraged their vast fortune to exert outsized influence over American politics. It also showed that their environmental and safety record was woefully at odds with their burnished public images as selfless philanthropists.

I had previously devoted the same amount of space in *The New Yorker* to profiling another such plutocratic donor, George Soros, a billionaire investor who spent a fortune underwriting liberal organizations and candidates. Soros hadn't liked the story, but he'd accepted that tough questions were to be expected from the press in a democracy. In contrast, when the *New Yorker* story on the Kochs came out, the brothers were enraged. Their company's general counsel, Mark Holden, later described the story as "a wake-up call," admitting, "We didn't have a response that was ready to go." Spearheading an aggressive damage-control effort, he soon sent a letter of complaint to the magazine. He was unable to identify any factual errors but argued that contrary to the article's title, "Covert Operations," there was nothing secretive or "covert" about them. Yet the Kochs, unlike Soros, had declined to grant *The New Yorker* an interview. Instead, after our story ran, David Koch denounced it in *The Daily Beast* as "hateful," "ludicrous," and "plain wrong." But his complaints lacked specificity, requiring no corrections, and so the magazine stood by the story, and we moved on. The calm, however, was deceptive.

In a squat Washington office building three blocks from the White House, a boiler room operation formed. Beginning in the summer of 2010, as the Kochs were ramping up spending on the midterm elections, half a dozen or so highly paid operatives labored secretly in borrowed office space in the back of the lobbying firm run by the former congressman J. C.

Watts. Their aim, according to a well-informed source, was to counteract *The New Yorker*'s story on the Koch brothers by undermining me. "Dirt, dirt, dirt" is what the source later told me they were digging for in my life. "If they couldn't find it, they'd create it."

Reprising the intimidating tactics that critics of Koch Industries had complained of for years, a private investigative firm with powerful political and law enforcement connections was retained. The firm, it appears, was Vigilant Resources International, whose founder and chairman, Howard Safir, had been New York City's police commissioner under the former mayor Rudolph Giuliani. The firm advertised itself as upholding "the highest standards of confidentiality and discretion."

It's uncommon for a private detective to be hired to conduct a retaliatory investigation into a reporter's character. It is after all the job of the press to cover politics. How much, if at all, the Kochs were personally involved in these activities remains unclear. Often private investigators are hired indirectly, working for law firms retained by the principals, so that they can claim attorney-client privilege, preserve deniability, and erase fingerprints. Asked whether he had investigated me, Howard Safir said only, "I don't comment. I don't confirm or deny it." His son, Adam Safir, who worked with him in the firm, also declined to comment. An effort to interview Charles and David Koch resulted in an e-mail from their company's spokesman, Steve Lombardo, saying simply, "We will have to decline." Asked in a follow-up e-mail whether the company had mounted a private investigation into me, he declined to respond.

However, clues leading back to the Kochs were everywhere. Sources described Goldfarb, Ellender, and other Koch Industries personnel as deeply involved in the project. Leading it, one source said, was Nancy Pfotenhauer, a longtime member of the Kochs' inner circle who has served as a Koch Industries spokesperson, as the head of its Washington office, and as the president of Americans for Prosperity.

I had no inkling about this until that fall, when, a few months after my story ran, a blogger called me to ask if I had heard the rumor that I was the target of some sort of cloak-and-dagger private detective's investigation. I laughed it off. At a Christmas party that winter, I was equally nonchalant when a former reporter pulled me aside with an odd warning. "This may be nothing," she said, but a private investigator she knew had mentioned there were a couple of conservative billionaires who wanted help digging up dirt on a Washington reporter. The reporter had written a story they disliked. "It occurred to me afterward that the reporter they wanted to investigate might be you."

These warnings flashed through my mind as I read the e-mail that Remnick forwarded from the *New York Post* reporter that afternoon in January. Kelly, the *Post* reporter, was hoping to get comment on "allegations" that he said were about to be published against me, claiming that I had "borrowed heavily" from other reporters' work. Before I had the chance to respond, though, a second set of e-mails reached both Remnick and me. This time the sender was Jonathan Strong, then a reporter at the online conservative news site *The Daily Caller,* whose editor, Tucker Carlson, was a senior fellow at the Cato Institute. Strong, too, it appeared, was about to publish a hit piece on me. His e-mails were ominous, asking Remnick outright whether my work fell "within the realm of plagiarism." He provided several samples of my writing and demanded an answer by ten o'clock the next morning.

Plagiarism ranks pretty high up on the list of crimes of moral turpitude in journalism. In a business where your name and credibility are everything, allegations like these could prove ruinous. Upon close inspection, though, it became clear that the allegations were inane and easily refutable. Someone, probably using a computer program, had mechanically sifted through almost a decade of my work and isolated quotations from officials, and other widely repeated phrases, to argue that "the structure and wording" were "quite close" to four other reporters' news stories. None of the supposedly purloined sentences were of any particular significance. This wasn't the sort of material anyone who actually knew anything about journalism would pay any attention to. Even sillier, in two of the four stories I was alleged to have "plagiarized," I had specifically given credit to the authors whose work *The Daily Caller* was claiming I'd stolen.

In twenty-five years of journalism, I'd made my share of spectacular mistakes, but no one had ever accused me of misappropriating their work. In fact, I'd always gone out of my way to credit others. But I also knew that if these charges weren't answered immediately, the truth would scarcely matter. Once the smear got into print, people would assume that there must have been *something* to it.

I was later told that by cooking up these charges, the boiler room operatives felt close to victory. "They thought they had you. They thought they were going to be knighted by the Kochs," said one source. Their search for dirt had started with my personal life, I was told, but when that turned up nothing truly incriminating, they moved on to plagiarism.

With only a few hours before these allegations were set to go online, all I could do was to try to get out the truth before the lies were spread. By midnight, I had reached three of the four authors from whom I was alleged to have plagiarized. All offered to make public statements supporting me and denying I had misappropriated their work. *The Daily Caller*'s reporter hadn't even interviewed them.

Lee Fang, a blogger for the liberal Web site *ThinkProgress* whose pathbreaking work on the Kochs I had cited in my story, issued a statement saying, "These accusations are without merit." He went on, "Ms. Mayer properly credited me in her story, and clearly did a ton of her own research. I have nothing but admiration for her integrity as a journalist."

Paul Kane, a reporter at *The Washington Post,* quickly looked up the story in question and sent me an e-mail saying, "Not only did you not steal from me, you Frickin' credited me in the VERY NEXT line." *The New Yorker* had even linked to his story online. And, I later learned, my husband, who was then an editor at *The Washington Post,* had edited the story that I supposedly stole. The allegations were becoming comical. The third reporter I reached also gave a statement saying she had no complaints. Later, the fourth did as well. If this was the best opposition research money could buy, it was pretty shoddy.

I sent the facts to *The Daily Caller,* which, after confirming them, dropped the story.

But Keith Kelly, to his credit, kept reporting. He tried to press the Koch spokesmen on whether they were behind the smear but, interestingly, got no response. He wrote a follow-up called "Smear Disappears," asking, "Who is behind the apparently concerted campaign to smear the New Yorker's Jane Mayer?" He noted, "The story is dead but the person or persons behind the allegations remains a shadowy mystery." He asked *The Daily Caller*'s editor, Carlson, who its source was, but Carlson claimed, "I have no clue where we got it."

There actually was a big clue. The plagiarism ploy had been timed to try to stop *The New Yorker* from nominating the Koch story for a National Magazine Award, according to the *New York Post.* And when *The New Yorker* went ahead and nominated the story anyway, the Kochs tried to stand in the way. Koch Industries' general counsel, Holden, sent a highly unusual letter to the board of the American Society of Magazine Editors, trying to stop it from picking my story for the prize. (The story didn't win anyway. *Que sera.*)

By then, as David Remnick told the *New York Post,* the

whole opposition research campaign seemed "pathetic." He added derisively, "I'm a little surprised to see a big-time operation behave like a bunch of Inspector Clouseaus."

The Kochs also went after Ed Crane, the Cato Institute head, who admitted to having been behind an unattributed quotation in my *New Yorker* story making light of Charles's "Market-Based Management" system. In response, shortly before the January 2011 summit, Charles invoked his ownership of Cato shares to force a management change, insisting that two longtime company loyalists, Nancy Pfotenhauer and Kevin Gentry, neither of whom was known as a deep libertarian thinker, join the think tank's board. Crane, who had co-founded Cato, was furious, but it was prelude to the final shake-up later that year in which Charles and David forced him out completely. David reportedly told Cato's chairman of the board, Robert Levy, that instead of producing esoteric intellectual theories, the ostensibly nonpartisan think tank should provide "intellectual ammunition that we can then use at Americans for Prosperity and our allied organizations" to influence elections.

If anything, the Kochs' ham-fisted reaction to criticism, and sense of aggrieved embattlement, seem to have only spurred their backers on, because by the time they left the guarded enclave near Palm Springs on February 1, 2011, the Koch coffers had $49 million more to spend. The bidding during the final fund-raising spree was so exuberant that one hotel staffer claimed he heard donors making pledges in increments of $5 million. With the House of Representatives safely delivered, the group was now on a roll, looking ahead to finishing off Obama once and for all in 2012.

First, though, there was a lot of discussion about how they could help the Republicans in the House, now that the GOP had the majority. Sean Noble, who continued as a contract political consultant to the Kochs, was pushing hard for them to start by helping Paul Ryan, the Wisconsin congressman who was the incoming chairman of the House Budget Committee.

For the big donors, Ryan was a superstar, a square-jawed, blue-eyed, earnest young Ayn Rand disciple described as "wonky" so often it seemed affixed to his title. His problem, though, was that his budget-slashing ideas scared the public, horrified liberals, and worried many Republicans, too. As he put it himself, "There's a lot of sharp knives in my drawer."

In the coming congressional session, Ryan planned to introduce a budget proposal that would serve as a blueprint for hard-line fiscal conservatives. No one expected it to pass in 2011, because the Democrats still held the Senate and the White House. But if Ryan gathered enough support, he could push the party hard to the right, tie Obama in knots, and provide a first draft for the GOP's 2012 platform. Tactically, a lot was riding on his success.

For several years, Ryan had been advocating radically deep cuts in government spending, including to Medicare and Medicaid, the two main government health programs for the elderly and the poor. He had also floated the idea of partially privatizing Social Security by introducing alternative private retirement accounts. He argued that the bloodletting was necessary for the country's fiscal health. The deficit, in his view, was reaching a crisis level, and these programs were unsustainable. His ideas were wildly popular with most of the wealthy donors. As the country's highest taxpayers, they would be the biggest beneficiaries of the tax savings produced by spending cuts. Moreover, none of them needed to rely on government social services for their health or welfare.

But many of Ryan's ideas were anathema to much of the middle class. When President George W. Bush had tried to privatize Social Security, a plan pushed by the Cato Institute, he had been forced to retreat in the face of overwhelming public opposition. The reality was that despite mobilizing the Tea

Party, the big conservative donors had a number of different priorities from the less affluent followers. Tea Party leaders had deliberately "fudged" their agenda on Social Security in order not to alienate the followers, according to one study. They talked in vague terms about keeping America from "going broke" but avoided specifics. Meanwhile, not one grassroots Tea Party supporter encountered by the study's authors argued for privatizing Social Security. Entitlement programs aiding the middle class were in fact so popular with most Americans that they were virtually sacrosanct. While rich free-market enthusiasts often favored replacing these programs with market-oriented alternatives, polls showed that virtually everyone else was adamantly opposed to the kinds of changes that Newt Gingrich candidly called "right-wing social engineering."

To popularize his radical budget plan, Ryan would need help, and Noble soon came up with a way for the donors to deliver it. He suggested they pay for expensive private polling and market testing to help Ryan fine-tune his pitch, as well as a campaign by "Astroturf" groups to create a drumbeat of public support. It was an intriguing idea, but it teetered on the edge of impropriety. Drafting the government's annual budget was a core congressional function.

At first, in the beginning of 2011, the donors were unenthused about the idea. Having already paid for an expensive election, they didn't understand why they now also needed to pay for polling and focus groups about government policy. But in the following months, this changed, and mysterious money from the Koch network started flowing. Much of it moved from the donors to a 501(c)(4) "social welfare" group cryptically called the TC4 Trust, working closely with a subgroup focused on budget issues called Public Notice. The TC4 Trust was little more than a UPS box in Alexandria, Virginia, but between 2009 and 2011 it reported revenue to the IRS of approximately $46 million and gave away some $37 million to other conservative nonprofit groups. It defined itself as a free-market advocacy group and filed papers with the IRS proclaiming that "the grant funds shall not be used for political activity." But it soon was paying for polling and a public advocacy campaign aimed at shaping and selling the Republican budget.

Ed Goeas, the president of the Tarrance Group, a Republican polling company that worked on the budget project, said that the challenge was to minimize political damage from cuts to entitlement spending. "It wasn't about developing policy," Goeas said, "it was about selling it." The solution, it appears, was to avoid the frank use of the word "cut" when talking about Medicare or Social Security. "There was discussion that you could deal with it as 'getting your money's worth out of the government,'" said Goeas. "You could talk about it as 'more effective'—but not as cutting it. It had to be more about 'efficiencies.' That was a large part of it," he said. Public Notice, which paid for the research, also mounted a public advocacy campaign describing the deficit as a looming catastrophe. "Public Notice was one of the Koch Brothers' groups," Goeas confirmed, adding that his firm worked "for it for three or four years" while simultaneously advising Ryan.

Ryan evidently proved eminently teachable. He was expert in the fine print of the budget but less certain about the public relations. So long as what emerged from these sessions was in line with his values, he was described as grateful for the help. Moreover, unlike most such advice, it came prepaid. As President Obama worked up his own budget proposal that spring, a process at the heart of governing, he had no idea that some of the richest people in the country, with huge stakes in the outcome, were partly paying to shape and sell the Republican alternative.

As the attention lavished on Ryan suggested, tax issues loomed large on the victorious donors' agenda. Dull though the mechanics can be, as Neera Tanden, the president of the liberal Center for American Progress, puts it, "When oligarchs control the levers of government, they get the spoils. It's litigated through tax policy."

Even before the Republicans formally took control of the House, the president felt forced into making concessions on tax issues vital to the donor class. In December 2010, he reached a deal that temporarily extended unemployment benefits to the millions of Americans still out of work, along with reducing payroll taxes and providing other help for the middle class. In exchange, Obama gave Republicans what they most wanted—an extension of the Bush-era income tax cuts that had disproportionately benefited the wealthy, which were slated to automatically expire.

Those cuts had lowered the top income tax rate from 39.6 percent to 35 percent. With bipartisan support, Bush had also slashed taxes on unearned income, most of which went to the rich. Taxes on dividends, for instance, were reduced dramatically from 39.6 percent to 15 percent. Taxes on capital gains, the overwhelming bulk of which were reaped by the wealthy, fell from 20 percent to 15 percent. As a result, many of the richest Americans were taxed at lower rates than middle- and working-class wage earners.

A 2008 study of the wealthiest four hundred taxpayers, for instance, showed that they earned an average of $202 million and paid an effective income tax rate of less than 20 percent. Fully 60 percent of their declared income derived from capital gains. In other words, the effective tax rate on earning $202 million was lower than the rate paid by Americans earning $34,501 a year.

The tax code hadn't always been so lopsided. As income grew increasingly concentrated at the top during the twentieth century, the tax code grew more generous to those with extreme wealth in response to the political pressure they put on lawmakers. The first peacetime income tax was enacted in 1894 as the result of William Jennings Bryan's Populist movement and applied to only the richest eighty-five thousand Americans out of a population of sixty-five million, or the top 0.1 percent. But the Supreme Court struck it down after the robber barons waged a proxy legal battle. Eighteen years later, the Sixteenth Amendment to the Constitution legalized the income tax, which in the beginning was only levied on the very rich. Rates were especially high in wartimes, when the taxes were seen as part of the patriotic duty of the privileged. During World War I, top earners paid a rate of 77 percent, and during World War II they paid a rate of 94 percent. (It was this tax that the Scaife family had avoided with its elaborate trusts and foundations.)

Soon, though, those at the very top succeeded in shifting the burden to those beneath them, so that by 1942 nearly two-thirds of the population paid income taxes. The rates remained relatively progressive for decades, with the top bracket paying a 50 percent rate in 1981. But the 1970s kicked off a three-decade-long "tax-cutting spree" during which the wealthiest 1 percent succeeded in getting their average effective federal tax rate slashed by a third, and the very, very richest, the 0.01 percent of the population, did even better, getting its effective federal tax rate cut in half. Unsurprisingly, the distribution of wealth in America grew increasingly skewed.

Critics argued that the extraordinarily rich had managed to shirk their fair share. But this was not how Charles Koch looked at it. He argued that "there is no 'fair share'" of the tax burden. The notion that cutting taxes on the wealthy shifted the burden to others, he said, was a false premise. Everyone's taxes should be cut, he argued. The aim, he said, was to shrink the government. "Our goal," he wrote in an impassioned essay in 1978, is "not to *reallocate* the burden of government; our goal is to *roll back* government."

From the standpoint of a radically antigovernment libertarian, paying lower taxes wasn't a matter of greed; it was a matter of principle. Libertarianism elevated tax avoidance into a principled crusade. Indeed, Koch argued that it was a moral act for the wealthy to cut their own taxes. As he put it in the same essay, "Morally, lowering taxes is simply *defending* property rights." It was, as the Libertarian Party platform put it in 1980, the responsibility of citizens to "challenge the cult of the omnipotent state."

Foster Friess, the Wyoming mutual fund manager who had joined political forces with the Kochs since the 1980s, depicted opposition to taxes as selfless too, but from a slightly different angle. He argued that the public benefited more when the wealthy paid less because the rich could do more good with their money than the government. "Wealthy people self-tax," he argued, by contributing to charities. "It's a question—do you believe the government should be taking your money and spending it for you, or do you want to spend it for you?" He argued, "It's that top 1 percent that probably contributes more to making the world a better place than the 99 percent."

Charles Koch, however, favored neither taxes nor charity. As he explained in a speech in 1999, "I agree with the 12th century philosopher, Maimonides, who defined the highest form of charity as dispensing with charity altogether, by enabling your fellow humans to have the wherewithal to earn their own living."

But according to the cultural critic and Jewish scholar Leon Wieseltier, who has taught several university courses on Maimonides, "This is false and tendentious and idiotic." He explains, "Maimonides did indeed prize the sort of charity that made its recipient more self-reliant, but he believed that the duty of charity is permanent" and that the responsibility to help the poor was "unequivocal and absolute." In fact, he points out, Maimonides declared that "he who averts his eyes from the obligation of charity is regarded as a villain."

While Koch and others in his group described their opposition to taxes as matters of pure principle, they put the Obama administration under constant pressure to accept tax cuts that directly increased their own wealth at the expense of everyone else. To reach the deal in December 2010, for instance, Republican negotiators insisted on cuts in estate taxes that would cost the Treasury $23 billion and save some sixty-six hundred of the wealthiest taxpayers an average of $1.5 million each.

The demand didn't materialize out of thin air. For years, some of the Republican Party's wealthiest backers, including the Kochs and the DeVoses, had been agitating to abolish what were cleverly dubbed "death taxes." The Kochs joined with sixteen of the other richest families in the country, including the Waltons of Walmart and the Mars candy clan, in financing and coordinating a massive, multiyear campaign to reduce and eventually repeal inheritance taxes. According to one 2006 report, these seventeen families stood to save $71 billion from the tax change, explaining why they willingly spent almost half a billion collectively, lobbying for it, beginning in 1998.

They were represented by a handful of front groups, including the American Family Business Institute, which strove to cast the tax break as necessary to preserve family farms. Unfortunately, in 2001, the group couldn't find a single family farm put out of business by the estate tax. After Hurricane Katrina, the same group scoured the country to find a storm victim whose heirs were hurt by the estate tax, in order to create some sympathy for its cause, but again failed to find a single one. In truth, only 0.27 percent of all estates were wealthy enough to be affected by estate taxes.

The lengths that some members of the Kochs' donor circle went to, hoping to ensure the biggest possible share of their family's fortunes, were impressive. The Koch brothers were far from alone in having litigated aggressively against their relatives. One member of their network during this period, Susan Gore, heiress to a piece of the Gore-Tex fabric fortune and founder of a conservative think tank called the Wyoming Liberty Group, was so intent on increasing her personal inheritance that she tried to legally adopt her ex-husband in order to claim that she had as many children as her siblings and thereby enlarge her portion of the family trust. But in late 2011, a judge rejected the seventy-two-year-old heiress's scheme, ruling that she could not count her former husband as her "son."

Although it enraged progressives, President Obama reluctantly consented to many of the Republicans' demands, including the enlarged exemptions from the estate tax. He had campaigned against extending the Bush tax cuts for those earning over $250,000 a year, but in December 2010, with the Republicans poised to take over the House, he tried to convince his disappointed supporters that this was the best deal they were likely to get for some time. "It used to be that you could govern by peeling off a couple of Republicans to do the right thing," he said, "but now, Glenn Beck and Sarah Palin are the center of the Republican Party—and there is no possibility of cooperation."

December's machinations were just the opening act, it turned out, in an unfolding drama in which Republicans in the House would eventually threaten to default on paying America's debts, potentially pitching the fragile U.S. economy into a calamitous free fall, in order to extort further tax and spending concessions favored by wealthy donors. All of this played out against a backdrop of growing economic inequality and stagnating social mobility. The United States, which idealized itself as a classless society in which everyone had the opportunity to get ahead, had in fact fallen behind many other rich nations in terms of intergenerational economic mobility, including such old-world, class-bound countries as France, Germany, and Spain.

Advancing the agenda of America's wealthiest winners under such circumstances would ordinarily be a hard sell. After all, in 2011, twenty-four million Americans were still out of work. The Great Recession had wiped out some $9 trillion in household wealth. But after forty years, the conservative nonprofit ecosystem had grown quite adept at waging battles of ideas. The think tanks, advocacy groups, and talking heads on the right sprang into action, shaping a political narrative that staved off the kind of course correction that might otherwise have been expected.

A key skirmish in this battle was the reframing of the history of the 2008 economic crash. From an empirical standpoint, it was hard to see it as anything other than a wipeout for the proponents of free-market fundamentalism and an argument for stronger government regulations. Like the Great Depression, it might have been expected to produce a backlash against those seen as irresponsible profiteers, resulting in more government intervention and a fairer tax system.

Joseph Stiglitz, the liberal economist, described the 2008 financial meltdown as the equivalent for free-market advocates to the fall of the Berlin Wall for Communists. Even the former Federal Reserve chairman Alan Greenspan, Washington's free-market wise man nonpareil, admitted that he'd been wrong in thinking Adam Smith's invisible hand would save business from its own self-destruction. Potentially, the disaster was a "teachable moment" from which the country's economic conservatives could learn. This is not what happened, however. They instead started with their preferred conclusion and worked backward to reach it.

In what the economic writer and asset manager Barry Ritholtz labeled Wall Street's "big lie," scholars at conservative think tanks argued that the problem had been too much government, not too little. The lead role in the revisionism was played by the American Enterprise Institute, whose board was stocked with financial industry titans, many of whom were free-market zealots and regulars at the Koch donor seminars.

Specifically, AEI argued that government programs that helped low-income home buyers get mortgages caused the collapse. Ritholtz noted that these theories "failed to withstand even casual scrutiny." There was plenty wrong with the government's quasi-private mortgage lenders, Fannie Mae and Freddie Mac, but numerous nonpartisan studies ranging from Harvard University's Joint Center for Housing Studies to the Government Accountability Office proved they were not a major cause of the 2008 crash. Yet by shifting the blame, Ritholtz noted, those "whose bad judgment and failed philosophy helped cause the crisis" could continue to champion the "false narrative" that free markets "require no adult supervision."

Self-serving research from corporate-backed conservative think tanks wasn't exactly news by 2011, but what was surprising, Ritholtz contended, was that "they are winning. Thanks to the endless repetition of the big lie." Phil Angelides, the chairman of the bipartisan commission that Congress set up to investigate the causes of the crash, was also taken aback by the revisionism. In an op-ed column, he tried to remind the public that it had been "the recklessness of the financial industry and the abject failures of policymakers and regulators that brought the economy to its knees." Instead, though, he said, "those at the top of the economic heap" were peddling "shopworn data" that had been "analyzed and debunked by the committee." He conceded that history was written by the winners and that by 2011, while much of the country lagged behind, most of the financial sector had bounced back and "the historical rewrite is in full swing."

Soon politicians backed by the same conservative donors who funded the think tanks were echoing the "big lie." Marco Rubio, a rising Republican star from Florida, for instance, who had defeated a moderate in the 2010 Republican Senate primary with the help of forty-nine donors from the June 2010 Koch seminar, soon proclaimed, "This idea—that our problems were caused by a government that was too small—it's just not true. In fact, a major cause of our recent downturn was a housing crisis created by reckless government policies."

Against this backdrop, on April 15, 2011, Ryan's budget

plan, now packaged as "The Path to Prosperity," came up for a vote in the House of Representatives. In the past, its prospects had been uncertain at best. Not just Democrats but many Republicans had deemed previous versions too harsh. A year earlier, Speaker of the House John Boehner had given it only lukewarm support. But by then the Republican caucus had moved far to the right, and the proposal had been repackaged. It now passed easily in the House 235–193, losing only four Republican votes but not attracting a single Democrat.

In the name of fixing Medicare, it shrank it to voucher-like "premium supports," with which senior citizens could buy private medical insurance. It also transformed Medicaid into a tattered patchwork of state-run block grants while cutting overall funding. Further, it repealed the Medicaid expansion that was a part of Obama's Affordable Care Act. At the same time, it reduced income taxes into two rates, cutting the top rate down to 25 percent—half of what it was when Ronald Reagan was elected. Theoretically, any losses were to be made up by eliminating deductions, but these were not specified. As the *New York Times* reporter Noam Scheiber summarizes it in *The Escape Artists: How Obama's Team Fumbled the Recovery,* Ryan's plan cut taxes for the wealthy by $2.4 trillion in comparison with Obama's proposed budget and then cut spending by $6.2 trillion. He describes it in short as "right-wing lunacy."

The most shocking aspect was its radical rewrite of America's social contract. To reduce the deficit, Ryan prescribed massive cuts in government spending, 62 percent of which would come from programs for the poor, even though these programs accounted for only about a fifth of the federal budget. According to a *New York Times* analysis of a similar, later version of Ryan's budget, 1.8 million people would be cut off food stamps, 280,000 children would lose their school lunch subsidies, and 300,000 children would lose medical coverage. Robert Greenstein of the liberal Center on Budget and Policy

Priorities called the plan "Robin Hood in reverse," arguing, "It would likely produce the largest redistribution of income from the bottom to the top in modern U.S. history."

The plan was successfully sold, nonetheless, winning a chorus of acclaim from conservative pundits and think tank scholars, whom the Republican leadership had treated to high-level policy briefings. Singing the plan's praise were the Cato Institute, the Heritage Foundation, and Grover Norquist's powerful antitax group, Americans for Tax Reform, which declared, "Paul Ryan's budget is what a REAL conservative budget looks like!" Many other nonprofit advocacy groups, like Public Notice, the 60 Plus Association, the Independent Women's Forum, and American Commitment, also chimed in for the drastic spending cuts. The clamor seemed multitudinous, but beneath the surface each of these groups shared a common aquifer—the pool of cash contributed by the Koch donor network.

A number of opinion writers also embraced Ryan as oracular. David Brooks, a moderately conservative *New York Times* columnist whose opinion Obama valued, declared Ryan's plan "the most courageous budget reform proposal any of us have seen in our lifetimes . . . His proposal will set the standard of seriousness for anybody who wants to play in this discussion. It will become the 2012 Republican platform, no matter who is the nominee."

The broader news media also echoed Ryan's claim that the federal deficit was the most pressing economic issue facing the country. As Freeland noted in *Plutocrats,* in April and May the five largest papers in the country published over three times more stories about the deficit than they did about jobs, even though unemployment was at 9 percent. "The right had succeeded in setting the terms of the economic debate. A good outcome for the 1 percent," she writes.

Ryan's success in convincing much of the Washington

media establishment that he was tackling hard problems, showing leadership, and bravely putting forth a plan to rescue entitlement programs while also fixing the country's daunting deficit threw the White House into a tailspin. It scrambled to put forth its own new alternative plan, which to the dismay of liberals called for additional cuts in spending beyond those the administration had already offered. Top political advisers to the president, like David Plouffe and Bill Daley, had long been preoccupied with looking centrist and winning independent voters, rather than catering to their liberal base, whom Plouffe had memorably dismissed as "bedwetters."

President Obama now proposed $4 trillion in spending cuts over the next twelve years, not all that far from the $4.4 trillion that Ryan had proposed. The proposal so distressed Hillary Clinton, then secretary of state, a colleague said, she had to go outside to get some air.

Then, in what came to be known as "the ambush," the White House invited Ryan to Obama's speech unveiling his counterproposal. With the congressman sitting in front of him, Obama lambasted Ryan's plan as "a vision that says we can't afford to keep the promises we made to our seniors . . . Put simply, it ends Medicare as we know it." Obama accused the Republicans of giving "more than $1 trillion in new tax breaks to the wealthy" and argued that it was "less about reducing the deficit than it's about changing the basic social compact in America."

Ryan was affronted at being attacked so publicly and personally. The breach of decorum became a mini-flap in Washington. Obama later told Bob Woodward that he hadn't known Ryan was there in the auditorium when he delivered his pointed speech. "We made a mistake," he confessed.

Out in the country, where people were less concerned with political etiquette than whether their benefits were about to be slashed, Ryan's proposed Medicare makeover proved immediately toxic. A Democratic underdog in a special congressional election in upstate New York clobbered the expected Republican winner by campaigning against Ryan's Medicare plan.

But the House Republicans were jubilant anyway. They had forced Obama to play their budget game. Instead of talking about jobs and spending, he was talking about the deficit and bargaining with them over how many trillions to cut. "*We* led. *They* reacted to *us*," exulted Kevin McCarthy, the House Republican whip. The donors were excited, too. Just the fact that Obama had been thrown on the defensive convinced those whose fortunes had helped pay for the Ryan plan that their investment was worth it.

By the late spring, the House Republicans had Obama in a bind on another issue as well. No sooner had the president reached a temporary budget agreement with the Republicans—one that included large Democratic concessions—than the self-styled "Young Guns," backed by the Tea Party faction in the House, forced a fight over raising the debt ceiling, a pro forma measure long used to authorize payment of the country's financial obligations. It looked as if the Tea Party radicals were protesting profligate spending, but in fact all they were doing was refusing to formally authorize payment of funds that Congress had already appropriated, in essence refusing to pay Congress's credit card bill after the previous year's shopping spree. In the end, their self-destructive fight hurt themselves more than anyone else, but meanwhile the radicals' willingness to pitch the U.S. government into default created a national crisis. The increasingly desperate standoff might produce chaos and dysfunction, but that prospect merely served the conservatives' antigovernment agenda. In the words of Mike Lofgren, a longtime Republican congressional aide, his party was becoming like "an apocalyptic cult."

If Congress failed to pay its bills, the country's AAA credit rating would be downgraded, potentially rocking markets, shaking business confidence, and worsening the painful recession. No one knew exactly how bad the consequences of default would be. Ordinarily, it would be unthinkable. Boehner had warned the insurgents in his caucus that they needed to "deal with it as adults." But Eric Cantor, the House majority leader and a founder of the Young Guns, seized on the debt ceiling vote as what he called "a leverage moment."

By 2011, the extremist upstarts had formed a powerful clique within the party's leadership and appeared itching to challenge Boehner's authority. Many owed more to the Kochs and other radical rich backers than they did to the party. The White House was under the misimpression that stolid business forces within the Republican Party would see the threat to the economy and force the radicals back from the edge. But while more traditional business interests, as represented by the U.S. Chamber of Commerce, took this stance, the right flank of the donor base was urging the Young Guns on to a showdown. In *The Wall Street Journal,* Stanley Druckenmiller, a billionaire hedge fund manager, described government default as less "catastrophic" than "if we don't solve the real problem," by which he meant government spending. And Charles Koch made clear in a March 2011 op-ed piece in *The Wall Street Journal* that he regarded any raise of the debt ceiling as simply a way to "delay tough decisions."

Pushing the Young Guns forward toward the financial cliff was Americans for Prosperity, the Kochs' political arm. Some forty other Tea Party and antitax groups also clamored for all-out war. Among the most vociferous was the Club for Growth, a small, single-minded, Wall Street–founded group powerful for one reason: it had the cash to mount primary challenges against Republicans who didn't hew to its uncompromising line. The club had developed the use of fratricide as a tactic to keep officeholders in line after becoming frustrated that many candidates it backed became more moderate in office. It discovered that all it had to do was threaten a primary challenge, and "they start wetting their pants," one founder joked. Its top funders included many in the Koch network, including the hedge fund managers Robert Mercer and Paul Singer and the private equity tycoon John Childs.

The Young Guns portrayed their opposition to compromise as a matter of pure principle, but beneath the surface huge vested interests were at play. The president and Boehner were close to negotiating what they called a "grand bargain" that anticipated closing some tax loopholes. The Young Guns were categorically opposed to reforms that might cut into the profits of hedge funds and private equity firms.

Cantor was especially protective of the carried-interest tax loophole. For him, the happiness of hedge fund and private equity titans was personal. He was among the House's top recipients of contributions from securities and investment firms. Three of the largest contributors to Cantor's two campaign funds in 2010 were financiers affiliated with the Koch network: Steven Cohen, the billionaire founder of the hugely lucrative hedge fund SAC Capital; Paul Singer, the multimillionaire head of the so-called vulture fund Elliott Management; and Stephen Schwarzman, the billionaire co-founder of the Blackstone Group. So although one study showed that the top twenty-five hedge fund managers earned an average of nearly $600 million a year and that closing this one loophole would raise $20 billion over the next decade, Cantor and the other rebels in the House who professed concern over the deficit "crisis" refused to back Boehner's proposed "grand bargain."

As tensions built in the increasingly calamitous debt ceiling stalemate, two sources say, Boehner traveled to New York to personally beseech David Koch's help. One former adviser to the Koch family says that "Boehner begged David to 'call off the dogs!' He pointed out that if the country defaulted, David's own investments would tank." A spokeswoman for

Boehner, Emily Schillinger, confirmed the visit but insisted, "Anyone who knows Speaker Boehner knows he doesn't 'beg.'" But the spectacle of the Speaker of the House, who was among the most powerful elected officials in the country, third in line in the order of presidential succession, traveling to the Manhattan office of a billionaire businessman to ask for his help in an internecine congressional fight captures just how far the Republican Party's fulcrum of power had shifted toward the outside donors by 2011.

In the final days of July, with default looming, Obama thought he was close to reaching a deal with Boehner. It was an abomination in the eyes of many Democrats because, among other features, it included cuts in projected Medicare and Medicaid spending. Obama had bought into the idea that cutting the deficit was of paramount importance and believed that the deal was necessary to stabilize the economy. He started preparing Democrats on the Hill for the painful news. Yet when the president called Boehner to formalize the agreement the night of July 21, to Obama's growing fury, with the clock ticking dangerously toward default, the Speaker didn't call him back. The president made multiple calls. He left messages. Almost an entire day passed. Finally, when Boehner called, it was to break off the talks, walk away, and then denounce Obama publicly.

"With no basis in fact," according to Thomas Mann and Norman Ornstein's study of congressional dysfunction, *It's Even Worse Than It Looks,* Boehner claimed that the president had reneged on the terms of their agreement. "I gave it my all," Boehner proclaimed. "Unfortunately, the president would not take yes for an answer."

Cantor later told the real story to Ryan Lizza of *The New Yorker.* Blowing up the grand bargain had been his idea. He said it was a "fair assessment" to say that in the critical final moments he had talked Boehner out of accepting the deal for purely political reasons. Cantor had argued, why give Obama a win? Why aid his reelection campaign by helping him look competent? It would be more advantageous for the Republicans to sabotage the talks, regardless of the mess it left the country in, and wait to see if the next year's presidential election brought them a Republican president who would give them a better deal.

The eventual result was what Lizza described as a "byzantine" arrangement in which in order to forestall default, both parties agreed to automatic spending cuts, imposed indiscriminately across the whole budget. No one believed the mindless cuts, which were called a "sequester," would ever get enacted. But in fact, when no other resolution could be reached, they were. The mechanism placed Obama in a fiscal straitjacket indefinitely. The chairman of the Congressional Black Caucus, Emanuel Cleaver, denounced the deal as "a sugar-coated Satan sandwich," which the House minority leader, Pelosi, amended to "a Satan sandwich with Satan fries on the side."

The political damage stretched far and wide. The nonpartisan Congressional Budget Office estimated that the sequester would cost the economy 750,000 jobs a year and hurt millions of Americans who were reliant on public services. Standard & Poor's downgraded America's credit rating for the first time in the country's history. The stock market plummeted, falling 635 points on the spot. The public, meanwhile, was so disgusted with Congress that polls registered the lowest approval rating in the history of such measurements. Obama's popularity also took a hit, dropping below the all-important 50 percent threshold for the first time. He was derided and belittled by both the Left and the Right. Internal polls called him "weak."

A political minority, responding to the interests of its extreme sponsors, had succeeded in rendering the most powerful democracy in the world dysfunctional. Thirty years after the Libertarian Party platform called for the "abolition of Medicare and Medicaid," the "repeal . . . of the increasingly oppressive Social Security System," and "the eventual repeal of all taxation," its billionaire backers had the upper hand.

At this point, Neera Tanden believes, the president finally understood what he was up against. "I think he came in truly trying to be post-partisan," she said. "I think it took the debt ceiling fight to make him see that they hated him more than they wanted to succeed. It was an irrational deal, driven by their funders." Two and a half years into his presidency, she said, "he finally realized they would rather kill him than save themselves."

CHAPTER TWELVE

Mother of All Wars: The 2012 Setback

ON A SOFT, SUMMERY NIGHT IN BEAVER CREEK, COLORADO, AT the end of June 2011, the Kochs mustered their troops once again for what Charles described as "the Mother of All Wars." The phrase, borrowed from the Iraqi dictator Saddam Hussein, hinted at the level of martial ferocity with which the billionaire brothers planned to approach the coming 2012 presidential campaign.

It would be the first presidential race after the Supreme Court's *Citizens United* decision. For those with the requisite financial resources, political spending was now as limitless as the open sky above the Bachelor Gulch Ritz-Carlton. Three hundred or so participants were there for the semiannual seminar, whose theme was "Understanding and Addressing Threats to American Free Enterprise and Prosperity." This time, the planners took extra precautions to keep the proceedings secret. A series of loudspeakers formed a fence around an outdoor pavilion in which the donors met, emitting static toward the outside world, to prevent eavesdropping. Or so they thought until a reporter for *Mother Jones,* Brad Friedman, obtained an audio recording of the weekend's highlights and published a transcript.

As they gathered in the foothills of the Rockies, the donors had ample reason for optimism. *The New York Times*'s resident number cruncher, Nate Silver, who handicapped political odds with the unsentimental eye of a racetrack bookie, was openly asking, "Is Obama toast?" After analyzing Obama's sagging approval rating and the economy's lagging indicators, he concluded that Obama had gone from "a modest favorite to win re-election to, probably, a slight underdog." If the Republicans chose a weak candidate or the economy miraculously revived, he noted, this could change. But if the challengers played it right, he predicted, Obama would go the way of the recent reelection losers Jimmy Carter and George H. W. Bush.

The choice of a strong Republican candidate, however, fifteen months before the next presidential election, was far from assured. Behind the scenes, Sean Noble, with the assent of the Kochs, had been furtively trying for months to persuade Paul Ryan to run for the White House. The billionaire backers were eager for him to apply his "sharp knives" to the federal budget. But Ryan had demurred. Neither he nor his wife relished a presidential marathon. "Wouldn't it be easier just to be picked as vice president?" he asked an emissary from the Kochs, in a meeting in the congressman's Washington office. "Because then it's only, like, two months."

With Ryan declining to run, the Kochs and their operatives searched anxiously for an alternative. Mitt Romney was obviously a serious contender, but they worried that he couldn't relate well enough to ordinary people to get elected. Polls showed that Romney, who had made a fortune in finance before his stint as governor of Massachusetts, fared dismally when voters were asked if he "cares about people like you." The search for a more promising candidate set off a torrid courtship of Chris Christie, the tough-guy governor of New Jersey. David Koch invited Christie to his Manhattan office, where the two spent almost two hours bonding over Christie's brawls with the unions and other liberal forces. The governor's scrappy blue-collar style, combined with his plutocrat-friendly economic policies, made him an almost irresistible prospect. By June, the Kochs had given Christie the keynote speaker slot at their seminar, where he could audition for his party's leading role in front of the people who could pay his way.

Rick Perry, the governor of Texas, who preceded Christie as a speaker, provided a perfect foil. In a prelude to Perry's later "oops" moment during the Republican debates, the governor made a poor impression on the numerically minded businessmen in the audience by displaying five fingers to illustrate a four-point plan, only to be left with one digit still waving in the air, programmatically unaccounted for.

In comparison, Christie was the political equivalent of his idol, Bruce Springsteen. David Koch personally introduced him, showering him with praise as not just a "true political hero" who "tells it like it is" but also "my kind of guy." Koch was especially effusive about the "courage and leadership" Christie showed in forging a bipartisan deal to cut future pension and benefit payments to New Jersey's unionized public sector employees. In exchange for these concessions, the Democrats and their union allies had obtained a promise from Christie to increase payments into the ailing funds. This tough-minded seeming "fix" vaulted Christie to national prominence. Four years later, a judge would rule that it was more like a bait and switch. The workers' benefits were cut, but the state, which was in an economic slump, reneged on its end of the bargain. In 2011, however, for the Kochs and their assembled allies, Christie was the cherished face of the future. "Who knows?" Koch teased, as the donors cheered, whistled, and hooted their approval during his introduction. "With his enormous success in reforming New Jersey, some day we might see him on a larger stage where, God knows, he is desperately needed!"

Christie soon brought the well-heeled crowd to its feet by casting low taxes on high-income earners as a populist cause. In a bravura performance, he described going to battle against what he called a "Millionaires Tax"—a 1 percent income tax increase on the state's top earners. "Take this back where it came from, 'cuz I ain't signin' it," he recounted telling the Democrats as the donors cheered. Christie had campaigned on making his state a superpower in wind energy, but his reversal and withdrawal from a regional program to reduce greenhouse gas emissions also drew cheers. When it came time for questions from the audience, the first speaker voiced the excitement in the room, saying, "You're the first guy I've seen who I know could beat Barack Obama," and then, amid laughter and applause, begged Christie to run.

But the dinner's main course was the fund-raising session led by Charles Koch. In a folksy midwestern voice, he appealed for contributions as if America's survival depended on it. After invoking Saddam Hussein's famous battle cry from the first Gulf War, Koch struck a more alarmist note. The stakes in the coming presidential campaign, he warned, were nothing short of "the life or death of this country." Not, he added with good humor, that he was trying to "put any pressure on anyone here, mind you. This is not pressure. But if this makes your heart feel glad and you want to be more forthcoming, so be it." Then, in a move guaranteed to put the squeeze on everyone else, he publicly identified and commended the largest donors to date. "What I want to do is recognize not all our great partners, but those partners who have given more than a billion—a mill—no, billion," at which point he caught and corrected himself. As the wealthy crowd knowingly guffawed at the easy confusion over a few extra zeros, Charles ad-libbed, "Well, I was thinking of Obama and his billion dollar campaign, so I thought we gotta do better than that." He went on, "If you want to kick in a billion, believe me, we'll have a special seminar just for you."

Charles then ticked off the names of the thirty-two donors who had contributed a million dollars or more during the previous twelve months. Nine were billionaires whose fortunes had landed them on *Forbes*'s list of the four hundred wealthiest Americans. Some, like the finance stars Charles Schwab, Ken Griffin, and Paul Singer, as well as Amway's Richard DeVos and the natural gas entrepreneur Harold Hamm, were fairly well-known. Many others, though, were members of the invisible rich—owners of enormously profitable private enterprises that rarely drew public attention. Two among the nine billionaires, for instance, John Menard Jr., whose fortune *Forbes* estimated at $6 billion, and Diane Hendricks, whose fortune the magazine valued at $2.9 billion, owned private building and home supply companies in Wisconsin and were not well-known outside the state, let alone in it. Many of the nonbillionaires whom Charles recognized were familiar faces in the Kochs' circle. There were the Popes from North Carolina, the Friess family from Wyoming, and the Robertsons of the Texas oil clan, as well as coal barons like Joe Craft and the Gilliams and members of the Marshall family, the only significant outside owners of Koch Industries' stock.

Charles then added, "Ten more will remain anonymous, including David and me. So we're very humble in that," he joked. More seriously, though, he declared that "the plan is, the next seminar, I'm going to read the names of the *ten* million"—not mere one million—dollar donors.

As he read the names of the generous, he made clear what he expected their money to buy. He promised those he referred to as his "partners" that "we are absolutely going to do our utmost to invest this money wisely and get the best possible payoff for you in the future of the country."

None of these thoughts were shared with the rest of the country. Far from the Supreme Court majority's assumption in the *Citizens United* case that political spending would be transparent, the Kochs and their partners took great pains to hide what they were up to. Indeed this was a selling point. Kevin Gentry, vice president of Koch Industries for special projects, who had overseen fund-raising for the brothers for years and who played the role of master of ceremonies at the seminars, assured the donors that weekend, "There is anonymity we can protect."

The Kochs had recently come up with a new and even cleverer way of masking the money. Rather than simply directing the funds through the maze of secretive nonprofit charities and social welfare groups that they had used during the 2010 campaign, they now established a more efficient method. They pooled much of the cash first in a form of nonprofit corporation that the tax code defined as a 501(c)(6), or a "business league." The advantage of this umbrella organization, which they named the Association for American Innovation (AAI), was that donations to it could be classified as "membership dues" and to some extent get deducted as business expenses. As with contributions to a 501(c)(4), the law protected the donors' anonymity. But as a business league, it fell outside the charitable trust purview of state attorneys general, further safeguarding the secrecy.

By the time the Beaver Creek seminar adjourned, the Kochs had collected some $70 million in new pledges. There is no public record showing specifically how these new funds were spent, but it appears that much of the money was directed into the new "business league," the Association for American Innovation. During 2011 alone, tax records show, the AAI, which soon changed its name to Freedom Partners, accumulated over a quarter of a billion dollars.

The new business league, which was at first run by Wayne Gable, the head of lobbying for Koch Industries, was less than candid with the Internal Revenue Service about its intentions. According to its founding documents, it told the IRS it "does not currently plan to attempt to influence any election" and in the future might do so but only to "an insubstantial" extent. From the start, however, the organization financed many of the same political front groups that the Kochs had mobilized in the 2010 midterms. This time, though, their underground guerrilla war against Obama was waged by a "business league" and treated as a partially tax-deductible business expense. From November 2011 to October 2012, the Kochs' new "business league" transferred $115 million to Sean Noble's Center to Protect Patient Rights and $32.3 million to David Koch's group, Americans for Prosperity.

In October 2011, Christie announced definitively that 2012 was not his year. The truism about the two parties was that when it came to choosing candidates, "Democrats fall in love, while Republicans fall in line." But 2012 was shaping up to be the exception. With power shifting from the centralized party professionals to rogue billionaires, top-down consensus was giving way to warring factions. Even within the Koch camp, there were divergent opinions. After the infatuation with Ryan, David Koch liked Christie. Charles Koch admired Mike Pence, then a congressman and later governor of Indiana. When Pence declined to get in the race, the Kochs hired his former chief of staff, Marc Short, as yet another political adviser. The donors, meanwhile, were all over the Republican lot. Noble was trying hard to herd everyone in one direction but failing.

Unsure what else to do, in late 2011 the Koch operatives made one of the first attack ads of the general election season. Sponsored by Americans for Prosperity, it slammed Obama as corruptly showering his friends with "green giveaways" such as Solyndra. AFP spent $2.4 million running the ad thousands of times in the key states of Florida, Michigan, Nevada, and Virginia. Sean Noble had sold the idea as a clean shot. But it caused a little problem. One of the Koch donors turned out to have invested in Solyndra and was not happy.

A subsequent Koch-created ad, aired by the American Future Fund, also proved problematic. The mysterious Iowa-based front group was a favorite choice for messages from which the Koch camp preferred to distance itself. Shot as populist rage against the "1 percent" was coalescing in the Occupy movement and protesters were marching on David Koch's apartment, the ad slyly attacked Obama for being too cozy with Wall Street. After quoting Obama calling Wall Street bankers "fat cats," it asked, "Guess who voted for the Wall Street bailout? His White House is full of Wall Street executives," it went on, as mug shots of Obama's advisers flashed by. The Kochs' political operatives tested the ad in fifteen separate focus groups. Once aired, it seemed to be a great success, getting over five million hits on YouTube. But some of the finance industry executives in the donor group were not amused by the political misdirection. "Why attack Wall Street?" they asked.

One donor, Peter Schiff, an attendee at the June Koch seminar, evidently didn't receive the new, populist talking points. A Connecticut financial analyst and broker, he barged into the midst of the Occupy movement's Manhattan encampment in October with a sign proclaiming, "I am the 1%. Let's talk." Subsequent video footage of him arguing in favor of eliminating the minimum wage and paying "mentally retarded" people $2 an hour made him a laughingstock on Jon Stewart's *Daily Show*. The Kochs' "Mother of All Wars" wasn't starting out all that much better than Saddam Hussein's.

The picture was far brighter in the key presidential battleground state of Wisconsin. There, the first-term governor, Scott Walker, had vaulted to national stardom by enacting unexpectedly bold anti-union policies. Walker exemplified the new generation of Republicans who had coasted to victory in 2010 on a wave of dark money, ready to implement policies their backers had painstakingly incubated in conservative nonprofits for decades.

For the Koch network, Walker's improbable rise was a triumph. Koch Industries PAC was the second-largest contributor to Walker's campaign. More important, the Kochs were an important source of funds to the Republican Governors Association, which Republicans used in Wisconsin and elsewhere in 2010 to work around strict state contribution limits. The Kochs' PAC had also contributed to sixteen state legislative candidates in Wisconsin, who all won their races, helping conservatives take control of both houses of the legislature and setting the stage for Wisconsin's dramatic turn to the right.

Walker had also benefited enormously from the philanthropy of two other archconservative brothers, the late Lynde and Harry Bradley, whose foundation had grown into an ideological behemoth in Milwaukee. Walker's campaign manager, Michael Grebe, was the Bradley Foundation's president. Think tanks had long supplied policy ideas to those in power. Some, like the liberal Center for American Progress, were led by well-known partisans who moved in and out of government. It was rare, though, to wear both hats simultaneously. But Grebe's dual role would have made his predecessor at the Bradley Foundation, Michael Joyce, proud. It was exactly the kind of hands-on political impact Joyce had sought when he set out to weaponize conservative philanthropy.

The Bradley Foundation's close ties to Walker were evident on his social calendar. Among his first private engagements after the election was a celebratory dinner with the foundation's board and senior staff at Bacchus, a stylish Milwaukee restaurant overlooking Lake Michigan. By then, Lynde and Harry Bradley's foundation had assets of over $612 million and had provided the playbook for many of Walker's policies.

Grebe denied his foundation had hatched the initiative that made Walker famous, his crackdown on the state employees' unions. But he applauded the move and had personally sent out fund-raising letters asking supporters to help Walker fight "the big government union bosses." The Bradley Foundation, meanwhile, in 2009, gave huge grants to two conservative Wisconsin think tanks developing plans to break the power of the state's public employee unions. As the *Milwaukee Journal Sentinel* noted in 2011, the Bradley Foundation was "one of the most powerful philanthropic forces behind America's conservative movement" and "the financial backer behind public policy experiments that started in the state and spread across the nation—including welfare reform, public vouchers for private schools and, this year, cutbacks in public employee benefits and collective bargaining." As Grebe later acknowledged about Walker's meteoric rise to *The New York Times,* "At the risk of being immodest, I probably lent some credibility to his campaign early on."

As a college dropout with no exceptional charisma or charm, Walker might not ordinarily have been marked for high office, but Americans for Prosperity, which had a large chapter in Wisconsin, had provided him with a field operation and speaking platform at its Tea Party rallies when he was still just the Milwaukee county executive. The Kochs' political organization had been fighting the state's powerful public employee unions there since 2007. The fight was freighted with larger significance. In 1959, Wisconsin had become the first state to allow its public employees to form unions and engage in collective bargaining, which conservatives detested in part because the unions provided a big chunk of muscle to the Democratic Party. "We go back a long way on this in Wisconsin, and in other states," Tim Phillips, the head of Americans for Prosperity, acknowledged to *Politico.* In the past, Phillips had spoken enviously of the unions as the Left's "army on the ground."

Walker's anti-union, antitax, and small-government message harmonized perfectly with the Kochs' philosophy and also served their business interests. Koch Industries had two Georgia-Pacific paper mills in the state, as well as interests in lumber mills, coal, and pipelines employing some three thousand workers.

Soon, a handful of Wisconsin's wealthiest magnates, who were part of the Koch donor network, started writing checks, too. John Menard Jr., for instance, the richest man in Wisconsin, was both a million-dollar donor at the Kochs' June 2011 summit and a million-and-a-half-dollar donor to the Wisconsin Club for Growth, an outside dark-money group boosting Walker. Like many of Menard's investments, the political contributions more than paid off. Once in office, Walker chaired a state economic development corporation that bestowed $1.8

million in special tax credits on Menard's business. Walker's administration also eased up on enforcement actions against polluters.

Seventy years old at the time Walker was elected, Menard had made a fortune, estimated at about $6 billion in 2010, from a chain of home improvement stores bearing his name, but until Walker entered the statehouse, his relationship with the government had been contentious, to say the least. According to a 2007 profile in *Milwaukee Magazine,* his company had more clashes with the state's Department of Natural Resources than any other firm in Wisconsin. Ultimately, his company and Menard personally paid $1.7 million in fines for illegally disposing of hazardous waste. In one memorable instance, his company reportedly labeled arsenic-tainted mulch as "ideal for playgrounds."

Menard's hostility to organized labor was pronounced. He imposed an absolute ban on hiring anyone who had ever belonged to a union. One employee described having to fire two promising management prospects because they had worked in high school as baggers for a unionized supermarket. Managers, meanwhile, were subject to 60 percent pay cuts if their stores became unionized. They also had to agree to pay fines of $100 per minute for infractions such as opening late and to submit any disputes to management-friendly arbitration rather than the courts. Menard also forbade employees to build their own houses, for fear they would pilfer supplies. When one employee got special permission to build a ramp-equipped home in order to accommodate a wheelchair-bound daughter (in exchange for a demotion and a large salary cut), he was fired. His offense was that his contractor was using building materials from a competitor.

Menard had a disputatious record on compensation and taxes as well. The IRS ordered him to pay $6 million in back taxes after he allegedly mischaracterized $20 million as salary, not dividends, deducting it as a business expense. In a separate case, the Wisconsin Supreme Court forced Menard to pay $1.6 million to a former legal counsel, a woman who was the sister of his girlfriend at the time, to compensate for gender discrimination and gross underpayment. The woman's lawyer described Menard as "a man without parameters, no limits, no respect for the law, and obviously no self-discipline."

That case was followed by another in which the wife of a former business associate whom Menard fired in 2011 accused him of retaliating against her husband because of her refusal to engage in a sexual threesome with the billionaire and his wife. A spokesman for Menard denied the allegation. Meanwhile, a second woman, the wife of a former Indianapolis Colts quarterback, claimed Menard fired her for rebuffing his sexual advances. The company spokesman denied this as well. All in all, Menard seemed an unlikely patron for Walker, who emphasized his Christian conservatism as the son of a Baptist preacher, but on economic policies there was a meeting of the minds. Moreover, Menard was famously press shy, and little of his involvement with Walker surfaced until years later.

Diane Hendricks, the richest woman in Wisconsin and another of the Kochs' million-dollar donors, might also have stayed beneath the radar except for a documentary filmmaker who fortuitously caught her on camera. Fifteen days after Walker was inaugurated, in January 2011, Hendricks was captured in what she thought was a private chat, urging the governor to go after the unions. Looking glamorous but impatient, the sixty-something widow pressed Walker to turn Wisconsin into a "completely red" "right-to-work" state. Walker assured her that he had a plan. He had kept voters in the dark about it during his campaign, but he confided to Hendricks that his first step was to "deal with collective bargaining for all public employees' unions." This, he assured her, would "divide and conquer" the labor movement. Evidently, this was what Hendricks wanted to hear. She had amassed a fortune estimated at $3.6 billion from ABC Supply, the nation's largest wholesale distributor of roofing, windows, and siding, which she and her late husband, Ken, founded in 1982. Despite her phenomenal success, Hendricks said she was worried that America was becoming "a socialist ideological nation." Soon after the governor reassured her that he shared her concern, Hendricks and her company began a series of record-setting contributions that would reportedly make her Walker's biggest financial backer.

When Walker "dropped the bomb" on the unions, as he put it, he effectively stripped most state employees of the right to bargain collectively on their pay packages. He singled out the public employees, and particularly teachers, whose average salary was $51,264, as causes of the state's deficit. Amid the doomsday talk about overindulged and under-contributing public workers who were bankrupting the state, one awkward fact went unmentioned. Thanks to complicated accounting maneuvers, Diane Hendricks, according to state records, did not pay a dime in personal state income taxes in 2010.

Lines were drawn in Madison. In a desperate attempt to deprive Republicans of the quorum necessary to pass Walker's anti-union bill, Democratic legislators fled the state. Angry activists stormed the legislature, thronged the streets, and lambasted Walker as the Kochs' anti-union stooge. Walker unwittingly lent credence to the caricature less than a month into his tenure by carrying on a long, cringe-worthy phone conversation with a prankster pretending to be David Koch, the contents of which were soon made public. In a phrase that said all too much, Walker enthusiastically signed off with the impostor by saying, "Thanks a million!"

As the furious backlash against Walker evolved into a prolonged and ultimately unsuccessful effort by his critics to recall him from office, the Kochs, who by then had become the face of the opposition, mounted a fierce counterattack. They used Americans for Prosperity and other vehicles to mobilize pro-Walker rallies and air thousands of "Stand with Walker" and "It's Working!" television and radio ads. They also utilized

Themis, a high-tech data bank they had developed, to help get out the vote.

After Walker triumphed in the recall fight, putting him in line for his ill-fated run for the White House in 2016, an independent counsel's investigation into possible campaign-finance violations disgorged a trove of e-mails revealing just how many hugely wealthy, out-of-state hidden hands were involved in his campaign to stay in office. The e-mails revealed advisers to Walker scheming to get the Kochs and allied donors to help him by donating to what purported to be an independent group, the Wisconsin Club for Growth. One e-mail suggested, "Take Koch's money." Another insisted that the governor should "get on a plane to Vegas and sit down with Sheldon Adelson." It went on, "Ask for $1m now." A third advised Walker that Paul Singer, the hedge fund mogul, would be at the same resort as he and insisted, "Grab him." Soon after, the Wisconsin Club for Growth received $250,000 from Singer.

At the helm of the Wisconsin Club for Growth, and thus at the center of the web, was an old ally of the Kochs', Eric O'Keefe. He was the same Wisconsin investor who had volunteered in David Koch's ill-fated Libertarian campaign for vice president, before going on to run the Sam Adams Alliance, which had played a seminal role in launching the Tea Party movement, and join the Cato Institute's board. Over the years, O'Keefe's various political gambits had also been greatly aided by the Bradley Foundation. According to one tally, it contributed over $3 million to groups directed or founded by O'Keefe between 1998 and 2012. The Bradley Foundation, meanwhile, tightened its ties to several members of the Kochs' circle. It soon added to its board both Diane Hendricks and Art Pope, the Kochs' longtime North Carolina ally, who also was on the board of Americans for Prosperity. The club that O'Keefe and the others belonged to was ingrown and small, but its reach was growing.

Richard Fink made clear what the stakes were for both

himself and his benefactors after the embarrassment of the trick phone call. "We will not step back at all," he proclaimed. "With the Left trying to intimidate the Koch brothers to back off of their support for freedom and signaling to others that this is what happens if you oppose the administration and its allies, we have no choice but to continue the fight." Fink defiantly claimed, "This is a big part of our life's work. We are not going to stop."

Buoyed by their success in Wisconsin, the Kochs began to focus in earnest on the presidential race. It had taken years, but by 2012 they were becoming a rival center of power to the Republican establishment. Political insiders who had once scoffed at them now marveled at the breadth of their political operation.

While amassing one of the most lucrative fortunes in the world, the Kochs had also created an ideological assembly line justifying it. Now they had added a powerful political machine to protect it. They had hired top-level operatives, financed their own voter data bank, commissioned state-of-the-art polling, and created a fund-raising operation that enlisted hundreds of other wealthy Americans to help pay for it. They had also forged a coalition of some seventeen allied conservative groups with niche constituencies who would mask their centralized source of funding and carry their message. To mobilize Latino voters, they formed a group called the Libre Initiative. To reach conservative women, they funded Concerned Women for America. For millennials, they formed Generation Opportunity. To cover up fingerprints on television attack ads, they hid behind the American Future Fund and other front groups. Their network's money also flowed to gun groups, retirees, veterans, antilabor groups, antitax groups, evangelical Christian groups, and even $4.5 million for something called the Center for Shared Services, which coordinated administrative tasks such as office space rentals and paperwork for the others. Americans for Prosperity, meanwhile, organized chapters all across the country. The Kochs had established what was in effect their own private political party.

Secrecy permeated every level of the operation. One former Koch executive, Ben Pratt, who became the chief operating officer of the voter data bank, Themis, used a quotation from Salvador Dalí on his personal blog that could have served as the enterprise's motto: "The secret of my influence is that it has always remained secret."

Robert Tappan, a spokesman for Koch Industries, defended the secrecy as a matter of security, because "Koch has been targeted repeatedly in the past by the Administration and its allies because of our real (or, in some cases, perceived) beliefs and activities concerning public policy and political issues," overlooking decades of secrecy from the John Birch Society onward.

This consolidation of power reflected the overall national trend of increasingly large and concentrated campaign spending by the ultra-wealthy in the post–*Citizens United* era. The spending, in turn, was a reflection of the growing concentration of wealth more generally in America. As a result, the 2012 election was a tipping point of sorts. Not only was it by far the most expensive election in the country's history; it was also the first time since the advent of modern campaign-finance laws when outside spending groups, including super PACs and tax-exempt nonprofit groups, flush with unlimited contributions from the country's richest donors, spent more than $1 billion to influence federal elections. And when the spending on attack ads run by nonprofits was factored in, outside spending groups might well have outspent the campaigns and the political parties for the first time.

The Koch network loomed as a colossus over this new political landscape. On the right, there were other formidable donor networks, including the one assembled by Karl Rove, but no single outside group spent as much. On its own, in 2012 the Kochs' network of a few hundred individuals spent at least $407 million, almost all of it anonymously. This was more than John McCain spent on his entire 2008 presidential bid. And it was more than the combined contributions to the two presidential campaigns made by 5,667,658 Americans, whose donations were legally capped at $5,000. *Politico*'s Kenneth Vogel crunched the numbers and discovered that in the presidential race the top 0.04 percent of donors contributed about the same amount as the bottom 68 percent. No previous year for which there were data had shown more spending by fewer people. The staggeringly lopsided situation made 2012 the starkest test yet of Louis Brandeis's dictum that the country could have either "democracy, or we may have wealth concentrated in the hands of a few," but not both.

The Kochs' growing clout was evident in a confidential internal Romney campaign memo dated October 4, 2011. Romney, like virtually every ambitious Republican in the country, was angling for David Koch's support. The memo described him plainly as "the financial engine of the Tea Party," although it noted that he "denies being directly involved."

Romney, it revealed, had hoped to woo Koch in a private tête-à-tête at the billionaire's beachfront mansion in Southampton, New York, over the summer. But to the campaign's dismay, Hurricane Irene had washed the meeting out. With the Iowa caucuses looming, and Chris Christie out of the race, Romney tried again in the fall.

Shortly after the memo was written, Romney took two controversial campaign stances that were guaranteed to please the billionaire brothers. First, he reversed his earlier position on climate change. In his 2010 book, *No Apology,* Romney had written, "I believe that climate change is occurring—the reduction in the size of global ice caps is hard to ignore. I also believe that human activity is a contributing factor." When he hit the campaign trail in June of 2011, Romney reiterated this view and stressed that it was "important for us to reduce our emissions of pollutants and greenhouse gases that may well be significant contributors to the climate change and the global warming that you're seeing." But at a rally in Manchester, New Hampshire, in late October, he suddenly declared himself a climate change skeptic. "My view is that we don't know what's causing climate change on this planet," he said. "And the idea of spending trillions and trillions of dollars to try to reduce CO_2 emissions is not the right course for us," he declared. By the time he accepted the Republican nomination in Tampa the following summer, Romney treated the notion of acting on climate change as a joke. "President Obama promised to begin to slow the rise of the oceans. And to heal the planet," he mocked. "My promise is to help you and your family."

A week after first reversing himself on climate change, Romney skipped a campaign event attended by every other Republican presidential candidate in Iowa in order to speak at Americans for Prosperity's annual Defending the American Dream summit in Washington. There he delivered a keynote address that could have passed as an audition for David Koch, who was in the audience. Romney had governed Massachusetts as a northeastern moderate, but now he unveiled a budget plan reminiscent of Paul Ryan's.

Soon afterward, Romney proposed to cut all income tax rates by one-fifth. According to the nonpartisan Tax Policy Center, Romney's proposal would save those in the top 0.1 percent an average of $264,000 a year, and the poorest 20 percent of taxpayers an average of $78. The middle class would get on average $791. Romney also proposed other items high on his donors' wish lists, including eliminating estate taxes, lowering the corporate tax rate, and ending taxes owed by companies that had shipped operations overseas. Taken as a whole, the Tax Policy Center said the proposal would add $5 trillion to the deficit over the next decade. Romney said he would make up the difference by closing unspecified tax loopholes.

Charles Koch often described his support for slashing taxes

as motivated by a concern for the poor. "They're the ones that suffer" from "bigger government," he argued in an interview with his hometown paper. Yet there was no getting around the fact that the numbers added up to a disproportionately huge gift to the already rich. "These guys all talk about the deficit, but there's not a single tax benefit for the wealthy they'll get rid of," Dan Pfeiffer, Obama's former communications adviser, later pointed out. "What really made them furious," he said, "was when we started talking about closing the loopholes for private jets!"

If these policy shifts were designed in part to win the Kochs' support, they succeeded. By July, David Koch not only embraced Romney but threw a $75,000-per-couple fund-raiser for him at his Southampton estate. Romney and Koch were described as exuding a "confident glow" as they and their wives descended the stairs following a private half-hour chat before the other guests arrived. A few weeks later, Romney chose Ryan as his running mate. The pick was opposed by Romney's campaign consultant, Stuart Stevens, and proved baffling to Obama because of the unpopularity of Ryan's extreme budget plan. But conservative donors, including David Koch and his wife, Julia, had lobbied for Ryan. It was one more indication that an invisible wealth primary was shaping the discourse and the field long before the rest of the country had the chance to vote.

With two of the largest fortunes in the world at their disposal—together worth an estimated $62 billion by 2012—Charles and David Koch were perfectly positioned to take advantage of the growing importance of money in American politics. Yet the presidential campaign still proved difficult for them to manage. With the eclipse of the party professionals by outside funders, virtually any novice with enough cash, including other donors in their own circle, could now disrupt the process.

As the presidential race began, Sean Noble was arguing to anyone in the Koch fold who would listen that it was time to "pull the trigger" on Newt Gingrich. The former Speaker of the House from Georgia had reinvented himself as a long-shot Republican presidential candidate. Even some of the conservatives who had been part of Gingrich's revolution in the House in the 1990s were privately begging the Koch operatives to act before Gingrich did irreparable damage to the other Republican candidates and the party. Gingrich was a brilliant force of entropy, dazzlingly eloquent on some occasions, utterly daft on others, and ruthlessly destructive to anyone in his path. For him, politics was total war, and he had the scars to prove it.

In preparation, Noble's firm quietly produced what it hoped was a lethal television ad using footage from a 2008 ad showing Gingrich sitting on a dainty love seat with Nancy Pelosi, agreeing that they needed to fight global warming. On the Republican side, it would have proved pure poison. But Noble couldn't get authorization to air it. The hesitation appeared related to the addition of Sheldon Adelson, the enormously wealthy casino mogul, to the Koch circle.

Sheldon Adelson, whom President George W. Bush once reportedly described as "this crazy Jewish billionaire, yelling at me," wasn't exactly the Kochs' type. He was a hard-right foreign policy hawk who was focused on ensuring the security of Israel. He had been a Democrat, but he shared the Kochs' antipathy toward labor unions, Obama, and redistributive income taxes. "Why is it fair that I should be paying a higher percentage of taxes than anyone else?" he once complained. Perhaps more important, with a fortune estimated in 2011 at $23.3 billion, the seventy-eight-year-old chairman of the Las Vegas Sands Corporation brought a lot of chips to the table. He could potentially increase the power of the Koch donor network exponentially. The Kochs had repeatedly invited Adelson to join their group but gotten nowhere. So when he finally showed up for the first time at their January 2012 summit in Indian Wells, California, they were not eager to trash his favorite candidate, who happened to be Gingrich.

"There were a lot of them who were pretty unhappy with Sheldon," a Koch confidant says, "but Newt pushed all his buttons." The odd couple had been friends for decades, bonding in the 1990s when Gingrich helped Adelson prevail in a bitter war to keep his casino operation, unlike the others in Las Vegas, union-free. They also shared a deep commitment to Israel's hard-line conservatives, especially its prime minister, Benjamin Netanyahu, with whom an associate says Adelson often spoke several times a week. Adelson had lavished millions of dollars on Gingrich during his precipitous ups and downs. Calling himself "just a loyal guy," Adelson continued that support after Gingrich was forced to resign from office in 1999 amid ethics charges and an insurrection within his own ranks. Long after the center of political gravity had shifted elsewhere, Adelson continued to loan Gingrich his private jets and contributed nearly $8 million to the nest of ventures that kept Gingrich employed.

But there was one touchy Israel-related issue on which the old friends disagreed. Adelson had long sought clemency for Jonathan Pollard, the Jewish American spy convicted of passing state secrets to Israel, who was serving a life sentence in federal prison. In the past, Gingrich had called Pollard "one of the most notorious traitors in U.S. history" and scuttled a Clinton-era deal to release him. If freed, Gingrich warned, Pollard might "resume his treacherous conduct and further damage the national security of the United States." But in December 2011, as Gingrich was heading into the Iowa caucuses in desperate need of cash, he switched his position. In an interview with the Jewish Channel, he announced that he now had "a bias in favor of clemency" for Pollard. Within weeks, Adelson donated $5 million to Gingrich's sputtering campaign, which otherwise in all likelihood would have fizzled out.

Adelson's cash temporarily revived Gingrich, unleashing a chain of unintended consequences. The pro-Gingrich super PAC used the casino magnate's money to purchase more than $3 million in advertising time in South Carolina. Then it aired a half-hour video called "King of Bain: When Mitt Romney Came to Town" that eviscerated Romney as a greedy, "predatory corporate raider." After the video was attacked, Gingrich called on the super PAC to take it down but not before he amplified the message by denouncing Bain Capital, the private equity company that Romney had co-founded, as "rich people figuring out clever ways to loot a company."

No left-winger could have made the case against high finance more convincingly. Romney became the face of "vulture capitalism," which was depicted as heartlessly cannibalizing what was left of the country's middle class. When Gingrich was finished with Bain, he went on to demand that Romney release his tax returns. As Noble had feared, the consequences of Gingrich at full throttle were disastrous for the Republicans.

Gingrich's attack on capitalist excess was underwritten by one of the richest men in the world whose international gambling empire was at that moment under federal criminal investigation for laundering money and foreign corrupt practices. Eventually, according to court testimony, Adelson's company paid a $47 million out-of-court settlement in the money-laundering case for failing to report a $45 million transfer of cash it made on behalf of a Chinese-Mexican businessman who was under investigation for drug trafficking. In another case, Adelson's former chief executive officer accused the mogul's subsidiary in Macao of consorting with organized crime figures and making excessive payments to a local official that might breach laws prohibiting U.S. citizens from engaging in corrupt practices overseas. Adelson described the allegations as "delusional and fabricated." But the legal cloud did little to enhance the image of the Koch network or the GOP. Instead of shoring up the Republican ticket, big money tainted the brand, prolonged the primaries, pushed the candidates to adopt their donors' pet issues, and, all in all, did the Democrats' work for them.

Romney did nothing to mitigate the "Richie Rich" caricature. After insisting that "corporations are people" and saying, "I like being able to fire people," he revealed details of a $250 million blind trust crammed with offshore investments in tax havens ranging from Switzerland to the Cayman Islands. His description of the $374,000 he made in speaking fees in 2010 as "not very much" sealed his image as hopelessly out of touch with ordinary Americans. The snapshot showing how the 1 percent lived became more toxic still when, under pressure from Gingrich, Romney released his tax returns, revealing that he had paid an effective tax rate of 14 percent on income of $21.7 million. It was less than half the rate paid by many middle-class wage earners. Gingrich trounced Romney in South Carolina, winning his first primary and proving that while the American public admired success, it also believed in fairness.

By the time the Romney campaign woke up to the threat posed by Gingrich, defeating him soundly in Florida, the damage had already been done. "With those attacks on Bain, he laid down the blueprint for Obama," lamented a conservative in the Kochs' circle.

Foster Friess, the multimillionaire mutual fund manager from Wyoming and longtime member of the Kochs' donor circle, was creating chaos, too. As Romney was trying to finish off Gingrich, Friess was spewing cash into a super PAC promoting Rick Santorum, a former senator from Pennsylvania who shared his zealous Christian conservatism. The nearly $1 million spent by Santorum's super PAC in Iowa vaulted him from footnote status into first place, assuring that his candidacy would continue far beyond its natural political shelf life. Friess, who seemed to love the spotlight almost as much as Santorum, joined the candidate in making a series of pronouncements about reproductive and gender issues that shocked many women. In the midst of an interview with the NBC correspondent Andrea Mitchell, for instance, Friess explained why he and Santorum took issue with the contraceptive coverage for women included in Obama's health-care plan. "Back in my day, they used Bayer aspirin for contraceptives," joked Friess. "The gals put it between their knees and it wasn't that costly." Mitchell, whose professional command was ordinarily unshakable, stammered, "Excuse me? I'm just trying to catch my breath from that, Mr. Friess, frankly."

By the time Santorum and Gingrich bowed out of the presidential race in the late spring, Friess had contributed $2.1 million and Adelson and his wife over $20 million to the campaigns of their respective favorites. The Democrats were ecstatic at the damage inflicted by the rogue donors. "We were killing them on contraception," says Jim Messina, Obama's campaign manager. "And we were winning on tax issues for the first time since 1996." Steve Schmidt, a Republican political operative, suggests that the shift from broad-based party funding to hugely wealthy outside donors turned the race into "an ideologically driven ecosystem." The candidates, he says, were "like these football players with their sponsors' names on their jerseys. If you have a single person responsible for your nomination, you owe them everything. You can say not, but it's determinative."

Jim Margolis, co-founder of GMMB, the campaign consulting company that worked for Obama's reelection, suggests that Romney would have fared better as a moderate, but his radical backers prevented it. "Romney's best strategy would have been to give Obama a golden watch and say basically, 'We all had such hope, he tried, but he didn't get it done. I can. I'm Mr. Fix-It. I know how to create jobs.' But Romney never successfully did that. Instead, he ran to the right." The Tea Party in 2010, and the donors behind it, stirred what Margolis calls "this supercharged Republican primary electorate. We didn't know how it would play out, but the likelihood of a moderate, appealing candidate emerging from this? Instead, they had Herman Cain, Michele Bachmann, Rick Santorum, and Newt Gingrich! That was a problem for Romney."

As the general campaign got under way, Obama too had to worry about rich donors. He had been itching to make economic fairness the center of his presidential campaign. But some of his advisers worried that populism was a dangerous force to play with in an era when both parties were increasingly reliant on hugely wealthy patrons. Obama, though, had sought the presidency in part because he hoped to alter the relationship between powerful financial interests and those who govern. "One of the reasons I ran for President," he had said, "was because I believed so strongly that the voices of everyday Americans—hardworking folks doing everything they can to stay afloat—just weren't being heard over the powerful voices of the special interests in Washington."

The Occupy movement had further emboldened him. So he decided to kick off his reelection campaign at the end of 2011 in the tiny town of Osawatomie, Kansas. There, in the place where Theodore Roosevelt had delivered a fiery speech in 1910 demanding that the government be "freed from the sinister influence or control of special interests," he tried to tackle the thorny issue of America's growing economic inequality.

Obama denounced the "breathtaking greed" that had led to the housing market's collapse, as well as the Republican Party's "you're-on-your-own economics." He also had some stinging words for big money's influence on politics. "Inequality distorts our democracy," he warned. "It gives an outsized voice to the few who can afford high-priced lobbyists and unlimited campaign contributions, and it runs the risk of selling out our democracy to the highest bidder."

The words were ringing. The audience cheered. The problem, though, was that no matter how keenly Obama wanted to address economic inequality, he was going to have to turn to his party's own billionaires and multimillionaires for help. Soon, in fact, Obama would set a record for the number of fund-raisers attended by an incumbent president. He continued to speak out, even directly to the donors, telling one small gathering of moguls that included Microsoft's co-founder Bill Gates, the richest man in America, "There are five or six people in this room *tonight* that could simply make a decision—this will be the next president—and probably at least get a nomination, if ultimately the person didn't win. And that's not the way things are supposed to work." But like it or not, Obama was, as one top progressive donor, the former head of the Stride Rite shoe company Arnold Hiatt, put it, "in a bind."

In an early 2012 meeting in the Roosevelt Room, his campaign manager, Jim Messina, shocked the president by sharing the bad news that they now expected outside Republican spending against him to reach $660 million.

"How sure are you?" Obama asked.

"Very sure," replied Messina.

Obama had reserved some of the harshest words of his presidency for the *Citizens United* ruling, saying that he couldn't "think of anything more devastating to the public interest." So he had steadfastly refused to encourage supporters to form an "outside" super PAC that could accept unlimited contributions on his behalf. "I think we need to switch our position," Messina said. "Until people understand it's important to you, they're not going to give."

Soon after, Obama bowed to the new economic reality and reversed himself. His campaign began encouraging supporters to give to the pro-Obama super PAC, Priorities USA. It wasn't the first time Obama had been rendered a hypocrite in order to raise funds. In 2008, after championing campaign-finance reform in the Senate, he broke his own pledge to accept public financing as a presidential candidate. Obama admitted that he suffered "from the same original sin of all politicians, which is: We've got to raise money." But he insisted that he would fight to reform the system: "The argument is not that I'm pristine, because I'm swimming in the same muddy water. The argument is that I know it's muddy and I want to clean it up."

The extent to which the same moneyed interests tainted both parties, though, became clear after Priorities USA aired its first television ad. It was an emotional tirade from a steel mill worker whose plant was closed down by Bain. "He'll give you the same thing he gave us: nothing. He'll take it all," the worker said of Romney. The Obama campaign then underscored the powerful message from the super PAC with its own ad, calling Romney a "job destroyer" and his firm "a vampire."

At the time, a number of thoughtful economists and academics from both ends of the political spectrum were deeply concerned about the finance industry's impact on the country's growing economic inequality. While high-earning executives particularly in the finance industry were prospering, wage earners were stagnating. Experts ranging from former Treasury secretary Lawrence Summers to the neoconservative theorist Francis Fukuyama worried that the trend was threatening the middle class and overwhelming the political system.

Yet when Obama's ads broached these crucial issues, Wall Street–linked Democrats erupted in anger. Steven Rattner, who had made millions at the investment bank Lazard Frères and whose wife was the former finance director for the Democratic Party, denounced the ads as "unfair." Harold Ford Jr., a former Democratic congressman from Tennessee who had migrated to Wall Street, protested that "private equity is a good thing in many, many instances." Cory Booker, the mayor of Newark, New Jersey, who was a rising star in the party and who had numerous supporters in the finance industry, went on national television and, to the fury of the White House, said "this kind of stuff is nauseating to me on both sides."

Bill Clinton dealt the final blow. In an interview on CNN,

he said, "I don't think we ought to get into the position where we say this is bad work—this is good work." From 2006 until 2009, Chelsea Clinton, the daughter of the former president, worked as an associate at Avenue Capital Group, a $14 billion private equity and hedge fund firm. Marc Lasry, co-founder of Avenue Capital, was a major Clinton supporter as well as a $1 million investor in a fund managed by the Clintons' son-in-law, Marc Mezvinsky. The Clinton administration had been rife with Wall Street tycoons. Now, as the Obama administration was teeing up Romney's rapacious business record as his key disqualification, Clinton summarily announced that Romney's "sterling business career crosses the qualification threshold." (At the time, Hillary Clinton reportedly disapproved of her husband's comment, privately saying, "Bill can't do that again.")

In response, the Obama campaign tailored its message more carefully. For the most part, rather than hammering Romney's wealth directly, it relied on sly symbolism to address the touchy issue of class. "There was too much blowback, so we used cues," says Margolis. "We showed him standing next to Trump's private jet."

Regardless of what the donor class thought, the anti-Bain ads proved among the most effective of the campaign. When nervous Obama campaign aides prescreened the ads in focus groups, "they kept telling us to relax! 'Stop asking if it's unfair,'" Margolis recalls. Evidently, the broad public was deeply uneasy about the winner-take-all ethic of corporate America. Yet, according to the Princeton University professor of politics Martin Gilens, because of the outsized influence that the affluent exert over the political process, "under most circumstances the preferences of the vast majority of Americans appear to have essentially no impact."

The perception gap between the donor class and the rest of the country was unceremoniously exposed in September when *Mother Jones* revealed a secret recording made that May by a member of the waitstaff at a high-end fund-raiser for Romney. Outrage spread as the public eavesdropped on Romney assuring wealthy supporters gathered for cocktails at a mansion in Boca Raton, Florida, that the votes of 47 percent of the population weren't of concern to him.

Romney's assertion came in response to a question about how he planned to "convince everybody you've got to take care of yourself." The subtext seemed to be that the country was rife with freeloaders. "My job is not to worry about those people. I'll never convince them they should take personal responsibility for their lives," Romney replied. "There are 47 percent of the people who will vote for the president no matter what." As he described them, they were people who were "dependent upon government, who believe they are victims, who believe government has a responsibility to care for them, who believe they are entitled to health care, food, to housing, you name it." These were "people who pay no income tax," he said, and so "our message of low taxes doesn't connect." He seemed to be implying that nearly half the country consisted of parasites.

This was no slip of the tongue. Romney was expressing what *The Wall Street Journal* described as the "new orthodoxy" within the Republican Party. In a new twist on the old conservative argument against government aid for the poor, it denigrated nearly half the country as what the *Journal* called "Lucky Duckies" freeloading off the rich. This startling theory held that because many members of the middle class and working poor received targeted tax credits, such as the earned income tax credit and the child tax credit, which reduced their income taxes to zero, they were "a nation of moochers," as the title of a book written by a fellow at the Wisconsin Policy Research Institute put it.

Behind the theory were several nonprofit organizations tied to the Kochs and other wealthy ideologues, including the Heritage Foundation and AEI. Foremost perhaps was the Tax Foundation, an antitax group founded in opposition to Roosevelt's New Deal that had been resurrected by Charles Koch's cash and directed for some time by Wayne Gable, the president of the Charles Koch Foundation and head of Koch Industries' Washington lobbying operation. As Scott Hodge, president of the Tax Foundation, explained it simply, there were "two Americas: the nonpayers and the payers."

Critics immediately pointed out that the theory ignored the many other taxes paid by lower- and middle-income Americans, including sales taxes, payroll taxes, and property and gas taxes, which took a disproportionately large share of their income. The theory also overlooked the unique circumstances of retirees, students, veterans, and the unwillingly unemployed. And it completely ignored the many tax breaks disproportionately enjoyed by the wealthy, from mortgage and charitable deductions to the preferential treatment for unearned income that kept Romney's income taxes at an effective rate of 14 percent. But the flattering distinction between "makers" and "takers" advanced by conservative think tanks and scholars had won great favor in wealthy, conservative circles. In fact, some conservatives who opposed virtually every other tax increase had started calling for new taxes on meager earners, ostensibly for the country's civic good. As *Slate*'s David Weigel cheekily wrote, "Republicans have finally found a group they want to tax: poor people."

The Blackstone billionaire Stephen Schwarzman made this argument nine months before Romney was caught saying essentially the same thing. When asked in a Bloomberg television interview if, given the dire state of the economy, his own taxes should be raised, Schwarzman, who was one of the most vigorous defenders of the carried-interest loophole, suggested that, to the contrary, the poor needed to pay more. "You have to have skin in the game," he said. "The concept that half of the public isn't involved with the income tax system is somewhat odd, and I'm not saying how much people should do, but we should all be part of the system." In addition to its political obtuseness, the comment betrayed complete ignorance of the history of the income tax, which began as a tax only on the 0.1 percent and was never designed to target the poor.

At the time, Schwarzman's comment got little attention. But when the rest of the nation learned from Romney's remarks that the superrich considered nearly half of them freeloaders, the reaction was explosive. Obama's internal polling numbers, which had hovered steadily in the range of 48 to 50 percent, shot up to 53 percent over Romney. The damage was even more pronounced in battleground states, where Romney's numbers plummeted. Within days, polls showed that fully 80 percent of the country had heard about the remark—more, one pollster said, than knew of the existence of North Korea.

The Obama campaign delightedly held its fire while Romney tried to explain but never disavowed it. Finally, after ten days, Obama's team went on the air with a new television ad slamming the 47 percent gaffe. It was not the original version the campaign had created. The first version, which never aired, cast Romney's remark against a backdrop of impoverished Americans whose woeful portraits seemed borrowed from Walker Evans or from Robert Kennedy's tour of Appalachia. But in the version that aired, the poor had been banished, replaced by the middle class. The ad now featured female factory workers wearing protective eye gear, a Latino construction worker near a ladder, redolent of upward mobility, and steely-eyed retired veterans in VFW hats. This wasn't just about the poor. By parroting his donors, Romney had cast the election, the "Mother of All Wars," as a fight between a tiny, privileged clique and virtually everyone else.

For the most part, the Kochtopus was more sensed than seen during the campaign, but one month before the election its elaborate funding mechanism came perilously close to exposure. In California, the Fair Political Practices Commission, the state's campaign ethics watchdog, demanded to know who was behind a suspicious $15 million donation aimed at influencing two controversial California ballot initiatives. One initiative would raise taxes on the wealthy, and the other would curb labor unions from spending money on politics. The donor purported to be an obscure Arizona nonprofit called Americans for Responsible Leadership, but California officials were not convinced this was the whole story. At the eleventh hour, they launched an investigation to learn more, because the state's stringent campaign laws required full donor disclosure.

Soon California authorities began to uncover an extraordinary dark-money shell game involving many of the same donors, operatives, and front groups associated with the Kochs. Overseeing it was Sean Noble, the Kochs' outside political consultant. His group, the Center to Protect Patient Rights, had passed the money from undisclosed individuals to the obscure Arizona nonprofit, which had sent it on without the donors' names to California. In between, there was a shuffle back and forth to another nonprofit in Arlington, Virginia, Americans for Job Security. As a result, the identities of the original sources of the contributions were masked. Among them was Charles Schwab, the Koch network regular, whose chatty e-mail to Charles Koch surfaced, asking for "several million" dollars for the California fight and promising to catch up on the golf course after the election. "I've committed an extra 2 million today making my total commitment 7 million," Schwab wrote. "I must tell you that Sean Noble from your group has been immensely helpful to our efforts."

The Kochs, according to one adviser, "panicked" as California investigators began unraveling Noble's money operation, which was entwined with their own. "They did it wrong, and they thought they had legal liability," he said. Details started emerging, such as a deposition from a California political consultant snared in the investigation who described how the scheme had begun with "some donors who were part of

Koch" who wanted to wage an antilabor fight in California, like the one in Wisconsin. "They liked the Koch model," the consultant, Tony Russo, explained, so they suggested that he work with Noble, whom Russo identified as the Kochs' "outside consultant."

After a lengthy investigation, Ann Ravel, the head of the California Fair Political Practices Commission, blasted the daisy chain of front groups as "definitely money laundering." The agency eventually imposed a record-breaking $1 million fine to settle the case. It exposed a "nationwide scourge of dark money nonprofit networks hiding the identities of their contributors," Ravel said in a public statement that also noted that the groups involved were tied to "the 'Koch Brothers' Network.'"

Koch Industries officials leaped in, stressing that the settlement had stipulated that the lawbreaking was "inadvertent, or at worst negligent," and that the Kochs had not personally donated money to influence the California ballot initiatives. Further, they argued, Noble was merely an independent contractor. "There is not a Koch *network* in the sense of we control these groups, I don't understand what that means," Mark Holden, the company's general counsel, told *Politico*'s Vogel, who pointed out that, to the contrary, Charles Koch had referred to "our network" himself, in his invitation to the 2011 donor seminar.

Following the embarrassing California investigation, which went on into late 2013, the Kochs began to ease Noble out. By then, Noble, the sunny avatar of small-town America, had left his wife for an office colleague and stirred additional bad publicity by charging almost $24 million for his and his firm's services in 2012. This was more than $1 for every $6 that the Center for Patient Rights spent, according to ProPublica. As the investigation grew in California, the Koch world expertly distanced itself. "They've spun it really well," said one of Noble's friends, who spoke on condition that he not be identified because he, too, feared retribution. "They've worked it hard. The truth? The guy who the billionaires hire to direct the money got caught breaking the law. Is he guilty? It's not Sean who is the problem—it's the enterprise—it's an illegal enterprise!"

In the final stretch of the campaign, it became clear that the presidential race was so close that the outcome would likely depend on voter turnout. Nowhere was this truer than in the state of Ohio, without which Romney couldn't rack up enough electoral votes to win. Here, too, the Kochs and other conservative philanthropists played a little-detected role.

Controversy about allegations of voter fraud had built to a boiling point all summer. Each side accused the other of dirty tricks, further poisoning and polarizing the political process. The chairman of the Republican National Committee, Reince Priebus, accused Democrats of "standing up for fraud—presumably because ending it would disenfranchise at least two of its core constituencies: the deceased and double voters." Democrats accused Republicans of deliberately reviving racist voter suppression tactics predating the civil rights movement. Bill Clinton declared, "It's the most determined effort to limit the franchise since we got rid of the poll tax and all the other Jim Crow burdens on voting." Impartial experts, meanwhile, like Richard Hasen, a professor of election law at the University of California in Irvine, regarded the allegations of fraud as the real fraud. After searching in vain to find a single case since 1980 when "an election outcome could plausibly have turned on voter impersonation fraud," he concluded the problem was a "myth."

Nonetheless, the alarmism resulted in legislative initiatives aimed at requiring voters to produce official photo IDs in thirty-seven states between 2011 and 2012. It also led to a national outbreak of mysterious citizen watchdog groups calling for crackdowns on election fraud. One such group, the

Ohio Voter Integrity Project, policed voter rolls for "irregularities" and then persuaded local election authorities to send summonses to suspect voters requiring them to prove their legitimacy at public hearings. Teresa Sharp, a fifty-three-year-old lifelong Democrat from the outskirts of Cincinnati, who received one such summons, discovered at the hearing that the self-appointed watchdog group had mistaken her address for a vacant lot. "My first thought," recalled Sharp, who is African-American, "was, Oh, no! They ain't messing with us poor black folks! Who is challenging my right to vote?"

The national outbreak of fear over voter fraud appeared a spontaneous grassroots movement, but beneath the surface there was a money trail that led back to the usual deep-pocketed right-wing donors. To target Sharp, for instance, the Ohio Voter Integrity Project had relied on software supplied by a national nonprofit, True the Vote, which itself was supported in different ways by the Bradley Foundation, the Heritage Foundation, and Americans for Prosperity.

True the Vote described itself as a nonprofit organization, created "*by* citizens *for* citizens," that aimed to protect "the rights of legitimate voters, regardless of their political party." But its founder, Catherine Engelbrecht, a Houston Tea Party activist, was guided by Hans von Spakovsky, a Republican lawyer and fellow at the Heritage Foundation who had made a career of challenging liberal voting rights reforms. Heritage had an ugly history on the issue. The think tank's founder, Paul Weyrich, had openly admitted, "I don't want everybody to vote." In 1980, he told supporters, "As a matter of fact our leverage in elections quite candidly goes up as the voting populace goes down."

Spakovsky's most recent book, *Who's Counting?,* which was filled with incendiary claims about voter fraud, was published by Encounter Books, a Bradley Foundation grantee, and co-authored by John Fund, another Heritage Foundation fellow. True the Vote, meanwhile, had received Bradley Foundation funds. Americans for Prosperity also gave the organization and the voter fraud issue a boost by featuring both Fund and Engelbrecht at its political events.

If the aim was to intimidate voters like Sharp, though, in her case, it backfired. When her name was called at the hearing, Sharp, who was accompanied by six other members of her family, walked to the front, slammed her purse and papers on the table, and asked, "Why are you all harassing me?" Later she said, "It was like a kangaroo court. There were, like, ninety-four people being challenged, and my family and I were the only ones contesting it! I looked around. The board members and the stenographer, they were all white people. The lady bringing the challenge—she was white." Sharp concluded, "I think they want to stop as many black people as they can from voting."

On Election Day, to the surprise of Romney and his backers, Democratic voters turned out in far bigger numbers than the Republicans expected. The Koch network had spent an astounding $407 million at a minimum, most of it from invisible donors. The operatives running the enterprise believed they were able to accurately anticipate how the vote would go, and right until the polls closed on November 6, they, like the Romney team, were convinced victory was at hand.

Sean Noble, who was already under a cloud because of the California campaign-finance scandal, was so sure of success that on Election Day he sent out a memo to the donors telling them that soon the rest of the country would know the good news that they already did, which was that Romney would be the next president. But around 4:30 that afternoon, Frank Luntz called. He said the exit polls didn't look right. But neither Noble nor anyone else among the big donor groups believed it yet.

At 11:12 p.m., NBC News called Ohio for Obama, projecting him as the election's winner. When Fox News followed suit, Karl Rove, who was a Fox News analyst as well as the founder of the American Crossroads independent campaign operation, threw a fit on the air. He had talked the rich into contributing $117 million to his super PAC, and many, many more millions in dark money, and had confidently assured them of a historic victory. It was "premature" for Fox to call the race, he insisted. Fox's number crunchers, however, held their ground. Romney had lost.

"What happened? We had bad data," a Koch insider conceded after it was over. They had counted on an electorate less diverse than the one that swept Obama into office in 2008. Instead, the 2012 voters were even more diverse. While the proportion of the electorate that was white and old fell, the participation by Hispanic, female, and young voters rose. Black voters, meanwhile, held steady, casting an overwhelming 93 percent of their votes for Obama. The America that the conservative donors were counting on was out of touch with the reality.

In a postelection phone call to his biggest contributors, Romney explained it a little differently. The problem, he said, was that Obama had in essence bribed supporters with government services. "What the president's campaign did was focus on certain members of his base coalition, give them extraordinary financial gifts from the government, and then work very aggressively to turn them out to vote."

Obama chuckled upon hearing of Romney's analysis. "He must have really meant that 47 percent thing," he told his aides.

In Bentonville, Arkansas, a few days later, Senator John McCain's private cell phone interrupted a meeting with Walmart's top executives by mechanically announcing the name of a caller trying to reach him. "Mitt Romney!" it squawked. "Mitt Romney!" Looking a little startled, McCain fished the phone out of his pocket and answered, rising to leave the room so that he could speak in privacy. When McCain returned, he explained to the curious executives that Romney had wanted advice on how to cope with losing the presidency. "I told him the first time, I did it all wrong," McCain related. "My wife talked me into taking a vacation in Tahiti. Worst Goddam mistake I ever made. The second time," he went on, "I just went right back to work. It was fine. I told him, 'Go back to work.'" The only problem, someone cracked, was that Romney, like those loafers in the 47 percent, had no job.

Commentators leaped to the conclusion that 2012 proved that money had little or no influence on elections. *Politico* changed the heading for a series it had been running on money in politics from "The Billion-Dollar Buy" to "The Billion-Dollar Bust?" With a final tally of approximately $7 billion in traceable spending on the presidential and congressional campaigns, it was the most expensive election in American history by far. One donor alone, Sheldon Adelson, who had vowed to spend "as much as it takes," had dumped nearly $150 million, $92 million of which was disclosed, and had still come up short. Approximately $15 million of that had reportedly gone to the Kochs' group, Americans for Prosperity.

All in all, super PACs and independent groups that could take unlimited contributions had spent a staggering $2.5 billion and, it seemed, changed nothing. Obama would remain in the White House, the Democrats would continue to dominate the Senate, and Republicans would continue to control the House.

Defeat on this scale did not sit well with the Kochs or their donors. "The donors were livid," recalls one adviser. Disappointed but ever persistent and methodical, Charles Koch sent out an e-mail to his network informing them that the next donor seminar would be postponed from January until April while he and his operatives analyzed what went wrong. "Our goal of advancing a free and prosperous America is even more difficult than we envisioned, but it is essential that we continue, rather than abandon, this struggle," he wrote.

The media's box score approach to politics, however, overlooked the many more subtle ways that money had bought influence. Hugely wealthy radicals on the right hadn't won the White House, but they had altered the nature of American democracy. They had privatized much of the public campaign process and dominated the agenda of one of the country's two major political parties. David Koch, in fact, attended the Republican National Convention as an alternate delegate, a sign of how much the party had changed. (Arguably he had changed too. At the convention, he gave an interview supporting gay marriage, demonstrating that on this issue he had come far from the day when he had participated in the scheme to blackmail his brother. The Kochs did not, however, put their financial clout behind promoting gay marriage, and David's private view had no visible influence on the Party.)

On a raft of other issues, though, including climate change, tax policy, entitlement spending, and undisclosed campaign contributions—which the Republican Party platform now embraced in a reversal from the past—the preferences of the Kochs and their political "partners" had prevailed. There was no more talk of strengthening the Clean Air Act, mockery of "Voodoo Economics," support for "compassionate conservatism," or expanding Medicare drug coverage, as there had been under the Bush presidencies. Government was a force for evil, not public good.

Contrary to predictions, the *Citizens United* decision hadn't triggered a tidal wave of corporate political spending. Instead, it had empowered a few extraordinarily rich individuals with extreme and often self-serving agendas. As the nonpartisan Sunlight Foundation concluded in a postelection analysis, the superrich had become the country's political gatekeepers. "One ten-thousandth" of America's population, or "1% of the 1%," was "shaping the limits of acceptable discourse, one conversation at a time."

Obama won, but he had few illusions that he had vanquished big money. "I'm an incumbent president who already had this huge network of support all across the country and millions of donors," he told a few supporters. It had enabled him to, as he put it, "match whatever check the Koch brothers want to write." But, he warned, "I'm not sure that the next candidate after me is going to be able to compete in that same way." Messina too was worried. "I think they erred badly with their strategy," he said. "But I don't think they're going to make the same mistake twice."

CHAPTER THIRTEEN

The States: Gaining Ground

THE DAY AFTER THE ELECTION, NO ONE WAS HANGING BLACK crepe at the Republican Party's state headquarters on Hillsborough Street in Raleigh, North Carolina. In Washington, pundits were proclaiming that Obama's reelection proved the failure of big money, but in North Carolina, Republicans were toasting its triumph at the state level. The REDMAP plan that Ed Gillespie had described at the Kochs' donor summit eighteen months earlier had worked remarkably well. Republicans had cemented their control of the state legislature and redrawn the boundaries of the congressional districts in North Carolina so artfully that despite getting fewer votes than the Democrats, they had won more congressional seats. The same pattern was repeated in enough other states that the Republicans were able to hold on to the House of Representatives, despite a bigger 2012 turnout nationwide for Democrats. It was a strange anomaly but not an accidental one.

For the Koch machine, North Carolina had become something of a test kitchen.

"A few years ago, the idea we had was to create model states," Tim Phillips, the president of Americans for Prosperity, explained in 2013. "North Carolina was a great opportunity to do that—more so than any other state in the region. If you could turn around a state like that, you could get real reform."

Phillips declined to say how much the Kochs' political organization had spent in North Carolina to help conservatives take power. "It was significant" is all he would say. "It was one of the states in which we were most active."

If the first phase of the project had been achieved by the

Republican takeover of North Carolina's state assembly in 2010, the second began in February 2011, when Tom Hofeller, a white-haired black belt in the dark art of carving congressional districts, or gerrymandering, as it was known, showed up at the Republican Party headquarters on Hillsborough Street.

There, a back room had been set aside for mapmaking.

The new census on which the congressional districts would be based hadn't even been released yet. But Hofeller was nothing if not thorough. The advent of computers had turned redistricting into an expensive, cynical, and highly precise science. Hofeller, the foremost practitioner on the Republican side, had professionalized the vast ideological sorting of the country into warring partisan camps. On his laptop was a program called Maptitude that contained the population details of every neighborhood, including the residents' racial makeup.

In the past, Hofeller had worked for the Republican Party. But by 2011, he was a private contractor, working for big outside money. Many of the financial details remained shrouded. But according to documents contained in a later lawsuit, he would eventually make ten trips to North Carolina to consult with local Republicans on how to create the largest number of safe seats possible. For his services, Hofeller would earn more than $166,000.

The process was closely guarded, and access to the room was tightly controlled. But at least one well-known figure was allowed into the inner sanctum. Art Pope, the multimillionaire discount chain store magnate who was the state's top political donor and a longtime ally of the Kochs', became a frequent adviser.

"We worked together at the workstation," one of the technical experts, Joel Raupe, said in a later legal deposition. "He sat next to me." Pope was a nonpracticing lawyer and held no elected office in the state, but the Republican leadership in the state legislature had quietly appointed him "co-counsel" to the politically sensitive project.

Gerrymandering was a bipartisan game as old as the Republic. What made it different after *Citizens United* was that the business of manipulating politics from the ground up was now heavily directed and funded by the unelected rich. To get the job done, they used front groups claiming to be nonpartisan social welfare groups, funded by contributions from some of the world's largest corporations and wealthy donors like the Kochs. The big outside money flowing into the most granular level of politics was transformative. "The Kochs were instrumental in getting the GOP to take over state legislatures," observed David Axelrod, Obama's erstwhile political adviser. "The GOP is top-down, but the Kochs had a different plan, which was to organize the grass roots. It's smart. There's no equivalent on the Democratic side," he admitted. "They're damn good organizers."

According to a report by ProPublica, Hofeller and his team were hired for the job by a dark-money group called the State Government Leadership Foundation. This was actually an offshoot of the group that Gillespie had used to run REDMAP, the Republican State Leadership Committee. But unlike the main group, the offshoot was a 501(c)(4) "social welfare" organization that could conceal the identities of its donors. Adding one more layer of security to the operation in North Carolina was a state-level dark-money group calling itself Fair and Legal Redistricting for North Carolina.

The work, like the funding, was stealthy. Hofeller kept a PowerPoint presentation on his computer with admonitions such as "Make sure your security is real." "Make sure your computer is in a PRIVATE location." He warned, "Emails are the tool of the devil." He also stressed that those working with him should "use personal contact or a safe phone!" "Don't reveal more than necessary." "BEWARE of nonpartisan, or bipartisan, staff bearing gifts," he added. "They probably are not your friends."

In theory, redistricting was supposed to reflect the fundamental democratic principle of one person, one vote. The shifting U.S. population was supposed to be equally distributed in accordance with the new census figures, across all 435 of the country's congressional districts. In a charade of fairness, Republican legislators overseeing the process in North Carolina crisscrossed the state to hold public hearings, gathering comments and suggestions from citizens about how the lines could best be drawn. "What we are here for is to basically hear your thoughts and dreams about redistricting," the chairman of the state senate committee in charge of the process told a crowd in Durham. In reality, however, Hofeller later admitted under oath that he never bothered to read the transcripts of the public testimony.

By the time Hofeller's team was done, the new map severely reduced the number of congressional seats that Democrats could win. To achieve that, the operatives had packed minority voters into three districts that already had a high concentration of African-American voters. This left more of the surrounding territory white and Republican, and the Democrats in those areas stranded. In effect, the new map had resegregated the state into congressional districts in which minority voters could dominate their own neighborhoods but were unlikely to see their party gain majority power in the state.

Progressive groups immediately filed suit, alleging that the new maps violated the Voting Rights Act, which prohibits discriminatory elections. Republican officials defended the maps as fair. Here, too, however, a flood of undisclosed cash spent by dark-money groups affiliated with Pope and other members of the Koch network influenced the course of events.

The case was headed to the state's supreme court where the Republicans held a 4–3 majority, making it likely that the Republican redistricting plan would get a friendly hearing. But before that could happen, the judges were up for reelection in 2012, and conservatives worried that one Republican incumbent appeared likely to lose. His Democratic challenger seemed poised to tip the court's political balance toward the Democrats, imperiling the Republican redistricting plan.

But a sudden wave of outside cash rescued Paul Newby, the Republican judge, just in time. Outside groups spent more than $2.3 million helping him, an unheard-of sum in such a judicial race. The money trail was dizzyingly complex, making it all but impossible for ordinary citizens to follow, but among those contributing were Gillespie's group, the Republican State Leadership Committee; Pope's company, Variety Wholesalers; and the Kochs' organization, Americans for Prosperity. The money paid for a barrage of media ads that touted the Republican judge's toughness on crime.

On Election Day, Newby was narrowly reelected. Soon afterward, the state supreme court upheld the Republican-led redistricting plan. In 2015, however, the U.S. Supreme Court ordered it to reconsider the case on the grounds that the minority-packed districts were racially discriminatory. But by then, the North Carolina delegation had become ensconced in the House of Representatives, where it added to the Republican majority as it mounted a new wave of radical resistance to the Obama administration's policies.

"The other side has killed us at that stuff," admitted Steve Rosenthal, a Democratic strategist with ties to the labor movement. By channeling donors' money to largely overlooked state and local races, Republicans succeeded not only in advancing their political agenda but in wiping out a generation of lower-level Democratic office holders who could rise in the future. And North Carolina was not the only place this happened. Successive midterm losses in 2010 and 2014 cumulatively cost the Democrats more than nine hundred legislative seats and eleven governorships, according to an analysis by the Democratic National Committee.

Gillespie's REDMAP plan had proved a stunning success. For years, North Carolina had been a politically divided, or "purple," state. It had backed Barack Obama's election in

2008 but not in 2012, when, seemingly overnight, it turned a deep shade of crimson. That November, Republicans added to their previous gains by winning the governorship and veto-proof majorities in both houses of the general assembly. It was the first time since Reconstruction that the Republican Party had complete control of the state's government. And thanks to Hofeller's expert maps, Republicans also now dominated the congressional delegation, whose makeup went from seven Democrats and six Republicans to nine Republicans and four Democrats in 2010.

But no one benefited more from the election than Art Pope. It transformed him from a backroom kingmaker in North Carolina into a very central public power. Almost as soon as Pat McCrory, the new Republican governor, was sworn in, he stunned many in the state by appointing his benefactor, Pope, to be the state's budget director. Voters had years before rejected Pope's one bid for statewide office, his run for lieutenant governor in 1992. The state legislature had also turned down repeated bids by Pope for appointive jobs, including membership on the state university system's board of governors. Pope was widely respected but not beloved. Richard Morgan, a Republican state legislator with whom he had a falling-out, described Pope as unpopular with colleagues because his attitude was "my way, or everyone else is wrong."

Now Pope was arguably the second most powerful official in North Carolina. As budget director, he had the governor's ear, a supermajority in both legislative chambers, and massive authority over which government functions would and would not get funded. Cutting government spending had long been his dream. Morgan recalled that as a state legislator Pope had spent long hours analyzing the numbers. "When he was done, there wasn't a bone buried in the budget Art hadn't dug up and chewed on." Now he had the chance to remake the whole state.

It is unusual for those wielding plutocratic power in America to exercise it directly, according to Jeffrey Winters, the political scientist specializing in oligarchy. Direct rule by the superrich invites a dangerous amount of scrutiny. Those who have used their vast fortunes to secure public office in the United States, like Michael Bloomberg, the former mayor of New York City, typically have made an effort not to appear to be ruling *as* oligarchs or *for* them. Pope clearly sensed the peril. He took care to say that he would waive the usual salary and only stay in office for a year. But questions about self-interest arose almost immediately. As North Carolina took a whiplash-inducing lurch in favor of the haves at the expense of the have-nots, it stirred a heated debate about the influence of big money in the state's politics in general and about the motives and financial designs of Art Pope in particular.

Within a few months, the legislature had overhauled the state's tax code and budget from top to bottom. On almost every issue, the legislature followed the right-wing playbook that had originated in two think tanks, the John Locke Foundation and the Civitas Institute, which were founded by Pope and largely funded by the Pope family's $150 million John William Pope Foundation. Critics described Civitas as Pope's conservative assembly line and a powerful force pushing the state's politics ever further to the right. Pope rejected the description. "It's not my organization," he protested. "I don't own it." The Pope family foundation, however, had supplied Civitas with more than 97 percent of its funding since its founding in 2005—some $8 million—and Pope sat on its board of directors. It also had supplied about 80 percent of the John Locke Foundation's funding. A good bit of the remainder came from tobacco companies and two Koch family foundations.

In fact, starting in the 1980s, Pope and his family foundation had invested $60 million in the systematic development of a conservative infrastructure in North Carolina that functioned as a "conservative government in exile," according to Dee Stewart, a Republican political consultant in the state.

The think tanks were 501(c)(3) organizations, enjoying

the same tax-exempt status as churches, universities, and public charities. Legally, these organizations were barred from participating in politics or lobbying to any substantial degree. Yet the lines were a blur. Top officers at the Pope-linked think tanks, for instance, cycled back and forth into Republican campaigns and Americans for Prosperity, where Pope was a director. The think tank personnel wrote model bills, which they previewed for legislators, and boasted of their clout in the general assembly. Pope was proud of the achievement, telling the conservative Philanthropy Roundtable, "In a generation, we've shifted the public-policy debate in North Carolina from the center-left to the center-right."

Besides the $60 million that Pope and his family foundation put into this ideological infrastructure, they gave more than $500,000 to state candidates and party committees in 2010 and 2012. In addition, Pope's company, Variety Wholesalers, gave nearly $1 million more to outside groups running independent campaigns during that period. In the state of North Carolina, Pope was, as one of his former political advisers, Scott Place, put it, "the Koch brothers lite."

The agenda this money was behind became apparent once the Republicans won control of North Carolina's general assembly. In a matter of months, they enacted conservative policies that private think tanks had been incubating for years. The legislature slashed taxes on corporations and the wealthy while cutting benefits and services for the middle class and the poor. It also gutted environmental programs, sharply limited women's access to abortion, backed a constitutional ban on gay marriage, and legalized concealed guns in bars and on playgrounds and school campuses. It also erected cumbersome new bureaucratic barriers to voting. Like the poll taxes and literacy tests of the segregated past, the new hurdles, critics said, were designed to discourage poor and minority voters, who leaned Democratic. The election law expert Richard Hasen declared, "I've never seen a package of what I would call suppressive voting measures like this." The historian Dan T. Carter, who specialized in southern history at the University of South Carolina, noted that when friends around the country asked if things in North Carolina were as bad as they looked from the outside, he was forced to answer, "No, it's worse—a lot worse."

Republicans claimed their new policies allowed residents to "keep more of their hard-earned money." But according to a fact-checking analysis by the Associated Press, the working poor were in line to pay more while the wealthiest gained the most. The North Carolina Budget and Tax Center scored the changes and found that 75 percent of the savings would go to the top 5 percent of taxpayers. The legislature eliminated the earned-income tax credit for low-income workers. It also repealed North Carolina's estate tax, a move that was projected to cost the state $300 million in its first five years. Yet the benefits of this tax break were so skewed to the wealthiest few that only twenty-three estates would have been big enough to qualify as of 2011, because the existing law already exempted the first $5.25 million of inheritance from taxation. (The Pope-funded Civitas Institute had first proposed many of these top-weighted tax cuts, with the assistance of its special adviser, Arthur Laffer, the controversial inventor of supply-side economics.)

At the same time, the legislature cut unemployment benefits so drastically that the state was no longer eligible to receive $780 million in emergency federal unemployment aid for which it would otherwise have qualified. As a result, North Carolina, which had the country's fifth-highest unemployment rate, soon offered the most meager unemployment benefits in the country.

The state also spurned the expanded Medicaid coverage for the needy that it was eligible for at no cost under the Affordable Care Act. This show of defiance denied free health care to 500,000 uninsured low-income residents. A study by health experts at Harvard and the City University of New York projected that the legislature's obstruction of these benefits would cost residents between 455 and 1,145 lives *a year.*

Art Pope was fond of the libertarian saying "There is no such thing as a free lunch," and in North Carolina his budget proved him right. To make up for the projected billion-dollar-a-year shortfall created by the many new tax cuts he helped to deliver, something had to give. So for savings, the legislators turned to the one institution that had distinguished North Carolina from many other southern states—its celebrated public education system.

The assault was systematic. They authorized vouchers for private schools while putting the public school budget in a vise and squeezing. They eliminated teachers' assistants and reduced teacher pay from the twenty-first highest in the country to the forty-sixth. They abolished incentives for teachers to earn higher degrees and reduced funding for a successful program for at-risk preschoolers. Voters had overwhelmingly preferred to avoid these cuts by extending a temporary one-penny sales tax to sustain educational funding, but the legislators, many of whom had signed a no-tax pledge promoted by Americans for Prosperity, made the cuts anyway.

North Carolina's esteemed state university system also took a hit. Ideological warfare infused the fight. Pope's network had waged a long campaign to slash spending, with employees of the John William Pope Center for Higher Education Policy, another Pope-created nonprofit, accusing the university system of becoming a "niche for radicals," describing the public funding as "a boondoggle," and demanding that the legislature "starve the beast." The center dug up professors' voting records in an effort to prove political bias. Once the Republican majority took over the legislature, it quickly imposed severe cuts that were projected to cause tuition hikes, faculty layoffs, and fewer scholarships, even though the state's constitution required that higher education be made "as free as practical" to all residents.

Bill Friday, a revered former president of the University of

North Carolina, confided not long before he died in 2012 that he was afraid the changes would put higher education out of reach for many poor and middle-income families. "What are you doing, closing the door to them?" he asked. "That's the war that's on. It's against the role that government can play. I think it's really tragic. That's what's made North Carolina different."

At the same time that Pope's network fought to cut university budgets, he offered to privately fund academic programs in subjects he favored, like Western civilization and free-market economics. A $500,000 gift that Pope made to North Carolina State University, for instance, funded lectures by conservatives. "I'm pretty sure we would not invite Paul Krugman," a professor who picked the speakers and was affiliated with the John Locke Foundation, acknowledged. Some faculty saw Pope's donations as a bid to buy academic control. "It's sad and blatant," said Cat Warren, an English professor at North Carolina State. Pope, she said, "succeeds in getting higher education defunded, and then uses those cutbacks as a way to increase leverage and influence over course content."

The John Locke Foundation also sponsored the North Carolina History Project, which aimed to reorient the state's teaching of its history by providing online lesson plans for high school teachers that downplayed the roles of social movements and government while celebrating what it called the "personal creation of wealth." In a similar vein, Republicans in the state senate passed a bill requiring North Carolina's high school students to study conservative principles as part of American history in order to graduate in 2015. The bill stressed the "constitutional limitations on government power to tax and spend." "It's all part of Pope's plan to build up more institutional support for his philosophy," said Chris Fitzsimon, director of NC Policy Watch, a liberal watchdog group.

But Pope became a lightning rod as his profile grew. The NAACP began holding weekly "Moral Monday" protests in the state capital against North Carolina's turn to the right and eventually began picketing the chain stores owned by Pope's company, Variety Wholesalers.

Even some Republicans in the state accused Pope of going too far. Jim Goodmon, the president and CEO of Capitol Broadcasting Company, which owned the CBS and Fox television affiliates in Raleigh, said, "I was a Republican, but I'm embarrassed to be one in North Carolina, because of Art Pope." Goodmon had deep ties to the state's conservative establishment. His grandfather A. J. Fletcher was among Jesse Helms's biggest backers. But Goodmon described the Pope forces as "anti-community," adding, "The way they've come to power is to say that government is bad. Their only answer is cut taxes." He concluded, "It's never about making things better. It's all about tearing the other side down."

Interviewed in a spare office overlooking a suburban parking lot that served as Variety Wholesalers headquarters in Raleigh, Pope dismissed those who were trying to paint him as extreme as misinformed. "If the left wing wants a whipping boy, a bogeyman, they throw out my name," he protested. "Some things I hear about this guy Art Pope—you know I don't like this guy Art Pope that they're talking about. I don't know him. If what they say were true, I wouldn't like a lot of things about me. But they're just not true."

In a nearly four-hour-long, lawyerly rebuttal, he argued that conservatives like himself were the underdogs in North Carolina and that his expenditures merely represented an effort to balance the score. He said that he was driven not by "narrow corporate interest" but by abstract idealism. He described himself as "politically a conservative" and a "classical liberal, philosophically." He acknowledged that the nonprofit groups he supported took many positions advantageous to his business, such as opposition to minimum wage laws. In fact, critics, like Dean Debnam, a liberal North Carolina businessman, accused Pope of exhibiting "a plantation mentality" by keeping "people working part time . . . He preys on the poorest of the poor, and uses it to advance the agenda of the richest of the rich," he charged. But Pope said he didn't take positions to enhance his bottom line. In the tradition of John Locke, he said, he just believed that society functioned best when citizens were rewarded with the wealth that their hard work produced.

Pope, who credited a summer program run by the Cato Institute for first exposing him to free-market theories, argued that the country's growing economic inequality was not a worry because "wealth creation and wealth destruction is constantly happening." All Americans, he said, had a fair chance at success. Citing Michael Jordan and Mick Jagger as examples, he asked, "Why should they be deprived of that money—why is that unfair?" He noted, "I'm not envious of the wealth that Bill Gates has," and added, "America does not have an aristocracy or a plutocracy."

The poor, he argued, were largely victims of their own bad choices. "Really, when you look at the lowest income, most of that is just simply a factor of age and marriage. If you're young and single—and God forbid if you're young and a single parent, and don't have a high school education—then your earnings will be low, and you'll be in the bottom twenty percent."

The constellation of nonprofit groups supported by Pope's fortune echoed this tough-luck message. For instance, a researcher at the Civitas Institute asserted that the poor in America lived better than "the picture most liberals like to paint." The researcher Bob Luebke cited a Heritage Foundation study showing that the poor often had shelter, a refrigerator, and cable television. "The media obsession with pervasive homelessness also appears a myth," he declared. John Hood, a bright protégé of Pope's who moved from the John Locke Foundation to become head of the John William Pope Foundation in 2015, stressed that "the true extent of poverty in North Carolina and around the country is woefully overestimated." Where poverty did exist, he asserted, it largely resulted from "self-destructive behavior."

Gene Nichol, the director of the Center on Poverty, Work, and Opportunity at the University of North Carolina School of Law, pointed out that one-third of the state's children of color lived in poverty, meaning they started at the bottom, long before they were old enough to make choices of their own. But Pope's network successfully pressured the university to eliminate the Center on Poverty in 2015 after Nichol criticized Republican policies.

Pope's own experience of poverty was limited. He grew up in a wealthy household, attended a private boarding school before the University of North Carolina and the Duke School of Law, and joined his family's discount store business, which was started by his grandfather and expanded by his father. But Pope often stressed, "I am not an heir." He explained that his father had demanded that he and his siblings buy stakes in the family-owned business. Like Charles Koch, and many others in their donor network, Pope believed that he had advanced to the helm of the company on his own merits. Those who knew Pope confirmed that he worked extremely hard and was obsessively frugal. But he also received many advantages from his parents, including hundreds of thousands of dollars in campaign contributions.

Scott Place, who served as campaign manager during Pope's one bid for statewide office, his unsuccessful 1992 run for lieutenant governor, recalled one transaction vividly, when Pope's father made a donation to his campaign. "He had his checkbook, and he was stroking the check. He said, 'How much?' Art says, 'Well, I guess $60,000.' The dad bitched. I was standing, thunderstruck. I said, 'That's a HUGE check!' The father responded, 'Well, it's Art's inheritance. I guess he can do whatever the hell he wants to with it.' It wasn't like, 'Go get 'em, son,'" Place recalled. "It was more like, 'Take the money and get out!'"

Before the campaign ended with Pope's defeat, records show that Pope's parents made uncollected "loans" to him of approximately $330,000, which, adjusted for inflation, would be more than half a million dollars today.

Place said of Pope, "He thinks that if you're poor, you're just not working hard enough. It's all about free enterprise. He probably did grow his daddy's business, and he is smart and politically shrewd. But he wasn't just born on third base. He started out within an inch of home plate." Place suggested, "Anybody can be politically effective if they have got almost a blank check."

David Parker, the chair of the North Carolina Democratic Party, accused Pope of glossing over the fact that he was born privileged. "All this talk of Protestant work ethic," he said, "but he made his money the old-fashioned way: his mother bore a son." He added, "We're all prisoners of Art Pope's fantasy world."

The ideological machine that Pope bankrolled in North Carolina was unusually powerful, but just one part of the multimillion-dollar system of interlocking nonprofit organizations conservatives had built in almost every state by the time Obama was reelected president. Because they were partial to federalism and suspicious of centralized power, the emphasis was natural. From the Civil War on through the civil rights movement, states' rights had been a conservative rallying cry, particularly in the South. Historically, it had often been bound up in racial animosities, with local jurisdictions resisting federal interference. Then, during the Reagan years, the movement took on a pro-corporate cast. While conservative business leaders such as Lewis Powell and William Simon organized corporate interests to counter the liberal public interest movement nationally, conservative allies set up similar organizations at the state and local levels. As one leader of this effort, Thomas A. Roe, an anti-union construction magnate from Greenville, South Carolina, reportedly declared to a fellow trustee at the Heritage Foundation during the 1980s, "You capture the Soviet Union—I'm going to capture the states."

Roe went on to found the State Policy Network in 1992, a national coalition of conservative state-based think tanks. By 2012, the network had sixty-four separate think tanks turning out cookie-cutter-like policy papers, including at least one hub in every state. In North Carolina, for instance, both of the think tanks founded by the Pope fortune were members. The organization's president, Tracie Sharp, described each as "fiercely independent." But behind closed doors, she likened the group's model to the global discount chain store Ikea. She told eight hundred members gathered for an annual meeting in 2013 that the national organization would provide them with a "catalogue" of "raw materials" and "services" so that local chapters could assemble the ideological products at home. "Pick what you need," she said, "and customize it for what works best for you."

In 2011, the State Policy Network's budget reached a sizable $83.2 million. Coordinating with the think tanks were over a hundred "associate" members that included conservative nonprofit groups like Americans for Prosperity, the Cato Institute, the Heritage Foundation, and Grover Norquist's Americans for Tax Reform, which the Kochs also helped to fund.

Adding clout to the Right's reach at the state level was the American Legislative Exchange Council. Weyrich's brainchild had grown impressively since the 1970s, when Richard Mellon Scaife had provided most of its start-up funding. Critics called it a conservative corporate "bill mill." Thousands of businesses and trade groups paid expensive dues to attend closed-door conferences with local officials during which they drafted model legislation that state legislators subsequently introduced as their own. On average, ALEC produced about a thousand new bills a year, some two hundred of which became state law. The State Policy Network's think tanks, some twenty-nine of which were members of ALEC, provided legislative research.

ALEC was in many ways indistinguishable from a corporate lobbying operation, but it defined itself as a tax-exempt 501(c)(3) "educational" organization. But to its allies, ALEC touted its transactional achievements. As one member-only newsletter boasted, ALEC made a "good investment" for companies. "Nowhere else can you get a return that high," it said. To avoid appearing bought off, lawmakers made sure not to mention the corporate origins of the model bills. But as the former Wisconsin state legislator (and later governor) Tommy Thompson admitted, "Myself, I always loved going to these [ALEC] meetings because I always found new ideas. Then I'd take them back to Wisconsin, disguise them a little bit, and declare that 'It's mine.'"

The Kochs were early financial angels of this state-focused activism. Koch Industries had a representative on ALEC's corporate board for nearly two decades, and during this time ALEC produced numerous bills promoting the interests of fossil fuel companies such as Koch Industries. In 2013 alone, it produced some seventy bills aimed at impeding government support for alternative, renewable energy programs.

Later the Kochs presented themselves as champions of criminal justice reform, but while they were active in ALEC, it was instrumental in pushing for the kinds of draconian prison sentences that helped spawn America's mass incarceration crisis. For years among ALEC's most active members was the for-profit prison industry. In 1995, for instance, ALEC began promoting mandatory-minimum sentences for drug offenses. Two years later, Charles Koch bailed ALEC out financially with a $430,000 loan.

In 2009, the conservative movement in the states gained

another dimension. The State Policy Network added its own "investigative news" service, partnering with a new organization called the Franklin Center for Government and Public Integrity and sprouting news bureaus in some forty states. The reporters filed stories for their own national wire service and Web sites. Many of the reports drew on research from the State Policy Network and promoted the legislative priorities of ALEC. Frequently, the reports attacked government programs, particularly those initiated by Obama. The news organization claimed to be a neutral public watchdog, but much of its coverage reflected the conservative bent of those behind it.

Professional journalists soon took issue with the Franklin Center's labeling of its content as "news." Dave Zweifel, editor emeritus of *The Capital Times* of Madison, Wisconsin, called the group's Web site in the state "a wolf in disguise" and "another dangerous blow to the traditions of objective reporting." The Pew Research Center's Project for Excellence in Journalism ranked Franklin's reports as "highly ideological." But Franklin's founder, Jason Stverak, was undeterred. He told a conservative conference that his organization, whose financing he refused to disclose, planned to fill the vacuum created by the economic death spiral in which many of the "legacy media" found themselves at the state level all over the country.

Cumulatively, these three groups created what appeared to be a conservative revolution bubbling up from the bottom to nullify Obama's policies in the states. But the funding was largely top-down. Much of it came from giant, multinational corporations, including Koch Industries, the Reynolds American and Altria tobacco companies, Microsoft, Comcast, AT&T, Verizon, GlaxoSmithKline, and Kraft Foods. A small knot of hugely rich individual donors and their private foundations funded the effort, too.

Much of the money went through DonorsTrust, the Beltway-based fund that erased donors' fingerprints. Fewer than two hundred extraordinarily rich individuals and private foundations accounted for the $750 million pooled by DonorsTrust and its sister arm, Donors Capital Fund, since 1999. Many were the same billionaires and multimillionaires who formed the Koch network.

This relatively small group of contributors to DonorsTrust provided 95 percent of the Franklin Center's revenues in 2011. The big backers behind DonorsTrust and Donors Capital Fund also put $50 million in the State Policy Network's think tanks from 2008 to 2011—a sum that goes far at that level. Whitney Ball, who ran DonorsTrust, and who was also a director on the State Policy Network's board, explained that during the Obama years, conservative donors saw "a better opportunity to make a difference in the states."

In the autumn of 2013, fallout from the conservative makeover of North Carolina reached far beyond state boundaries. An obscure Republican freshman congressman from one of the newly gerrymandered districts helped set in motion the process that led to the shutdown of the federal government. The episode became an object lesson in the way that the radicalized donor base in the Republican Party was polarizing politics to an extent that would have been almost unthinkable just a few years earlier.

Until his election in 2012, Mark Meadows had been a restaurant owner and Sunday-school Bible teacher in North Carolina's westernmost corner. Previously, the rural, mountainous Eleventh Congressional District had been represented by a former NFL quarterback and conservative Democrat named Heath Shuler. But gerrymandering had removed so many Democrats from the district that Shuler retired rather than wasting time and money on what was clearly a hopeless race, all but handing over the seat to Meadows.

After only eight months in office, Meadows made national headlines by sending an open letter to the Republican leaders of the House demanding they use the "power of the purse" to kill the Affordable Care Act. By then, the law had been upheld by the Supreme Court and affirmed when voters reelected Obama in 2012. But Meadows argued that Republicans should sabotage it by refusing to appropriate any funds for its implementation. And, if they didn't get their way, they would shut down the government. By fall, Meadows had succeeded in getting more than seventy-nine Republican congressmen to sign on to this plan, forcing Speaker of the House John Boehner, who had opposed the radical measure, to accede to their demands.

Meadows later blamed the media for exaggerating his role, but he was hailed by his local Tea Party group as "our poster boy" and by CNN as the "architect" of the 2013 shutdown. The fanfare grew less positive when the radicals in Congress refused to back down, bringing virtually the entire federal government to a halt for sixteen days in October, leaving the country struggling to function without all but the most vital federal services. In Meadows's district, day-care centers that were reliant on federal aid reportedly turned distraught families away, and nearby national parks were closed, bringing the tourist trade to a sputtering standstill. National polls showed public opinion was overwhelmingly against the shutdown. Even the *Washington Post* columnist Charles Krauthammer, a conservative, called the renegades "the Suicide Caucus."

But the gerrymandering of 2010 had created what Ryan Lizza of *The New Yorker* called a "historical oddity." Political extremists now had no incentive to compromise, even with their own party's leadership. To the contrary, the only threats faced by Republican members from the new, ultraconservative districts were primary challenges from even *more* conservative candidates.

Statistics showed that the eighty members of the so-called Suicide Caucus were a strikingly unrepresentative minority. They represented only 18 percent of the country's population and just a third of the overall Republican caucus in the House.

Gerrymandering had made their districts far less ethnically diverse and further to the right than the country as a whole. They were anomalies, yet because of radicalization of the party's donor base they wielded disproportionate power.

"In previous eras," Lizza noted, "ideologically extreme minorities could be controlled by party leadership. What's new about the current House of Representatives is that party discipline has broken down on the Republican side." Party bosses no longer ruled. Big outside money had failed to buy the 2012 presidential election, but it had nonetheless succeeded in paralyzing the U.S. government.

Meadows of course was not able to engineer the government shutdown by himself. Ted Cruz, the junior senator from Texas, whose 2012 victory had also been fueled by right-wing outside money, orchestrated much of the congressional strategy. A galaxy of conservative nonprofit groups funded by the party's big donors, meanwhile, promoted Meadows's petition while also organizing a state-based campaign of massive resistance to Obamacare so fierce it was likened to the southern states' defiance of the Supreme Court's 1954 decision in *Brown v. Board of Education*. Like the segregationists, they refused to accept defeat.

Much of America was taken by surprise by such radical action. But conservative activists had been secretly drawing up various sabotage schemes for some time.

The raw anger behind this radicalism was evident in an address given by Michael Greve, a law professor at George Mason University, at an American Enterprise Institute conference in 2010. Greve was the chairman of the Competitive Enterprise Institute—an antiregulatory free-market think tank in Washington funded by the Bradley, Coors, Koch, and Scaife Foundations, along with a roster of giant corporations—and a fervent opponent of Obamacare. "This bastard has to be killed as a matter of political hygiene," he declared.

"I do not care how this is done, whether it's dismembered,

whether we drive a stake through its heart, whether we tar and feather it and drive it out of town, whether we strangle it," he went on. "I don't care who does it, whether it's some court some place, or the United States Congress. Any which way, any dollar spent on that goal is worth spending, any brief filed toward that end is worth filing, any speech or panel contribution toward that end is of service to the United States."

The radical resistance didn't end after the Supreme Court upheld the law in the spring of 2012 and the public reelected Obama that fall. Instead the right wing regrouped. As *The New York Times* later reported, a "loose-knit coalition of conservative activists" began gathering in secret in Washington to plot how else they could disrupt the program. The meetings produced a "blueprint to defund Obamacare" signed by some three dozen conservative groups who called themselves the Conservative Action Project. Their leader was the former attorney general Edwin Meese III, an aging standard-bearer of the conservative movement who held the Ronald Reagan chair at the Heritage Foundation, served on the board of directors at the Mercatus Center at George Mason University, and was a frequent attendee at the Koch donor summits. One scheme was the initiative that Meadows eventually championed, to hold up congressional funds for the health-care program.

Another scheme was a massive "education" campaign to stir noncompliance with the federal law, both on the part of state officials, like those in North Carolina who refused to set up insurance exchanges, and by citizens. Freedom Partners Chamber of Commerce, the Koch network's "business league," financed much of the fight. It used its youth-oriented front group, Generation Opportunity, to post online advertisements featuring a tasteless cartoon version of Uncle Sam jumping between the legs of a young woman undergoing a gynecological exam to spread fear about the government's interference in private health-care matters. (The Kochs' front group seemed to have no such qualms about government intrusion into reproductive health issues.) The organization also sponsored student-oriented protests at which mock Obamacare insurance cards were burned like draft cards during the Vietnam War. The disinformation campaign spread fear and confusion. News reports reflected a widespread belief, particularly in desperately poor areas, that the government was setting up "death panels."

In the summer and fall of 2013, as Meadows was gathering co-sponsors for his open letter, Americans for Prosperity spent an additional $5.5 million on anti-Obamacare television ads. Asked about this later, Tim Phillips stressed that his group merely wanted to repeal rather than defund the health-care law. But either way, he acknowledged that the Kochs' political organization was not giving up. It planned to spend "tens of millions" of dollars on a "multi-front effort" against the law, he said.

As part of that effort, Americans for Prosperity pressured states to refuse the free, expanded Medicaid coverage included in the program, which meant denying health-care coverage to four million uninsured adults. They also pressured state officials across the country into refusing to set up their own health-care exchanges, as anticipated by the law. Meanwhile, the Cato Institute and the Competitive Enterprise Institute promoted the theory that it was illegal for the federal government to step in where the states failed to act—an interpretation of the law contradicted by both the Republican and the Democratic legislators who drafted it. This nonetheless formed the basis for the second legal challenge to the Affordable Care Act to reach the Supreme Court, *King v. Burwell,* which in the summer of 2015 also proved unsuccessful.

(The Kochs and their allies had already played a largely unnoticed role in quietly financing the first legal challenge to the health-care law to reach the Supreme Court. Officially, the lawsuit was brought by the National Federation of Independent Business. But the NFIB was talked into signing up as the plaintiff at a Heritage Foundation event in 2010. Afterward, the Kochs' organization Freedom Partners, DonorsTrust, Karl Rove's dark-money group Crossroads GPS, and the Bradley Foundation all helped to fund the NFIB.)

Phillips maintained that the conservative groups were vastly outspent in the health-care fight by the law's supporters. "It's David versus Goliath," he claimed. But according to Kantar Media's Campaign Media Analysis Group, which tracks spending on television ads, $235 million was spent on ads demonizing the law in the two years following its passage. Only $69 million was spent on ads supporting it.

In the run-up to the government shutdown, the Heritage Foundation played a major role too. In 2013, Senator Jim DeMint of South Carolina had resigned his Senate seat to become president of the organization, and under his leadership it became an increasingly radical and aggressive faction within the Republican Party. As part of the new aggressiveness under DeMint, Heritage created a dark-money 501(c)(4) arm called Heritage Action that could engage directly in partisan warfare, into which the Koch network put $500,000. (John Podesta, the head of the liberal Center for American Progress, came up with this new wrinkle, which he called a way to create "a think tank on steroids." In 2010, Heritage copied it.)

Heritage Action stunned Republican moderates by attacking those who declined to sign Congressman Meadows's open letter to "defund Obamacare." The internecine warfare was so heated that Heritage Action was kicked out of a Republican congressional caucus in which the think tank had long been welcome. But the pressure tactics were "hugely influential," David Wasserman, a nonpartisan expert for the respected *Cook Political Report,* told the *Times*. "When else in our history has a freshman member of Congress from North Carolina been able to round up a gang of 80 that's essentially ground the government to a halt?"

After the 2012 election political leaders in both parties had expressed hope that the partisan battles would subside so that the government could finally tend to the serious economic, social, environmental, and international issues demanding urgent attention from the world's richest and most powerful nation. Speaker of the House Boehner made it clear to the extremists in his party that it was time to back off. "The president was reelected," he reminded them. "Obamacare is the law of the land."

Yet less than a year later, the country was held hostage in another futile fight over Obamacare. As congressional leaders met with Obama at the White House on October 2, 2013, in what turned out to be an unsuccessful effort to reach a deal that could avert the disastrous shutdown, Obama pulled the Speaker aside.

"John, what happened?" the president asked.

"I got overrun, that's what happened," he replied.

A bipartisan compromise eventually enabled the government to reopen. Boehner, in a rare moment of candor for Washington, then singled out the real people responsible for the meltdown. Self-serving, extreme pressure groups, he said, were "misleading their followers" and "pushing our members in places where they don't want to be. And frankly I just think they've lost all credibility."

But if their fortunes were radicalizing American politics from the roots up, the Kochs and Art Pope saw it as progress. In North Carolina, Pope had a message for his growing chorus of critics: "I am not going to apologize for making the decisions on how I spend my generation's money."

CHAPTER FOURTEEN

Selling the New Koch: A Better Battle Plan

AS THE HOUSELIGHTS DIMMED AND THE INTRODUCTORY COUNtry music faded to an expectant hush, four aging white men in dark business suits appeared from behind the curtains in a large auditorium and one by one took their turns at the lectern to prove that they were in fact, as the title of the program that day advertised, "the smartest guys in the room."

It was March 16, 2013, and at the annual Conservative Political Action Conference the heads of Washington's most influential conservative think tanks—the closest thing the movement had to wise men or witch doctors—were gathered on one stage to diagnose how the election of 2012 had gone so wrong and deliver a cure. Edwin Feulner was there, with a dapper gold pocket square, the grand old man of the Heritage Foundation. So was Lawson Bader, the bald and bearded leader of the scrappy Competitive Enterprise Institute. John Allison was there too, looking every inch the southern banker he had been until recently, before leaving the helm of BB&T for that of the Cato Institute. The scene-stealer, though, was Arthur Brooks, the president of the American Enterprise Institute.

Gaunt, with a salt-and-pepper beard, a receding hairline, and the heavy black-rimmed glasses of an intellectual, Brooks had traded an earlier career as a French horn player for a job hitting just the right conservative notes. He had a knack for phrasing and timing and for boiling down complicated material into engaging and accessible nuggets, as he did that day.

"There's only one thing you need to know," Brooks said about 2012. "I know it makes you sick to your stomach," he added. But one statistic, he said, explained why conservatives had lost: only a third of the public agreed with the statement that Republicans "care about people like you." Further, only 38 percent believed they cared about the poor.

Conservatives had an empathy problem. This mattered, Brooks explained, because, as a recent study by Jonathan Haidt, a psychologist at NYU's Stern School of Business, had shown, Americans universally agreed with the statement that "fairness matters." In a nod to his conservative audience, Brooks repeated, "I know it makes you *sick* to think of that word 'fairness.'" But Americans, he said, also universally believed that "it's right to help the vulnerable."

Unfortunately, in the view of the American public, Brooks explained further, the Democrats were "the 'fairness guys.' They're the 'helping-the-poor' guys. Who are we? We're the 'money guys'!"

If conservatives wanted to win, he exhorted his audience, they had to improve their image. It wasn't a policy problem, he assured everyone. Conservative policies, he maintained, still offered the best solutions. It was a messaging problem. To persuade the public, they needed more compassionate packaging. "In other words," Brooks said, "if you want to be seen as a moral, good person, talk about fairness and helping the vulnerable." He added, "You want to win? Start fighting for people! . . . Lead with vulnerable people. Lead with fairness! . . . Telling stories matters. By telling stories, we can soften people. Talk about people, not things!"

Some sharp-eyed conservatives, such as Matthew Continetti, gently mocked Brooks's prescription, suggesting that "maybe it's also the content of the message" that was a problem. Perhaps, he suggested archly in *The Weekly Standard,* the public wasn't wrong to question whether "corporate tax reform" of the type backed by the business elite "would allow the poor to operate on a level playing field with Alcoa and Anheuser-Busch." But as the Kochs assessed the damage after 2012 and began planning their next moves, they embraced Brooks's advice.

They then launched what was essentially the best public relations campaign that money could buy. Underlying it all was the simple point that Brooks had stressed. If the "1 percent" wanted to win control of America, they needed to rebrand themselves as champions of the other "99 percent."

By supplying the research necessary for this political makeover, Brooks was providing one of the key services for which AEI and the other conservative think tanks in Washington were founded. "Conservative think tanks, which are almost exclusively funded by very wealthy people, are the front line of the income-defense industry," observed the political scientist Jeffrey Winters. Brooks, in his CPAC session, put it another way. As he faced an audience filled with the defeated foot soldiers of the conservative movement, he said, "We in the think tanks assist you. We run the idea guns to you!"

After the humiliating presidential defeat of 2012, there was no doubt that the Kochs and the other outsized spenders in their club were in desperate need of new ammunition. Opponents had vilified them relentlessly. One Koch Industries employee recalled, "We had such serious image problems and morale problems, when you said 'Koch,' you might as well have said you work for the devil."

These problems worsened at the start of 2014 as Harry Reid, the Democratic majority leader in the U.S. Senate, began attacking the Kochs almost daily from the Senate floor for, as he put it in one outburst, "trying to buy America. It's time that the American people spoke out against this terrible dishonesty of these two brothers, who are about as un-American as anyone that I can imagine."

Many would have backed down in the face of such public pressure, but the Kochs were determined to double down. "We're going to fight the battle as long as we breathe," David Koch had declared in *Forbes*.

Around the time that Reid began his attacks, the Kochs hired a new chief of communications, Steve Lombardo, a former chair of Burson-Marsteller's U.S. public affairs and crisis practice in Washington, who had previously burnished the image of tobacco companies, among others. At the time, they were still in the midst of a rigorous postmortem, trying to pinpoint where their political operation had gone wrong.

The Republican National Committee was also assessing its failings. In an unusually candid and self-critical public exegesis, it found among other things that out-of-control spending by outsiders was overwhelming the candidates, giving rich donors too much influence. "The current campaign finance environment has led to a handful of friends and allied groups dominating our side's efforts. This is not healthy. A lot of centralized authority in the hands of a few people at these outside organizations is dangerous for our Party," it warned.

The Kochs' analysis was kept secret, but in May 2014 a hint of their thinking surfaced when *Politico* got ahold of a "confidential investor update" sent by Americans for Prosperity to its big donors. It tracked closely with Arthur Brooks's view that the problem had more to do with packaging than content. "We consistently see that Americans in general are concerned that free-market policy—and its advocates—benefit the rich and powerful more than the most vulnerable in society," the memo from Americans for Prosperity lamented. "We must correct this misconception."

Soon after, more information leaked out. On June 17, 2014, a young, little-known blogger and Web producer named Lauren Windsor, who hosted an online political news program called *The Undercurrent*, began posting a series of audiotapes of the secret sessions that had taken place just days before, during the Kochs' semiannual donor summit. Windsor had been libertarian herself. But she had lost her job in the 2008 financial crash and, with it, her faith in free markets. By the time the Kochs and their circle gathered at the St. Regis Monarch Beach resort outside Laguna Beach, California, on Friday, June 13, Windsor had become a crusader against the corrupting influence of big money in politics. Working with an unnamed source who attended the conference, she was eager to spill the Kochs' secrets. The tapes she began revealing didn't disappoint.

A number of news stories resulted from these tapes. But as it turned out, there was at least one more that Windsor didn't release because of its poor audio quality. If anything, it provided an even more stunning picture of the scope and audacity of the Kochs' designs on the country, as well as their effort during this period to recast themselves, in order to appear less threatening.

On Sunday, June 15, the donors came together in the Pacific Ballroom of the five-star oceanfront resort for a confidential post-lunch seminar titled "The Long-Term Strategy: Engaging the Middle Third." As he took the floor, Richard Fink, who was introduced as Charles Koch's "grand strategist," provided a fascinating and at times startling tour through the new political plan. In some ways, no one in the Koch empire was more on the hook for the failures of 2012 than Fink, the brothers' longtime consigliere. Fink was executive vice president and a director of the board of Koch Industries, as well as a board member of Americans for Prosperity. After the election, he had thrown himself into the kind of unsparing internal review for which the company was known. It included an analysis of twenty years of research into political opinions, based on 170,000 surveys taken both in the United States and abroad, as well as many meetings and focus groups. Its conclusion, Fink told the donors, was that if they were to win over America, they needed to change.

"We got our clocks cleaned in 2012," Fink began. "This is a long-term battle." The challenge, he said he had learned, was that the country was divided into three distinct parts. The first third already supported the Kochs' conservative, libertarian vision. Another third, the liberals, whom he referred to as "collectivists," using the old John Birch Society term, were beyond the Kochs' reach. "The battle for the future of the country is who can win the hearts and minds of the middle third," Fink said. "It will determine the direction of the country."

The problem, he said, was that free-market conservatives had lost the all-important "middle third." This segment of the American population tended to believe that liberals cared more about ordinary people like themselves. In contrast, he said, "big business they see as very suspicious . . . They're greedy. They don't care about the underprivileged."

Assuming that he was among friends, Fink readily conceded that these critics weren't wrong. "What do people like you say? I grew up with pretty much very little, okay? And I worked my butt off to get what I have. So," he went on, when he saw people "on the street," he admitted, his reaction was, "Get off your ass and work hard, like we did!"

Unfortunately, he continued, those in the "middle third"—whose votes they needed—had a different reaction when they saw the poor. They instead felt "guilty." Instead of being concerned with "opportunity" for themselves, Fink said, this group was concerned about "opportunity for other people."

So, he explained, the government-slashing agenda of the Koch network was a problem for these voters. Fink acknowledged, "We want to decrease regulations. Why? It's because we can make more profit, okay? Yeah, and cut government spending so we don't have to pay so much taxes. There's truth in that." But the "middle third" of American voters, he warned, was uncomfortable with positions that seemed motivated by greed.

What the Koch network needed to do, he said, was to persuade moderate, undecided voters that the "intent" of economic libertarians was virtuous. "We've got to convince these people we mean well and that we're good people," said Fink. "Whoever does," he said, "will drive this country."

Fink was brutally honest about how unpopular the right-wing donors' views were. "When we focus on decreasing government spending," he said, and "decreasing taxes, it doesn't do it, okay? They're not responding, and don't like it, okay?"

But, he pointed out, if anyone in America knew how to sell something, it should be those in the Koch network. "We get business—what do we do?" he asked. "We want to find out what the customer wants, right? Not what we want them to buy!"

The Kochs' extensive research had shown that what the American "customer" wanted from politics, alas, was quite different from their business-dominated free-market orthodoxy. It wasn't just that Americans were interested in opportunity for the many, rather than just for themselves. It also turned out, Fink acknowledged, that they wanted a clean environment and health and high standards of living, as well as political and religious freedom and peace and security.

These objectives would seem to present a problem for a group led by ultrarich industrialists who had almost single-handedly stymied environmentalists' efforts to protect the planet from climate change. The extraordinary measures that the Kochs and their allies had taken to sabotage the country's first program offering affordable health care to millions of uninsured citizens might also seem to be problematic. Their championship of tax breaks for heirs, hedge fund managers, offshore accounts, and other loopholes favoring the rich, along with their opposition to welfare, the minimum wage, organized labor, and funding public education, also would seemingly fly in the face of the middle third's interest in widening opportunity.

These political problems would seem to have been compounded by new statistics showing that the top 1 percent of earners had captured 93 percent of the income gains in the first year of recovery after the recession.

But rather than altering their policies, those in the Koch network, according to Fink, needed a better sales plan. "This is going to sound a little strange," he admitted, "so you'll have to bear with me." But to convince the "middle third" of the donors' good "intent," he said, the Koch network needed to reframe the way that it described its political goal. What it needed, he said, was to "launch a movement for well-being."

The improved pitch, he said, would argue that free markets were the path to happiness, while big government led to tyranny and fascism. His reasoning went like this: Government programs caused dependency, which in turn caused psychological depression. Historically, he argued, this led to totalitarianism. The minimum wage, he said, provided a good example. It denied the "opportunity for earned success" to 500,000 Americans who, he estimated, would be willing to work for less than the federal minimum standard of $7.25 per hour. Without jobs, "they've lost their meaning in life," said Fink. This, he warned, had been "a very big part of the recruitment in Germany during the '20s." Thus, he argued to an audience that included many of the country's billionaires, minimum wage laws could be described as leading to the kinds of conditions that caused "the rise and fall of the Third Reich."

Freedom fighters, as Fink labeled the donors, needed to explain to American voters that their opposition to programs for the poor did not stem from greed, and their opposition to the minimum wage wasn't based on a desire for cheap labor. Rather, as their new talking points would portray it, unfettered free-market capitalism was simply the best path to human "well-being."

Charles Koch had expressed similar sentiments in a recent interview with the *Wichita Business Journal*. In it, he said, "The poor, okay, you have welfare, but you've condemned them to a lifetime of dependency and hopelessness." Like Obama, he said, "We want 'hope and change.' But we want people to have the hope that they can advance on their own merits, rather than the hope that somebody gives them something." In the same interview, Koch described, without any self-consciousness, how he had recently promoted his son, Chase, to the presidency of Koch Fertilizer and how at "every step, he's done it on his own." The possibility that his son, like he and his brothers, Richard Mellon Scaife, Dick DeVos, and the Bechtel boys, to name just a few in his network, might have benefited from a job in the family's business or a huge inheritance, rather than having been "condemned . . . to a lifetime of dependency and hopelessness," because "somebody" had given "them something," seemed not to have crossed his mind.

To "earn the respect and good feeling" of those whose support they needed, Fink went on to explain during his talk, the Kochs would also form and publicize partnerships with unlikely allies. This would counteract critics who claimed they were negative or divisive. For instance, he told the donors, they were going to hear about the Kochs' partnerships with the United Negro College Fund and with the National Association of Criminal Defense Lawyers, the latter of which they had been financially supporting for several years. Later that afternoon, in fact, Fink was joined in another panel discussion, titled "Driving the National Conversation," with Michael Lomax, president of the United Negro College Fund, along with Norman Reimer, executive director of the National Association of Criminal Defense Lawyers. Fink explained that by reaching across the partisan divide, the Kochs could present their group as offering America "a positive vision." He said it would demonstrate that "the other side creates divisiveness, but we solve problems."

There were in fact more than a few connections between the defense bar and the Koch network. A surprising number of the donors had been ensnared in serious legal problems. Not only had the Kochs faced environmental, workplace safety, fraud, and bribery allegations; many others in their group had legal issues too. At that moment, Renaissance Technologies, the hedge fund co-directed by Bob Mercer, who had become an increasingly active member of the Koch network, was still under investigation by the Internal Revenue Service for avoiding more than $6 billion in taxes between 2000 and 2013. In a 2014 Senate inquiry, Democratic senator Carl Levin denounced the company's accounting as a "pretty stunning bit of phony and abusive tax machinations." A company spokesman acknowledged the complicated accounting method but maintained it was "appropriate under current law."

Meanwhile, SAC Capital, Steven Cohen's huge hedge fund, had been under criminal investigation for years while its managing director, Michael Sullivan, belonged to the Koch network, performing as a featured speaker at one seminar. In the end, neither Cohen nor Sullivan was charged with criminal wrongdoing, but after eight SAC employees pleaded guilty to or were convicted of insider trading, the government accused Cohen of turning "a blind eye to misconduct" and in a settlement slapped his firm with a $1.8 billion fine, the largest such fine in history.

In his own remarks at the donor summit, Reimer described the criminal justice system as "overly abusive, overly inclusive" and suggested that "there probably isn't a single person in this group who doesn't have a friend, a relative or a co-worker, a neighbor, someone you care about who hasn't been caught up in the criminal justice system in this country." He was closer to the mark than he probably knew.

As hoped for, these bipartisan moves soon stirred positive headlines outside the Kochs' tight circle, creating exactly the kind of image overhaul they had in mind. Obama's senior adviser, Valerie Jarrett, surprised those familiar with the Kochs' full record by inviting Mark Holden, the general counsel of Koch Industries, to meet with her and other top officials about the issue in the White House, enabling the Kochs to appear above "divisiveness," just as Fink had planned. Particularly effective was their joining an alliance for criminal justice reform with a number of progressive groups, including the

Center for American Progress. Washington's premier liberal think tank regarded the partnership as a means of adding financial and political clout to the cause of poor and minority inmates. But the Kochs had long had other kinds of perpetrators in mind. The platform of the Libertarian Party in 1980—the year David Koch ran on its ticket—called for an end to the prosecution of all tax evaders. The Kochs also objected vociferously to the many environmental crimes with which they had been charged.

Holden acknowledged in an interview that the Kochs became active in criminal justice reform when the Clinton Justice Department charged Koch Industries in 2000 with environmental crimes. "It was hell," recalled Holden. He said Charles Koch saw the prosecution as "government overreach" and grew concerned more generally about the issue.

But far from an abusive prosecution of the powerless, the 2000 case was initiated by the Koch employee in Corpus Christi, Texas, who blew the whistle on the company for trying to cover up the fact that it was, as she put it, "hemorrhaging benzene"—a known carcinogen—into the air. This was the case that David Uhlmann, the prosecutor and later law professor, had described as "one of the most significant cases ever brought under the Clean Air Act." The company was not falsely accused. It paid a $20 million fine, thereby avoiding jail time for its employees. The ability of the Kochs to spin this fifteen years later into a campaign for bipartisan, populist social reform—one aimed at weakening the government's prosecutorial powers—was a masterful bit of self-promotion.

Holden, who had been a prison guard early in his career, spoke feelingly in public about the country's over-incarceration of underprivileged prisoners. Whether the Kochs truly shared his views or merely saw criminal justice reform as a means of weakening the government's hand against corporate crime, and whitewashing their own image, remained to be seen. Skeptics pointed out that the Kochs continued to support numerous candidates—including Scott Walker, whom David Koch named in 2015 as their favorite presidential candidate until he dropped out—who had records on criminal justice issues that completely belied the Kochs' professed concern. They also noted that the Kochs only championed a corporate campaign against "check the box" forms, requiring job seekers to disclose prior criminal convictions, after Koch Industries got in trouble with the federal government for failing to reveal its own criminal record.

Nonetheless, the $25 million grant from Charles's foundation to the United Negro College Fund just before the June 2014 summit began was winning them positive headlines. "Increasing well-being by helping people improve their lives has long been our focus," said Charles in a prepared public statement about the donation.

His use of the new buzz phrase "well-being" seemed almost offhand. But during another session at the summit that June, a speaker explained to the donors just how deliberate and politically disarming the term was. James Otteson, a conservative professor of political economy at Wake Forest University, called it "a game changer." In fact, he told the donor group that he was planning to build a "well-being" center at Wake Forest, where he already was executive director of the BB&T Center for the Study of Capitalism.

One anecdote, he said, illustrated "the power of framing" free-market theories as a movement to promote well-being. He recounted that a colleague, whom he described as a prominent "left wing political scientist" who "rails" against Republicans and capitalism, had been so entranced by the idea of studying the factors contributing to human well-being that he had said, "You know, I'd even be willing to take Koch money for that." Upon hearing this, the donors laughed out loud. "Who can be against well-being? The framing is absolutely critical," Otteson exclaimed.

The idea of sugarcoating antigovernment, free-market ideology as a nonpartisan movement to enhance the quality of life had clear advantages. And Otteson's success at penetrating academia with the approach was especially encouraging to the group. The growing emphasis on academia as a delivery system for the donors' conservative ideology and as a long-range strategy to change the country's political makeup was, in fact, another major focus of the donor summit.

As the Olin and Bradley Foundations had demonstrated, and as Charles Koch's early blueprint for advancing libertarianism showed, winning the hearts and minds of college students had long been a core strategy on the right. That weekend, Kevin Gentry, the conference's emcee, who was vice president for special projects at Koch Industries and vice president of the Charles Koch Foundation, described academia as "a great investment" and "an area—for this group—this seminar network—that is a significant competitive advantage" and an important component of the Kochs' ambitious designs.

As Ryan Stowers, vice president of the Charles Koch Foundation, recounted to the donors, in the 1980s, when Charles Koch and Richard Fink first tried to use Hayek's model of production as a means of manufacturing political change, it seemed far-fetched to try to convert academia into a source of free-market ideology. There were so few free-market scholars in America, Stowers said, that Charles could barely find enough to hold a conference. But with "courage, investment, and leadership," from Charles and the other donors, he said, "we've built a robust, freedom-advancing network" of nearly five thousand scholars in some four hundred colleges and universities across the country.

A breakthrough, Stowers related, was the creation of some two dozen privately funded academic centers, the flagship of which was the Mercatus Center at George Mason University. As a 2015 report by one of the nonprofits connected to Art Pope explained, private academic centers within colleges and universities were ideal devices by which rich conservatives could replace the faculty's views with their own. "Money talks loudly on college campuses," it noted. As an example, the report profiled the trailblazing record of John Allison, the former Cato Institute chairman, who had overseen grants to sixty-three colleges when running the BB&T bank. All of these programs were required to teach his favorite philosopher, the celebrator of self-interest Ayn Rand.

But as earmarked grants proliferated, controversy over academic freedom grew, increasing the need for slicker marketing. By 2014, the various Koch foundations alone were funding pro-corporate programs at 283 four-year colleges and universities. At Florida State University, where a Koch foundation grant in 2008 gave the foundation a say on faculty hires, criticism erupted into a public fight. Students complained that the Koch influence was nefarious and omnipresent. Jerry Funt, an undergraduate, said that in the public university's introductory economics course, "We learned that Keynes was bad, the free-market was better, that sweatshop labor wasn't so bad, and that the hands-off regulations in China were better than those in the U.S." Their economics textbook, he said, was co-written by Russell Sobel, the former recipient of Koch funding at West Virginia University who had taught that safety regulations hurt coal miners. The textbook, which Funt described as arguing that "climate change wasn't caused by humans and isn't a big issue," had been given an F by an environmental group. But when critics raised objections, the Kochs defended their purchase of influence over public universities as merely providing "fresh" college thinking.

The Kochs were also directing millions of dollars into online education, and into teaching high school students, through a nonprofit that Charles devised called the Young Entrepreneurs Academy. The financially pressed Topeka school system, for instance, signed an agreement with the organization which taught students that, among other things, Franklin Roosevelt didn't alleviate the Depression, minimum wage laws and public assistance hurt the poor, lower pay for women was not discriminatory, and the government, rather than business, caused the 2008 recession. The program, which was aimed at low-income areas, also paid students to take additional courses online.

At the June summit, Stowers stressed to the donors that this "investment" in education had created a valuable "talent pipeline." Assuming the thousands of scholars on average taught hundreds of students per year, he said, they could influence the thinking of millions of young Americans annually. "This cycle constantly repeats itself," he noted, "and you can see the multiplier effect it's had on our network since 2008."

In summation, Gentry stressed to the donors, "So you can see, higher education is not just limited to an impact on higher education." The students were "the next generation of the freedom movement," he said. "The students that graduate out of these higher-education programs populate the state-based think tanks and the national think tanks." And, he said, they "become the major staffing for the state chapters" of the "grassroots" groups. Those with passion were encouraged to become part of what he called the Kochs' *"fully integrated network."* At this point, he paused and said, "I got to be careful how I say this." He paused again. "They populate our *program.*"

The reason Gentry had to be careful was that the Kochs described their educational activities to the IRS as nonpolitical charitable work, qualifying them for tax breaks and anonymity. Yet what Gentry was describing could scarcely be more political. It was a full-service political factory. As he addressed the donors, cajoling them to "invest" more, he couldn't resist adding further detail. "It's not just work at the universities with the students," he went on. "It's building the state-based capabilities, and *election* capabilities, and *integrating* this talent pipeline. So you can see how this is useful to each other over time. No one else has this infrastructure. We're very excited about doing it!"

Evidently, the donors were enthused, too. By the time the

summit ended on June 17, the Kochs had set a fund-raising goal of $290 million. It was an audacious and, at the time, unprecedented sum for any outside group to spend in a midterm election.

"I know on the one hand this is crazy; $290 million is an extraordinary figure," Gentry acknowledged, shortly before the final pledges were made. But he told the secret gathering, "We've come a long way from where we were seven or eight years ago." He added, "You know, we're trying to do this in a businesslike way for you all, because, literally, you all are our investors."

Eight days later, the Charles Koch Institute hosted what it called its Inaugural Well-Being Forum at the Newseum in Washington. Among the panelists was Professor James Otteson from Wake Forest. In an online essay, Charles explained that his foundation's "Well-Being Initiative" aimed to "foster more conversation about the true nature of well-being." Displayed prominently beneath his byline was a quotation from Martin Luther King Jr. No mention was made of King's vision of well-being, which included labor unions, national health care, and government employment for those needing jobs.

Among the five members on the advisory board to Charles Koch's new Well-Being Initiative was Arthur Brooks, whose discovery that conservatives needed to be seen as more caring had deeply influenced the Kochs. By then, Brooks had moved beyond an earlier book he had written—which, like Mitt Romney, divided Americans into "makers" and "takers"—and turned out a new one that defined free enterprise as a path to happiness. Unhappiness, according to Brooks, "had a strong link" to "economic envy," such as the kind of thinking that pushes for higher taxes on the very rich. *The New York Times* deemed Brooks's theories on this print-worthy enough to publish in its opinion section. Evidently, the new well-being trope was gaining traction.

As they recast themselves in public as nonpartisan reformers, the Kochs' increasingly aggressive private political machine geared up for the 2014 election. The ultimate prize was control of the U.S. Senate. If Republicans could capture the majority in the upper chamber and hold on to the House, they would dominate Congress, controlling the legislative agenda and creating a formidable roadblock to President Obama.

But the Kochs had reached an important conclusion during their post-2012 autopsy. "They decided that the Republican Party's infrastructure wasn't worth a damn, and if they wanted it to be done better, they'd have to do it themselves," said the Koch Industries employee who had described the company's image problems during this period.

It might seem a radical and troubling step for a couple of billionaire businessmen who had never been elected to any office, and had no formal allegiance to anything other than their massive, private multinational company, to decide to supplant one of the country's two political parties. But in his interview with the *Wichita Business Journal,* Charles shrugged it off nonchalantly. Asked why he was so involved in politics, he likened himself to the golfer Lee Trevino, who, he said, explained his reason for winning tournaments by saying, "Well, somebody has got to win them, and it might as well be me." Charles added, "There doesn't seem to be any other large company trying to do this, so it might as well be us. Somebody has got to work to save the country." Far from being some sort of evil Svengali, he said his primary role at Americans for Prosperity was this: "I write a check." He added, "Listen, if I could do everything that's attributed to me, I would be a very busy boy."

As the Kochs' donor network poured a record amount of money into the 2014 midterm elections, Charles continued to portray himself, and probably to think of himself, as a disinterested patriot. In an op-ed piece in *The Wall Street Journal* that spring, he described himself as involved in politics only reluctantly and recently. Dating his activism to the founding of the biannual donor seminars, he asserted that he'd only been politically engaged for a decade. But after tallying up the $7 million or so that the Kochs had poured into politics more than a decade earlier, the nonpartisan fact-checking group PolitiFact judged his claim to be "false."

A longtime associate who declined to be named, exclaimed, "He has been trying since the 1970s to get his Libertarian Revolution going!" Charles might have started as a bookish idealist who disdained conventional politics, but at each step of the way he had learned from his failures and moved closer to the center of power. He was disciplined and methodical. After 2012, for instance, he had systematically studied not only his own side's weaknesses but also the other side's strengths. "He's learned a lot from the Democrats, particularly about using grass roots," said the associate. "For Charles, politics is another form of science—just dealing with people, not molecules."

Inside the Obama White House, as the 2014 midterm elections approached, David Simas, director of the Office of Political Strategy and Outreach, began to suspect that the Kochs had reverse engineered the data analytics that the Obama effort used in 2012. The implications, a White House official said, were, in a word, "huge."

Computers had transformed the business of winning elections into a rapidly changing high-tech competition for massive amounts of voter data. Realizing that its data operation had fallen woefully behind in 2012, the Koch network took serious remedial action. Freedom Partners, as the Koch donors now referred to themselves, quietly made a multimillion-dollar investment in i360, a state-of-the-art political data company, which then merged with the Kochs' troubled data collection effort, Themis. Soon the operation had hired a hundred staffers and assembled detailed portraits of 250 million U.S.

consumers and over 190 million active voters. Field workers for the Kochs' many advocacy groups were armed with handheld devices on which they constantly updated the data. Their political operatives could then determine which voters were "persuadable" and bombard them with personalized communications aimed at motivating them to vote or to stay home.

The Kochs' development of their own data bank marked a pivotal moment in their relationship with the Republican Party. Until then, handling the voter files had been a core function of the Republican National Committee. But now the Kochs had their own rival operation, which was by many accounts easier to use and more sophisticated than that of the RNC. Several top Republican candidates started to purchase i360's data, even though they were more expensive, because they were better. With little other choice, in 2014 the RNC struck what it called a "historic" deal to share data with the Kochs. But the détente was reportedly strained. By 2015, the acrimony had broken out into the open as Katie Walsh, the chief of staff at the RNC, all but accused the Kochs of usurping the Republican Party.

In an extraordinary public rebuke, she told *Yahoo News,* "I think it's very dangerous and wrong to allow a group of very strong, well-financed individuals who have no accountability to anyone to have control over who gets access to the data when, why and how."

Michael Palmer, the president of i360, punched back, saying, "We believe that a robust marketplace . . . is a healthy way to advance past the single monopoly model that has failed the Republican Party in recent presidential elections." Having embraced the Kochs' free-market ideology and their right to spend unlimited money, the Republican Party was now ironically finding itself sidelined and perhaps imperiled by the rapaciousness of its own big donors. Alarmed, a source "close to the RNC" told *Yahoo,* "It's pretty clear that they don't want to work with the party but want to supplant it."

If in 2012 the Kochs had rivaled the Republican Party, by

2014 they had in many ways surpassed it. "They're building a party from outside to take over the party—they're doing it by market segments—it's like a business plan," observed Lisa Graves, the head of the Center for Media and Democracy, a liberal watchdog group that studied the mechanics of political manipulation.

Americans for Prosperity had expanded its ground game to 550 paid staffers, with as many as 50 in a single pivotal state like Florida, as *Politico* reported. Other Koch-backed advocacy groups, such as Generation Opportunity and the LIBRE Initiative, planted grassroots organizers wherever there were hotly contested elections. The Koch constellation also added Aegis Strategic, an organization that aimed to recruit and train candidates. This way the Koch network could avoid the kinds of flaky misfits who had plagued Republicans in 2012. As he watched their progress, Axelrod was impressed. "They aggressively corrected the problems they had last time with terminal foot-in-mouth disease," he said. "It showed."

On November 4, 2014, the investors of the Koch network finally got their money's worth. Election Day proved a Republican triumph. The GOP picked up nine seats in the Senate, winning full control of both congressional chambers. Beltway pundits proclaimed President Obama a "lame duck" whose presidency they said was, for all intents and purposes, over. From this point on, they predicted, he would be largely relegated to playing defense against conservatives' efforts to roll back everything his administration had done before.

The election was as big a victory for ultrarich conservative donors as it was for the winning Republican candidates. As the *Times* noted, the conservative outside groups had "retooled and revamped" during the previous year and a half and emerged as the preeminent forces in the election. There had never been a costlier midterm election, nor one with more outside money.

And the largest overall source fueling this explosion of private and often secret spending was the Koch network. All told, it poured over $100 million into competitive House and Senate races and almost twice that amount into other kinds of activism.

Four years into the *Citizens United* era, the numbers were more numbing than shocking. The only suspense in each election cycle was the factor by which the spending had multiplied over the previous one. Mark McKinnon, a centrist political consultant who had advised both Republicans and Democrats, declared, "We have reached a tipping point where mega donors completely dominate the landscape."

A few of the biggest spenders were now Democrats, like the California hedge fund magnate turned environmental activist Tom Steyer. The $74 million he spent trying to elect candidates who pledged to fight global warming made him the largest disclosed donor in 2014. While this added some ideological diversity, it did nothing to dilute the concentration of wealth that now influenced elections. The 100 biggest known donors in 2014 spent nearly as much money on behalf of their candidates as the 4.75 million people who contributed $200 or less. On their own, the top 100 known donors gave $323 million. And this was only the disclosed money. Once the millions of dollars in unlimited, undisclosed dark money were included, there was little doubt that an extraordinarily small and rich conservative clique had financially dominated everyone else.

"Let's call the system that *Citizens United* and other rulings and laws have created what it is: an oligarchy," declared McKinnon. "The system is controlled by a handful of ultra-wealthy people, most of whom got rich from the system and who will get richer from the system."

From the Republic's earliest days, the wealthy had always dominated politics, but at least since the Progressive Era the public, through its elected representatives, had devised rules to keep the influence in check. By 2015, however, conservative legal advocates, underwritten by wealthy benefactors and aided by a conservative majority on the Supreme Court, had led a successful drive to gut most of those rules. It was no longer clear if the remaining checks on corruption were up to the task. It had long been the conceit in America that great economic inequality could coexist with great social and political equality. But a growing body of academic work suggested that this was changing. As America grew more economically unequal, those at the top were purchasing the power needed to stay there.

Among the new power brokers, few if any could match the political clout of the Kochs. The reach of their "integrated network" was unique. One reflection of their singular status was their relationship with the new majority leader of the Senate, Mitch McConnell. Only a few months before assuming that position, McConnell had been an honored speaker at their June donor summit. There, he had thanked "Charles and David" and added, "I don't know where we would be without you." Soon after he was sworn in, McConnell hired a new policy chief—a former lobbyist for Koch Industries. McConnell then went on to launch a stunning all-out war on the Environmental Protection Agency, urging governors across the country to refuse to comply with its new restrictions on greenhouse gas emissions.

Three of the newly elected Republicans who joined the Senate in 2014 had also attended the secret Koch meeting in June, where they, too, had gushed over their sponsors. The leaked tapes of the event caught Joni Ernst, for instance, who had previously been, by her own account, a "little-known state senator from a very rural part of Iowa," crediting the Kochs with transforming her, like Eliza Doolittle, into a national star. "Exposure to this group and to this network and the opportunity to meet so many of you," she said, were what "really started my trajectory."

Charles Koch's trajectory had been a longer climb, but it was hard not to marvel at how far he, too, had come from the days when he had haunted the John Birch Society bookstore in Wichita and teetered with the Freedom School and the Libertarian Party on the outermost fringe of political irrelevance. The force of his will, combined with his fortune, had made him one of the most formidable figures in modern American politics. Few had waged a more relentless or more effective assault on Americans' belief in government.

He and his brother had built and financed a private political machine that had helped cripple a twice-elected Democratic president and begun to supplant the Republican Party. Educational institutions and think tanks all over the country promoted his worldview, doubling as a talent pipeline. A growing fleet of nonprofit groups mobilized public opinion behind his agenda. The groups trained candidates and provided the technological and financial assistance necessary to run state-of-the-art campaigns. The money they could put behind their chosen candidates was seemingly limitless. Congressmen, senators, and presidential hopefuls now flocked to their secret seminars like supplicants, eager to please them in hopes of earning their support.

Rare was the Republican candidate who wouldn't toe the Kochs' line. John Kasich, the iconoclastic governor of Ohio, prompted an angry walkout by some twenty donors at the Kochs' April 2014 summit for criticizing the Koch network's position against Medicaid expansion. In answer to Randy Kendrick, who had questioned his pro-Medicaid position, Kasich retorted, "I don't know about you, lady. But when I get to the pearly gates, I'm going to have an answer for what I've done for the poor." He added, "I know this is going to upset a lot of you guys, but we have to use government to reach out to people living in the shadows." The Kochs never invited Kasich back again.

Donald Trump, the New York real estate and casino magnate whose unorthodox bid for the Republican nomination flummoxed party regulars, was also left off the Kochs' invitation list. In August 2015, as his rivals flocked to meet the Koch donors, he tweeted, "I wish good luck to all of the Republican candidates that traveled to California to beg for money etc. from the Koch Brothers. Puppets?" Trump's popularity suggested that voters were hungry for independent candidates who wouldn't spout the donors' lines. His call to close the carried-interest tax loophole, and talk of the ultrarich not paying its share, as well as his anti-immigrant rants, made his opponents appear robotically subservient, and out of touch. But few other Republican candidates could afford to ignore the Kochs.

Among their most astonishing feats, the Kochs had succeeded in persuading hundreds of the other richest conservatives in the country to give them control over their millions of dollars in contributions, in effect making them leaders of a conservative billionaires' caucus. Most of the other partners, as they called themselves, were silent. Their names rarely if ever appeared. When, in response to criticism, the Kochs invited the media to cover snippets of their summits, they insisted that the reporters agree not to name the other donors. Yet this secretive, unelected, and unaccountable club was changing the face of American politics.

Charles Koch denied he had ever given any dark money. "What I give isn't 'dark.' What I give politically, that's all reported," he told CBS News in a 2015 interview. "It's either to PACs or to candidates. And what I give to my foundations is all public information." Perhaps he believed it, but during the previous five years alone, he, his brother David, and their allies had contributed over $760 million to mysterious and ostensibly apolitical nonprofits such as the Freedom Partners Chamber of Commerce, the Center to Protect Patient Rights, and the TC4 Trust. From there the money had been disbursed to dozens of other nonprofits, some of which were little more than mailboxes, which had then spent the funds promoting the donors' political interests both directly in elections, and indirectly in countless other ways. As for the transparency of Charles Koch's foundations, two of them had made grants of nearly $8 million between 2005 and 2011 to DonorsTrust, whose stated purpose was to mask the money trail.

"It's extraordinary. No one else has done anything like it," said Rob Stein, the Democratic activist who tried to create a progressive counterweight called the Democracy Alliance. "It takes an enormous amount of money, and many years, to do what the Kochs have done. They're deeply passionate. They're disciplined, and they're also ruthless."

In an interview, Brian Doherty, libertarianism's historian, said of the Kochs, "There are few policy victories you can lay directly at their feet." But he suggested that "if you look at the larger eco-system of libertarianism they were absolutely key." Because of them, he said, "the general sense of valuing Free Markets—the intellectual zeitgeist—now recognizes libertarianism in a way it never did twenty years ago."

Less than a decade later, the influence of the Kochs and their fellow "radicals for capitalism" extended well beyond just zeitgeist. They still might not have been able to take credit for many positive legislative accomplishments, but they had proven instrumental in obstructing those of their opponents. Despite the radicalism of their ideas, which had developed in a direct line from the John Birch Society, the Kochs had fulfilled Charles's 1981 ambition not just to support elected politicians, whom he regarded as mere "actors playing out a script," but to "supply the themes and words for the scripts."

By 2015, their antigovernment lead was followed by much of Congress. Addressing global warming was out of the question. Although economic inequality had reached record levels, raising taxes on the runaway rich and closing special loopholes that advantaged only them were also nonstarters. Funding basic public services like the repair of America's crumbling infrastructure was also seemingly beyond reach. A majority of the public supported an expansion of the social safety net. But leaders in both parties nevertheless embraced austerity measures popular with the affluent. Even though Americans overwhelmingly opposed cuts in Social Security, for instance, the Beltway consensus was that to save the program, it needed to be shrunk.

Obama's Affordable Care Act had survived, and polls showed that it was growing in popularity. But after nonstop battering, and the Obama administration's own serious fumbles, its reputation, and Obama's, had been damaged, even though the country's health-care costs and medical coverage, like the economy as a whole, were far better off than before he took office. Unemployment was down, and incomes and markets were up. Yet faith in government reached new lows. Obama could make progress on his environmental and other goals by taking executive actions, but in Congress ambitious new programs were out of the question.

Equally hopeless, it seemed, was campaign-finance reform. An overwhelming bipartisan majority of Americans disapproved of the amount of money in politics and supported new spending restrictions. Yet the Republican Party was now overrun by minority views, including opposition to virtually all limits on campaign spending, that seemed outlandish when the Kochs expressed them in 1980.

The radical rightists in Congress had gained so much sway by September 2015 that they effectively forced the resignation of House Speaker John Boehner, whom they had threatened to depose for not acceding to their latest demands. Leading the charge against Boehner had been Representative Mark Meadows, the North Carolina Tea Party Republican whose election had been greased by gerrymandering and other help from dark-money groups. On his way out, Boehner took a parting shot at "false prophets" and "groups here in town" who "whipped people into a frenzy believing they could accomplish things that they know, they know are never going to happen."

Conventional political wisdom measured power on the basis of election outcomes, chalking up 2012 as a loss for the Kochs, 2014 as a win, and 2016 as a test whose results remained to be seen. But this missed the more important story. The Kochs and their ultra-wealthy allies on the right had become what was arguably the single most effective special-interest group in the country.

The Kochs hadn't done it on their own. They were the fulfillment of farsighted political visionaries like Lewis Powell, Irving Kristol, William Simon, Michael Joyce, and Paul Weyrich. They were also the logical extension of the legacies of earlier big right-wing donors. John M. Olin, Lynde and Harry Bradley, and Richard Mellon Scaife had blazed the path by the time the Kochs rose to the pinnacle of their power.

During the 1970s, a handful of the nation's wealthiest corporate captains felt overtaxed and overregulated and decided to fight back. Disenchanted with the direction of modern America, they launched an ambitious, privately financed war of ideas to radically change the country. They didn't want to merely win elections; they wanted to change how Americans thought. Their ambitions were grandiose—to "save" America as they saw it, at every level, by turning the clock back to the Gilded Age before the advent of the Progressive Era. Charles Koch was younger and more libertarian than his predecessors, but, as Doherty observed, his ambitions were if anything even more radical: to pull the government out "at the root."

The weapon of choice of these wealthy activists was philanthropy. The early concerns that private foundations would become undemocratic forces of elite political power were long forgotten a century later. Leapfrogging beyond a failed political experiment by the liberal Ford Foundation in the late 1960s, the conservative rich created a new generation of hyper-political private foundations. Their aim was to invest in ideology like venture capitalists, leveraging their fortunes for maximum strategic impact. Because of the anonymity that charitable organizations provided, the full scope of these efforts was largely invisible to the public. The conservative philanthropists were, as Edwin Meese once said of Scaife, the "unseen hands."

As they began to gain ground, their war spread from "beachheads" in academia and law to corporate front groups purporting to represent public opinion. At each step, they hired the smartest and slickest marketers that money could buy, policy entrepreneurs like Frank Luntz who were skilled at popularizing the agenda of wealthy backers by "framing" their issues in more broadly appealing terms. As their efforts grew increasingly political, the funders continued to cloak these projects under the mantle of philanthropy. Few of the sponsors of this radical reorientation of American thinking were known to the public. Some carved their names in the institutions they built or attached them to the academic chairs they underwrote. But they rarely ran for office, and when they did, they even more rarely won. They exercised their power from the shadows, meeting in secret, hiding their money trails, and paying others to front for them. The dark-money groups masquerading as "social welfare" organizations during the Obama era were merely the latest iteration of a privately funded, nonprofit ideological war that had begun forty years earlier.

These political philanthropists defined themselves as selfless patriots, motivated by public, not private, gain. In many instances, they were likely sincere. Almost all gave generously not just to political projects but also to the arts, sciences, and education and, in some cases, directly to the poor. But at the same time, it was impossible not to notice that the political policies they embraced benefited their own bottom lines first and foremost. Lowering taxes and rolling back regulations, slashing the welfare state, and obliterating the limits on campaign spending might or might not have helped others, but they most certainly strengthened the hand of extreme donors with extreme wealth. "Giving back," as Peter Buffett, the son of the legendary billionaire financier Warren Buffett, observed, "sounds heroic." But he noted, "As more lives and communities are destroyed by the system that creates vast amounts of wealth for the few," philanthropists were frequently left "searching for answers with their right hands" to problems that they had "created with their left." Whether their motives were virtuous or venal, in the course of a few decades a handful of enormously rich right-wing philanthropists had changed the course of American politics. They created a formidable wealth defense movement, which had become a sizable part of what Buffett dubbed "the charitable-industrial complex."

Much as they had achieved by 2015, there was still a major item on the Kochs' shopping list: the White House. Anyone paying attention knew that 2014 was just a trial run for the presidential race in 2016. Phil Dubose, the former Koch Industries manager who spent twenty-six years working for the Kochs before testifying against them in court, had no doubt that they now had their sights on all three branches of government. "What they want is to get their own way," he said. "They call themselves libertarians. For lack of a better word, what it means is that if you're big enough to get away with it, you can get away with it. No government. If it's good for their business, they think it's good for America. What it means for the country," he added, speaking from his modest home in rural Louisiana, "is it would release the dogs. The little people? They'd get gobbled up."

On the last weekend of January 2015, as was their custom, the Kochs again convened their donor summit at a resort in

Rancho Mirage, outside Palm Springs, California. Marc Short, the president of Freedom Partners, acknowledged that "2014 was nice, but there's a long way to go." To get there, according to one ally, that weekend Charles and David Koch each pledged to give $75 million. If so, their contributions would still represent a mere fraction of the network's new fund-raising goal announced that weekend. This time, the Koch network aimed to spend $889 million in the 2016 election cycle. The sum was more than twice what the network had spent in 2012. It rivaled the record $1 billion that each of the two major political parties was expected to spend, securing their unique status as a rival center of gravity. The Kochs could afford it. Despite their predictions that Obama would prove catastrophic to the American economy, Charles's and David's personal fortunes had nearly tripled during his presidency, from $14 billion apiece in March 2009 to $41.6 billion each in March 2015, according to *Forbes*.

To Fred Wertheimer, Washington's battle-hardened liberal crusader against political corruption, the sum was almost beyond belief. "Eight hundred and eighty-nine million dollars? We've had money in the past, but this is so far beyond what anyone has thought of it's mind-boggling. This is unheard of in the history of the country. There has never been anything that approaches this."

Wertheimer was a public interest lawyer who had been waging an uphill battle to stem the rising tide of money in politics since the Watergate days. From his perspective, the country's democratic process was in crisis. "We have two unelected multibillionaires who want to control the U.S. government and exercise the power to decide what is best for more than 300 million American people, without the voices of these people being heard." He added, "There is nothing in our constitutional democracy that accepts that two of the richest people in the world can control our destiny."

As was clear from the more than $13 million a year that Koch Industries spent lobbying Congress, the Kochs had enormous financial stakes in the U.S. government. The idea that they and their allies were spending nearly $1 billion for completely selfless reasons strained credulity. Of course, money wasn't always the determinant of American elections, but there was little doubt that if the American presidency was on the auction block in 2016, the Kochs hoped to make the winning bid.

In an interview with *USA Today,* another instance in which he said that all he wanted was to "increase well-being in society," Charles Koch bristled at the idea that he was motivated by an interest in boosting his bottom line. "We are doing all of this to make more money?" he asked. "I mean, that is so ludicrous."

Some of course might have used the same adjective to describe the two-decade-long legal battle that he and his brothers waged against each other after each inheriting hundreds of millions of dollars, in order to get a bigger share. But sharing was never easy for Charles Koch. As a child, he used to tell an unfunny joke. When called upon to split a treat with others, he would say with a wise-guy grin, "I just want my fair share—which is all of it."

AUTHOR'S NOTE

In many ways, the research on this book began three decades ago when I arrived in Washington to cover Ronald Reagan's presidency for *The Wall Street Journal*. During the intervening years, I've interviewed countless political players in all forms of public life, from presidents to voters, and watched as American politics increasingly has been shaped by an ever-rising tide of private money. This book is based on hundreds of interviews conducted during the past five years with a wide range of sources spanning from the main characters and their family members, friends, and ideological allies to their business associates and political competitors.

In an ideal world, every interview would be conducted on the record. Several of the sources to whom I owe the most, however, have asked to have their names withheld. I apologize in advance to readers for not being able to fully identify these sources, but where possible I have tried to indicate their expertise and outlook, and where not possible I have tried to be scrupulous in vetting their accounts for accuracy. I also regret that several of the major characters in this saga were unreachable. Some, such as Richard Mellon Scaife, provided access to some of their papers, while others, such as Charles and David Koch, declined to participate or, like John M. Olin and Lynde and Harry Bradley, had long since passed away.

Dozens and dozens of other named sources, though, took time from their busy lives, and in some cases risked reprisal, to help me tell this story. I am immensely grateful to all of them. I also am hugely indebted to the authors of the hundreds of outstanding books, articles, studies, and news stories on which I drew. At the risk of accidentally leaving some out or of bogging readers down, I have tried to give credit in the text or the notes.

In addition, I want to give special thanks to those on whose writing I leaned most heavily. There is no way that I could have written this book without the path-blazing work of the Center for Media and Democracy, the Center for Public Integrity, the Center for Responsive Politics, Democracy 21, ProPublica, Mike Allen, Neela Banerjee, Nicholas Confessore, Clayton Coppin, Brian Doherty, Robert Draper, Lee Fang, Michael Grunwald, John Gurda, Mark Halperin, Dale Harrington, John Heilemann, Eliana Johnson, John Judis, Robert Kaiser, Andy Kroll, Chris Kromm, Charles Lewis, Robert Maguire, Mike McIntire, John J. Miller, Kim Phillips-Fein, Eric Pooley, Daniel Schulman, Theda Skocpol, Jason Stahl, Peter Stone, Steven Teles, Kenneth Vogel, Leslie Wayne, Roy Wenzl, and Bill Wilson.

Many, many others were essential to this enterprise as well, but none more so than my brilliant editor at Doubleday, Bill Thomas; my ever-resourceful literary agent at ICM, Sloan Harris; and the amazing team at *The New Yorker* that shepherded into print the original 2010 article on the Koch family that inspired this book: David Remnick, Daniel Zalewski, and the heroic checking department. I owe huge thanks also to those who helped with the book's exhausting research and fact-checking: Andrew Prokop and Ben Toff. There are no others with whom I'd rather share a foxhole.

NOTES

INTRODUCTION

6 As a former member: Charles Koch was an acolyte of Robert LeFevre, whom Brian Doherty, the libertarian author of *Radicals for Capitalism: A Freewheeling History of the Modern American Libertarian Movement* (Public Affairs, 2007), described in an interview with the author as "an anarchist figure who won Charles's heart." For more on LeFevre, see chapter 2.

7 For the most part: During Ronald Reagan's presidency, which I covered for *The Wall Street Journal,* there were constant divisions between the establishment Republicans and the conservative purists, whom many in the Reagan White House still regarded with suspicion as outliers.

7 George Soros: See Jane Mayer, "The Money Man," *New Yorker,* Oct. 18, 2004.

7 "The Kochs are on a whole": Jane Mayer, "Covert Operations," *New Yorker,* Aug. 30, 2010.

9 "there was a sense": John Podesta, interview with author.

10 "the mercantile Right": Craig Shirley, interview with author.

10 "It was obvious": Matthew Continetti, "The Paranoid Style in Liberal Politics: The Left's Obsession with the Koch Brothers," *Weekly Standard,* April 4, 2011.

12 "When W. Clement Stone": Dan Balz, "'Sheldon Primary' Is One Reason Americans Distrust the Political System," *Washington Post,* March 28, 2014.

12 "We're not a bunch": Continetti, "Paranoid Style in Liberal Politics."

12 Participants at the summits: See Kenneth R. Vogel, *Big Money: 2.5 Billion Dollars, One Suspicious Vehicle, and a Pimp—on the Trail of the Ultra-rich Hijacking of American Politics* (Public Affairs, 2014), for an excellent account of the Koch seminars.

13 In order to foil: Michael Mechanic, "Spying on the Koch Brothers: Inside the Discreet Retreat Where the Elite Meet and Plot the Democrats' Defeat," *Mother Jones,* Nov./Dec. 2011.

13 "There is anonymity": Vogel, *Big Money.*

13 the combined fortunes: Known participants at Koch seminars worth $1 billion or more as of 2015 valuations include the following:

Charles Koch: $42.9 billion
David Koch: $42.9 billion
Sheldon Adelson: $31.4 billion
Harold Hamm: $12.2 billion
Stephen Schwarzman: $12 billion
Philip Anschutz: $11.8 billion
Steven Cohen (represented by Michael Sullivan): $10.3 billion
John Menard Jr.: $9 billion

Ken Griffin: $6.5 billion
Charles Schwab: $6.4 billion
Richard DeVos: $5.7 billion
Diane Hendricks: $3.6 billion
Ken Langone: $2.9 billion
Stephen Bechtel Jr.: $2.8 billion
Richard Farmer: $2 billion
Stan Hubbard: $2 billion
Joe Craft: $1.4 billion
Elaine Marshall, whose fortune was estimated at $8.3 billion in 2014, dropped off *Forbes*'s list of billionaires in 2015. When her estimated 2014 worth is added to the cumulative fortunes of the known participating billionaires during the Obama presidency, the total tops $222 billion.

14 The gap between: Jacob S. Hacker and Paul Pierson, *Winner-Take-All Politics: How Washington Made the Rich Richer—and Turned Its Back on the Middle Class* (Simon & Schuster, 2010), says in 2007 that the top 1 percent of earners took home 23.5 percent of the country's income, when capital gains and dividends were factored in.

14 Liberal critics: See Chrystia Freeland, *Plutocrats: The Rise of the New Global Super-rich and the Fall of Everyone Else* (Penguin, 2012), 3.

14 "We are on the road": Paul Krugman, speaking in an interview with Bill Moyers about Thomas Piketty's book *Capital in the Twenty-First Century*. "What the 1% Don't Want Us to Know," BillMoyers.com, April 18, 2014.

15 "Wealth begets power": Joseph E. Stiglitz, "Of the 1%, by the 1%, for the 1%," *Vanity Fair*, May 2011.

15 Thomas Piketty: Thomas Piketty, *Capital in the Twenty-First Century*, trans. Arthur Goldhammer (Belknap Press/Harvard University Press, 2014).

16 "disconnect themselves": Mike Lofgren, "Revolt of the Rich," *American Conservative*, Aug. 27, 2012.

16 Only one full guest list: The list was published by the Web site *Think-Progress*, on October 20, 2010, in a news story by Lee Fang. In 2014, *Mother Jones* published an additional partial list.

17 vulture fund: See Ari Berman, "Rudy's Bird of Prey," *Nation*, Oct. 11, 2007, regarding the New York State legislature enacting legislation to aid his pursuit of repayment. In addition, Singer sought help from the U.S. courts in pressuring Argentina to repay him at a profit for bonds on which the country had defaulted.

18 In the wake of the 2008 market crash: According to David Carey and John E. Morris, *King of Capital: The Remarkable Rise, Fall, and Rise Again of Steve Schwarzman and Blackstone* (Crown Business, 2010), "The catalysts that spurred Congress to action were Schwarzman's birthday gala and the looming Blackstone IPO, say people who followed the congressional discussions."

19 three domestic servants soon sued him: Christie Smythe and Zachary Mider, "Renaissance Co-CEO Mercer Sued by Home Staff over Pay," *Bloomberg Business*, July 17, 2013.

19 The sum was so scandalously large: Ken Langone, whose wealth *Forbes*

estimated at $2.9 billion as of 2015, argued that Grasso's pay was reasonable, an argument that eventually prevailed in court.

19 "if it wasn't for us fat cats": Mark Halperin and John Heilemann, *Double Down: Game Change 2012* (Penguin, 2013), 194.

19 "an even wealthier man": "Richard Strong's Fall Came Quickly," Associated Press, May 27, 2004.

20 "prepaids done slightly differently": David Cay Johnston, "Anschutz Will Cost Taxpayers More Than the Billionaire," *Tax Notes: Johnston's Take,* Aug. 2, 2010.

21 By 2009, DeVos's son: "DeVoses May Pay a Price for Hefty Penalty; Record Fine Presents Problems; Lawyers Say They Will Appeal," *Grand Rapids Press,* April 13, 2008.

21 "largest private hoard": Daniel Fisher, "Fuel's Paradise," *Forbes,* Jan. 20, 2003.

22 Later, Massey was bought: In 2015, Alpha Natural Resources, the country's fourth-largest coal company, filed for bankruptcy protection.

22 Harold Hamm: Josh Harkinson, "Who Fracked Mitt Romney?," *Mother Jones,* Nov./Dec. 2012.

23 Further, in the summer of 2008: Koch Industries argued that it was in compliance with the trade ban because it had used a foreign subsidiary to help Iran build the largest methanol plant in the world. By using offshore employees as a cutout, Koch Industries adhered to the letter of the law while evading the intent of a U.S. trade ban that had been in place since 1995. Asjylan Loder and David Evans, "Koch Brothers Flout Law Getting Richer with Secret Iran Sales," *Bloomberg Markets,* Oct. 3, 2011.

24 Paternalistic and family-owned: For an excellent history of Bechtel, see Sally Denton, *Profiteers: Bechtel and the Men Who Built the World* (Simon & Schuster, forthcoming).

24 But when a former company pilot: In 2010, Stewart, his wife, daughter, and two others were killed in a helicopter crash that investigators reportedly believed was caused when his five-year-old daughter, who was sitting in the cockpit, kicked the controls.

25 He understood how to sell: Sean Wilentz, "States of Anarchy," *New Republic,* March 30, 2010.

27 In hopes of staving off: TARP details come from Hank Paulson, *On the Brink: Inside the Race to Stop the Collapse of the Global Financial System* (Headline, 2010), chaps. 11–13.

28 Among the groups now listed: On October 1, 2008, the day of the Senate vote, Senator John Thune's office released a list of groups that supported the bailout, and AFP was on that list: http://www.thune.senate.gov/public/index.cfm/press-releases?ID=8c603eca-77d3-49a3-96f5-dfe92eacda06.

28 A source familiar: In his book, *Democracy Denied* (BenBella Books, 2011), Phil Kerpen, who was a top Koch operative at Americans for Prosperity, admitted that although he "hated the bill," "I was genuinely frightened that our financial system would disintegrate."

29 "the fight of their lives": Bill Wilson and Roy Wenzl, "The Kochs' Quest to Save America," *Wichita Eagle,* Oct. 15, 2012.

29 "like to slice and dice": Barack Obama, Keynote Address, Democratic National Convention, July 27, 2004.

CHAPTER ONE: RADICALS

34 Koch fought back: The most thorough account of the legal issues appears in Clayton A. Coppin, "A History of Winkler Koch Engineering Company Patent Litigation and Corruption in the Federal Judiciary." Unpublished. Commissioned by Koch Industries, shared with author.

34 "The fact that the judge": Koch family associate in interview with author.

34 But by 1932: Alexander Igolkin, "Learning from American Experience," *Oil of Russia: Lukoil International Magazine,* 2006.

34 Fred Koch continued to provide: The reference to one hundred units is attributed to the "Economic Review of the Soviet Union" as quoted in a report titled "Why the Soviet Union Chose the Winkler-Koch Cracking System" by Clayton A. Coppin, commissioned by Koch Industries.

35 Wood River Oil & Refining: Koch Industries' Web site, History Timeline.

35 "enjoyed its first real": Charles G. Koch, *The Science of Success: How Market-Based Management Built the World's Largest Private Company* (John Wiley & Sons, 2007), 6.

35 During the 1930s: Fred Koch's business trips to Germany were described by a family member.

35 Archival records document: Rainer Karlsch and Raymond Stokes, *Faktor Öl* [The oil factor] (Beck, 2003).

35 "agent of influence": Davis was never charged with criminal wrongdoing. After he died in 1941, a Justice Department investigation implicating him was covered up, according to Dale Harrington, *Mystery Man: William Rhodes Davis, American Nazi Agent of Influence* (Brassey's, 1999), 206.

35 The president of the American bank: Ibid, 14. Charles Spencer of the Bank of Boston refused to have anything to do with the deal. Instead, he foisted it off on lower officers at the bank who were less scrupulous.

36 "Gentlemen, I have reviewed": Ibid., 16.

36 personally autograph a copy: Ibid., 19.

36 "deeply committed to Nazism": Ibid., 18.

36 "produce the high-octane gasoline": Ibid., 19.

37 "was hugely, hugely important": Peter Hayes, interview with author.

37 "Winkler-Koch benefited directly": Raymond Stokes, interview with author.

37 "Although nobody agrees": Fred Koch to Charles de Ganahl, Oct. 1938, in Daniel Schulman, *Sons of Wichita: How the Koch Brothers Became America's Most Powerful and Private Dynasty* (Grand Central, 2014), 41–42.

39 The nanny's iron rule: Descriptions of the nanny are based on interviews with a knowledgeable source who asked not to be identified in order to maintain ongoing relations with the family.

40 "My father was fairly tough": Bryan Burrough, "Wild Bill Koch," *Vanity Fair,* June 1994.

40 "a real John Wayne type": John Damgard, interview with author.

40 Koch emphasized rugged pursuits: Interview with Koch family cousin.

41 "By instilling a work ethic": Charles G. Koch, *Science of Success,* 9.

42 "Father wanted to make": Maryellen Mark, "Survival of the Richest," *Fame,* Nov. 1989.

42 Clayton Coppin: Coppin worked at the Program in Social and Organizational Learning, based at George Mason University, which was largely funded by the Koch family.

43 Portia Hamilton: Hamilton was a 1940 graduate of Columbia University who wrote popular newspaper columns on psychology suggesting that child's play and Rorschach tests could shed light on inner turmoil. In one column, "Troubled Little Minds," *Milwaukee Sentinel,* April 3, 1949, she described a little girl who received "too much love" from her parents and grandparents.

44 His mother made clear: Wayne, "Survival of the Richest."

44 "I pleaded with them": Brian O'Reilly and Patty de Llosa, "The Curse on the Koch Brothers," *Fortune,* Feb. 17, 1997.

44 "I hated all that": Charles Koch reminisced about his school years in an interview with Jason Jennings, posted on Koch Industries' Web site.

44 Eventually, Culver expelled him: The expulsion is described by both Wayne, "Survival of the Richest," and Coppin's unpublished study commissioned for Bill Koch, "Stealth: The History of Charles Koch's Political Activities, Part One," a copy of which was shared with the author.

44 As punishment, Charles's father: Charles Koch, interview with Jennings. Charles Koch's reminiscence of his father, from interview with Jennings.

44 "Father put the fear": O'Reilly and de Llosa, "Curse on the Koch Brothers."

44 "Charles spent little": Coppin, "Stealth."

44 "There was a lot of strife": Coppin, interview with author.

45 "I think he thought": Roy Wenzl and Bill Wilson, "Charles Koch Relentless in Pursuing His Goals," *Wichita Eagle,* Oct. 14, 2012.

45 "As soon as we arrived": Elizabeth Koch, "The World Tour Compatibility Test: Back in Tokyo, Part 1," *Smith,* March 30, 2007, http://www.smithmag.net.

45 "staring down that dark well": Elizabeth Koch, "The World Tour Compatibility Test: Grand Finale," *Smith,* May 3, 2007, http://www.smithmag.net.

45 "When you are 21": Kelley McMillan, "Bill Koch's Wild West Adventure," *5280: The Denver Magazine,* Feb. 2013.

46 "Never did such good advice": O'Reilly and de Llosa, "Curse on the Koch Brothers."

48 "you won't be very controversial": Lee Fang, *The Machine: A Field Guide to the Resurgent Right* (New Press, 2013), 100.

48 "utterly absurd": FBI memo, March 15, 1961, addressed to C. D. DeLoach (assistant FBI director), uncovered through a Freedom of Information Act request filed by Ernie Lazar.

48 An alphabet soup: Fang, *Machine,* 97.

49 "collectivists": Charles Koch, "I'm Fighting to Restore a Free Society," *Wall Street Journal,* April 2, 2014.

49 "a very intelligent, sharp man": Fang, *Machine,* 96.

49 "the spirit of Moscow": Ibid., 102.

50 Instead of winning: Some conservatives have argued that Goldwater's candidacy clarified and strengthened the GOP, but others, like Michael Gerson in "Goldwater's Warning to the GOP," *Washington Post,* April 18,

2014, regard his candidacy as disastrous for Republicans, partly because it repelled future generations of minority voters.

50 Before the emergence: Fang, *Machine.*

50 "it bordered on anarchism": Rick Perlstein, *Before the Storm: Barry Goldwater and the Unmaking of the American Consensus* (Nation Books, 2009), 113.

51 "there are certain laws": Wenzl and Wilson, "Charles Koch Relentless."

51 Early on, the Internal Revenue Service: Coppin, "History of Winkler Koch," 29.

51 He remained vehemently opposed: Wilson and Wenzl, "Charles Koch Relentless."

51 Among other strategies: Gary Weiss, "The Price of Immortality," *Upstart Business Journal,* Oct. 15, 2008; "Estate Planning Koch and Chase Koch (Son of Charles Koch): Past, Present, and Future," *Repealing the Frontiers of Ignorance,* Aug. 4, 2013, http://repealingfrontiers.blogspot.com.

51 "So for 20 years": Weiss, "Price of Immortality."

52 he arranged to pass his fortune: In his letters, Fred Koch described his concerns about children given family fortunes at young ages who disowned their fathers, according to Coppin.

52 "It was pretty clear": Gus diZerega lost touch with Charles and eventually abandoned his right-wing views, becoming a political science professor and writer on spiritual and other matters. He nonetheless credits Charles with opening his mind to political philosophy, which set him on the path to academia.

52 "LeFevre was an anarchist figure": Brian Doherty, interview with author.

53 As the journalist: Mark Ames, "Meet Charles Koch's Brain," *NSFWCorp,* Sept. 30, 2013. See also George Thayer, *The Farther Shores of Politics: The American Political Fringe* (Simon & Schuster, 1967). As also recounted by Donald Janson, "Conservatives at Freedom School to Prepare a New Federal Constitution," *New York Times,* June 13, 1965, LeFevre claimed in a memoir that he took dictation from saints, drove at sixty miles per hour for twenty miles with his eyes shut, and left his physical body behind while traveling through the air to Mount Shasta, where he met Jesus Christ.

53 The school taught a revisionist version: The description of the Freedom School's curriculum is based on interviews with three former attendees, including Gus diZerega, the other two of whom asked to remain anonymous.

54 bastion of "ultraconservatism": Janson, "Conservatives at Freedom School to Prepare a New Federal Constitution."

54 Charles Koch was so enthusiastic: Clayton Coppin believes that the elder Fred Koch agreed to Charles's request that he attend the Freedom School for a week in exchange for Charles's agreement to support the John Birch Society.

55 Charles was so incensed: "Toe the line" is based on the recollection of a source close to the Kochs.

55 James J. Martin: Martin wrote for the Institute for Historical Review's publication, *The Journal of Historical Review,* and his book *The Man Who Invented "Genocide": The Public Career and Consequences of Raphael Lemkin* was published in 1984 by the Institute for Historical Review. In an inter-

view with the author, Deborah Lipstadt, author of *Denying the Holocaust: The Growing Assault on Truth and Memory* (Plume, 1994), said, "One cannot be officially affiliated with the IHR and regularly publishing in its pages if one is not a Holocaust denier."

55 "It was a stew pot": Gus diZerega, interview with author.

55 As Angus Burgin describes: Angus Burgin, *The Great Persuasion: Reinventing Free Markets Since the Depression* (Harvard University Press, 2012), 88.

56 Hayek touted it as the key: Phillips-Fein writes, "The great innovation of Hayek and von Mises was to create a defense of the free market using the language of freedom and revolutionary change. The free market, not the political realm, enabled human beings to realize their liberty . . . [T]he free market, not the welfare state, was the true basis of meaningful opposition to fascism." Kim Phillips-Fein, *Invisible Hands: The Making of the Conservative Movement from the New Deal to Reagan* (Norton, 2009), 39–40.

56 By the time LeFevre died: In 2010, a spokesman for Koch Industries tried to distance the family from the Freedom School, insisting Charles and David had never been LeFevre's "devotees," as I described them in the 2010 *New Yorker* story "Covert Actions." The spokesman said, "In fact they have had no contact with him since the 1960's." However, as Mark Ames first reported, Charles Koch sent LeFevre a friendly letter in 1973 asking for LeFevre's approval of his plan to personally take over another libertarian organization to which LeFevre had ties, the Institute for Humane Studies.

57 The private life of the younger Frederick: Deposition of William Koch.

59 "homosexual blackmail attempt": O'Reilly and de Llosa, "Curse on the Koch Brothers."

59 "Charles' 'homosexual blackmail'": Schulman, *Sons of Wichita,* 130. Schulman describes the blackmail scheme as taking place after the senior Fred Koch died, but that is not the way it is described in Bill Koch's deposition.

59 wealthiest man in Kansas: See Coppin, "Stealth."

60 Koch Industries acquired the majority share: The Kochs bought the Pine Bend Refinery from J. Howard Marshall II, whose family members became virtually the only outside investors in Koch Industries, retaining a 15 percent share. Marshall became tabloid fodder at the age of eighty-nine for marrying Anna Nicole Smith, who at the time was a memorably zaftig twenty-six-year-old stripper and *Playboy* model.

60 "This single Koch refinery": David Sassoon, "Koch Brothers' Activism Protects Their 50 Years in Canadian Heavy Oils," *InsideClimate News,* May 10, 2012.

61 "Here I am one of the wealthiest": Leslie Wayne, "Brothers at Odds," *New York Times,* Dec. 7, 1986.

61 "an iron hand": Bruce Bartlett (an economist who formerly worked for the National Center for Policy Analysis, a Dallas-based think tank that the Kochs funded), interview with author.

61 In 1983, Charles and David bought out: Schulman, *Sons of Wichita*, 142.

62 Unlike his brothers, Frederick preferred: Among Frederick Koch's donations was a $3 million gift to restore the Swan, a Shakespearean theater

in Stratford-upon-Avon. He attended the opening, at which Queen Elizabeth personally officiated, but requested that she not mention his name.

63 He lived lavishly: Rich Roberts, "America 3 Win No Bargain Sail," *Los Angeles Times,* May 17, 1992.

63 He, too, barely spoke: Bill Koch broke his silence to speak with Charles at his twin David's birthday party and at a visit to Bohemian Grove, the exclusive men's social retreat in Northern California.

63 "in a fifty-fifty deal": See Louis Kraar, "Family Feud at Corporate Colossus," *Fortune,* July 26, 1982.

64 "When you're the only one": Weiss, "Price of Immortality."

64 "the cheapest person": *Park Avenue: Money, Power, and the American Dream,* PBS, Nov. 12, 2012.

65 "It's going to cost them": Interview with author. For more on David Koch's resignation from WNET's board, see Jane Mayer, "A Word from Our Sponsor," *New Yorker,* May 27, 2013.

65 Later clashes: The Oil, Chemical, and Atomic Workers union called a strike at Koch's Pine Bend Refinery that lasted nine months starting in January 1973. According to Coppin, "Stealth," "If he could have Charles Koch would have eliminated the union from his refinery."

66 "Ideas do not spread": Charles Koch, "The Business Community: Resisting Regulation," *Libertarian Review,* Aug. 1978.

66 Around the same time: Coppin, "Stealth," describes the conference and quotes from the papers given there at length.

69 The brothers took an even: Charles Koch "liked the idea of being in control of things even though he is not recognized as being in control," David Gordon, a fellow libertarian activist, told *Washingtonian* magazine. Luke Mullins, "The Battle for the Cato Institute," *Washingtonian,* May 30, 2012.

69 "David Koch ran in '80": Grover Norquist, interview with author.

70 But at the Libertarian Party convention: Marshall Schwartz, "Libertarians in Convention," *Libertarian Review,* Nov. 1979.

71 "It tends to be a nasty": See Mayer, "Covert Operations."

71 "They weren't really on my radar": Richard Viguerie, interview with author.

CHAPTER TWO: THE HIDDEN HAND

73 "the leading financial supporter": Robert Kaiser, "Money, Family Name Shaped Scaife," *Washington Post,* May 3, 1999, A1.

74 "You fucking Communist": Karen Rothmyer, "Citizen Scaife," *Columbia Journalism Review,* July/Aug. 1981.

74 In 2009, however: Richard Scaife shared a copy of his memoir with the author and authorized the use of all requested material, other than a small portion dealing with a litigious divorce, some details about which do not appear here.

75 "Nowadays there are no": Lionel Trilling, *The Liberal Imagination: Essays on Literature and Society* (Viking, 1950), xv.

75 "He's the originator": Christopher Ruddy, interview with author.

75 In 1957, *Fortune* ranked: Rothmyer, "Citizen Scaife."

76 "How beautifully he summed up": Richard Mellon Scaife, "A Richly Conservative Life," 282.

76 "a gutter drunk": Kaiser, "Money, Family Name Shaped Scaife."

77 "My father—he was suckin'": Burton Hersh, *The Mellon Family: A Fortune in History* (Morrow, 1978).

77 "a lightweight": Kaiser, "Money, Family Name Shaped Scaife."

77 "My political conservatism": Scaife, "Richly Conservative Life," 20.

77 "He was concerned": Ibid., 21.

78 "Alan Scaife was terribly worried": Kaiser, "Money, Family Name Shaped Scaife."

78 "From top to bottom": Isaac William Martin, *Rich People's Movements: Grassroots Campaigns to Untax the One Percent* (Oxford University Press, 2013), 25.

79 His Union Trust bank: Ibid., 34.

79 In an effort to win: Ibid., 45. Mellon argued that if taxes were lowered on the rich, they would be less inclined to invest in tax-exempt bonds, thereby spurring greater revenue for the Treasury and, coincidentally, for financial institutions like the Mellon Bank.

79 Sixty years later: The Gerald R. Ford Library contains a June 11, 1975, memorandum from Bob Golden, of the American Enterprise Institute, to Dick Cheney, at the Ford White House, to which is attached a copy of an academic paper by Jude Wanniski on which is scrawled the title "Santa Claus Theory."

79 Once in public office: John B. Judis, *The Paradox of American Democracy: Elites, Special Interests, and the Betrayal of the Public Trust* (Routledge, 2000).

79 "cut the tax rates on the richest": Isaac William Martin, *Rich People's Movements,* 64.

79 Not only did his economic theories: Judis, *Paradox of American Democracy,* 46.

80 "I don't know what": Scaife, "Richly Conservative Life," 61.

80 "equality of sacrifice": See Kenneth F. Scheve Jr. and David Stasavage, "Is the Estate Tax Doomed?," *New York Times,* March 24, 2013. They note that "equality of sacrifice" was a term used by John Stuart Mill and grew from the nineteenth century into an argument in favor of progressive taxation, particularly in financing wars.

81 "When I can't sleep": Scaife, "Richly Conservative Life," 6.

81 "making each other totally miserable": Robert Kaiser and Ira Chinoy, "Scaife: Funding Father of the Right," *Washington Post,* May 2, 1999, A1.

83 "The first priority": Scaife, "Richly Conservative Life," 43.

83 "Isn't it grand": Ibid., 46.

85 Today, they are commonplace: John D. Rockefeller met secretly with President William Taft in an effort to get his support for the creation of the Rockefeller Foundation, but regardless of the effort the U.S. Senate rejected the idea in 1913, according to Rob Reich's paper "Repugnant to the Whole Idea of Democracy? On the Role of Foundations in Democratic Societies" (Department of Political Science, Stanford University, for the Philanthropy Symposium at Duke University, Jan. 2015), 5.

86 "represent virtually by definition": See Ibid, 9.

86 By 1930, there were approximately: Ibid., 7.

86 "completely irresponsible institution": Richard Posner likens perpetual charitable foundations to hereditary monarchies. He suggests that they may be a useful form of self-taxation by the rich but also questions why they should enjoy tax breaks, particularly in the case of foundations run by businessmen who are simultaneously polishing the image of their companies. See "Charitable Foundations—Posner's Comment," *The Becker-Posner Blog*, Dec. 31, 2006, http://www.becker-posner-blog.com.

87 "The result": Scaife, "Richly Conservative Life," 66.

87 "advance ideas that I believe": Ibid., 58.

87 "This was the beginning": Ibid., 70.

88 Carrying out this attack: In *The Rise of the Counter-establishment: From Conservative Ideology to Political Power* (Times Books, 1986), Sidney Blumenthal made the term "counter-establishment" famous and for the first time told much of the early intellectual history of the movement.

89 "Attack on American Free Enterprise System": For more on the origins and impact of Lewis Powell's memorandum, see Phillips-Fein, *Invisible Hands*, 156–65.

89 "We didn't have anything": Piereson's comments were made in a panel discussion with Gara LaMarche at an Open Society Institute forum, Sept. 21, 2006.

90 "lay siege to corporations": Staughton Lind, quoted in Phillips-Fein, *Invisible Hands*, 151.

91 Powell's defense of the tobacco companies: See Jeffrey Clements, *Corporations Are Not People* (Berrett-Koehler, 2012), 19–21.

91 Income in America: Isaac William Martin, *Rich People's Movements*, 155.

92 Powell called on corporate America: Some have questioned whether too much has been made of Powell's memo. Mark Schmitt of *The American Prospect* wrote in 2005, "The reality of the right is that there was no plan, just a lot of people writing their own memos and starting their own organization."

92 "single-minded pursuit": Phillips-Fein, *Invisible Hands*, 164.

92 "tax-exempt refuge": For more on Buchanan's memo, see Jason Stahl, *The Right Moves: The Conservative Think Tank in American Political Culture Since 1945* (University of North Carolina Press, forthcoming), 93.

93 "the artillery": James Piereson comments at Open Society Institute's Forum, Sept. 21, 2006.

94 One of them: Feulner was a member of the Mont Pelerin Society, an Austrian economics club that Hayek co-founded and attended and that was almost entirely underwritten by American businessmen.

94 described himself openly as a "radical": David Brock, *Blinded by the Right: The Conscience of an Ex-conservative* (Crown, 2002), 54.

94 After reading Powell's memo: Lee Edwards, *The Power of Ideas: The Heritage Foundation at 25 Years* (Jameson Books, 1997).

94 "I do believe": See Dan Baum, *Citizen Coors: A Grand Family Saga of Business, Politics, and Beer* (William Morrow, 2000), 103. Weyrich added, "Coors is the kind of guy who thinks you can write your congressman and get something done."

95 Convinced that radical leftists: Ibid.

96 Scaife's money soon followed: Before founding Heritage, Feulner had worked at the Center for Strategic and International Studies, which was almost single-handedly funded by Scaife in its early years, so he would have recognized Scaife's potential as a backer.

96 "Coors gives six-packs": Kaiser and Chinoy, "Funding Father of the Right."

96 "free from any political": Judis, *Paradox of American Democracy,* 122.

96 "The AEIs and the Heritages": Ibid., 169. Leaders of conservative foundations such as William Simon might have perceived themselves as merely providing political balance and copying the activism of liberal foundations, but the political scientist Steven Teles pointed out in an interview with the author that there were key differences. The boards of the earlier establishment foundations such as Ford tended to be centrist, while those at the new conservative foundations like Olin tended, he says, to be "ideologically-aligned" and more likely to embrace grant making as a form of movement building.

97 "a scholarly institute": Adam Curtis, "The Curse of Tina," BBC, Sept. 13, 2011.

97 The Sarah Scaife Foundation: Martin Gottlieb, "Conservative Policy Unit Takes Aim at New York," *New York Times,* May 5, 1986.

98 "As you well know": L. L. Logue to Frank Walton (Heritage Foundation), Nov. 16, 1976, folder 16, Weyrich Papers, University of Montana.

99 "'big business' pressure organization": Jason Stahl, "From Without to Within the Movement: Consolidating the Conservative Think Tank in the 'Long Sixties,'" in *The Right Side of the Sixties: Reexamining Conservatism's Decade of Transformation,* ed. Laura Jane Gifford and Daniel K. Williams (Palgrave Macmillan, 2012), 105.

99 Powell and others: See Stahl, *Right Moves.* Stahl describes the way that the conservative think tanks upended the notion of expertise with the concept of political balance. He also describes the Ford Foundation's donation to AEI.

99 fight criticism that it was liberal: In 1976, in a move that rocked staid philanthropic circles, Henry Ford II resigned in protest from the board of the foundation bearing his family name, arguing that it wasn't sufficiently pro-business.

100 "That was quite the heist": The note from the friend to William Baroody Jr. is described in Stahl, *Right Moves.*

100 "Funders increasingly expect": Steven Clemons, "The Corruption of Think Tanks," Japan Policy Research Institute, Feb. 2003.

100 "We've become money launderers": Claudia Dean and Richard Morin, "Lobbyists Seen Lurking Behind Tank Funding," *Washington Post,* Nov. 19, 2002.

101 "socialism out and out": Phillips-Fein, *Invisible Hands,* 174.

101 "I saw how right-wing ideology": Brock, *Blinded by the Right,* 77.

101 "the unseen hand": Many of these details are drawn from Michael Joseph Gross, "A Vast Right-Wing Hypocrisy," *Vanity Fair,* Feb. 2008.

101 "I don't think he had": Kaiser, "Money, Family Name Shaped Scaife."

102 "With political victory": Ibid.

102 "We did what comes naturally": Gross, "Vast Right-Wing Hypocrisy."

102 According to Scaife's son: Ritchie denied the marijuana anecdote, but Scaife confirmed it in ibid.

102 "Ritchie loves Dick": Ibid.

103 "Wife and dog missing": Ibid.

104 "had particularly in mind": Edwards, *Power of Ideas.*

104 "can order people done away with": John F. Kennedy Jr., "Who's Afraid of Richard Mellon Scaife?," *George,* Jan. 1999.

106 "the development of a well-financed cadre": Cited in Nicholas Confessore, "Quixotic '80 Campaign Gave Birth to Kochs' Powerful Network," *New York Times,* May 17, 2014.

106 Koch Industries had just become: Ibid.

106 Its start-up funding: Michael Nelson, "The New Libertarians," *Saturday Review,* March 1, 1980.

107 "I said my bank account": Ed Crane, interview with author.

107 "Ed Crane would always call": Mullins, "Battle for the Cato Institute."

107 "serve as a night watchman": Schulman, *Sons of Wichita,* 106.

108 In fact, after Watergate: Stahl, in *Right Moves,* quotes an AEI official making this argument to business leaders after Watergate.

108 list of the Heritage Foundation's sponsors: Box 720, folder 5, Clare Boothe Luce Papers, Library of Congress.

108 "that the think tanks": Piereson comment, Open Society forum.

108 Americans' distrust of government: Judis, *Paradox of American Democracy,* 129.

109 The labor movement: For an excellent, detailed description of labor's congressional setbacks, see Hacker and Pierson, *Winner-Take-All Politics,* 127.

109 "We are basically a conduit": Phil McCombs, "Building a Heritage in the War of Ideas," *Washington Post,* Oct. 3, 1983.

109 "ALEC is well on its way": George Archibald to Richard Larry, Feb. 3, 1977, Weyrich Papers.

110 "the Golden Rule": See Alexander Hertel-Fernandez, "Funding the State Policy Battleground: The Role of Foundations and Firms" (paper for Duke Symposium on Philanthropy, Jan. 2015).

110 Weyrich was particularly adept: Randall Balmer, a historian of American religion, argues in his book *Redeemer: The Life of Jimmy Carter* (Basic Books, 2014) that the conventional wisdom, which holds that the backlash against *Roe v. Wade* created the Christian Right, is wrong. Instead, he suggests, it was evangelicals' opposition to integration that truly launched the movement. Weyrich, he suggests, brilliantly seized on evangelicals' anger at Jimmy Carter's refusal to grant tax-exempt status to Bob Jones University because it had an explicit whites-only admissions policy.

110 According to Feulner: Dom Bonafede, "Issue-oriented Heritage Foundation Hitches Its Wagon to Reagan's Star," *National Journal,* March 20, 1982.

110 He slashed corporate: Congress cut the effective federal income tax rate on the top 1 percent of earners from 31.8 percent in 1980 to 24.9 percent in 1985. In contrast, Congress raised the effective rates on the bottom four-fifths of earners from 16.5 percent to 16.7 percent. It wasn't a big tax increase for the vast majority of Americans, but it was a substantial tax cut for the wealthy. As a result, from 1980 to 1985, after-tax income in the top 5 percent of earners increased, while it decreased for everyone else, accord-

ing to Judis, *Paradox of American Democracy,* 151. See also Daniel Stedman Jones, *Masters of the Universe: Hayek, Friedman, and the Birth of Neoliberal Politics* (Princeton University Press, 2012), 265.

111 Scaife, who by then had donated: Ed Feulner describes the scope of Scaife's giving in the Luce Papers.

111 "I was lucky": Scaife, "Richly Conservative Life," 22.

CHAPTER THREE: BEACHHEADS

112 uprising at Cornell University: An excellent report on the protest appears in Donald Alexander Downs, *Cornell '69: Liberalism and the Crisis of the American University* (Cornell University Press, 1999).

112 "the most disgraceful": David Horowitz, "Ann Coulter at Cornell," Front PageMag.com, May 21, 2001.

113 "The catastrophe at Cornell": John J. Miller, *A Gift of Freedom: How the John M. Olin Foundation Changed America* (Encounter Books, 2006).

113 "saw very clearly": John J. Miller, *How Two Foundations Reshaped America* (Philanthropy Roundtable, 2003), 16.

114 "These guys, individually": Lizzy Ratner, "Olin Foundation, Right-Wing Tank, Snuffing Itself," *New York Observer,* May 9, 2005.

114 Each side would argue: James Piereson, for instance, who regards hugely well-endowed, establishment nonprofit organizations such as the Ford Foundation as liberal, argues that the Right has been routinely outspent by the Left.

115 "saving the free enterprise": Olin's general counsel was Frank O'Connell, a labor lawyer who was famously tough on unions.

115 Olin followed closely: This account of Olin's history draws extensively on Miller, *Gift of Freedom.*

117 In the summer of 1970: E. W. Kenworthy, "U.S. Will Sue 8 Concerns over Dumping of Mercury," *New York Times,* July 25, 1970, 1.

117 Subsequently, the Justice Department: The Olin Corporation dumped mercury into a landfill known as the 102nd Street site, which was also used by the Hooker Chemicals and Plastics Corporation.

117 Eventually, the Olin Corporation: The maximum fine for each of the seven misdemeanor convictions was $10,000, thus the maximum fine in total was $70,000. "Olin Fined $70,000," Associated Press, Dec. 12, 1979.

118 For decades, Saltville: "End of a Company Town," *Life,* March 26, 1971. See also Tod Newcombe, "Saltville, Virginia: A Company Town Without a Company," Governing.com, Aug. 2012.

118 "They all knew the dangers": Harry Haynes, interview with author.

119 Dangerous levels of mercury: Virginia Water Resources Research Center, "Mercury Contamination in Virginia Waters: History, Issues, and Options," March 1979. See also EPA Superfund Record of Decision, Saltville Waste Disposal Ponds, June 30, 1987.

120 *Life* magazine produced: "End of a Company Town."

120 "It's a ghost town": Shirley "Sissy" Bailey, interview with author.

120 "Common sense should have": Stephen Lester, interview with author.

121 "It is possible": James Piereson, e-mail interview with author.

121 "The Olin family": William Voegeli, e-mail interview with author.
121 "My greatest ambition": Quoted in Ratner, "Olin Foundation, Right-Wing Tank, Snuffing Itself."
122 "with definite left-wing attitudes": John M. Olin to the president of Cornell, 1980, in Teles, *Rise of the Conservative Legal Movement,* 185.
122 "It was like a home-study course": Miller, *Gift of Freedom,* 34.
122 By the late 1960s, Ford: James Piereson describes the Ford Foundation's leading role as liberal activist philanthropists in an incisive essay, "Investing in Conservative Ideas," *Commentary,* May 2005.
123 "almost identical": Miller, *How Two Foundations Reshaped America,* 13.
123 "Since the 60's, the vast bulk": William Simon, *A Time for Truth* (Reader's Digest Press, 1978), 64–65.
124 "What we need": Miller, *Gift of Freedom,* 56.
124 "Capitalism has no duty": Simon, *Time for Truth,* 78.
125 "They must be given grants": Miller, *Gift of Freedom,* 57.
125 "Joyce was a true radical": Ralph Benko, interview with author.
126 "because they were emulated": Teles, *Rise of the Conservative Legal Movement,* 186.
126 "The only way you're going": Miller, *How Two Foundations Reshaped America,* 17.
126 "the most influential schools": James Piereson, "Planting Seeds of Liberty," *Philanthropy,* May/June 2005.
127 Princeton's Madison Program: Miller, *Gift of Freedom.*
127 "a savvy right-wing operative": Max Blumenthal, "Princeton Tilts Right," *Nation,* Feb. 23, 2006.
127 "perhaps we should think": Piereson, "Planting Seeds of Liberty."
127 the CIA laundered: Most of the CIA funds arrived from an organization called the Dearborn Foundation. The Olin Foundation then disbursed the funds to a Washington, D.C.–based organization called the Vernon Fund.
127 the press exposed the covert propaganda: In 1967, *Ramparts* magazine blew the cover on the covert CIA program. Additional reports revealed that the CIA had been secretly funneling money through as many as a hundred private foundations in the country that were acting as front groups and passing the money on covertly to Cold War anti-Communist projects. Some of the money was spread to domestic groups such as the National Student Association. Liberal organizations, including teachers' unions, acted as fronts too.
128 Soon the Olin Foundation was investing: Miller, *Gift of Freedom.*
128 "a wine collection": James Barnes, "Banker with a Cause," *National Journal,* March 6, 1993.
129 "Lott's claimed source": Adam Winkler, *Gunfight: The Battle over the Right to Bear Arms in America* (Norton, 2011), 76–77.
129 Another Olin-funded book: See Jane Mayer and Jill Abramson, *Strange Justice: The Selling of Clarence Thomas* (Houghton Mifflin, 1994), for a more thorough analysis of Brock's role in the confrontation between Thomas and Hill.
130 "If the conservative intellectual movement": Miller, *Gift of Freedom,* 5. Also Miller's defense of Lott's research as "rigorous," 72.
130 "On the right, they understood": Steve Wasserman, interview with author.

131 "John Olin, in fact, was prouder": Miller, *Gift of Freedom.*

131 "I saw it as a way": Jason DeParle, "Goals Reached, Donor on Right Closes Up Shop," *New York Times,* May 29, 2005.

132 "If you said to a dean": Teles, *Rise of the Conservative Legal Movement,* 189.

132 "was considered a marginal": Ibid., 108.

132 In 1985, however, the foundation: Miller, *Gift of Freedom,* 76.

133 "the most important thing": Paul M. Barrett, "Influential Ideas: A Movement Called 'Law and Economics' Sways Legal Circles," *Wall Street Journal,* Aug. 4, 1986.

133 "the most successful": Teles, *Rise of the Conservative Legal Movement,* 216.

133 "taking advantage of students' financial need": Alliance for Justice, *Justice for Sale: Shortchanging the Public Interest for Private Gain* (Alliance for Justice, 1993).

134 A study by the nonpartisan: Chris Young, Reity O'Brien, and Andrea Fuller, "Corporations, Pro-business Nonprofits Foot Bill for Judicial Seminars," Center for Public Integrity, March 28, 2013.

134 Federalist Society: The $5.5 million figure from Olin represents funding over two decades, as reported by Miller, Gift of Freedom, 94.

135 All of the conservative justices: For a more complete index of influential members of the Federalist Society, see Michael Avery and Danielle McLaughlin, *The Federalist Society: How Conservatives Took the Law Back from Liberals* (Vanderbilt University Press, 2013).

135 "it possibly wouldn't exist": Miller, *How Two Foundations Reshaped America,* 29.

135 "one of the best investments": Miller, "A Federalist Solution," *Philanthropy,* Fall 2011. Irving Kristol was among the earliest fund-raisers for the Federalist Society.

135 a key $25,000 investment: The Olin Foundation eventually donated a total of $6.3 million to the Manhattan Institute.

136 "It was a classic case": Charles Murray, interview with author.

136 Critics said it overlooked: For a fuller analysis of *Losing Ground,* see Thomas Medvetz, *Think Tanks in America* (University of Chicago Press, 2012), 3.

136 "It took ten years": Ibid., 5.

137 Among them was the *Dartmouth Review:* Louis Menand, "Illiberalisms," *New Yorker,* May 20, 1991.

137 ABC correspondent Jonathan Karl: Karl was the first network television journalist invited by the Kochs to moderate a political panel discussion during a seminar for their donors, which he did in January 2015. ABC's decision to participate in the otherwise-closed event stirred criticism and controversy but created a precedent when the *Politico* columnist Mike Allen moderated a candidates' forum at a Koch fund-raising conference in August 2015, accepting an invitation that the CNN correspondent Jake Tapper turned down on principle.

137 "We've got money": Many details regarding the history of the creation of the Bradley Foundation are drawn from John Gurda's *Bradley Legacy,* which was commissioned by Michael Joyce and published in 1992 by the Lynde and Harry Bradley Foundation.

138 During the next fifteen years: Patricia Sullivan, "Michael Joyce; Leader in Rise of Conservative Movement," *Washington Post,* March 3, 2006.

138 At least two-thirds: According to James Barnes, "Banker with a Cause," *National Journal,* March 6, 1993, 564–65, well over two-thirds of the $20 million that the Bradley Foundation doled out each year went to "conservative intellectual" support.

138 Continuing the strategic emphasis: Katherine M. Skiba, "Bradley Philanthropy," *Milwaukee Journal Sentinel,* Sept. 17, 1995.

138 "Typically, it was not just": According to Bruce Murphy, Joyce spent $1 million subsidizing Murray's writing of *The Bell Curve.* Murphy, "When We Were Soldier-Scholars," *Milwaukee Magazine,* March 9, 2006.

139 "the chief operating officer": Neal Freeman, "The Godfather Retires," *National Review,* April 18, 2001.

140 "package for public consumption": "The Bradley Foundation and the Art of (Intellectual) War," Autumn 1999, was a twenty-page confidential memo prepared for the foundation's November 1999 board meeting, a copy of which was obtained by the author.

140 The event that multiplied: Allen-Bradley's trustees had initially valued the company at $400 million, although they later enlarged the valuation, according to a wonderful article on the sale of Allen-Bradley by James B. Stewart, "Loss of Privacy: How a 'Safe' Company Was Acquired Anyway After Bitter Infighting," *Wall Street Journal,* May 14, 1985.

140 The deal created: Ibid.; Gurda, *Bradley Legacy,* 153.

140 "symbol of a military": Peter Pae, "Maligned B-1 Bomber Now Proving Its Worth," *Los Angeles Times,* Dec. 12, 2001.

140 Rockwell waged a strenuous: Winston Williams, "Dogged Rockwell Bets on Reagan," *New York Times,* Sept. 30, 1984. The B-1 would prove useless until 2001, when, after the government spent an additional $3 billion retrofitting the planes, they were finally deployed for conventional use in Afghanistan. A Congressional Research Service report in 2014, however, described the planes as "increasingly irrelevant."

141 "teetered on the edge": Gurda, *Bradley Legacy,* 92.

142 "Karl Marx was a Jew": Bryan Burrough, *The Big Rich* (Penguin, 2009), 211.

142 "the two major threats": Gurda, *Bradley Legacy,* 115.

142 In 1966, a federal judge: Ibid., 131.

144 "deprive future generations": Rich Rovito, "Milwaukee Rockwell Workers Facing Layoff Reach Agreement," *Milwaukee Business Journal,* June 27, 2010.

144 "the most polarized": See Craig Gilbert, "Democratic, Republican Voters Worlds Apart in Divided Wisconsin," *Milwaukee Journal Sentinel,* May 3, 2014.

144 leaving Milwaukee: For more on Milwaukee, see Alec MacGillis's insightful piece, "The Unelectable Whiteness of Scott Walker," *New Republic,* June 15, 2014.

145 "overarching purpose": In a 2003 speech at Georgetown University, Michael Joyce said, "At Olin and later at Bradley, our overarching purpose was to use philanthropy to support a war of ideas to defend and help recover the political imagination of the [nation's] founders."

CHAPTER FOUR: THE KOCH METHOD

146 "He wasn't always": Doreen Carlson, interview with author.
146 "He was practically swimming": Ibid.
147 "I was a young guy": Tom Meersman, "Koch Violations Arouse Concerns," *Minneapolis Star Tribune*, Dec. 18, 1997.
147 Afterward, numerous scientific studies: David Michaels, *Doubt Is Their Product* (Oxford University Press, 2008), 76, provides an excellent discussion of benzene, illustrating the oil industry's efforts to block its regulation.
147 Four federal agencies: A list of agencies classifying benzene as a carcinogen appears in Loder and Evans, "Koch Brothers Flout Law Getting Richer with Secret Iran Sales."
147 "I didn't even know": Meersman, "Koch Violations Arouse Concerns."
147 "socialistic": Charles Koch's 1974 speech as cited in Confessore, "Quixotic '80 Campaign Gave Birth to Kochs' Powerful Network."
148 "I'm looking for some accountability": Meersman, "Koch Violations Arouse Concerns."
149 "We should *not* cave": Charles Koch, "Business Community."
149 "unceasingly advance": Ibid.
150 "Libertarianism is supposed to be": Tom Frank, interview with author.
150 "The refinery was just hemorrhaging": Loder and Evans, "Koch Brothers Flout Law Getting Richer with Secret Iran Sales."
150 Rather than comply: At first, the company had installed a new antipollution device, but when it proved deficient, instead of addressing the problem, the company disconnected the apparatus and falsified the record.
151 Defenders of Koch Industries: John Hinderaker, a frequent defender of the Kochs, calls Barnes-Soliz "a poor employee who, anticipating termination, asserted false claims against her employer in order to set up a lawsuit," in his Oct. 6, 2011, entry on PowerLineBlog.com.
152 "The government's case": David Uhlmann, interview with author, and additional comments from him in Sari Horwitz, "Unlikely Allies," *Washington Post,* Aug. 15, 2015.
152 For her whistle-blowing: Barnes-Soliz's account is derived from Loder and Evans, "Koch Brothers Flout Law Getting Richer with Secret Iran Sales."
152 According to two statements: Carnell Green, interviews with Richard J. Elroy, Sept. 18, 1998, and April 15, 1999; a copy of Elroy's report was obtained by the author.
153 soil samples were later taken: According to the analysis done by Cirrus Environmental's laboratory, one sample contained 180 parts per million of mercury and the other 9,100 parts per million. The legal limit is 30 parts per million. Green's OSHA complaint went nowhere because it was filed past the deadline, according to his statement.
154 "Green was just a nice": Jim Elroy, interview with author.
154 "They're always operating": Schulman, *Sons of Wichita,* 216; Angela O'Connell, interview with author.
154 "repeatedly lied": Schulman, *Sons of Wichita,* 215.
155 "for the next four or five years": Author interview with David Nicastro.
155 In court papers: Filings relating to a 1997 petition for a protective order,

Charles Dickey et al. v. J. Howard Marshall III, describe Koch Industries as "among the best clients" of the private investigative firm Secure Source, run by Charles Dickey and David Nicastro. "Over the past three years they performed numerous investigations for Koch Industries and its numerous entities," a filing on behalf of the firm states. By 2000, the firm had been dissolved following a legal settlement between the partners.

155 "They lie about everything": Angela O'Connell, interview with author.

156 "There were times": Schulman, *Sons of Wichita,* 226, gives a full account of these cases.

156 These misdeeds paled: A vivid and meticulously researched account of the Smalley case appears in ibid., 211.

157 Koch Industries offered Danny: Ibid., 214, writes that Smalley "wanted the opportunity to sit on the witness stand" so that he could make "Charles and David Koch understand just what they had taken from him."

157 "I'm not saying": Ibid., 218.

157 An investigation: The information about the National Transportation Safety Board report is based on Loder and Evans, "Koch Brothers Flout Law Getting Richer with Secret Iran Sales."

157 "Swiss cheese": Ibid.

158 "Koch Industries is definitely responsible": Schulman, *Sons of Wichita,* 219.

158 "They said, 'We're sorry'": "Blood and Oil," *60 Minutes II,* Nov. 27, 2000.

159 "quietly enraged": Senate committee member, interview with author.

159 In fact, the other companies: The allegation that other companies turned Koch Industries in is according to a former official involved in the Senate investigation.

159 His specialty had been: Elroy had compiled much of the evidence against Koch Industries, using two-hundred-millimeter lenses to photograph Koch employees as they gathered oil from scattered wells, and then he went door-to-door, he said, saying, "I'm from the FBI, and I want to talk to you about the oil you've been stealing. Are you taking it down the road and selling it?" He said that many replied, "No, the company makes us do it." The company's lawyer adamantly denied his allegations.

160 According to the Senate report: The November 1989 report by the Special Committee on Investigations of the Select Committee on Indian Affairs of the U.S. Senate documents that a Koch employee "went so far as to interview the ex-wife" of a Senate investigator and that "Koch also attempted to look into the backgrounds of Committee staff."

160 Kenneth Ballen: Ballen established a nonprofit organization, Terror Free Tomorrow, to which William Koch made a contribution in 2007, but had no personal relationship with any of the Kochs during the period when the hearings were under way.

160 "It wasn't like politics": Kenneth Ballen, interview with author.

160 Don Nickles: Nickles received large campaign contributions from Koch Industries over the years; see Leslie Wayne, "Papers Link Donations to 2 on Senate Hearings Panel," *New York Times,* Oct. 30, 1997. In 2014, Koch Industries' Public Sector division hired Nickles's lobbying company to fight campaign-finance reform; see Kent Cooper, "Koch Starts Lobbying on Campaign Finance Issue," RollCall.com, June 9, 2014.

161 "We don't know who": Wick Sollers, interview with author.

161 "It's very intimidating": Robert Parry, "Dole: What Wouldn't Bob Do for Koch Oil?," *Nation,* Aug. 26, 1996.

161 "I did not want my family": "Blood and Oil."

162 Nickles recommended the appointment: The previous U.S. attorney had resigned.

162 "You can say this": Author interview with Nancy Jones.

163 "not even aware": Nickles's and Leonard's denials were obtained by Phillip Zweig and Michael Schroeder, "Bob Dole's Oil Patch Pals," *BusinessWeek,* March 31, 1996. The U.S. Bureau of Indian Affairs, like the grand jury, found no actionable wrongdoing stemming from the Senate's report. However, *BusinessWeek* notes that key members of the Osage tribe, who had defended Koch Industries, later felt they and the Bureau of Indian Affairs had been duped. The magazine reported that "Charles O. Tillman Jr., principal chief of the Osage tribe, wrote in a Nov. 29, 1994, letter to Senator John McCain (R-Ariz.), a member of the investigative committee: 'We are left with the inescapable conclusion that the Bureau of Indian Affairs was more concerned with putting a lid on your committee's findings than in providing us with the truth.'"

163 "I was surprised": Zweig and Schroeder, "Bob Dole's Oil Patch Pals."

163 "You have to have intelligence": Burrough, "Wild Bill Koch."

164 "It was to find anything": Republican operative, interview with author.

165 Becket Brown International: See Gary Ruskin, "Spooky Business: Corporate Espionage Against Nonprofit Organizations," Nov. 20, 2013.

165 "That blows my mind": Barbara Fultz, interview with author.

166 "They were just mis-measuring crude": Phil Dubose, interview with author.

167 He denied defrauding: "If the producers believe your measurements are not as accurate as somebody else's, they're going to take volume away from you," Charles Koch testified. "Tulsa Okla. Jury Hears Last Day of Testimony in Oil-Theft Trial," *Tulsa World,* Dec. 11, 1999.

168 "It was the first time": Phil Dubose, interview with author.

168 although in 2010 the company: "Toxic 100 Air Polluters," Political Economy Research Institute, University of Massachusetts Amherst, 2010, www.peri.umass.edu/toxicair_current/.

168 In 2012, the Environmental Protection Agency's database: See the EPA's Toxic Release Inventory data bank, 2012. The company's ranking among the top thirty for all three forms of pollution was described by Tim Dickinson, "Inside the Koch Brothers' Toxic Empire," *Rolling Stone,* Sept. 24, 2014.

170 "disgusting": James Huff, interview with author.

170 "surprised": Harold Varmus, interview with author.

171 "involved in improper payments": Loder and Evans, "Koch Brothers Flout Law Getting Richer with Iran Sales."

171 "It is beyond spectacular": See Mayer, "Covert Operations."

CHAPTER FIVE: THE KOCHTOPUS

172 "What a jackass": Bill Wilson and Roy Wenzl, "The Kochs' Quest to Save America," *Wichita Eagle,* Oct. 13, 2012.

172 "creepy when you have to deal": Ed Crane, interview with author.

173 As Fink later described it: A version of Richard Fink's paper "The Structure of Social Change" appeared under the title "From Ideas to Action: The Roles of Universities, Think Tanks, and Activist Groups," *Philanthropy* 10, no. 1 (Winter 1996).

173 the Kochtopus: According to David Gordon, a libertarian at the Von Mises Institute, who was involved at Cato during its early years, the name was coined by Samuel Edward Konkin III, whom he describes as an "anarcho-libertarian."

174 "so brutalized by the process": W. John Moore, "The Wichita Pipeline," *National Journal,* May 16, 1992.

174 "corporate defense": Parry, "Dole."

174 "It was the investigation": Brian Doherty, interview with author.

174 "Establishment" politician: David Koch's views on Bob Dole, according to his brother Bill, as quoted in Parry, "Dole."

174 Dole reportedly helped: For more on the Kochs and Dole, see the excellent piece by Zweig and Schroeder, "Bob Dole's Oil Patch Pals."

175 Had it passed: For more on the legislative wheeling and dealing, see Center for Public Integrity, *The Buying of the President* (Avon Books, 1996), 127–30.

175 Koch Industries did succeed: Dan Morgan, "PACs Stretching Limits of Campaign Law," *Washington Post,* Feb. 5, 1988.

175 "I've always believed": Charles Green, "Bob Dole Looks Back," *AARP Bulletin,* July/Aug. 2015.

175 "I see the White House": William Rempel and Alan Miller, "Donor Contradicts White House," *Los Angeles Times,* July 27, 1997.

176 The conservative Republican: In his history of Charles Koch's "Stealth" political operation, Coppin writes, "It was believed by members of the investigating committee that Koch Industries used economic Education Trust and Citizens for the Republic as front organizations to hide Koch's paying for the anti-Docking ads."

176 the Federal Election Commission: Elizabeth Drew, *The Corruption of American Politics: What Went Wrong and Why* (Carol, 1999), 56.

176 Carolyn Malenick: Malenick acknowledged that the scheme had pushed the envelope in new ways but insisted that Triad merely balanced the money spent legally by labor unions. The notion that labor had a spending advantage was commonplace among conservatives, although, according to Drew (Ibid.), in 1996 business outspent labor by as much as twelve times. See the FEC judgment against Malenick: http://www.fec.gov/law/litigation/final_judgment_and_order_02CV1237.pdf.

177 What made the Koch family's: Of course, liberals give huge quantities of money, too. Their most prominent donor during these years, the financier George Soros, runs the Open Society Foundations, which have spent as much as $100 million a year in America. Soros has also made huge private contributions to various Democratic outside groups, triggering fines for campaign-finance violations in 2004. But the causes Soros backs—such as decriminalizing marijuana and strengthening civil liberties—don't benefit his fortune in obvious ways according to Michael Vachon, his spokesman, who argues that "none of his contributions are in the service of his own economic interests." For more on Soros, see Mayer, "Money Man."

177 "unprecedented in size": See Charles Lewis et al., "Koch Millions Spread Influence Through Nonprofits, Colleges," Investigative Reporting Workshop, July 1, 2013.

177 "My overall concept": Moore, "Wichita Pipeline."

178 "Who else would give": Teles, *Rise of the Conservative Legal Movement,* 239.

178 "In recent years": Moore, "Wichita Pipeline."

179 the Kochs' multidimensional political spending: See Mayer, "Covert Operations."

179 Only the Kochs know: Private foundations are legally required to publicly disclose their grants, but the recipients have no obligation to disclose the identities of their donors. Thus if the recipients pass the donations to secondary groups, the money trail becomes obscured.

180 "a shell game": Koch associate, interview with author.

181 Rothbard called the putsch: David Gordon, "Murray Rothbard on the Kochtopus," LewRockwell.com, March 10, 2011.

181 "cannot tolerate dissent": The Rothbard memo is described in Schulman, *Sons of Wichita,* 156–57.

182 "staunchly anti-regulatory center": Al Kamen, "I Am OMB and I Write the Rules," *Washington Post,* July 12, 2006, A13.

183 "a lobbying group disguised": Coppin, "Stealth," pt. 2.

183 "Of all the teachers": *The Writings of F. A. Harper* (Institute for Humane Studies, 1979).

183 Anxious at one point: Charles's micromanagement at IHS and the Cato Institute is described in a richly reported article by Mullins, "Battle for the Cato Institute."

184 "all human behavior": Robert Lekachman, "A Controversial Nobel Choice?," *New York Times,* Oct. 26, 1986.

184 "libertarian mecca": Julian Sanchez, "FIRE vs. GMU," Reason.com, Nov. 17, 2005.

184 Liberals, however, regarded: According to the Mercatus Center's Web page, it "does not receive financial support from George Mason University or any federal, state, or local government." Yet Mercatus is headed "by a faculty director who is appointed by the provost of George Mason University."

185 "almost a Marxist faith": Daniel Fisher, "Koch's Laws," *Forbes,* Feb. 26, 2007.

186 "In that, I echo Martin Luther": Charles Koch, acceptance speech for the Richard DeVos award, at the Council for National Policy in Naples, Fla., Jan. 1999. Cited in Fang, *Machine,* 120.

186 "He thinks he's a genius": Ed Crane, interview with author, 2010. Crane's comment on Charles Koch appeared unattributed when first published in *The New Yorker,* but when asked, Crane confirmed to David Koch that he was the source, a fact that has been widely published since.

186 "Richie exploited MBM": Cato official interview with author. Richard Fink declined to be interviewed, according to Steve Lombardo, a spokesman for Koch Industries.

187 "Koch has been constantly": Thomas McGarity, interview with author.

187 The EPA, she argued: Susan Dudley, the Mercatus fellow who concocted the pro-smog argument against the Clean Air Act, became the head of the Office of Information and Regulatory Affairs in the George W. Bush

administration, overseeing the development and implementation of all federal regulations.

189 By 2015, according to an internal list: The colleges and universities with programs subsidized by Koch family foundations as of August 2015 appear here: http://www.kochfamilyfoundations.org/pdfs/CKF UniversityPrograms.pdf.

189 "After a whole semester": Heather MacDonald, "Don't Fund College Follies," *City Journal* (Summer 2005).

189 Charles Koch's foundation gave additional: IRS 990 forms for the Charles G. Koch Charitable Foundation; Lee Fang, "Koch Brothers Fueling Far-Right Academic Centers at Universities Across the Country," *ThinkProgress,* May 11, 2011.

189 The foundation required the school: According to the Charles Koch Foundation grant, "Prior to the extension of any offer for the Donor Supported Professorship Positions [professors hired with Koch grants], the Dean of the College of Business and Economics, in consultation with professor Russell Sobel or his successor, shall present the candidate's credentials to CGK Foundation." In addition, the foundation insisted on the right to withdraw funding from any professor hired by its grant who displeased it.

189 The Kochs' investment: For more on the Kochs' coal interests, see http://www.kochcarbon.com/Products.aspx.

190 "Are workers really better off": Evan Osnos, "Chemical Valley," *New Yorker,* April 7, 2014.

190 "We support professors": John Hardin, "The Campaign to Stop Fresh College Thinking," *Wall Street Journal,* May 26, 2015.

190 "entire academic areas": John David, "WVU Sold Its Academic Independence," *Charleston Gazette,* April 23, 2012.

191 "Even great ideas": Charles Koch's 1999 speech at the Council on National Policy, ibid.

191 "What we needed was a sales force": Continetti, "Paranoid Style in Liberal Politics."

CHAPTER SIX: BOOTS ON THE GROUND

196 In a revealing private letter: DeMille Foundation correspondence appears in Sophia Z. Lee, *The Workplace and the Constitution: From the New Deal to the New Right* (Cambridge University Press, 2014), chap. 3. The first quotation is from Donald MacLean (DeMille Foundation) to Joseph C. Fagan (Wisconsin State Chamber of Commerce), Oct. 13, 1954. The second quotation is from MacLean to Reed Larson, Aug. 15, 1956.

196 Although the Kochs were the founders: See Dan Morgan, "Think Tanks: Corporations' Quiet Weapon; Nonprofits' Studies, Lobbying Advance Big Business Causes," *Washington Post,* Jan. 29, 2000.

198 "I can't prove it": Dan Glickman, interview with author.

198 "Our belief is that the tax": "Politics That Can't Be Pigeonholed," *Wichita Eagle,* June 26, 1994.

198 CSE's ads: David Wessel and Jeanne Saddler, "Foes of Clinton's Tax-Boost Proposals Mislead Public and Firms on the Small-Business Aspects," *Wall Street Journal,* July 20, 1993, A12.

198 "They can fly under the radar": Morgan, "Think Tanks."
198 "The split was about control": Dick Armey, interview with author.
200 Phillips was not charged: Phillips's organization, the Faith and Family Alliance, passed cash to Abramoff's gambling clients on at least one documented occasion.
200 "Grover told me Ralph": Bruce Bartlett, interview with author.
201 "I'm gonna be for that guy": Tim Phillips, transcript of an unpublished interview with the documentary filmmaker Alex Gibney, April 19, 2012.
201 "I was intrigued by the idea": Ibid.

CHAPTER SEVEN: TEA TIME

203 a former futures trader: Rick Santelli was a vice president of Drexel Burnham Lambert.
204 The immediate provocation: The Homeowner Affordability and Stability Plan was a temporary relief package for homeowners facing an $8 trillion loss in housing wealth after the market's alarming 2008 collapse.
204 Ross, a personal friend: Ross in October 2014 hosted a party to celebrate David Koch. Mara Siegler, "David Koch Celebrated by Avenue Magazine," *New York Post,* Oct. 2, 2014.
204 His private equity company: For more on Ross's interests in home mortgages, see Carrick Mollenkamp, "Foreclosure Tsunami Hits Mortgage-Servicing Firms," *Wall Street Journal,* Feb. 11, 2009.
204 Critics would later point out: Before Obama took office, Bush's Treasury secretary, Henry "Hank" Paulson, had already spent $125 billion on bank bailouts, and an additional $20 billion was in the pipeline.
205 "The Boston Tea Party": Michael Grunwald, *The New New Deal: The Hidden Story of Change in the Obama Era* (Simon & Schuster, 2012), 280.
205 "It was the guy in Chicago": Fink's protestations were made to *The Wichita Eagle* as well as to the *Frum Report*'s Tim Mak. He acknowledged the Kochs had been asked to fund the Tea Party, but he said none of the activists' proposals met their standards, which required well-defined goals and measurable timelines and benchmarks.
205 "I've never been to a tea-party event": Andrew Goldman, "The Billionaire's Party," *New York,* July 25, 2010.
205 "Oh, *please*": Elaine Lafferty, "'Tea Party Billionaire' Fires Back," *Daily Beast,* Sept. 10, 2010.
205 "a new strain of populism": Mark Lilla, "The Tea Party Jacobins," *New York Review of Books,* May 27, 2010.
206 "mass rebellion": Theda Skocpol and Vanessa Williamson, *The Tea Party and the Remaking of Republican Conservatism* (Oxford University Press, 2012).
206 "The problem with the whole libertarian movement": Jane Mayer, "Covert Operations," *New Yorker,* Aug. 30, 2010.
208 "I think that's actually": Wilson and Wenzl, "Kochs' Quest to Save America."
208 "a never-ending campaign": Vogel, *Big Money,* 42.
209 "If we had run more ads": See Frank Rich, "Sugar Daddies," *New York,* April 22, 2012, on Simmons's quotation, which was derived from an inter-

view with *The Wall Street Journal*'s Monica Langley, "Texas Billionaire Doles Out Election's Biggest Checks," March 22, 2012.

209 "There was a growing sense": Daschle interview with *Frontline*, "Inside Obama's Presidency," Jan. 16, 2013.

209 "nothing more, and nothing less": Daniel Schulman reports, for instance, that the brothers were involved on such a detailed level in Americans for Prosperity, they employed the outside political operatives who created the group's ads. Schulman, *Sons of Wichita*, 276.

210 "Bankers, brokers and businessmen": Charles G. Koch, "Evaluating a President," KochInd.com, Oct. 1, 2010.

210 "prolonged and deepened": Charles Koch's disparagement of the New Deal appears in Charles Koch, "Perspective," *Discovery: The Quarterly Newsletter of the Koch Companies*, Jan. 2009, 12.

211 The company that syndicated: Kenneth Vogel of *Politico* broke the story of the payments to Limbaugh, Mark Levin, and Glenn Beck. Kenneth P. Vogel and Lucy McCalmont, "Rush Limbaugh, Sean Hannity, Glenn Beck Sell Endorsements to Conservative Groups," *Politico*, June 15, 2011.

211 "We're not here to cut deals": Grunwald, *New New Deal*, 142.

212 "If the Purpose of the Majority": Ibid., 142–43.

212 "In the past, it was rare": Steve LaTourette (who retired at the end of the 2012 session), interview with author.

213 "What they said": Grunwald, *New New Deal*, 145.

214 "It was stunning": Ibid., 190.

215 "They turned on Obama so early": Bill Burton, interview with author.

216 Five years later, a survey: Justin Wolfers, "What Debate? Economists Agree the Stimulus Lifted the Economy," *New York Times*, July 29, 2014.

217 TaxDayTeaParty.com: Fang, *Machine*, 32.

217 The founder of the Sam Adams Alliance: Fang, in ibid., describes Rich as the founder of the Sam Adams Alliance. Rich declined to respond to interview requests.

218 Rich in particular: See, for instance, Russ Choma, "Rich Rewards: One Man's Shadow Money Network," OpenSecrets.org, June 19, 2012.

218 He almost invariably declined: Howard Rich failed to respond to several attempts I made to reach him for comment as well.

218 "My 32 years": Marc Fisher, "Wisconsin Gov. Scott Walker's Recall: Big Money Fuels Small-Government Fight," *Washington Post*, March 25, 2012.

218 But after the referendum succeeded: Dan Morain, "Prop. 164 Cash Trail Leads to Billionaires," *Los Angeles Times*, Oct. 30, 1992.

219 "the Kochian deep pockets": Sarah Barton, The Ear, *Rothbard-Rockwell Report*, July 1993.

219 "a prairie fire of populism": Timothy Egan, "Campaign on Term Limits Taps a Gusher of Money," *New York Times*, Oct. 31, 1991.

219 "I ignited the spark": Ibid.

220 But an investigation: Bill Hogan, "Three Big Donors Bankrolled Americans for Limited Government in 2005," Center for Public Integrity, Dec. 21, 2006.

220 "We're not going to be shut up": Jonathan Rauch, "A Morning at the Ministry of Speech," *National Journal*, May 29, 1999. In the summer of 2008:

Eric Odom provided his own account of these events, insisting the Tea Party was a spontaneous outpouring but ignoring the issue of who funded the Sam Adams Alliance or Rob Bluey. Odom, "The Tea Party Conspirators and the Real Story Behind the Tea Party Movement," *Liberty News*, Aug. 30, 2011.

220 "a card-carrying member": Ben Smith and Jonathan Martin, "BlogJam: Right-Wing Bluey Blog," *Politico*, June 18, 2007.

220 They sent out Twitter messages: All summer long, as oil and gasoline prices hit highs, energy industry moguls including Larry Nichols, chairman of the giant Oklahoma oil and gas company Devon Energy, who attended the Kochs' donor summits, had been pushing hard to expand offshore drilling. Several other Koch network members, including the Las Vegas casino owner Sheldon Adelson, Dick Farmer of Cintas, and Stan Hubbard of Hubbard Broadcasting, were also involved, funding a pro-drilling front group called American Solutions, run by Newt Gingrich.

222 He noted that Americans for Prosperity: Lee Fang's early report questioning whether the Tea Party was an "Astroturf" movement manufactured in Washington led the way in getting the press to look more closely. His first major story was "Spontaneous Uprising?," *ThinkProgress*, April 9, 2009.

222 "It was very much a put-up job": Thomas Frank, interview with author.

222 "I was a member of the Tea Party": Peggy Venable, interview with author.

224 "spent hours and hours on the phone": Dick Armey, interview with author.

225 "We thought it would be a useful tool": Dick Armey, interview with author about Glenn Beck payments. See also Vogel and McCalmont, "Rush Limbaugh, Sean Hannity, Glenn Beck Sell Endorsements to Conservative Groups."

225 Beck, whose views were shaped: Sean Wilentz, "Confounding Fathers," *New Yorker*, Oct. 18, 2010.

225 "That rant from Santelli": Frank Luntz, interview with author.

225 "In an atmosphere primed": John B. Judis, "The Unnecessary Fall," *New Republic*, Aug. 12, 2010.

226 professed to be discomfited: A source who spoke at length with Fink shared his thinking with the author.

226 "the most radical president": Continetti, "Paranoid Style in Liberal Politics."

227 "It was hard for me to believe": "Obama's Interview Aboard Air Force One," *New York Times*, March 7, 2009.

228 forced to refund $32 million: Purva Patel, "Woodforest Bank to Hand Back $32M in Overdrafts," *Houston Chronicle*, Oct. 13, 2010.

228 Daschle was expected to become: Daschle was named to serve a dual role as HHS secretary and White House health czar but was forced to withdraw due to a controversy about unpaid taxes in early February.

229 She and a handful of other multimillionaires: The ballot initiative, which had been drafted by the Goldwater Institute, was narrowly defeated in November 2008.

230 "What organizations are doing this?": Eliana Johnson, "Inside the Koch-Funded Ads Giving Dems Fits," *National Review Online*, March 31, 2014.

232 "I can't tell you": Kim Barker and Theodoric Meyer, "The Dark Money Man," ProPublica, Feb. 14, 2014.

232 Fact-checkers later revealed: "Dying on a Wait List?," FactCheck.org, Aug. 6, 2009.

233 "If you want an assassination": Peter Hart, interview with author.

233 "The think tanks became the creators": Frank Luntz, interview with author.

233 In playing this role: In his book *Rich People's Movements,* Isaac William Martin describes the historic role of "policy entrepreneurs."

234 a conservative idea hatched: For more on Republican support of the individual mandate, see Ezra Klein, "A Lot of Republicans Supported the Individual Mandate," *Washington Post,* May 12, 2011.

235 "We knew we had to make": Johnson, "Inside the Koch-Funded Ads Giving Dems Fits."

235 "create a movement": Amanda Fallin, Rachel Grana, and Stanton Glantz, "To Quarterback Behind the Scenes, Third-Party Efforts: The Tobacco Industry and the Tea Party," *Tobacco Control,* Feb. 2013.

236 it had mocked Al Gore's environmental jeremiad: Antonio Regalado and Dionne Searcey, "Where Did That Video Spoofing Gore's Film Come From?," *Wall Street Journal,* Aug. 3, 2006.

236 Pretty soon: David Kirkpatrick, "Groups Back Health Reform, but Seek Cover," *New York Times,* Sept. 11, 2009.

237 "This year has been really": Dan Eggen, "How Interest Groups Behind Health-Care Legislation Are Financed Is Often Unclear," *Washington Post,* Jan. 7, 2010.

237 "public education programs": Ken Vogel, "Tea Party's Growing Money Problem," *Politico,* Aug. 9, 2010.

237 "We met for 20 or 30 years": Bill Wilson and Roy Wenzl, "The Kochs' Quest to Save America," *Wichita Eagle,* Oct. 3, 2012.

238 Not only had he been invited: Mark Holden, the general counsel to Koch Industries, described Noble as "an independent contractor" and "a consultant" to the company, in an interview with Kenneth Vogel, *Big Money,* 201.

238 "pack the hall": Lee Fang, "Right-Wing Harassment Strategy Against Dems Detailed in Memo," *ThinkProgress,* July 31, 2009.

238 "We packed these town halls": Johnson, "Inside the Koch-Funded Ads Giving Dems Fits."

239 "couldn't have done it": Grover Norquist, interview with author.

240 "I thought on health care": One of the few in the media to question whether the Tea Party protests were, as he put it, "orchestrations of incivility" rather than a brand-new widespread movement was Rick Perlstein, who warned in an essay in *The Washington Post,* "Conservatives have become adept at playing the media for suckers." He argued that "the tree of crazy," as he called the far-right protesters, was ever present in American politics, but in the past a more robust press corps, as well as more responsible conservatives, such as William F. Buckley, had "unequivocally labeled the civic outrage represented by such discourse 'extremist'—out of bounds." See Rick Perlstein, "Birthers, Health Care Hecklers, and the Rise of Right-Wing Rage," *Washington Post,* Aug. 16, 2009.

240 "wasn't really tracking": David Axelrod, interview with author.

240 When fewer than sixty-five thousand: Some dispute the crowd estimate.

240 Membership in the Liberty League: See Kevin Drum, "Old Whine in New Bottles," *Mother Jones,* Sept./Oct. 2010.

241 330,000 activists: Devin Burghart, "View from the Top: Report on Six National Tea Party Organizations," in *Steep: The Precipitous Rise of the Tea Party,* ed. Lawrence Rosenthal and Christine Trost (University of California Press, 2012).

242 It was hard not to notice: Lee Fang first noted the similarity between the pageantry at the Defending the American Dream Summit and that at presidential nominating conventions. Fang, *Machine,* 121.

CHAPTER EIGHT: THE FOSSILS

244 "The change wrought": National Security Strategy, Washington, D.C. (Office of the President of the United States, 2010), 8, 47.

244 "we face risks": American Association for the Advancement of Science, Climate Science Panel, "What We Know," 2014.

244 Mann wasn't particularly political: Mann told Neela Banerjee, "I started out as a scientist who didn't think there was much of a role to play in public policy." Banerjee, "The Most Hated Climate Scientist in the US Fights Back," *Yale Alumni Magazine,* March/April 2013.

245 "What we didn't take into account": Michael Mann, interview with author.

245 "it's like the switch from whale oil": Ibid.

246 He owned, by one count: Fisher, "Fuel's Paradise."

246 Only the U.S. government: Neela Banerjee, "In Climate Politics, Texas Aims to Be the Anti-California," *Los Angeles Times,* Nov. 7, 2010.

247 "unleash what became known": Daniel Yergin, *The Quest: Energy, Security, and the Remaking of the Modern World* (Penguin, 2011), 328–29.

247 The Kochs, too: For more on the Kochs' fracking investments, see Brad Johnson, "How the Kochs Are Fracking America," *ThinkProgress,* March 2, 2012.

248 If the world were to stay: See "Global Warming's Terrifying New Math," by Bill McKibben, *Rolling Stone,* July 19, 2012. He explains that scientists believe the earth can tolerate the burning of roughly 565 more gigatons of carbon dioxide by mid-century, but that informed estimates place the currently untapped carbon reserves at 2,795 gigatons.

249 As early as 1913: The history of the oil depletion allowance is described in Robert Bryce, *Cronies* (PublicAffairs, 2004).

249 As Robert Caro recounts: "A new source of political money, potentially vast, had been tapped," Caro writes, "and Lyndon Johnson had been put in charge of it." Robert Caro, *The Path to Power* (Vintage Books, 1990), 637.

249 "the deep-tissue insecurity": Bryan Burrough, *The Big Rich: The Rise and Fall of the Greatest Texas Oil Fortunes* (Penguin, 2009), 204.

250 "the restoration of the supremacy": Ibid., 138.

250 Cullen's political ambitions: Ibid., 220, bases his assertion that Cullen was the largest contributor in 1952 on research by the University of North Carolina professor Alexander Heard.

250 "to succeed in politics": Ibid., 210.

251 What he discovered: Fighting the science of climate change was not the

only issue these groups and candidates focused on, but it was the single issue they all had in common.

251 His research showed: The Kochs outspent ExxonMobil in their funding of nonprofit groups, not politicians.

251 "kingpin of climate science denial": See "Koch Industries, Secretly Funding the Climate Denial Machine," Greenpeace, March 2010.

251 "campaign to manipulate": Robert J. Brulle, "Institutionalizing Delay: Foundation Funding and the Creation of U.S. Climate Change Countermovement Organizations," *Climate Change* 122, no. 4 (Feb. 2014): 681–94.

253 Between 1999 and 2015: Whitney Ball died in August 2015, and in a tribute that appeared in *National Review,* James Piereson wrote that from its founding in 1999 DonorsTrust had given away $750 million. Donors Trust announced that Lawson Bader, CEO of the Competitive Enterprise Institute, who had been vice president of the Mercatus Center at George Mason University, would succeed her.

254 "We just have this great big unknown": Andy Kroll, "Exposed: The Dark-Money ATM of the Conservative Movement," *Mother Jones,* Feb. 5, 2013.

255 "There's a better scientific consensus": As quoted by Ross Gelbspan, "Snowed," *Mother Jones,* May/June 2005, and requoted by Michaels, *Doubt Is Their Product,* 197.

255 the plan was the brainchild: Chris Mooney, *The Republican War on Science* (Basic Books, 2006), 83.

255 "central cog": "Global Warming Deniers Well Funded," *Newsweek,* Aug. 12, 2007.

256 Leading the charge: Fred Seitz had previously distributed $45 million from R. J. Reynolds to scientists willing to defend tobacco. Fred Singer had attacked the EPA's assertion that secondhand smoke was a health hazard. The financing for Singer's work was a grant from the Tobacco Institute, a group supported by cigarette companies. The money was filtered, though, through a nonprofit organization called the Alexis de Tocqueville Institution. Singer's work on secondhand smoke took place during the 1990s. Tax records show that between 1988 and 2002, the Alexis de Tocqueville Institution received $1,723,900 from the Bradley, Olin, Scaife, Philip M. McKenna, and Claude R. Lambe Foundations.

256 "yet, for years the press": Naomi Oreskes and Erik M. Conway, *Merchants of Doubt* (Bloomsbury Press, 2010), 9.

256 As late as 2003: Poll numbers attributed to Theda Skocpol, *Naming the Problem: What It Will Take to Counter Extremism and Engage Americans in the Fight Against Global Warming* (Harvard University, Jan. 2013).

257 It quickly drew criticism: Dr. Steven C. Amstrup, chief scientist with Polar Bears International and a U.S. Geological Survey polar bear project leader for thirty years, explained that estimates of the size of the polar bear population in past decades were nothing more than guesses, but their grim future was a certainty if nothing was done to preserve their habitat, which he said was undeniably "disappearing due to global warming." Further, in 2008 polar bears became the first vertebrate species listed under the Endangered Species Act as threatened by global warming. See also Michael Muskal, "40% Decline in Polar Bears in Alaska, Western Canada Heightens Concern," *Los Angeles Times,* Nov. 21, 2014.

257 "There are more polar bears": Ed Crane, interview with author. For more on the polar bear controversy, see "Koch Industries, Secretly Funding the Climate Denial Machine."

258 Without disclosing it: See Justin Gillis and John Schwartz, "Deeper Ties to Corporate Cash for Doubtful Climate Researcher," *New York Times,* Feb. 22, 2015.

258 Yet from that moment on: Mann and his co-authors had been openly cautious about their findings, noting that because there were no temperature records kept a thousand years ago, they had been forced to use "proxy" methods, which included less than optimal techniques such as studying ice cores and tree rings.

258 Koch Industries' political action committee: Between 2005 and 2008, KochPAC made federal contributions totaling $4.3 million, in comparison with ExxonMobil's $1.6 million, according to FEC reports.

258 The company's expenditures: Koch Industries spent $857,000 on lobbying in 2004, which grew to $20 million by 2008, according to the Center for Public Integrity. See John Aloysius Farrell, "Koch's Web of Influence," Center for Public Integrity, April 6, 2011.

259 As the Harvard political scientist: Skocpol, *Naming the Problem.*

259 At the time, Morano was working: When he promoted the "Swift Boat" story questioning John Kerry's Vietnam War record, Morano worked as a reporter for Cybercast News Service, a project of the Media Research Center, which the Scaife family foundations funded, among others.

259 "You've got to name names": See Robert Kenner's 2014 documentary film, *Merchants of Doubt.*

259 "We had a lot of fun": Ibid.

259 "the 'climate con'": Banerjee, "Most Hated Climate Scientist in the US Fights Back."

260 "State political veterans": Tom Hamburger, "A Coal-Fired Crusade Helped Bring Bush a Crucial Victory," *Wall Street Journal,* June 13, 2001.

260 "case study in managing": Barton Gellman, *Angler* (Penguin, 2008), 84.

260 Cheney used his influence: The *Los Angeles Times* broke the story of Cheney's influence on the fracking exemption, noting that his former company Halliburton had interests in fracking. Tom Hamburger and Alan Miller, "Halliburton's Interests Assisted by White House," *Los Angeles Times,* Oct. 14, 2004.

261 In all, the Bush energy act: The subsidies were tallied by Public Citizen, "The Best Energy Bill Corporations Could Buy," Aug. 8, 2005.

261 41 percent of the American public: Gallup poll; see Skocpol, *Naming the Problem,* 72. Gore's acclaim is described in Eric Pooley, *The Climate War* (Hachette Books, 2010).

262 "Climate denial got disseminated": Skocpol, *Naming the Problem,* 83.

262 the climate problem was real: McCain made these comments in the second presidential debate; see Pooley, *Climate War,* 297.

264 leases on over a million acres: Steve Mufson and Juliet Eilperin, "The Biggest Foreign Lease Holder in Canada's Oil Sands Isn't Exxon Mobil or Chevron. It's the Koch Brothers," *Washington Post,* March 20, 2014.

264 Koch Industries alone: The 300 million tons of carbon dioxide figure comes from Brad Johnson, "Koch Industries, the 100-Million Ton Car-

bon Gorilla," *ThinkProgress,* Jan. 30, 2011, and is cited in Fang, *Machine,* 114.

265 "The Earth will be able": Goldman, "Billionaire's Party."

265 Rather than fighting global warming: For an excellent report on Koch Industries' lobbying, see Farrell, "Koch's Web of Influence."

265 "The Obama budget proposes": Fang, *Machine,* 115.

266 "I rode more hot-air balloons": Jim Rutenberg, "How Billionaire Oligarchs Are Becoming Their Own Political Parties," *New York Times Magazine,* Oct. 17, 2014.

266 Reams of faxes arrived: Kate Sheppard, "Forged Climate Bill Letters Spark Uproar over 'Astroturfing,'" *Grist,* Aug. 4, 2009.

266 Later one of the disruptive members: See Fang, *Machine,* 176.

267 Mike Castle: Pooley, *Climate War,* 406.

267 "go ask the unicorns": Ibid., 393.

267 The process wasn't pretty: For an authoritative account of the cap-and-trade fight in the House, see ibid.

268 Quietly funding it: See Steven Mufson, "New Groups Revive the Debate over Climate Change," *Washington Post,* Sept. 25, 2009.

268 As soon as Obama's EPA: For more on the dispute, and a statement by John Nielsen-Gammon, Texas's state climatologist, see David Doniger, "Going Rogue on Endangerment," *Switchboard* (blog), Feb. 20, 2010.

269 One posted a report: Marc Sheppard, "UN Climate Reports: They Lie," *American Thinker,* Oct. 5, 2009.

269 "A miracle has happened": The Web site on which the contrarian wrote was Climate Audit.

269 "The blue dress moment": Chris Horner, "The Blue Dress Moment May Have Arrived," *National Review,* Nov. 19, 2009.

270 "a crucial tipping point": Tim Phillips was speaking about the Climategate leaks at the Heritage Foundation on October 26, 2010, as reported by Brad Johnson, Climate Progress, Nov. 27, 2010. Phillips did all he could to exploit the situation, staging an Americans for Prosperity protest in Copenhagen outside the United Nations conference on climate change, where he declared, "We're a grassroots organization . . . I think it's unfortunate when wealthy children of wealthy families . . . want to send unemployment rates in the United States to twenty percent." See Mayer, "Covert Operations."

270 The facts, when fully understood: Neela Banerjee provides a very clear and detailed analysis of the leaked e-mails in her profile of Mann, "Most Hated Climate Scientist in the US Fights Back."

272 As Mann recounts in his book: Mann writes that the Southeastern Legal Foundation demanded information from the National Science Foundation about its grants to him and his colleagues at Penn State. The Landmark Legal Foundation, he writes, sued to obtain personal e-mails he sent to colleagues at other schools who had collaborated on his hockey stick research. Michael E. Mann, *The Hockey Stick and the Climate Wars* (Columbia University Press, 2012), 229.

272 "a vicious S.O.B.": Vogel and McCalmont, "Rush Limbaugh, Sean Hannity, Glenn Beck Sell Endorsements to Conservative Groups"; John

Goodman, "Talk Radio Reacts to Politico on Cain; Mark Levin Criticizes Ken Vogel," *Examiner,* Nov. 2, 2011.

272 "I don't know why": "Levin to Female Caller: 'I Don't Know Why Your Husband Doesn't Put a Gun to His Temple,'" *Media Matters,* May 22, 2009.

272 "and the other advocates": Mark Levin, *Liberty and Tyranny* (Threshold, 2010), 133.

275 Almost half of those polled: Cited in Kate Sheppard, "Climategate: What Really Happened?," *Mother Jones,* April 21, 2011.

275 "I have come to conclude": Ryan Lizza, "As the World Burns," *New Yorker,* Oct. 11, 2010.

276 "Gridlock is the greatest friend": Kenner, *Merchants of Doubt.*

276 "The influence of special interests": Lizza, "As the World Burns."

CHAPTER NINE: MONEY IS SPEECH

279 One associate said: A social acquaintance of David Koch's, interview with author.

280 "difficult to see": Richard Posner, "Unlimited Campaign Spending—A Good Thing?," *The Becker-Posner Blog,* April 8, 2012.

280 "it gave rich people": Jeffrey Toobin, "Republicans United on Climate Change," *New Yorker,* June 10, 2014. Also see his "Money Unlimited," *New Yorker,* May 21, 2012.

281 In a growing backlash: See Elizabeth F. Ralph, "The Big Donor: A Short History," *Politico,* June 2014.

284 After news of their involvement: Dale Russakoff and Juan Williams, "Rearranging 'Amway Event' for Reagan," *Washington Post,* Jan. 22, 1984.

284 "They're not a business": "Soft Soap and Hard Sell," *Forbes,* Sept. 15, 1975.

285 In 1980, Richard DeVos: In "Rearranging 'Amway Event' for Reagan," Russakoff and Williams write that "DeVos, former finance chairman of the Republican National Committee, gave $70,575 in independent expenditures; Van Andel, former chairman of the U.S. Chamber of Commerce, chipped in $68,433."

285 By 1981, their titles: Ibid.

285 DeVos, the son of a poor: See Andy Kroll's excellent piece on the DeVos family, "Meet the New Kochs: The DeVos Clan's Plan to Defund the Left," *Mother Jones,* Jan./Feb. 2014.

285 The scandal exploded: Kitty McKinsey and Paul Magnusson, "Amway's Plot to Bilk Canada of Millions," *Detroit Free Press,* Aug. 22, 1982.

286 In 1989, Amway paid: Ruth Marcus, "Amway Says It Was Unnamed Donor to Help Broadcast GOP Convention," *Washington Post,* July 26, 1996.

286 "We were losing": Russakoff and Williams, "Rearranging 'Amway Event' for Reagan."

286 The DeVos family nonetheless: For statistics on the DeVos's spending, see Kroll, "Meet the New Kochs."

286 "There's not a Republican president": Ibid.

286 "a little-known club": David Kirkpatrick, "Club of the Most Powerful Gathers in Strictest Privacy," *New York Times,* Aug. 28, 2004.

287 "the doers": On March 22, 2005, Paul Weyrich said on C-SPAN (http://www.c-span.org/video/transcript/?id=7958) that the Council for National Policy, "in the words of Rich DeVos, brings together the doers with the donors."

287 Her father, Edgar: Jeremy Scahill, *Blackwater: The Rise of the World's Most Powerful Mercenary Army* (Nation Books, 2007), 78.

287 "the world's most powerful": Erik Prince, a swashbuckling former navy SEAL officer, soon ran into professional legal trouble. He eventually moved abroad and changed the company's name to escape its reputation as an international outlaw after its guards were charged with murder for gunning down seventeen civilians during the Iraq War.

288 "a spending edge": John David Dyche, *Republican Leader: A Political Biography* (Intercollegiate Studies Institute, 2009).

288 "Money, money, money": John Cheves, "Senator's Pet Issue: Money and the Power It Buys," *Lexington Herald-Leader,* Oct. 15, 2006.

288 "If we stop this thing": Michael Lewis, "The Subversive," *New York Times Magazine,* May 25, 1997.

289 "The relationship between": Marcus Owens was interviewed by Jon Campbell, who first wrote about the unusual relationship between Bopp and the James Madison Center in "James Bopp Jr. Gets Creative: How Does the Conservative Maestro of Campaign Finance Fund His Legal Work?," Slate.com, Oct. 5, 2012.

289 "Soft money": Betsy DeVos, "Soft Money Is Good: Hard-earned American Dollars That Big Brother Has Yet to Find a Way to Control," *Roll Call,* Sept. 6, 1997.

290 In 2004, Democratic-aligned outside groups: Trevor Potter, "The Current State of Campaign Finance Laws," *Brookings Campaign Finance Sourcebook,* 2005.

290 Leading the pack: For more on Soros's spending in the 2004 presidential election, see Mayer, "Money Man."

290 "was really Jim": David Kirkpatrick, "A Quest to End Spending Rules for Campaigns," *New York Times,* Jan. 24, 2010. Theodore Olson, a far better litigator than Bopp, argued the crucial oral argument in front of the Supreme Court.

291 "We had a 10-year plan": Ibid.

291 With his shaggy gray: Stephanie Mencimer, "The Man Who Took Down Campaign Finance Reform," *Mother Jones,* Jan. 21, 2010. Mencimer recounts that in 2008 the U.S. District Court judge Royce Lamberth "actually laughed at Bopp."

291 Clint Bolick, a pioneer: See Teles, *Rise of the Conservative Legal Movement,* 87.

292 While polls consistently showed: According to a poll conducted by ABC News on February 17, 2010, eight out of ten Americans surveyed opposed the Supreme Court's *Citizen United* decision.

292 "I would not have been": Bradley Smith, interview with author.

293 The litigation, meanwhile: Robert Mullins, "Racine Labor Center: Meeting Place for Organized Labor on the Ropes," *Milwaukee Business Journal,* Dec. 23, 1991.

293 He had been the Senate's premier: In 2002, Senators Russell Feingold and

John McCain, Republican of Arizona, co-authored the Bipartisan Campaign Reform Act, known as McCain-Feingold, which *Citizens United* largely undid.

293 "This Supreme Court decision": "Changes Have Money Talking Louder Than Ever in Midterms," *New York Times,* Oct. 7, 2010.

294 "not true": Technically, *Citizens United* said nothing about what foreign corporations could do, so some nonpartisan fact-checkers said Alito was right to object to Obama's description of the ruling as opening the doors to foreign spending. But the *Citizens United* decision did open a way for U.S. subsidiaries of foreign corporations to spend unlimited sums in American campaigns.

294 "It unshackled the big money": David Axelrod, interview with author.

CHAPTER TEN: THE SHELLACKING

295 Although Brown was a low-profile: See Brian Mooney, "Late Spending Frenzy Fueled Senate Race," *Boston Globe,* Jan. 24, 2010. The total spending by Brown and his opponent, Martha Coakley, in the Senate race was roughly equal, but while Coakley benefited from a large amount of cash from conventional Democratic Party committees, Brown got no money from GOP committees. The $2.6 million in contributions he got from outside conservative groups, which was almost $1 million more than Coakley got from outside spending groups, played a crucial role in filling this gap.

296 Two of the most active: According to Steve Leblanc's report for the Associated Press, Feb. 19, 2010, the American Future Fund spent $618,000 against Martha Coakley, and Americans for Job Security—a group that would receive $4.8 million from the Center to Protect Patient Rights in 2010—spent $460,000 on ads against Coakley. Together with the U.S. Chamber of Commerce's $1 million in last-minute ads, those three groups made up the bulk of the $2.6 million spent by conservative outside groups in the last twelve days of the campaign.

296 "We thought we had it won": Participant who spoke on the grounds that he not be identified, interview with author.

297 Its clients ranged: Ed Gillespie said he never supported the individual mandates, even though his firm represented the coalition of companies that suggested the plan. See James Hohmann, "Ed Gillespie's Steep Slog to the Senate," *Politico,* Jan. 13, 2014.

297 Within weeks, he set out: Vogel, *Big Money,* 47, describes the meeting at the Dallas Petroleum Club in greater detail.

298 "People call us": Ken Vogel, "Politics, Karl Rove and the Modern Money Machine," *Politico,* July/August 2014.

298 "It was all conceived": Glenn Thrush, "Obama's States of Despair: 2010 Losses Still Haunt," *Politico,* July 26, 2013.

299 By the end of 2010: See Olga Pierce, Justin Elliott, and Theodoric Meyer, "How Dark Money Helped Republicans Hold the House and Hurt Voters," ProPublica, Dec. 21, 2012.

299 "It was three yards": See Nicholas Confessore, "A National Strategy Funds State Political Monopolies," *New York Times,* Jan. 12, 2014.

299 In the previous decade: The $40 million spending figure is according to an analysis of tax records by Democracy NC, a progressive government watchdog group.

300 "He was a terrible candidate": Bob Geary, interview with author, which first appeared in Jane Mayer, "State for Sale," *New Yorker,* Oct. 10, 2011.

300 "I'm not a charismatic": Art Pope, interview with author, which first appeared in ibid.

301 Under his guidance: See Ted Gup, "Fakin' It," *Mother Jones,* May/June 1996. He writes that homemade-looking placards were in fact FedExed to the smokers' rights groups from the tobacco company executives in Winston-Salem, North Carolina.

301 In 1994 alone: Peter Stone describes the organization of smokers' rights groups in his piece, "The Nicotine Network," *Mother Jones,* May/June 1996.

302 In 2012, he pleaded guilty: Ellis pleaded guilty in June 2012 to a felony charge of making an illegal campaign contribution. In the plea deal, he received four years of probation and was fined $10,000. He says it is his understanding that following the probationary period, in 2016, further adjudication may dismiss the charge.

302 "The grass roots was designed": Jim Ellis, interview with author.

302 At a second Capitol Hill rally: Sam Stein, "Tea Party Protests—'Ni**er,' 'Fa**ot' Shouted at Members of Congress," *Huffington Post,* March 20, 2010.

303 "You know they're gonna": Halperin and Heilemann, *Double Down,* 13.

303 "We made a deliberate": Johnson, "Inside the Koch-Funded Ads Giving Dems Fits."

304 About a third of this: The forms showed TC4 sending money to what accountants call "disregarded entities," so that instead of appearing to go to CPPR, it went to two phantom limbs called Eleventh Edition LLC and American Commitment. See Viveca Novak, Robert Maguire, and Russ Choma, "Nonprofit Funneled Money to Kochs' Voter Database Effort, Other Conservative Groups," OpenSecrets.org, Dec. 21, 2012.

304 Previously, they had given: The main such "social welfare" group the Kochs supported prior to 2010 was Americans for Prosperity, which they only moderately funded during the Bush years. Instead, they had donated mostly to what the IRS defined as charitable organizations, or 501(c)(3)s, for which they could take tax deductions and which were more strictly barred from electoral politics.

305 For example, at the end of 2010: The Center for Responsive Politics first reported on the fact that the Center to Protect Patient Rights reported no spending on politics in its 2010 IRS 990 tax form. Kim Barker did an excellent, extensive report later, "How Nonprofits Spend Millions on Elections and Call It Public Welfare," ProPublica, Aug. 18, 2012, describing the phenomenon in further detail.

305 Yet it granted $103 million: These spending figures cover the years 2009 to 2011 and include the TC4 Trust.

305 In 2006, only 2 percent: These sums were calculated by the Center for Responsive Politics and exclude spending by party committees.

305 "The political players": Barker, "How Nonprofits Spend Millions on Elections and Call It Public Welfare."

306 Some joked that they attended: Steven Law said several attendees, including himself, "went so they could tell their friends they went to Karl Rove's house." Joe Hagan, "Goddangit, Baby, We're Making Good Time," *New York*, Feb. 27, 2011.

306 "the birthplace of a new": Vogel, *Big Money*, 49.

306 Working closely with both: Bloomberg reported, for instance, that in 2009 and 2010 the health insurance industry secretly funneled over $86 million into the U.S. Chamber of Commerce for attack ads. Drew Armstrong, "Health Insurers Gave $86 Million to Fight Health Law," Bloomberg, Nov. 17, 2010.

306 "there wasn't one race": Vogel, *Big Money*, 53.

307 "in order of the likelihood": Eliana Johnson, "Inside the Koch-Funded Ads Giving Dems Fits," NationalReview.com, March 31, 2014.

308 Efforts to track down: Jim Rutenberg, Don Van Natta Jr., and Mike McIntire, "Offering Donors Secrecy, and Going on Attack," *New York Times*, Oct. 11, 2010.

308 "has no purpose": Mike McIntire, "Under Tax-Exempt Cloak, Political Dollars Flow," *New York Times*, Sept. 23, 2010.

308 In addition, Noble directed millions: In 2010, Noble's CPPR distributed $31 million—just under half of its funds—to five conservative groups that then spent similar amounts on TV ads targeting fifty-eight House Democratic candidates. The groups were the American Future Fund ($11.6 million), the 60 Plus Association ($8.9 million), Americans for Job Security ($4.8 million), Americans for Tax Reform ($4.1 million), and Revere America ($2.3 million). CPPR provided at least one-third of the budget raised by each of those five groups that year. CPPR's next-largest expenses were $10.3 million for "communications and surveys" and $5.5 million to Americans for Limited Government, which sent out mailings attacking House Democrats.

309 "For the first time": Pooley, *Climate War*, 406.

309 "The Koch brothers went after me": Rick Boucher, interview with author.

311 McCarthy was an old hand: Larry McCarthy declined to comment.

311 "Larry is not just": Floyd Brown, interview with author, which first appeared in Jane Mayer, "Attack Dog," *New Yorker*, Feb. 13, 2012.

311 "serial offender": Geoff Garin, interview with author, which first appeared in ibid.

312 "a war": Jonathan Alter, "Schwarzman: 'It's a War' Between Obama, Wall St.," *Newsweek*, Aug. 15, 2010.

312 "You have no idea": James B. Stewart, "The Birthday Party," *New Yorker*, Feb. 11, 2008.

313 A 2007 *Wall Street Journal* profile: Henry Sender and Monica Langley, "How Blackstone's Chief Became $7 Million Man," *Wall Street Journal*, June 13, 2007.

313 The media sensation: Even business publications ran columns blasting the loophole. See Martin Sosnoff, "The $3 Billion Birthday Party," *Forbes*, June 21, 2007.

313 over $6 billion a year: Randall Dodd, "Tax Breaks for Billionaires," Economic Policy Institute, July 24, 2007.

314 "Hedge funds really need": Asness's open letter was written earlier, in May 2009, and was criticizing Obama for demonizing hedge funds for not going along with his administration's attempt to restructure Chrysler. See Clifford Asness, "Unafraid in Greenwich Connecticut," *Business Insider*, May 5, 2009.

315 "the closest thing": Andrew Miga, "Rich Spark Soft Money Surge—Financier Typifies New Type of Donor," *Boston Herald*, Nov. 29, 1999.

315 According to later reports: See Michael Isikoff and Peter Stone, "How Wall Street Execs Bankrolled GOP Victory," NBC News, Jan. 5, 2011.

315 eleven were on *Forbes*'s list: They were as follows:

Charles Koch: $44.7 billion
David Koch: $44.7 billion
Steve Schwarzman: $11.3 billion
Philip Anschutz: $11 billion
Ken Griffin: $7 billion
Richard DeVos: $5.8 billion
Diane Hendricks: $3.6 billion
Ken Langone: $2.9 billion
Steve Bechtel: $2.7 billion
Stan Hubbard: $2 billion
Joe Craft: $1.4 billion

316 "target-rich": Paul Abowd, "Donors Use Charity to Push Free-Market Policies in States," Center for Public Integrity, Feb. 14, 2013.

316 By the end of the meal: Kenneth Vogel and Simmi Aujla, "Koch Conference Under Scrutiny," *Politico*, Jan. 27, 2011.

317 "one hell of a wake-up call": See Sam Stein, "$200 Million GOP Campaign Avalanche Planned, Democrats Stunned," *Huffington Post*, July 8, 2010.

317 "It was clear": Anita Dunn, interview with author.

317 As late as May: David Axelrod, conversation with author, May 2010.

318 "dropped on me": Bruce Braley, interview with author, which first appeared in Mayer, "Attack Dog."

319 In 2010, Americans for Prosperity: See Fang, *Machine*, 174. He describes attending the 2010 Conservative Political Action Conference and seeing attendees taught to use video cameras "to harass Democratic officials until their inevitable outbursts were caught on tape." He writes that several conservative groups held training sessions in the ambush video technique, according to attendees at their functions, including Americans for Prosperity, FreedomWorks, and American Majority.

320 Only in 2011 did it surface: See Ben Smith, "Hedge Fund Figure Financed Mosque Campaign," *Politico*, Jan. 18, 2011. Smith credits his colleague Maggie Haberman with figuring out the money trail.

321 "I voted to help build": Mayer, "State for Sale."

322 Pope was instrumental: The racially charged ad was produced by the North Carolina Republican Party. Pope said that he was not involved in its creation, but he and three members of his family gave the Davis campaign a $4,000 check each—the maximum individual donation allowed by state

law. Pope told ProPublica that his $200,000 donation to Real Jobs NC was not for the REDMAP operation, or redistricting work. A lawsuit filed after the election concerning the redistricting effort, however, revealed that Pope consulted on how the borders were drawn. See Pierce, Elliott, and Meyer, "How Dark Money Helped Republicans Hold the House and Hurt Voters."

323 "We didn't have that before 2010": Mayer, "State for Sale."
323 "Those ads hurt me": Ibid.
324 "If you put all of the Pope groups": Ibid.
324 "People throw around terms": Art Pope, interview with author, which first appeared in Mayer, "State for Sale."
326 "The Obama team": Thrush, "Obama's States of Despair."
326 "We lost all hope": David Corn, *Showdown: The Inside Story of How Obama Fought Back Against Boehner, Cantor, and the Tea Party* (William Morrow, 2012), 44.
327 The conventional wisdom: See a more detailed description of the debate over blaming dark money in ibid., 40.
329 "a 5,700-square-foot, eight-bedroom house": Jonathan Salant, "Secret Political Cash Moves Through Nonprofit Daisy Chain," Bloomberg News, Oct. 15, 2012.

PART THREE: PRIVATIZING POLITICS

331 "There's class warfare all right": Ben Stein, "In Class Warfare, Guess Which Class Is Winning," *New York Times,* Nov. 26, 2006.

CHAPTER ELEVEN: THE SPOILS

333 whose donor network had spent: The figure $130.7 million represents the 2009–2010 spending by the Center to Protect Patient Rights ($72 million), the TC4 Trust ($38.5 million), and Americans for Prosperity ($38.5 million), deducting the money passed back and forth among these three nonprofits to avoid double counting, as reported by the groups' IRS filings.
333 "Charles and David Koch no longer": Tom Hamburger, Kathleen Hennessey, and Neela Banerjee, "Koch Brothers Now at Heart of GOP Power," *Los Angeles Times,* Feb. 6, 2011.
335 those with massive financial resources: Freeland, *Plutocrats.*
335 "The more Republicans depend": Lee Drutman, "Are the 1% of the 1% Pulling Politics in a Conservative Direction?," Sunlight Foundation, June 26, 2013.
335 "radicalization of the party's donor base": For more on the implications of the "rise of the radical rich," as Frum terms it, see David Frum, "Crashing the Party: Why the GOP Must Modernize to Win," *Foreign Affairs,* Sept./Oct. 2014.
335 "took the biggest leap": Skocpol, *Naming the Problem,* 92.
336 Now the new Republican leadership: The contributions and influence of the Kochs over the committee were first detailed by Hamburger, Hennessey, and Banerjee, "Koch Brothers Now at Heart of GOP Power."

336 signed an unusual pledge: Lewis et al., "Koch Millions Spread Influence Through Nonprofits, Colleges."

336 "No Climate Tax" pledge: See Eric Holmberg and Alexia Fernandez Campbell, "Koch Climate Pledge Strategy Continues to Grow," Investigative Reporting Workshop, July 1, 2013.

337 By then, the 1980 Superfund law: For more on the defunding of the Superfund program, see Charlie Cray and Peter Montague, "Kingpins of Carbon and Their War on Democracy," Greenpeace, Sept. 2014, 26.

338 "rejected in a class action suit": See "Crossett, Arkansas—Fact Check and Activist Falsehoods," KochFacts.com, Oct. 12, 2011.

338 "All along our street": David Bouie was interviewed in Robert Greenwald's film, *Koch Brothers Exposed,* produced by Brave New Films.

338 Two years earlier: See "The Smokestack Effect," *USA Today,* Dec. 10, 2008.

338 Of this total output: See EPA's Toxic Release Inventory databank. By 2013 Koch Industries had improved its standing so that it ranked as the country's tenth-largest toxic polluter, out of eight thousand companies required by law to register with the EPA.

338 "The investment banks": Continetti, "Paranoid Style in Liberal Politics."

338 Another defender: The University of Kansas political science professor Burdett Loomis told the *Washington Post,* "I'm sure he would vigorously dispute this, but it's hard not to characterize him as the congressman from Koch." See Dan Eggen, "GOP Freshman Pompeo Turned to Koch for Money for Business, Then Politics," *Washington Post,* March 20, 2011.

339 Within weeks, Pompeo: *The Washington Post* first wrote about Pompeo's championing of the Kochs' legislative priorities. Ibid.

339 Koch Industries' lobbying disclosures: See the Sunlight Foundation's Influence Explorer data, http://data.influenceexplorer.com/lobbying/?r#aXNzdWU9RU5WJnJlZ2lzdHJhbnRfZnQ9a29jaCUyMGluZHVzdHJpZXM=.

339 "naked belly crawl": Robert Draper, *When the Tea Party Came to Town* (Simon & Schuster, 2012), 180.

340 "It hurts to be tossed out": Robert Inglis, interview with author.

340 "an unconstitutional power grab": Fred Upton and Tim Phillips, "How Congress Can Stop the EPA's Power Grab," *Wall Street Journal,* Dec. 28, 2010.

340 "a wish list": Leslie Kaufman, "Republicans Seek Big Cuts in Environmental Rules," *New York Times,* July 27, 2011.

340 "rips the heart out": "A GOP Assault on Environmental Regulations," *Los Angeles Times,* Oct. 10, 2011.

341 Contrary to the partisan hype: Solyndra went bankrupt, as did several other firms supported by the huge government loan guarantee program, but as National Public Radio reported, despite $780 million in losses from defaults on loans, the program made $810 million in interest, yielding a $30 million profit. Jeff Brady, "After Solyndra Loss, U.S. Energy Loan Program Turning a Profit," NPR, Nov. 13, 2014.

341 A huge investor: Dixon Doll's firm, DCM, invested in Abound Solar.

341 "like night and day": Hamburger, Hennessey, and Banerjee, "Koch Brothers Now at Heart of GOP Power."

341 "If you look": Coral Davenport, "Heads in Sand," *National Journal,* Dec. 3, 2011.
342 "citizen's arrest": Kenneth P. Vogel, "The Kochs Fight Back," *Politico,* Feb. 2, 2011.
343 "spumed and sputtered": Golf partner of the Kochs, interview with author. The Kochs laying blame on the media for death threats and the need for bodyguards is based on author interviews with two of their interlocutors.
343 "They somehow thought": Vogel, "Kochs Fight Back."
343 Michael Goldfarb: See Jim Rutenberg, "A Conservative Provocateur, Using a Blowtorch as His Pen," *New York Times,* Feb. 23, 2013. See more at http://rightweb.irc-online.org/profile/center_for_american_freedom/#_edn13.
343 Later, he founded: When the Kochs signed him on, Goldfarb was vice president of a public relations firm called Orion Strategies, LLC. *The Washington Free Beacon* was published by a nonprofit organization that hid its donors, called the Center for American Freedom. Its chairman was Goldfarb. Its 990 IRS disclosure shows that the Goldfarb-led nonprofit reported paying one for-profit vendor for public relations work: his own firm, Orion Strategies, LLC.
343 "Do unto them": See Matthew Continetti, "Combat Journalism: Taking the Fight to the Left," *Washington Free Beacon,* Feb. 6, 2012.
344 "I mean no disrespect": Eliza Gray, "Right vs. Write," *New Republic,* Feb. 22, 2012.
344 "tactics that have helped": See Kenneth Vogel, "Philip Ellender: The Kochs' Unlikely Democratic Enforcer," *Politico,* June 14, 2011.
345 "a wake-up call": Liz Goodwin, "Mark Holden Wants You to Love the Koch Brothers," *Yahoo News,* March 25, 2015.
346 It's uncommon for a private detective: In a story about the company's unusually aggressive dealings with reporters, in which *The Washington Post* described me as "the Kochs' Public Enemy No. 1," their spokesmen said only that the brothers had "no knowledge" of the plagiarism allegations made against me. See Paul Farhi, "Billionaire Koch Brothers Use Web to Take on Media Reports They Dispute," *Washington Post,* July 14, 2013.
347 This time the sender: Friess later said he had no involvement in the proposed investigative story on me.
350 "intellectual ammunition": See Schulman, *Sons of Wichita,* 320, which quotes Robert Levy, then Cato's chairman, describing David Koch's telling him that he wanted more "ammunition" for Americans for Prosperity and to support the Republican Party.
350 If anything, the Kochs' ham-fisted reaction: Kenneth Vogel and Tarini Parti, "Inside Koch World," *Politico,* June 15, 2012.
350 The bidding during the final: Interview with a guest at the resort during the seminar weekend.
351 "There's a lot of sharp knives": Halperin and Heilemann, *Double Down,* 346.
352 Tea Party leaders: See Skocpol and Williamson, *Tea Party and the Remaking of Republican Conservatism.*
352 While rich free-market enthusiasts: For more on the differences in the

policy preferences of the rich and others concerning entitlement spending, see Martin Gilens, *Affluence and Influence: Economic Inequality and Political Power in America* (Princeton University Press and Russell Sage Foundation, 2012), 119.

352 It was an intriguing idea: Chapter 7 of the House of Representatives' ethics manual bans all "unofficial office accounts" including "in-kind contribution of goods and services for official purposes." Specifically, members are prohibited from accepting "volunteer services" from paid political consultants "pertaining to the development and implementation of [the member's] legislative agenda."

352 Much of it moved: Overseeing the project at TC4 Trust, and later at a subgroup called Public Notice, was the same operative, a former Bush administration press officer named Gretchen Hamel, who had given a presentation at the January 2011 Koch seminar titled "Framing the Debate on Spending."

352 The TC4 Trust was little more: OpenSecrets.org did the groundbreaking reporting on the TC4 Trust. See, for instance, Novak, Maguire, and Choma, "Nonprofit Funneled Money to Kochs' Voter Database Effort, Other Conservative Groups."

353 "It wasn't about developing policy": Ed Goeas, interview with author.

353 As President Obama worked up: Paul Ryan's eventual pitch, which was found misleading by several nonpartisan fact-checkers, claimed that it was Obama, not he, who planned to cut Medicare. In reality, Obama's health-care act anticipated steady increases in Medicare spending but predicted a future reduction in the *rate* of increase, thanks to projected savings. Obama critics soon echoed the line of attack, though. Rush Limbaugh, for instance, claimed on his radio show, "Paul Ryan doesn't rape Medicare to the tune of $500 billion! Your guy did!"

354 "When oligarchs control": Neera Tanden, interview with author.

354 A 2008 study: For the study of the four hundred top taxpayers and tax rates during the twentieth century, see James Stewart, "High Income, Low Taxes, and Never a Bad Year," *New York Times,* Nov. 2, 2013.

354 Fully 60 percent: A concise and illuminating report on capital gains taxes, from which the statistics here are drawn, is Steve Mufson and Jia Lynn Yang, "Capital Gains Tax Rates Benefiting Wealthy Feed Growing Gap Between Rich and Poor," *Washington Post,* Sept. 11, 2011. They note that 80 percent of capital gains during the previous twenty years went to just 5 percent of Americans, of which half were among the wealthiest 0.1 percent of the population.

355 Soon, though, those at the very top: Jeffrey A. Winters, *Oligarchy* (Cambridge University Press, 2011), 228.

355 "tax-cutting spree": See Hacker and Pierson, *Winner-Take-All Politics,* 48.

355 "Our goal": Charles Koch, "Business Community."

356 "Wealthy people self-tax": Friess as quoted by Freeland, *Plutocrats,* 246–47.

356 "I agree with": Charles Koch's speech to the Council for National Policy, Jan. 1999.

356 "This is false": Leon Wieseltier, interview with author.

357 According to one 2006 report: Public Citizen and United for a Fair Economy, *Spending Millions to Save Billions: The Campaign of the Super Wealthy*

to Kill the Estate Tax, April 2006, http://www.citizen.org/documents/EstateTaxFinal.pdf.

357 One member of their network: Cris Barrish, "Judge Shuts Down Heiress' Effort to Alter Trust with Adoption Plot," *Wilmington News Journal,* Aug. 2, 2011.

358 "It used to be": Corn, *Showdown,* 76.

359 "failed to withstand": Barry Ritholtz, "What Caused the Financial Crisis? The Big Lie Goes Viral," *Washington Post,* Nov. 5, 2011.

361 "right-wing lunacy": Noam Scheiber, *The Escape Artists: How Obama's Team Fumbled the Recovery* (Simon & Schuster, 2011).

361 According to a *New York Times* analysis: These projections of the fallout from cuts in Ryan's budget refer to its 2012 iteration and appeared in Jonathan Weisman, "In Control, Republican Lawmakers See Budget as Way to Push Agenda," *New York Times,* Nov. 13, 2014.

362 "Robin Hood in reverse": See Jonathan Chait, "The Legendary Paul Ryan," *New York,* April 29, 2012.

362 "the most courageous": David Brooks, "Moment of Truth," *New York Times,* April 5, 2011.

362 "The right had succeeded": See Freeland, *Plutocrats,* 265. She writes, "In April and May of 2011, when unemployment was 9 percent, . . . the five largest papers in the country published 201 stories about the budget deficit and only sixty-three about joblessness."

363 "We made a mistake": Bob Woodward, *The Price of Politics* (Simon & Schuster Paperbacks, 2013), 107.

364 A Democratic underdog: The race in New York's Twenty-Sixth Congressional District was won by the Democrat, Kathy Hochul.

364 But the House Republicans: See Draper, *When the Tea Party Came to Town,* 151.

364 "*We* led": Ibid.

364 The donors were excited: The assertion that the donors felt their investment was worth it is based on an interview with someone familiar with their thinking, who asked not to be identified.

364 "an apocalyptic cult": Thomas E. Mann and Norman J. Ornstein, *It's Even Worse Than It Looks: How the American Constitutional System Collided with the New Politics of Extremism* (Basic Books, 2012), 54.

365 "deal with it as adults": Naftali Bendavid, "Boehner Warns GOP on Debt Ceiling," *Wall Street Journal,* Nov. 18, 2010.

365 "if we don't solve": Frum, in "Crashing the Party," describes Stanley Druckenmiller's position as "amazing" and radical.

365 "delay tough decisions": In addition, Koch-backed advocates had long argued against closing the carried-interest loophole. In 2007, when Congress debated closing it, Adam Creighton, a Koch fellow at the Tax Foundation, a research group supported by Charles Koch, argued that "this is not going to raise tax revenue at all."

366 "they start wetting their pants": Stephen Moore, former Club for Growth president. Matt Bai, "Fight Club," *New York Times Magazine,* Aug. 10, 2003.

366 The president and Boehner: In the grand bargain, Obama would agree to cut spending in exchange for the debt ceiling extension and for the

Republicans "cleaning out the garbage" in the tax code, as Boehner put it. Boehner wouldn't agree to raise tax rates, but he would agree to eliminate some tax loopholes.

366 He was among the House's top: See Alec MacGillis, "In Cantor, Hedge Funds and Private Equity Firms Have Voice at Debt Ceiling Negotiations," *Washington Post,* July 25, 2011.

366 So although one study: The 2006 study is cited in Hacker and Pierson, *Winner-Take-All Politics,* 51.

366 "Boehner begged David": Author interviews with family adviser, a congressional source, and Emily Schillinger.

367 "With no basis in fact": Mann and Ornstein, *It's Even Worse Than It Looks,* 23.

367 Cantor later told: Ryan Lizza, "The House of Pain," *New Yorker,* March 4, 2013.

369 "I think he came in truly trying": Neera Tanden, interview with author.

CHAPTER TWELVE: MOTHER OF ALL WARS

370 Or so they thought: Brad Friedman, "Inside the Koch Brothers' 2011 Summer Seminar," *The Brad Blog,* June 26, 2011.

370 *The New York Times*'s resident: Nate Silver, "Is Obama Toast? Handicapping the 2012 Election," *New York Times Magazine,* Nov. 3, 2011.

371 "Wouldn't it be easier": Halperin and Heilemann, *Double Down,* 345.

372 Four years later: For more on Christie's record, see Cezary Podkul and Allan Sloan, "Christie Closed Budget Gaps with One-Shot Maneuvers," *Washington Post,* April 18, 2015, A1.

372 "Who knows?": Friedman, "Inside the Koch Brothers' 2011 Summer Seminar."

372 Christie had campaigned: See Joby Warrick, "Foes: Christie Left Wind Power Twisting," *Washington Post,* March 30, 2015.

375 From the start: Freedom Partners made grants of $1 million or more in 2012 to the following groups:

Center to Protect Patient Rights: $115 million
Americans for Prosperity: $32.3 million
60 Plus Association: $15.7 million
American Future Fund: $13.6 million
Concerned Women for America Legislative Action Committee: $8.2 million
Themis Trust: $5.8 million
Public Notice: $5.5 million
Generation Opportunity: $5 million
Libre Initiative: $3.1 million
National Rifle Association: $3.5 million
U.S. Chamber of Commerce: $2 million
American Energy Alliance: $1.5 million

375 David Koch's group: Technically, the Kochs' spokesmen insisted that David Koch was only chairman of the Americans for Prosperity Foundation, but in his introduction of David Koch during the June 2011 seminar

Kevin Gentry seemed to describe him simply as "chairman of Americans for Prosperity."

377 For the Koch network: The Koch Industries PAC donated $43,000 to Walker's gubernatorial campaign, and David Koch donated $1 million to the Republican Governors Association in 2010.

378 Some, like the liberal: John Podesta, the founder of the Center for American Progress, in 2015 signed on as the chairman of Hillary Clinton's presidential campaign.

378 "the big government": See Jason Stein and Patrick Marley, *More Than They Bargained For: Scott Walker, Unions, and the Fight for Wisconsin* (University of Wisconsin Press, 2013), 37.

378 The Bradley Foundation: See Patrick Healey and Monica Davey, "Behind Scott Walker, a Longstanding Conservative Alliance Against Unions," *New York Times,* June 8, 2015. The paper reported that in 2009 the Bradley Foundation gave a grant of $1 million to the Wisconsin Policy Research Institute and provided one-third of the budget of the MacIver Institute, both of which drew up lists of proposals for the incoming governor, at the top of which was curbing the power of the state employee unions. The MacIver Institute had numerous ties to the Wisconsin chapter of the Koch advocacy group Americans for Prosperity. Three members of the MacIver Institute's board also served as directors of Americans for Prosperity in Wisconsin. One of these, David Fettig, was a Koch seminar attendee as well.

378 "one of the most powerful": Daniel Bice, Bill Glauber, and Ben Poston, "From Local Roots, Bradley Foundation Builds a Conservative Empire," *Milwaukee Journal Sentinel,* Nov. 19, 2011.

379 As a college dropout: In 2010, an offshoot of Americans for Prosperity calling itself Fight Back Wisconsin organized Tea Party rallies across the state featuring Scott Walker, who was then Milwaukee county executive. Later, the secretly funded group helped him get out the vote. Meanwhile, in a bit of philanthropic back-scratching, the Bradley Foundation in 2010 gave $520,000 to the Americans for Prosperity Foundation.

379 "We go back": Adele M. Stan, "Wall Street Journal Honcho Shills for Secret Worker 'Education' Program Linked to Koch Group," *Alternet,* June 3, 2011.

379 Once in office: See Michael Isikoff, "Secret $1.5 Million Donation from Wisconsin Billionaire Uncovered in Scott Walker Dark-Money Probe," *Yahoo News,* March 23, 2015. Laurel Patrick, Walker's press secretary, issued a strong denial to *Yahoo News* concerning any favoritism shown Menard. She denied that the governor had provided any special favors for Menard and said Walker was "not involved" in the decision to award his firm tax credits, which were approved by the Wisconsin Economic Development Corporation for expansions of existing facilities in order to create jobs. (She also noted that Menard's firm had been awarded $1.5 million in tax credits in 2006 under Democratic Gov. James Doyle. State records show these were reduced to $1 million when the company failed to meet its full job-creation requirements.)

380 According to a 2007 profile: See Mary Van de Kamp Nohl, "Big Money," *Milwaukee Magazine,* April 30, 2007.

380 One employee described: Ibid.

381 That case was followed: See Bruce Murphy, "The Strange Life of John Menard," UrbanMilwaukee.com, June 20, 2013. Donald Trump's wife, Melania, also filed a separate $50 million suit against John Menard, claiming damages from his cancellation of a promotional deal with her line of skin care products. Menard's lawyers described the Trump deal as void.

382 Soon after the governor: Diane Hendricks donated $10,000, the maximum allowable amount, to Walker's campaign in 2011, while her company donated $25,000 to the Republican Governors Association. In 2012, she donated $500,000 to fight the effort to recall Walker. In 2014, she donated $1 million to Wisconsin's Republican Party.

382 Thanks to complicated accounting: According to an account by Cary Spivak, "Beloit Billionaire Pays Zero in 2010 State Income Tax Bill," *Milwaukee Journal Sentinel,* May 30, 2012, the tax director for Hendricks's company, ABC Supply, described her zero personal state income tax payment as an anomaly, stemming from the reclassification of her company from an S corporation, in which she had paid the taxes, to one in which the company paid the $373,671 state tax bill for the second half of 2010.

382 Walker unwittingly lent: The prank phone caller was Ian Murphy. For his account, see "I Punk'd Scott Walker, and Now He's Lying About It," *Politico,* Nov. 18, 2013.

383 After Walker triumphed: See Adam Nagourney and Michael Barbaro, "Emails Show Bigger Fund-Raising Role for Wisconsin Leader," *New York Times,* Aug. 22, 2014.

383 According to one tally: See Brendan Fischer, "Bradley Foundation Bankrolled Groups Pushing Back on John Doe Criminal Probe," Center for Media and Democracy's PR Watch, June 19, 2014.

384 "We will not step back": Schulman, *Sons of Wichita,* 304.

385 "The secret of my influence": Novak, Maguire, and Choma, "Nonprofit Funneled Money to Kochs' Voter Database Effort, Other Conservative Groups."

385 "Koch has been targeted": Matea Gold, "Koch-Backed Political Network Built to Shield Donors," *Washington Post,* Jan. 5, 2014.

385 This consolidation of power: Total traceable election spending by all candidates, parties, and outside groups reached $7 billion, while the amount spent by independent groups and super PACs reached $2.5 billion, of which $1.25 billion came from traditional PACs and $950 million came from super PACs with unlimited contributions. In comparison, $1.576 billion was spent by the Democratic and Republican Parties, according to the Federal Election Commission's report "FEC Summarizes Campaign Activity of the 2011–2012 Election Cycle," April 19, 2013. Spending by "outside political committees" topped party spending for the first time, according to the FEC commissioner Ellen Weintraub's statement, Jan. 31, 2013.

385 On its own: I reached the sum of $407 million by adding up disclosures, but Matea Gold, in her excellent post-2012 feature on the Koch network's spending, cites the figure $400 million. See Gold, "Koch-Backed Net-

work, Built to Shield Donors, Raised $400 Million in 2012 Elections," *Washington Post,* Jan. 5, 2014.

386 *Politico*'s Kenneth Vogel: See Vogel, *Big Money,* 19.

386 No previous year: For statistics on the increasing concentration of donations, see Lee Drutman, "The Political 1% of the 1% in 2012," Sunlight Foundation, June 24, 2013.

386 "the financial engine": Hayley Peterson, "Internal Memo: Romney Courting Kochs, Tea Party," *Washington Examiner,* Nov. 2, 2011.

387 There he delivered a keynote: For details of Romney's budget speech, see Donovan Slack, "Romney Proposes Wide Cuts to Budget," *Boston Globe,* Nov. 5, 2011.

388 "They're the ones that suffer": "Quotes from Charles Koch," *Wichita Eagle,* Oct. 13, 2012.

388 "These guys all talk": Dan Pfeiffer, interview with author.

388 "confident glow": Schulman, *Sons of Wichita,* 341.

389 "Why is it fair": For George W. Bush's comment about Adelson, and Adelson's comment on income taxes, see the groundbreaking piece by Connie Bruck, "The Brass Ring," *New Yorker,* June 30, 2008.

390 The odd couple had been friends: See Vogel, *Big Money,* 79.

390 "a bias in favor": Jewish Channel, Dec. 9, 2011.

390 Within weeks, Adelson donated: Sheldon Adelson said of Gingrich's statement, "Read the history of those who call themselves Palestinians, and you will hear why Gingrich said recently that the Palestinians are an invented people." By the time Adelson's money arrived, Gingrich had finished fourth in Iowa, and he was about to be buried in New Hampshire. Adelson later pressed Romney to switch his position on Pollard, but Romney resisted. Romney did, however, sit next to Adelson at a fund-raiser in Israel at which he suggested that Palestinians were culturally inferior to Israelis.

391 "delusional and fabricated": Chris McGreal, "Sheldon Adelson Lectures Court After Tales of Triads and Money Laundering," *Guardian,* May 1, 2015.

393 "We were killing them": Jim Messina, interview with author.

393 "an ideologically driven": Steve Schmidt, interview with author.

395 "There are five or six people": Obama spoke in February 2012 at the home of the Costco co-founder Jeff Brotman according to Vogel, *Big Money,* vii.

395 "in a bind": Arnold Hiatt, interview with author.

395 In an early 2012 meeting: Messina's conversation with Obama as described in Halperin and Heilemann, *Double Down,* 314.

396 Experts ranging: Summers and Fukuyama expressed their concerns in a fascinating essay by Thomas Edsall, "Is This the End of Market Democracy?," *New York Times,* Feb. 19, 2012.

397 "Bill can't do that": Hillary's private disapproval is recounted in Halperin and Heilemann, *Double Down,* 381.

397 "under most circumstances": Gilens, *Affluence and Influence,* 1.

398 "new orthodoxy": Jonathan Weisman, "Huntsman Fires at Perry from the Middle," *Wall Street Journal,* Aug. 21, 2011.

399 "Republicans have finally found": Dave Weigel, "Republicans Have Finally Found a Group They Want to Tax: Poor People," *Slate,* Aug. 22, 2011.

401 "They did it wrong": Koch Industries adviser who asked not to have his name disclosed because he continues to work with the company. Interview with author.
401 "some donors who were part": Deposition of Tony Russo, State of California Fair Political Practices Commission Investigative Report, Aug. 16, 2013.
402 "There is not a Koch *network*": Vogel, *Big Money*, 201.
402 This was more than $1: See Barker and Meyer, "Dark Money Man."
404 "My first thought": Teresa Sharp, interview with author.
404 "I don't want everybody to vote": Ari Berman, *Give Us the Ballot: The Modern Struggle for Voting Rights in America* (Farrar, Straus and Giroux, 2015), 260.
404 Spakovsky's most recent book: Encounter Books was founded in 1998 with a $3.5 million grant from the Bradley Foundation to publish "serious non-fiction." In an interview with the author, Hans von Spakovsky denied that he was motivated either by racial discrimination or by partisan gain. "I believe in having fair elections," he said. "My interest is in making sure that the person who people vote for the most wins." See Jane Mayer, "The Voter-Fraud Myth," *New Yorker,* Oct. 29, 2012.
404 True the Vote, meanwhile: True the Vote was forced to return the funds it received from the Bradley Foundation after the IRS had not yet granted the organization tax-exempt status.
406 "What the president's campaign": Romney's November 14, 2012, call to his contributors is described in Halperin and Heilemann, *Double Down,* 468.
407 Approximately $15 million: Peter Stone first revealed the size of the Adelsons' contributions to Americans for Prosperity in his piece "Watch Out, Dems: Sheldon Adelson and the Koch Brothers Are Closer Than Ever," *Huffington Post,* June 14, 2015.
407 "Our goal of advancing": According to Robert Costa, "Kochs Postpone Post-election Meeting," *National Review Online,* Dec. 11, 2012, Charles Koch's e-mail to his donor network said, "We are working hard to understand the election results, and, based on that analysis, to re-examine our vision and the strategies and capabilities required for success."
408 David Koch, in fact: Charles Koch continued to maintain, "I'm neither Republican nor Democrat," even though his political operation was fused with that of his brother.
408 "One ten-thousandth": Drutman, "Political 1% of the 1% in 2012."
408 "I'm an incumbent president": Vogel, *Big Money,* viii.

CHAPTER THIRTEEN: THE STATES

410 The same pattern was repeated: This mathematically odd outcome had only occurred twice before in the past century.
410 "A few years ago": Tarini Parti, "GOP, Koch Brothers Find There's Nothing Finer Than Carolina," *Politico,* May 11, 2013.
410 Phillips declined to say: Nationally, the Koch network's main bank, Freedom Partners, poured $32.3 million into Americans for Prosperity in 2012. But how much of this went into North Carolina remained undisclosed.

411 For his services: The State of North Carolina paid Hofeller an additional $77,000 as well.

411 "We worked together": Raupe is quoted in an excellent ProPublica investigative piece by Pierce, Elliott, and Meyer, "How Dark Money Helped Republicans Hold the House and Hurt Voters."

412 "The Kochs were instrumental": David Axelrod, interview with author.

412 According to a report: Pierce, Elliott, and Meyer, "How Dark Money Helped Republicans Hold the House and Hurt Voters."

412 "Make sure your security": See Robert Draper, "The League of Dangerous Mapmakers," *Atlantic*, Oct. 2012.

413 In reality, however: Hofeller's failure to read the public hearing transcripts was attributed by ProPublica to court documents, and ProPublica noted that Hofeller declined to comment further.

413 But before that could happen: The Democratic challenger was Sam Ervin IV, a rising star who shared the name of his famous grandfather, a former North Carolina senator who won national acclaim during the Watergate hearings.

414 The money trail: ProPublica traced over $1 million back to Gillespie's Republican State Leadership Committee. Pope's company, Variety Wholesalers, contributed some of this cash. The RSLC's role was hidden behind a new group that sprang up, calling itself Justice for All NC. This group in turn donated $1.5 million to a super PAC called the North Carolina Judicial Coalition.

414 Successive midterm losses: Nicholas Confessore, Jonathan Martin, and Maggie Haberman, "Democrats See No Choice but Hillary Clinton in 2016," *New York Times*, March 11, 2015.

415 Almost as soon: Pat McCrory attended events for Americans for Prosperity before declaring his candidacy for governor in 2012, and once he did declare, AFP spent $130,000 in mailers benefiting his campaign.

415 "my way, or everyone else": Richard Morgan, interview with author, which first appeared in Mayer, "State for Sale."

415 "When he was done": Ibid.

415 It is unusual: Winters, *Oligarchy*, xi.

416 "conservative government in exile": Matea Gold, "In NC Conservative Donor Sits at the Heart of the Government He Helped Transform," *Washington Post*, July 19, 2014.

417 Yet the lines: Jack Hawke, a Republican political operative, for instance, moved back and forth between the presidency of the Civitas Institute and the campaigns of the Republican governor Pat McCrory.

417 "the Koch brothers lite": Scott Place, interview with author.

417 "I've never seen": Lynn Bonner, David Perlmutt, and Anne Blythe, "Elections Bill Headed to McCrory," *Charlotte Observer*, July 27, 2013.

418 "No, it's worse": Dan T. Carter, "State of Shock," *Southern Spaces*, Sept. 24, 2013.

419 So for savings: See ibid.

419 The assault was systematic: Spending on public schools in North Carolina was reduced to $7.5 billion in 2012–2013 from $7.9 billion in 2007–2008, despite the state's rapidly growing population, according to Rob Chris-

tiansen, "NC GOP Rolls Back Era of Democratic Laws," *News Observer,* June 16, 2013.

420 "What are you doing": Bill Friday, interview with author, which first appeared in Mayer, "State for Sale."

420 "I'm pretty sure": Stephen Margolis (the former chair of NC State's economics department), interview with author. See ibid.

420 "It's sad and blatant": Mayer, "State for Sale."

420 "constitutional limitations": David Edwards, "NC GOP Bills Would Require Teaching Koch Principles While Banning Teachers' Political Views in Class," *Raw Story,* April 29, 2011.

421 "I was a Republican": Jim Goodmon, interview with author, which first appeared in Mayer, "State for Sale."

421 opposition to minimum wage laws: In an interview with the author, Roy Cordato, a vice president at the John Locke Foundation, argued that "the minimum wage hurts low-skilled workers, by pricing them out of the market," and that concern about worker exploitation was "the kind of thinking that comes from Karl Marx." In Cordato's view, "any freely made contracts among consenting adults should be legal," including those involving prostitution and the sale of dangerous drugs. He said he supported child-labor laws but opposed what he called "compulsory education" for minors.

422 "a plantation mentality": Dean Debnam, interview with author, which first appeared in Mayer, "State for Sale."

422 "wealth creation and wealth destruction": Ibid.

423 "He had his checkbook": Scott Place, interview with author.

424 David Parker: interview with author, which first appeared in Mayer, "State for Sale."

425 "You capture the Soviet Union": Ed Pilkington and Suzanne Goldenberg, "State Conservative Groups Plan US-Wide Assault on Education, Health, and Tax," *Guardian,* Dec. 5, 2013.

425 "Pick what you need": See Jane Mayer, "Is Ikea the New Model for the Conservative Movement?," *New Yorker,* Nov. 15, 2013.

425 In 2011, the State Policy Network's budget: See "Exposed: The State Policy Network," Center for Media and Democracy, Nov. 2013. The report is thorough and well documented and makes the point on page 3 that the organization helped to spread the Kochtopus's "financial tentacles across the states."

426 On average, ALEC produced: For ALEC's track record on introducing bills, see Cray and Montague, "Kingpins of Carbon and Their War on Democracy," 37.

426 "Nowhere else can you get": The quotations from the ALEC members' newsletter and from Thompson appear in Alexander Hertel-Fernandez, "Who Passes Businesses' 'Model Bills'? Policy Capacity and Corporate Influence in U.S. State Politics," *Perspectives in Politics* 12, no. 3 (Sept. 2014).

426 Two years later: For more on ALEC, see ALECExposed.org, produced by the Center for Media and Democracy.

427 "a wolf in disguise": Dave Zweifel, "Plain Talk: 'News Service' Just a Wolf in Disguise," Madison.com.

427 "legacy media": Jason Stverak spoke about the "vacuum" at a Heritage

Foundation conference, "From Tea Parties to Taking Charge," April 22–23, 2010.

427 Much of the money went through: For one of the best analyses of the finances of DonorsTrust, see Abowd, "Donors Use Charity to Push Free-Market Policies in States."

428 The big backers: See "Exposed: The State Policy Network," 18.

428 "a better opportunity": Abowd, "Donors Use Charity to Push Free-Market Policies in States." According to "Exposed: The State Policy Network," 19–20, inadvertent disclosures by just two State Policy Network think tanks, in Massachusetts and Texas, revealed major deposits from Koch Industries and the Koch family foundations. David Koch's personal contribution of $125,000 in 2007 to the Massachusetts-based member of the State Policy Network, the Pioneer Institute, showed that he was the single largest donor to the group that year. A similar mistaken disclosure by the Texas Public Policy Foundation revealed that Koch Industries contributed over $159,000 to the think tank in 2010, while one of the Koch family foundations contributed over $69,000.

429 "historical oddity": See Ryan Lizza, "Where the G.O.P.'s Suicide Caucus Lives," *New Yorker,* Sept. 26, 2013.

430 Big outside money: Kenneth Vogel, in *Big Money,* 211, makes much the same point, writing, "Nearly eleven months after the biggest of the big-money mostly failed to get its way at the ballot box, the shutdown battle was proof that the 2010 and 2012 spending sprees were having more impact than ever on the way American government functioned."

430 A galaxy of conservative: Todd Purdum, "The Obamacare Sabotage Campaign," *Politico,* Nov. 1, 2013.

430 "This bastard has to be killed": Linda Greenhouse, "By Any Means Necessary," *New York Times,* Aug. 20, 2014.

431 "loose-knit coalition": Sheryl Gay Stolberg and Mike McIntire, "A Federal Budget Crisis Months in the Planning," *New York Times,* Oct. 5, 2013.

431 The meetings produced: In his article "Meet the Evangelical Cabal Orchestrating the Shutdown," *Nation,* Oct. 8, 2013, Lee Fang notes that the Conservative Action Project was closely affiliated with the secretive Council on National Policy and had been meeting in Washington since at least 2009.

431 Freedom Partners: Stolberg and McIntire, "Federal Budget Crisis Months in the Planning," suggested that Freedom Partners spent $200 million in the fight against health care, but this figure represents other spending by the group as well.

432 News reports reflected: Jenna Portnoy, "In Southwest Va., Health Needs, Poverty Collide with Antipathy to the Affordable Care Act," *Washington Post,* June 19, 2004.

432 As part of that effort: The figure of four million uninsured adults blocked by the states refusing to expand Medicaid comes from the Kaiser Family Foundation. Rachel Garfield et al., "The Coverage Gap: Uninsured Poor Adults in States That Do Not Expand Medicaid—an Update," Kaiser Family Foundation, April 17, 2015.

432 Meanwhile, the Cato Institute: See Alec MacGillis's profile of the Cato

Institute's Michael Cannon for a revealing look at the think tank's behind-the-scenes role. MacGillis, "Obamacare's Single Most Relentless Antagonist," *New Republic,* Nov. 12, 2013.

432 This nonetheless formed: See Robert Pear, "Four Words That Imperil Health Care Law Were All a Mistake, Writers Now Say," *New York Times,* May 25, 2015.

432 But the NFIB was talked: The NFIB called itself "America's leading small business association," and in previous years most of its funding had come from its small-business members. But starting in 2010, the year it agreed to act as the plaintiff in the court challenge, outside money from some very big fortunes started filling its coffers. In 2012, the year the case reached the Supreme Court, as CNN first reported, the NFIB received more money from Freedom Partners than from any other single source. In addition, from 2010 until 2012, DonorsTrust supplied over half of the budget for the NFIB's legal center. The Bradley Foundation donated funds, too.

The combined millions of dollars in contributions paid for some of the most brilliant litigators in the country to advance arguments that Josh Blackman, a conservative law professor who wrote *Unprecedented,* a book on the case, admitted seemed "crazy" in the beginning. Yet because of the efforts of a few activists bankrolled by wealthy ideological entrepreneurs, the challenge went from the fringe to one vote short of victory in the Supreme Court. For more, see Blackman, *Unprecedented: The Constitutional Challenge to Obamacare* (PublicAffairs, 2013).

433 "It's David versus Goliath": Stolberg and McIntire, "Federal Budget Crisis Months in the Planning."

433 $235 million was spent: For Kantar Media statistics on ad spending, see Purdum, "Obamacare Sabotage Campaign."

433 "When else in our history": Stolberg and McIntire, "Federal Budget Crisis Months in the Planning."

434 "The president was reelected": Boehner, interview with Diane Sawyer, ABC News, Nov. 8, 2012.

434 "John, what happened": See John Bresnahan et al., "Anatomy of a Shutdown," *Politico,* Oct. 18, 2013.

434 "I am not going to": Art Pope, interview with author.

CHAPTER FOURTEEN: SELLING THE NEW KOCH

436 "maybe it's also the content": Matthew Continetti, "The Double Bind: What Stands in the Way of a Republican Revival? Republicans," *Weekly Standard,* March 18, 2013.

437 "Conservative think tanks": Jeffrey Winters, interview with author.

437 "We're going to fight": Daniel Fisher, "Inside the Koch Empire," *Forbes,* Dec. 24, 2012.

437 Around the time that Reid: See John Mashey, "Koch Industries Hires Tobacco Operative Steve Lombardo to Lead Communications, Marketing," DeSmogBlog.com, Jan. 10, 2014.

438 "The current campaign finance": Republican National Committee, Growth and Opportunity Project, March 13, 2013, 51.

438 "We consistently see": See Kenneth Vogel, "Koch Brothers' Americans for Prosperity Plans $125 Million Spending Spree," *Politico,* May 9, 2014.

441 These political problems: See Annie Lowrey, "Income Inequality May Take Toll on Growth," *New York Times,* Oct. 16, 2012.

442 "The poor, okay": See Bill Roy and Daniel McCoy, "Charles Koch: Business Giant, Bogeyman, Benefactor, and Elusive (Until Now)," *Wichita Business Journal,* Feb. 28, 2014.

444 Michael Sullivan: Asked whether Steven Cohen and Michael Sullivan contributed money to the Kochs' political efforts, Mark Herr, a spokesman for Point72, Cohen's new hedge fund, said, "We don't comment or offer guidance on political donations."

444 Obama's senior adviser: Holden met in the White House with Jarrett, the domestic policy director, Cecilia Muñoz, and the White House counsel, W. Neil Eggleston, on April 16, 2015. Subsequently, Obama defended the Kochs' involvement on criminal justice reform issues, though he disparaged them not long afterward for opposing government support for renewable energy. Charles Koch described himself as "flabbergasted" by the president's criticism.

445 "It was hell": Goodwin, "Mark Holden Wants You to Love the Koch Brothers."

445 "hemorrhaging benzene": Loder and Evans, "Koch Brothers Flout Law Getting Richer with Secret Iran Sales."

446 Nonetheless, the $25 million: Some liberal groups, like AFSCME, criticized the United Negro College Fund for taking money from the Kochs, whom it accused of breaking public employees' unions that had provided employment to many minorities.

447 As a 2015 report: Jay Schalin, *Renewal in the University: How Academic Centers Restore the Spirit of Inquiry,* John William Pope Center for Higher Education, Jan. 2015.

448 By 2014, the various Koch foundations: The number 283 comes from ibid., 17.

448 "We learned that Keynes": Jerry Funt, interview with author.

448 Russell Sobel: Sobel became a teacher at the Citadel after abruptly leaving West Virginia University in 2012. Sobel was also a visiting fellow at the South Carolina Policy Council, part of the State Policy Network, and was affiliated with the Mercatus Center, the Cato Institute, the Fraser Institute, the Tax Foundation, and programs partly funded by grants from the Kochs at Troy University in Alabama and Hampden-Sydney College in Virginia.

448 But when critics raised: See Hardin, "Campaign to Stop Fresh College Thinking."

448 Young Entrepreneurs Academy: *The Huffington Post* published a newsmaking story on the Kochs' incursions into high schools. See Christina Wilkie and Joy Resmovits, "Koch High: How the Koch Brothers Are Buying Their Way into the Minds of High School Students," July 21, 2014.

450 Displayed prominently: Beneath his byline, Charles appended a quotation from Martin Luther King Jr.: "We are caught in an inescapable network of mutuality."

450 No mention was made: In his essay on the Well-Being Initiative, Charles Koch offered some of his own theories on the topic. As he saw it, the world had been divided for 240 years between those who believed government could make one happy and those who sought fulfillment through self-reliance. The split began with the French Revolution, continuing through the Russian Revolution, and on through tyrannical states like North Korea, he said. He contrasted these "collectivists" with the United States, whose founders, he said, "chose a very different path."

But two American historians who read his essay found it full of factual flaws. Rather than opposing the French Revolution, Founding Fathers like Thomas Jefferson greatly admired it. Moreover, as the Princeton professor Sean Wilentz noted in an interview with the author, the U.S. Constitution was inspired by the European Enlightenment and calls for the government to "promote the general welfare." Further, the Georgetown University professor Michael Kazin noted that far from being laissez-faire, the federal government had been intervening in support of public welfare since before the Civil War, often in aid of businesses. "The Koch version of history is a complete fairy tale," he said in an interview with the author.

450 By then, Brooks had moved: See Chris Young, "Kochs Put a Happy Face on Free Enterprise," Center for Public Integrity, June 25, 2014, which was the first report describing their embrace of "well-being" as a public relations gambit.

451 "Well, somebody has got to win": Roy and McCoy, "Charles Koch."

452 But after tallying up: Louis Jacobson, "Charles Koch, in Op-Ed, Says His Political Engagement Began Only in the Last Decade," PolitiFact.com, April 3, 2014.

453 The Kochs' development: The Democratic National Committee had undergone a somewhat similar transformation a decade earlier when about a hundred investors, including George Soros, combined forces to fund the creation of a nonparty political data and analytical firm called Catalist. In contrast to i360, Catalist was a co-op, formed by constituent groups in the progressive political sphere, such as labor unions and environmental groups. It was owned by a trust, and if it were sold, its charter required its investors to donate any profits to charity.

453 "I think it's very dangerous": See Jon Ward, "The Koch Brothers and the Republican Party Go to War—with Each Other," *Yahoo News,* June 11, 2015.

454 "They're building a party": Lisa Graves, interview with author.

454 Americans for Prosperity had expanded: See Mike Allen and Kenneth P. Vogel, "Inside the Koch Data Mine," *Politico,* Dec. 8, 2014.

454 "They aggressively corrected": David Axelrod, interview with author.

454 "retooled and revamped": See Nicholas Confessore, "Outside Groups with Deep Pockets Lift G.O.P.," *New York Times,* Nov. 5, 2014.

455 "We have reached": Mark McKinnon, "The 100 Rich People Who Run America," *Daily Beast,* Jan. 5, 2015.

455 A few of the biggest: Tom Steyer's organization was called Next Generation.

455 The 100 biggest known donors: According to *Politico,* 501(c) groups dis-

closed $219 million in campaign spending to the Federal Election Commission, 69 percent of which was by conservative groups. But this *disclosed* spending was a fraction of all of the 501(c) political spending during the 2014 midterm elections. One single Koch-backed 501(c) group, Americans for Prosperity, alone spent $125 million. See Kenneth Vogel, "Big Money Breaks Out," *Politico,* Dec. 29, 2014.

456 As America grew more: See Eduardo Porter, "Companies Open Up on Giving in Politics," *New York Times,* June 10, 2015, who writes that "unbridled spending" could create the "nightmare situation" where "those at the pinnacle of American society purchase the power needed to preserve the yawning inequities of the status quo."

456 Among the new power brokers: Koch Industries spent over $13 million lobbying Congress in 2014, as well as making over $3 million in political action committee contributions, according to OpenSecrets.org. https://www.opensecrets.org/lobby/clientsum.php?id=D000000186&year=20, https://www.opensecrets.org/pacs/lookup2.php?strID=C00236489&cycle=2014.

456 Soon after he was sworn in: See Lee Fang, "Mitch McConnell's Policy Chief Previously Lobbied for Koch Industries," *Intercept,* May 18, 2015.

456 Three of the newly elected: The other two freshman Republican senators expressing thanks at the Kochs' 2014 June summit were Colorado's Cory Gardner and Arkansas's Tom Cotton.

457 John Kasich, the iconoclastic governor: Neil King Jr., "An Ohio Prescription for GOP: Lower Taxes, More Aid for Poor," *Wall Street Journal,* Aug. 14, 2013; and Alex Isenstadt, "Operation Replace Jeb," *Politico,* June 19, 2015.

458 "What I give isn't 'dark'": Charles Koch interview with Anthony Mason, *CBS Sunday Morning,* Oct. 12, 2015. Yet as Paul Abowd revealed in his investigative report on DonorsTrust, "Donors Use Charity to Push Free-Market Policies in States," Center for Public Integrity, Feb. 14, 2013, "The Knowledge and Progress Fund, a Wichita, Kansas–based foundation run by Charles Koch . . . gave almost $8 million dollars to Donors Trust between 2005 and 2011. Where the funds ended up is a mystery." In addition, he reported, the Charles G. Koch Foundation also filtered small grants through DonorsTrust.

458 "over $760 million": This figure is according to Robert Maguire, an investigator at the Center for Responsive Politics. This included $64 million to groups in the Koch network, such as the American Future Fund, 60 Plus, and Americans for Prosperity in 2010, $407 million to the network in 2012, and pledges of $290 million to the network in 2014, according to Peter Stone's report, "Koch Brothers Unveil New Strategy at Big Donor Retreat," *Daily Beast,* June 13, 2014.

459 "It's extraordinary": Rob Stein, interview with author.

459 "There are few policy victories": Brian Doherty, interview with author.

459 "actors playing out": Ibid.

460 Even though Americans: Just 6 percent of Americans wanted Social Security cut, according to Lee Drutman, and a slight majority wanted the program's benefits increased; see Drutman, "What Donald Trump Gets About the Electorate," *Vox,* Aug. 18, 2015.

460 "false prophets": John Boehner's interview with John Dickerson on *Face the Nation,* CBS News, Sept. 27, 2015.

463 "Giving back": Peter Buffett, "The Charitable-Industrial Complex," *New York Times,* July 26, 2013.

463 Anyone paying attention: Confessore, "Outside Groups with Deep Pockets Lift G.O.P.," *New York Times,* Nov. 5, 2014.

463 "What they want": Phil Dubose, interview with author.

464 To get there: The information on the Kochs' pledges of $75 million is based on an interview with one source who is politically allied with them on several projects.

464 This time, the Koch network: James Davis, a spokesman for Freedom Partners, emphasized that the $889 million budget covered not just electoral spending but the whole universe of ideological spending by the Koch network, including think tanks, advocacy groups, voter data, and opposition research.

464 "Eight hundred and eighty-nine million dollars": Fred Wertheimer's interview with the author. Wertheimer's nonprofit organization Democracy 21 had been supported by grants from George Soros's Open Society Foundations. Wertheimer had nonetheless criticized Soros's use of big money on elections.

464 As was clear: According to OpenSecrets.org's tally of lobbying records, Koch Industries spent $13.7 million on lobbying in 2014, https://www.opensecrets.org/lobby/clientsum.php?id=D000000186&year=2014.

465 "We are doing all of this": Fredreka Schouten, "Charles Koch: We're Not in Politics to Boost Our Bottom Line," *USA Today,* April 24, 2015.

INDEX